CAMBRIDGE STUDIES IN EARLY MODERN HISTORY

# Rome in the Age of Enlightenment

This is the only scholarly work in the English language on the city of Rome in the Age of the Enlightenment, and the only book in any language to treat this fascinating city in all its multifarious aspects. Professor Gross combines extensive archival research with the latest findings of other scholars to produce a uniquely rounded portrait of the papal capital, elegantly illustrated with contemporary engravings by Piranesi and others. The book is divided into two sections, in the first of which Professor Gross discusses the material and institutional structures of the city, including its demography, economy, food supply, and judicial systems. The second considers aspects of intellectual, cultural, and artistic life. Professor Gross contends that ancien-regime Rome not only witnessed a decline in Counter-Reformation fervour, but that this decay resulted in a marked dissonance in the political, social, and cultural life of the city.

CAMBRIDGE STUDIES IN EARLY MODERN HISTORY

*Edited by Professor J. H. Elliott, The Institute for Advanced Study, Princeton, Professor Olwen Hufton, Harvard University, and Professor H. G. Koenigsberger*

The idea of an "early modern" period of European history from the fifteenth to the late eighteenth century is now widely accepted among historians. The purpose of the Cambridge Studies in Early Modern History is to publish monographs and studies which will illuminate the character of the period as a whole, and in particular focus attention on a dominant theme within it, the interplay of continuity and change as they are presented by the continuity of medieval ideas, political and social organization, and by the impact of new ideas, new methods and new demands on the traditional structures.

For a list of other titles in this series please see the end of the volume

# Rome in the Age of Enlightenment

The post-Tridentine syndrome and the ancien regime

HANNS GROSS

*Professor in the Department of History,*
*Loyola University of Chicago*



*The right of the University of Cambridge to print and sell all manner of books was granted by Henry VIII in 1534. The University has printed and published continuously since 1584.*

CAMBRIDGE UNIVERSITY PRESS

*Cambridge*
*New York Port Chester*
*Melbourne Sydney*

Published by the Press Syndicate of the University of Cambridge
The Pitt Building, Trumpington Street, Cambridge CB2 1RP
40 West 20th Street, New York, NY 10011, USA
10 Stamford Road, Oakleigh, Melbourne 3166, Australia



First published 1990

Printed in Great Britain by the University Press, Cambridge

*British Library cataloguing in publication data*

Gross, Hanns
Rome in the Age of Enlightenment: the post-Tridentine syndrome and the ancien regime. – (Cambridge studies in early modern history)
1. Italy. Rome, 1527–1798
I. Title
945'.63207

*Library of Congress cataloguing in publication data*

Gross. Hanns. 1928–
Rome in the Age of Enlightenment: the post-Tridentine syndrome and the ancien regime / Hans Gross.
p. cm. – (Cambridge studies in early modern history)
Bibliography
ISBN 0 521 37211 9
1. Rome (Italy) – Civilization – 18th century. I. Title.
II. Series.
DG812.4.G76 1990
945'.632 – dc 20 89-992 CIP
ISBN 0 521 37211 9

VN

To Donald F. Lach

With profound affection
and appreciation

# Contents

*List of illustrations* *page* vii
*Preface*

Introduction 1

I THE MATERIAL AND INSTITUTIONAL STRUCTURES

1 The city 15
2 The government: state and city 40
3 The population 55
4 The economy 88
5 Public finance and currency 116
6 The Agro Romano 152
7 Food supply 175
8 Poor relief and health 196
9 Law enforcement and criminal justice 214
10 Education 232

II ASPECTS OF ROME'S INTELLECTUAL AND CULTURAL LIFE

11 Intellectual life 247
12 Jansenism as a Roman phenomenon 270
13 Literature 286
14 Antiquarianism and neoclassicism 310
15 Painting and sculpture 331
Epilogue 366

*Bibliography* 371
*Index* 393

# Illustrations

PLATES


1 The port of the Ripetta on the Riber, by Giovanni Battista Piranesi *page* 24
2 The Piazza di Spagna with the Spanish Steps, by Giovanni Battista Piranesi 26
3 The facade of S. Maria Maggiore, by Ferdinando Fuga 31
4 The Palazzi di Campidoglio with the Church of the Aracoeli on the left, by Giovanni Battista Piranesi 50
5 The Old Forum, Rome's cattle market, by Giovanni Battista Piranesi 188
6 Msgr. Prospero Lambertini, later Pope Benedict XIV, by Pier Leone Ghezzi (Courtesy Vatican Library) 240
7 Celestino Galiani, by Pier Leone Ghezzi (Courtesy Vatican Library) 253
8 Faustina Maratta Zappi, by Pier Leone Ghezzi (Courtesy Vatican Library) 290
9 Gian Vincenzo Gravina, by Pier Leone Ghezzi (Courtesy Vatican Library) 292
10 Baron Philipp von Stosch, by Pier Leone Ghezzi (Courtesy Vatican Library) 317
11 The nave of St. John Lateran with the statues of the twelve Apostles (Courtesy Archivi Alinari) 358
12 Tomb of Pope Clement XIV, by Antonio Canova (Courtesy Loyola University of Chicago Archive) 363


MAPS


1 Rome in 1775/77, divided into rioni (anonymous) 16
2 Environs of Rome in 1755 according to a map by Christoforo Maire and Ruggero Giuseppe Boscovich 154

# Preface

The genesis of this work dates back to the year of 1974 when I taught at the Rome Center of Liberal Arts of Loyola University of Chicago. There I discovered that no history or comprehensive account in the English language existed for the city of Rome during the period of the ancien regime. There were indeed books on Roman art, which had played so significant a role in European culture. But the only history of the city was in Italian, Vittore Emanuele Giuntella's rather brief *Roma nel Settecento* (Bologna, 1971), a work that was written out of a genuine love for Rome but that left many areas of its life untouched. This deficiency was symptomatic of the state of research on Rome at the time, which, in comparison with the scholarship of so many other urban areas north of the Alps and even in northern Italy, was still in its infancy. Fortunately, further progress has been made in the intervening period, although there is still some way to go to bring our knowledge of Rome and its inhabitants up to the level of other urban centers. Nevertheless I believe the time has come for an overall account of Rome during a crucial period in European history. With this intention I set out to write this book. Its primary purpose, therefore, is to give us a panoramic view of the various facets and activities of the Eternal City.

Whereas there is a lack of general histories of Rome during the last decades of the ancien regime, there is none of interpretation. In the late nineteenth and early twentieth century, Italian historiography, given its *Risorgimento* bias, dismissed the city under papal rule as an example of inefficiency and hopeless decadence. More recently efforts have been made to rectify the picture and rescue the city's reputation. These endeavors centered on the economic sphere, where the emphasis has been on the reforms, or more often attempted reforms, undertaken by the various popes. I believe the truth lies somewhere in between the two extremes. This book is thus the start of a quest for an explanation. It must be admitted that, even though the papal government was on occasions in the van of reform, there was no consistently applied program of reform and the isolated efforts lacked cohesion and frequently failed to achieve their goals. Yet to charge it with being irretrievably retrograde, willfully reactionary and inept does not do full justice to the condition either. What we find is rather a gradual loss of energy and integrative force that stems from a more subtle malaise, which I termed the Post-Tridentine Syndrome. Not being a semantic purist, I understand by Post-Tridentine the era when the zeal and the perspective of the Counter Reformation, normally associated with the goals and achievements of the Council of Trent and the activities of the Society of Jesus, had waned and were in the process of disappearing.

In order to judge this Rome fairly, an occasional comparison with other cities is called for. These comparisons will help us put the papal capital in the context of the wider development. But they should not be taken as an attempt at writing a comparative urban history.

My first debt is to the memory of the late Professor Eric Cochrane. His rigorous but honest criticism and his helpful and kindly advice did a great deal to improve and recast the contents of this work, although the final version may not have followed his own views.

A work of this scope also owes much to the living. My gratitude extends to Loyola University of Chicago, which on two occasions granted me paid leaves of absence, once during the academic year 1976/77 to do research in Rome and again during the spring semester of 1983 to write up the first version. To the directors and staffs of the various archives and libraries in Rome, who tried to help a groping researcher unacquainted with their rich resources, goes out a special thanks. Their names are too many to recite here. At various times I was helped by graduate assistants in transcribing and coding the often undecipherable *stati delle anime* lists in preparation for the computerized study; in particular I would mention Signora Carmela Martino-Gallinella, who pioneered this effort with singular devotion. My colleagues in the history department at Loyola University exercised admirable patience with me during the years this work was in gestation. To two of them I am in special debt: Professor Robert Birely, S.J., for critically reading parts of the earlier chapters and for his constant encouragement to carry through the project when circumstances seemed unfavorable, and to Professor Jo Hays for reading and advising me on the section about scientific thought and activity in Chapter 11. I also appreciate the work of the editorial staff at the Cambridge University Press.

Finally, this work owes more than can ever be put in words to my step-mother, Rose Gross, who has been a tower of strength and support to me for all these years.

# Introduction

About seventy years ago one of the founders of modern urban studies, Robert Ezra Park, claimed that "the city is a state of mind, a body of customs and traditions, and of unorganized attitudes and sentiments that inhere in those customs and are transmitted with this tradition."[1] Contemporary urbanologists may find this description too intangible for their approach. The historian, however, cannot help feeling that Park has caught some of the essence of urban history. The nature and character of a city must be sought not only in its distinct traits, social, political, economic, but in its spirit and ethos which both grows out of these traits and interacts with them, while transcending them. A city creates its own spirit, not independently of its parts but beyond them, and this spirit grows, evolves, and changes over time.

Rome is a fine example of this notion. The grandeur that was Rome never rested wholly, even during the heyday of the ancient Empire, in the elements that made up the city. When the city was laid low in the Middle Ages, the idea outshone its physical reality. The Renaissance brought Rome a new glory and a new character. Starting with the return of the papacy in the fifteenth century following the Great Schism until the French Revolution, the city of Rome may be said to have shared with much of western Europe three stages in its development, the Renaissance, the baroque, and the ancien regime, each with its distinctive ethos.

This work focuses on the city's ancien-regime phase, which started late in the seventeenth century and reached its maturity in the eighteenth. For the elite of western Europe, the city played the role of a cultural model, a role it shared with Paris and in the realm of art it probably surpassed the City of Lights. The influx of foreigners into the Eternal City no longer consisted of pilgrims only, although they continued to make up a large proportion of the foreigners in Rome, especially during Holy Years, but of tourists who came to see the remains of the ancient city and admire its art, perhaps with some private amusement at the side. They came to drink in what they perceived to be the culture of Rome and broaden their education. Alongside them were the artists, who either visited or settled for an extended period and then took the influence of Rome and its art back home. By way of these, Roman culture, or what went for Roman culture, formed a significant element in eighteenth-century European culture.

The English were to assume a special role in this diffusion of Roman influence. It

[1] Quoted in H. J. Dyos (ed.), *The Study of Urban History* (London, 1966), 1.

all began with the institution of the Grand Tour. Back in Elizabethan England the Grand Tour had already been recognized as a means for gathering information which could be turned to the nation's advantage and for training young gentlemen to take their places in the world. The first reference to a Grand Tour in English only dates, however, from 1679, the year Richard Lassels' *An Italian Voyage, or a Compleat Journey through Italy* was published posthumously. Lassels, a classical scholar and an enthusiastic connoisseur of painting, found a congenial profession of escorting well-to-do and noble young Englishmen through Italy, which nearly always ended with a visit to Rome.[2] This fashion would become so popular and widespread that in 1734 a small private society of gentlemen who had travelled in Italy was formed with the purpose "of encouraging at home a taste for those objects which had contributed so much to their entertainment abroad." Initially it was no more than a gathering for social and convivial intercourse, but after a year or two it became evident that not conviviality but the love of art, with the ambition of fostering the same sentiment in others, was destined to be the ruling principle of the Society of Dilettanti.[3]

By that date the vogue for Italian, and particularly Roman, art and antiquities had already made its influence felt. Its inroads can be most clearly discerned. From the time of Inigo Jones, who had visited Italy on two occasions in 1613–1614 in the suite of the young Earl of Arundel, the Palladian style had spread in England. But that style is arguably Venetian, and it was not until the time of Robert Adam, following his long sojourn in Italy in the 1750s, that a new variation of classicism inspired by the ancient Roman models of temples, baths, and triumphal arches began to dominate the architectural taste.[4] Adam, too, spent his time in Italy gathering ideas for the interior decoration of houses as much as for their outward appearance.

The average English tourist in Rome usually wanted some memento of his travels, be it either in the form of a personal record such as a portrait with some recognizable ruin in the background, or of a romantic landscape painting, or more preferably of some ancient remain, a bust, a bas relief, or a copy of some well-known antique. These demands encouraged a brisk trade in antiquities and works of art, keeping the Roman art dealers and antiquarians in business.

Important as the individual demand was, greater significance must be attached to the more extensive patrons. In the area of works of art, Sir Thomas Isham, a gentleman from Northamptonshire, and the fifth Lord Exeter stand out in the later seventeenth century. Sir Thomas left England in 1676 and spent nearly eighteen

[2] Geoffrey Trease, *The Grand Tour* (London, 1967), 1–3, 10; Christopher Hibbert, *The Grand Tour* (New York, 1969), 10; Robert Enggass, *Early Eighteenth-Century Sculpture in Rome* (2 vols.; University Park, Penn. and London, 1976), 1:10.

[3] Lionel Cust and Sir Sidney Colvin, *History of the Society of Dilettanti* (2nd enlarged ed.; London, 1914), 1–6.

[4] Hibbert, *The Grand Tour*, 239–42; John Fleming, *Robert Adam and His Circle in Edinburgh and Rome* (Cambridge, Mass., 1962), 193, 267.

months in Italy. There, advised mainly by a priest called Bruno Talbot, he commissioned a number of contemporary paintings, all of which were carried out in Rome. Lord Exeter was a collector on a far larger scale. He spent two periods in Rome between 1680 and 1685, where he bought Marattas, Gaullis, and other works by Roman painters. He is believed to have introduced Carlo Maratta to other members of the English nobility.[5]

In the early eighteenth century the tempo of acquisition increased. In 1712, the fourteen-year-old Thomas Coke, later the first Earl of Leicester, an orphan with an annual spendable income of £10,000, left England for a projected course in architectural studies with Giacomo Leoni in Rome. During his stay in Rome he met the antiquarian Francesco de' Ficoroni, who advised him on his first purchases of ancient statuary in anticipation of rebuilding his ancestral estate of Holkham Hall. He also came to know William Kent, who had shown enough promise as a painter for his patrons to subsidize a period of study in Italy. Kent was to discover that he could do better as an architect and, at the finish, he did even better as a designer of gardens. Under Kent's guidance, Coke was to make his generous art purchases. Although Coke returned to England in 1718, it was not until 1734 that he was ready to translate his Italian experience into building Holkham Hall. At the end of the 1740s he sent the son of his architect, Matthew Brettingham, Jr., for further acquisitions to Rome.[6]

Other collectors of antiquities were to follow. Henry Howard, since 1738 Earl of Carlisle, met Ficoroni in Rome in 1717 when 23 years old. Howard inherited Castle Howard, which had been in building since 1700 according to plans by John Vanbrugh. There he exhibited about a hundred pieces of ancient art, some probably from Ficoroni's own collection. In 1764 Henry Temple, later Viscount Palmerston, acquired in Rome a collection of antiques for his residence at Broadlands.[7]

But only a relatively small proportion of English country houses owned antiquities; preference was given to collecting paintings. Here, too, the influence of Rome was marked, even if the modality was somewhat different. The English tourist bought up works of painters and sculptors such as Correggio, Guido Reni, Guercino, and the Caracci, who were much more admired in the eighteenth century than they are today. Many of the paintings were probably fakes, purchased at absurdly inflated prices in Rome, but they were the spur to the formation of many fine art collections in Britain.

The demand for portraiture was even more pervasive. At its height any tourist who could afford it would seek out Carlo Maratta and Gaulli, and, at a later point in time, Pompeo Batoni. British artists, however, gradually acquired the skill. It was

[5] Francis Haskell, *Patrons and Painters. A Study in the Relations between Italian Art and Society in the Age of the Baroque* (London, 1963), 195–98.

[6] Trease, *The Grand Tour*, 136–39; Hansgeorg Oehler, "Das Zustandekommen einiger englischen Antikensammlungen im 18. Jahrhundert," in H. Beck, P. C. Bohl, *et al.* (eds.), *Antikensammlungen im 18. Jahrhundert* (Berlin, 1981), 296–98. [7] Ibid., 299–302.

no new thing for a young British painter to journey to Italy and there eke out his money by copying the old masters or by absorbing knowledge of Graeco-Roman sculpture in the hope of forming a profitable association with some wealthy British visitor, who would patronize him on his return. Some of the earliest of these painters, such as Hugh Howard, who had been a pupil of Maratta in the 1690s, and William Kent, a student of Benedetto Luti, showed little signs of Italian influence. But the next generation of leading British portraitists in Rome came under the influence of Francesco Fernandi, a somewhat elusive figure who worked outside the orbit of the official Accademia di San Luca, but enjoyed the patronage of Cardinal Imperiali. He specialized in teaching his art, of Marattesque derivation, to foreigners. Among his British pupils were Allan Ramsay and William Hoare. His one known Italian pupil was significantly Pompeo Batoni, who, we know, became the favorite portrait painter of British gentry. It is not by chance, therefore, that we find complementary qualities in Batoni and Ramsay.[8]

The classical age of British painting, which owed its success to the benign eye of George III and the genius of Sir Joshua Reynolds, bore all the marks of Roman influence. Reynolds sailed for Italy in 1750 and stayed in Rome until 1752. Unlike Ramsay, his art and mind were formed not by the teaching of contemporary Italian painters, but by his daily communion with the long tradition of art from the Antique through Raphael and Michelangelo. On his return he determined to elevate the British portrait tradition by marrying it, as far as possible, to the Roman Grand Style. In the 1760s he set his career in naturalizing this taste in England, an effort that culminated in the foundation of the Royal Academy in 1768. Not surprisingly the Society of Dilettanti would take an active interest in the success of the Royal Academy.[9]

About the same time that Reynolds left Rome, Richard Wilson, one of the co-founders of the Royal Academy, followed suit. Wilson fills much the same place in the development of landscape painting in Britain that Reynolds does in portraiture. Both appeared on the scene when the ground had already been broken for the establishment of a new style. The man to introduce the seventeenth-century Roman tradition of landscape painting into Britain was John Wootton, who had spent the early 1720s in Rome, where he had fallen under the spell of Gaspard Dughet and Claude Lorrain, the two classic masters responsible for evolving the Roman landscape tradition. On his return he introduced the Gaspardesque style into Britain. Until then a landscape was either a piece of decorative furniture or a record of an actual scene. It was Wilson's accomplishment to infuse the landscape in

[8] Hibbert, *The Grand Tour*, 238–39; Anthony M. Clark, "Batoni's Professional Career and Style," in Henry A. Millon (ed.), *Studies in Italian Art and Architecture. Fifteenth through Eighteenth Centuries* (Cambridge, Mass. and London, 1980), 332; Ellis K. Waterhouse, *Painting in Britain, 1530 to 1790* (Baltimore, 1953), 122–23, 151–53.

[9] Ibid., 157–59; Cust and Colvin, *Society of Dilettanti*, 57.

Britain with the value of an independent work.[10] Thomas Jones, who had studied with Wilson and was himself in Rome between 1776 and 1783, was to carry on the Italian landscape tradition in Britain.[11]

England's absorption of Roman culture was a comparatively uncomplicated process. It was largely a simple exchange of ancient and modern objects of art against cash on the one hand and the acquisition of taste and skills needed for the various branches of Roman art on the other. The Romans, for their part, were happy to endure the eccentricities and heresies of Englishmen in the expectation of prestige and, more importantly, financial gain. The relationship between Roman culture and France was a great deal more ambivalent. As France grew increasingly powerful and self-assured, criticism and hostility toward Italian art became more pronounced. Bernini's failure in Paris in 1664/65 marked the turning point in the Italian prestige in France. Italian participation in building and decorating Versailles was almost negligible. The establishment by Louis XIV in 1666 of the French Academy in Rome would actually carry the rivalry between official French art and Roman culture into hostile territory. Its declared purpose was to enable French artists to share with the Italians the privilege of studying the masterpieces of the past and thus eventually to replace them. For, despite their hostility, in the inmost French consciousness classical still meant Roman. The history of the Académie française à Rome was to be a checkered one and, although there was frequently close collaboration between Italian artists in Rome and the Academy, even to the extent of a formal link between Rome's own Accademia di San Luca and the French sister institute, yet by the end of the century there can be little doubt that the crown had passed to Paris.[12]

With such an attitude there was naturally less eagerness for Frenchmen to visit Rome, and in comparison to Englishmen few actually did so, although those that did included some distinguished persons such as Montesquieu. The turning point occurred in the middle of the century. Madame de Pompadour unwittingly became the instigator of this movement when, in 1749, she named her brother M. de Vaudières, later the Marquis de Marigny, director-general of buildings. Wanting him to acquire a thorough knowledge indispensable to the exercise of his office, she sent him in December to Italy to familiarize himself with its artistic beauty. He was accompanied by the architect Jacques Germain Soufflot, the engraver Charles-Nicolas Cochin, and the abbé Leblanc, who acted as chronicler of the expedition. The trip lasted two years. In the wake of M. de Vaudières the worlds of art and finance in France were seized with an urge to see Rome in the second half of the

10 Waterhouse, *Painting in Britain*, 114, 172–73; W. G. Constable, *Richard Wilson* (Cambridge, Mass., 1953), 35–36, 80–81, 85, 96; *Settecento a Roma. Mostra, 19 marzo – 31 maggio 1959* (Rome, 1959), 229–30.

11 Ibid., 129.

12 Haskell, *Patrons and Painters*, 188–89; Michelangelo Cagiano de Azevedo, *Il gusto nel restauro delle opere d'arte antiche* (Rome, 1948), 35–36.

eighteenth century. Great tax farmers and everyone else who could afford to indulge a whim set out for Italy. The trip, too, is popularly credited as marking the beginning of the classical revival, set in opposition to the prevailing rococo, although that change in all probability occurred earlier in France.[13]

The influence of Rome on Germany is more difficult to estimate, in part because of the divided nature of the country. It is true the Germans had a certain idealized romantic attraction to the land where the lemon blossoms. But there are indications that their interest in Roman culture became more serious with the passing of time. For example, in 1606, the young Franz-Christoph Khevenhüller on his Grand Tour spent three days in Rome, whereupon he claimed to have seen everything worthwhile. In contrast another Khevenhüller, Count Franz Anton, in a letter of introduction to Cardinal Alessandro Albani for a noble cousin of his, around the middle of the eighteenth century, strongly commended a thorough study of Rome, "where all the unique objects are to be found, that deserve the worthy attention of a young gentleman."[14] Even more profound at times was the scholarly contact. In 1689 the young Gottfried Wilhelm Leibniz stayed at Rome, where he was received into the Accademia Fisico-matematica and was first introduced by a Jesuit, Grimaldi, to Chinese studies. He exchanged scientific knowledge with Giovanni Ciampini and Francesco Bianchini.[15] From then on the number of German tourists, including scholars of the caliber of Goethe and Herder, began to increase. During the pontificate of Pius VI, the visits by princely and noble personages, some of whom were to become patrons of Roman culture, grew in frequency.[16]

Rome was also receptive to German artists. As early as 1675 the Accademia di San Luca admitted German painters to membership.[17] In return, Italian artists, particularly those trained in Rome, would enrich the artistic life of Germany. In Vienna, the Liechtenstein family, which had come into wealth from the expropriations that followed the Protestant defeats in the Habsburg dominions, turned into important patrons of Italian art.[18] The Roman painter Gregorio Guglielmo, who had studied at home in association with such names as Conca, Trevisani, and Benefial, arrived in Germany shortly after 1750. He spent time working in Dresden in 1753, in Vienna in 1755 and at the Schönbrunn palace in

[13] M. Albert Tornézy, *Bergeret et Fragonard. Journal inedit d'un voyage en Italie, 1773–1774. Précedé d'une étude* (Paris, 1895), 1–51; Michel N. Benisovich, "Ghezzi and the French Artists in Rome," *Apollo*, N.S. 63 (1967), 345.

[14] Eva-Marie Csáky-Loebenstein, "Studien zur Kavalierstour österreichischer Adeligen im 17. Jahrhundert," *Mitteilungen des Instituts für österreichische Geschichtsforschung*, 79 (1971), 420; Friedrich Noack, *Das Deutschtum in Rom seit dem Ausgang des Mittelalters* (2 vols.; Berlin and Leipzig, 1927), 1:171.

[15] Ibid., 1:191–92. See more about Ciampini, Bianchini, and the Accademia Fisico-matematica in Rome in Chapter 11.

[16] Ludwig Freiherr von Pastor, *Geschichte der Päpste seit dem Ausgang des Mittelalters* (16 vols., Freiburg im Breisgau, 1930–1933); 16, pt 3: 68–73, 80; Noack, *Deutschtum in Rom*, 1:170–86; Emilia Morelli (ed.), *Le lettere di Benedetto XIV al Card. de Tencin dai testi originale* (3 vols.; Rome, 1955–65), 2:359–60, 363–64. [17] Ibid., 1:210. [18] Haskell, *Patrons and Painters*, 194.

1760–61, in Berlin in 1764, and in Augsburg in 1766–67, before he left for Russia.[19] The famous Marmorbad at Cassel is another remarkable contribution of eighteenth-century Roman art to Germany. The academy of drawing at Mannheim founded by the Elector Charles Theodore in 1752 was consciously modelled on the Accademia di San Luca by its director, the Flemish sculptor Peter Anton van Verschaffelt, who had spent fourteen years in Rome. These are but disparate examples of the importance of Roman culture in the German-speaking areas. Unlike England and even France, however, there are no discernible patterns of diffusion of either contemporary Roman art and culture or of interest in Roman antiquity. Much depended on the interests and whims of individual territorial rulers, such as the Habsburgs, the Hohenzollerns, and the Wettins.[20]

One could go beyond Britain, France, and Germany to trace the rays of Roman culture that penetrated European civilization in the course of the eighteenth century. It has left its traces in Spain, Sweden, and Russia, just to name a few of the more outstanding examples. However, this image which Rome projected on the European scene through its cultural impact has been refracted by our – and contemporary – preoccupation with the glory of its classical past, the antiquarian remains of which continued to attract the curious and the scholarly, and with the grandeur of its art, still associated with the genius of the Renaissance and the achievement of the high baroque.

The true nature of its state, that state of mind which is a city as Park defined it, cannot be found in the macrocosmic image that Rome projected at large, but must be examined in the state of its people, its institutions and, perhaps most sensitive of all, the cultural and intellectual life within its gates. These are the principal focus of this work.

The time frame chosen for the examination is the period which started late in the seventeenth century and reached its fullness in the eighteenth century. It is the period that is broadly identified with the term ancien regime in western Europe. The principles or characteristics we usually attribute to it were taken from the France of Louis XIV and his later imitators throughout the Continent. Its salient features were absolutism, paternalism, and privilege. Each of these traits can be found in Rome as well. Having failed to maintain its civic independence, the capital of the Papal States had become subordinated to the papal government and its administration was little more than a department of state. We may argue about the measure of power that a reigning pope wielded in person, but the absolute nature of his government can hardly be in doubt.

Paternalism was the hallmark of papal rule. Although deprived of all opportunity

19 *Settecento a Roma*, 122.

20 For collections of Roman antiquities by the Brandenberg rulers, see Gerald Heres, "Der Neuaufbau des Berliner Antikenkabinetts im Jahre 1703," in H. Beck, P. C. Bol, *et al.* (eds.), *Antikensammlungen im 18. Jahrhundert* (Berlin, 1981), 187–98; and Klaus Parlasca, "Die Potsdamer Antikensammlung im 18. Jahrhundert," in ibid., 211–29; Enggass, *Early Eighteenth-Century Sculpture*, 1:77–80; *Settecento a Roma*, 153.

to exercise independent decision-making, no urban population was pampered more than that of Rome. Other cities may have enjoyed more efficient government and, to a degree, a more progressive, if not more enlightened, social policy, but none provided such a broad range of support for its urban dwellers, all the way from almsgiving to ensuring the adequacy of its food supply. This care, occasioned by a fear of unrest, appeared to have its desired effect. Bread riots, if not unknown, were rare and subdued. The Romans gladly sacrificed power for a sense of security.

Privilege is usually thought of in terms of the special rights and exemptions granted to the nobility and the church under an absolute government. While the church obviously enjoyed a unique, though ambivalent, status within the Papal States, the nobility had been deprived of a great deal of power, including much of the feudal jurisdiction around Rome. This is not to argue the measure of fiscal privilege it still enjoyed. Our concern, however, is with the privilege of the city and its inhabitants. For in Rome it was not class or order, but the city itself that became the seat of privilege. The Romans enjoyed considerable exemptions from financial levies and duties. We have already noted their favored status in the matter of food supply. The countryside was robbed of its own produce to satisfy the Roman demand; the food prices were subsidized so that the urban folk could eat more cheaply than the producers.

It may well be argued that elements described as distinctive of this historical phase can already be detected in the preceding baroque era and, even earlier, in the Renaissance. Certainly absolutism, paternalism, and privilege did not suddenly burst upon the scene at the close of the seventeenth century. Paolo Prodi recently attempted to show that the papacy spearheaded the creation of modern absolute government since the Renaissance.[21] Virtually no new major administrative or financial institution surfaced during the period under review. Nor are these features solely confined to Rome. In fact, they are more often associated with France, Spain, and Germany than with Rome. This leaves us with the basic question of what made Rome distinctive during this period. It is probably best answered by a brief consideration of the phase immediately preceding it, the baroque.

The baroque, although it began with a definition of an artistic style,[22] has become closely associated with an epoch in history and its ethos, the Catholic Counter Reformation, as viewed across the broad spectrum of political, ideological, social, and cultural manifestations. It is true, of course, that not all baroque is religious in nature or aspiration. Nor indeed is it exclusively confined to Catholicism. Yet within the context of Rome, which became the seat and directing center of the Counter Reformation, the age of the baroque is spiritually and artistically identified with the Counter Reformation and its most visible symbols – the decisions and the message of the Council of Trent and the activities of the

[21] Paolo Prodi, *Il sovrano pontifice. Un corpo e due anime: la monarchia papale nella prima età moderna* (Bologna, 1982).

[22] Heinrich Wölfflin, *Renaissance and Baroque*, translated by Kathrin Simon (Ithaca, N.Y., 1966).

Society of Jesus. We need not stress that the first distinctively baroque structure in Rome was the Jesuit church of the Gesù. This Counter Reformation or, as I will loosely use the term, Tridentine spirit was not only directed against the enemies and external threats to the faith, but its zeal and fervor acted as an integrating force in the Catholic world at large, and even more so in the heart of the Catholic world, Rome. It provided the needed energy and incentive; but it did more than that, it subordinated all aspects of life and government, in various degrees, to an overarching ideology. José Antonio Maravall has suggested, quite rightly in my opinion, that the culture of the baroque was an attempt to integrate and guide the various strands of life, political, cultural, economic, social, to impose order on society, by all means available.[23] As long, therefore, as the spirit of Trent prevailed, the papal rule within the Papal States, and particularly its capital, showed a remarkable cohesiveness. Even where there were setbacks, abroad or at home, or when there were severe financial burdens, the effects over time were minimized or, at least, did not appear to produce an extended crisis. In the realm of art, Roman baroque, the embodiment of this spirit, ruled supreme with Gian Lorenzo Bernini as its outstanding exponent.

This Tridentine spirit, however, would gradually dissipate and with its disappearance came a shift in the as yet largely inarticulated attitudes and sentiments. It may be asserted, with a measure of justification, that this change began at the death of Pope Urban VIII in 1644. But Innocent XI, whose pontificate lasted from 1676 to 1689, showed enough zeal for the cause of the church, both at home and abroad, to count as a Tridentine pope, despite the evident loss of power the papacy had suffered since the Peace of Westphalia. With the death of Innocent in 1689 and of Bernini in 1682 the curtain definitely was drawn on the Tridentine period. Leaving aside the brief reign of the Ottoboni pope, Alexander VIII, the new age would therefore start with Innocent XII in 1691.[24] His formal abolition of official nepotism and new approach to pauperism are both signs of a changed outlook.

Art historians have detected iconographical changes symptomatic of the transition. The tomb of the exiled Queen Christina of Sweden at St. Peter's is one of the indications. Christina, daughter of the Protestant champion Gustavus Adolphus and a convert to Catholicism, was considered a living symbol of the triumph of faith over heresy. Her tomb was begun in 1697 at the request of Innocent and finished in 1702. The monument features an enormous relief showing the queen abjuring the throne. Concealed against a column in an almost inaccessible spot is a small relief devoted to Religion driving out Heresy.[25] Bernini would not have approved. Even the iconography of a secular composition of his, such as the

[23] José Antonio Maravall, *Culture of the Baroque. Analysis of a Historical Structure*, translated by Terry Cochran (Minneapolis, 1986), 35–36, 57–58.

[24] Raymond J. Maras, *Innocent IX. Pope of Christian Unity* (Notre Dame, Ind., 1984).

[25] Enggass, *Early Eighteenth-Century Sculpture*, 1:13.

Four Rivers fountain on the Piazza Navona, is distinguished by its predominantly Christian symbolism, the universality of Faith. In stark contrast we have Salvi's eighteenth-century creation, the Trevi fountain, an essentially pagan design whose animating principle is water.[26]

Actually a premonition of Rome's changed position may be detected much earlier, at the time of Alexander VII (1655–67), whose plan for rebuilding Rome was geared no longer to the convenience of the pious pilgrim, but with an eye to attracting the cultured or would-be cultured gentleman, who might be, but was not necessarily, a Catholic.[27] By 1714 this policy was openly articulated. Clement XI, on the occasion of presenting five Egyptian vases to the conservators at the Campidoglio, enunciated his goals. It was, he said, his special concern to provide for the glory and luster of the Eternal City, so that the many foreigners visiting it would admire not only churches and other sanctuaries, but also the most important remains of antiquity.[28]

Not all the impact of the new circumstances would be felt immediately. Sometimes the process of secularization became drawn out. The Congregazione dei Virtuosi, a confraternity of artists created in the characteristic Counter Reformation atmosphere that prevailed at its foundation in 1543, had as its two main purposes the promotion of good works and the use of fine arts to glorify religion. These objectives were responsible for the nature of the exhibitions it held each year at the Pantheon. But these exhibitions too came to an end sometime before 1764.[29] Even more symptomatic of the turn of events over the previous decades was the almost simultaneous suppression of the Jesuits, the standard bearers of the Tridentine spirit, and the establishment of what was to become the Museo Pio-Clementino in 1769 by Clement XIV. In it the heathen gods came to life again in their pagan shrines, marking the final triumph of pagan classicism.[30]

What do these changes indicate in practical terms and how did they affect the history of Rome and the life of its people during this ancien regime phase? We have stressed the concentrated energy that the direction of the Counter Reformation gave to the policies of the papal government and the cohesiveness it provided for the functioning of its institutions. Once this spirit suffered fatigue or was totally dissipated, not only did Rome lose a sense of direction – one could almost say, with a little exaggeration, its *raison d'être* – but a degree of disorder, an absence of cohesion and a dissonance becomes apparent. This phenomenon of a gradual degradation of culture may best be diagnosed as entropy. Entropy, originally a concept in physics,

[26] John A. Pinto, *The Trevi Fountain* (New Haven and London, 1986), 232.

[27] Richard Krautheimer, *Roma Alessandra. The Remapping of Rome under Alexander VII, 1655–1667* (Poughkeepsie, N.Y., 1982), 31–32.

[28] Wolfgang Liebenwein, "Der Portikus Clemens' XI. und sein Statuenschmuck. Antikenrezeption und Kapitolsidee im frühen 18. Jahrhundert," in H. Beck, P. C. Bol, *et al.* (eds.), *Antikensammlungen im 18. Jahrhundert* (Berlin, 1981), 76. [29] Haskell, *Patrons and Painters*, 126.

[30] Hans von Steuben, "Das Museo Pio-Clementino," in H. Beck, P. C. Bol. *et al.* (eds.), *Antikensammlungen im 18. Jahrhundert* (Berlin, 1981), 149.

was the measure of the amount of energy no longer capable of conversion into work. To put it rather unscientifically, it was a qualitative loss of energy; the energy which had been previously organized and focused on the central task of the papacy now tended to be distributed more broadly over many interests and more divergent goals, none of which were to reach the intensity, the breadth and overarching importance of its previous single obsessive zeal. Loss of energy is translated into a deficiency of cohesive force. Hence it has become customary to identify entropy as a measure of disorder. The vision of harmonious striving for order throughout nature is disturbingly contradicted. Single elements tend to behave in complete independence from each other, producing an absence of form and pattern, or simply an improbable arrangement of elements; a degradation involving the break-up of shape and the dissolution of functional contexts. Much of that has become characteristic of the state of Rome in this period. While there were numerous individual and isolated efforts at reform, there is no detectable overall policy and goal, no grand vision. Indeed, entropy allows for such reversals of direction as are implied by attempts at reform but at the cost of losing additional energy, which leads to further weakening. It is this entropy which must be held responsible for an increasing compartmentalization of life in Rome and makes it sometimes difficult to put one sphere into a meaningful relationship with another.[31] Yet random elements that are released from this break-up can be picked up to the benefit of other cultural elements as we have noted at the start by tracing the influence of Roman culture that was exerted on the rest of eighteenth-century Europe.

Through examining the "unorganized attitudes and sentiments," in the words of Robert Park, we may, however, discover the condition of ancien-regime Rome, which I have entitled the Post-Tridentine Syndrome.[32] The characteristic of this syndrome will be a slow and gradual loss of active energy, marked, among other features, by a perceptible, if not always overt, secularization and the loss of the associative mode of action inspired and inculcated at Trent, with intermittent efforts at reversing the trend. In general, there is a certain amount of inertia and disorder, but no wilfull retrogression. In other words, the weakness is not clerical government per se, as used to be asserted by anticlericals, but as clerical government that had lost its overall integrative vision and direction. Whether we approve that direction and vision is immaterial to the theme.

The book is divided into two parts. The first ten chapters are devoted to the

[31] Nicholas Georgescu-Roegen, *The Entropy Law and the Economic Process* (Cambridge, Mass., 1971), 3–12, 142, 277; Rudolf Arnheim, *Entropy and Art. An Essay on Disorder and Order* (Berkeley, Los Angeles and London, 1971), 1–3, 7–8, 12–15; Jeremy Rifkin, *Entropy. A New World View* (New York, 1980), 35–37; Daniel Hershey and Hsuan-Hsien Wang, *A New Age-Scale for Humans* (Lexington, Mass. and Toronto, 1980), 19–24.

[32] As indicated earlier I am consciously using the terms "Tridentine" and "Post-Tridentine" in an unconventional sense. In my usage, "Tridentine" applies to the whole ethos and spirit that pervaded the Catholic Counter Reformation, of which the Council of Trent was simultaneously the central event and the principal symptom. "Post-Tridentine" then refers to the period when the spirit and zeal of the Counter Reformation was on the wane.

material and institutional structures. The second part deals with selected aspects of the intellectual and cultural life in the city. Inevitably this latter section differs from the first. For learning, literature, and art has always been borne by an elite. In ancien-regime Rome this hiatus was particularly marked. Its culture was not rooted in the populace, with the possible exception of the opera. There was an estrangement from culture by the masses, partly because Rome by its cosmopolitan character attracted talents from beyond its borders, while its natives often lacked the needed education.[33] Nevertheless the same Post-Tridentine Syndrome was apparent in both the city at large and its culture. It formed the common overarching bond of its eighteenth-century history. To that extent the elements making up Roman life in the ancien-regime phase shared a similar experience.

[33] Vittorio Emanuele Giuntella, *Roma nel Settecento* (Bologna, 1971), 135–37.

# PART I

# The material and institutional structures

I

# The city

"Rome leaves me with the impression of a provincial town in comparison to Paris," so the French financier Bergeret de Grancourt tells us of his visit to the papal capital in 1773.[1] And not without justification. For although the circumference of Rome formed by the Aurelian wall, 19 km in length, which enclosed 13.66 sq. km, made it just a little smaller than Paris, the population within its walls amounted to only a fraction of the great metropolis on the Seine and occupied only about a fifth of the available surface area in the city.[2] The same traveller elaborated in his initial impressions:

> The first sight of the city at the Porta del Popolo is not very marvellous, and it is only close to the city that the road becomes passable. There are few streets such as the Via del Corso which are passable . . . but there are beautiful palaces . . . filled with fine paintings and rareties . . . We lodged at the Piazza di Spagna, which is not far from the entrance by the Porta del Popolo. This piazza, like all the piazze in this country, is a space rather than a consolidated arrangements of buildings.

In other words, Rome possessed no Place Royale.

In spite of the criticism of such academically minded Frenchmen as Bergeret, the Rome of the eighteenth century was regarded as one of the best laid-out cities in Europe. Its appearance was the result of the dynamic and ardent building construction ranging over three distinct periods, the medieval, the Renaissance, and the baroque, with a modest contribution at the time of the ancien regime.

The medieval city was crowded together in the plain along the Tiber, the Porta del Popolo, the ancient forum and the district of Trastevere on the right bank. In contrast to the city of antiquity, which had grown from the settlements on its hills, it was firmly anchored to the river. The houses lining the streets of this medieval Rome may have been remodelled time and time again, to be sure, but the essential street system remained intact and the majority of the old streets and alleys in the

1 M. Albert Tornézy, *Bergeret et Fragonard*, 139.

2 Ibid., 136–37; Giuliano Friz, *Consumi, tenore di vita e prezzi a Roma dal 1770 al 1900* (Rome, 1980), 13–14. Even as late as 1841 only 27.1 percent of the surface area was built on. Fiorella Bartoccini, *Roma nell'Ottocento. Il tramonte della "città santa." Nascita di una capitale* (Bologna, 1985), 135.

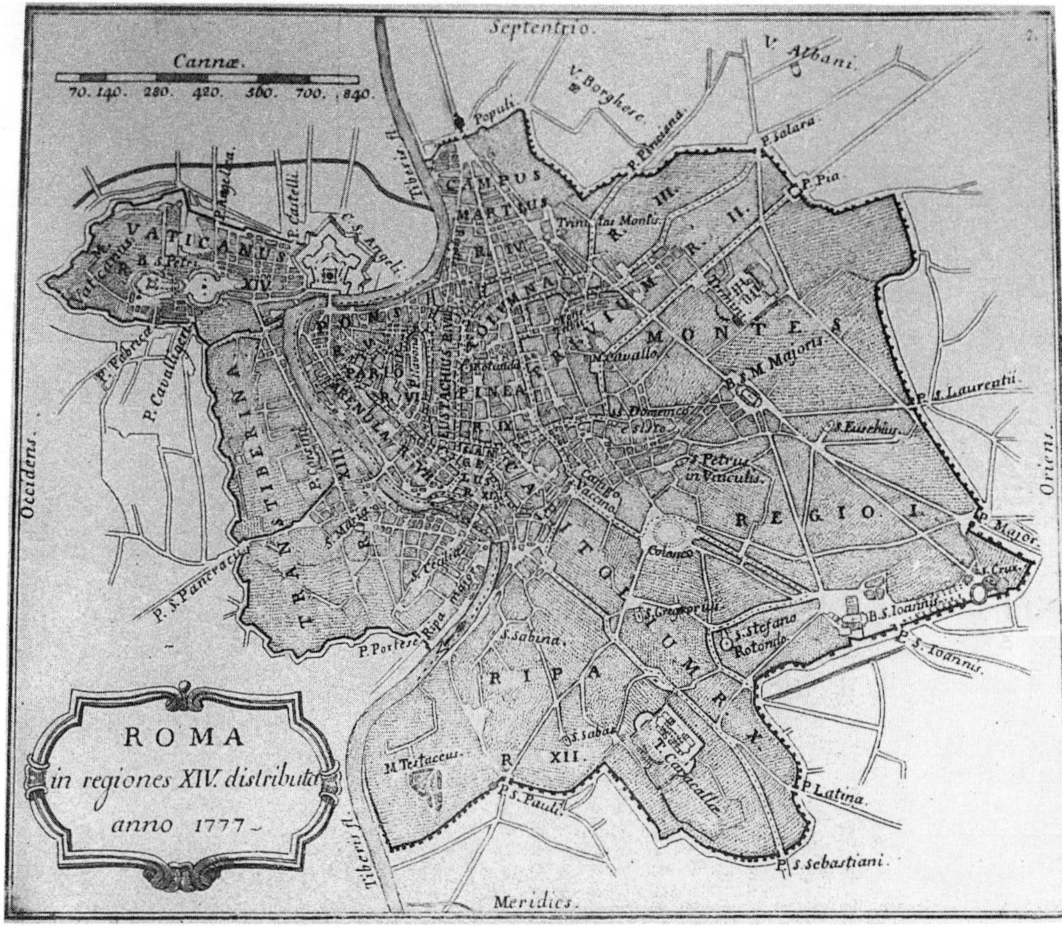


Map 1 Rome in 1775/77, divided into rioni

urban core, from the Corso to the Tiber bend south of the Tiber island, still retained the crooked directions and often the width of their medieval predecessors.[3]

The Rome which attracted the attention of the urban planners was superimposed upon this medieval framework. It was the result of more than two centuries of building activities by a number of popes. Notwithstanding the contrasting characters of the Renaissance popes and their frequently discontinuous building policies, there was a basic continuity and even a sort of regular evolution in Roman urbanism. Underlying the building activities of these popes, beside their family interests, were two motives: to beautify the city and to drive wide straight roads through the overcrowded quarters linking up the principal churches. The preoccupation with the beautiful was the thread that tied the construction of churches and palaces to the policy and work of urban planning; palaces and streets, churches and aqueducts, houses and obelisks were to beautify the residence of the vicar of Christ. And this beauty was conceived as a homage to God. Pope Nicholas V, who dreamed of transforming Rome, explained to the assembled cardinals on his deathbed the motives for his actions. Because of the fragility of the faith of the masses, he claimed, it was important to consolidate their faith with the spectacle of material grandeur. In the process, the popes invested the city gradually with an imperial aura.[4]

But any urban plan came up against the difficulties peculiar to the papal city. The site of Rome is naturally chaotic. The capital of the Catholic world lacked an internal unity and had no central place that could act both as the secular and spiritual heart of the city. The old commercial centers, the Campo dei Fiori and Piazza Navona, did not coincide with the religious and political centers, the Lateran, the Vatican, and the Campidoglio, which were on the periphery of the city.

Undeterred, the earliest papal planners at the time of the Renaissance, beginning with Nicholas V, who was inspired by Leon Battista Alberti, and Sixtus IV pursued twin objectives: to bring the city toward the east in order to extend it over the heights and valleys where the air was healthier and the danger of flooding less, and to facilitate the access of pilgrims to the Vatican, which entailed improving the approach roads. The centerpiece of the first project was the Via del Corso – then called Via Lata – which linked up the two ancient consular roads, the Via Flaminia and the Via Cassia, with the medieval core in the bend of the river. It gradually became the axis of the new urban quarter. Leo X with the Via Ripetta in 1513 and Clement VII with the Via del Babuino for the Jubilee year of 1525 completed around this axis of the Via Lata the famous trident arrangement with its terminal

3 Krautheimer, *Roma Alessandrina*, 1–2; Giorgio Fiocca, "Struttura urbana e controllo sociale a Roma nel '700 e nel primo '800: mobilità sociale, paesaggio urbano ed enti di sorveglianza pontifici," in Ercole Sori (ed.), *Città e controllo sociale in Italia tra XVIII e XIX secolo* (Milan, 1982), 381.

4 Christoph Luitpold Frommel, "Papal Policy: The Planning of Rome during the Renaissance," *The Journal of Interdisciplinary History*, 17 (1986), 364; Maurice Andrieux, *Daily Life in Papal Rome in the Eighteenth Century*. Translated by Mary Fitton (London, 1968), 18–19; Jean Delumeau, *Vie économique et sociale de Rome dans la seconde moitié du XVIe siècle* (2 vols.; Paris, 1957–59), 1:247–50.

apex at the Piazza del Popolo, a limited application of the radial-concentric scheme favored by Renaissance urban theorists. It was to become the most imitated model in European city planning.

The other objective emerged in the aftermath of some pilgrims being crushed in the press around Ponte Sant'Angelo in the Holy Year of 1450. In order to remove possible danger to the pilgrim for the next Holy Year of 1475, Sixtus IV constructed a bridge, which was named after him Ponte Sisto, to bypass Ponte Sant'Angelo. Julius II, advised no doubt by Bramante, began construction of an access road, the Via Giulia, on the the left bank of the Tiber and the Via Lungara on the right bank, also with pilgrims in mind.[5]

Simultaneously with these developments, the pontiffs embarked upon an ongoing program of embellishing the city. The first need was for a papal residence. The Lateran palace, the traditional seat of the Roman bishop some distance from the medieval town, was partly in ruins. So Nicholas V opted for building the modern Vatican in 1447. The last of this complex of edifices, the new Vatican palace, which today overlooks St. Peter's Square, was begun in 1589. The work progressed in record time and was almost completed by the end of the century.

But the popes were not solely concerned with their official residences. They also encouraged Renaissance prelates to build sumptuous family palaces at the expense of the church.

The Farnese pope Paul III continued the process of improving the appearance of the city by setting the construction of the modern Campidoglio in motion. The project was meant to put the growing papal dominance over the municipal magistracy in visible terms. The Palace of the Conservators, the last of the three palaces on the Capitoline hill, was only finished in the reign of Innocent X (1644–55).[6]

In spite of all these accomplishments in building and street planning, Rome at the very end of the Renaissance, say about 1560, still retained much of the character of a medieval city. It was left to Gregory XIII and, even more, to his successor Sixtus V, to give us the baroque city. These two pontiffs started to stamp the imprint of the new Tridentine aims of the church upon the city's plan. In so doing they did not turn away from the traditions of their predecessors, but amplified them. The criteria were those of Sixtus IV, to build straight thoroughfares connecting the seven basilicas of the Eternal City for the convenience of the pilgrims, while at the same time modernising and embellishing the urban environment.

Gregory XIII prepared the ground for his successor by joining the basilica of St. John Lateran to that of Santa Maria Maggiore. Sixtus V constructed what was then one of the largest thoroughfares in Rome which went from the church of SS. Trinità

[5] Ibid., 1:298–301; Paolo Portoghesi, *Roma barocca* (2 vols.; Bari, 1973), 1:63–64.

[6] Frommel, "Papal Policy: The Planning of Rome," 40, 43, 48; Rodolfo Lanciani, *Storia degli scavi di Roma e notizie intorno le collezioni romane di antichità* (4 vols.; Rome, 1902–12), 2:4, 18–77, 236; Delumeau, *Vie économique et sociale de Rome*, 1:263–69, 272–73, 292–95.

dei Monti to the church of S.Croce in Gerusalemme in a straight line of 2.78 km, of which more than one-half was over hilly ground. With the death of Sixtus V in 1590, the plan to regulate the system of roads in the city was abandoned and, apart from some lesser street modifications, not taken up again until Rome became the capital of a unified Italy in 1870.[7]

The Vatican long had a reputation as an unhealthy spot. It probably rested on no more than the sharp change of temperature felt at nightfall after the heat of the day, but which can be dangerous for elderly men. Gregory XIII, consequently, decided to build a modest residence on top of the Quirinal hill in 1583, to enjoy the natural amenities of the place and the healthfulness of the air. Under Sixtus V, the architect Domenico Fontana enlarged the structure, which under its popular name of Monte Cavallo became the favorite residence of the popes until it was taken over by the kings of the house of Savoy.[8]

The whole project on the Quirinal, however, was part of a larger policy, that of repeopling the hilly area of Rome, the *monti*, a region inhabited in ancient times, but deserted since the Norman incursions in the tenth and eleventh centuries. The idea was old. Nicholas V had already granted tax exemptions to persons who would inhabit the region. But it was only in the second half of the sixteenth century, after adequate water supply was made available that the interest of the authorities in this area began to take concrete form. Sixtus V made a concerted effort at attracting the population to the monti and grouping them around the basilica of Santa Maria Maggiore and the Quirinal palace. In order to induce people to move to the Via Pia and adjoining streets he held out various incentives: proprietors were exempt from certain taxes and from penalties for building infringements.

This move toward the monti was accompanied by a shift in the residence of foreigners in Rome. They had preferred to live in the Borgo around the Vatican and the region along the Tiber. But after 1555 they began to move to the area extending east from the Via del Corso to the slopes of the Pincio. Artists were the first to make the move, among them Rubens, Claude Lorrain, and Poussin. In time the more affluent strangers congregated in the area now comprehended under the name of Piazza di Spagna, where many inns and furnished apartments became available.[9]

Changes in the field of housing and town planning came about thanks in part to the existence of norms for building construction that were laid down during these early phases and remained in force until 1870. The norms rested on the principle of public expropriation. In 1480 Sixtus IV first stated that principle in his bull

[7] Ibid., 1:313, 316, 320; Portoghesi, *Roma barocca*, 1:64–74; Vincenzo Golzio, *Palazzi romani dalla rinascita al neoclassico* (Bologna, 1971), 21–22; John Moore, *A View of Society and Manners in Italy* (2 vols.; London, 1781), 1:395–96.

[8] Konrad Escher, *Barock und Klassizismus. Studien zur Geschichte der Architektur Roms* (Leipzig, 1910), 11; Lanciani, *Storia degli scavi*, 4:96–98; Delumeau, *Vie économique et sociale de Rome*, 1:271–72.

[9] Ibid., 1:310–12, 322; Portoghesi, *Roma barocca*, 1:73; Pastor, *Geschichte der Päpste*, 14, pt 2: 1094–95; Lanciani, *Storia degli scavi*, 3:101, 103–10.

*Amplificatio jurisdictionis*. In return for expropriation the owners were entitled to receive just compensation. Gregory XIII consolidated the existing provisions in his law *De aedificis* in 1574. This decree became the instrument by which the appearance of Rome was gradually changed. Its first purpose was to facilitate the cutting of new streets and the widening and straightening of existing alleys. Its second concern was devoted to the problem of enlarging housing units by acknowledging the right of forced acquisition of adjoining property subject to compensation. Neighbors were given the right of preemption. In effect, the legislation laid the groundwork for the progressive enlargement of housing units.

With the regulatory foundation thus in place by the end of the sixteenth century, there was a housing boom in the following century, which became a source of employment and of capital investment in real estate. After the completion of the Renaissance and baroque framework of streets and slum clearance, a new expansion toward the northeast followed. This process of renewal in the seventeenth century, which by the grandeur of its scale and the rapidity with which it was carried out astonished its contemporaries, affected both ecclesiastical and aristocratic building as well as ordinary dwelling or tenant houses. For with the help of the above building criteria the little one-family house with a shop on the ground floor of earlier times was very slowly giving way to a domicile usually of four to five stories with two rental apartments on each floor. This development was a building enterprise almost without history, except that we can see from the consecutive plans of seventeenth-century Rome the network of streets filling up, especially in Trastevere and the zone around the Quirinal. With the death of Alexander VII in 1667 the rate of building began to slacken again.[10]

Thereafter the urban physiognomy continued to change gradually and virtually imperceptibly, often by petty alterations of masonry, the closing and opening of passageways, the elimination of windows belonging to neighboring houses, all for the purpose of increasing living space. In some areas, however, a more visible expansion of housing would continue, predominantly in the valley which rises from the Trevi fountain to the Piazza Barberini, along the present-day Via del Tritone, and the zone of the Suburra, stretching from the Quirinal to the Oppio. As a rule, popular housing there was constructed on the lower ground, while aristocratic and monastic buildings were erected on the elevations. Along the valley of the Tritone the Via Pia was lined by the Quirinal and the residences of the Albani, the Barberini, the Costaguti, the Gonzaga, and the Rospigliosi, interspersed by houses belonging to the Carthusians, the Carmelites, the Jesuits, and the Trinitarians and by convents for Dominican, Capuchin, and Carmelite nuns. The number of religious houses in the area was only a reflection of their prevalence in eighteenth-century

[10] Portoghesi, *Roma barocca*, 1:64–68; Delumeau, *Vie économique et sociale de Rome*, 1:230–34; C. Paolo Scavizzi, "Le condizioni per lo sviluppo dell'attività edilizia a Roma nel sec. XVII: la legislazione," *Studi Romani*, 18 (1969), 160–63, 171; Petrocchi, *Roma nel Seicento*, 56; Italo Insolera, *Roma. Immagini e realtà dal X al XX secolo* (Rome and Bari, 1980) 284.

Rome, where it was estimated that there were 240 monasteries for male religious and 73 convents for female religious and, out of a total of 440 villas, vineyards, and the orchards, 132, that is about a third, belonged to religious institutions.[11]

This activity contrasts with what was happening in Bologna at the same time, where the urban picture was little altered since the Renaissance.[12] Nevertheless, all these changes had only modified superficially the medieval layout of the original inhabited area, the *abito*, as late as the time of the Chigi pope, Alexander VII (1655–67). Contrary to previous approaches to town planning, Alexander aimed at attacking the very core of the old town. Working with Gian Lorenzo Bernini and Pietro da Cortona he wanted to carry on the process of embellishing Rome, together with turning it into a truly modern city. Modern urbanism, as he understood it, required spacious squares with regular boundaries, long, straight streets and commodious, well-lit palaces. Open areas and their bordering structures were to complement one another. His building program had certain practical considerations, however. It would stimulate employment in the building trades, relieve traffic congestion, and attract tourists, who in turn would bring business and funds to the innkeepers and others willing to rent out apartments. Rome's traffic problems in the seventeenth century were nearly as bad as they are today. Since the 1560s coaches had replaced the sedan chairs and litters. By the middle of the seventeenth century, coaches had become status symbols. Up to 200 coaches met Queen Christina of Sweden on her arrival in 1655. But the streets of Rome were hard to negotiate and quarrels over precedence were frequent. Alexander, therefore, planned to adapt the streets and piazze for coach traffic, including St. Peter's Square, although he did not think of it primarily as a parking lot.

Alexander's overall master plan was to be an interplay of stage design and city planning. At the core were to be *teatri*, showpieces consisting of piazze and streets in which both modern buildings and ancient monuments would jointly reflect the glories of *Roma antica e moderna*. These teatri would break up the urban fabric of the old city in a clearly conceived pattern. With few exceptions they would line up along the route travelled by important visitors on their entry to Rome: the Piazza del Popolo, where Alexander was building the two churches; the Piazza Colonna with the column of Marcus Aurelius and the new Chigi palace; the Corso, where Alexander removed all ugly spots; Piazza San Marco, far narrower than today's Piazza Venezia, whence the Campidoglio came into view. The route then passed along the widened westward street toward the churches of the Gesù and Sant'Andrea della Valle, in front of which a small square was laid out, and on to the Piazza Monte Giordano adjoining Borromini's clock tower near the Chiesa Nuova. On the other side of the Tiber, Bernini designed and enclosed St. Peter's Square

[11] Fiocca, "Struttura urbane e controllo sociale," 338; Insolera, *Roma*, 316–18; Mario Battaglini, "La soppressione dei conventi nella Repubblica romana giacobina," *Palatino*, 1–3 (1965), 13.

[12] Anna Maria Matteucci, *Carlo Francesco Dotti e l'architettura bolognese del Settecento* (Bologna, 1969), 2–3.

with its colonnades in the form of a courtyard to enhance the grandeur of the basilica and to give the tourist or pilgrim an opportunity to collect his thoughts. Alexander's plans clearly point to a change in the direction of urbanistic goals. While they were meant to add to the splendor of Rome and its sovereign, the other motive was no longer so much the glory of the faith and the concern for the pilgrims, but the convenience and pleasure of the tourists, the display of the art and architecture of antiquity and the baroque.[13]

With Alexander VII urban planning on a grand scale had reached its apogee in Rome. The ancien regime was a less favorable period, and Venice and Naples – where the government would open up new arterial streets[14] – surpassed Rome in this respect. What there was of building activity was largely concerned with adding to public structures and with renovating or embellishing churches.

The first among the ancien-regime popes, Innocent XII, carried on the primarily secular tradition established by Alexander VII, albeit with a less grandiose vision. He restricted himself almost exclusively to the functional needs of the city and was the only one among that series of popes concentrating on large public works who did not build a church. His favorite architect was Carlo Fontana. A native of the Ticino, he arrived in Rome around 1650, where he became in turn assistant to Pietro da Cortona and Bernini.

Innocent XII commissioned Fontana to transform the unfinished palace of Montecitorio into the seat of the law courts. The project of concentrating the various tribunals in one spot had a long ancestry. In 1508 Julius II first mooted the idea and Bramante drew up a plan for a Palazzo dei Tribunali, which would have been the first real office building in Rome since antiquity. But this attempt at centralization was hardly acceptable to the old Roman republicans, who still guarded the privileges left to them. So it was not until 1694, when republican liberties were truly dead, that the project was resumed. Bernini had begun a family palace for the Ludovisi, which was never completed. Innocent chose it for the location of his law courts. It was the only opportunity the architect had to embark on a work comparable to the great building projects of the middle years of the seventeenth century. The variations which Fontana suggested to the original structure of Bernini were few, but significant. They were all details which took away from the palace the feeling of a noble family residence and tended to characterize it as a public building. To approach the palace, henceforth known as the Curia Innocenziana, the Via degli Uffici del Vicario was improved.[15]

Innocent's attention also turned toward improving the untidy and rather

[13] Krautheimer, *Roma Alessandrina*, 1–18, 30.

[14] Claudia Petraccone, *Napoli dal '500 all '800. Problemi di storia demografica e sociale* (Naples, 1974), 133.

[15] Valerio Mariani, *Le chiese di Roma dal XVII al XVIII secolo* (Bologna, 1963), 147; Aldo De Rinaldis, *L'arte in Roma dal Seicento al Novecento* (Bologna, 1948), 49–50; Lina Montalto, *Un mecenate in Roma barocca* (Florence, 1955), 269–76; Pastor, *Geschichte der Päpste*, 14, pt 2: 1091–93; Frommel, "Papal Policy: The Planning of Rome," 51–53; Portoghesi, *Roma barocca*, 1: 125; 2: 567–73, 590–95.

primitive state of the port of the Ripa Grande, the entry to Rome by water for ships coming upstream. He built warehouses and supplied the port with other necessary equipment. He had Fontana convert the old temple of Neptune at the Ripa into a customs house for the commodities coming by sea, the Dogana di mare. For goods entering overland, he had the Dogana di terra constructed behind the colonnade of the temple of Hadrian in the Piazza di Pietra. As part of the building program he finished work on the slope of the Tre Pile, which became an access road for carriages to the Piazza del Campidoglio.[16]

His most significant undertaking was the gigantic Ospizio Apostolico di San Michele, work on which was started in 1693. This complex of buildings is probably a unique example of the centralization or concentration of public social functions, caritative and penal, within a unified structure, a concrete step in the papal government's assumption of municipal functions. For this purpose, Innocent XII chose a huge expanse of land on the Tiber, on the periphery of Rome, close by the port of Ripa Grande, but beyond the last houses in Trastevere. A relative of his, Msgr. Tommaso Odescalchi, had already opened there an asylum for orphans and abandoned children in 1686. These children without family were followed in 1703 by delinquent youths, for whom a reformatory school was set up.

The Albani pope, Clement XI, was to carry on the program of public works of his predecessor. In 1708 a new wing was started for sheltering the elderly of both sexes. Clement XI also installed a manufacture for working wool and a workshop for tapestry in which more than 200 people, mainly women, found employment. This aspect of setting up state factories in places where the state had concentrated a needy and poor work force would spread elsewhere in eighteenth-century Europe, although as we shall see later it did not bring the hoped-for benefits in Rome. Long after Clement's time, a prison for fallen women, *traviate*, on a design by Ferdinando Fuga, was added in 1735 and finally a wing for poor unmarried girls, *zitelle*, in 1790–94. The whole edifice was organized around a series of courtyards, the Cortile delle arti, dei ragazzi, dei vecchi and so forth, each devoted to a particular activity. Its facade was one of neat simplicity, which with its unending series of similar windows became a backdrop to the picturesque disorder of the port of the Ripa Grande.[17]

Clement XI would also finish Innocent XII's work of laying out the ports on the Tiber. He turned his attention to the port which handled the shipping that came downriver from northern Lazio and Umbria, at the Ripetta. This port had actually existed for centuries, but in its original state it was but a gash in the urban texture, which exposed the bed of the river with its steep bank. In 1703, Alessandro Specchi, the most active and visible of Fontana's students, began the construction of the stage-set port with its wharves and flights of steps at a cost of about 60,000 scudi. The work took two years. During this time Rome was shaken by earthquakes which

[16] Insolera, *Roma*, 279–83. [17] Ibid., 276–78.

1 The port of the Ripetta on the Tiber, by Giovanni Battista Piranesi

occasioned the collapse of the two arches in the second row of the Colosseum. The rubble recovered from the ground was immediately incorporated into the new structure. In planning his project, Specchi had to take account of an asymmetrical backdrop composed of the church of San Girolamo degli Schiavoni, some small palazzi and the more distant layer of the Palazzo Borghese. He succeeded in reorganizing the inchoate mass into an organic expression geometrically determined, with elegantly inflected lines, which fitted into the whole urban layout and, from a town planner's view, provided the city with a very interesting spatial nodal point. In the nineteenth century, however, the port had to give way to the new river embankments and the Ponte Cavour.

Under Clement XI, the development of the Suburra, already referred to, went ahead. He was to have the distinction of opening up the last new street in Rome until the following century. The Strada Clementina, linking the Piazza Zingari to the Vicola Cimarra, a distance of less than 100 m, was cut through a block of houses that had remained untouched for almost two centuries.[18]

The same pontiff was also responsible for getting another important project on the way, although it would only be completed in 1726 under Benedict XIII. Between 1717 and 1720 various plans were drawn up for the construction of the Spanish Steps. Specchi, together with Francesco De Sanctis, and others submitted their ideas. De Sanctis' plan was eventually chosen by Innocent XIII and building

[18] Ibid., 283.

started in 1723. The purpose was to connect the church of SS. Trinità dei Monti and its piazza at the top of the Pincio, a nodal point for the network of streets that had been built in the monti in the late sixteenth century, with the Piazza di Spagna, then divided into two triangular spaces, below. Until that time only an unpaved, tree-lined path had led up the slope. The area, however, had assumed increasing importance since it had become the favorite center for foreign tourists and residents. The choice of building steps, rather than a ramp for vehicular traffic, at a time when the exact opposite policy was carried out at the Campidoglio had a special meaning. It signified the final abandonment of Sixtus V's most important road network, that from Santa Croce in Gerusalemme to the Piazza del Popolo, and, with it, the rejection of the plan to connect the old quarters of the city with that of the villas and the green belt on the fringes. Thus one more idea of Tridentine Rome was silently buried. Instead the stairs determined the future direction, the concern for visibility and views and the convenience of the strolling public. De Sanctis applied a precise iconographic program for the steps, derived from the title of the church above; he divided the stairs into groups of three. Not everyone approved of the new structure: Montesquieu, for one, thought it a bad piece of work. Two years after completion, in September 1728, the collapse of a retaining wall, weakened by flooding, smashed the steps. Filippo Raguzzini presented an expert appraisal for the restoration and may actually have been responsible for rebuilding them.[19]

Benedict XIII was left with continuing the work of providing Rome with the social institutions it needed, a work which Innocent XII and Clement XI had so energetically started. He focused on the sector of public hospitals. The pope enlarged the hospice of the Trinità dei Pellegrini, near Ponte Sisto, built and run by the Oratorians. The hospice received patients discharged from other hospitals for short-term care and convalescence, and, in so doing, relieved their case load and indirectly increased their capacity. With this enlargement in 1725 the hospice was able to accommodate two thousand convalescents of both sexes.

At the same time a new hospital, that of San Gallicano, for those suffering from venereal and skin diseases, was built. It was the largest edifice to be erected in Trastevere after the complex of San Michele and from every point of view a model for public buildings at the time. It answered all the demands of hygiene in its day. The architect was Raguzzini. A Neapolitan by birth, he was called by Benedict XIII to Rome together with other master masons whom the pope had known and with whom he had worked in his old see of Benevento. Raguzzini planned and realized the structure in little more than eighteen months. If the hospital played a conspicuous role in the history of sanitary engineering, it was also of great

[19] Ibid., 284; Portoghesi, *Roma barocca*, 2:605–12, 621–30; Roberto Gabetti, "Architettura italiana del Settecento," in *Storia dell' arte italiana* (Turin, 1982), part 2a, vol. 20, 2:678–79; Jean Arnaud, *L'Académie de Saint-Luc à Rome. Considérations historiques depuis son origine jusqu'à nos jours* (Rome, 1886), 55; Maurice Andrieux, *Les Français à Rome* (Paris, 1968), 165–66; Timon H. Fokker, *Roman Baroque Art. The History of a Style* (2 vols.; London, 1938), 1:320–21; Montesquieu, *Voyages:* VII, "Rome" and IX, "Rome (second séjour)" in *Oeuvres complètes de Montesquieu*, 2:1102, 1122–23.

2 The Piazza di Spagna with the Spanish Steps, by Giovanni Battista Piranesi

importance in the history of architecture. Beyond being a model of balanced masses and cheerful plastic linear decorations, it was a most successful example of accommodation to the requirements of its environment in all but one respect.

Different from San Michele, San Gallicano did not rise on vacant land, but in the midst of compact blocks of buildings, necessitating much demolition. This process was not limited to houses, but involved three streets. As a consequence only one road that ran right through Trastevere, the Lungaretta, was left intact. The Trasteverines now experienced an inversion. The urbanistic projects carried out during the Renaissance had tied them to the central districts, or *rioni*, of Rome on the other bank of the Tiber by way of the Ponte Sisto and the Tiber island, eliminating their isolation on the end of the medieval city. Now this project cut them off once more and tended to push them again to the periphery.[20]

Raguzzini was also responsible for one of the finest miniature pieces of town planning at the time, the Piazza di San Ignazio, built in 1726–27, a marvellous creation of Rome's indigenous rococo. The Roman rococo differed from its French counterpart by its faithfulness to the old Roman *gravitas* and by its classical roots. The aim was to give a meaningful layout to the space facing the great facade of the church, this time not by building edifices for public use but by constructing ordinary dwelling houses several stories high. Here, in the center of Rome, before the enormous mass of the Jesuit church, these small palazzi with their twisting features rose to create a compact ambience, yet airy because of the successful effects of spatial illusion, elegant even though the decorations are sober. The geometric scheme did not have the coherence of the port of the Ripetta: it resulted rather from the tangential union of three ovals, the largest one of which determined the curvature of the central palazzetto and the lateral ones. Everything in the piazze and the alleys tended toward the achievement of a stylistic unity. The design, however, was met with bitter hostility, not only from academic critics who, apart from their instinctive hatred of the Beneventines, dismissed Raguzzini as a "Gothic" architect, but also from the Roman public, who could not understand his intimistic style.[21]

If Raguzzini's appearance in Rome marked the first stark departure from the Roman culture rooted in Bernini, his influence was not very profound, for his difficult balancing act between a native heritage and the ability to absorb an acquired one could not be maintained for long. In the interval the historical arch of the baroque school ended in Rome. A new generation of sufficient homogeneity took its place. Its epigones were champions of a return to Renaissance classicism, of a *neo-cinquecentismo*. Among their number were two Tuscans, Alessandro Galilei and Ferdinando Fuga, who significantly first made their mark in Rome in the reign

[20] Insolera, *Roma*, 284–86.

[21] Mario Rotili, *Filippo Raguzzini e il rococo romano* (Rome, 1951), 7, 11–17, 30–56, 64–86, 96; Mariani, *Le chiese di Roma dal XVII al XVIII secolo*, 185, 217, 222–30; Portoghesi, *Roma barocca*, 2:675–77, 685–95, 702–03, 870; De Rinaldis, *L'arte in Roma*, 33–34; Escher, *Barock und Klassizismus*, 63; Gabetti, "Architettura italiana del Settecento," 681.

of Clement XII, of the Florentine Corsini family. To Fuga we owe three public buildings. The architect, who had spent some of his earlier years in Rome, departed for Naples and Palermo in 1726. About three years later Clement recalled him to complete and transform the complex of palaces on the Quirinal. Together with lesser-known participants, Fuga built the small palace of the Secretariat of the Ciphers. In comparison to this rather simple building, the Palace of the Consulta, erected between 1732 and 1734, is remembered as one of the greatest works of Fuga. Because of the disorder caused by the erratic building history on the Quirinal, it was decided to give the piazza more dignity by constructing a magnificent stage-set in the form of the Consulta palace. Fuga was conscious of the importance of the task, which for the first time in eighteenth-century Rome offered him the opportunity to raise a great public building from the ground up. With the fine intuition of an urban planner, he conceived the facade as a set design for the piazza. The other utilitarian structure in which he revived his theme of bare simplicity was the house of correction for women at San Michele a Ripa.[22]

But Clement XII's best-known public structure was the Trevi fountain. The history of that fountain goes back to Nicholas V's ambitious program of urban renewal. With the assistance of Leon Battista Alberti, he renovated and restored the Trevi fountain as the terminus and principal urban display of the Acqua Vergine in 1453. It is difficult to determine precisely the results of Alberti's intervention, for between 1641 and 1643, Bernini, who had been appointed architect of the Acqua Vergine in 1629, razed the Renaissance fountain and many houses standing behind the site of the old fountain in order to make room for his monumental display. It was never completed and for almost a century the undistinguished appearance stimulated the imagination of successive popes and generations of artists.

Soon after his election on 12 July 1730, Clement ordered a competition (*concorso*) for designing the Trevi fountain. This *concorso* took place almost simultaneously with that for the Lateran facade; it was won by Alessandro Galilei. The Roman architectural establishment was so angry that this plum went to a Florentine that the pope appointed a secret congregation to handle the Trevi competition in a less public fashion. After a complicated decision-making process that took more than two years, Nicola Salvi's design was chosen, probably to pacify the native Roman school of which Salvi was a younger representative. Salvi's architecture constituted an acceptable compromise between the reforming style of the Tuscan architects, especially Galilei, favored by the Corsini and the tradition of late baroque classicism espoused by the Roman architectural profession. Because of a conflict with the Conti family, relatives of the previous pope Innocent XIII, a typical instance of strife between rival papal families which was so rife in Rome, there was

[22] Giuntella, *Roma nel Settecento*, 108; Roberto Pane, *Ferdinando Fuga* (Naples, 1956), 14–56; Portoghesi, *Roma barocca*, 2:807–14; De Rinaldis, *L'arte in Roma*, 50–52; Anthony Blunt, "Architecture," in *The Golden Age of Naples. Art and Civilization under the Bourbons, 1734–1805* (2 vols.; Detroit and Chicago, 1981), 1:35–36, 41.

another delay before the work could finally start in 1734. Two years later the imposing facade, including the central niche and the two lateral wings, stood complete, but the sculpture, the central group of which was entrusted to Giovanni Battista Maini, still had to be installed. When Clement XII died, he left 40,000 scudi to finish the work. The task was entrusted to Benedict XIV who, conscious of the papal government's financial position, neither initiated an ambitious building program nor welcomed the heritage of unfinished monuments passed on to him. On 24 August 1743, in the presence of this reluctant pope, the waters of the Acqua Vergine were allowed to flow again into the newly finished basin.

Meanwhile Salvi was overtaken by a crippling paralysis, which brought about his death in 1751, followed a year later by that of Maini. After another long hiatus work was resumed with the accession of Clement XIII in 1758 under the direction of Gian Paolo Panini's son, Giuseppe. Several new sculptors were engaged; among these Pietro Bracci was responsible for the central sculptural group, including the Oceanus figure, and Filippo Della Valle carved the allegorical statues occupying the lateral niches. At last, on 22 May 1762, everything was ready for the final inauguration.[23]

As we noted in the Introduction, Salvi had created a distinctively pagan theme for his design; nothing less than the role of water as the primary animating principle of all nature, both in its benign as in its destructive form. At the same time he created grand theater in stone, not unlike the contemporary operatic composition of his fellow Arcadian, Metastasio.[24]

While all this public building activity was going on, very few major ecclesiastical edifices were put up. The most important projects were generally completions of what the previous age had planned or carried forward. In part this absence of church building may be accounted for by the increasing shortage of financial resources. But the decline cannot be wholly divorced from the exhaustion of the Tridentine zeal and its attendant diminution of devotion. It is perhaps not without significance that most of the projects focused on new facades. The facades could be interpreted as creating the backdrop to the theater of the city and the desire to improve the urban landscape in order to make it more attractive to the new type of tourist.

The series of great eighteenth-century church restoration opened with the rebuilding of the ancient basilica of SS. Apostoli in 1702. It gave Francesco Fontana, the son of Carlo, his first important professional opportunity after having worked in the shadow of his father. The new church, while retaining the dimensions of the old church which had fallen into a state of dilapidation, preserved nothing of

[23] Portoghesi, *Roma barocca*, 2:829–38; Costanza Gradara, *Pietro Bracci, scultore romano, 1700–1773* (Milan, 1920), 76–79; Mario Rinaldi, *Due secoli di musica al Teatro Argentina* (2 vols.; Florence, 1978), 1:142; Gabetti, "Architettura italiana del Settecento," 679–80; B. N. Ro., Fondo Vittorio Emanuele, ms. 580; Pinto, *Trevi Fountain*, 28–61, 98, 121–89, 248–49; Antonino Santangelo, "La scultura," in *Il Settecento a Roma. Mostra a Roma, 19 marzo – 31 maggio, 1959* (Rome, 1959), 35–37; Fokker, *Roman Baroque Art*, 1:323–26. [24] Pinto, *Trevi Fountain*, 166–68, 223–24, 234.

the old fabric, but rather constituted a variant on the model of S. Giovanni de' Fiorentini and Sant'Ignazio.[25]

But some of the greatest ecclesiastical commisions of the century were carried out during the pontificate of Clement XII and went to the two Tuscan architects whom the Corsini pope had called to Rome. Discussion about a new facade for St. John Lateran had started at the end of 1699, the year that Cardinal Benedetto Pamphilj had become archpriest of the basilica. The previous plans by Borromini had been lost, providing a new challenge to architects. The cardinal, who had amply endowed his church with statuary and, in 1729, a new portal, had as early as 1714 proposed a bond issue to meet the expenses for the new facade and, when it was launched, contributed handsomely to it. In 1732 a competition was held and, among the 23 architects who entered, the jury chose Alessandro Galilei. A former architect to the grand duke of Tuscany, he had spent some years in England, where he had become a disciple of Christopher Wren and John Vanbrugh, before he arrived in Rome. The result of his experience can be traced in the very beautiful facade of the Lateran basilica.

The monumental facade with the loggia was an attempt to synthesize two very different stylistic approaches: in this we find both Galilei's merit and limitations. There is little doubt that his solution is one of the most classical statements of the eighteenth century and reveals a style thoroughly developed by way of *neo-cinquecentismo* and Michelangelo. This splendid bit of architecture, which fused grandeur and a harmonious variety of effects, presents us with a charming recovery of classical rhythms until we arrive at the gigantic terminal balustrade with the enormous statues, each 7 m tall, dominated by the Christ Blessing in the center. It was precisely this last concept, still in the baroque tradition – it was suggested by Cardinal Albani, who was concerned with fitting the work into the existing Roman milieu – that allowed Galilei to crown his masterpiece with a picturesque theme. So the two trends in eighteenth-century architecture, classical aspirations and baroque pictorialism, are displayed in one and the same piece of work, in a perfect meeting in which both perform their expressive function without provoking annoying conflicts and stylistic inconsistencies.

Galilei's sensitivity to proportional and stylistic values was also stated with great originality in the facade of another Roman church, S. Giovanni de' Fiorentini, which he took in hand in 1734. The beautiful facade with its two orders of Corinthian colonnades marks the end of the long and complex building history of the church for which Michelangelo himself had drawn up the plans, but which were later lost. In the seventeenth century, Carlo Maderno and his colleagues took up the

[25] Golzio, *Palazzi romani dalla rinascita*, 16–17; Portoghesi, *Roma barocca*, 2:731–32, 757–64; Mariani, *Le chiese di Roma dal XVII al XVIII secolo*, 172–73. For an extended treatment of the ecclesiastical building program of Clement XI see Christopher M. S. Johns, "The Art Patronage of Pope Clement XI Albani and the Paleochristian Revival in Early Eighteenth Century Rome" (Unpublished dissertation. University of Delaware, June 1985). Johns' thorough treatment tends to overemphasize the religious motivation of Clement's work at the expense of his more secular preoccupations.

3 The facade of S. Maria Maggiore, by Ferdinando Fuga

work; but the facade for which the Florentine lilies and Medician emblems had been sculpted in the sixteenth century by Simone Mosca had to wait another century to be planned and finally built.[26]

Like all major architects of those years, the other Tuscan, Fuga, had taken part in the competition for the facade of St. John Lateran, the commission of which went to Galilei. He was, however, to be compensated by executing another major ecclesiastical work, the new facade of Santa Maria Maggiore. The year after his election, Benedict XIV, although generally critical of spending money on ecclesiastical construction,[27] wanted to give a new arrangement to the facade of the

[26] Mariani, *Le chiese di Roma dal XVII al XVIII secolo*, 182–88; Portoghesi, *Roma barocca*, 2:843–46; Escher, *Barock und Klassizismus*, 46, 133–35; Montalto, *Un mecenate in Roma barocca*, 434–46; Arnaud, *L'Académie de Saint-Luc à Rome*, 58–59; Gabetti, "Architettura italiana del Settecento," 680; ASR, Camerale II, antichità e belle arti, busta 3, fasc. 123.

[27] Morelli (ed.), *Lettere di Benedetto XIV*, 2:321 (14 October 1750).

basilica and thereby bring to a conclusion the protracted building process of this venerable edifice which dated back to the time of Sixtus III. Throughout the seventeenth century the ancient structure was being surrounded by new buildings. Now Fuga, in what proved to be his masterpiece, had the task of finishing the plans first envisioned by Paul V of producing a view worthy of this revered goal of pilgrimages and processions. The problem that Fuga faced was to make the portico tie together the more recent lateral additions with the principal facade. At the same time he was required to preserve the existing mosaics by Filippo Rusuti on the outside wall. At the cost of 82,232.46 scudi he arrived at a solution, which consisted of creating the balcony of blessing and the two symmetrical portals. The work was finished in 1743.[28]

The last of the series of major restorations of basilicas, that of S. Croce in Gerusalemme, has sometimes been described as the swan song of Roman baroque architecture. The ancient church, on the east side across from St. John Lateran, housed the relics thought to have been brought back by St. Helena from her journey to the Holy Land. It had experienced radical changes throughout the Middle Ages and the Renaissance until it acquired its present-day aspect. The work was entrusted to the Sicilian Domenico Gregorini, a student of the famed Filippo Juvara. Gregorini associated in this work a fellow-countryman of his, Pietro Passalacque, who until that time had only a modest achievement to his credit. The most important part of the restoration was without doubt the facade tied organically to a large elliptical porch. To counterbalance the smaller dimensions of this church in relation to the large basilica across the square the architects sought to ensure a certain independence by following the lines of Borromini.[29]

In 1764–65, Giambattista Rezzonico was appointed grand prior of the order of Malta. He asked Giovanni Battista Piranesi, already renowned for his etchings of classical and contemporary Rome, to transform the church of the Priorate on the Aventine and lay out the villa and the small piazza in front of it. The church of the Priorato, of sixteenth-century origin, was a modest structure made up of an empty rectangle with internal niches at the sides according to a popular Renaissance scheme and an apse at the end. Piranesi retained the existing outline, but converted it to a building in a transitional style. In the facade, the pediment of which was destroyed during alterations, Piranesi's classical aspirations of Venetian and Palladian origins, the sharp and elegant treatment of lines, so opposed to the baroque, asserted themselves. But whereas Galilei had achieved a harmonious

[28] Pane, *Fuga*, 84–92; Mariani, *Le chiese di Roma dal XVII al XVIII secolo*, 194–96; Portoghesi, *Roma barocca*, 2:807, 821–25; De Rinaldis, *L'arte in Roma*, 53; Arnaud, *L'Académie de Saint-Luc à Rome*, 60–61; Pastor, *Geschichte der Päpste*, 16, pt 1:112–13; Carl Justi, *Winckelmann und seine Zeitgenossen* (3 vols.; 5th ed.; Cologne, 1956), 2:185; ASR, Camerale 1, fabbriche, busta 1555.

[29] Escher, *Barock und Klassizismus*, 135–36; Mariani, *Le chiese di Roma dal XVII al XVIII secolo*, 196–99; Portoghesi, *Roma barocca*, 2:769–77.

compromise between Roman baroque and classical nostalgia, in Piranesi they still tend to do battle.[30]

With the pontificate of Clement XII the short period of ecclesiastical building in Rome had reached its apogee. Of course, a number of small private commissions, of which the church of the Priorato was perhaps the most important, were still executed. In general, however, lack of funds and other interests and preoccupations diverted the attention of the subsequent popes from improving the image of the city. Benedict XIV's concerns with the papacy's international standing and the threatening budget crisis, Clement XIII's preoccupation with the century's worst food crisis,[31] which began just as Piranesi's Priorato was being built, and the conflict with the Bourbon governments that ended with the suppression of the Jesuits, a conflict that dragged on through the reigns of Clement XIII and Clement XIV, took priority in the minds of these popes. But, above all, such interests as they had was turned from the physiognomy of the capital and toward its archeological patrimony, an interest that very much coincided with the spirit that prevailed in the last decades of the century.

Consonant with that interest the major building work of Clement XIV's pontificate was the Vatican museum of classical antiquities, later the Museo Pio-Clementino, for which Michelangelo Simonetti was chosen as architect in 1771. On his death in 1787 he was succeeded by Giuseppe Camporesi. The vast hall of the museum was to be the first evidence of the forms and formal elements of ancient buildings. The design by Simonetti and Camporesi demonstrates an uncertainty of style in terms of decoration. Certain parts, Camporesi's Hall of Muses and the statue court of the Belvedere with its pilasters and Ionic pillars wreathed in garlands, were still in the traditional style. The Rotunda, on the other hand, gave Simonetti an opportunity to imitate the dome of the Pantheon. Simonetti's overall achievement is remarkable; yet his work cannot be said to accord in all points with the neoclassical language which had come into vogue by that date.[32]

Only during the time of Pius VI do we note a limited revival of building. In his belated, and what turned out to be ruinous, endeavour to revive the glory of the Renaissance, this pope began work in 1778 on building the sacristy of St. Peter's with Carlo Marchionni as architect. Since the time of Alexander VII there had been talk of erecting this needed edifice, which sixteenth-century planners had placed to the left side of the basilica. But it was not until 1715 that a public competition for plans was first held and the young Filippo Juvara, then in Rome, was declared the

[30] De Rinaldis, *L'arte in Roma*, 56–58; Mariani, *Le chiese di Roma dal XVII al XVIII secolo*, 234–38; Escher, *Barock und Klassizismus*, 84–85. [31] See Chapter 7.

[32] Carlo Ceschi, *Le chiese di Roma dagli inizi del neoclassico al 1961* (Bologna, 1963), 28; Louis Hautecoeur, *Rome et la renaissance de l'antiquité à la fin du XVIIIe siècle* (Paris, 1912), 130–32; Jonathan Scott, *Piranesi* (New York, 1975), 222; Wolfgang Liebenwein, "Der Portikus Clemens' XI. und sein Statuenschmuck," 104.

winner. Thereafter other plans were developed, especially during the pontificate of Clement XII. Yet it took until 1776 before Pius VI chose from among the different plans that by Carlo Marchionni.

The work entailed huge expenses and a large amount of demolition, but Marchionni was able to give his structure a remarkable functionality, and an elegant balance of elements. For the sacristy actually consisted of two buildings with different functions, the sacral part, that is the sacristy proper, and a six-story residential building, which contained the living quarters and offices of the chapter of St. Peter's. Although each part had its own roof and facade, Marchionni may take credit for the skill in combining both segments into an organic whole in its external appearance.

The building, which was completed in 1784, by which time the neoclassical revival had asserted itself, has sometimes been dismissed as a dreary and confused work, which had no other merit than that of a transitional structure between baroque and Renaissance classicism that failed to meet expectations. In fairness to Marchionni it should be said that he was less concerned about conforming to the changes of style that were going on around him than in retaining the freedom to select the style that most suited his individual taste or the character of his subject. Much of the coolness with which the work has been received may be attributed to the fact that it arose alongside the masterpieces of Bramante and Michelangelo, with which it could not bear comparison. But viewed as a building separate from the Vatican basilica, it seems a refined jewel box.[33] Its cost, however, would add significantly to the crushing burden of debt that weighted down the papal government in the last years of the ancien regime.

Pius VI was the last of the pontiffs to build a family palace on a grandiose scale. By some counts there were as many as 337 palaces in the city. But, beside the Palazzi Altieri, Borghese, Chigi, Colonna, Farnese, Fiano, Pamphilj, Ruspoli, and Sciarra, monumental buildings that remained virtually unchanged in the families whose names they bore, there were no more than sixty which appear to have been made for residences of nobles rather than commoners. Within the Roman context the importance of these palaces lies in the role they played in town planning. Inasmuch as their construction was preceded by a kind of reclamation of the area, destroying slums and hovels, eliminating evil-smelling alleys, opening up spaces and squares,

[33] Johns, "Art Patronage of Pope Clement XI Albani," 187–90; Rudolf Berliner, "Zeichnungen von Carlo und Filippo Marchionni," *Münchner Jahrbuch der Bildenden Kunst* (1958–59), 281–82, 285, 368, 395 n. 98; Mattia Loret, "Attività ignota di Filippo Juvara a Roma," *Critica d'Arte* (1936), 200–201. Escher, *Barock und Klassizismus*, 37, 46, 85–86; Mariani, *Le chiese di Roma dal XVII al XVIII secolo*, 216–17; Portoghesi, *Roma barocca*, 2:753, 860; Ceschi, *Le chiese di Roma dagli inizi del neoclassico*, 28; B. CORS., ms. no. 1173, ff. 2–10; Gabetti, "Architettura italiana del Settecento," 682.

the new palaces renovated entire quarters, greatly improving the esthetic appeal, without, however, obeying any preordained urban plan.[34]

Just as the financial constraints curtailed expenditure on public and ecclesiastical buildings during the ancien regime, so they affected the incomes of many aristocratic families. Consequently very few new palazzi were put up. There were some, of course; Alessandro Specchi, for instance, built the De Carolis palace on the Corso. More often old palaces were renovated or given new facades.

One of the best examples of the latter is the Palazzo Corsini. In 1736 Cardinal Neri Corsini, nephew of Clement XII, commissioned Fuga with transforming and enlarging the fifteenth-century Palazzo Riario in the Lungara, once the residence of Queen Christina of Sweden; the cardinal planned to set up his picture gallery and extensive library in the new building. The need to preserve a good part of the old Renaissance structure, which had already more or less determined the relationship between the external surfaces, was a heavy encumbrance for the architect. By accepting the old divisions facing the Via Lungara as they existed, Fuga was limited in his choices. He simply repeated his motif of plastic projections for each which produced a rather monotonous serialization. He had more success with the rear portion with its broad green area extending to the slope of the Gianicolo. In contrast to the front view there was the grandiose effect of the internal space, from the tripartite vestibule to the staircase. On crossing the entrance the visitor is struck by a complex of pilasters, arches, and vaults strictly tied together and symmetrical, into which light penetrates from the bottom and the sides. Thus the internal arrangement of the palace met the principal requirements for convenience and lighting.[35]

If the Corsini palace is an indicator that the spirit of nepotism had not been fully extinguished, the Palazzo Braschi proclaimed it more boldly. In 1790 Pius VI acquired the rundown Palazzo Santobono in the Piazza Navona by the statute of Pasquino at an estimated cost of 60,000 scudi and converted it with a *neo-cinquecentismo* facade into a residence for his nephew, Luigi Onesti-Braschi. But at this point the shadow of the French Revolution was already hanging over the papal capital and the history of the building really belongs to the next age.[36]

Not all people in Rome lived in palazzi, although some of these palaces sheltered a large number and great variety of them. The outstanding example is the Farnese palace, whose average population in the eighteenth century was around 80. From

[34] BL, Egerton ms. 2798, chap. 7; Vicchi, *Vincenzo Monti. Le lettere e la politica in Italia dal 1750 al 1820 (Trienno 1778–80)* (Fusignano, 1885), 60–61; Charles de Brosses, *Le Président De Brosses en Italie. Lettres familières écrites d'Italie en 1739 et 1740* (Paris, 1861), 2:10–11; Golzio, *Palazzi romani dalla rinascita*, 19.

[35] Portoghesi, *Roma barocca*, 2:819–21; Escher, *Barock und Klassizismus*, 49.

[36] ASR, Miscellanea famiglia, busta 30, fasc. 14.

1735 to 1775 it was as high as 143.[37] Although accurate statistics are hard to come by, one source claimed that there were about 36,000 dwellings in eighteenth-century Rome; each was not necessarily a house, of course.[38] Very few genuinely medieval houses had survived. Those that did were narrow, low, and comparatively deep. Their street front was rarely wider than 5 m, their height at the most two or three low stories, 8 m or so, all told, on lots sometimes as small as 10.6 sq. m. Their facades might be nondescript with but a door on the ground floor. Not infrequently a porch or portico carried by columns – spoils were plentiful among the ruins – took up as much as half the depth of the ground floor. As time passed, adjoining houses bought up by more affluent owners were fused into a single complex, linking connecting doorways and stairs, notwithstanding the difference in height and floor level.[39]

The buildings in Rome were generally very solid, because the volcanic soil provided a firm foundation. And there was an abundance of building materials. The favorite stone of the Romans, like that of their ancient forebears, was travertine from Tivoli, an ivory-colored limestone of very fine grain; soft when first mined in the quarry, it soon became very hard, weather resistant, and capable of bearing heavy loads. Another stone, called *peperino*, greyish-brown or ashen-colored depending upon its provenance, was less beautiful, less homogeneous, more porous than travertine, but it was also very much employed in the great buildings and cost less. In composition it was a form of modified volcanic tufa, drawn from the seams on the Via Appia. Other stones of volcanic origin and inferior quality were also used at different times in Roman buildings. For decorative or statuary uses basalt, granite, and porphyry, coming from as far away as Greece and Egypt, although most of it stripped from older ruins, were preferred. Marble, when it was imported at all, came from Carrara. Since the end of the ancient republic the Romans used brick only for exceptional purposes. In the finest buildings it was employed for outer facings. Tiles were of excellent quality thanks to the seams of white and red clay behind the Vatican.

Lime was the primary auxiliary building material. Much of it was of good quality and was obtained from the white semi-crystalline limestone, *palombino*, found in the mountains of Tivoli and Palestrina, and the Aniene valley. During and after the Renaissance, however, much lime came from ancient buildings and monuments. But by the middle of the seventeenth century (1658) most lime came from outside the gates and standards of weight, price, and provenance were being set in Rome. Some time in the eighteenth century it was estimated that the normal consumption of lime amounted to about 50,000 loads a year, each load weighing 133.2 kg and

37 Geneviève Michel, "Vie quotidienne au Palais Farnèse (XVIIe – XVIIIe siècle)," in Ecole française de Rome (ed.), *Le Palais Farnèse* (2 vols.; Rome, 1981), 2:551.

38 Andrieux, *Daily Life in Papal Rome*, 51.

39 Richard Krautheimer, *Rome, Profile of a City, 312–1308* (Princeton, N.J. 1980), 293–94; Delumeau, *Vie économique et sociale de Rome*, 1:284–86; Montesquieu, *Voyages. Oeuvres complètes*, 2:1102; Tornézy, *Bergeret et Fragonard*, 146–47; Philippe Petit-Radel, *Voyage historique, chorographique, et philosophique dans les principales villes de l'Italie en 1811 et 1812* (2 vols.; Paris 1815), 2:529–30.

costing 60 scudi; 40,000 of these loads were used by masons, the rest went to tanners, whitewashers, and others. In place of sand, Romans used pozzolana, gravel of volcanic origin, often reddish-brown in color, which was found in plenty both inside the city and the surrounding countryside.[40]

The process of replacing the one-family unit with the tenement house with its many floors accelerated toward the end of the seventeenth century and produced in certain spots a pronounced increase in the density of residential dwellings. Trastevere was one such location, where in some parishes it resulted in the paradox of overcrowding and empty flats. The vacant dwellings were due to the poor, underemployed inhabitants being unable to pay their rent. This was confirmed by the report of an architect who was commissioned by the Apostolic Chamber in 1744 to evaluate the state of housing in the Trasteverine parish of S. Salvatore a Ponte Rotto. He established that less than half of the rental dwellings were occupied and that rooms for the most part were inhabited by poor folks, from whom one could never demand nor expect that they pay their rents and remain solvent. On the other hand, we have the phenomenon of dwellings filled with totally unrelated persons; the only thing these had in common was their will to survive. Such nuclei were usually formed by widows or recent immigrants, who, faced with financial difficulties, tended to crowd together for mutual support.[41]

In general rents were moderate in comparison to the cost of food and even to income. In modest dwellings they came to a little above 10 baiocchi per room a month. But to the poor struggling Roman it was just the last burden and frequently remained unpaid. In San Salvatore the rent for a two-room apartment, with an area of about 41 sq. m on the second floor with access by way of an outside staircase, was 30 baiocchi monthly, making it 3.60 scudi a year. Two rooms with a direct entrance from the street, together with a store and a cellar, came to 12 scudi annually. Rents, however, varied usually not on the basis of rooms, but rather the location of the house and floor, even within the same neighborhood. Yet any attempt at arriving at a sure estimate is frustrated by the fact that, in keeping with the Roman spirit of charity, rents were sometimes remitted or reduced because of hardship.

Although the population density in Rome increased from 283.5 people per sq. km in 1701 to 325.3 in 1782 and the population outstripped the rate for building new units, the rents remained fairly steady until 1789. Those that the Doria Pamphilj family drew from a house in the Salita di Marforio between 1763 and 1789 enable us to document this stability. The annual rent for two rooms on the second floor (the

40 Gioacchino De Angelis d'Ossat, "Materiali da costruzione in Roma e nel Lazio," in Federico Millosevich (ed.), *Le scienze fisiche e biologiche in Roma e nel Lazio* (Rome, 1933), 126–29, 133–35; Delumeau, *Vie économique et sociale de Rome*, 1:286–88; Petit-Radel, *Voyage historique*, 2:35–36; Joseph Jérôme de Lalande, *Voyage d'un françois en Italie, fait dans les années 1765 et 1766* (8 vols.; Paris, 1786), 5:51–52; ASR, Camerale II, arti e mestieri, busta 25.

41 Anna Lepre, "Agricoltura e manifattura in un rione di Roma nel seicento e nel settecento," *Studi Romani*, 25 (1977), 366–68; Portoghesi, *Roma barocca*, 1:87–89; Vicchi, *Vincenzo Monti (1778–1780)*, 44.

Roman *primo piano*) of this superior residence came to 24 scudi; there were apparently six rooms available on that floor. The third floor also went for 24 scudi. It has been suggested that the reason for the stability of these moderate rents was to be found in the fact that unfurnished property in Rome was to a large extent in the hands of religious institutions. These, having need for a steady cash income, rather than sell the houses preferred to rent them out on long, or even permanent, leases. Hence the rents for these leases stayed even when prices rose. Their rent then served to establish a kind of maximum ceiling for other landlords.[42]

Some tenants appear to have been very recalcitrant in their payments. A certain Franco Vicolani, who moved into two rooms on the second floor of the house in the Salita di Marforio on January 1786, two years later owed 22.55 scudi. No wonder he disappeared without trace and an order of payment went out for him. Francesco Conti, a tenant since 1763 on the third floor for 24 scudi a year, moved out on 3 September 1778, owing back rent for 96.20 scudi. A law suit was pending. This habit of not paying rent reached up the ranks: a Viterbese nobleman, Conte Tobia Fani Ciotti, was 192.52 scudi in arrears for a house in the Piazza Morgana belonging to the Doria Pamphilj in which he lived between 1788 and 1793. Some *sbirri* were sent after him to Toscanella, until his wife paid up in *cedole*, worthless no doubt. So accustomed had the landlord become to this practice that he made a special note when one of his tenants, a certain Baldassare Massa, paid regularly.[43]

Not all movement in the city, however, involved absconding debtors. There is some evidence to demonstrate considerable elasticity of residence. Although the permanent influx of people to Rome in the eighteenth century did not create new nuclei of habitation from a topographical point of view, a study of the areas around the Piazza di San Lorenzo in Lucina, and the Via Ripetta and Via Macelli within the parish of S. Lorenzo in Lucina, the most populous in Rome, for the years 1750–55, 1765–70, and 1785–90, shows that the annual mobility of families averaged 30 percent of the total. Over a five-year period this came to between 60 and 70 percent. Admittedly these variations were very great, probably because of the density of the area. But in the parish of S. Maria in Monticelli, the resident population renewed itself wholly or almost so every ten years between 1720 and 1800. The reasons for the move of what appear to have been primarily nuclear families from one residence to another, whether within the same parish or to another, is difficult to determine. It may be due to a weak economic structure, whereby families in search of work moved closer to where they believed better opportunities existed. At least, it would seem this was the case with physicians and surgeons. In the parish of S. Maria in Traspontina it is rare that one lived more than ten years in the same house, while

[42] Friz, *Consumi, tenore di vita e prezzi*, 121; Claudio Schiavoni and Eugenio Sonnino, "Popolazione e territorio nel Lazio, 1701–1811," in Società italiana di demografia storica, *La popolazione italiana nel Settecento* (Bologna, 1979), 221.

[43] Lepre, "Agricoltura e manifattura in un rione," 368–70; ADP, Roma, amministrazione, busta 89.16.2 and 5, and busta 89.22.

frequently they stayed no longer than two years. Between 1720 and 1810 only 7 percent of the physicians remained more than ten years, 13 percent more than five years and the other 80 percent changed residence within three years. Possibly the closeness of the hospital of Santo Spirito accounted for a merely temporary stay during their internship or apprenticeship.[44]

Rome's building history in this period reflects its general evolution during the post-Tridentine period. The early years indicate a measure of continuity from the previous age; but a distinct change in direction toward catering primarily for the city's secular needs occurred, which was accompanied by a blurring of the vision of what the city represents. By mid-century financial and other woes finally put an end even to this limited process. Admittedly, Clement XII and, at even greater cost, Pius VI tried to reverse the trend. Their efforts, while enhancing the appearance of parts of the city, only contributed to its further exhaustion. The change did not seem to affect the ordinary citizens immediately. They had already been deprived of the most important instrument for determining their city's future, access to a self-governing magistracy. The continuing expansion of the temporal papal power had not halted before the Aurelian wall.

[44] Fiocca, "Struttura urbane e controllo sociale," 383–84, 387.

2

# The government: state and city

In the past decades a polite polemic has been carried on between those historians, Jean Delumeau and Paolo Prodi among them, who see in the development and consolidation of the Papal States in early modern times a process analogous to what occurred in other Italian and European states, and those, like Mario Caravale, who note instead a strong resistance to such development marked by the persistence of local divisions, the privileges of the little annexed states and various communities and the failure of an emergence of an indigenous lay ruling class.[1]

The reason behind these differing views is the fact that there really was not one Papal State but, as the English rendering put it, there were the Papal States, each unit of which was governed differently. In 1766 the contiguous temporal domains of the church consisted of thirteen provinces, extending from the duchy of Ferrara and the Bolognese in the north to Lazio and Marittima in the south; to these must be added the papal enclaves of Benevento and Pontecorvo within Neapolitan territory and Avignon and the Comtat Venaissin in France.

Most of these provinces had their own local traditions and administrations, depending upon the circumstances under which they became part of the papal territory. The Romagna, Umbria, and the duchy of Urbino, which had only been annexed in 1631 at the death of its last duke, each had a legate at the head of its provincial administration, as did the Marches of Ancona, which also had their own system of laws. There was a cardinal legate at Ferrara, and the duchy had an ambassador in Rome until about 1738. Probably the most extreme case of devolution was Bologna. The city and its immediate surroundings cherished a long and strong republican and anticurial tradition, which went back to Renaissance times. This republicanism was embodied by the senate established by Julius II in 1507. In fact, at the start of the eighteenth century there was even a movement to secede, which faded when the city's autonomy was fully acknowledged by Popes Clement XII and Benedict XIV. The constitutional arrangement resembled a dyarchy, where the senate, controlled by a narrow oligarchic group, corporately wielded the actual power, whereas the pope as the constitutional head became the guarantor of the constitutional balance. Only the personal union of a common

[1] Delumeau, *Vie économique et sociale de Rome*; Prodi, *Il sovrano pontifice*; Mario Caravale and Alberto Caracciolo, *Lo Stato pontificio da Martino V a Pio IX* (Turin, 1978).

sovereign, the pope, bound the city to the Papal States. Its separateness was symbolically underlined by the completion of the road linking the city with Florence in 1762. Henceforth Bologna was bound commercially and intellectually to Tuscany and the north rather than to Rome.[2]

To complicate matters, all legations and provinces were interspersed with baronial fiefs and *castelli*, each with its own jurisdiction, and with free municipalities or communities exercising their ancient papal or imperial privileges. One of the main tasks of the papal government, therefore, was to preserve the difficult equilibrium between centralization and local autonomy. It appears that during the first forty years of the eighteenth century the competences of the central congregations, the courts, the taxing authorities, all of which made up the Roman curia in the administrative and judicial sphere, were increasing. But this was more the result of outward contingencies than of conscious, well-ordered planning. Yet this centralization often only concealed some of the more pronounced differences in the economic and political conditions among the various parts of the Papal States.[3]

Another peculiarity of the Papal States has to be kept in mind before we can proceed to a study of the constitution and central institutions of this unique polity. In theory, canon law was the law in the juridical order of the state, a law whose primary purpose was the salvation of souls and whose intent was to subordinate, in the arrangement of its diverse public and private institutions, material to spiritual ends. This notion had been explicitly confirmed in many official documents since 1567.[4] Although some of this missionary fervor had abated by the close of the seventeenth century, the strong tie between church and state with its inherent contradictions, this mixture of spiritual and temporal power, would over a prolonged period become a very great obstacle to the successful evolution of an absolute state and a concerted effort at thoroughgoing reform.[5]

This and other reasons given below will make the papacy in the period of the ancien regime seem less like the absolutism that we normally associate with a monarchy of the type Louis XIV had established. Pope Benedict XIV once joked: "The pope commands, the cardinals do not obey, and the people do what they

[2] Paolo Colliva, "Bologna dal XIV al XVIII secolo: 'governo misto' o signoria senatoria?" in Aldo Berselli (ed.), *Storia della Emilia Romagna* (Bologna, 1977), 22–31; Alfeo Giacomelli, "Carlo Grassi e le riforme bolognesi del Settecento. 1: L'età lambertiniana." *Quaderni culturali bolognesi*, 3 (1979), 5, 37–38; Luigi Dal Pane, *Economia e società a Bologna nell'età del Risorgimento. Introduzione alla ricerca* (Bologna, 1969), 344–45; Giovanni Ricci, *Bologna* (Rome and Bari, 1980), 113; Maria Valeria Cristoferi, "Fieri e mercati," in Aldo Berselli (ed.), *Storia della Emilia Romagna* (Bologna, 1977), 184–85.

[3] Lalande, *Voyage d'un françois en Italie*, 3:15–17; Caravale and Caracciolo, *Lo Stato pontificio*, 450, 457, 536.

[4] Giovanni Ancarani, "A proposito del movimento culturale riformatore settecentesco nello Stato Pontificio," *Jus*, N.S. 13 (1962), 475–76.

[5] Enrico Stumpo, *Il capitale finanziario a Roma fra cinque e seicento. Contributo alla storia della fiscalità pontificia in età moderna (1570–1660)*. (Milan, 1985), 22; Luigi Dal Pane, *Lo Stato Pontificio e il movimento riformatore del Settecento* (Milan, 1959), 85–86.

wish." Beneath the obviously humorous overstatement, this remark showed an astute assessment of the conditions existing in his day. The Papal States had clearly not been immune to the general tendency of the Italian states to move toward absolutist centralized rule. Paolo Prodi had recently demonstrated that in his *Il sovrano pontificie*. But the earlier diagnosis by the French historian Louis Madelin of Rome as an aristocratic republic fallen into an ineffectual despotism comes closer to reality. Originally the Sacred College of cardinals, an electoral and governmental body, made the Papal States a kind of aristocratic republic at the head of which a chief elected for life, the pope, reigned by delegation. For quite some time, however, the college of cardinals had virtually ceased to claim its erstwhile rights of deliberation and control, except on occasions when the cardinals felt their special interests as a group were threatened. Indeed, some cardinals, candidates for the tiara themselves, hoping to profit one day from the papal power, let it willingly expand and consolidate.

Nevertheless there were built-in safeguards against any plenary absolutism by the pope. For one thing the temporal power rested on feeble props: the army was a caricature, the police was frequently an object of mockery and disdain, the system of law enforcement was chancy. All of this produced a certain degree of anarchy and confusion.

The popes were also hampered by the dual nature of their office. The solicitude of being the vicar of the merciful Christ, even on the earthly throne, put the pope under the obligation of gentleness, which sometimes provoked him to mitigate in practice the rigors he had put into the law.[6]

Added to this was the debilitating effect of the conflicting triple goals of papal policy: the pope's duties as the spiritual head of the Catholic world, his effective power as a ruler of a small Italian state, and his private and family predilections; the financial burden of all of which had to be borne almost wholly out of the revenues from his modest territory.[7] The sum of all this was, as Montesquieu observed when visiting Rome, that the popes had more authority outside their state than within. "The vicar of Christ is very great and the prince is very small."[8]

Actually Montesquieu ignored the serious erosion in papal authority and prestige in the course of the eighteenth century outside the borders of the Papal States. It started with a diplomatic faux-pas by Clement XI. While the conclave electing Clement was still in progress, Philip of Anjou claimed the Spanish throne in accordance with the will of Charles II of Spain. The new pope responded by

[6] Stuart Woolf, *A History of Italy, 1700–1860. The Social Constraints of Political Change* (London, 1979), 63; Louis Madelin, *La Rome de Napoléon. La domination française à Rome de 1809 à 1814* (2nd ed.; Paris, 1906), 46; Andrieux, *Daily Life in Papal Rome*, 25–26.

[7] Delumeau, *Vie économique et sociale de Rome*, 2:843.

[8] Jean-Baptiste de Secondat, Baron Montesquieu, "Voyages," in *Oeuvres complètes de Montesquieu*, under the direction of M. André Masson (Paris, 1950), 2:1103.

sending his congratulations to Philip V on the assumption of his throne in Madrid, an action which understandably was regarded as a partisan and provocative step in Vienna. To deny subsequently the recognition of the kingdom of Naples and Sicily to Philip was not enough to pacify Emperor Leopold I. The incident disqualified the pope and the papacy from acting as impartial mediators between the two most important Catholic ruling families, the Bourbons and the Habsburgs, for virtually the rest of the century, and made the Papal States themselves a theater of military conflict.[9] Evidence for this progressive debilitation is provided by the next major war in Europe, that of the Polish Succession. At its start in 1733, Clement XII proffered his services as mediator in the hope of preventing conflict among Catholic powers, only to find that the papal voice no longer carried much weight in European politics. Indeed, the Papal States, although nominally neutral, were subjected to a series of three invasions by both Spanish and imperial armies even more disastrous than that under Clement XI, while the pope was constantly forced to make concessions, especially to the Bourbons, whose troops appeared in Ostia and Rome. At its conclusion Rome emerged as if it had lost the war.[10] The third and last scourge befell during the War of the Austrian Succession, when the states of the church once more endured the martyrdom of neutrality.[11]

To bring the traditional policy of the papacy more in line with the Europe that had emerged through the struggles and changes of the first half of the eighteenth century, Benedict XIV saw himself obliged to make a number of accommodations, usually in the form of concordats. In 1741 he concluded concordats with Sardinia and Naples, and in 1753 with Spain, while he reached a more tacit agreement with Tuscany. The sum total of these agreements was a recognition on the part of the Roman curia of the regalistic claims within the Catholic states. Economically the result was a clear loss for the already deficit-ridden Papal States, which now could count only upon smaller remittances from abroad.[12]

But the retreat of the popes did not end there. The conflict between Jansenists and Jesuits, which had reached the papal capital before the middle of the century, would turn into a contest between the Catholic powers and the Holy See. After the Jesuits had been expelled from Portugal, the Bourbon powers put pressure on Benedict XIV's successor, Clement XIII, to suppress the order. It became a bitter

[9] Pastor, *Geschichte der Päpste*, 15:14–21; Caravale and Caracciolo, *Lo Stato pontificio*, 458–61, 465; Enggass, *Early Eighteenth-Century Sculpture*, 1:11–12.

[10] Ibid., 1:16; Pastor, *Geschichte der Päpste*, 15:651–61; Caravale and Caracciolo, *Lo Stato pontificio*, 465–66 (in future the work will be credited to Caracciolo only since he wrote the part of the book covering this period); Franco Venturi, *Settecento riformatore*. 1: *Da Muratori a Beccaria* (Turin, 1969), 9–10; Franco Valsecchi, *L'Italia nel Settecento dal 1714 al 1788* (Milan, 1959), 477–81.

[11] Pastor, *Geschichte der Päpste*, 16, pt 1:63, 73–79, 103; Caracciolo, *Lo Stato pontificio*, 457–58; Valsecchi, *Italia nel Settecento*, 481–85; Venturi, *Settecento riformatore*, 1:104–06.

[12] Ibid., 1:111–12; Pastor, *Geschichte der Päpste*, 15:663–71; 16, pt 1:41–53; Emilia Morelli, "Benedetto XIV. Uomo e pontifice," in *Tre Profili* (Rome, 1955), 3–4.

power struggle, in which eventually Clement XIV was coerced to comply in 1773.[13] Thereafter the Catholic powers became the spector that would haunt the pontiffs until the greater danger of the French Revolution overtook them.[14]

With the prestige of the papal authority under attack, there was a temptation among incumbents to promote the interests of the family. Innocent XII's bull *Romanum decet pontificem* of 22 June 1692, which forbad popes to enrich their relatives with the property of the church and suppressed a group of well-endowed offices that had been traditionally held by the *nipoti*, the papal nephews, was to be a step in the right direction and helped to eliminate a source of heavy drain on the papal treasury.[15] Nevertheless there were still ways that some of the pontiffs, such as the Albani pope Clement XI from Urbino, the Florentine Corsini pope Clement XII, the Venetian Rezzonico pope Clement XIII, and, most blatantly of all, the last eighteenth-century pope, Pius VI Braschi, had at their disposal to promote the fortunes of their families and the interests of their compatriots in Rome.[16] Of course, in no case, with the possible exception of Pius VI, could the extent of their nepotism and political patronage be compared to that of earlier pontiffs. The material resources simply were not available. But where other means failed, there were always cardinals' hats to bestow and the family could share in the privileges and authority of the college of cardinals.

In theory, the Sacred College of cardinals was invested with all the administrative powers. Although it has recently been argued, not unjustly, that it had lost the character of a senate at the end of the sixteenth century,[17] there are evidences that, while its regular meetings had disappeared, the cardinals guarded their prerogative jealously. When Benedict XIII summoned the provincial synod of Rome in 1725, to which only the local bishops were invited, a commission of cardinals protested the exclusion of their college. The pope immediately backed down.[18] Normally, however, the cardinals served on special commissions or congregations or held administrative offices, rather than acted as a body. One of the weaknesses of the administration by cardinals was that they performed so many and such different functions in turn that they were never long enough in one office to master its technique and routine. The other was that of actual or potential conflict of interest.

13 B. N. Ro., Fondo Gesuitico, ms. 196, no. 24; B. CORS., ms. 1891, pt 2, f. 305f; ms. 1533, f. 349; Girolamo Amati (ed.), *Alcune lettere dell'abate Antonio Niccolini a Monsignore Giovanni Bottari intorno la corte di Roma, 1724–1761* (Bologna, 1867), 20–21, 23–25; Enrico Dammig, *Il movimento giansenista a Roma nella seconda metà del secolo XVIII* (Vatican City, 1945), 390; Pastor, *Geschichte der Päpste*, 16, pt 2:228–44; Valsecchi, *Italia nel Settecento*, 834–42; Andrieux, *Daily Life in Papal Rome*, 194–96. 14 See Chapter 12.

15 Pastor, *Geschichte der Päpste*, 14, pt 2:1087–89, 1128–29; Petrocchi, *Roma nel Seicento*, 87.

16 Prodi, *Il sovrano pontifice*, 169–85.

17 For example, in 1783 a Rezzonico was cardinal *camerlengo*, and Giovanni Albani held the post of prefect of the annona. Nicola Maria Nicolai, *Memorie, leggi, ed osservazioni sulle campagne e sull'annona di Roma* (3 vols.; Rome, 1803), 1:317.

18 Luigi Fiorani, *Il Concilio Romano del 1725* (Rome, 1977), 38.

Not only did some cardinals have their eye on the papal throne themselves, but others had family connections abroad or represented the interests and were in the pay of foreign powers. For example, Cardinal Federigo Lante was the son of a French princess and had most of his fortune in France.[19] Others acted as protectors of an outside power within the curia. Alessandro Albani was both cardinal protector for the Austrian rulers and, because of his business contacts, represented English Hanoverian interests. His function as protector may have been quite legitimate, but it becomes more questionable when a key papal administrator, the governor of Rome, Cardinal Caprara, is reported in 1767 to have been receiving an annual pension of 1,000 scudi from France with the obvious intention of keeping the French government informed of any intrigues, especially during periods of conclave. It was in those times that the residences of cardinals became the rival centers of power and intrigue, both on behalf of the Catholic powers and for those who were looking for future preferment.[20]

The primary method by which cardinals exercised their share in the temporal power was by their membership in the congregations which had jurisdiction over the affairs of state. These congregations present an almost impenetrable maze to the uninitiated. They frequently complemented and encroached upon each other; some concerns were administered by several congregations collaterally.

The internal administration was chiefly under the jurisdiction of three permanent congregations: the Consulta, the Buon Governo, and the Economica. The Consulta, first set up by Sixtus V and presided over by the secretary of state, was a real council of state and functioned as a sort of collective ministry of the interior, without whose agreement the secretary of state would rarely act. Yet this council was completely deprived of any oversight or administration affecting the city of Rome and its surrounding territories. The power of the Consulta was hemmed in and sometimes opposed by the second congregation, the Buon Governo. It was empowered to regulate and control the administration of the communities, that is, the municipalities in the provinces, on the one hand, and to protect them and individuals against abuses by the Consulta and its agents, on the other. Yet its main functions remained economic. The third congregation, the Economica, a later creation, was the council of finances presided over by the cardinal *camerlengo*. As it was called on to check and, if need be, revise the decisions of the Buon Governo in matters pertaining to the budget of the communities, it constituted a new wheel in this system of a hundred heads where everybody was controlled, thwarted, and entangled. Added to these and other permanent congregations were innumerable

[19] Morelli (ed.), *Lettere di Benedetto XIV*, 1:113 (20 September 1743).

[20] B. N. Ro., Fondo Gesuitico, ms. 1363; Maurice vicomte de Boutry, *Choiseul à Rome. Lettres et memoires inedites, 1754–1757* (Paris, 1895), 278; Laurie Nussdorfer, "City Politics in Baroque Rome, 1623–1644" (Unpublished dissertation. Princeton University, January 1985), 3, 361.

specially commissioned ones, *ad hoc* bodies, busily set up to discuss projects or confront sudden problems.[21]

Below the pope, the two ministers who governed were the cardinal secretary of state and the cardinal camerlengo. Minister of state for foreign affairs by the will of the pope, president by law of the Consulta, and thereby minister of the interior, head of the military organization, intimate counsellor and sometimes the sole confidant of the sovereign with whom he shared lodgings, the secretary of state was, in fact, prime minister. The camerlengo retained no less a share of the authority. He was rarely a creature of the pope, since his position was a lifetime one. During the long interregnum between each pontificate, the *sede vacante*, he managed the conclave, from which charge he derived great moral authority. As hierarchical superior of the treasurer general he was the most influential member of the Apostolic Chamber and the Economica, making him a triple minister of finance, of agriculture, and of commerce and public works. These two ministers, then, adroitly balanced and neutralized each other.[22]

The offices which made up the Apostolic Chamber (Reverenda Camera Apostolica) formed the massive financial organism of the state, which looked after the temporalities. But here again we come across the confused administration. In theory, the camerlengo was the supreme head of the Chamber and the minister of finance; the Economica was the treasury and the Chamber the audit office. In reality, the state's finances, with some important exceptions, were in the hands of one man only: the treasurer general, a distinguished prelate close to receiving the cardinal's hat, who was authorized to bypass the camerlengo and deal with the sovereign on his own about the budget, the imposition of levies, or the advisability of expenditure and the administration of the public debt. The treasurer also had jurisdiction over all offenses pertaining to financial and commercial matters, including usury. Normally, these judicial functions were entrusted to the auditor of the Chamber, who exercised them through assessors. Under Benedict XIV the treasurer general accumulated some other functions as a result of the pope's reform of the accounting system. These reforms created two new – or revised – organs within the Apostolic Chamber, an office of receipt (*depositaria generale*) and an office of audit (*computisteria*) for gathering and drawing up the annual account.[23]

Attached to the Apostolic Chamber were a group of prelates collectively known

[21] Madelin, *Rome de Napoléon*, 50–53; Elio Lodolini, *L'archivio della S. Congregazione del Buon Governo (1592–1847). Inventario* (Rome, 1956), XIII–XV, XIX–XXIV; Delumeau, *Vie économique et sociale de Rome*, 2:617–18; Philippe comte de Tournon-Simiane, *Etudes statistiques sur Rome et la partie occidentale des Etats Romains* (2 vols.; 2nd ed.; Paris, 1855), 2:33–34; Caracciolo, *Lo Stato pontificio*, 451; Valsecchi, *Italia nel Settecento*, 458–59.

[22] Madelin, *Rome de Napoléon*, 49–50; Andrieux, *Daily Life in Papal Rome*, 26–27; David Silvagni, *La corte pontificia e la società romana nei secoli XVIII e XIX* (4 vols.; Rome, 1971), 71–72.

[23] Madelin, *Rome de Napoléon*, 53–54; Armando Lodolini, *L'archivio di Stato di Roma. Epitome di una guida degli archivi dell'administrazione centrale dello Stato pontificio* (Rome, 1960), 177–79; Lalande, *Voyage d'un françois en Italie*, 4:460–62, 468–71; Jacques Casanova de Seingalt, *Histoire de ma vie* (Wiesbaden and Paris 1960–62), 2:242 n. 22.

as the *chierici* of the Chamber. Their existence can be traced back to before 1444, at least. They had been the principal assistants to the camerlengo in the discharge of his temporal duties. With the passing of time, however, the chierici were given individual responsibilities by filling prefectures, presidencies and commissariats. Two such charges, those of the treasurer general and auditor of the Apostolic Chamber we have already noted. Among the most important of the others were those presiding over the *annona*, the principal organ for grain and bread supply in the district of Rome, and the *grascia*, its administrative counterpart for meat and oil. The remaining dealt with roads, water supply, port facilities and river navigation, the mint, prisons, the military, and the archives. Beside them some lesser magistracies were attached to the Chamber, several of which were legal offices.[24]

At one count there were something like a hundred different ministries, each with a regular staff and a mob of lesser functionaries. To this huge crowd must be added the staffs of the papal palaces, the Lateran, Vatican, and Quirinal, who down to the humblest stable boy had official rank. It is impossible to arrive at an exact figure, but by some conjectures this group together with their families amounted to between 70,000 and 80,000, undoubtedly an exaggerated figure, since estimates for the 1840s, when Rome's population was larger, only come to between 40,000 and 45,000, that is, to about 5 to 6 percent of the population. Nevertheless the figure is large enough to crowd the city with place seekers; careerism became the besetting sin of the Roman court, against which such fervent preachers as Paolo della Croce and Leonardo da Porto Maurizio inveighed with little effect. It was carried on quite brazenly.[25]

This crowd of officials was headed and directed by the prelates, between 200 and 250 in number. The prelature was the only way open to the higher echelons in papal government. No consistent study has yet been made of the social composition of this body. In the interval we can only provide some more general impressions on this administrative elite. It had its origin probably among the nobility, greater and lesser, and the more affluent bourgeoisie from all over Italy. The reason for this assumption lies in the fact that they shared a common educational experience. Most of them had attended the colleges or institutions of secondary education founded throughout Italy, including Rome, in the sixteenth and seventeenth centuries by religious orders, Barnabites, Piarists, Scolopians, Oratorians, but above all Jesuits. These colleges had a structured educational program, frequently, although by no means always, based on the Jesuit *Ratio studiorum*. The political content of the pedagogy was rooted in the service of an aristocratic ideology. Its aspiration was to produce the ideal gentleman. At the same time the orders strove to produce an

[24] Leone Vicchi, *Vincenzo Monti (1778–1780)* 103–05; Emmanuel Pierre Rodocanachi, *Les Institutions communales de Rome sous la papauté* (Paris, 1901), 253; Giuseppe Mira, "Note sui trasporti fluviali nell'economia dello Stato Pontificio nel XVIII secolo," *Archivio della società romana di storia patria*, 77 (1954), 31 n. 1; Tournon, *Etudes statistiques sur Rome*, 2:37.

[25] Madelin, *Rome de Napoléon*, 73–75; Andrieux, *Daily Life in Papal Rome*, 28; Montesquieu, "Voyages," 2:1099; Bartoccini, *Roma nell'Ottocento*, 135.

educational program suitable for all the needs of a ruling social class. Its students came from all over the Catholic world. The Clementino in Rome educated young boarders from Denmark, Spain, Germany, Sweden, Ireland, Switzerland, and Austria. A study of 332 Bolognese students who graduated from Jesuit colleges in Parma, Bologna, Siena, and Modena showed that 56 percent of them entered the civil magistracy in Bologna, and 74, that is 22 percent of the total, became clerics, of which 39 percent entered the hierarchy, one becoming a pope and others bishops and cardinals.[26] This shared educational experience opened the way to power. The young graduate put on the black cassock of the *abate*. Anxious to rise, after a short stint in lesser offices, he became a domestic prelate, a *ponente* of a congregation, a chierico of the Apostolic Chamber, an auditor in one of the tribunals, or an attaché to a nunciature. Some advanced to the higher prelatures, auditors of the court of the Rota, nuncios, secretaries of the great congregations, and the three highest offices reserved for non-cardinals: papal auditor, treasurer general, and governor of Rome. At that point the doors to the cardinalate were opened.[27]

For laymen, of whatever rank, positions of great authority were barred. Apart from a handful of openings in the military, the best prospects for advancement were among the lawyers, who could find employment as assessors, procurators, and advocates in the innumerable tribunals, one of which was attached to every papal organ of government. Since this proliferation of jurisdictions with their attendant conflicts provided plenty of business, there was no lack of lawyers. By one estimate there were something like 1,200 of them in a city with a population that reached 166,000 at the most, that is a ratio of one for almost every 140 persons. Whereas in other countries, France most prominently, the opposition to the old regime was to be found among their ranks, in Rome the lawyers became the most fervent lay partisans of a regime that provided them with fruitful opportunities of gainful employment.[28]

This barrier for service also affected the secular nobility. In Rome the lay elite, whether aristocratic or civic, was not directly attached to the monarchical administration as in secular states. The great nobility, whether of feudal or of papal origin, was limited to a few families, less than one hundred, to which every new pope added another.[29] A lesser nobility was almost non-existent in the capital, although it abounded in the provinces. Many of the great nobles bore proud names such as Aldobrandini, Barberini, Altieri, Borghese, Colonna, Orsini, Odescalchi, Sforza-Cesarini, Doria Pamphilj. But unless a member of any of these families could become a cardinal, which appears not to have been too difficult, judging by the number of times their names appear among the Sacred College, they had no direct share in the administration. That is not to say, of course, that they played no role

[26] Gian Paolo Brizzi, *La formazione della classe dirigente nel Sei-Settecento. I seminaria nobilium nell'Italia centro-settentrionale* (Bologna, 1976), 6, 23, 33–34, 70 n. 27, 160–69.

[27] Madelin, *Rome de Napoléon*, 74. [28] Ibid., 61–64.

[29] Friz, *Consumi, tenore di vita e prezzi*, 21, 44–45; Nussdorfer, "City Politics in Baroque Rome," 357.

whatsoever. Together with many of the cardinals they formed a social elite enjoying many of the perquisites of a court aristocracy. They acted as hosts to noble visitors, were granted exemption from import duties. It is difficult to establish their true wealth, apart from the amount of land they held – some of these noble families still prefer to guard their records after more than two hundred years – but there are indications that some noble families, alongside their peers in Bologna,[30] suffered economic difficulties, partly through mismanagement and extravagance, as in the case of the Albani,[31] or because of the vagaries of the agricultural economy. Others, such as the Borghese, were wealthy enough to withstand adverse circumstances.[32] Virtually no self-made men joined the ranks of the high nobility in the course of the eighteenth century by virtue of their banking and financial dealings, as did for instance the Chigi in the sixteenth century, not even the merchant-banker Girolamo Belloni, in spite of his widespread connections and the acquisition of the marquisate and fief of Oliveto in 1750.[33] Only at the very end of the century, from about 1785, did Giovanni Torlonia succeed in raising his family in the social scale by the not too scrupulous conduct of his banking business. He received an imperial patent of nobility in 1794. The history of his family belongs to the nineteenth century.[34]

The international connections of these noble families, in part due to their family ties and in part through holdings abroad, may have been to some advantage to the papacy. We know, of course, that the head of the house of Colonna served as *connestabile* of the king of Naples and the Doria Pamphilj family had contacts with Genoa, which they could exploit when the times required it. Thus, when the French revolutionary armies imposed an indemnity of thirty million livres tournois on the Papal States by the Peace of Tolentino in February 1797, Principe Andrea IV Doria Pamphilj obtained a loan of four million livres for the state from Genoa on his own collateral.[35] Within the country, however, their official functions were relegated to sitting on advisory panels alongside others on matters where their interests, if not always their expertise, could be of use, such as those that affected the running of the annona and the grascia.[36] It is not surprising that this exclusion from the exercise of power provoked some unrest in their ranks, especially among the younger generation. It was surely a symptom of their dissatisfaction with the papal regime that the former Principe Giuseppe Spada accepted command of the new National Guard on the day after the proclamation of the Jacobin republic on 15 February 1798, and other noblemen, such as Francesco Santacroce, assumed

30 Giacomelli, "Carlo Grassi e le riforme bolognesi," 86 n. 229.
31 Morelli (ed.), *Lettere di Benedetto XIV*, 2:241. 32 See Chapter 6.
33 Alberto Caracciolo, *L'albero dei Belloni. Una dinastia di mercanti del Settecento* (Bologna 1982), 101–02.
34 Noack, *Deutschtum in Rom*, 1:266–68; Werner Körte, *Der Palazzo Zuccari in Rom. Sein Freskenschmuck und seine Geschichte* (Leipzig, 1935), 54.
35 ADP, 87:39:1. 36 Nicolai, *Memorie, leggi ed osservazioni*, 1:vii.

4 The Palazzi di Campidoglio with the Church of the Aracoeli on the left, by Giovanni Battista Piranesi

colonelcies, whereas the young Francesco Maria Sforza Cesarini shared in the clandestine preparation of one of those ceremonial trees celebrating liberty.[37]

Not only was the secular court nobility cut off from an effective share in government, but the ancient magistracy of Rome, which still bore proudly the title of Popolo Romano, was also deprived for most purposes of power. The latter's fate paralleled that of its counterparts in most capital cities during the age of the baroque, among them Paris. It had become a mere appendage of the monarchy it served, thereby losing its vaunted autonomy.[38]

The history of Rome's civic magistracy goes back to the restoration of the Roman senate in 1193, at the close of the pontificate of Innocent II. Almost immediately a conflict broke out between the senate and the pope, and by 1363 the creeping process whereby the papacy very gradually seized control over the organization of the municipal administration on the Campidoglio began. It has recently been suggested that Michelangelo's monumental project for the Campidoglio with its three palaces reflecting the hierarchical nature of papal rule, and the dominance of the Palazzo dei Senatori, which was started in 1560, "marks the architectural defeat of republican autonomy, the final consequences of papal appropriation of the city."[39] More properly, it was the symbolic harbinger of what was yet to come. The formal assumption of the functions of the urban government of the papal authorities may perhaps be dated from 1646, when the senator was first appointed by papal brief. But the process would not be completed in the baroque age and dragged on for another century.[40]

What remained of the municipal government of Rome during the period of the ancien regime consisted of the senator, the three conservators, the prior of the *caporioni*, with a token secret council and a host of minor functionaries, including musicians and trumpeters. In its outline the administration had been fixed by the statutes of Gregory XIII in 1580. At the head of this Capitoline magistracy was the

[37] Antonio Cretoni, *Roma Giacobina. Storia della Repubblica Romana del 1798–99* (Rome, 1971), 45–52, 57–58. The continued privileged status and even the influence which the lay aristocracy of Rome still appeared to enjoy in the eighteenth century cannot be explained within the context of the city, where it was obviously deprived of power apart from holding honorific offices. The explanation probably lies in the outlying territories, such as the Romagna, where the papal government traded economic, social, and communal privileges with the local nobility in return for overall centralized control. If the nobility outside the capital, therefore, enjoyed this exceptional position, the greater houses in Rome itself, many of whom owned land in those provinces, could not be denied it. Cesarina Casanova, *Le mediazioni del privilegio. Economia e potere nelle legazioni pontificie del'700* (Bologna, 1984), 21–60. Only in the nineteenth century, with the increasing laicization of the administration, did the nobility reenter the government, and after 1846 they virtually dominated the municipal government of Rome in conjunction with the upper bourgeoisie, albeit under papal control. Bartoccini, *Roma nell'Ottocento*, 142, 167–80.

[38] Maravall, *Culture of the Baroque*, 114, 117–18.

[39] Frommel, "Papal Policy: the Planning of Rome," 62–64.

[40] Arturo Bassotti, *La magistratura capitolina dal secolo XIV al secolo XIX* (Rome, 1955), 5–8, 34; Luigi Guasco, *L'Archivio Storico del comune di Roma* (Rome, 1919), 61–63; Rodocanachi, *Les Institutions communales de Rome*, 332.

senator of Rome. Although his name recalls the ancient senate, his office was primarily judicial and resembled more that of a *podestà* of medieval Italian tradition. According to the city's ordinances the incumbent had to be a foreigner. This rule was maintained in the eighteenth century, except for Mario Frangipani (1712–37) from Nemi. Although the senator was in theory an integral part of the Roman magistracy on all public occasions, he really represented the authority of the sovereign rather than that of the Popolo Romano by virtue of his appointment by papal brief. He symbolized the unity of city and ruler. During the ancien regime his effective jurisdiction was shrinking at the expense of the governor's tribunal. Mostly minor offenses and lawsuits affecting retail commerce and consumer matters continued to occupy his time.[41]

The three conservators, who had first appeared in 1368, although subject to papal confirmation, were chosen from among the local patriciate and represented more directly the interests and needs of the Roman people. They were likened by contemporaries to either the ancient Roman consuls or aediles. Although the conservators did not necessarily have to be Romans, the Roman nobility became intimately tied to these municipal offices as a substitute for their exclusion from papal government at large. The duties of the conservators were wide and, in theory, still included the preservation of the city's religious and artistic patrimony, that is, churches and ancient monuments and relics, cleaning roads, and inspecting weights and measures. Many of their functions, however, had been eliminated when the chierici of the Chamber were given these particular charges. For the time being, the conservators also had the right to issue diplomas granting Roman citizenship, but the significance of such privilege would be diminished as both the power and the prestige of the Popolo Romano was reduced. The number of Roman patricians entitled to hold the higher municipal offices was limited. Perhaps the most important duty remaining to them was in connection with the provisioning of Rome. In conjunction with the president of the grascia, the papal organ supervising meat and oil supply, they fixed the selling price for meat and other commodities in the city.[42]

As for the two councils of the municipal government, the public council (Consiglio pubblico), which represented all the Roman citizens, already poorly attended during the pontificate of Urban VIII in the first half of the seventeenth century, had passed into oblivion by now. The private council (Consiglio segreto), membership of which was confined to actual former officeholders at the Campidoglio, had also been diminished in its powers. It had to refer all its proposals

[41] Ibid., 333–36; Lalande, *Voyage d'un françois en Italie*, 4:465–67; Nussdorfer, "City Politics in Baroque Rome," 13–25; Friz, *Consumi, tenore di vita e prezzi*, 23 n. 5.

[42] Rodocanachi, *Les Institutions communales de Rome*, 336–40; Delumeau, *Vie économique et sociale de Rome*, 2:600–02; Nussdorfer, "City Politics in Baroque Rome," 45–47, 174; Carlo Mistruzzi, "La nobiltà nello Stato pontificio," *Rassegna degli archivi di stato*, 23 (1963), 238.

to the pope. At best it could still act as a mouthpiece of the Roman population. But there is little actual evidence of that available.[43]

The loss of prestige can be attributed to the restriction imposed upon those eligible to hold office at the Campidoglio on the one hand and the receding jurisdiction of the Capitoline tribunals, to which we have already referred, on the other hand. During the baroque period, under Urban VIII, entry into the civic oligarchy that controlled municipal offices was still fairly open, at least in comparison to other major cities. Place of birth, for instance, was no bar to access, although the civic patriciate predominated. Citizenship was readily obtainable. And those at the top, such as the conservators, could still extend valuable patronage, either in the form of minor offices or other favors, to the mass of the ordinary folk. But by the eighteenth century the Popolo Romano became more exclusive. The occasion was Benedict XIV's decree *Urbem Romam* of 1746. By this time the number of diplomas of citizenship had become so prolific that there was hardly a family that did not possess one. He determined that no one was to arrogate for himself the honor and privilege of Roman noble unless he was entered into the Golden Book. To qualify the person had to be able to demonstrate that he and his ancestors had possessed noble rank for a whole secular century in Rome or another Italian city. The number of such families came to 180. From among those Benedict chose the names of sixty families to form the inner circle of Noble Roman Conscript Citizens. These could prove an unblemished nobility for two hundred years on all four sides of their grandparents and had established their domicile in the city. Families of popes were also inscribed in the book, but members of the medieval feudal nobility were expressly excluded. The sum of these provisions deprived the Capitoline magistracy of much of its popular attraction. Instead of acting as a socially integrative institution and as a hub of an upwardly mobile citizenry, access became restricted, and, with the attendant diminution of power, it lost most of its appeal.[44]

Even before this blow to the *Popolo Romano*, the governor of Rome had replaced the authority of the Capitoline magistrates. This prelate, although not ordinarily a cardinal, dealt directly with the pope and served almost as his third minister, the minister of Rome, alongside the secretary of state and the camerlengo. As well as the general administrator of the city he was its head of police and supreme judge. The institution dates back to 17 January 1436, when Pope Eugene IV had to flee the city. From that day 126 incumbents held the office, the majority of whom were raised to the cardinalate after their tenure. With the office of governor, a responsibility charged to a cleric, the pope imposed upon Rome a high magistracy completely loyal to him. The gubernatorial jurisdiction grew and developed constantly over

[43] Rodocanachi, *Les Institutions communales de Rome*, 319, 345–47; Bassotti, *La magistratura capitolina*, 8; Nussdorfer, "City Politics in Baroque Rome," 134–35.

[44] Ibid., 90, 164–65; Mistruzzi, "La nobiltà nello Stato pontificio," 225, 237–38.

time. So Pius V, in 1570, for instance, decreed that any sentence, edict, or provision which emanated from the governor in the pope's name had the full force of law.

In civil matters, the competence of the governor remained rather modest, limited, in fact, to trying and settling suits involving persons of humble station, and cases of servants, workmen, and agricultural laborers being cheated of their wages. He lost even this when the pope appointed a special *giudice dei mercenari* to handle the latter.

In addition to his judicial function the governor had a rather ragged, incompetent police force of sbirri at his disposal. Yet the authority of the governor was great enough, as we have seen, for foreign powers to be anxious to have a friendly incumbent.[45]

But the governor was by no means master in his own house. He had to contend with many other competing jurisdictions, the most prominent of which was that of the cardinal vicar. Third among the cardinals in dignity, he was the deputy of the pope as bishop of Rome. In theory his jurisdiction extended only to matters of worship and morals over a territory which included Rome and all the lands within ten Roman miles (14,895 m) of its walls, but his tribunal also settled disputes among lay people by way of conciliation. The cardinal vicar represented in Rome what in a smaller community a parish priest would have been: the father and universal corrector. The tolerated Jews, the heretics passing through, the Catholics of doubtful faith, all who committed moral offenses or religious transgressions sooner or later came under the eye of the vicariate. There was scarcely a family in Rome which did not at some time or other experience the judgment of the cardinal vicar or his deputy, the vicegerent.[46]

Since the close of the seventeenth century, then, we can say that such independent municipal spirit that had survived in Rome during the previous centuries had largely been dissipated. It does not mean, of course, that the individual Roman had lost his civic pride. But the government was effectively in the hands of papal appointees, frequently outsiders and on their way to becoming cardinals, who probably shared a common ethos and a common educational background, but who often lacked the experience of running a city the size and character of Rome, and certainly would not have that intimate feeling for the well-being of its people. What follows is a picture of how the city and its services fared under their rule, from the economy to education, from food supply to public welfare. But before we examine how the city functioned, we need to take a closer look at the people who inhabited it and note any significant demographic changes.

[45] Niccolò Del Re, *Monsignore Governatore di Roma* (Rome, 1972), 11, 18–26, 37, 45–50; Lalande, *Voyage d'un françois en Italie*, 4:462–65; BL, Egerton ms. 3798, chap. 18; Andrieux, *Daily Life in Papal Rome*, 27; Rodocanachi, *Les Institutions communales de Rome*, 348–50; Giuntella, *Roma nel Settecento*, 14 n. 3; Vicchi, *Vincenzo Monti (1778–1780)*, 118.

[46] Ibid., 106–07; Casanova, *Histoire de ma vie*, 2:364–65 n.9.

3

# The population

During the period of the ancient Antonine emperors, Rome had an estimated population of between 1,200,000 and 1,600,000 people distributed over an area roughly within the bounds of the later Aurelian wall. But those were halcyon days. By the fourth century the number had shrunk to about half a million. After further decline and decay Procopius tells us that only five hundred men were left at the end of the Gothic wars, an improbable claim. Although the figure may have swollen to perhaps 90,000 under Gregory the Great, when refugees flocked into the city from the countryside to escape the Lombards, the influx was only temporary. For after the removal of the papacy to Avignon the number of inhabitants may have fallen to as low as 17,000. But most of these figures are only conjectural. There is nothing to go on prior to the first real census made in 1527, when the city counted over 55,000 inhabitants, this after a century of rapidly rising prosperity and expansion. In 1600 it reached 109,729, which amounted to a density of about 80.33 per hectare. In the course of the seventeenth century the population grew erratically to 135,089 in 1699. By the 1770s Rome with a population of more than 158,000 had become Italy's second most populous capital city, greatly surpassed by Naples with 337,210 (1763), but somewhat larger than Venice with 140,286 (1780) and Milan with 117,134 (1780), and much larger than Florence with 78,537 (1784).[1]

During the eighteenth century there were several censuses in the Papal States, mainly for fiscal purposes, but for most of our statistics we do not rely upon these, rough as they are, but on the *stati delle anime*. In brief, the *stati delle anime* were the annual lists of Easter communicants in each parish of the city. Although some early records in individual Roman parishes go back to the time of the Council of Trent, it was the *Rituale Romano* of Paul V, issued in June 1614, which standardized and codified the method of keeping these books. By 1650 the *stati delle anime* were being kept throughout all the Roman parishes.

These records had a social purpose. They set up the parish priest as censor of morals and warden of the poor. Whether the priest could meet these obligations remains another question. Certainly, by compiling the *stati delle anime* the priest

[1] Jérôme Carcopino, *Daily Life in Ancient Rome*, translated by E. O. Lorimer (New Haven and London, 1962), 20; Krautheimer, *Rome, 312–1308*, 231–32; Petrocchi, *Roma nel Seicento*, 56; Vicchi, *Vincenzo Monti (1778–1780)*, 70; Petraccone, *Napoli dal'500 all'800*, 135–36; Franco Venturi, "Napoli nell'anno della fame," *Rivista storica italiana*, 85 (1973), 436; Herman Büchi, *Finanzen und Finanzpolitik Toskanas im Zeitalter der Aufklärung, 1737–1790* (Berlin, 1915), 224; Karl Julius Beloch, *Bevölkerungsgeschichte Italiens* (2nd ed.; 2 vols.; Berlin, 1965), 2:148.

enabled the bishop to perform his Tridentine duty of keeping watch over the spiritual life of his diocese. In the case of Rome the secretariat of the cardinal vicar required annually detailed, as well as summarized, information on the composition of the population in the individual parishes. It needed to have a clear picture of the poor to be admitted to relief and, given the contemporary preoccupation with matters pertaining to morality and sound doctrine, of the non-communicants, whores, concubines, prisoners, and even heretics and Turks.[2]

The parish, therefore, became the prime unit for this type of record keeping, a feature which coincided with the growth of the importance of the parish in Catholic life in general and Roman life in particular. When in the later Middle Ages the ecclesiastical magistracy gradually reasserted itself at the expense of the authority of the Campidoglio, the territorial organization moved from the rioni to the parishes. But in 1566 the parish in Rome was still disorganized and, from an ecclesiastical and territorial point of view, not even well defined. Between 1566 and 1569 the Cardinal Vicar Giacomo Savelli, on orders from Pius V, carried through a reform and a reorganization of the parishes. At the time, Rome, with a shrunken population, had 130 parishes, the smaller ones almost without parishioners. Savelli drastically reduced their number. The number of parishes and their size continued to fluctuate thereafter, however, making exact secular studies of them difficult. Starting with 81 parishes in 1695, they reached the maximum for the century of 86 in 1715, and finally settled at 82 in 1766.

Given the uncertain relationship between parishes and rioni during the era of the ancien regime, no reliable population statistics for individual rioni can be reconstructed on the basis of the *stati delle anime*. It will only become easier after the reform of Leo XII in 1824, which established a clear correspondence between parishes and rioni.[3]

In contrast to the registers for baptisms, deaths, and marriages, which remained more or less complete, the majority of the *stati delle anime* records that have come down to us have gaps and breaks in the annual series. All these lacunae have not been caused by records being lost or destroyed. It is more likely either that the parish priest failed to perform his duty or, if he did carry out his obligation, did not follow the prescribed techniques of record keeping. Other factors also reduced the usefulness of the records. Religious houses, for instance, were generally indicated in the *stati delle anime*, but very often without any description of the persons living there. This fact can be explained by a certain resistance on the part of the regular orders to the presumed meddling by the parochial and curial authorities.

[2] Carla Sbrana, Rosa Traina, and Eugenio Sonnino, *Gli "stati delle anime" a Roma dalle origini al secolo XVII. Origini, consistènze, contenuti* (Rome, 1977), 23, 27, 46–47, 51–53, 57, 82, 88–89, 98, 104, 348–49; Francesco Corridore, *La popolazione dello Stato Romano* (Rome, 1906), 13–14.

[3] Sbrana *et al.*, *Gli "stati delle anime" a Roma*, 22–23, 117–18, 120–23, 346; Giggi Zanazzo, *Tradizioni popolari romane. Usi, costumi, e pregiudizi del popolo di Roma* (Turin and Rome, 1907–10), 166; Giuliano Friz, *La popolazione di Roma dal 1770 al 1900* (Rome, 1974), 40.

In addition to keeping their own annual books on individuals and households, the parish priests also had to send summaries (*sommari*) of the composition of the parochial population under fixed categories to the secretariat of the cardinal vicar. The data thus collected from all parishes were copied onto four large double pages; from these the secretariat made a summary of the data submitted by all the parishes of the city. But every year the office of the vicariate also prepared a general register which contained the year-by-year totals for the previous ten years.

Unless we venture upon the gigantic task of analyzing baptismal and death records, the *stati delle anime* are our sole source for studying the population patterns of Rome during the ancien regime, notwithstanding the uneven way the data were collected. While they are better records than many other cities of its size possessed, these numbers should be regarded more as measures of magnitude than as absolute figures.

At the base of any demographic study lies the size of the population. We shall, therefore, start with the annual figures as given in the summaries (Table 1).[4]

Behind the erratic numbers, which may in part be attributable to computational errors or the constant ebb and flow of outsiders, we are able to detect a pattern in the population growth of Rome throughout the eighteenth century and beyond. Starting with 130,826 people in 1695, the number began to increase gradually until it shot up suddenly in 1700 to 149,447. This figure was artificially swollen by the influx of pilgrims for the Holy Year. But then came the early years of Clement XI's pontificate, plagued with earthquakes, floods, epidemics, grain shortages, and the War of the Spanish Succession. With some exceptions, a steady overall decline in the population followed until about 1713, with its low point of 132,104 in 1705. Thereafter the figures begin to rise steadily, with minor fluctuations until about 1797, reaching artificial heights during the Jubilees of 1725, 1750, and 1775. Yet each of these Holy Years appears to have given a boost to future population growth.

In some respects the pattern of population growth approaches the hypothesis which the French demographer Jacques Dupaquier propounded concerning the demographic "take-off" in western Europe, making allowance that his pattern was based primarily on France. Dupaquier advanced two stages in the demographic

[4] The statistics for the population table and for the subsequent tables were collated from following sources:

i From the ten-year summaries (*sommari*) derived from ASR, Camerale II, popolazione, status animarum, busta 7 (1697–1706, 1731–40), busta 8 (1754–63), busta 9 (1771–80, 1776–85), busta 10 (1783–93, 1781–90); B. N. Ro., Fondo Gesuitico, ms. 1667 (1688–97, 1701–10, 1706–15, 1707–16, 1722–31, 1728–37); B. N. Ro., Fondi minori, varia, ms. 478 (1725–34, 1743–52, 1745–54, 1754–63, 1765–74, 1775–84).

ii From the annual summaries by parishes derived from ASR, Camerale II, popolazione, status animarum, busta 7 (1701, 1702, 1703, 1706, 1740), busta 8 (1750, 1760, 1763, 1765, 1770, 1777), busta 9 (1780, 1785), busta 10 (1790, 1793); B. N. Ro., Fondo Gesuitico, ms. 1667 (1715, 1719, 1725, 1737); B. N. Ro., Fondi minor, varia, ms. 478 (1734, 1752, 1763, 1764).

To fill up some of the gaps, especially after 1793, I have used Philippe comte de Tournon-Simiane, *Etudes statistiques sur Rome*, 1:272–78, and Friz, *La popolazione di Roma*, 137, table 1.

Table 1

| Year | Population | Year | Population | Year | Population |
|---|---|---|---|---|---|
| 1695 | 130,826 | 1737 | 149,180 | 1779 | 162,242 |
| 1696 | 131,603 | 1738 | 147,119 | 1780 | 163,423 |
| 1697 | 133,894 | 1739 | 146,750 | 1781 | 161,898 |
| 1698 | 133,824 | 1740 | 146,080 | 1782 | 162,805 |
| 1699 | 135,089 | 1741 | No record | 1783 | 163,993 |
| 1700 | 149,447 | 1742 | No record | 1784 | 161,552 |
| 1701 | 141,784 | 1743 | 147,476 | 1785 | 162,452 |
| 1702 | 138,568 | 1744 | 147,432 | 1786 | 163,956 |
| 1703 | 134,528 | 1745 | 149,396 | 1787 | 164,595 |
| 1704 | 133,625 | 1746 | 151,188 | 1788 | 165,441 |
| 1705 | 132,104 | 1747 | 149,361 | 1789 | 163,034 |
| 1706 | 132,176 | 1748 | 151,713 | 1790 | 162,982 |
| 1707 | 132,128 | 1749 | 152,872 | 1791 | 163,093 |
| 1708 | 134,562 | 1750 | 157,881 | 1792 | 162,427 |
| 1709 | 134,262 | 1751 | 154,568 | 1793 | 165,316 |
| 1710 | 132,610 | 1752 | 153,811 | 1794 | 166,948 |
| 1711 | 132,974 | 1753 | 153,667 | 1795 | 164,586 |
| 1712 | 133,829 | 1754 | 153,130 | 1796 | 166,417 |
| 1713 | 132,567 | 1755 | 153,912 | 1797 | 166,280 |
| 1714 | 134,050 | 1756 | 153,843 | 1798 | 151,657 |
| 1715 | 136,287 | 1757 | 152,748 | 1799 | 149,026 |
| 1716 | 137,958 | 1758 | 154,058 | 1800 | 153,004 |
| 1717 | 136,383 | 1759 | 155,184 | 1801 | 146,384 |
| 1718 | 136,293 | 1760 | 157,085 | 1802 | 144,212 |
| 1719 | 137,729 | 1761 | 157,458 | 1803 | 140,003 |
| 1720 | 133,832 | 1762 | 158,819 | 1804 | 136,762 |
| 1721 | 134,254 | 1763 | 156,449 | 1805 | 134,973 |
| 1722 | 138,067 | 1764 | No record | 1806 | 136,356 |
| 1723 | 139,894 | 1765 | 158,095 | 1807 | 136,854 |
| 1724 | 142,348 | 1766 | 157,868 | 1808 | 136,268 |
| 1725 | 148,155 | 1767 | 159,760 | 1809 | 123,033 |
| 1726 | 145,937 | 1768 | 158,847 | 1810 | 128,850 |
| 1727 | 145,981 | 1769 | 158,906 | 1811 | 121,608 |
| 1728 | 143,990 | 1770 | 158,443 | 1812 | 117,882 |
| 1729 | 144,620 | 1771 | 159,675 | 1813 | 130,505 |
| 1730 | 145,494 | 1772 | 158,849 | 1814 | 128,384 |
| 1731 | 146,148 | 1773 | 158,563 | 1815 | 128,997 |
| 1732 | 149,674 | 1774 | 160,896 | 1816 | 129,128 |
| 1733 | 149,771 | 1775 | 165,047 | 1817 | 131,356 |
| 1734 | 151,334 | 1776 | 163,316 | 1818 | 133,812 |
| 1735 | 150,665 | 1777 | 163,100 | 1819 | 134,161 |
| 1736 | 150,749 | 1778 | 162,442 | 1820 | 135,046 |

growth: the first one between 1650 and 1720 was marked by periodic crises of mortality, but recovered its losses partially through increased births, especially in the rural zones, and the second one from 1720 to 1790 where disasters were less frequent, the rate of mortality falls, but the increasing population finds life more difficult. Some signs of this crisis were an increase in the frequency of celibacy and a later age for first marriages, a swelling of the marginal population of vagrants and the poor, and a shrinking in real wages. Because of the slower tenor of life in Rome, not all these characteristics nor the cut-off points coincide exactly with those in France, but we shall note some similiarities.[5]

Compared to its populous neighbor to the south, Naples, Rome's demographic growth appears modest. Naples experienced at 64 percent increase between 1688 and 1742, whereas Rome's was only 14.2 percent between 1695 and 1745. From 1742 to 1765 the Neapolitan population grew by 10 percent and the Roman one by 5.8 percent. In contrast it should be borne in mind that Naples experienced a serious demographic crisis as a result of the famine of 1764, which accounted for a loss of 26,041 souls, while in Rome the size of the population was not greatly affected by the disaster. The subsequent period of 1765–97 saw a rate of increase of 29 percent in Naples, but only 18.3 percent in Rome. The years thereafter showed an even more marked difference. Naples gained 3.12 percent in its population between 1797 and 1804. In Rome, on the other hand, the French occupation, compounded by the dismal internal economic, social, and political conditions, including the epidemics, the famine of 1799, and the flooding of 1804, actually registered an 18.3 percent loss, with a population that had sunk to 117,382 souls. Recovery only set in in 1817–18.[6]

However, Naples is an exceptional case which fits the pattern of southern Italy, where the population growth between 1700 and 1800 was in the range of 46.9 percent, well above the average of 34.9 percent for Italy as a whole. The central zone, however, only marked a rise of 29.8 percent.[7] Yet Rome's growth rate lagged behind that for its own geographical zone and certainly for that of the whole of Italy, which itself was one of the lowest in Europe, when compared to a rate of about 40 percent for France, 48.4 percent for Germany and Austria, 54 percent for Scotland, 57 percent for England and Wales, and 64 percent for Spain.[8] The papal capital's growth can only really be compared to a city such as Bologna. Bologna, according to a census carried through by Clement XI in 1701, had a population of 63,346. By

[5] Jacques Dupâquier, "Il problema della crescita demografica nel XVIII secolo. Lo stato della ricerca in Francia," in Società italiana di demografia storica, *La popolazione italiana nel Settecento* (Bologna, 1979), 148–49.

[6] The percentages of Naples were calculated from Petraccone, *Napoli dal'500 all'800*, 130–43; Venturi, "Napoli nell'anno della fame," 436, 439; Patrick Chorley, *Oil, Silk and Enlightenment. Economic Problems in XVIIIth Century Naples* (Naples, 1965), 15; Athos Bellettini, "L'evoluzione demografica dell'Italia nel quadro europeo del Settecento. Analogie e particularità," in Società italiana di demografia storica, *La popolazione italiana nel Settecento* (Bologna, 1979), 50–52.

[7] Ibid., 23–24. [8] Ibid., 17–18.

1718 it had reached 65,000, at which figure it stayed until the middle of the century. Finally in 1791, it touched 71,000, that is, a 12.8 percent increase, compared to a 15.03 percent growth for Rome in the same period.[9]

The population growth of the papal capital lagged behind that of the provinces of the Papal States. This characteristic it shared with other capital cities. Whereas the population of Rome decreased by 5.1 percent between 1701 and 1708, it grew during the same period in the provinces, admittedly only by a minute 0.64 percent. Between 1736 and 1768, there was a growth rate of 19.32 percent in the provinces, but only of 5.13 percent in the city. For the subsequent period, between 1769 and 1782, the respective estimates are 6.87 percent and 2.39 percent. Thus in the period between 1701 and 1799, when the population of the whole of the Papal States grew from 1,900,000 to 2,300,000, marking an increase of 21 percent, their capital in contrast grew by only 5.11 percent. This trend duplicates one in the northern neighbor Tuscany, where the demographic process in the eighteenth century was also one of populating the countryside. With the exception of Livorno and Pisa, the other major urban centers there lost ground to the agricultural areas and small rural towns.[10]

The ratio of the population of the capital to the provinces of the Papal States was on the average about 7.5 percent or one-thirteenth. In comparison the population of Naples and its suburbs was something over a tenth of the total population of the kingdom, and that of Florence, the capital to the north, almost one-twelfth of that of Tuscany. Even London's population was just over one-sixteenth. On the other hand, that of Paris was only a thirty-sixth and Vienna's a mere seventy-second. Yet, notwithstanding the examples of Paris and Vienna, Rome cannot really be considered a top-heavy capital.[11]

For our purposes, however, Rome's population has to be broken down into its constituent elements to give us an idea of the people of the city, who determined its character and way of life, and created its problems. What strikes one first of all is the fact that in Rome males outnumbered females. Its ecclesiastical nature as the center of Catholicism can explain this phenomenon, but it may have been augmented by a considerable amount of celibacy among laymen and by male tourists flocking to the city. Rome was not alone in the large number of male celibates. Among the Milanese patriciate, between 1700 and 1749, 50.5 percent were still unmarried by the age of 50 and between 1750 and 1799 36.5 percent (compared to only 34.5 percent and 13 percent for females respectively). Among the Florentine patriciate in the eighteenth century, 38 percent of the males were still unmarried at the age of 50, as against 14

9 Athos Bellettini, *La popolazione di Bologna dal secolo XV all'unificazione italiana* (Bologna, 1961), 42, 48, 192–216; Dal Pane, *Economia e società a Bologna*, 20–21; Giacomelli, "Carlo Grassi e le riforme bolognesi," 13.

10 The percentages for the papal provinces were calculated on the basis of Corridore, *La popolazione dello Stato Romano*, 21–22, 25–27; Bellettini, *La popolazione di Bologna*, 181; Bellettini, "L'evoluzione demografica dell'Italia," 47; Büchi, *Finanzen und Finanzpolitik Toskanas*, 224.

11 Schiavone and Sonnino, "Popolazione e territorio nel Lazio," 204.

Table 2

| Years | No. of females | Years | No. of females | Years | No. of females |
|---|---|---|---|---|---|
| 1696–1700 | 70.43 | 1736–1740 | 76.98 | 1776–1780 | 80.5 |
| 1701–1705 | 72.23 | 1741–1745 | 79.66 | 1781–1785 | 82.64 |
| 1706–1710 | 72.58 | 1746–1750 | 78.75 | 1786–1790 | 84.64 |
| 1711–1715 | 75.77 | 1751–1755 | 78.69 | 1791–1795 | 81.13 |
| 1716–1720 | 73.11 | 1756–1760 | 79.5 | 1796–1800 | 85.11 |
| 1721–1725 | 75.1 | 1761–1765 | 79.54 | 1801–1805 | 90.92 |
| 1726–1730 | 76.6 | 1766–1770 | 80.12 | 1806–1810 | 90.85 |
| 1731–1735 | 76.98 | 1771–1775 | 82.75 | 1811–1815 | 93.98 |

percent of the females.[12] The reason for this has been attributed to the system of primogeniture, whereby the eldest sons took over the estate and the younger were left with small pensions. In Rome, the practice by laymen, usually scholars and minor literati, of assuming the dress and habits of an abate without becoming priests, in order to acquire social standing in a society where ecclesiastic status conferred a certain amount of prestige, might be a contributing factor. Whatever the reasons, and they are probably a combination of several, Table 2 shows the number of females per hundred males broken down into five-year periods. The century clearly indicates a steady and impressive increase in the proportion of women in the Roman population. The figures become particularly significant after 1796, which is the time of the first Roman republic and Napoleonic rule, an era of forced secularization in the old Papal States. By the same token, the sudden interruption of growth in the period of 1791–95 may possibly be explained by the influx of clerical refugees escaping the French Revolution. Yet Rome stands in contrast to other Italian cities, such as Turin, Naples, and even Milan, despite what happened to its patricians, where there was either a permanent or intermittent predominance of females. In Bologna, for instance, in the course of the eighteenth century there were about 110.8 females to every 100 males and the ratio remained fairly stable throughout the period. On the other hand, Rome's experience seems to accord with what was happening in other large centers of Lazio, only to a more pronounced degree.[13]

Its population, like that of any city, was profoundly marked by the natural demographic movements of births, deaths, and, by extension, marriages. When we

[12] Marzio Barbagli, *Sotto lo stesso tetto. Mutamenti della famiglia in Italia dal XV al XX secolo* (Bologna, 1984), 198, tab. IV. 24.

[13] Friz, *La popolazione di Roma*, 67–68. In one representative parish in Naples, Sant'Anna di Palazzo, the ratio of males to females, in 1757 and 1804, was about 95 males to 100 females; Petraccone, *Napoli dal '500 all '800*, 159–60; Bellettini, *La popolazione di Bologna*, 61, table 7.

Table 3

| Years | Births per 1,000 | Years | Births per 1,000 | Years | Births per 1,000 |
|---|---|---|---|---|---|
| 1696–1701 | Not recorded | 1736–1740 | 32.6 | 1776–1780 | 33.27 |
| (1702)–1705 | 28.15 | 1741–1745 | 33.06 | 1781–1785 | 33.84 |
| 1706–1710 | 31.35 | 1746–1750 | 32.23 | 1786–1790 | 33.76 |
| 1711–1715 | 30.77 | 1751–1755 | 33.66 | 1791–1795 | 32.47 |
| 1716–1720 | 31.57 | 1756–1760 | 33.38 | 1796–1800 | 34.44 |
| 1721–1725 | 31.79 | 1761–1765 | 31.78 | 1801–1805 | 30.99 |
| 1726–1730 | 30.31 | 1766–1770 | 29.89 | 1806–1810 | 35.33 |
| 1731–1735 | 32.58 | 1771–1775 | 31.76 | 1811–1815 | 32.14 |

look upon the birthrate it should be noted that usually only baptized infants were recorded as births; those unfortunates who died before they were baptized were not recorded. Yet, while the *stati delle anime* give us no data about perinatal mortality, the practice in Catholic lands of having infants, especially sick ones, baptized as soon as possible after birth minimizes that factor in the statistics (Table 3).

The average birth rate remained fairly steady between 30.0 and 33.9 per thousand, making it lower than that of most Italian cities. Turin had, on the average, 39.1 births per thousand annually between 1761 and 1800, Naples had 37.7 per thousand in 1707 and 34.9 per thousand in 1742, Florence 35.5 in the 1740s and 37.2 in 1761, and Bologna roughtly 34.4 per thousand between 1729 and 1800. Rome was on a level with Venice, which had an average annual birth rate of 32.32 per thousand in the course of the eighteenth century.

In some years when the birth rate departed from the norm it was probably affected by external factors. The early years of Clement XI's pontificate, we need not repeat, were disastrous and so the birth rate was abnormally low. Another period of suffering was that of 1763–66 with the horrendous famine. It was marked by a low birth rate of 29.89 per thousand. On the other hand, the first Roman republic, in spite of the famine of 1799, gave a temporary boost to births as did Napoleon's occupation a decade later.

But births have to be balanced by deaths, and in this Rome's record was not a happy one (Table 4). Over the whole period from 1702, when data were first given, to 1815, the average annual death rate was 40.53 per thousand, that is, it exceeded the birth rate by 6.84 per thousand. In Venice, not one of the more vibrant cities of Italy at the time, as we have seen, the death rate only exceeded the birth rate by 2.48 per thousand. In Turin, in fact, between 1761 and 1800, there were 3.4 births per

Table 4

| Years | Deaths per 1,000 | Years | Deaths per 1,000 | Years | Deaths per 1,000 |
|---|---|---|---|---|---|
| 1696–1701 | Not recorded | 1736–1740 | 41.62 | 1776–1780 | 39.95 |
| (1702)–1705 | 24.86 | 1741–1745 | 47.24 | 1781–1785 | 48.43 |
| 1706–1710 | 38.12 | 1746–1750 | 40.32 | 1786–1790 | 43.82 |
| 1711–1715 | 36.05 | 1751–1755 | 42.99 | 1791–1795 | 38.58 |
| 1716–1720 | 40.26 | 1756–1760 | 38.09 | 1796–1800 | 48.81 |
| 1721–1725 | 39.13 | 1761–1765 | 41.17 | 1801–1805 | 59.65 |
| 1726–1730 | 39.79 | 1766–1770 | 47.92 | 1806–1810 | 34.50 |
| 1731–1735 | 37.29 | 1771–1775 | 34.53 | 1811–1815 | 29.06 |

thousand a year more than deaths and in the urban areas of the state of Milan, between 1773 and 1781, we have 0.5 per thousand more births.[14]

Thus the natural demographic balance of Rome was more unfavorable than in most Italian cities. Between 1702 and 1815, there were only nineteen years – six of them in the early nineteenth century – when there were more births than deaths (1702–04, 1706–07, 1719, 1722, 1735, 1756–57, 1774–75, 1778; 1809–15, except 1812). Overall only during the Napoleonic period does Rome really start having an excess of births over deaths, although the 1756–57 and the 1774–78 periods were quite favorable. Particularly fearful, on the other hand, was the period 1766–70, when deaths exceeded births by 18.03 per thousand, that is, by 60.32 percent, as well as the years 1781, when they exceeded by 26.46 per thousand (72.14 percent) and 1783 by 25.98 per thousand (79.1 percent). Some of the high death rates corresponded more or less to periods of famines and epidemics of infectious diseases during the century.[15]

Marriages were only recorded since 1793 and thus do not help us much to fill out the demographic picture (Table 5). Obviously under the short-lived republican regime there was a marriage boom. It corresponded with the experience of Naples under its republican regime in 1799 and of Paris in the early years of the French

[14] Lorenzo del Panta and Massimo Livi-Bacci, "Le componenti naturali dell'evoluzione demografica nell'Italia del Settecento," in Società italiana di demografia storica, *La popolazione italiana nel Settecento* (Bologna, 1979), 76–77, 82; Bellettini, *La popolazione di Bologna*, 132, table 26; 136, table 28. I would agree with Del Panta and Livi Bacci that there was a slightly higher frequency of mortality crises in the central-south zone of Italy, including Rome, than in Tuscany and the north (p. 98).

[15] Oddo Casagrandi, *La popolazione, le nascite, le morti negli ultimi due secoli a Roma. (Studio demografico-statistico)* (Rome, 1903), 20.

Table 5

| Year | Marriages per 1,000 pop. | Year | Marriages per 1,000 pop. | Year | Marriages per 1,000 pop. |
|---|---|---|---|---|---|
| 1793 | 9.16 | 1799 | 11.26 | 1805 | 10.79 |
| 1794 | 8.58 | 1800 | 7.48 | 1806 | 8.90 |
| 1795 | 8.07 | 1801 | 6.73 | 1807 | 8.60 |
| 1796 | 8.62 | 1802 | 6.99 | 1808 | 10.40 |
| 1797 | 9.70 | 1803 | 6.79 | | |
| 1798 | 11.72 | 1804 | 8.76 | | |

Revolution from 1789 to 1794 (14.9 per thousand). It certainly exceeded the average ratio of marriages in Italy as a whole at the end of the eighteenth century, which was between 8.5 and 9 per thousand.

What Rome lost by its excessive death rate would normally have to be replaced by immigration. Hence data on immigration patterns would be valuable. But here the *stati delle anime* help us little. What we have are statistics worked out by Giuliano Friz, which, however, only start with 1770 (Table 6). The migratory movements in the earlier years here recorded followed a fairly regular rhythm, without abnormal oscillations, especially between 1779 and 1788, the last peaceful decade of eighteenth-century Rome, when immigrants exceeded emigrants by an average of 15.4 per thousand. Thereafter the figures reflect the political vicissitudes of the time. The 27.11 per thousand influx in 1794 marks the Terror in France with the flight of the clergy and aristocracy. The 79.82 per thousand emigration in 1798 follows the founding of the Jacobin republic in Rome and the attendant exodus, voluntary or forced, of the papal–clerical establishment, which returned in 1800 after the collapse of the French puppet regime, producing a 60.41 per thousand immigration figure. Probably some Jacobin sympathizers or suspects left during the following year. The same picture is repeated in 1809 and 1813 with the Napoleonic occupation and evacuation respectively.

In addition to the permanent population, Rome has always sheltered an enormously large floating population. The city had been, and still continued to be, the homeland of pilgrims, but under the ancien regime it also became the goal of the young aristocrat on his Grand Tour, the artist and art lover, as well as of less respectable characters; in short, it was the city of foreigners, the *patria mundi* it boasted of being. Yet only those who were in the city during the time of the census taking would have been included in the records and, even then, some of the more transient ones may not have been registered. We can only conjecture that they would have added a thousand or two a year to the regular population, perhaps double that during a Holy Year and much less in periods of epidemial, political or

Table 6

| Year | Excess of | | Excess per 1,000 population | |
|---|---|---|---|---|
| | Immigrants | Emigrants | Immigrants | Emigrants |
| 1770 | 1,216 | | 7.67 | |
| 1771 | 2,866 | | 17.95 | |
| 1772 | | 240 | | 1.51 |
| 1773 | 875 | | 5.52 | |
| 1774 | 1,961 | | 12.19 | |
| 1775 | 3,729 | | 22.59 | |
| 1776 | | 2,175 | | 13.32 |
| 1777 | 865 | | 5.30 | |
| 1778 | | 939 | | 5.78 |
| 1779 | 2,108 | | 12.99 | |
| 1780 | 3,056 | | 18.70 | |
| 1781 | 2,759 | | 17.04 | |
| 1782 | 2,119 | | 13.02 | |
| 1783 | 2,673 | | 16.30 | |
| 1784 | 1,756 | | 10.87 | |
| 1785 | 1,559 | | 9.59 | |
| 1786 | 2,839 | | 17.44 | |
| 1787 | 2,618 | | 15.91 | |
| 1788 | 3,627 | | 21.92 | |
| 1789 | | 885 | | 5.43 |
| 1790 | 1,982 | | 12.16 | |
| 1791 | 2,235 | | 13.66 | |
| 1792 | | 564 | | 3.47 |
| 1793 | 3,614 | | 21.86 | |
| 1794 | 4,526 | | 27.11 | |
| 1795 | | 1,177 | | 7.15 |
| 1796 | 3,801 | | 22.84 | |
| 1797 | 1,098 | | 6.60 | |
| 1798 | | 12,106 | | 79.82 |
| 1799 | | 2,475 | | 16.84 |
| 1800 | 9,242 | | 60.41 | |
| 1801 | | 3,886 | | 23.13 |
| 1802 | 5,425 | | 37.62 | |
| 1803 | 1,203 | | 8.59 | |
| 1804 | 4,402 | | 32.19 | |
| 1805 | | 369 | | 2.73 |
| 1806 | 2,199 | | 16.13 | |
| 1807 | 1,329 | | 9.71 | |
| 1808 | | 6 | | 0.04 |

Table 6 – *Continued*

| | Excess of | | Excess per 1,000 population | |
|---|---|---|---|---|
| Year | Immigrants | Emigrants | Immigrants | Emigrants |
| 1809 | | 13,600 | | 110.56 |
| 1810 | 3,950 | | 30.66 | |
| 1811 | | 8,727 | | 71.77 |
| 1812 | | 3,060 | | 25.96 |
| 1813 | 12,182 | | 93.35 | |
| 1814 | | 2,560 | | 19.94 |
| 1815 | 345 | | 2.67 | |

economic crises. Among the residents of the city, non-Catholics, with the exception of Jews, formed a negligible proportion, usually less than 0.1 percent. There was also a seasonal descent of laborers from the Abruzzi and the dioceses of Sora and Sulmona in Naples, who by definition cannot be counted easily and may have amounted to several more thousand people.[16] Finally, Rome harbored a garrison of troops fluctuating between 3,530 and 4,370 men.[17]

To summarize the natural demographic movement of Rome, we can say that despite the fact that the gap between deaths and births widened (between 1751 and 1775 there were 8.85 more deaths per thousand annually than births, while between 1776 and 1800 the difference grew to 10.36 per thousand), the population saw a fairly steady growth, reaching its maximum of 166,948 in 1794. The difference between the indigenous population and the ultimate size of its population had to be bridged by the immigration of outsiders; hence Rome's increasing openness to non-natives and the important role they played both in its everyday life and its cultural life.

We have already remarked in the previous chapter that Rome's rents remained steady. The same holds true for the size of households. The first of the categories into which the *stati delle anime* are divided is formed by the problematic expression *casa e famiglia*. For purposes of census taking, it appears certain that not the natural family, but the number of all those cohabiting was counted. Such a unit may have embraced on occasions individuals who were not related and were not even

[16] Friz, *La popolazione di Roma*, 26–27, 47 and 51; Jacques Revel, "Le grain de Rome et la crise de l'annone dans la seconde moitié du XVIIIe siècle," in *Mélanges de l'Ecole française de Rome. Moyen Age, temps moderne* (1972), 223–24; Giorgio Rossi, *L'Agro di Roma tra '500 e '800. Condizioni di vita e lavoro* (Rome, 1985), 9. In 1853 the number of seasonal workers was estimated at 20–30,000 a year. This seems too high a figure for the previous century. Besides, not all of them would be present in the city at the same time. Bartoccini, *Roma nell'Ottocento*, 230.

[17] Andrea Da Mosto, *Milizie dello Stato Romano (1600–1797)* (Città di Castello, 1914), 212–19.

Table 7

| Years | Number of persons per household | Years | Number of persons per household | Years | Number of persons per household |
|---|---|---|---|---|---|
| 1696–1700 | 4.5 | 1731–1735 | 4.53 | 1766–1770 | 4.35 |
| 1701–1705 | 4.25 | 1736–1740 | 4.48 | 1771–1775 | 4.35 |
| 1706–1710 | 4.23 | 1741–1745 | 4.46 | 1776–1780 | 4.13 |
| 1711–1715 | 4.13 | 1746–1750 | 4.58 | 1781–1785 | 4.18 |
| 1716–1720 | 4.27 | 1751–1755 | 4.41 | 1786–1790 | 4.16 |
| 1721–1725 | 4.6 | 1756–1760 | 4.28 | 1791–(1793) | 4.22 |
| 1726–1730 | 4.48 | 1761–1765 | 4.42 | | |

permanent residents, but happened to be there on the day the parish priest or his assistant came around. It could be the equally considerable cases of secular clergy that made up individual *famiglie*. In short, we are dealing with a household. With this assumption we can crudely estimate the average number of people in a Roman household over most of the eighteenth century (Table 7).[18] By this form of calculation the average number of people in a household over the whole period would come to about 4.35. There is no indication that the household density increased with Rome's growing population. In fact, it was higher at the start of the century than at the close, and certainly maintained an elevated level between 1721 and 1775. The lack of any usable records for the history of common housing in Rome makes it impossible to estimate the actual density of living space available. It may just be the case, although not likely, that fewer people living in a household at the close of the century subsisted in much more crowded conditions than the larger households in its middle years. Only a closer look at the composition of individual parishes may help us to have a better idea of the various forms a Roman household can take. But before we do so we must consider the role of a very important segment, the ecclesiastical one, in the papal capital's population.

As the center of universal Catholicism we naturally expect the clerical population to form a considerable proportion of the inhabitants of Rome. The figures, however, do not really bear out our expectations or, for that matter, the picture many travellers have handed down to us. It is clear that the ecclesiastical influence, given the very nature and form of government of the Papal States, far surpassed the numerical weight of its clerical population.

In Table 8, where the percentage of the clerical population to the inhabitants of the city as a whole is given, grouped in five-year periods, we not only counted

[18] The sources for this table are the same as those in note 4.

Table 8

| Years | % of clerical population | Years | % of clerical population | Years | % of clerical population |
|---|---|---|---|---|---|
| 1696–1700 | 6.88 | 1736–1740 | 6.87 | 1776–1780 | 5.64 |
| 1701–1705 | 7.33 | 1741–1745 | 6.46 | 1781–1785 | 5.36 |
| 1706–1710 | 6.77 | 1746–1750 | 6.51 | 1786–1790 | 5.12 |
| 1711–1715 | 7.11 | 1751–1755 | 6.46 | 1791–1795 | 4.85 |
| 1716–1720 | 7.41 | 1756–1760 | 6.27 | 1796–1800 | 3.54 |
| 1721–1725 | 7.15 | 1761–1765 | 6.19 | 1801–1805 | 3.30 |
| 1726–1730 | 6.91 | 1766–1770 | 6.04 | | |
| 1731–1735 | 6.69 | 1771–1775 | 5.58 | | |

secular and regular priests including bishops, but also nuns and seminarians.[19] Thus the share of the clerical population until 1740 hovered between 6.7 and 7.5 percent of the total, which is about one to every 15 or 16 persons. Then the percentage began to decrease until the French Revolution, except for a very slight temporary upswing during the Reign of Terror owing to the influx of émigré priests. From the restoration on it was to stay at a proportion roughly constant to the population of the city at 3.5 percent. This compared well with Bologna, which had an average of roughly 5.8 percent between 1708 and 1791, although it would drop precipitously to 0.8 percent in 1799. But Bologna was atypical. For we are confronting an overall decline of the ecclesiastical population throughout Italy and, indeed, Catholic Europe. Until the end of the seventeenth century the ecclesiastical population of Italy increased, an increase powered no doubt by the Tridentine reforms. This tendency stopped in the first half of the eighteenth century. The arrest occurred even before the states by way of concordats or other dispositions took control over entry into holy orders. In some cases this tendency to decline of the clerical population assumed sweeping proportions in the second half of the eighteenth century. In Tuscany the number of religious persons, regulars, seculars, and nuns dropped from 3.15 to 2.28 per hundred inhabitants between 1745 and 1784, in the kingdom of Naples from 2.84 to 1.72 between 1766 and 1796, in the state of Milan from 1.98 to 0.84 between 1771 and 1799, and in the Terraferma of Venice from 1.78 to 1.43 between 1766 and 1790.[20] Rome, as we see, was not spared

[19] The same sources were used as for notes 4 and 18.

[20] Bellettini, *La popolazione di Bologna*, 58–59, table 6; Del Panta and Livi-Bacci, "Le componenti naturali dell'evoluzione demografica," 127–29 and 128, table 30. For a thorough treatment of the decline in clerical vocations in the area of Lombardy, see Xenio Toscani, *Il clero lombardo dall'ancien regime alla restaurazione* (Bologna, 1979). Toscani's Introduction (pp. 15–41) provides a fine summary on the state of research into the problem by Italian and French historians.

Table 9

| Years | No. of regulars | Years | No. of regulars | Years | No. of regulars |
|---|---|---|---|---|---|
| 1696–1700 | 1.32 | 1731–1735 | 1.36 | 1766–1770 | 1.51 |
| 1701–1705 | 1.34 | 1736–1740 | 1.39 | 1771–1775 | 1.25 |
| 1706–1710 | 1.5 | 1741–1745 | 1.46 | 1776–1780 | just below 1 |
| 1711–1715 | 1.28 | 1746–1750 | 1.29 | 1781–1785 | .97 |
| 1716–1720 | 1.49 | 1751–1755 | 1.4 | 1786–1790 | 1.06 |
| 1721–1725 | 1.44 | 1756–1760 | 1.37 | 1791–(1793) | 1.06 |
| 1726–1730 | 1.46 | 1761–1765 | 1.63 | | |

this effect. The phenomenon is not negligible, but is a clear indication of the dissipation of the Tridentine spirit and, as we have argued, leaves its traces throughout Roman life in general, in the effectiveness of its policies and attempted reform and its overall cultural direction, not to speak of its social effects on families. The last, however, will not become noticeable until the generation of the French Revolution.

It has also been argued that the secular clergy felt the winds of change before the regulars, that is, those belonging to religious orders or societies. In Rome, unlike most other cities, regulars nearly always outnumbered the seculars, who made up the majority of the parish priests and chaplains in private houses (although about one-third of the parishes were in charge of regulars). Table 9 compares the number of regular priests to one secular priest.

Only during the decade of 1776 to 1785, possibly because of the increase in the number of secular priests, was there a rough balance between the two groups. In general, the number of secular priests tended to oscillate between 2,300 and 2,900, somewhat toward the lower number during the earlier part of the century and the higher in the latter. But from 1774 (3,292) until 1788 (3,101), their number remained above the 3,000 level. Still, their growth lagged behind that of the population as a whole. The predominance of regulars may be related to the complaint by the seculars that all positions of advancement in church and state were given to regulars. Whether their influence was the cause or the effect of their greater numbers is not clear.[21] During the years of Jubilee, however, the secular priests, often chaperoning their flock, made their presence more noticeably felt; sometimes it affected the following year also. In 1700 their number amounted to 3,016 and rose to 3,824 the following year; in 1725 there were 3,064, and in 1750 3,514, and in 1775 3,573.

[21] See Chapter 12.

Table 10

| Years | % of nuns in female population | Years | % of nuns in female population | Years | % of nuns in female population |
|---|---|---|---|---|---|
| 1696–1700 | 3.4 | 1731–1735 | 2.91 | 1766–1770 | 2.41 |
| 1701–1705 | 3.25 | 1736–1740 | 2.89 | 1771–1775 | 2.18 |
| 1706–1710 | 3.29 | 1741–1745 | 2.6 | 1776–1780 | 2.15 |
| 1711–1715 | 3.32 | 1746–1750 | 2.63 | 1781–1785 | 2.17 |
| 1716–1720 | 3.26 | 1751–1755 | 2.75 | 1786–1790 | 2.01 |
| 1721–1725 | 3.31 | 1756–1760 | 2.7 | 1791–(1793) | 2 |
| 1726–1730 | 3.13 | 1761–1765 | 2.57 | | |

The number of nuns and sisters fluctuated between 1,700 and 2,000 until it began to drop to about 1,500 and below from 1771 onwards (with the exception of 1774, 1778, and 1783). What may be surprising, given all the inducements the papal authorities and private charities held out to poor girls to enter the religious life, is the fact that the number of nuns remained so small in relation to the overall female inhabitants of Rome (Table 10), sometimes only half of what the percentage of the total ecclesiastical population in the whole urban population was. Probably the prospects that a clerical career held out for male religious were more attractive.

Not only did the percentage of nuns among the women of Rome remain low, but their share was constantly falling, especially since 1741. It would further corroborate the general decline in religious vocation. But it has another significance. Taken together with the growing proportion of women in relation to men, it probably represents a modest indication of the greater independence, if not importance, of women in Roman life under the ancien regime. And women play a key role in every household.

The best way to gain an insight into the Roman household is to study it from the original *stati delle anime*.

For this purpose we have chosen three parishes and made a more in-depth examination of the individuals recorded on the parish lists for Easter communion, from which ultimately the *stati delle anime* were compiled. The three parishes were SS. Apostoli in the rione of Trevi, S. Salvator ai Monti in the Monti, and S. Maria in Traspontina in the Borgo, which included the Castel Sant'Angelo within its bounds. These parishes were located in three representative sections of the city, but there is no pretense that they form a scientific sample. The years chosen for the analysis were 1700, 1730, 1770, and 1800 (except in the case of S. Maria in Traspontina, where the 1700 and 1800 lists were not available, but had to be substituted by a 1697 and 1801 list), in order to see if and what changes occurred in the course of the century.[22]

The number of households in a single house are given as percentages of the total number of households in any year (Table 11). (There were also houses with more than seven households.) These figures definitely indicate a trend away from single-household houses to multi-household houses (except for the quirk of S. Salvator ai Monti in 1730, where nonetheless four- and five-household buildings were on the increase). Even though the number of palaces in the parish of SS. Apostoli may be responsible in part for the trend there, the increase of this phenomenon is clearly marked in S. Maria in Traspontina, where 2.7 percent of the houses contained ten households and 1.8 percent eleven households, and confirms the change in the type of popular housing during the second half of the eighteenth century, which has been described in the first chapter.

Since we are dealing with households it is now possible to gain a closer look at their composition. The first point of interest is to see the number of people that make up each household (expressed in percentages of the total number of households in the parish that year) (Table 12). Leaving aside the question of single-person households, into which we will look more closely below, there is a predominance of two- to four-person households in all parishes, with a slight overall tendency for these to increase over the century. Small households frequently point to nuclear families, that is, to two parents and their children, or just a married couple (Table 13).

These statistics do not indicate a clear trend toward ever more nuclear families in these parishes, and probably in Rome as a whole. In fact, leaving aside the year 1800 immediately following the marriage boom and secularization of the Jacobin republic, the percentage of nuclear families reached its highest point in 1730. We cannot verify the point, but we suspect the population growth and the lag in new housing units in the subsequent years, to which we referred earlier, may have caused people other than nuclear family members to move together into one household. This would be an unusual departure; for since the end of the fourteenth

22 The data, as indicated in the text, have been compiled from the original books of the census takers in the three parishes for the years mentioned. These are deposited in the Archivo Segreto del Vicariato di Roma. I am grateful to the various graduate assistants who have helped me intermittently in deciphering and transcribing the information in readiness for the computer. I owe a special debt of gratitude to Mr. Peter Conlin formerly of the Sociology Department of Loyola University of Chicago, for preparing for me the program for aggregating the data on individuals into households. Unfortunately the *stati delle anime* do not help us to estimate the economic conditions of households. I am aware that a full exploitation of these records would enable us to glean much more information, but, as scholars on the spot admit, this would require a team of researchers. Fiocca, "Strutture urbane e controllo sociale," 389.

Table 11

| Number of households in one house | SS. Apostoli | | | | S. Salvator ai Monti | | | | S. Maria in Traspontina | | | |
|---|---|---|---|---|---|---|---|---|---|---|---|---|
| | 1700 | 1730 | 1770 | 1800 | 1700 | 1730 | 1770 | 1800 | 1697 | 1730 | 1770 | 1801 |
| 1 | 59.0 | 53.3 | 38.5 | 27.4 | 54.7 | 57.2 | 51.0 | 41.2 | 61.2 | 58.9 | 42.6 | 37.0 |
| 2 | 19.5 | 20.5 | 19.9 | 20.5 | 21.7 | 17.5 | 22.1 | 18.8 | 18.7 | 17.5 | 14.3 | 18.1 |
| 3 | 8.3 | 11.6 | 14.7 | 15.3 | 10.7 | 9.7 | 12.4 | 11.8 | 10.5 | 8.6 | 9.8 | 11.1 |
| 4 | 5.3 | 7.6 | 9.7 | 10.9 | 5.0 | 6.3 | 6.4 | 7.6 | 7.2 | 6.7 | 6.5 | 9.9 |
| 5 | 2.0 | 3.4 | 4.8 | 8.4 | 2.2 | 4.2 | 4.0 | 6.7 | 1.7 | 3.3 | 4.9 | 7.2 |
| 6 | 1.9 | 2.2 | 4.6 | 5.8 | 3.1 | 2.1 | 1.5 | 3.5 | 0.5 | 2.5 | 2.0 | 3.3 |
| 7 | 1.9 | 0.6 | 1.8 | 3.9 | 1.0 | 1.2 | 0.9 | 2.6 | 0.1 | 1.1 | 1.7 | 1.8 |

Table 12

| Number persons in one household | SS. Apostoli | | | | S. Salvator ai Monti | | | | S. Maria in Traspontina | | | |
|---|---|---|---|---|---|---|---|---|---|---|---|---|
| | 1700 | 1730 | 1770 | 1800 | 1700 | 1730 | 1770 | 1800 | 1697 | 1730 | 1770 | 1801 |
| | 368 households | 361 households | 443 households | 480 households | 430 households | 450 households | 479 households | 462 households | 198 households | 227 households | 294 households | 211 households |
| 1 | 16.3 | 14.1 | 16.5 | 8.1 | 15.3 | 9.8 | 11.9 | 9.3 | 6.2 | 7.2 | 22.4 | 12.3 |
| 2 | 21.9 | 18.3 | 22.8 | 21.0 | 22.1 | 17.4 | 20.9 | 17.3 | 20.2 | 24.2 | 23.8 | 34.1 |
| 3 | 19.3 | 20.2 | 17.6 | 18.5 | 18.4 | 17.0 | 20.3 | 19.0 | 22.8 | 21.6 | 20.1 | 22.7 |
| 4 | 14.1 | 18.0 | 14.0 | 15.6 | 12.1 | 17.4 | 15.2 | 16.9 | 17.6 | 18.9 | 15.0 | 16.6 |
| 5 | 9.8 | 10.2 | 9.0 | 11.2 | 9.8 | 12.8 | 11.5 | 13.4 | 11.9 | 11.5 | 10.2 | 5.2 |
| 6 | 6.3 | 6.6 | 7.2 | 9.0 | 6.0 | 9.8 | 7.1 | 8.2 | 11.4 | 9.7 | 3.1 | 6.6 |
| 7 | 4.0 | 5.5 | 5.2 | 4.8 | 5.8 | 8.5 | 5.4 | 6.1 | 4.1 | 3.5 | 2.7 | 2.4 |
| 8 | 3.5 | 1.9 | 2.9 | 5.2 | 5.1 | 2.4 | 3.5 | 4.8 | 3.1 | 1.8 | 1.0 | — |
| 9 | 2.3 | 1.4 | 2.0 | 2.3 | 3.0 | 2.0 | 2.3 | 2.2 | 0.5 | 1.8 | 0.7 | — |
| 10 | 1.3 | 1.4 | 0.7 | 2.3 | 0.7 | 0.9 | 0.4 | 1.5 | — | — | 0.7 | — |
| 11 | — | — | — | — | 0.7 | 1.1 | 0.4 | 1.1 | 1.0 | — | — | — |

Table 13

| Nuclear families | SS. Apostoli | | | | S. Salvator ai Monti | | | | S. Maria in Traspontina | | | |
|---|---|---|---|---|---|---|---|---|---|---|---|---|
| | 1700 | 1730 | 1770 | 1800 | 1700 | 1730 | 1770 | 1800 | 1697 | 1730 | 1770 | 1801 |
| No. | 113 | 136 | 136 | 189 | 153 | 202 | 186 | 207 | 68 | 98 | 110 | 74 |
| % | 28.4 | 37.7 | 30.7 | 39.4 | 35.6 | 43.9 | 38.8 | 47 | 35.2 | 43.2 | 37.4 | 35.1 |

Table 14

| | SS. Apostoli | | | | S. Salvator ai Monti | | | | S. Maria in Traspontina | | | |
|---|---|---|---|---|---|---|---|---|---|---|---|---|
| | 1700 | 1730 | 1770 | 1800 | 1700 | 1730 | 1770 | 1800 | 1697 | 1730 | 1770 | 1801 |
| No. of households with children | 174 | 199 | 208 | 301 | 218 | 290 | 271 | 293 | 111 | 145 | 161 | 122 |
| % of total households | 43.7 | 55.1 | 47 | 67.7 | 50.7 | 63 | 56.6 | 63.4 | 57.5 | 63.9 | 54.8 | 57.8 |

Table 15

| | SS. Apostoli | | | | S. Salvator ai Monti | | | | S. Maria in Traspontina | | | |
|---|---|---|---|---|---|---|---|---|---|---|---|---|
| | 1700 | 1730 | 1770 | 1800 | 1700 | 1730 | 1770 | 1800 | 1697 | 1730 | 1770 | 1801 |
| No. of households with non-relatives | 102 | 66 | 108 | 125 | 85 | 70 | 34 | 73 | 63 | 34 | 21 | 13 |
| % of total households | 25.6 | 18.3 | 24.4 | 26 | 19.8 | 15.2 | 7.1 | 15.8 | 32.6 | 15 | 7.1 | 6.2 |

century it has been the general practice among the urban population in north-central Italy to set up a separate residence after marriage.[23]

What percentage of family households – not necessarily nuclear – had children in them? Here a caveat is called for, namely that under the term children we are not dealing with a particular age group, but a grade of relationship, sons and daughters of the heads of the household, including foster and step-children, some of whom were well past their youth (Table 14). Again the households with children in the parishes (qualified by those of SS. Apostoli), like the nuclear family households, reached its high point in 1730. The reason for this last phenomenon is difficult to ascertain, given the variety of the ages for the children. We may surmise that it lies with the depressed figures for 1770, which followed immediately after the disastrous famine years of 1764 to 1767. If this is correct then we can assume that the number of households with children grew gradually over the century, which, in conjunction with other demographic factors, such as the decline in clerical vocation, would suggest that Rome was distinctly becoming a more secular city.

It would take a whole book simply to analyze some of the strange configurations of relationship that can be found within a Roman household. But a significant number of households had non-relatives, servants, secretaries, and lodgers living in them, and a few of them were made up wholly of unrelated persons, including some small religious houses or lodgings of immigrants or itinerant workers (Table 15).

Apart from SS. Apostoli, the number of households containing or consisting of non-relatives generally did not surpass 20 percent and was usually much lower than that. The higher percentage at SS. Apostoli must be credited to the fact that that parish contained an unusual number of palaces of nobles and cardinals, which were more likely to shelter servants, attendants, or even other important lodgers than the other two more plebeian parishes. The same point is reflected if we just choose the households containing servants (Table 16).

A comparison of the two last tables not only shows that a very significant number of non-relatives in the household were not servants, but that the overall share of non-relatives that were servants declined in relation to the other non-relatives over the course of the century. This holds especially true for a poor parish such as S. Maria in Traspontina, where the percentage of live-in servants over the whole period tended to decrease in relation to the other households, and less so in a more affluent parish such as SS. Apostoli.

In general, the number of servants living in a household was much less than one might expect in a city where people laid so much stress on external ostentation and display. Perhaps this situation becomes more striking when we break down the

[23] Barbagli, *Sotto lo stesso tetto*, 515. A random sampling of 1,112 cases by Barbagli for the mid-eighteenth century in Rome came up with 54 percent of nuclear families. It would still make Rome the last in percentages of nuclear families after Parma (1765) with 66 percent, Florence (1810) with 65 percent, Bologna (1807) with 63 percent, Lucca (1809) with 61 percent, and Perugia (1733) with 59 percent. Barbagli, *Sotto lo stesso tetto*, 172–73, tables IV. 8 and 9.

Table 16

| | SS. Apostoli | | | | S. Salvator ai Monti | | | | S. Maria in Traspontina | | | |
|---|---|---|---|---|---|---|---|---|---|---|---|---|
| | 1700 | 1730 | 1770 | 1800 | 1700 | 1730 | 1770 | 1800 | 1697 | 1730 | 1770 | 1801 |
| No. of households with servants | 64 | 45 | 60 | 65 | 53 | 38 | 7 | 25 | 2 | 8 | 2 | 4 |
| % of total households | 16.1 | 12.5 | 13.5 | 13.5 | 12.3 | 8.3 | 1.5 | 5.4 | 1 | 3.5 | 0.7 | 1.9 |

Table 17

| No. of servants in one household | SS. Apostoli | | | | S. Salvator ai Monti | | | | S. Maria in Traspontina | | | |
|---|---|---|---|---|---|---|---|---|---|---|---|---|
| | 1700 % | 1730 % | 1770 % | 1800 % | 1700 % | 1730 % | 1770 % | 1800 % | 1697 % | 1730 % | 1770 % | 1801 % |
| 0 | 83.9 | 87.5 | 86.5 | 86.5 | 87.7 | 91.7 | 98.5 | 94.6 | 99 | 96.5 | 99.3 | 98.1 |
| 1 | 8.3 | 6.9 | 9.3 | 10.0 | 8.1 | 5.4 | 1.0 | 4.5 | 1.0 | 3.1 | 0.7 | 1.9 |
| 2 | 4.0 | 3.3 | 3.4 | 2.7 | 2.3 | 1.7 | 0.2 | 0.6 | — | 0.4 | — | — |
| 3 | — | 0.6 | 0.5 | 0.8 | 0.7 | 0.9 | 0.2 | 0.2 | — | — | — | — |
| 4 | 1.5 | 0.6 | 0.26 | — | — | — | — | — | — | — | — | — |
| 5 | — | — | — | — | 0.7 | — | — | — | — | — | — | — |

household once more by the number of servants in them (again in percentages of the total households). Of course, we also have to bear in mind that there were numerous domestics and servants in Rome who did not live in, but headed their own households or were members of other households, among them in particular stable hands, coachmen, cooks, and stewards. This fact, however, should not vitiate the overall picture seriously (Table 17). So even when a household had resident servants, it had only one in most cases. From further statistical analysis, there was only a minimal decline in the absolute number of live-in servants by the end of the century with a slight propensity toward households with no servants at all. More significant perhaps appears to be the shift from a male-dominated domestic staff to a slight female majority, a transformation that would probably have been slower in the more aristocratic areas such as SS. Apostoli (Table 18). This decline in the size of the domestic labor force, especially among males, although small, Rome appears to have shared with most of Italy. It could have had some social importance and exerted its impact on the life and ethos of the city. By putting young people of impressionable age into the homes and service of a family of a different social status a potent process of social integration was set in motion. The practice of bringing different social groups into contact had an homogenizing effect, transmitting language and beliefs. In Rome, at least, it formed the best educational experience. By depriving young people of this harmonizing education, a further note of dissonance, however minute, was added to the age.[24]

The tendency to stay in one-person households, which many people regard as a special characteristic of highly developed urbanized societies of our time, was in reality widely spread in Italian cities since the fifteenth century, and Rome was no exception. We shall take a closer look at this phenomenon in our parishes (Table 19). Given the fluctuations which such a type of household can experience at different times and places, the average here comes close to 12.5 percent, an impressive figure. Who were these lonely people? We need to determine what proportion was widowed, had never married, or possibly was left deserted, since divorce was obviously impossible in the capital of Catholicism in the eighteenth century (Table 20). Although the widowed element formed a large portion of the single-person households, in S. Maria in Traspontina sometimes even the majority, yet the bulk of the one-person households seems to have been made up of single persons. From the above percentages it would appear then that the solitary member of a household, in most cases, was a single male, occasionally, but not as a rule, a cleric (Table 21). The fact that the single male household predominated particularly in the more aristocratic parish of SS. Apostoli appears to correspond with what we noted earlier about the prevalence of male celibacy among the Milanese and Florentine patriciate.[25]

Since the census takers provided more detail about the head of the household

[24] Ibid., 341–42. [25] See this chapter, pp.60–61.

Table 18

| Sex of servants | SS. Apostoli | | | | S. Salvator ai Monti | | | | S. Maria in Traspontina | | | |
|---|---|---|---|---|---|---|---|---|---|---|---|---|
| | 1700 | 1730 | 1770 | 1800 | 1700 | 1730 | 1770 | 1800 | 1697 | 1730 | 1770 | 1801 |
| Male No. | 115 | 57 | 44 | 34 | 87 | 30 | 5 | 17 | 1 | 23 | 28 | 2 |
| % | 75.2 | 55.3 | 40 | 51.5 | 71.3 | 46.9 | 35.7 | 45.19 | 50 | 88.5 | 82.4 | 40 |
| Female No. | 38 | 46 | 66 | 32 | 35 | 34 | 9 | 20 | 1 | 3 | 6 | 3 |
| % | 24.8 | 44.7 | 60 | 48.2 | 28.7 | 53.1 | 64.3 | 54.1 | 50 | 11.5 | 17.6 | 60 |

Table 19

| | SS. Apostoli | | | | S. Salvator ai Monti | | | | S. Maria in Traspontina | | | |
|---|---|---|---|---|---|---|---|---|---|---|---|---|
| | 1700 | 1730 | 1770 | 1800 | 1700 | 1730 | 1770 | 1800 | 1697 | 1730 | 1770 | 1801 |
| No. of single-person households | 63 | 49 | 72 | 39 | 64 | 34 | 59 | 45 | 11 | 16 | 61 | 24 |
| % of total households | 16.3 | 14.1 | 16.5 | 8.1 | 15.3 | 9.8 | 11.9 | 9.3 | 6.2 | 7.2 | 22.4 | 12.3 |

Table 20

| Marital status, single-person household | SS. Apostoli | | | | S. Salvator ai Monti | | | | S. Maria in Traspontina | | | |
|---|---|---|---|---|---|---|---|---|---|---|---|---|
| | 1700 | 1730 | 1770 | 1800 | 1700 | 1730 | 1770 | 1800 | 1697 | 1730 | 1770 | 1801 |
| Single | 48.9 | 74.1 | 89.4 | 70.3 | 56.8 | 50.0 | 52.2 | 75.6 | 38.5 | 77.2 | 51.3 | 38.4 |
| Widowed | 36.9 | 24.1 | 10.6 | 27.0 | 35.3 | 50.0 | 47.8 | 19.5 | 61.5 | 22.7 | 46.3 | 46.2 |
| Married | 4.6 | 1.9 | — | 2.7 | 7.8 | — | — | 4.9 | — | — | 1.3 | 15.4 |

Table 21

| Sex of single person household | SS. Apostoli | | | | S. Salvator ai Monti | | | | S. Maria in Traspontina | | | |
|---|---|---|---|---|---|---|---|---|---|---|---|---|
| | 1700 | 1730 | 1770 | 1800 | 1700 | 1730 | 1760 | 1800 | 1697 | 1730 | 1770 | 1801 |
| Male | 49.2 | 70.4 | 80.5 | 70.3 | 55.7 | 48.5 | 50.8 | 59.6 | 23.1 | 68.2 | 64.1 | 60 |
| Female | 50.8 | 29.6 | 19.5 | 21.7 | 4.3 | 51.5 | 49.2 | 40.4 | 76.4 | 31.8 | 35.9 | 40 |

Table 22

| | SS. Apostoli | | | | S. Salvator ai Monti | | | | S. Maria in Traspontina | | | |
|---|---|---|---|---|---|---|---|---|---|---|---|---|
| | 1700 | 1730 | 1770 | 1800 | 1700 | 1730 | 1770 | 1800 | 1697 | 1730 | 1770 | 1801 |
| No. of households with female head | 65 | 43 | 74 | 106 | 64 | 87 | 74 | 83 | 44 | 31 | 42 | 50 |
| % of total households | 16.3 | 11.9 | 16.7 | 22.1 | 14.9 | 18.9 | 15.4 | 18 | 22.8 | 13.7 | 14.3 | 23.7 |

Table 23

| Marital status of head of household | SS. Apostoli | | | | S. Salvator ai Monti | | | | S. Maria in Traspontina | | | |
|---|---|---|---|---|---|---|---|---|---|---|---|---|
| | 1700 | 1730 | 1770 | 1800 | 1700 | 1730 | 1770 | 1800 | 1697 | 1730 | 1770 | 1801 |
| Married | 53.3 | 68 | 57.8 | 64.2 | 69.8 | 71.5 | 69.7 | 71.7 | 64.5 | 73 | 74.3 | 71 |
| Widowed | 20.3 | 18 | 21.9 | 22.9 | 18.6 | 21.3 | 21.5 | 20.9 | 20.3 | 17.6 | 19.1 | 26.3 |
| Single | 26.4 | 14 | 20.4 | 12.8 | 11.6 | 7.3 | 8.8 | 7.4 | 15.1 | 9.4 | 6.4 | 2.7 |

than the rest of the members of a household and since in many cases, if not all, the head was also the principal breadwinner, it behooves us to examine a bit more closely the nature and characteristics of this person.

Among the heads of these multi-person households were a number of females (Table 22). Over the century, in the three parishes together, almost one-sixth (17.39 percent) of all multi-person households were headed by a woman, and the number had distinctly increased by the end of the century to a little more than a fifth (21.27 percent), which would be consonant with the overall growth of the proportion of women in the total population.

When examining the marital status of all heads of households (in percentages of the total), the results are very much what one would expect (Table 23). The majority of the households were headed by married persons, followed at some distance by those headed by widowed people, who usually amounted to roughly a third of the married persons. Only in the parish of SS. Apostoli was there an abnormal percentage of households headed by single persons, which may be attributed once more to the clerical and aristocratic elements living there.

Where did these heads of households come from? We can only give here crude percentages based on broad geographical regions (Table 24). Making allowance for the rather sketchy data available, we can make certain general conclusions. The majority of immigrant heads of households had moved in from the area immediately surrounding the capital itself. Indeed there is evidence that the population in some areas around Rome, especially in the hilly areas, had grown considerably and some of the surplus may have sought employment or help in the city.[26] The unusually high influx in 1800–01 was probably due to the immediate aftermath of the bloody fighting which ended the Jacobin republic and the famine of 1799, when people flocked into the city for safety and food. The greater part of the remaining immigrant heads came from the poorer provinces of the Papal States to the north, Umbria, the Romagna, and especially the Marches of Ancona. The few Bolognese at SS. Apostoli were probably more affluent residents. The main point of origin from outside the Papal States was Naples and the province of Campania surrounding it. These heads of households could possibly be migrant laborers who had settled down, but there were also priests and artists in their ranks. Like the Bolognese, those who came from Florence and Tuscany remained in the more patrician parish of SS. Apostoli. The census takers had difficulty in distinguishing between Swiss, Burgundians, and Germans. Many of them were employed as cooks and confectioners, some were artists.

There are also some statistics available on the age distribution of the population for these parishes (Table 25). The age distribution remained remarkably steady. It would be fair to say that the typical inhabitant of the three parishes was a person between the ages of 28 and 31. In most of the years studied the largest age group

[26] Rossi, *L'Agro di Roma*, 98–101.

Table 24

| Place of origin of head of household | SS. Apostoli | | | | S. Salvator ai Monti | | | | S. Maria in Traspontina | | | |
|---|---|---|---|---|---|---|---|---|---|---|---|---|
| | 1700 | 1730 | 1770 | 1800 | 1700 | 1730 | 1770 | 1800 | 1697 | 1730 | 1770 | 1801 |
| Rome | 24.6 | 38.6 | 74.7 | 48.1 | | | 56.5 | 64.7 | | 14.9 | 56.3 | 60.2 |
| Lazio | 6.0 | 9.0 | 2.7 | 30.1 | | | 15.4 | 10.1 | | 7.5 | 4.3 | 11.5 |
| Umbria | 3.0 | — | 1.8 | 3.8 | | | 3.6 | 2.9 | | — | 2.1 | 3.5 |
| Marches | 6.6 | 6.5 | 5.0 | 3.8 | | | 3.4 | 4.7 | | 9.0 | 8.3 | 4.0 |
| Romagna | 4.8 | 1.6 | 0.5 | 4.4 | | | 1.1 | 1.1 | | 4.5 | 2.4 | 1.0 |
| Bolognese | — | 3.9 | 3.2 | — | | | — | — | | — | 1.1 | — |
| Abruzzi | — | — | — | — | | | 0.9 | 0.8 | | — | 0.8 | — |
| Naples & Campania | 2.4 | 2.9 | 1.4 | 1.9 | | | 1.6 | 4.7 | | — | 1.6 | 3.5 |
| Florence & Tuscany | 4.8 | 5.5 | 1.4 | 1.3 | | | 1.6 | — | | — | 2.9 | — |
| Lucca | — | — | 1.8 | — | | | 1.1 | — | | 6.0 | 1.3 | 1.0 |
| Milan | — | 2.9 | 0.5 | 4.4 | | | 3.2 | 2.1 | | 3.0 | 1.1 | 2.0 |
| Como | — | 3.2 | 0.5 | — | | | — | 0.5 | | — | 1.3 | — |
| Venice & Veneto | 3.0 | — | — | — | | | 1.1 | 0.8 | | 4.5 | — | |
| Genoa | — | — | — | — | | | — | 1.1 | | 10.4 | — | — |
| Swiss & Burgundian | 10.2 | 2.3 | 0.5 | 1.3 | | | — | — | | — | — | — |
| German | — | — | — | — | | | — | — | | 4.5 | 1.9 | — |

Table 25

| age groups | SS. Apostoli | | | | S. Salvator ai Monti | | | | S. Maria in Traspontina | | | |
|---|---|---|---|---|---|---|---|---|---|---|---|---|
| | 1700 | 1730 | 1770 | 1800 | 1700 | 1730 | 1770 | 1800 | 1697 | 1730 | 1770 | 1801 |
| 1–10 | 15.3 | 20.5 | 16.5 | 19.2 | 19.1 | 20.2 | 17.7 | 21.0 | 23.1 | 23.4 | 20.4 | 19.3 |
| 11–20 | 16.4 | 15.2 | 16.6 | 15.8 | 19.5 | 20.1 | 19.3 | 18.4 | 16.5 | 14.5 | 16.5 | 17.2 |
| 21–30 | 21.7 | 19.1 | 20.5 | 17.3 | 20.2 | 17.8 | 17.6 | 18.2 | 23.1 | 19.0 | 16.3 | 20.4 |
| 31–40 | 17.6 | 17.8 | 13.4 | 15.7 | 16.4 | 13.1 | 16.2 | 14.7 | 18.6 | 15.3 | 16.9 | 14.7 |
| 41–50 | 12.6 | 11.9 | 14.2 | 12.7 | 11.1 | 12.4 | 13.0 | 12.5 | 9.1 | 11.6 | 12.4 | 14.3 |
| 51–60 | 10.2 | 8.5 | 9.3 | 10.5 | 8.3 | 8.6 | 9.4 | 9.2 | 6.3 | 9.2 | 9.6 | 9.2 |
| Above 60 | 6.2 | 7.0 | 9.5 | 8.2 | 5.4 | 7.8 | 6.9 | 6.0 | 3.3 | 7.0 | 7.9 | 4.9 |
| Mean age | 30.97 | 29.55 | 31.47 | 30.82 | 28.39 | 29.06 | 29.80 | 28.51 | 26.24 | 28.92 | 30.90 | 28.92 |
| Median | 29.49 | 28.55 | 28.77 | 29.38 | 26.15 | 25.47 | 28.07 | 25.46 | 25.41 | 27.60 | 29.24 | 27.29 |

found in the parishes was between 21 and 30 (babies of less than one year of age were usually not counted). The population was growing slightly older until the very end of the century, when a rejuvenation occurred, probably the result of the burst of marriages during the republican period we noted earlier. The fact that the mean age, as well as the older age groups, were in general a little higher in the parish of SS. Apostoli than in the other two more working-class parishes may bear out the travellers' remark that cardinals and their like lived to a good old age in Rome; although it is worth reiterating that in virtually all parishes the population was mixed. In general, a Roman enjoyed a reasonably long life, once he or she had succeeded in surviving the years of early infancy and childhood. Octogenarians were not unknown in the parish lists; there were even nonagenarians and one centenarian.[27]

These results give us an indication of the general demographic trends and some of the characteristics of its households. In all they show that Rome still remained an open city that needed, and was ready to receive, outsiders in its bosom. The natural demographic movement lagged a little behind north and central Italy, but reflected many of the features found elsewhere. Two of these features are of particular relevance to the creation of a Roman environment that differed from the Tridentine spirit: a significant decrease in the proportion of the ecclesiastical element in its population and consequently a small, but nevertheless detectable, increase in the demographic role of the female population. At the same time the drop in the proportion of male domestics may have had somewhat of an adverse effect on the homogeneous ethos that prevailed in the city. In other words, while it is frequently argued that the Counter Reformation at large produced a hierarchical society, there was one aspect of it in which it associated all classes in one effort and one mentality. The master–servant relationship was a useful conduit for spreading this common ethos. Unfortunately the *stati delle anime* give us no clue to the economic conditions of the Roman household. We can only study the finances and economy of Rome in general.

There was one element of the permanent population that has been left out consistently from the contemporary records: the Jews. Although numerically small, they were a long-established part of Roman life, even though the period of the ancien regime was not one of the brightest epochs of Christian–Jewish symbiosis in the city.

While it is true that Jews had to live apart in wretched quarters in their ghetto and wear distinctive dress, the popes as a group showed themselves among the most lenient of all rulers, with the possible exception of those of Tuscany, where Jews found an unusual oasis of peace and prosperity. The papal sovereigns normally

[27] The population of Parma, however, lived longer: 11 percent of its people in 1765 were 60 years or over. Barbagli, *Sotto lo stesso tetto*, 175, table IV. 11.

extended them a degree of liberty of conscience, albeit within a very confining set of regulations, that few other rulers allowed them. The same cannot be always said of the Roman populace, for whom an attack on the ghetto had become a ritual exercise.[28]

The number of Jews in Rome under the ancien regime is difficult to establish with certainty. The first reliable official census of Jews only took place in 1809, under Napoleon; it put the number at 3,076, that is, 2.5 percent of the size of the Christian population. A local census of 1656 showed that 4,127 people lived in the ghetto. In 1697 the cardinal vicar claimed that 9,000 to 10,000 Jews existed in the Eternal City. According to a survey made in 1732 the number had risen to 12,000. But perhaps a more credible basis was the survey Raimondo Basi made in 1734 at the behest of the Apostolic Chamber; it put the Jewish community at 4,060 persons over the age of four (approximately 2.8 percent of the whole population). The lower 1809 figure was the consequence of the large emigration to Tuscany following the papal restoration.[29]

The Jewish community was subjected to constant demographic losses. Endemic disease caused by the proximity of the ghetto to the Tiber, the constant humidity of the ground and lack of fresh air created ravages in their ranks. Another loss was due to emigration. The popes, however, did not like to see their Jewish subjects transfer their activity and their possessions away from Rome; for a long time they placed a crippling tax on emigrants. The third loss was by conversion. While its frequency cannot be compared to that of Spain, where more draconian methods of conversion were used, there were nevertheless between five and ten conversions annually. So the Jewish community on the Tiber would have disappeared were it not for its great natural fertility, as well as the fresh influx from outside.

Jewish fertility was much higher than that of the Catholic population around them. Levels of birthrate around 50 per thousand were not uncommon prior to the nineteenth century. This may be attributable to the very low age at marriage of the girls, which many writers fix at less than 20. This age would have been more than five years younger than that of Catholic women. Both these factors, high birthrate and early marriage, are usually indicators of poverty and lack of proper social conditions. The birthrate, in spite of a continuous high infant mortality – little more than a quarter of those born reached their sixth birthday – offset in part the losses of the Jewish community. Toward the end of the century Jewish ages at marriage tended to rise closer to the Catholic level and, concomitantly, the birthrate also declined a little, but still remained somewhat high in the wretched conditions of the

28 Andrieux, *Daily Life in Papal Rome*, 86; Emanuel Pierre Rodocanachi, *Le Saint Siège et les Juifs. Le ghetto à Rome* (Paris, 1891), 3. For conditions in other parts of Italy, including Tuscany, see Renzo De Felice, "Il problema ebreico in Italia," *Rassegna storica del Risorgimento*, 40 (1953), 342–51.

29 Rodocanachi, *Le Saint Siège et les Juifs*, 12, 68–70; Attilio Milano, *Ricerche sulle condizioni economiche degli ebrei a Roma durante la clausura nel ghetto (1555–1838)* (Città di Castello, 1931), 79–80; B. CORS., ms. 1479, ff. 34–35.

Table 26

| Date | Capital declared (scudi) | Date | Capital declared (scudi) | Date | Capital declared (scudi) |
|---|---|---|---|---|---|
| 1701 | 174,000 | 1736 | 98,014 | 1766 | 73,291 |
| 1712 | 110,041 | 1741 | 89,343 | 1771 | 72,051 |
| 1716 | 116,675 | 1746 | 81,582 | 1776 | 68,379 |
| 1721 | 118,771 | 1751 | 85,493 | 1781 | 50,817 |
| 1726 | 115,318 | 1756 | 78,662 | | |
| 1731 | 109,024 | 1761 | 68,748 | | |

Roman ghetto. Between 1771 and 1775 it was 41.6 per thousand and between 1796 and 1800, 44.1 per thousand, compared to 31.76 per thousand and 34.44 per thousand respectively for the Catholic population of Rome. During the short-lived emancipation under Napoleon, it dropped to 35.6 per thousand (between 1811 and 1815), much closer to the general 32.14 ratio.[30]

The miserable circumstances in which the Roman Jews found themselves at the time of the ancien regime stemmed at least in part from papal policy in earlier centuries. By the end of the sixteenth century the parameters limiting Jewish life and economic activity had been set both legally and, with the establishment of the ghetto, concretely. With the papal edict of 1682 forbidding the Jews to lend money on interest the last blow which was to foreshadow the economic ruin of the community was struck. The sum of all the prohibitions upon the Jewish community found its natural sequel on the threshold of the ancien regime in the unofficial bankruptcy of Roman Jewry in 1698.[31]

The financial and economic situation in the ghetto further deteriorated in the course of the eighteenth century, when, with the exception of Clement XIV, all popes showed hostility to the Jews. It reached its nadir in 1755, and the official Jewish communal authority formally declared bankruptcy when its debt reached the total of 279,425.20 scudi.

At the same time the private wealth of Rome's Jews was rapidly shrinking. Table 26, based upon the sworn statements of his financial state, including the worth of his

[30] De Felice, "Il problema ebreico," 341–42; Massimo Livi-Bacci, *A History of Italian Fertility during the Last Two Centuries* (Princeton, 1977), 41–43; Zanazzo, *Tradizioni popolare romani. Usi, costumi*, 186–87; Cracas, *Diario ordinario*, 5127 (30 May 1750).

[31] Delumeau, *Vie économique et sociale de Rome*, 1:99–100, 217, 488–90; Milano, *Ricerche sulle condizioni economiche degli ebrei*, 5–8, 25–27; B. N. Ro., Fondo Vittorio Emanuele, ms. 928, 2–4; Léon Poliakov, *Les Banquiers juifs et le Saint-Siège du XIIIe au XVIIIe siècle* (Paris, 1967), 249–57.

property in Rome and outside, his furnishings, jewelry, and clothing, which each Jew had to give every five years, illustrates their impoverishment. It should be compared to the roughly 500,000 scudi that were declared during the pontificate of Urban VIII.[32]

Perhaps the only consolation for the Roman Jews was the fact that they did not suffer financial and economic hardship alone. The overall economy of the city of Rome was itself in an unsatisfactory state; some of its sectors were distinctly antiquated. And the economic situation, in turn, reflected unfavorably on the finances, both of the papal government and, ultimately, of the population, despite the deliberate policy of shielding the citizens from much of its ill-effects.

[32] Milano, *Ricerche sulle condizioni economiche degli ebrei*, 26, 29, 33, 44–51, 56–58, 60–62, 82; Rodocanachi, *Le Saint Siège et les Juifs*, 261–64; A.Cap.R., no. 22, cred. XVIII, 49.

# 4

# The economy

In 1684 the trade and payment deficit was put at a staggering five million scudi with a further loss of 1,300,000 scudi as a result of the unadjusted gold–silver ratio and the haphazard debasement of various coins. By 1786 it was suggested that in normal times the imports into the Papal States exceeded the exports threefold in value. Whatever the true figures might be, and exact statistics are virtually impossible to come by, the trend is clear. There was something radically at fault with the whole economic set-up of the Papal States, that would not let them compete on an equal footing with their foreign rivals. In this chapter we shall concentrate on Rome and its economy, only departing outside where appropriate.[1]

The Papal States shared with the other Italian states the negative effects of a general decline since the start of the seventeenth century. The most serious effects, which varied with the different regions of the state, but were apparent everywhere, included: an economy based largely on agriculture with no or little capital accumulation, incapable, therefore, of promoting productive investments; scarcity of capital, or at least capital available for realizing new productive industrial activity; a manufacturing activity still at the level of the craftsman and artisan, characterized by a constantly declining productivity while other parts of Europe were entering the period of protoindustrialization;[2] and, finally, a market paralyzed and discouraged by political divisions and local barriers, by lack of communications, by desultory brigandage, and by an almost total absence of credit facilities.[3]

Even the most progressive region of the Papal States, Bologna, did not remain

1 ASR, Famiglie diverse, Cavaletti, busta 1, vol. XII, no. XI; BL, Egerton ms. 3798, chap. 4.

2 Rome, in common with other parts of Italy, although not Lombardy and Piedmont, failed to enter in the course of the eighteenth century the stage of production which is currently labelled protoindustrialization. It lacked a truly entrepreneurial class that would have harnessed a rural cottage industry, based on the contiguous provinces, for the economic benefit of the city. Cf. Myron P. Gutmann, *Toward the Modern Economy. Early Industry in Europe, 1500–1800* (New York, 1988), 115–49.

3 Nicola La Marca, *Saggio di una ricerca storico-economica sull'industria e l'artigianato a Roma dal 1750 al 1849* (Padua, 1969), 12–15. A short discussion on the overall economic decline in Italy, with most of the emphasis on the north, is found in Frederick Krantz and Paul M. Hohenberg (eds.), *Failed Transitions to Modern Industrial Society. Renaissance Italy and Seventeenth Century Holland. Proceedings of the First International Colloquium of the Interuniversity Centre for European Studies, April 18–20, 1974* (Montreal, 1975), 8–34; Carlo M. Cipolla, "The Economic Decline of Italy," in Brian Pullan (ed.), *Crisis and Change in the Venetian Economy in the Sixteenth and Seventeenth Centuries* (London, 1968), 127–45.

unaffected by this economic retardation. In the course of the eighteenth century it suffered a gradual deindustrialization. Although the Bolognese economy claimed to be a mixed one, it consisted preponderately of the hemp and silk industry. Once Bologna possessed a virtual monopoly over the supply of these raw materials in Italy and the technology of working them, thereby controlling an ample slice of the world market. But the monopoly came to an end when a silk industry arose in Piedmont in 1630 and then spread to Venice, Zurich, Lyons, and England, so that between 1713 and 1750 the city lost 53 silk mills, 52.2 percent of its total. Similarly, the success of the agrarian sector in exporting raw hemp cheaply without restriction destroyed the domestic industry.[4]

Rome's economy suffered even more disadvantages. The transportation network did not favor trade. The Tiber was not navigable for sea-going craft or, for that matter, for large shipping from upstream; a lateral canal between Umbria and the sea was needed. The roads were still the fine old Roman consular roads that resounded to the footsteps of the legions, but, left too often without proper maintenance, their huge flagstones were brittle, worn, and disjointed. Although the coastline was long, the ports were few in number and of little importance. The harbors of Montalto, Corneto, and Porto d'Anzio sheltered mainly fishing boats. Fiumicino could accommodate ships of 190 metric tons. The only suitable port for the city was Civitavecchia.

Finding liquid capital indispensible for launching any productive initiative was almost impossible. Wealth was not lacking in Rome, but it was either tied up in land or in *luoghi di monte* (government bonds), or was immobilized in the coffers of religious establishments, who applied it generously to relieve hardship, support hospitals and shelters, and build chapels. For example, Giovanni Andrea Doria Pamphilj, at his death in December 1764, left total assets of 2,956,436.13 scudi, of which 25 percent were in *luoghi di monte*, but only 5.7 percent of which in Roman *luoghi*, contrasted to 8.8 percent in Genoese investments, and 24.2 percent in property, both rural and urban.[5] By some counts the ecclesiastical fortune made up an estimated six-tenths of the Roman wealth, while the nobles possessed another three-tenths, leaving one-tenth to be divided among more modest hands.

The nobles, even if rich in lands, palaces, villas, and art treasures, had little ready cash, and what they had was often deposited abroad. Although a few noble families in the sixteenth and seventeenth centuries exploited the mineral wealth in their holdings with indifferent results, by the turn of the seventeenth century a Borghese or a Braschi would have been shocked if anyone tried to persuade him to subsidize a model farm. As for small industrial ventures, if nobles took any part at all, they were normally the lesser and more recently ennobled, such as Cavaliere Sampieri.

4 Giacomelli, "Carlo Grassi e le riforme bolognesi," 12–20; Dal Pane, *Economia e società a Bologna*, 88, 254–59, 288, 293, 334.

5 ADP, 86.56.3. Over 24 percent of the Doria Pamphilj fortune was invested abroad, not counting the *luoghi*.

The bourgeoisie, insignificant in numbers as it was, had never recovered from being blocked in its effort to expand around the start of the seventeenth century. About 1600 there existed in Rome a middle class which had a certain capacity for capital accumulation. But it found no future, since the papal government of the Counter Reformation failed to take hold of the opportunity to turn the Rome of its time into an industrial city. Instead, the considerable capital which the city possessed then was diverted to a large degree to building construction, and the Roman bourgeoisie, with its capacity for saving and investing in productive enterprises, turned away from work and, following the example of the magnates, had little option but to invest its money in *luoghi di monte* and *vacabili*.

To this must be added the historic function of the city, that of the directive center of the entire Catholic community, with the papal court and an urban aristocracy which for centuries had enriched itself, not through trade and industry, but through benefices and other ecclesiastical revenues. Even more than most capitals in Europe, Rome was a city of consumption and not production, seat not only of a nobility, with its great landed possessions and what little was left of its feudal privileges, but of a middle class, such as it was, which had come to see its possibility of social advancement by entering public employment, and of an urban lower class, often of rural extraction, which frequently found its only means of livelihood in the service of great families and the princes of the church or, in the absence of which, in begging and public assistance.

The final obstacle to the rise of a native industry in Rome was the competition by religious institutions and hospices, which set up their own workshops. They not only enjoyed certain tax exemptions and could make use of outlets for marketing their own goods not available to private entrepreneurs, among them public institutions such as the papal establishment, but, worse still, they disposed of an unpaid labor force or, at least, one below cost. All these factors, together with the lack of modern efficient machinery, the large number of transit tolls and duties, and an unskilled labor force, constituted a barrier to the achievement of a truly indigenous industrial activity.[6]

As a consequence, what little there was of Roman industry was not concentrated. Even though one may come across some "industrialist" or artisan who possessed more than one workshop, he did not succeed to monopolize the sector, unless he were granted a special monopoly or *privativa*, a well meant incentive to introduce new industries, the effect of which was usually that of a constraint on trade. These were as a rule owners of water mills used not only for milling grain and making

[6] Delumeau, *Vie économique et sociale de Rome*: 76–77; Giuntella, *Roma nel Settecento*, 72–73; Andrieux, *Daily Life in Papal Rome*, 76–77; Renzo De Felice, *Aspetti e momenti della vita economica di Roma e del Lazio nei secoli XVIII e XIX* (Rome, 1965), 275, 278–79; La Marca, *Saggio di una ricerca storico-economica*, 15–20; Ida Rossodivita, "Appunti per una storia della popolazione di Trastevere nel Settecento," *Studi Romani*, 23 (1975), 160; Madelin, *Rome de Napoléon*, 41–43; Cipolla, "The Economic Decline of Italy," 137–40.

paper but also for preparing paints, tobacco, and for tanning. Most workshops, however, were family concerns carried on personally by the owner with the help of his family and, at the most, one or two laborers. Labor, given the appalling number of the poor, was generally cheap, but left much to be desired technically. It was these craftsmen with their little shops resounding with brisk activity that gave the Roman neighborhoods their local color. Under these conditions the products of manufacture were few and almost all consumed on the spot. The bulk of the industrial export, such as it was, consisted of raw materials and a few processed goods.

Rome's craftsmen, with some important exceptions, were still organized as in so many European cities in guilds and corporations (*università*), which had degenerated from valid instruments for the propagation and specialization of the various arts and crafts into conservative tools of blind selfishness, intent only upon combatting any means of competition which could harm in some way the interests of their members. The only difference was that whereas in the period of the ancien regime the power of the guilds was challenged elsewhere, in Rome these associations seemed to have reached the apogee of their influence, at least in the early part of the eighteenth century.

The system of guilds in Rome went back to the Middle Ages with the appearance of a *mercanzia* composed of thirteen *arti*. In the middle of the thirteenth century, the different categories of *mercatores*, starting with the innkeepers, shoemakers, and masons began to separate into distinct corporations. This process was halted by the exile of the popes at Avignon and the troubles of the Great Schism, and only regained its momentum in the fifteenth century.

By the eighteenth century Rome had 92 guilds, or 130 if you include the religious confraternities associated with the various crafts. No other city in Italy, not even Milan or Florence, where the guilds under the last Medici ruler, Gian Gastone, were still able to resist the grand ducal policy of economic control, had so many or better organized ones at the time. Yet they were constantly subject to the intervention of papal power, not only in their relationship with the public, in regulating their privileges and limiting their rights, but also in their organic life, such as drafting and amending their statutes, arbitrating internal discords, and maintaining their hierarchical structure. This intervention might be direct, by papal decree, or more often it emanated from representatives of papal power, the cardinal camerlengo, the governor of Rome, and the heads of the grascia and annona. The last two were particularly concerned with the guilds active in the city's food supply. The establishment of a general tariff of prices, as well as the surveillance of those corporations involved in clothing, luxury items, and the arts, was reserved for the cardinal camerlengo.

But, apart from government intervention, the corporate system imposed its own constraints on trade and limited individual initiative. To take one such example, several masters could possess a workshop jointly, but with few exceptions, among them tailors and soapmakers, no one was allowed more than one. Some guilds also limited the overall number of workshops and stores for their particular trade and the distance that had to be preserved between each shop. Such distance would vary from trade to trade: the blacksmiths, who branched off into several specialities, had to be 25 meters apart, the sellers of acquavita 40 meters, the pharmacists 400 meters. More burdensome were what in modern union language would be termed the jurisdictional divisions. The shoemakers were only permitted to make new shoes, while the cobblers had to restrict themselves to repairs. The makers of candles had to obtain their tallow exclusively from the city's butchers. They were prohibited from procuring it elsewhere. It does not take a great deal of imagination to see that such rules opened up avenues of innumerable jurisdictional disputes and masses of petty law suits for the already litigious Romans.[7]

The history of the guilds during the ancien regime is everywhere filled with the accounts of the restrictive admission policies imposed by the master craftsmen, which resulted in keeping the journeymen from ever achieving their independence and thus creating a disaffected class of artisanal proletarians. The Roman story bears similarities to the general trend, but with modifications which were significant enough to obviate the worst effects of such a situation. Beginning in the seventeenth century, in the crafts that produced the greatest income for its members the guildsmen were making access progressively more difficult. Some corporations tended to transform themselves into a kind of closed caste reserved only to relatives of their members. This happened to the corporation of the *rigattieri*, the secondhand dealers, when they assumed the sale of all furnishings, and likewise to the corporations of the fishmongers and gilders. On the other hand, as the revenues of such università as the agricultural laborers and money lenders, who were only engaged in occasional activities, shrunk, the reverse occurred. They dropped their barriers to admission.

For the Roman journeymen and apprentices, who had to wait for the realization of their dream of becoming masters, two types of organizations were open: those dependent and those independent of the corporations of their master craftsmen. In their first the apprentices had their own officials, their own funds, and, as it appears, their own statutes, but remained subject to the regulations of their masters' guilds.

[7] La Marca, *Saggio di una ricerca storico-economica*, 15; Delumeau, *Vie économique et sociale de Rome*, 1:368–70; Gonippo Morelli, *Le corporazioni romane di arti e mestieri dal XIII al XIX secolo* (Rome, 1937), 22–23; Emanuel Pierre Rodocanachi, *Les Corporations ouvrières à Rome depuis la chute de l'Empire romain* (Paris, 1894), 1:i, xxix–xxi; Luigi Dal Pane, *Storia del laboro in Italia dagli inizi del secolo XVIII al 1815* (2nd ed.; Milan, 1958), 380 n. 31; Alberto Canaletti-Gaudenti, *Delle corporazioni artigiane nella storia economica di Roma del secolo XVIII* (Rome, 1914), 4; Furio Diaz, *Il Granducato di Toscana. I Medici* (Turin, 1976), 529–30. For examples of jurisdictional disputes and limitations on the exercise of trade see, inter alia, ASR, Camerale II, arti e mestieri, busta 4; busta 6, fasc. 10, 13; busta 7, fasc. 14; busta 12, fasc. 26, 27; busta 14, fasc. 33; busta 20, fasc. 44; busta 21; busta 22, fasc. 47; busta 23, fasc. 50; busta 34, fasc. 72, 73; busta 38, fasc. 83; busta 39, fasc. 86; busta 43, fasc. 90; busta 44, fasc. 91; busta 45, fasc. 92; A. Cap. R., no. 33, cred. XIII, bandi e editti, 121.

Sometimes, however, these associations were totally independent of their masters' guilds, as in the case of the *vermicellari* – retail pasta makers – tailors, shoemakers, and goldsmiths. Then the association assumed a class character, from which the masters were strictly excluded. With such an organization, legally recognized, behind them the edge was taken off some of the worst frustrations of a journeyman's existence. Whenever apprentices failed to gain recognition for a regular corporation they simply united to form a confraternity for religious purposes, which acted as a cover for their activities. This explains the favor the institution of the religious confraternity enjoyed among them. In contrast, in Florence the dissolution of the confraternities in 1785 was to deprive the masses of the principal safety valve for siphoning off their social and economic discontent.

The ties between religion and the craft guilds, under whatever name they masqueraded, were probably closer in Rome than elsewhere. The seat of these economic institutions was in their church, the building of which belonged completely to the università or was erected at their expense. In it, they carried on all their civic, economic, artistic, and spiritual activities. Each corporation had a cardinal protector, some among them future popes, such as Clement XII, who before his elevation was protector of the *speziali* – grocers and druggists – Clement XIII, who had been protector of the blacksmiths, secondhand dealers, and wine merchants, Clement XIV of the booksellers, and Pius VI of the innkeepers. Sometimes it was difficult to distinguish their lay activities from their religious ones. Their members bore the expenses of the great feast days of their patron saint, on which they sumptuously decorated the altar, the chapel, and the church for a worship service that was marked with pomp. They took part in religious processions. Yet the benefit was reciprocal; some of these guilds owed their existence and survival, occasionally their flourishing condition, to the special requirements of religious life and worship. Carpentry, carving, gilding ornaments, lamps, wax, silk, the making of gold and silver ribbons, absorbed to an unusual degree the resources and capacity of the Roman artisanat.

As the eighteenth century proceeded the corporative system became more stifling and the guilds more egocentric and jealous of their privileges. Unlike the more vigorous approach of Pietro Leopoldo's administration in Tuscany, where the whole guild structure was abolished in 1770, the Roman government, perhaps chastened by Turgot's failure in France, did not dare to tackle the problem head on by abolishing them. Instead it tried to reshape them to suit the new demands. The organs of government commissioned to carry through this reform were quickly paralyzed by the resistance they encountered. So the abolition of these bodies had to await the formal action of Pius VII at the dawn of the nineteenth century. Reform began with the suppression of the guilds connected with the annona on 2 February 1800, and with the grascia on 11 March 1801. A decree of 16 December of that year fixed the principles for suppressing all the guilds, but actually carried it into effect for only some of them. The congregation of the Economica was then charged with continuing the work of reform. It swept away most of the remaining guilds on 2 June 1806. The suppression of the corporations was an integral part of Pius VII's legislation in favor of free trade within the Papal States and in this light can be viewed as a continuation of the policy of Pius VI.[8]

Delumeau's pithy description, "Such was the destiny of Rome: to import primary commodities, food, and industrial products – and to export truth and art," held true for the ancien regime as much as for the sixteenth century, except that with the waning of the Counter Reformation fervor the export of art, both culturally and materially, assumed the preponderance. Both art and truth drew the pilgrims to their respective shrines in the Eternal City and so encouraged tourism, an invisible export not to be underestimated in the local economy. It was to these tourists and their noble Roman hosts that the shops producing luxury items, such as perfumery, artificial flowers, and objects of religious cult, were catering.

Leaving aside the essential and personal trades, Rome's artisanal industry concentrated in three sectors – building, the products of animal raising, such as textiles and leather, and the skills involving artistic elements. There is some overlapping, of course. The building industry from the point of view of the overall economy is not usually productive of exchangeable values and was less so in the circumstances of the ancien regime, where it was often employed in ecclesiastical construction and maintenance.

The most important product of sheep raising was wool. As for the other derivative trades, there was the use of hides for tanning and the making of gloves. With its large flocks of sheep there was an ample wool supply. In 1813 Tournon calculated the complete production in Lazio at 750,000 kg; of this about 300,000 was spun and woven locally and 100,000 kg carded and felted on the spot. The working of wool took place above all in the city.

The population required great quantities of cloth. So, if any major industry had a chance to succeed in Rome, it was this one, with its local source of the primary raw material and the alum of Tolfa, equalling the best in Europe, not far away. Although the *arte della lana*, the woollen guild, had been very prosperous in medieval Rome, it was clearly in decline by the middle of the sixteenth century. In spite of intermittent efforts by Pius V and Sixtus V the craft failed to keep up in quality and skill with its competitors. With other avenues of earning a living socially more acceptable, both the entrepreneurial spirit and the incentive to acquire the requisite skills were generally missing. In 1622 there were a mere 82 weavers in the Eternal City, whose output was unable to meet the domestic demand, not to speak of providing for the export trade. This number contrasted with the 878 weavers in Florence in 1604.

[8] Delumeau, *Vie économique et sociale de Rome*, 1:134, 287–88; Morelli, *Le corporazioni romane*, 13–14; Giuntella, *Roma nel Settecento*, 73–75; Valsecchi, *Italia nel Settecento*, 451–52; Eric Cochrane, *Florence in the Forgotten Centuries, 1527–1800* (Chicago, 1973), 402, 449; Petit-Radel, *Voyage historique*, 2:522–24.

With the start of the ancien regime at a moment when the Florentine *arte della lana* was feeling the marks of decline, new efforts were made by Innocent XII and Clement XI to resuscitate the Roman textile industry. Their endeavors centered on the woollen factory set up at San Michele a Ripa in Trastevere. The principal purpose of the organizers of this plant was to make it a trade school which would turn out a goodly number of apprentices, but at the same time it was also planned to increase the national production of woollen cloth, by supporting the workshop with all kinds of privileges and assistance. Alas, during the first year of the school's existence disorders arose, provoked by an open rift between the Piarist fathers, who had been put in charge of the whole project, and the master craftsmen, who had been called from Florence both to direct the factory and train the youths in the technical skills. The tension at times erupted into genuine revolts among the apprenticed youths.

When Montesquieu visited Rome in 1729 he found the quality of the woollen cloth to be poor. The Romans had attempted something beyond their means and their product became more expensive than the cloth imported from abroad. They had put too much wool into a piece so that the wool cost more than the cloth was sold for and the resultant fabric was coarse in the opinion of Montesquieu's informant. Leone Pascoli expressed a similar view and advised these quasi-religious institutions to stop making woollen cloth and apply themselves to more delicate textiles.

The Ospizio di San Michele, of course, was not the only institution engaged in making woollen cloth. There were looms in the Conservatorio Pio, the Conservatorio delle Mendicanti, and the orphanage attached to the hospital of Santo Spirito. The total output of the Mendicanti went to the prison administration and that of Santo Spirito was used on the premises. The cloth woven at the Conservatorio Pio, in lease to two enterprising manufacturers, was of better quality than that of San Michele.[9]

Papal endeavors did not end with the institutional promotion of the woollen industry. From Clement XI to Clement XII there was a deliberate effort to encourage woollen manufacture under the shelter of a protectionist policy. In 1719, and then repeated in 1720, 1721, 1725, 1730, and 1737, legislation prohibiting the import of foreign cloth was published, legislation, by the way, that had been tried with not much success in the previous century. The Apostolic Chamber also contributed its share by advancing free loans of money for the introduction of new manufactures of woollens. As a result of these measures, which were by no means totally effective, one pamphleteer at the time of Clement XIII claimed that in Rome

[9] Delumeau, *Vie économique et sociale de Rome*, 1:381, 501–04; Lanciani, *Storia degli scavi*, 4:155; Lepre, "Agricoltura e manifattura in un rione," 361–63, 366; Diaz, *Il Granducato di Toscana*, 1:486–89; Michele Fatica, "La reclusione dei poveri a Roma durante il pontificato di Innocenzo XII (1692–1700)," *Ricerche per la storia religiosa di Roma*, 3 (1979), 175–76; Rossodivita, "Appunti per una storia della popolazione," 155–57; Montesquieu, *Voyages. Oeuvres complètes*, 2:1189–90; La Marca, *Saggio di una ricerca storico-economica*, 40–41; De Felice, *Aspetti e momenti della vita economica*, 102–04.

alone more than 20,000 poor persons lived off the trade, inclusive of such secondary processes as dyeing, compared to roughly 17,000 to 18,000 in Florence (1765). The Roman figure is probably exaggerated, but it does point to the importance of the trade in the life of the city.

For the rest of the century the industry made some progress, in part through the government's efforts to modernize it, especially at the time of Pius VI, when Fabrizio Ruffo was treasurer general. Contacts were made with Frenchmen for introducing new processes and mechanical devices. In 1783, the Avignonese François Auber and François Landri proposed a machine for spinning made up of thirty spindles worked by one person only. The experiment was a success and the Apostolic Chamber agreed to have more built. Two years later, eleven of these machines were set up in Rome and three in Civitavecchia. Yet, the Roman industry remained ignorant of the really important technological breakthroughs associated with the Industrial Revolution even when they had become known elsewhere. In 1809 there was not a single loom with a flying shuttle in the city. What the local industry lacked, therefore, was technical know-how and an entrepreneurial class. Like the antiquated silk industry in Naples, it was unable to compete with the products from the north.

The proprietors of the greater manufactures of this period were almost all artisans who had succeeded through tireless labor to make a fortune out of their trade, but still had not acquired the mentality and the spirit of the industrial entrepreneur, incapable as they were of facing the least risk in the management of their enterprises. In 1809 there were 34 "factories" making woollen cloth, equipped with a total of 456 looms, that is an average of 14 looms per plant. For this industry nine fulling mills in Rome and another eleven on the Acqua Mariana in the immediate neighborhood were available.[10]

Among the more important derivatives of the woollen industry were the tapestries of the Ospizio di San Michele a Ripa, set up at the time of Clement XI. Some claim that the founder was the Fleming De Mignot, creator of the famous tapestry of the Virgin and Child in 1715; others assert it was the Frenchman Jean Simonet, who established the school in association with the painter Andrea Procaccini. Whoever it might have been, the tapestries of San Michele could hold their own with the more famous Gobelins of France during the first half of the eighteenth century. At the end of the century, however, the industry was in deep crisis. Production languished almost completely, because the traditional clientele,

[10] Petrocchi, *Roma nel Seicento*, 51; De Cupis, *Le vicende dell'agricoltura e della pastorizia nell'Agro Romano. L'annona* (Rome, 1911), 358–59; La Marca, *Saggio di una ricerca storico-economica*, 49–51; De Felice, *Aspetti e momenti della vita economica*, 225–30; Enzo Piscitelli, "Fabrizio Ruffo e la riforma economica dello Stato Pontificio," *Archivio della società romana di storia patria*, 74 (1971), 118–19; Tournon, *Etudes statistiques sur Rome*, 2:7–8; Rossodivita, "Appunti per una storia della popolazione," 156–57; Chorley, *Oil, Silk and Enlightenment*, 178, 198–200; Cochrane, *Florence in the Forgotten Centuries*, 401; ASR, Camerale II, commercio e industria, busta 13; ASR, Camerale II, arti e mestieri, busta 18, fasc. 40; A.Cap.R., no. 7, cred. VII, editti e bandi, 113.

the high prelates and aristocracy, had other things to occupy their minds than that of embellishing palaces.[11]

Silk making was an ancient art in Italy, dating from the ninth century, when there was a workshop in Lucca. In Rome, unlike Naples and Florence where it was a major industry, it never succeeded in taking root. The manufacture of silk was carried on in a few small workshops in the eighteenth century. Although an edict of 27 May 1778 speaks of a considerable number of Romans, both within and outside the city, engaged in silkworm breeding and unwrapping cocoons, spinning fibers, and weaving cloth, the silk industry never remotely approached the importance of the wool industry. It certainly did not employ anywhere near the 8,500 silk workers of Florence. In 1781, the number of licensed masters, it was stated, was 31 and licensed workmen about 85. But many of those working silk looms had not passed their competency tests.

Since 1772 the government constantly tried to rectify the situation by encouraging the introduction of the manufacture of fine French silk and velvet, generally with little or no success. The principal manufacture appeared to be mainly concentrated in two spinning mills of a very antiquated type in Trastevere, one at San Pietro in Montorio on the Acqua Paolo belonging to the Conservatorio delle Pericolanti, and the other, further down the slope at the Porta Settimiana, attached to the Conservatorio delle Cenciose. In both the raw silk was spun and twisted, but the shortage of raw materials slowed down the work.[12]

The working of linen and hemp was widespread, although limited in quantity, in Rome and all of Lazio. The spinning by distaff and spindle was the most universal craft among the needy classes in the city and the countryside. Weaving in Rome, as might be expected, was done on looms of obsolete design. It resulted in a good enough product, but one that obviously could not compete with the import and could only be used for popular and coarse clothing. The better class linen came from Germany. The hemp was used for rope making to supply the home market. During Napoleonic times the cities of Rome and Viterbo between them had 120 rope makers.

As for cotton, in spite of the provisions made under Pius VI, giving preference and subsidies to the cultivation of cotton in the Roman Campagna, especially along the Tyrrhenian littoral, and the working of the commodity in Rome, this branch was in anything but a flourishing condition at the end of the ancien regime. Spinning was imperfect and very expensive, while weaving was only carried on in

[11] La Marca, *Saggio di una ricerca storico-economica*, 41–42; De Felice, *Aspetti e monumenti della vita economica*, 230–31; Rossodivita, "Appunti per una storia della popolazione," 157; ASR, Camerale II, arti e mestieri, busta 9, fasc. 19.

[12] Delumeau, *Vie économique et sociale de Rome*, 1:504–10; La Marca, *Saggio di una ricerca storico-economica*, 42; De Felice, *Aspetti e momenti della vita economica*, 231–35; Rossodivita, "Appunti per una storia della popolazione," 158; Cochrane, *Florence in the Forgotten Centuries*, 401; Vicchi, *Vincenzo Monti (1778–1780)*, 204–5; ASR, Camerale II, arti e mestieri, busta 7, fasc. 15; busta 37, fasc. 79; ASR, Camerale II, commercio e industria, busta 13.

five establishments, of which the most important was undoubtedly the one set up by Clement XIV among the ruins of the Baths of Diocletian, of whose checkered career we shall have occasion to speak more in this chapter.[13]

The Roman countryside, traditionally rich in sheep and cattle, nourished a leather industry which for centuries had been one of the most flourishing in the city. Roman leather and hides were the first in Italy and, since the sixteenth century, in general demand abroad. But the diffidence and sluggishness, so typical of the Roman economy in general, in taking advantage of technical progress, began to make itself felt with pernicious consequences. Added to this was the drawn-out jurisdictional dispute between the two branches of leather workers, the *vaccinari* and the *pellari*. While they frittered away their time on internal squabbles, the local production of treated hides sank into a position of clear inferiority to foreign production. Consequently the export of tanned products was reduced; the raw leather and the hides were sold abroad where they were finished by the newest technical method only to be reimported again. By 1810 this absurd need to export raw hides and import tanned leather was estimated to cause a loss of 25,000 scudi annually.[14]

The making of musical instruments, although almost wholly of the character of a craft, was likewise highly regarded and enjoyed a great degree of prosperity. Roman pianos were good, as were the string instruments. There were four workshops for pianos, one of which was in the Via del Corso and another in the Via Condotti; string instruments were made by Giuseppe Argelli. But the best were the wind instruments produced by Domenico Biglioni in the Via dei Banchi Vecchi. From an economic standpoint the most important and prosperous branch was the production of musical strings made from the gut of sheep. With Naples, Rome shared almost a monopoly of this product, which was one of the glories of its economy. The craft, which had arisen in the fifteenth and sixteenth centuries, took root in the Eternal City thanks to the quality of the raw material and the protection of the government. The strings were soon in demand throughout Europe. In the seventeenth century there were about twenty small factories for musical strings, a number eventually fixed by papal decree. Some time at the close of the eighteenth century eighteen of these joined into one great firm, Pica-Tofanini and Company, with its studio in the Piazza di Napoli. Two smaller independent workshops survived. But the industry was in eclipse. Whereas Pica-Tofanini employed more

[13] La Marca, *Saggio di una ricerca storico-economica*, 42–43; De Felice, *Aspetti e momenti della vita economica*, 235, 272; Rossodivita, "Appunti per una storia della popolazione," 158; Tournon, *Etudes statistiques sur Rome*, 2:2–4; BL, Egerton ms. 3798, chap. 5.

[14] ASR, Camerale II, arti e mestieri, busta 6, fasc. 10; busta 44, fasc. 91; busta 45, fasc. 92; De Felice, *Aspetti e momenti della vita economica*, 251, 254–55; La Marca, *Saggio di una ricerca storico-economica*, 44, 49–51; Piscitelli, "Fabrizio Ruffo e la riforma economica," 120–21; William Witmore Story, *Roba di Roma* (London, 1871), 35.

than sixty hands in 1793 alone, the three firms together only had 25 employees in 1809.[15]

Most of the corporations connected with the river traffic on the Tiber were located in Trastevere. Although papal statutes and bulls prohibited unlicensed monopolies, these were in fact able to create all kinds of monopolies for their own advantage. The coopers and waggoners claimed the exclusive right of hauling wine and other merchandise unloaded at the Ripa Grande. The bargees and ferrymen were charged with bringing ashore the persons and goods which arrived at the Ripa Grande. The old college of brokers, or *sensali*, at the Ripa and the Ripetta, once powerful and wealthy, was suppressed by Clement XI in 1717 and its authority to levy imports on the transportation of goods transferred directly to the Apostolic Chamber.[16]

Apart from the clearly defined professions, Rome had what may be called a large population of "floating" trades. Many of these would fall under the category of street vendors who hawked their wares from door to door. There were something like 260 different kinds of such vendors. Roman leisureliness and the southern sun could have encouraged the development of such ambulatory trade, much of which can be classed as Rome's underground economy. Special licenses were granted to women and men who, without fixed store, went through the city selling old wares, but these articles had to be in such condition that the Monte di Pietà would accept them in pawn. But, license or no, the tinkers and coppersmiths of Rome were constantly augmented by foreign competitors coming from as far afield as Naples and the Trentino, as well as by local gypsies, who roamed the streets, much to the chagrin of the natives.[17]

We have no figure on the overall number of domestic employees of all categories, from kitchen maid to coachman, from lady in attendance to secretary or steward of the house. If the number who lived in a household that was given in Chapter 3 appears low, it should be borne in mind that a greater part did not live in, but had their own households or lived at home. As long as there were such openings available the fathers, whatever their social status, lived in the hope that their children would always find a place in the house of a prince or a cardinal, thereby forgetting the total lack of security that domestic employment provided against sickness, old age, and the loss of job.

15 ASR, Camerale II, arti e mestieri, busta 6, fasc. 10; busta 12, fasc. 27; Delumeau, *Vie économique et sociale de Rome*, 1:129; De Felice, *Aspetti e momenti della vita economica*, 47; Scott, *Piranesi*, 226; Giuseppe Roberti, "La musica in Italia nel secolo XVIII secondo le impressioni di viaggiatori stranieri," *Rivista musicale italiana*, 7/8 (1900–1901), 8:536.

16 Rossodivita, "Appunti per una storia della popolazione," 161; ASR, Camerale II, arti e mestieri, busta 11, fasc. 22; busta 35, fasc. 77.

17 ASR, Camerale II, arti e mestieri, busta 7, fasc. 14; busta 12, fasc. 26; busta 34, fasc. 72; busta 38, fasc. 83; A.Cap.R., no. 33, cred. XIII, bandi e editti, 121; Delumeau, *Vie économique et sociale de Rome*, 1:383.

Another uncounted group were the rural laborers who hired out their services to the landed proprietors. Much of Rome, it should be remembered, still consisted of vineyards, meadows, and park land, and just outside the gates were more vineyards and the large estates or *tenute*. These laborers lived in the peripheral rioni such as Trastevere and Monti. Their employment was often seasonal. Included in their number were smallholders and sharecroppers, that is, peasants who had a little bit of land to cultivate, but the yield of whose fields was not enough to support their family. These already constituted a privileged class, entrance into which would allow a higher standard of life. Above them was a handful of urban tenant farmers who had succeeded in obtaining the leasehold of some land, notably a vineyard, belonging to a noble or a monastery.

We know virtually nothing of the largest of the submerged sectors of Rome's population, the poor and the unemployed, except from the point of view of objects of Christian charity. There are no statistical figures available and it is doubtful whether the papal government had any idea. A report of 8 November 1810 on public order in Rome claimed that more than 2,000 working families were without work, which could mean as many as 15,000 to 20,000 persons were impoverished. But what about the greater number who never worked? By some conjectures, almost a quarter of the population of the state were beggars. More research on Rome's underworld of the poor is needed.

Last, but by no means least, is the share of work done by women, which was of considerable importance, since women played a vital part in the agricultural work of the "internal Campagna." Many devoted themselves to the domestic textile industry or effectively helped the men of the family in running their small craftshops or in the conduct of trade.[18]

Given the grim economic and financial conditions, it is not surprising that the ancien regime period would see a flood of pamphleteering on economic matters. Indeed, because censorship and the absence of a political newspaper press made political criticism impossible within the Papal States, some of the most active minds in public affairs turned to the economy and public finance. The files of various papal organs of government are filled with economic critiques and projects to improve the situation. We are dealing with the Roman counterpart of the reform movement in other Italian states, which in a qualified respect anticipated theirs.

In spite of their often nebulous and contradictory formulations, the bulk of the thinkers concurred with the idea that full freedom of trade, at least within the bounds of a single state, should be promoted by the abolition of the different kinds of duties and the adoption of uniform weights and measures,[19] as well as currency.

[18] Rossodivita, "Appunti per una storia della popolazione," 154–55; Joseph Gorani, *Rom und seine Einwohner am Ende des XVIII. Jahrhunderts* (Riga, 1794), 64–65; Andrieux, *Daily Life in Papal Rome*, 77; La Marca, *Saggio di una ricerca storico-economica*, 21, 53; Friz, *La popolazione di Roma*, 77.

[19] Nicolai, *Memorie, leggi, ed osservazioni*, 3:306–07.

Behind the work of most lurked a general premise which, as it turned out, was founded on a false assumption. It was the conviction that the Papal States enjoyed a privileged position by nature, which ought to make them the richest and most flourishing state in Italy, whereas the prevailing condition appeared in strident antithesis to this view. From this outlook naturally flowed a propensity to exaggerate and magnify the wealth of their natural resources. The writers tended to regard as fertile regions which were, and still are, not. They overlooked the obstacles in the way of introducing prospering industries. This defect was shared by almost all would-be reformers, be they mercantilists, physiocrats, or advocates of a free market. The majority of these writers, however, were government officials who became after about 1750 the followers of the economic theory then in fashion, namely physiocracy, and who, therefore, regarded land as the only true source of wealth and free trade as the surest way of achieving progress. Less agreement appeared in their ranks over measures to be taken in favor of industry.

One of the little known works, more relevant to the city of Rome than most of their kind, was a memorandum by Leonardo Libri, an official of the Apostolic Chamber for forty years, which was written some time during the year 1721, following the death of Clement XI. The writing probably reflected the thinking in Roman administrative circles. It followed the failure of the *congregazione del Sollievo*. Libri was concerned that the cameral officials simply did not have sufficient knowledge of the economic facts and statistics. He proposed to revive the congregation as a fact-finding commission, and put two merchants on it. His outlook was still mercantilistic, for he held to the notion that the happiness and greatness of a prince rested on the number of his subjects. The problem, as he saw it, was one of capital. Although it was not essential for the prince to provide the capital himself, it was his obligation to steer private capital toward the most useful sector in the economy; money ought to be moved into investment in industry instead of into *luoghi di monte* and the purchase of foreign products. There was an air of protectionism about his work. Perhaps no author after Libri ever emphasized the importance of the industrial sector as much as he. In contrast, he paid only scant attention to the Agro Romano.[20]

The first widely read author on economic matters at the time was Leone Pascoli. A Perugian by birth, after studying law in Rome he became secretary to the papal *Rota*. Then he spent some time in Ravenna, Florence, and Perugia, before returning to the papal capital to take up his own law practice. Because of his links to the Spanish ambassador, Pascoli was obliged for a time to leave the city again. He travelled in Spain and France; in the latter he witnessed the disaster inflicted upon its economy by John Law's experiment. He admired Holland and went as far as Danzig. On his return trip he stayed in northern Italy, where he saw Turin and observed the river traffic on the Po, never failing to make repeated sorrowful

[20] ASR, Camerale II, annona, discorsi e studi, busta 1; La Marca, *Saggio di una ricerca storico-economica*, 22–24; Dal Pane, *Lo Stato Pontificio e il movimento riformatore*, 111–26.

comparisons with the Papal States. Pascoli drew from his stay outside Italy both the literary model for his work and the inspiration for his economic and social program. There were indeed many *Etats de la France* and *Present State of Great Britains*, which he could have come across. Based on them Pascoli constructed a program which was rigidly protectionist, even prohibitionist, aimed at the development of manufactures in the States of the Church.

His principal work was his *Testamento politico d'un academico fiorentino*. It was probably written in 1723 and read to Innocent XIII in manuscript the following year, although it was not published until 1733. Many ideas in this work were also to be found among writers of memoranda and planners, but the author differed from them in that they had almost all addressed the congregations and appropriate government offices, without ever appealing to the public. Although a protectionist abroad, Pascoli advocated freedom of internal trade and the doing away with all barriers, such as transit tolls and duties, at home. He proposed the abolition of all indirect taxation, replacing it with two direct taxes, the *estimo*, an imposition on capital, whether in the form of real estate or money, and the *testatico*, an income tax. Another target of his attack was monopolies which impeded economic growth. In conjunction with this he called for the abolition of the two government bureaux in charge of Rome's food supply, the annona and the grascia, and a reduction in the government's role of providing sufficient supplies for consumption.

What was particularly modern in Pascoli's outlook was the value he attached to the individual interest and the profit motive. Certainly it was not a developed theme in his book, but its mere appearance in a treatise dealing with the Papal States was striking. His idea of setting up a stock exchange on the Campidoglio, preposterous as it may seem to us today, was an extension of this same preoccupation. Pascoli did not identify wealth with money or make it coincide with the riches of the ruler alone. In his view it was produced by and for society, which employed all the factors of production, labor, land, and capital in a fundamental interdependency. So, in a way, Pascoli was a transitional figure. He was born too soon to affirm absolute economic liberty, his protectionism is witness to that, yet he had overcome many of the fears and restraints which hedged in the traditional mercantilists.

After the 1730s it proved no longer feasible to realize in its entirety the program which Pascoli had championed in his *Testamento politico*, but between 1740 and 1743 he put down a kind of commentary and restatement of his principal work under the title of *Codicillo del Testamento politico*. It was a program of work for Benedict XIV, who thought highly of him, but did not or could not make use of his plans.[21]

[21] Ibid., 144–45, 208–9, 225–29, 233–35; Venturi, *Settecento riformatore*, 1:98–99, 101–2; Franco Venturi, "The Enlightenment in the Papal States," in *Italy and the Enlightenment. Studies in a Cosmopolitan Century*. Translated by Susan Corsi (London, 1972), 226–29; Oscar Nuccio, "La precettistica economica di Leone Pascoli (1674–1744)," *Studi Romani*, 27 (1979), 287–92, 300; Furio Diaz, *Francesca Maria Gianni dalla burocrazia alla politica sotto Pietro Leopoldi di Toscana* (Milan, 1966), 32.

Under Benedict XIV the publications on economic matters became more frequent and continued to multiply in volume until the time of Pius VI; although it may be said that with Pascoli the tone and direction of the local reformist tradition had already been set. The banker Girolamo Belloni was the administrator of the *dogana* in Rome from 1730 to 1737. He was thus involved in private as well as public affairs. In 1750 Belloni published his *Dissertazione sopra il commercio*. His goal was monetary stability; he was convinced that the majority of people who live off commerce were hurt by devaluation and that the true gold–silver ratio should be set by the market place and the conditions of trade in Europe. Any attempt on the part of the state to fix this ratio by decree violated natural law. The trade balance he found to be at the root of the shortage of cash in the Papal States. The measures proposed by Belloni to "convert a whole people from idleness to industrious activity" were those of the traditional mercantilist: freedom and incentives for exports, a ban on all non-essential foreign goods, abolition of tax farming, and the social recognition of the role of the big merchants. However, he did not possess the ability of offering an energetic and bold program of reform and only suggested an unorganized series of slow improvements.[22]

Belloni's monetarist approach to the economic problem was, as so much else in his work, not novel. The chronic monetary malaise and the absence of tender provoked other authors to take an intelligent look at the economic problems of their age and its social implications. One of these pamphleteers was the Venetian Gianfrancesco Scottoni, who, in 1770, attributed the appalling poverty to the papacy's parasitical relationship with other countries – he came upon this discovery at a time when it was almost no longer true. His hope was that the ever-increasing conflict between the curia and the Italian and other European states would end in a slowing down or even cessation of the flow of gold, which for centuries had been pouring into Rome. When no more money was coming in, the Romans would have to begin to work. Then, and only then, could Rome hope for her revival.[23]

In the early years of Pius VI's reign, from 1775 to 1780, when free trade in agricultural products was being introduced in Tuscany and attempts at liberalization started in Lombardy as well as in other Habsburg territories, we notice an intensification of agronomic propaganda in Rome. For two years, 1776 and 1777, Luigi Riccòmanni, a lawyer born in the nearby Sabina, made the capital the chief center for his agrarian campaign with his *Diario economico di agricoltura, manifattura, e commercio*. Realizing that in France Colbert's policy had encouraged farm workers to desert the countryside and become producers of luxury goods, to the detriment of French agriculture, Riccòmanni was put before the difficult alternative of choosing between an agrarian and an industrial policy. Somewhat

[22] Alberto Caracciolo, *L'albero dei Belloni*, 112–21; Venturi, *Settecento riformatore*, 1:449–53; B.CORS., ms. 1590, f. 15; ms. 1591, f. 25. Belloni's *Dissertazione spora il commercio* can be found in ASR, Famiglie diverse, Cavaletti, busta 2, and in *Scrittori classici italiani di economica politica* (Milan, 1802), Parte moderna, 2:3–153.

[23] Venturi, "Enlightenment in the Papal States," 240–41.

cautiously, he opted for an agrarian policy, in his view the necessary precondition for a general improvement. He was well disposed to physiocratic ideas, but also followed closely attempts to introduce new industries, particularly woollen manufacture, which he discussed at length in his *Diario economico*. In it, he found confirmation for his own conviction that it was not gold but improved cultivation of land, active and enlightened industry, regular work, wisely distributed among members of the body politic, which constituted the true wealth of nations.[24]

The dreams and projects of economic writers and planners are seldom adopted in their totality; on occasion they are even received with hostility. In any case, there is no guarantee that their implementation assures success, as Turgot's ill-fated economic reforms in France in 1776 and the marked reversion to a protectionist policy in Tuscany under the influence of Gianni in 1788 proved. Rome was no exception. The authorities were caught between the protectionism favored by the Roman producers and the economic liberalism advocated by the merchants. The government usually inclined toward a protectionist policy, but with considerable qualifications, fearing that by restricting imports too rigidly the local industry would not be able to satisfy all the consumer demand, and would be exposed to foreign retaliation.

An example of this approach was an edict by Clement XI, on 7 August 1719, forbidding the importation of cheap cloth from Naples, Germany, France, and the countries to the north in order to protect the domestic product, a measure that was confirmed several times subsequently. But under pressure from Vienna textiles from the hereditary Habsburg lands were exempted in 1731, and in 1732–33, amid threats of retaliation against Avignon by France, the whole matter of import restrictions had to be reconsidered. A solution was arrived at by the cardinals in 1735, which put a duty of 20 percent on the import of low-quality cloth, and one of 12 percent on finer textiles; both imposts, however, were limited to the territory of Rome.

With Benedict XIV the question of economic reform revived. In this field he set the overall concept which was to guide papal policy until Pius VII. His own legislation, however, barely succeeded in cutting into the foundations of those institutions which were so deeply entrenched in the customs and traditions of the Papal States. For his actions provoked a fierce resistance which even the pontiff's will failed to break. His most memorable achievement was the introduction of free

[24] Nuccio, "Precettistica economica di Pascoli," 301; Venturi, *Settecento riformatore*, 2:322; Cochrane, *Florence in the Forgotten Centuries*, 399, 449; Furio Diaz, *Gianni*, 36–39, 53–59; Alexander Grab, "The Politics of Subsistence. The Liberalization of Grain Commerce in Austrian Lombardy under Enlightenment Despotism," *Journal of Modern History*, 57 (1985), 186–90, 204; Venturi, "Enlightenment in the Papal States," 246–49; Dal Pane, *Lo Stato Pontificio e il movimento riformatore*, 166–75; Büchi, *Finanzen und Finanzpolitik Toskanas*, 168, 183, 187; Gaetano Gasparoni, *Settecento italiano. Contributo alla storia della cultura.* 1: *L'abate Giovanni Cristoforo Amaduzzi* (Padua, 1941), 72.

circulation of grain at home, twenty years before the slow thrust toward free trade started in Tuscany and Lombardy, after the great famine. In 1748, Benedict issued the bull *Quo die*, which allowed the free trade of agricultural products within his dominions. But its effectiveness was severely limited because it exempted the areas under the jurisdiction of the annona and the grascia, that is, Rome and its environment.[25]

Not until Pius VI became pope would reform be resumed. He had already formulated plans to that end when he was Clement XIII's treasurer general. To gather up-to-date information on the economic conditions in the state, he ordered the treasurer general, Msgr. Guglielmo Pallotta, to undertake a tour of inspection and present a report. On 21 September 1775, Pallotta, accompanied by officials of the accountant general's office, Giovanni Cristiano de Miller and Francesco Simonetti, set off on the first stage of their trip.

As a result of the tour the pope appointed, on 27 July 1778, a special congregation to study the report and make appropriate recommendations. Within less than six months, the congregation issued its first decision: the prohibition of tolls and transit duties exacted by "privileged" individuals, and the approval of an order by the prefect of the Buon Governo to draw up a cadaster. These actions were supplemented in 1786 by the establishment of a protective customs barrier on the frontiers of the Papal States. The tariff was evidently modelled on that of the *dogana* in Rome. It laid down a sliding scale which ran from 60 percent ad valorem duty for printed linen and cotton cloth to 5 percent for raw materials used in local manufactures. However, the plan failed to establish the principle of a unified customs barrier. Bologna and Ferrara, which had always enjoyed a measure of autonomy, were not included until 1790, only to be excluded again almost immediately afterwards. The free ports of Ancona and Civitavecchia constituted another gap in the protective wall. The same edict favored Roman industry by putting an additional surtax on many commodities made abroad which were brought to the capital.[26]

A tariff policy on its own proved insufficient to put the Roman economy back on its feet. At this point new personalities in the papal administration enter the picture. Pallotta was elevated to cardinal; the pope may have considered him too attached to the past and out of touch with his new ideas. He was replaced by a chierico of the

25 ASR, Camerale II, camerlengato e tesorierato, progetti diversi, busta 16; Giuntella, *Roma nel Settecento*, 44–48; Dal Pane, *Lo Stato Pontificio e il movimento riformatore*, 149–56, 203–04, 239–43; Büchi, *Finanzen und Finanzpolitik Toskanas*, 168, 183, 187, 262–66; Diaz, *Gianni*, 36–39; Cochrane, *Florence in the Forgotten Centuries*, 399, 449; Grab, "Politics of Subsistence," 188–90, 200–06, 208; Stefano Dini, "Nuove ricerche intorno al'abolizione delle gabelle di transito nello Stato della Chiesa," *Rassegna storica del Risorgimento*, 72 (1985), 267–95.

26 Dal Pane, *Lo Stato Pontifio e il movimento riformatore*, 255, 288–89; Piscitelli, "Fabrizio Ruffo e la riforma economica," 75–82; Giuntella, *Roma nel Settecento*, 49–50; Venturi, "Enlightenment in the Papal States," 259; La Marca, *Saggio di una ricerca storico-economica*, 32–33; ASR, Camerale II, zecca, busta 33.

Apostolic Chamber, Fabrizio Ruffo, an offspring of the Neapolitan branch of the Colonna family. There were long-standing ties of affection binding the pope to the Ruffo family; hence, Ruffo enjoyed the pope's full confidence.

As treasurer general, Ruffo concentrated his activities along three lines: speeding up the tax reform, trying to solve the monetary crisis, and developing agriculture, industry, and commerce. Unlike Pius VI, Ruffo did not think that changes in the tax system by themselves would be enough to bring the monetary circulation in order and stimulate a revived economy, but they were for him part of one whole and he proceeded at the same time with all three. In matters strictly financial Ruffo generally limited himself to the intelligent execution of measures already adopted, whereas in the area of increased productivity he showed himself more original. In his agricultural and industrial policy Ruffo's aim was to defend domestic production against foreign competition, while eliminating as much as possible the obstacles in the way of local industry.

Ruffo was assisted by Giovanni Cristiano de Miller. Probably English by birth and once an official to the archbishop of Mainz, de Miller belonged to the group of Lorrainers and Germans who transplanted to Tuscany to seek their fortune during the reign of Grand Duke Francesco Stefano, the husband of Empress Maria Theresa. Dismissed from his government post in 1774, de Miller arrived in Rome to enter papal service. It is not easy to pinpoint his exact role in the tangle of the general plan of economic renewal, but it is certain he played an important part behind the scenes. His personality was deeply stamped by his conviction of the omnipotence of the state, which in practice resulted in tireless planning, in trying without much consideration many different experiments, in plunging into great expense with little probability of positive results. He believed that the Papal States, unlike England, could only be reformed from above. The state would have to supply everything and to combine economic measures at every step with technical directives. De Miller placed his emphasis on the manufacturing processes and the industrial component in preference to the purely agricultural sector.[27]

Documentary materials reveal the importance, if not the exact role, of de Miller in the work of direction, preparation, and execution of the economic reforms of Pius VI. A memorandum, probably of the year 1794, refers to at least 15 economic operations entrusted to him by treasurers Pallotta and Ruffo between 1777 and 1793. There were probably another nine additional ones, not listed. First he was given the general task of regulating the poor, which resulted in the establishment of houses of correction, *reclusori*, for the idle poor and work houses for the deserving poor. But well beyond such social measures, the government launched what in Roman terms could only be called a massive effort to build up a diversified industry,

[27] La Marca, *Saggio di una ricerca storico-economica*, 30–32; Piscitelli, "Fabrizio Ruffo e la riforma economica," 70–72, 88–94, 107–30; Gorani, *Rom und seine Einwohner*, 354–58; Dal Pane, *Lo Stato Pontificio e il movimento riformatore*, 402–409, 423, 436; Venturi, "Enlightenment in the Papal States," 258–61.

by the use of two incentives, the grant of special franchises or *privativa*, an old device, and the extension of subsidies and loans.

To cap the endeavour, Ruffo set up a *Congresso accademico di agricoltura, manifattura e commercio*, an academy similar to others established in the eighteenth century under the auspices of prominent enlightened and progressive persons, which, however, in this case did not limit its action to the theoretical field. Supporting the policy of the government, it not only granted numerous subsidies but also large prizes, up to two hundred scudi, for all those who would promote knowledge that could contribute to the greater prosperity of the state. It also maintained a chemical laboratory in the Castel Sant'Angelo under the direction of Dr. Giuseppe Giacinto Bussani, who received a *privativa* for the manufacture of oil of vitriol for medicinal purposes.

To assist the development of industry in general the Apostolic Chamber disbursed between 26 March 1785 and the end of 1794 a total of 161,158.845 scudi, broken into the following annual figures (in scudi):[28]

| | | | |
|---|---|---|---|
| 1785 | 4,105.575 | 1790 | 26,256.36 |
| 1786 | 18,380.71 | 1791 | 18,589.685 |
| 1787 | 16,009.99 | 1792 | 18,589.685 |
| 1788 | 20,965.995 | 1793 | 4,208.18 |
| 1789 | 22,813.06 | 1794 | 5,894.365 |

A total of 42,988.955 scudi of this sum was in interest-free loans and 63,447.615 scudi in interest-bearing loans; 23,622.105 scudi of the loans had already been repaid by the end of 1794. The annual figures of disbursement clearly indicate that the most active period of the extraordinary effort fell between 1786 and 1792; by 1793 the economic crisis and inflation put a brake to it.

Where did this support go to? The largest recipient of this aid was the nascent textile industry – nascent in the sense that it fostered new enterprises. Between 1789 and 1793 woollen cloth and blanket manufactories received a total of 19,965.08 scudi. Particular attention was paid to spreading, and hopefully improving, spinning throughout the country, spinning of all kinds, particularly linen, cotton, and hemp. Schools for spinning were set up in Rome, Montefiascone, Todi, Bologna, Montalto, Subiaco, and elsewhere. A total of 20,112.58 scudi was spent on them, of which Rome with 6,062.76 scudi received the lion's share. In addition, another 7,389.675 went for the acquisition of wooden spinning machines.

Silk was also on the list of the Apostolic Chamber, for which Rome received 8,331.64 scudi. Beside silk cloth, there was silk sewing thread, silk stockings, and mixed silk and cotton cloth. As early as 1777 the Frenchman Julien Guttin from

28 ASR, Camerale II, commercio e industria, busta 1; busta 2; busta 7, fasc. 29; busta 12, fasc. 59; busta 13; busta 14, fasc. 69; ASR, Camerale II, arti e mestieri, busta 5; busta 37, fasc. 79; A.Cap.R., no. 22, cred. XVIII, 201.

Lyons was enticed to introduce the secret of dyeing silk the French way into Rome. He entered into partnership with the merchants Francesco and Antonio Canale, who contributed 15,000 scudi which the Apostolic Chamber matched with an equal sum. The making of muslin of the Swiss model was franchised to Xaver Spiller and his associates in 1794.

Sometimes the papal government reversed the process; instead of trying to attract foreigners to come to Rome and introduce the secrets of their trade, it would send out Romans to learn the skills abroad. This was the case when six weavers went to Turin to learn the art of making fine cloth the Dutch fashion. The project cost the Chamber 2,767.78 scudi. After about a year, having learned the skill, they returned home with some of the special machinery and were immediately put to diffusing their expertise throughout the Papal States.

Unfortunately, manufactures promoted and subsidized by the state only too often ended up in disaster, in which the authorities had to pick up the cost. Yet even these enterprises helped to stir the stagnant waters, posing problems and attempting solutions.

In 1794, when Fabrizio Ruffo had to leave the treasury under the pressure of the opposition to his reforming activities to become cardinal, de Miller's Roman career came to an end. In the following year, the economist Nicola Corona was to launch a vigorous attack on the protectionist policies of Ruffo and de Miller. Corona was prepared to take a step back and join up with the agricultural tradition of the physiocrats, seeing all progress in terms of an improvement in the lives of the peasants and agrarian techniques; first the fields, then manufacture; first the fight against luxury and privilege and then the development of industries.[29]

Before leaving government intervention in the Roman economy there is one case which deserves closer examination, because it was probably the only instance of an industrial enterprise of eighteenth-century Rome in the modern sense of the term. As already indicated, the working of cotton in the city was limited. Among the cotton shops were two which concentrated on printed cotton, calico, called *calancà* locally. One local workshop, Belli and Lazzari, was well managed and had its own market, namely the Jewish community, which absorbed most of its output. The other establishment, the *calancà* works amid the ruins of the Baths of Diocletian, was the state's great effort at promoting industry and productivity in the city.

The choice of a factory for cotton can be explained by the fact that its finished product was in demand by all strata of society. For cotton, which up to this time had been exclusively an article of luxury, now had become democratized and the feverish demand for the new material passed from consumer to producer. In the absence of an indigenous cotton industry, the manufactured products of the material had to be wholly imported from abroad, thereby contributing to the drain

[29] Dal Pane, *Lo Stato Pontificio e il movimento riformatore*, 433–36; Venturi, "Enlightenment in the Papal States," 261–63; La Marca, *Saggio di una ricerca storico-economica*, 35–36.

of money. One of the principal sources, North America, just recovering from its struggle for independence, was unable to send cotton at the customary quantity to the old continent, thus highlighting the need for the Papal States to make themselves at least partially independent from abroad to satisfy the continuously growing demand for cotton goods.

The choice of location for the works fell upon the old monastery of the Somasci fathers built upon the ruins of the Baths of Diocletian. After overcoming initial difficulties in adapting the structure for a factory and staffing it – for in spite of the claim that the factory was set up to find work for Rome's unemployed, the purpose was largely compromised by the fact that outside laborers were accepted – the treasurer general and the managers set the beginning of production for July 1774.

The start was inauspicious. Notwithstanding the noble efforts of the workmen brought in from outside, the product could not compete with that produced by the English, French, and Swiss, who could rely on an experience of many years and an amazing technical know-how that enabled them to sell the same product at much lower prices; for example, a piece of foreign calico with colored background cost only 3.90 scudi against the 8 scudi price for the Roman product. But the price was not the only problem. The stipulations in the original plan were not met. Instead of the 48 tables for printing as foreseen, only 23 were in effective operation, which caused some of the primary material to lie idle in the warehouse for years. The Apostolic Chamber, moreover, had given no advance consideration to the human element. Convicts were used for some jobs with the clear intention of reducing the cost of labor. Not surprisingly, continuous thievery and other forms of dishonesty were rife, which was a further blow to the uncertain balances of the factory. To this must be added a growing increase in the price of cotton. The logical consequence of all these negative factors was that the amount of sales and profits, which were never too encouraging, continued to shrink. The gross profits were given in 1775 at 7,973 scudi, they rose to 8,000 scudi in 1777 and 13,790 in 1778, but by 1779 they started to fall to 12,604 scudi, and were reduced to a mere 3,696 scudi in 1783 and only 1,783 scudi in 1786.

In the meantime, there were problems with the management of the works. The Apostolic Chamber, in search for adequate technical direction and better management of the labor force, made a contract in 1776 with two Swiss, Henri Guynet and Ferdinand Borel. The fact that the Swiss canton of Neuchâtel was in the forefront of the innovations that had produced a qualitative jump in the production of printed cloth probably dictated their choice. The immediate advantage of the two Swiss to Rome was that of access to new patterns (until then the practice was to copy those from imported cloth) and of careful bookkeeping. They also brought plans for further improvements. The biggest change, as it turned out, was to come in labor relations. The old system was limited by the corporative tradition, an embryonic form of workers' control, in which the rule was to acknowledge the autonomy of the skilled laborers and respect the hierarchy of workers. But the authority of the Swiss over the labor force was significantly extended. They tried to bring the individual habits of the skilled workman in line with the best qualitative efficiency of production. The outcome was a revolt – since strikes were not yet regarded as a legitimate practice – of the skilled laborers, the first such modern type of industrial dispute in Rome's history.

From the very commencement of the cotton printing factory, efforts were made to have it independent from abroad for the supply of cotton and cotton cloth. New experiments in growing cotton in Lazio, in the regions of Civitavecchia and Terracina were made. In spite of initial optimism, it became evident that the cultivation of cotton would not take root, since the peasants themselves were averse to growing it, being more interested in obtaining direct sustenance from cereal production than in a product that could be sold to one purchaser only, the state. Besides, the soil of Lazio was unsuitable for such cultivation. Cotton needs good quality soil, deep and permeable, and a constant and dry climate. Imagine, therefore, what chance it had of growing in the area of Civitavecchia, by the sea. The sole result of the experiment was a bad product at a high price. Similarly the numerous attempts at setting up workshops in Civitavecchia and even at the Baths of Diocletian themselves to produce the unfinished cotton cloth needed to make *calencà* were unsuccessful owing to the want of adequate machinery and technical skills.[30]

At the end of 1794 the Apostolic Chamber was at last persuaded of the uselessness of carrying on the direct management of the factory and considered itself fortunate to sign an agreement with Messrs. Acquaroni, Torlonia, and Stampa to lease the plant in return for a rent of 300 scudi and a seventh part of the profit. But the hope nurtured by the three leaseholders quickly turned into an unattainable dream in view of the Revolutionary events which compromised the fortunes of the factory. Hence they asked for and obtained a cancellation of their contract at the close of 1801. After several other leaseholders took over and abandoned the works, and a stint of direct intervention in 1810 by Tournon, Napoleon's prefect in Rome, also proved unsuccessful, the first and only major industrial enterprise in the city during the ancien regime folded in 1812, the victim, as almost all the economic ventures of the papal government, of inexperience, mismanagement, and ineptitude.[31]

These last three words give us some clue to the overall failure to provide a coherent economic policy. Doubtless, some popes were well-intentioned and hoped to revive the fortunes of the Papal States. Clement XI, for instance, issued about

[30] Nicola La Marca, "La manifattura statale delle Terme di Diocleziano da Clemente XIV e Pio VI al prefetto de Tournon," *Capitolium*, 44 (1969), 21, 27–28, 31–32; ASR, Camerale II, commercio e industria, busta 1, fasc. 2; busta 14, fasc. 69.

[31] La Marca, *Saggio di una ricerca storico-economica*, 88–90; De Felice, *Aspetti e momenti della vita economica*, 236; La Marca, "La manifattura statale delle Terme," 19–33; Mariana D'Amelia, "'Intrapredenti, lavoranti e Camera Apostolica': Potere e protesta in una fabbrica del '700," *Movimento operaio e socialista*, 11 (1979), 318–26, 329–32, 335–45; De Cupis, *Vicende dell'agricoltura nell'Agro Romano*, 363; ASR, Camerale II, commercio e industria, busta 2, fasc. 5.

thirty decrees on economic matters between 1701 and 1721. Benedict XIV attempted free-trade reforms and Pius VI was the most active of all, as we have seen. Yet each pope appeared to react to an existing situation rather than carry through a total program. Several reasons may be suggested. The very basic reason, of course, lay in the ambition of each pope to pursue his own policy rather than follow on that of his predecessor. The absence of a consensus on both the resources of the state and on the priority of its needs contributed its share of the blame. Even the pamphleteers were unable to agree on whether to stress industry or agriculture, whether to promote free trade or champion protectionism, whether to opt for mercantilism or physiocracy. How much more undecided was an inexperienced curial bureaucracy. Torn, even buffeted, between opposing economic interests, popes and ministers failed to push through an effective policy. Although Benedict XIV, for example, loosened the system of a controlled market by introducing internal free trade of grain and other commodities in 1748, probably because of the pressure of the small population growth, it remained largely ineffective. Other concerns, mainly external and financial, were more urgent than reforms that would provoke internal resentment. Pius VI's economic projects, his cadaster and customs reforms, as we shall see, fared little better. Besides, when these reforms were being mooted, Rome's financial chaos had reached such proportions that only a revival of the entrepreneurial spirit could have turned the tide of industry from the rocks of financial disaster. Such revival, in the face of post-Tridentine lassitude, was probably impossible to expect; the large vision, and with it the energetic leadership, was missing. Moreover, among the ranks of those who could conceivably have ventured their capital, bankers, financiers, treasurers, many had succumbed to bankruptcy amid the financial disorder.[32]

If financiers, such as the bankers Belloni and Argenvilliers, felt the impact of the adverse economic conditions in Rome, how did the average Roman fare? An exhaustive study of wages, particularly in relation to the cost of living for ancien-regime Rome still remains a desideratum. In 1796 the poet Vincenzo Monti, writing home to his brother Cesare, claimed that for 10 scudi a month a decent man on his own could not live more than ten days in the city. Of course, this was already on the threshold of the gigantic leap in prices, which became first noticeable in 1795 and really took off in 1797. If we were to reduce the sum to one scudo a day, we can still compare it to the complaint of the abate Onorato Caetani (1742–96), a curial employee, who found it difficult to manage on a salary of 30 scudi a month. But he was one of the lucky ones, for official salaries in Rome were low. In 1804, when prices were stabilized on the average at a level 30 percent higher than in pre-republican days, the superintendant at the *grazia* only earned 30 scudi a month, a

[32] La Marca, *Saggio di una ricerca storico-economica*, 25 n. 1; Cristoferi, "Fieri e mercati," 171; Schiavoni and Sonnino, "Popolazione e territorio nel Lazio," 198; Caracciolo, *Lo Stato pontificio*, 477–78; Morelli (ed.), *Lettere di Benedetto XIV*, 2:157, 160, (14 and 21 May 1749).

junior clerk in his office 12 scudi, the health inspector 18 scudi, and most scribes, porters, beadles and menials between 4 and 7 scudi, some even less.[33]

A successful artist, however, could make a good living. Pompeo Batoni charged in the 1740s and 1750s 30 scudi for a half-length and 60 scudi for a full-length portrait, and by the 1780s he was able to demand 100 scudi and 200 scudi respectively. At that date even a portrait by one of his better pupils fetched 100 scudi. He was still cheap compared to the £100 (400 scudi) priced by Gainsborough and the £200 by Joshua Reynolds.[34]

Such income contrasts with the ordinary craftsman. A cabinet maker, probably a journeyman, earned 17.5 baiocchi a day, which if he worked 25 days (that is, more than the normal number given the many religious holidays) would amount to only 4.375 scudi a month. This income would be wholly inadequate for a minimum standard of living. In general, unskilled workers, small craftsmen, and gardeners made about 15 to 30 baiocchi a day (3.75 to 7.5 scudi a month). At the woollen works at San Michele a Ripa in 1717/18, the director earned 15 scudi a month, the custodian of the warehouse 12 scudi, the calenderer 7 scudi and the principal bookkeeper only 6 scudi. Most of the laborers' wages were reckoned by piece work, but a workman without specialization made about 15 baiocchi a day. The wages of the printers at the calico works at the Baths of Diocletian were set by the Apostolic Chamber in 1784 at 7 scudi a week, compared to 25 scudi for the director and the cashier, 7 scudi for the polisher, and 2.20 scudi for the student laborer. Female labor, on the other hand, was exploited. A female spinner made a scudo and a half a month, less than 5 baiocchi a day, whereas the laundress in the French Academy in Rome received 74 baiocchi a month in 1781, when the director asked permission to raise the sum to one scudo.

The staffs of noble households were frequently in a favored position. In the household of Cardinal Orsini, for instance, the agent had a monthly salary of 15 scudi, which was later raised to 18.33 scudi, although a large part of the latter's remuneration came in kind, in the form of bread, wine, and firewood. The principal coachman received 14 scudi, the secretaries between 8 and 11 scudi, the house physician and surgeon 12.50 each. The master of the household and most of the gentlemen employees had salaries around 10 scudi. The butlers and chamberlains had to be satisfied with 8 scudi. The wages of the ordinary servants, including outriders, were usually 6 scudi, and those of the houseboys and pages 5 scudi. These compensations were obviously competitive with those earned in other jobs and even other households. In the Farnese palace in 1741, the stable boy only received a scudo a month and the legal agent had to be satisfied with 6 scudi, a little less than the architect and the first coachman. The salaries of the resident and the secretary-steward were indeed generous, 600 scudi and 300 scudi a year respectively. But low wages were boosted by gratuities, the *mancie*, which by time-honored custom

[33] Alfonso Bertoldi (ed.), *Epistolario di Vincenzo Monti*, 422; Friz, *Consumi, tenore di vita e prezzi*, 146–47 n. 4. [34] Clark, "Batoni's professional career," 336–37.

domestic staff were entitled to claim from visitors, and the customary bonuses at Christmas and the Feast of Assumption (*Ferragusta*).[35]

Balanced against those earnings have to be the essential expenditures of individuals and families. It should be borne in mind that for the local population Rome was not a cheap city in which to live. Prices, when not controlled, were much higher than in the other cities of the Papal States. According to the official statistics for the decade of 1785 to 1795, when, under Ruffo's administration, prices held steady and occasionally dropped a little, a *rubbio* of grain cost 7.85 scudi in Rome, compared to 6.95 in Bologna, 6.15 in Ferrara, and only 5.25 in Frosinone. Similarly, a hundred *libbre* of grapes for making wine cost 70 baiocchi in Rome, but only 36 baiocchi in Bologna, 20 in Frosinone, and 15 in Ferrara.[36]

For purposes of consumption the Romans can be divided into two groups, with the second forming two subgroups. In the first category was the privileged, numerically restricted circle of high churchmen, nobles, and a few wealthy, not yet ennobled individuals, who together with their families amounted to 3,000 to 4,000 people. The remaining 96 to 97 percent of the population can be subdivided into those who disposed a little more than was strictly necessary to meet the basic needs of sustenance and those who either did not or could scarcely dispose of the indispensible minimum to survive. About 10,000 to 12,000 may be assumed to make up the superior subgroup, comprising the lower clergy, government employees with monthly salaries above 15 scudi, physicians, shopkeepers with their own store, a part of the artisanat, and skilled craftsmen. To the inferior subgroup belonged the absolute majority of the inhabitants of the capital, which was over 90 percent of the population. The estimated distribution of expenses of the two subgroups is shown in the following table.[37]

| | Subgroup with income above 15 scudi monthly | Subgroup with income below 15 scudi monthly |
|---|---|---|
| Food | 80–90% | 95% |
| Clothing | 3–7% | 2% |
| Dwelling | 4–6% | 2% |
| Other expenses | 2–4% | 1% |
| Savings | 1–3% | |

[35] Luigi Fiorani, "Il secolo XVIII," in Fiorani *et al.*, *Rite, ceremonie, feste e vita del popolo nella Roma dei Papi* (Bologna, 1970), 224; Archille Agnati (ed.), "Ricerche di cinematica storia. Il movimento dei prezzi nello Stato della Chiese dal 1740 al 1800," *Il Giornale degli economisti e annali di economia* (1968), 754–57; Lepre, "Agricoltura e manifattura in un rione," 362–63; D'Amelia, "'Intrapredenti, lavoranti e Camerale Apostolica,'" 356–57; La Marca, *Saggio di una ricerca storico-economica*, 84–85; Henri Lapauze, *Histoire de l'Académie de France à Rome* (Paris, 1924), 389; Friz, *Consumi, tenore di vita e prezzi*, 147; Michel, "Vie quotidienne au Palais Farnèse," 2:532–35; Story, *Roba di Roma*, 65–66; ASR, Tribunale del governatore, miscell. artisti, busta 5, fasc. 493; ASR, Camerale II, Conti dell'entrata e dell'uscita, busta 5, lib. 22; A.Cap.R., Archivio Orsini, serie 2, rollo di salariati.

[36] Piscitelli, "Fabrizio Ruffo e la riforma economica," 138–39.

[37] Friz, *Consumi, tenore di vita e prezzi*, 143–45.

Table 27a. *Monthly food budget for a family of four with income above 15 scudi*

| Produce | Total quantity | Average cost (scudi & baiocchi) minimum | Average cost (scudi & baiocchi) maximum |
|---|---|---|---|
| Bread | kg 40.7 | 1.80 | 2.40 |
| Pasta, rice, flour | kg 10.2 | 0.60 | 1.20 |
| Dried legumes | kg 4.4 | 0.40 | 0.50 |
| Beef | kg 3.0 | 0.36 | 0.70 |
| Lamb & mutton | kg 1.0 | 0.08 | 0.15 |
| Pork | kg 1.0 | 0.12 | 0.24 |
| Preserved fish | kg 0.7 | 0.05 | 0.10 |
| Pecorino cheese | kg 1.4 | 0.16 | 0.20 |
| Eggs | no. 40 | 0.05 | 0.06 |
| Fresh vegetables & fruit | | 0.32 | 0.47 |
| Oil or lard | lit. 5.6 | 0.66 | 0.82 |
| Vinegar | lit. 5.5 | 0.48 | 0.60 |
| Wine | lit. 50.2 | 1.80 | 2.40 |
| Salt | kg 1.4 | 0.12 | 0.16 |
| Total expense | | 7.00 | 10.00 |

The share of income destined to satisfy the need of food was noticeably higher than the 60 percent estimated for Holland in the middle of the seventeenth century and the 74 percent for England's non-agricultural labor force at the end of the eighteenth century, exceeding even the 80 percent for northern France before 1700.[38]

To approach a diet needed to maintain a healthy balance, a family of four, two adults and two children, would have to spend about 10 scudi a month. Tables 27a and 27b will give us a look at the average Roman food bill during the later part of the eighteenth century. The first shows an expenditure at the maximum level, those who earned about 15 scudi or slightly less, and the second those of the inferior subgroup.[39]

The latter table indicates that it was possible for those whose economic capacity was less to make do with food of inferior quality, spending 8, 7, or even $5\frac{1}{2}$ scudi. But such a budget already shows serious nutritional gaps. We can thus conclude, taking in all expenditures, that 15 scudi a month marked the limit of modest comfort for a family of four, whereas 7 scudi indicated the true poverty level, or the level when the

[38] Carlo Cipolla, *Before the Industrial Revolution. European Society and Economy, 1000–1700* (New York, 1976), 30 tables 1–9.

[39] Friz, *Consumi, tenore di vita e prezzi*, 153–55. The tables are taken from p. 154, prosp. 6.

Table 27b. *Monthly budget for family of four with less than 15 scudi income*

| Produce | Total quantity | Average cost (scudi & baiocchi) | |
|---|---|---|---|
| | | minimum | maximum |
| Bread | kg 40.7 | 1.20 | 1.80 |
| Pasta, rice, flour | kg 8.7 | 0.50 | 1.00 |
| Dried legumes | kg 3.4 | 0.30 | 0.40 |
| Buffalo meat, & inferior pork; giblets | kg 5.1 | 0.30 | 0.60 |
| Preserved fish | kg 1.4 | 0.10 | 0.30 |
| Pecorino cheese | kg 0.7 | 0.08 | 0.10 |
| Ricotta, provatura | kg 0.7 | 0.04 | 0.05 |
| Eggs | no. 40 | 0.05 | 0.06 |
| Fresh vegetables & fruit | | 0.36 | 0.53 |
| Oil or lard | lit. 4.6 | 0.54 | 0.67 |
| Vinegar | lit. 7.3 | 0.64 | 0.80 |
| Wine | lit. 41.0 | 1.30 | 1.70 |
| Salt | kg 1.0 | 0.90 | 0.09 |
| Total expense | | 5.50 | 8.00 |

family could not meet the minimum diet and was plunged into physiological hunger, that is, an absence of the chief necessities for the normal continuation of life and work. Alas, when we compare this with the wage scales above, it would appear that all too many Romans were in such plight.

Fortunately, there were mitigating circumstances which allowed Romans with low basic wages to have a minimally adequate diet. Among these were the complex system of public and private assistance, the close rapport between city and countryside, where some members of the family came from the country, and the additional earnings and gratuities that Rome's "underground" economy produced and which to this day lack any statistical record.[40]

However, if the individual Roman's hardship could be mitigated in some measure, these resources were not always available to the papal government, which found itself in financial straits throughout the century. Its effort to shield the population from the worst effects of these difficulties in the face of increasing currency and food supply problems would eventuate in near bankruptcy at the close of the ancien regime.

[40] Bartoccini, *Roma nell'Ottocento*, 188–89.

# 5

# Public finance and currency

The fiscal and financial condition was indeed one of the weaknesses of the city or, more properly, of the papal government, a weakness which it shared with most other ancien-regime administrations. With the growing curial control financial affairs became the concern of the central organs of the state rather than of the municipal magistracy on the Campidoglio. Admittedly a few taxes were still levied by the city in the name of and for the needs of the municipality, but these were not very significant. Since the sixteenth century they consisted essentially of the *gabella dello studio*, a tax on retail sale of wine coming from outside, and the *quattrino della carne*, a tax on the retail sale of meat. But even these were largely appropriated in advance. With the *gabella dello studio*, for example, the Capitoline Chamber had to meet the faculty salaries and maintenance costs of its university, the Sapienza. With the little that was left of the two imposts, to which were added the annual tribute of the Jews and the meager sums collected from fines on consumer fraud, the municipality had to pay decent salaries to its largely redundant personnel. Consequently the Capitoline Chamber was completely unable to meet its commitments and maintain its corporative traditions and pomp. The pope had to come to the aid of the Popolo Romano and the Apostolic Chamber made itself responsible for a portion of the expenses, to the tune of about 4,423 scudi annually.[1]

To establish Rome's fiscal state, therefore, we have to look beyond the muncipality into the fiscal accounts of the papal government, an area fraught with innumerable complexities. The papal budgets form the basis of any study of public finances. These are more correctly balance sheets of the papal government, for, unlike modern budgets, we are not dealing with projections but with *post-factum* financial statements. Furthermore, we are faced with only a limited revelation of the true state of the papal finances. For they are not really the balance books of the state as a whole, but more narrowly the accounts of the Apostolic Chamber. Many other institutions, most prominent among them the annona, the administration for roads and water supply (*strade e acqua*), and, to a limited degree, the Apostolic Palace, not to speak of the legations of Bologna and Ferrara, had their own budgets, which were approved in special congregations. For a complete examination of the public

[1] Delumeau, *Vie économique et sociale de Rome*, 1: 12–13; 2: 751–53; Georg Lutz, "Zur Papstfinanz von Klemens IX. bis Alexander VIII. (1667–1691)." *Römische Quartalschrift für christliche Altertumskunde und Kirchengeschichte*, 74 (1979), 70.

revenue and expenses all these special budgets, together with other extraordinary budgets, as well as the ecclesiastical revenues and expenditures, which although largely separate, nevertheless at times overlap with the temporal finances, would have to be studied together, an enormously complicated task which has hardly begun.

A further caution has to be exercised when looking at these balances. Even as they stand they lack budgetary rigor and precision. For not all the theoretical revenue of the Apostolic Chamber was recorded; considerable sums were kept back locally in the various provinces by the private tax farmers, euphemistically named provincial treasurers, and other local organs, and therefore do not appear on the books at all. Since many of these tax farmers were foreigners, predominantly Florentines, an appreciable proportion of the money collected ended up abroad. The losses incurred through tax evasion and smuggling, often encouraged by the abuse of immunities, must have been also considerable if we are to judge from neighboring Tuscany. Nevertheless, our interest in the *conti dell'entrata e dell'uscita*, as these balances are called, consists not only in the fact that they deal with the greater part of the financial movement of the state, but also for the exceptional regularity and length of data the series provided for about two centuries.[2]

The principal account books of the *depositaria generale*, the central receipt office of the Apostolic Chamber, which was the agency responsible for implementing the new balance sheets, are still in existence. They go back with some gaps to 1528, but their content until 1735 is somewhat uneven. In 1735 Clement XII started to reform the accounting system, a process that was continued by Benedict XIV in 1746. Like Pompeo Neri in Tuscany, struggling against the administrative anarchy of the Tuscan finances left over from the Medici rulers and perpetuated by the regency government of Francesco Stefano, or the Bourbon rulers in Naples, these popes were conscious of the relationship between reform in economic matters and reform in the financial administration; before you can contemplate setting out on any organic reform you have to put your financial house in order. Such housecleaning involved the arduous task of replacing the numerous sets of written records of the various treasuries by a more unified method of administration and record keeping in order to enable the government to know the state of its finances without undue delays.

As a consequence of these changes the structure of the balances and the individual entries are not uniform throughout the period, but they are similar

[2] Alberto Caracciolo, "I bilanci dello Stato ecclesiastico fra XVI e XVIII secolo. Una fonte e alcune considerazioni," in *Méthodologie de l'histoire et des sciences humaines. Mélanges en l'honneur de Fernand Braudel* (Toulouse, 1973), 99–100; Lutz, "Zur Papstfinanz von Klemens IX.," 40–42; Stumpo, *Il capitale finanziario a Roma*, 99; Jean-Claude Waquet, "Aux marges de l'impôt. Fraudeurs et contrebandiers dans la Toscane du XVIIIe siècle," in Ecole française de Rome, *La fiscalité et ses implications sociales en Italie et en France aux XVIIe et XVIIIe siècles* (Rome, 1980), 84, 94.

enough to enable us with some prudence to construct a comparison over time. The monetary unit used was the Roman scudo and its fractions, a money of account.[3]

With these reservations we are able to formulate a list of annual balances for the period, making allowances for the gaps, particularly during the earlier part and again during the last decade (Table 28).[4]

At first sight these balances appear modest enough, even exemplary, if we compare them, for instance, with the housekeeping in Tuscany under the last Medici. These left in 1738 a revenue of 558,923 scudi against an expenditure of 674,587, that is, a deficit of 17.15 percent, a shortfall which Rome never experienced until the collapse of 1793. In fact, the favorable picture could be extended. From the time of Sixtus V to Urban VIII the revenue column had stayed between 1,500,000 and 1,800,000 scudi. Then there was a jump, raising the budget by almost a million scudi. This trend was very marked when the budget deficit reached the then alarming figure of 190,000 scudi in 1673 under Clement X. In the early years of the eighteenth century a small, if erratic, contraction occurred, especially in the difficult years of Clement XI's pontificate, but not enough to eliminate a reasonable surplus for many of those years. At the end of Benedict XIII's reign, from about 1729 or so there was regularly a negative balance until Benedict XIV ascended the papal throne.

But Rome was not alone. Bologna, too, experienced an annual current expense deficit during this period of about 65,000 lira (about 13,000 scudi).[5] Benedict XIV's economics not only managed, after initial difficulties, to reduce the budget further, but during much of his reign to produce a modest surplus. While the lean balances continued until about 1770, the period of surpluses drew to an end by 1758. The pontificate of Clement XIII was especially hard hit by the drawn-out famine and this is reflected in some of the deficits, notably in 1767. Following his reign, which ended in 1769, there appeared once more a spell of recovery, with a series of surpluses between 1771 and 1788, intermittently broken up by a year or two of losses. One of the weaknesses of these balances, however, is that they do not tell us

[3] Delumeau, *Vie économique et sociale de Rome*, 2:852–55; Dal Pane, *Lo Stato Pontificio e il movimento riformatore*, 157–59; Wolfgang Reinhard, *Papstfinanz und Nepotismus unter Paul V (1605–1621)* (2 vols.; Stuttgart, 1974), 1:2 n. 4, 3–4; Caracciolo, *Lo Stato Pontificio a Pio IX*, 501; Diaz, *Il Granducato di Toscana*, 540; Büchi, *Finanzen und Finanzpolitik Toskanas*, 90–91, 109–12; Cochrane, *Florence in the Forgotten Centuries*, 349–51. For the problem of money of account in general and the actual devaluation of money of account in Europe over extended periods, see Fernand P. Braudel and Frank Spooner, "Prices in Europe from 1450 to 1750," in *The Cambridge Economic History of Europe*. Vol. 4: *The Economy of Expanding Europe in the Sixteenth and Seventeenth Centuries* (Cambridge, 1967), 378–82, and 438 fig. 5. Since it is at this stage almost impossible to establish the stability of the Roman scudo, I have not attempted to account for possible fluctuations.

[4] Unless otherwise stated, the data for this and the subsequent tables are derived from ASR, Camerale II, Conti dell'entrata e dell'uscita, buste 3–15. In the earlier years of the century the figures do not always coincide exactly, and on one or two occasions there is even some uncertainty about the exact financial year involved. I then had to use informed judgment.

[5] Giacomelli, "Carlo Grassi e le riforme bolognesi," 58–59, 67.

what the papal financial administration did with the Apostolic Chamber's surplus or how it covered the years of deficit.

With the accession of Pius VI in 1775 the negative balances again became more frequent. But it would be true to say that none of these changes were in any way out of the ordinary; indeed, they were normal oscillations as might be expected, given the various factors involved, such as the personal style of the ruler, the hazards of war, and the even greater uncertainties of the weather.

Up to this point, therefore, the apparently stable finances of the papal government form a distinct contrast to the financial difficulties and even bankruptcies of some of the great monarchies of Europe and Italian states. Only in the 1790s would the grand projects of Pius VI bring out into the open, with deficits making up 28.8 percent and 38.4 percent of the expenditure in 1793 and 1796 respectively, what acute observers had feared years before.

The reality of the situation behind the facade of the relative stability of the Apostolic Chamber's budget can only be explained by the fact that we are face to face with a budget shrunk to the minimum, unalterable in its main parts, rarely burdened by extraordinary expenses, such as those for the acquisition of extra food supplies or for public works, a balance which rather than stimulating the economy contributed to keeping it suppressed.

The data on the budget requires, therefore, a closer examination to establish first the various sources of revenue and then the expenditure in terms of the numerous demands made on the temporal government of the church. At the base of the papal system of taxation we had the grants or concessions (*appalti*) made to the private tax farmers in the provinces as well as in Rome for collecting the dues and duties on behalf of the Apostolic Chamber. For the papal government was to retain this uneconomical method throughout the century, although neighboring Tuscany had abolished it by 1768 and in Lombardy taxes were already brought under the central control of royal officials in 1760. Excluding Rome and the administrative district around it, known as the *distretto*, there were eight provinces for tax purposes, and the duchy of Benevento. The contributions of the provinces to the revenue of the Apostolic Chamber amounted to the percentage of the total revenue shown in Table 29.[6]

The contributions from the provinces, which had made up more than half of the total cameral revenue in the early part of the century, settled at about 44 to 45 percent in the later 1730s. From 1769 to 1785 the proportion tended to rise a little bit again, only to oscillate during the last years of the century. The northern provinces of the Marches of Ancona and the Romagna contributed the largest share.

[6] Included in the calculations are the amounts designated under the heading *Stato Ecclesiastico* in the balances. Lutz, "Zur Papstfinanz von Klemens IX.," 81; Diaz, *Gianni*, 193–96; Büchi, *Finanzen und Finanzpolitik Toskanas*, 173; Carlo Capra, "Alcuni aspetti del riordinamento tributario in Lombardia nell'età teresiana," in Ecole française de Rome, *La Fiscalité et ses implications sociales en Italie et en France aux XVIIe et XVIIIe siècles* (Rome, 1980), 4–5.

Table 28

| Year | Revenue | Expenditure | Surplus | % of surplus | Deficit | % of deficit |
|---|---|---|---|---|---|---|
| 1669 | 2,612,129.48 | 2,711,189.12 | — | — | 99,059.64 | 3.65 |
| 1689 | 2,511,883.60 | 2,052,424.23 | 459,459.37 | 18.29 | — | — |
| 1691 | 2,321,139.00 | 2,220,984.00 | 100,155.00 | 43.14 | — | — |
| 1692 | 2,322,781.00 | 2,247,769.00 | 75,011.00 | 3.23 | — | — |
| — | — | — | — | — | — | — |
| 1706 | 2,469,00.515 | 2,896,225.08 | — | — | 472,224.565 | 14.75 |
| — | — | — | — | — | — | — |
| 1708 | 2,055,284.14 | 1,886,017.62 | 169,266.52 | 8.24 | — | — |
| — | — | — | — | — | — | — |
| 1712 | 2,446,677.735 | 2,346,011.73 | 100,666.005 | 4.11 | — | — |
| — | — | — | — | — | — | — |
| 1715 | 2,719,650.425 | 2,439,308.13 | 280,341.29 | 10.31 | — | — |
| 1716 | 2,390,488.89 | 2,322,803.975 | 67,684.913 | 2.83 | — | — |
| — | — | — | — | — | — | — |
| — | — | — | — | — | — | — |
| 1723 | 2,716,650 | 2,439,308 | 277,342 | 10.20 | — | — |
| — | — | — | — | — | — | — |
| 1729 | 2,317,397.49 | 2,447,585.39 | — | — | 130,187.90 | 5.32 |

| | | | | | | |
|---|---|---|---|---|---|---|
| 1730 | 2,395,394.90 | 2,423,493.40 | — | — | 28,098.50 | 1.16 |
| 1731 | 2,485,009.20 | 2,511,752.765 | — | — | 26,744.56 | 1.06 |
| 1732 | 2,488,625.265 | 2,685,845.805 | — | — | 195,220.54 | 7.27 |
| 1733 | 2,412,925.74 | 2,621,528.44 | — | — | 208,602.70 | 7.96 |
| 1734 | 2,422,917.685 | 2,715,214.495 | — | — | 292,296.32 | 10.77 |
| 1735 | 2,368,761.52 | 2,506,192.81 | — | — | 137,431.28 | 5.48 |
| 1736 | 2,395,459.91 | 2,494,718.81 | — | — | 99,258.90 | 3.98 |
| 1737 | 2,342,468.28 | 2,490,364.66 | — | — | 147,896.38 | 3.94 |
| 1738 | 2,483,921.13 | 2,496,761.68 | — | — | 12,840.55 | 0.51 |
| 1737 | 2,599,524.67 | 2,660,538.42 | — | — | 62,913.75 | 3.36 |
| 1740 | 2,622,051.145 | 2,797,153.715 | — | — | 175,102.57 | 6.26 |
| 1741 | 2,701,178.00 | 2,668,731.62 | 32,441.33 | 1.20 | — | — |
| — | — | — | — | — | — | — |
| 1744 | 2,276,289.66 | 2,152,549.94 | 123,739.72 | 5.44 | — | — |
| 1745 | 2,251,342.32 | 2,127,817.915 | 123,524.4 | 5.49 | — | — |
| 1746 | 2,220,128.12 | 2,135,862.34 | 84,265.78 | 3.80 | — | — |
| 1747 | 2,157,836.535 | 2,131,983.21 | 25,853.32 | 1.20 | — | — |
| 1748 | 2,187,443.18 | 2,116,797.675 | 70,643.50 | 3.23 | — | — |
| 1749 | 2,178,268.01 | 2,144,036.52 | 34,231.485 | 1.57 | — | — |

Table 28 – *Continued*

| Year | Revenue | Expenditure | Surplus | % of surplus | Deficit | % of deficit |
|---|---|---|---|---|---|---|
| 1750 | 2,349,687.03 | 2,086,592.385 | 263,094.645 | 11.20 | — | — |
| 1751 | 2,154,269.245 | 2,085,937.00 | 73,332.245 | 3.40 | — | — |
| 1752 | 2,166,740.055 | 2,122,961.61 | 43,778.455 | 2.02 | — | — |
| 1753 | 2,149,196.755 | 2,309,671.91 | — | — | 160,476.16 | 6.95 |
| 1754 | 2,128,098.00 | 2,180,623.24 | — | — | 52,525.24 | 2.41 |
| 1755 | 2,057,884.455 | 2,123,266.09 | — | — | 65,377.63 | 3.08 |
| 1756 | 2,150,477.39 | 2,111,816.805 | 38,660.585 | 1.80 | — | — |
| 1757 | 2,164,084.375 | 2,107,734.97 | 56,549.395 | 2.61 | — | — |
| 1758 | 2,113,935.86 | 2,270,639.21 | — | — | 154,703.35 | 6.80 |
| 1759 | 2,167,444.32 | 2,181,371.17 | — | — | 11,928.85 | 0.50 |
| 1760 | 2,093,293.59 | 2,232,415.215 | — | — | 139,121.655 | 6.23 |
| 1761 | 2,062,242.92 | 2,168,924.09 | — | — | 106,681.17 | 4.92 |
| 1762 | 2,108,108.50 | 2,205,773.89 | — | — | 105,665.39 | 4.78 |
| 1763 | 2,091,837.63 | 2,153,720.63 | — | — | 61,883.00 | 2.87 |
| 1764 | 2,154,272.22 | 2,248,683.105 | — | — | 94,410.885 | 4.20 |
| 1765 | 2,149,992.92 | 2,210,821.50 | — | — | 60,828.59 | 2.75 |
| 1766 | 2,121,499.09 | 2,193,243.66 | — | — | 71,744.575 | 3.27 |
| 1767 | 2,133,244.38 | 2,302,663.335 | — | — | 169,418.955 | 7.36 |
| 1768 | 2,148,112.27 | 2,225,519.40 | — | — | 77,407.13 | 3.48 |
| 1769 | 2,248,253.24 | 2,307,346.51 | — | — | 61,093.27 | 2.65 |

| | | | | | | |
|---|---|---|---|---|---|---|
| 1770 | 2,217,566.195 | 2,331,888.53 | — | — | 114,322,535 | 4.99 |
| 1771 | 2,243,275.905 | 2,209,014.56 | 34,231.35 | 1.53 | — | — |
| 1772 | 2,376,836.945 | 2,280,825.94 | 96,011.02 | 4.04 | — | — |
| 1773 | 2,286,020.205 | 2,273,106.335 | 12,913.87 | 0.56 | — | — |
| 1774 | 2,346,620.315 | 2,327,845.615 | 18,774.70 | 0.80 | — | — |
| 1775 | 2,446,810.365 | 2,420,276.83 | 26,533.535 | 1.08 | — | — |
| 1776 | 2,343,254.255 | 2,433,266.595 | — | — | 90,012.345 | 3.70 |
| 1777 | 2,341,666.51 | 2,300,882.605 | 40,783.905 | 1.74 | — | — |
| 1778 | 2,346,132.125 | 2,365,289.42 | — | — | 19,157.30 | 0.81 |
| 1779 | 2,423,550.08 | 2,350,151.16 | 73,389.92 | 3.03 | — | — |
| 1780 | 2,327,798.19 | 2,367,951.65 | — | — | 40,153.46 | 1.72 |
| 1781 | 2,375,224.375 | 2,336,389.18 | 38,835.195 | 1.64 | — | — |
| 1782 | 2,383,156.85 | 2,404,714.08 | — | — | 21,557 | 0.90 |
| 1783 | 2,336,156.10 | 2,338,852.21 | — | — | 2,696.12 | 0.12 |
| 1784 | 2,341,769.40 | 2,334,871.86 | 6,897.54 | 0.29 | — | — |
| 1785 | 2,378,066.435 | 2,223,947.985 | 54,218.45 | 2.28 | — | — |
| 1786 | 2,420,326,935 | 2,376,470.42 | 43,848.515 | 1.81 | — | — |
| 1787 | 2,247,996.215 | 2,358,270.035 | — | — | 110,273.82 | 4.68 |
| 1788 | 2,598,161.73 | 2,447,105.215 | 151,056.515 | 5.81 | — | — |
| 1789 | 2,447,604.42 | 2,575,577.105 | — | — | 121,972.685 | 4.74 |
| 1790 | 2,331,097.09 | 2,508,119.41 | — | — | 177,022,32 | 7.06 |
| 1791 | 2,351,744.24 | 2,529,648.83 | — | — | 177,904.595 | 7.03 |
| 1792 | 2,485,646.095 | 2,740,596.375 | — | — | 255,950.28 | 9.34 |
| 1793 | 2,330,425.875 | 3,276,325.325 | — | — | 945,899.48 | 28.81 |
| — | — | — | — | — | — | — |
| 1796 | 1,824,362.095 | 2,961,267.37 | — | — | 1,136,905.275 | 38.39 |

Table 29

| Year | % of contribution | Year | % of contribution | Year | % of contribution | Year | % of contribution |
|---|---|---|---|---|---|---|---|
| — | — | 1748 | 45.61 | 1764 | 44.91 | 1791 | 42.08 |
| 1706 | 63.95 | 1749 | 45.35 | 1765 | 44.61 | 1792 | 46.78 |
| — | — | 1750 | 41.11 | 1766 | 44.88 | 1793 | 46.77 |
| 1708 | 59.99 | 1751 | 44.48 | 1767 | 43.93 | — | — |
| — | — | 1752 | 43.52 | 1768 | 44.60 | 1796 | 44.39 |
| 1715 | 53.33 | 1753 | 43.64 | 1769 | 47.45 | 1780 | 45.72 |
| 1716 | 56.09 | 1754 | 43.64 | 1770 | 47.23 | 1781 | 46.98 |
| — | — | 1755 | 44.70 | 1771 | 47.71 | 1782 | 46.89 |
| 1735 | 51.22 | 1756 | 44.07 | 1772 | 44.65 | 1783 | 47.02 |
| — | — | 1757 | 43.76 | 1773 | 46.25 | 1784 | 47.23 |
| 1739 | 44.65 | 1758 | 44.97 | 1774 | 43.59 | 1785 | 45.80 |
| — | — | 1759 | 44.45 | 1775 | 43.11 | — | — |
| 1744 | 44.12 | 1760 | 43.70 | 1776 | 46.07 | 1788 | 39.70 |
| 1745 | 44.59 | 1761 | 45.64 | 1777 | 45.84 | 1789 | 44.75 |
| 1746 | 44.50 | 1762 | 43.58 | 1778 | 46.24 | 1790 | 42.24 |
| 1747 | 45.48 | 1763 | 44.23 | 1779 | 42.10 | | |

The Marches were responsible for roughly 11 to 14 percent and the Romagna 8 to 10 percent.[7]

It would have been interesting to estimate the per capita incidence of taxation in Rome and compare it with the provinces, since the discussions among contemporaries are laced with the alleged inequity of the treatment of the periphery in relation to the capital. In actual fact, Rome saw its fiscal burden practically doubled between the end of the sixteenth century and 1660/70, from an annual average of 300,000 scudi to one above 600,000 scudi largely collected through indirect taxes. By 1672 the contribution of the city came to 580,581 scudi with another 32,750 from the distretto around it. About the same sum, however, was returned to the city by the Apostolic Chamber. Toward the end of the seventeenth century a progressive

[7] Caracciolo, "I bilanci dello Stato ecclesiastico," 100–02; Caracciolo, *Lo Stato pontificio*, 516–17.

Table 30

| Year | Revenue (in scudi) | % of total revenue | Year | Revenue (in scudi) | % of total revenue | Year | Revenue (in scudi) | % of total revenue |
|---|---|---|---|---|---|---|---|---|
| 1706 | 500,000 | 20.25 | 1749 | 466,309.23 | 21.41 | 1771 | 411,814.63 | 18.36 |
| — | — | — | 1750 | 619,763.58 | 26.38 | 1772 | 410,724.79 | 17.30 |
| 1708 | 460,000 | 22.38 | 1751 | 457,860.105 | 21.10 | 1773 | 399,495 | 17.48 |
| — | — | — | 1752 | 453,399.565 | 20.93 | 1774 | 441,080.06 | 18.80 |
| 1715 | 545,375.97 | 20.05 | 1753 | 443,441.94 | 20.63 | 1775 | 460,123.83 | 18.80 |
| 1716 | 466,413.39 | 19.51 | 1754 | 457,130.32 | 21.48 | 1776 | 437,502.47 | 18.67 |
| — | — | — | 1755 | 432,916.245 | 21.04 | 1777 | 436,815.96 | 18.65 |
| 1729 | 450,539.68 | 18.81 | 1756 | 447,848.615 | 20.83 | 1778 | 430,313.41 | 18.34 |
| — | — | — | 1757 | 432,205.125 | 19.97 | 1779 | 432,629.87 | 17.85 |
| 1731 | 439,000 | 17.67 | 1758 | 431,989.685 | 20.42 | 1780 | 457,782.84 | 19.67 |
| — | — | — | 1759 | 431,098.90 | 19.87 | 1781 | 426,076.97 | 17.93 |
| 1733 | 415,539 | 17.22 | 1760 | 437,020.99 | 20.80 | 1782 | 408,790.37 | 17.15 |
| — | — | — | 1761 | 414,412.275 | 20.09 | 1783 | 411,180.01 | 17.60 |
| 1735 | 557,216.52 | 23.52 | 1762 | 423,291.96 | 20.08 | 1784 | 399,965,515 | 17.08 |
| — | — | — | 1763 | 432,980.085 | 20.23 | 1785 | 373,447.38 | 15.70 |
| 1739 | 502,079.11 | 19.31 | 1764 | 436,575.325 | 20.27 | 1786 | 428,674.095 | 17.71 |
| — | — | — | 1765 | 430,164.775 | 20.00 | 1787 | 433,709,92 | 19.20 |
| 1744 | 455,931.50 | 20.20 | 1766 | 405,587.085 | 19.12 | 1788 | 449,926.35 | 17.32 |
| 1745 | 479,093.09 | 21.28 | 1767 | 426,211.715 | 19.98 | 1789 | 430,023.425 | 17.57 |
| 1746 | 447,694.43 | 20.17 | 1768 | 403,070.35 | 18.76 | 1790 | 438,142.08 | 18.80 |
| 1747 | 449,598.065 | 20.84 | 1769 | 400,257.63 | 17.80 | 1791 | 425,129.625 | 18.03 |
| 1748 | 451,600.255 | 20.65 | 1770 | 399,341.535 | 18.00 | 1792 | 411,159.895 | 16.54 |
| | | | | | | 1793 | 375,669.215 | 16.10 |
| | | | | | | — | — | — |
| | | | | | | 1796 | 244,485.32 | 13.40 |

alleviation of the fiscal burden for the capital commenced, with the reduction, if not abolition, of some of the more burdensome gabelles.[8]

Yet the variety of contributions on the one hand and exemptions on the other for both the city and the distretto make any detailed calculation extremely complex and unreliable. The largest contribution of Rome to the cameral budget came from customs duties, the *dogana generale*; for most of the century the basic rate was 12 percent of the value on merchandise that came into the city from outside the state by

8 Stumpo, *Il capitale finanziario a Roma*, 98, 147, 158–59; Nicolai, *Memorie, leggi, ed osservazioni*, 2:79–81.

way of the sea, 9 percent for foreign merchandise that entered overland, and 6 percent for merchandise from within the state. But the actual imposition could vary greatly, since frequently extra fees and tolls were added. For instance, in 1731 the total payment was raised to about 30 percent. Yet, unlike Florence, the local nobility still enjoyed certain privileges; a good part of the food supply for noble houses in the seventeenth and early eighteenth century, which came from outside Rome, was exempt from the *dogana*. Allowing for these qualifications, we have a partial list of the income of the *dogana* and its proportional share in the total revenue of the Apostolic Chamber (Table 30).

Viewed in terms of monetary revenue, the income from the *dogana* as a whole was fairly high during the first two decades of the century, between about 450,000 and 500,000 scudi. It then began to fall until its administration was entrusted to the Roman banker Girolamo Belloni, on his terms, in 1730, when it was more or less stabilized.[9] By the 1740s the income remained within the limits of 400,000 to 450,000 scudi a year, apart from an occasional exceptional year, such as that of the Jubilee of 1750. A serious drop only occurred in 1793, with the rapid collapse of the papal economy. From the point of view of the contribution to the cameral income in general, the share of the *dogana* after it had been 19 and 21 percent from the 1730s to 1765 started a very slow decline until the end of the century. Still, it formed a healthy 18.8 percent in 1790 compared to only 6.5 percent in neighboring Naples. If the decline could have been attributed to a decrease in foreign imports, which were being replaced by home-made Roman products, it would have been a welcome boost to the local economy. Alas, the indicators do not point in that direction.[10]

Most of the rest of the revenues of the Apostolic Chamber came from taxes and gabelles and the rents of *appalti* and concessions. Some Romans paid some taxes; but even in the spendthrift reign of Pius VI they never amounted to a half, perhaps a little more than a quarter, of the twelve livres tournois (c. 2.26 scudi) the French were paying annually or the 20 lire (c. 2.87 scudi), which has been calculated as the individual tax burden of a Milanese in about 1770, not to speak of the £1.25 sterling (c. 5.46 scudi) that fell on an Englishman. The only direct levy affected property owners. The poorer classes had to pay virtually nothing at all in the form of direct taxes.[11]

The reason for these apparently low taxes is that the papal rulers seemed to prefer indirect taxes over direct taxes. One of the earliest of these indirect taxes was the

[9] Caracciolo, *L'albero dei Belloni*, 70–77.

[10] ASR, Famiglie diverse, Cavaletti, busta 2, vol. XIII, nos. XXXII, XXXVI; ASR, Camerale II, arti e mestieri vaccinari e macellari, busta 43, fasc. 90; Montalto, *Un mecenate in Roma barocca*, 73–75; Büchi, *Finanzen und Finanzpolitik Toskanas*, 65, 285; Lodovico Bianchini, *Della storia delle finanze del Regno di Napoli* (3 vols.; Naples, 1835), 3: 171–74. For a breakdown of the constituent parts of the *dogana generale*, see Girolamo Belloni's account from October to December 1732, in B. CORS., ms. 2547, no. 8.

[11] Capra, "Il riordinamento tributario in Lombardia," 15–16. To calculate exchange rates, I have used Giuseppe Felloni, *Gli investimenti finanziari genovesi in Europa tra il Seicento e la Restaurazione* (Milan, 1971), 503.

*macinato*, imposed on the sale of flour to bakers, which went back to the Renaissance pope Clement VII; Paul IV in 1555 introduced the *quattrino della carne*, which, as implied, amounted to one quattrino per Roman pound (*libbra*) of meat sold. After a number of vicissitudes these taxes were either revived or consolidated by Clement XI in 1708 in conjunction with his larger program of taxation known as the *tassa del milione*, which was planned to support an army of 20,000 new recruits during the War of the Spanish Succession. After the failure of the *tassa del milione* some of these taxes survived, that on the retail sale of meat until 1724; the *macinato* was used to shore up the finances of the ailing annona.

One of the more profitable sources of revenue for the Apostolic Chamber was the monopoly on tobacco. It began to be contracted out to farmers in the middle of the seventeenth century. But its collection posed so many difficulties that the government did not favor it. There was a great deal of smuggling. The concession was usually joined with that for local gin – acquavita – another source of profit, since it was estimated that about 1,500 barrels a year were consumed in Rome. The revenue from the tobacco monopoly was 29,300 scudi at the start of the century and rose to 102,846.42 scudi in 1744, then falling slightly to about 90,000 scudi in 1753–54, until Benedict XIV replaced it with a substitute when he found that the cost of trying to stop smuggling had begun to absorb all the profits. The substitute brought in about 86,000 scudi to the Apostolic Chamber. The acquavita monopoly was worth about 8,000 scudi, but was quickly reduced to 5,000 and even less until it was suppressed altogether in 1773. Among the variety of lesser taxes were ones on carriages in Rome, on hay and straw for animal fodder, and on wine. The last had to be paid by the innkeepers of the city, of whom there were about 160.[12]

In addition to the revenues from various taxes and duties the Chamber received, some of the privileged bodies, corporations and craft guilds had to make their own contributions. Between 1744 and 1796, their total annual payments to the Chamber averaged out at only 35,859 scudi.[13]

In the light of the complexity, if not the confusion, of the various sources of income, some kind of rationalization was indeed needed. In Rome, as elsewhere in Italy and in France, voices were calling for a reform of the system of revenue. They fell into two kinds: those who wanted to do away with the monopoly or *appalto* systems, and those who proposed an improved method of taxation. The appalti, which created monopolies primarily to fill the coffers of the treasury, were an

12 ASR, Camerale II, strade, busta 2; ASR, Camerale II, camerlengato e tesorierato, progetti diversi, buste 17 and 18; ASR, Camerale II, arti e mestieri, locandieri, albergatori, busta 28, fasc. 62; busta 29, fasc. 63; ASR, Camerale II, neve e ghiaccio busta 1; B. CORS., ms. 2547, no. 4; BL, Egerton ms. 3798, chap. II; Luigi Nina, *Le finanze pontifice sotto Clemente XI (Tassa del milione)*, (Milan, 1927), 27, 87–102, 106–18, 145–49, 173–77; Petrocchi, *Roma nel Seicento*, 44, 47–49; De Cupis, *Vicende dell'agricoltura nell'Agro Romano*, 297; Nicolai, *Memorie, leggi, ed osservazioni*, 2:86–88; 3:95; Montesquieu *Voyages. Oeuvres complètes*, 2:1181; Lalande, *Voyage d'un françois en Italie*, 5:20–21, 300, 302.

13 Ibid., 5:292; Delumeau, *Vie économique et sociale de Rome*, 2:882–84; Nina, *Le finanze pontifice sotto Clemente XI*, 210–26.

impediment to the development of industry. An early opponent of appalti, Clement XII charged a special congregation with a thorough review of the principal appalti of the Apostolic Chamber. The resistance which this first attempt at eliminating the appalti most harmful to the state's economy encountered was so strong that its results were nil. Related to this effort was a proposal, whose beginnings go back to the seventeenth century, to abolish the divers gabelles and indirect taxes in the city and replace them with flat rates to be paid by the different kinds of merchants and craftsmen. It was claimed that this would eliminate the army of tax farmers and customs officials, prevent smuggling and fraud, and attract business to Rome. Along the same lines, but spelled out more precisely, were the fiscal proposals of the economic author Leone Pascoli. He urged the abolition of all taxes and tolls within the country and the establishment of a tariff barrier at the borders; indirect taxes were to be limited to duties for foreign imports and to a select few monopolies given in appalto. We have already seen that it would take a long time before such proposals were implemented. In the meantime the Papal States would lose the reforming initiative to its neighbor to the north. With the accession of Grand Duke Pietro Leopoldo in 1765 the tax appalto was done away with in 1768 and Francesco Maria Gianni carried through a reform of taxation based on consumption in 1785.[14]

One source of income, outside the regular cameral budget, needs mention, not only because it was lucrative, but also because of the role it played in the social life of all classes in Rome: the lottery or *lotto*. Lotteries existed in Rome before the state took them over. Anyone might organize a lottery and the gambler was offered no guarantee or protection. This was a cause of scandal, as well as loss of money to the state, as Muratori had shown later. So Clement X made an effort to control the business by setting up an appalto for the so-called lotto of Genoa and Milan in Rome, upon which the people spent an estimated 100,000 scudi a year in the middle of the seventeenth century. The sterner pontiffs at the end of the century, however, forbad the lottery altogether. In 1731 Clement XII added the threat of excommunication in a final attempt to wipe out the vice. The Romans at once turned to lotteries functioning in other cities of Italy. So within barely six months the same pope reversed himself and reintroduced the lottery, putting it under the management of the state. The first draw of the official lottery took place at the Piazza di Campidoglio on 14 February 1732. Its apparent success probably served as a model to the Tuscan lottery, which was reintroduced under Francesco Stefano's government in 1739.

Although the treasurer general was at first resolved to gain nothing from the lottery, seemliness demanded that good works should benefit. The profits were divided between public works, churches, and charitable institutions. During the

[14] Ibid., 188–210, 608–09, 636–47; Rodocanachi, *Les corporations ouvrières à Rome*, 1:iii; La Marca, *Saggio di una ricerca storico-economica*, 28–29; Oscar Nuccio, "Precettistica economica di Pascoli," 27 (1979), 295–98; Diaz, *Gianni*, 193–96, 205–08; Büchi, *Finanzen und Finanzpolitik Toskanas*, 109–12, 455.

first six years of existence, the balance sheet of the Roman lottery showed 1,980,897.60 scudi in the credit ledger. Of this sum 97,241.80 scudi went to various institutions for propagating the Catholic faith, 160,690.035 scudi for building churches, religious houses, and hospitals in Rome and the provinces, and 720,308.22 scudi to embellishing the city of Rome, restoring its antiquities, opening up new streets and cleaning aqueducts. Of this last sum, 423,312.40 scudi alone was spent on the facade of St. John Lateran, and 44,000 on that of San Giovanni de' Fiorentini. The Trevi fountain was allocated 94,435.26 scudi.[15] A total of 103,789.25 scudi was spent on the acquisition of statues for the Capitoline museum and 11,000 on ancient coins for the Vatican library. Only 29,000.22 remained for the opening up of new streets and the cleaning of aqueducts. The share of the Apostolic Chamber came to 259,124.60. But from that sum 230,060.35 scudi were diverted to building the new palace of the Consulta on Montecavallo and 24,520 to the women's prison at San Michele a Ripa. With Bologna receiving 500 scudi, the Chamber was left with a meager 4,044.25 scudi at its disposal.

The lottery was not strictly speaking, therefore, a part of the cameral budget. In 1770 the operation was officially *incamerato* and the Apostolic Chamber from then on derived an annual revenue of between 80,000 and 82,000 scudi, about 3 percent of its total income. Yet much of the revenue from the lottery continued to be spent in the traditional way; for example, between 1770 and 1782, 333,736.825 scudi went to meet the expenses of the Vatican museum.

Leaving aside any immediate financial gain, however, the effect of the lottery on the Roman economy was harmful. It gave the Romans yet one more excuse for doing no work, while living in the expectation of the miracle that would make them wealthy overnight. It took out of circulation the immense sums they invested, which could have been employed much more productively.[16]

The Holy See also used to have access to resources of which its neighbors were deprived, the spiritualities, the greater part of which never showed up in the cameral balances. The total spiritual revenues for the ninety years between 1570 and 1660 can be roughly calculated at 100,475,000 scudi, that is, an annual average of about 1,116,380 scudi. These revenues consisted mainly of what was collectively called the *spogli*, that is, estates of clerics who died intestate and revenues from vacant benefices which all devolved upon the papacy, and from the income from the datary. The datary, established in the middle of the fifteenth century, is best defined

15 Pinto, *Trevi Fountain*, 173 states that "in the decade between 1732 and 1742 more than 58,000 scudi from the lottery were spent on the Trevi fountain." This sum is much smaller than that found in B.CAS., ms. vol. 2381, which estimates that from 1732 through March 1738 93,435.26 scudi were diverted from the *lotto* funds to building the fountain.

16 Idem.; ASR, Camerale II, camerlengato e tesorierato, progetti diversi, buste 18 and 19; A.Cap.R., vol. 33, cred. XIII, editti e bandi, 102, 150, 154; B. N. Ro., Fondo Vittorio Emanuele, ms. 603, ff. 8–10; Andrieux, *Daily Life in Papal Rome*, 83–84; Filippo Clementi, *Il carnevale romano nelle cronache contemporanee dalle origini al secolo XVIII* (2 vols.; Città di Castello, 1939), 2:52; Büchi, *Finanzen und Finanzpolitik Toskanas*, 107; Cochrane, *Florence in the Forgotten Centuries*, 249–50.

as the general *curia graziosa* of the pope for all grants of grace and favor, such as dispensations from canon law in areas of sacerdotal and matrimonial law, as well as grants of indulgences. In addition, there were regular revenues from the diocese of Rome, the chancellery and the secretariat of briefs, and other extraordinary levies, such as the Turkish "tithe" imposed on the Italian clergy. Most of the more regular spiritual revenues stayed in Rome in the form of payments to the curial bishops and prelates; scarcely 25 percent was paid to those holding office outside Rome. Almost a similar percentage was assigned to the datary.

The income of the datary, however, presents us with more difficulties, for theoretically it was regarded as the pope's privy purse, over which he could dispose at his discretion. In the seventeenth century some of it was used for the regular recurrent alms the pope gave; other parts went to meet the annual payment of ecclesiastical loans (*Monte Dataria*) and a portion to supplement the needs of the Apostolic Chamber.[17]

But if the Apostolic Chamber gained some from the revenue of the datary on the one hand, it probably lost more through the ruinous system of the cardinal nephews or *nipoti*. In the ninety years from 1570 to 1660, the system cost the Papal States altogether about 31 million scudi, not all paid by the Chamber admittedly, but an appreciable amount was in *luoghi di monte*, for which the Chamber had to pay interest. From 1670 to 1676 the Apostolic chamber paid the papal relatives a sum of about 1,200,000 scudi in various forms and Alexander VIII's nepotism cost it no less than 700,000 scudi, which probably raised the public debt by another 250,000 scudi.[18]

Innocent XII's abolition of nepotism came just in time to offset some of the losses in spiritual revenues. For the end of the seventeenth century saw a drop in these sources. In 1728 the Roman pamphleteer Leone Pascoli gave the figure of 700,000 scudi for all the foreign revenues of Christian Rome, which would fall to 300,000 scudi after the middle of the century. This loss had its repercussions. In 1609 the datary had transferred 159,000 scudi to supplement the budget of the Apostolic Chamber. The records of the datary for the eighteenth century have not yet been studied. But in the period between 1773 and 1782 the annual average paid by the datary to the Chamber came to 14,000.03 scudi, less than one-eleventh of what it had been about 170 years earlier. To this sum was also added the income from the secretariat of briefs, which averaged out at 45,069.05 scudi a year over the decade of 1762–71. In the seventeenth century it, together with the revenue of the papal chancellery, came to 290,000 scudi a year. At that time another 70,000 scudi a year came from the collectories of the *spogli* in Italy, Spain, and Portugal, which were no longer available by the latter part of the eighteenth century. These figures are

[17] Delumeau, *Vie économique et sociale de Rome*, 2:768–70, 824–27; Reinhard, *Papstfinanz und Nepotismus unter Paul V*, 1:6–12; Stumpo, *Il capitale finanziario a Roma*, 49, 54, 215.

[18] Ibid., 207, 275; Lutz, "Zur Papstfinanz von Klemens IX.," 87, 89.

enough to show that the revenues from Catholicism abroad, once one of the mainstays of paper power, had shrunk to insignificance.[19]

One of the principal reasons for the diminishing payments from abroad was the ever-growing power of the national rulers, who succeeded in wringing out concessions from an enfeebled papacy, usually in the form of concordats that deprived the pontiffs of the rights they once exercised over and within the national churches. The most prominent case was that of Spain. In the concordat of 1763 the Holy See surrendered its right of appointment to 52 specific benefices for which the Spanish king, Charles III, made a one-time payment of 233,333 scudi to the pope, which invested at 3 percent would yield a pitiful 7,000 scudi annually. As compensation for the loss of his other claims the king transferred gold bullion to the value of 1,333,333 scudi, an impressive sum at one time, but only a pittance for the long-term needs of the Papal States.

While not so crass, the losses from Naples were also palpable. The concordat with Naples in 1741, too, called for the abandonment of claims to ecclesiastical benefices and their pensions, in return for which the Holy See received 20,000 ducats in Neapolitan money every year. The situation reached its nadir in 1790, when as a result of the French Revolution and the conflict over the civil constitution of the clergy, the remaining source of income to the datary from France was cut off, which ultimately aggravated the already critical financial plight.[20]

While the credit side of the ledger does not indicate a vibrant, expanding economy, the debit columns call forth some dark forebodings such as were not uncommon in the era of the ancien regime. An analysis of the expenditure of the Apostolic Chamber will reveal that the bulk of it went on only two items – interest on the *luoghi di monte* and on the *uffici venali vacabili* (Table 31).[21]

To understand the figures we have to look more closely at the two items which together formed the equivalent of the public debt of the Papal States. The greater of the two were the *monti*, both the name and the principle of which were borrowed from Florence, which adopted this device for raising money in 1345. Not surprisingly then it was a Medici pope, Clement VII, who first instituted it in Rome in 1526 to finance the War of the Holy League of Cognac against the Turks. A *monte* was in effect an issue of government – sometimes private – bonds or *luoghi* at 100

19 ASR, Camerale II, camerlengato e tesorierato, progetti diversi, busta 18; Madelin, *Rome de Napoléon*, 54–56; Stumpo, *Il capitale finanziario a Roma*, 166, 175, 183.

20 Corridore, *La popolazione dello Stato Romano*, 24; B. N. Ro., Fondo Gesuitico, ms. 107, fasc. 10, and ms. 303, fasc. A; Silvagni, *La corte pontificia*, 2:68; Lodovico Bianchini, *Storia delle finanze del Regno delle Due Sicilie*, ed. by Luigi de Rosa (Naples, 1971), 3:361–62; Sir Marcus Cheke, *The Cardinal de Bernis* (London, 1958), 265–66; Woolf, *History of Italy, 1700–1860*, 142; Andrieux, *Daily Life in Papal Rome*, 69–70; Pastor, *Geschichte der Päpste*, 16, pt 3:505.

21 The data are derived from the same sources as in note 4, except that the figures for 1691 and 1693 were supplemented from Lutz, "Zur Papstfinanz von Klemens IX.," 79, table 1.

Table 31

| Year | Interest on *luoghi di monti* | Interest on *vacabili* | Total interest | % of total expenditure |
|---|---|---|---|---|
| 1691 | — | — | 1,270,342 | 57.20 |
| 1693 | — | — | 1,275,577 | 56.20 |
| 1706 | 1,247,388.63 | 176,825.60 | 1,424,164.23 | 49.17 |
| — | — | — | — | — |
| 1708 | 1,257,066.99 | 173,525.60 | 1,430,592.59 | 75.85 |
| — | — | — | — | — |
| 1712 | 1,272,390.58 | 135,994.21 | 1,408,384.79 | 60.03 |
| — | — | — | — | — |
| 1716 | — | — | 1,408,889.165 | 60.65 |
| — | — | — | — | — |
| 1729 | 1,277,863 | 177,914.32 | 1,455,777.32 | 60.07 |
| — | — | — | — | — |
| 1733 | 1,290,788.71 | 177,914.32 | 1,468,703.03 | 56.02 |
| — | — | — | — | — |
| 1735 | 1,291,860.37 | 177,914.37 | 1,469,774.74 | 58.65 |
| — | — | — | — | — |
| 1739 | 1,341,550.43 | 177,914.37 | 1,519,464.80 | *c.*56.28 |
| 1740 | 1,343,999.98 | 177,914.37 | 1,521,914.35 | 54.41 |
| — | — | — | — | — |
| 1744 | 1,284,360.995 | 107,227.26 | 1,391,588.255 | 64.65 |
| 1745 | 1,280,592.18 | 88,698.67 | 1,369,885.05 | 64.38 |
| 1746 | 1,275,103.46 | 87,742.02 | 1,362,845.48 | 63.81 |
| 1747 | 1,268,936.40 | 87,742.02 | 1,356,678,42 | 63.63 |
| 1748 | 1,267,088.68 | 87,742.02 | 1,354,830.70 | 64.00 |
| 1749 | 1,265,996.975 | 97,795.41 | 1,353,792.385 | 63.14 |
| 1750 | 1,265,383.045 | 87,742.02 | 1,353,125.07 | 64.85 |
| 1751 | 1,265,419.47 | 87,742.02 | 1,353,161.49 | 64.87 |
| 1752 | 1,265,387.17 | 87,742.02 | 1,353,129.19 | 63.74 |
| 1753 | 1,256,337.56 | 87,742.02 | 1,344,079.58 | 58.19 |
| 1754 | 1,240,725.05 | 87,902.08 | 1,328,627.13 | 60.92 |
| 1755 | 1,235,151.515 | 87,742.02 | 1,322,863.535 | 62.30 |
| 1756 | 1,241,639.515 | 87,742.02 | 1,329,381.535 | 62.95 |
| 1757 | 1,240,615.48 | 87,742.02 | 1,328,357.50 | 63.02 |
| 1758 | 1,239,353.65 | 87,742.02 | 1,327,095.67 | 58.45 |
| 1759 | 1,238,864.60 | 87,742.02 | 1,326,606.62 | 60.82 |

Table 31 – *Continued*

| Year | Interest on *luoghi di monti* | Interest on *vacabili* | Total interest | % of total expenditure |
|---|---|---|---|---|
| 1760 | 1,233,855.595 | 87,742.02 | 1,321,597.615 | 59.20 |
| 1761 | 1,233,341.545 | 87,742.02 | 1,321,083.57 | 60.91 |
| 1762 | 1,238,640.90 | 87,742.02 | 1,326,382.92 | 60.13 |
| 1763 | 1,236,762.095 | 87,742.02 | 1,324,504.115 | 61.50 |
| 1764 | 1,236,260.74 | 87,742.02 | 1,324,002.76 | 58.80 |
| 1765 | 1,240,504.765 | 87,742.02 | 1,328,246.785 | 60.08 |
| 1766 | 1,248,957.525 | 87,742.02 | 1,331,699.545 | 60.72 |
| 1767 | 1,246,100.74 | 87,742.02 | 1,333,842.76 | 57.90 |
| 1768 | 1,247,580.685 | 87,662.02 | 1,335,242.705 | 60.00 |
| 1769 | 1,253,907.685 | 87,662.02 | 1,341,569.705 | 58.08 |
| 1770 | 1,258,033.135 | 87,662.02 | 1,345,695.155 | 57.71 |
| 1771 | 1,263,943.27 | 87,662.02 | 1,341,605.29 | 61.19 |
| 1772 | 1,267,680.63 | 87,662.02 | 1,355,342.65 | 59.42 |
| 1773 | 1,270,663.715 | 87,662.02 | 1,358,325.73 | 59.76 |
| 1774 | 1,271,630.575 | 87,662.02 | 1,359,292.595 | 58.39 |
| 1775 | 1,272,862.89 | 87,662.02 | 1,360,524.91 | 56.21 |
| 1776 | 1,282,194.89 | 87,662.02 | 1,369,856.91 | 56.30 |
| 1777 | 1,283,106.97 | 87,662.08 | 1,370,769.05 | 59.58 |
| 1778 | 1,282,997.345 | 87,662.08 | 1,370,659.365 | 57.95 |
| 1779 | 1,282,901.425 | 87,662.08 | 1,370,563.445 | 58.32 |
| 1780 | 1,282,797.96 | 87,662.08 | 1,370,460.04 | 57.88 |
| 1781 | 1,282,601,04 | 87,662.08 | 1,370,263.12 | 58.65 |
| 1782 | 1,282,823.52 | 87,662.08 | 1,370,485.6 | 56.99 |
| 1783 | 1,282,959.555 | 87,662.08 | 1,370,621.635 | 58.60 |
| 1784 | 1,284,047.805 | 87,662.08 | 1,371,709.885 | 58.75 |
| 1785 | 1,283,800.46 | 87,662.08 | 1,371,462.54 | 61.67 |
| 1786 | 1,284,811.825 | 87,662.08 | 1,372,473.055 | 57.75 |
| 1787 | 1,288,057.625 | 87,662.08 | 1,375,719.705 | 58.34 |
| 1788 | 1,289,957.595 | 87,662.08 | 1,377,619.675 | 56.30 |
| 1789 | 1,291,854.295 | 87,662.08 | 1,379,516.375 | 53.56 |
| 1790 | 1,294,820.70 | 87,662.08 | 1,382,482.78 | 55.12 |
| 1791 | 1,303,060.08 | 87,662.08 | 1,390,722.685 | 54.90 |
| 1792 | 1,319,530.09 | 87,662.08 | 1,407,192.17 | 51.35 |
| 1793 | 1,336,351.115 | 87,662.08 | 1,424,013.195 | 43.46 |
| — | — | — | — | — |
| 1796 | 1,389,390.14 | 88,638.90 | 1,478,029.04 | 49.91 |

scudi each, with occasionally also half shares of 50 scudi, pledged against a clearly defined source of annual revenue. The *luoghi di monte* yielded an annual interest. The issue was then sold en bloc by the Apostolic Chamber to a bank or a consortium of bankers. From this sale the papacy often made a profit produced by competitive bidding among bankers. The bankers in turn put up the bonds for public sale at a commission, at least equal to 1 percent. These *luoghi* could then be resold by the holders. There was an extremely active market for them in Rome and throughout Italy. With the exception of the religious mendicants, every person was able to acquire shares in a *monte*, including members of religious orders of both sexes and even those declared juridically incompetent.[22]

Delumeau has estimated that the amount borrowed between 1526 and 1603, including those *monti* set up by private individuals with papal consent, amounted to close to 13 million scudi, almost all contracted after 1550. The borrowing would continue. By the end of the pontificate of Urban VIII in 1644 the Apostolic Chamber alone was believed to have been in debt for 8 million gold scudi, which can be roughly converted to 63,192,890 scudi of account.[23]

Alexander VII (1655–67) began the process of putting some order into the confused situation by consolidating the *monti*. He set up three *monti*, to the total value of 12,138,200 scudi at 4 percent and used the greater part of this sum to extinguish earlier *monti* which bore higher rates of interest. But by this time the golden age of papal finances, which some writers have placed between 1570 and 1660, had come to an end.[24] Under Clement IX (1667–69) and Clement X (1670–76) there was a series of dangerous budget deficits, which compelled Innocent XI to undertake some measures that would mark a temporary turning point in papal financial policy. Without appreciable increases in taxation or other imposts, Innocent proceeded by saving on papal household expenditure and in the central administration, foremost by abolishing posts and sinecures from which papal relatives profited. These steps took their full effect in 1678, when the expenditure in the budget fell by almost 100,000 scudi and revenue rose by even more. Nevertheless, interest payments continued to show a tendency to rise, so that if the balance of the budget were to stay the same within a few short years there would once again be a deficit. This threat probably moved Innocent XI to carry through the long-discussed plan to lower the general interest rate for the *luoghi di*

22 Delumeau, *Vie économique et sociale de Rome*, 2:783–90; Reinhard, *Papstfinaz und Nepotismus unter Paul V*, 1:16–17.

23 This figure was calculated from data given in Delumeau, *Vie économique et sociale de Rome*, 2:280. At another place Delumeau gave the public debt at the time of the death of Urban VIII in 1644, immediately following the War of Castro (1642–44), at thirty million. Jean Delumeau, *L'Alun de Rome, XVe–XIXe siècles* (Paris, 1962), 163. Petrocchi, *Roma nel Seicento*, 77, roughly agrees with the latter estimate, quoting a figure of 35 million scudi. Stumpo, *Il capitale finanziario a Roma*, 172, 249, 259, gives the nominal capital value of *monti* issued by the Apostolic Chamber at more than 33 million scudi in 1658 and of the *uffici venali vacabili* at 6,238,950 scudi in 1660, making the debt at close to forty million.

24 Stumpo, *Il capitale finanziario a Roma*, Viii.

*monte*. He performed the complicated operation of consolidating the system of *monti* and simultaneously converting them to 3 percent interest by setting up the Monte di San Pietro at 3 percent, composed of 209,271 *luoghi* at 100 scudi, and offering the creditors either payment in cash at 100 scudi per old *luogo* or an exchange for the new *monte*. The subsequent abrupt reduction in interest payment that followed, estimated at between 350,000 and 400,000 scudi, produced in the next four or five years extremely large surpluses. As in so many other endeavors, Rome led the way in the attempt to consolidate the public debt.[25] The reform-minded Habsburg administration in Lombardy, for example, would only start on the process in 1750, and Pietro Leopoldo of Tuscany converted the interest of those *luoghi* with high yields down to 3 percent as late as 1770.

But the extraordinary favorable situation would not endure. Before the close of Innocent XI's reign the threatening conflict with Louis XIV and, to a lesser extent, the Turkish campaign, produced a rise in military expenditure. New *monti* were issued. By 1722 the invested capital would rise by another 12,216,915 scudi. Nevertheless, the pontiff did leave an improved legacy to the ancien regime, at least for a while. The number of monti was reduced and rationalized and less of the cameral revenue was absorbed in paying interest on them. Whereas in 1595 64.37 percent were absorbed in paying interest on the debts, in 1691 the percentage fell to 54.73 percent. Although the burden on the public debt was reduced proportionally over the seventeenth century, yet the situation had deteriorated because the incoming money continued to be tied up in paying for the interest in the debts already contracted and there was no margin for new operations.

The eighteenth century was to bring no relief. The interest burden, as Table 30 shows, was to remain between 1,200,000 and 1,300,000 scudi until 1790, except for the years around 1739/40. From 1791 it began to rise rather steeply.[26] In a folder at the Archivio di Stato di Roma, there are records of the various *monti* launched in the eighteenth century. They are not in very good order and cannot be regarded as complete. Nevertheless they provide us with a guide to the size of the loans (in scudi) which the papacy assumed under the different pontiffs.[27]

| | |
|---|---|
| Innocent XII | 275,503.37 |
| Clement XI | 4,648,527.42 |
| Innocent XIII | 357,000.00 |
| Benedict XIII | 678,140.35 |
| Clement XII | 3,039,728.56 |

25 Lutz, "Zur Papstfinanz von Klemens IX.," 78, 81–86.

26 Giuseppe Felloni gives slightly higher figures. He used different sources for his calculation: ASR, Monti Camerali, registro 3,713 and various registri between 1,151 and 1,443, supplemented by ASR, luoghi di monte, busta 10. His nominal annual interest burden on *monti* are 1,331,288 scudi for 1723, 1,425,781 scudi for 1744, 1,388,972 for 1765, and 1,494,146 for 1786. Felloni, *Investimenti finanziari genovesi in Europe*, 166–67 table 40; 172.

27 ASR, Camerale II, luoghi di monte, busta 11.

| | |
|---|---|
| Benedict XIV | 924,856.79 |
| Clement XIII | 1,482,204.12 |
| Clement XIV | 565,246.26 |
| Pius VI (until 1782) | 1,540,625.565 |
| (1785–94) | 2,234,000.00 |

The records indicate that the value of the *luoghi* tended to rise in the course of the century. They sold at the start of the century at 119 scudi for a 100-scudi *luogo* and by the 1730s reached 127 scudi. By the end of the century a few even fetched as much as 129 scudi.

Before we can accept the above figures at face value several facts have to be noted. Not all the *monti* were issued to meet the cameral debt, although many were. During the pontificate to Clement XI a great deal of money was raised to aid the Christian powers in their war against the Turks and, in 1701, to meet the expenses caused by the poor harvest; Clement XII wanted to help the war-ravaged areas of Bologna and Ferrara in 1735, repair the hospital of Santo Spirito, as well as improve the streets and beautify the city of Rome. Benedict XIV repaired the aqueducts, in particular the Acqua Vergine. Clement XIII had to take precautionary measures in the face of the epidemic which had broken out in Dalmatia and he improved the flow of the Tiber. Finally, Pius VI needed money for his great building project of a sacristy for St. Peter's and the drainage of the Pontine marshes. These and other such financial burdens did not always fall directly upon the Apostolic Chamber, but they added to the growing public debt of the state. A few of these *monti* were probably simply loans to pay off older loans and so did not directly increase the debt. Still, 15,141,561.87 scudi of loans over approximately a hundred years, that is, an annual average of over 151,000 scudi, if not quite as spectacular as in previous centuries, was considerable. It does not compare well with the total Tuscan debt – admittedly, that of a smaller state – of 12,778,000 scudi in 1746, which was then considered oppressive.[28]

The system of *monti*, however practical it may have appeared at its inception to the government, had its negative aspects, one of which was the enormous drain on the financial resources of the state, in particular through the outflow of capital. Very frequently, the purchasers of a whole issue of a *monte* were foreigners, in the forefront among them Genoese. In the last five years of the sixteenth century Genoese financiers succeeded in displacing Florentine bankers by infiltrating the core of the papal administration and started to invest more widely in the *monti*. In the course of the following century the influx of Genoese capital, while still copious, probably slowed down. At the beginning of the eighteenth century, however, the Genoese presence in the papal public debt was still very extensive. In the second

[28] ASR, Camerale II, camerlengato e tesorierato, progetti diversi, busta 19; Reinhard, *Papstfinanz und Nepotismus unter Paul V*, 1:79, 141–45; Petrocchi, *Roma nel Seicento*, 76–77; Lalande, *Voyage d'un françois en Italie*, 5:19–20; Felloni, *Gli investimenti finanziari genovesi in Europa*, 163–65; Diaz, *Gianni*, 239–44; Büchi, *Finanzen und Finanzpolitik Toskanas*, 83–86.

half of that century there was actually a slight but distinct process of liquidation of the Genoese investment. Whereas the Genoese held in both 1725 and 1745 about 6,400,000 scudi's worth of *luoghi di monte* and another half a million in *uffici venali vacabili*, making a total of 6,900,000 scudi – roughly 12.5 percent of the cameral debt – it shrunk to 5,300,000 scudi in *monti* and 300,000 in *vacabili* in 1765, for a total of 5,600,000 (c. 10.4 percent), and to 5 million in *monti* and 200,000 in *vacabili* in 1785, for a total of 5,200,000 scudi (c. 9.4 percent). The consequence was that, in 1725 and 1745, 217,000 scudi went to Genoa in interest payment by the Apostolic Chamber, which was then reduced to 174,000 scudi in 1765 and 160,000 scudi in 1785. But it was conservatively believed that around one million scudi went abroad annually in interest from various securities throughout the state, including those of Bologna and Ferrara.

It is rather surprising that so many foreigners should still be interested in shares that yielded only 3 percent, but it may be that the appreciation of the value of the *luogo* during the first half of the century and the apparent permanence of the papal establishment attracted them. After 1750, however, solidity gave way to preference for a higher interest rate.

Another drawback to the system of *monti* involved the public financial institutions of Rome, the Monte di Pietà and the Banco di Santo Spirito. In many instances when a *monte* was launched, these two were compelled by the government to acquire a fixed number of *luoghi*, proportionally divided between them, whether they so desired or not. Such acquisitions would constitute a passive element in their holdings.

In fact, some attempts at extinguishing the *monti* were being made sporadically. For instance, between 1732 and February of 1740, a total of 211,493.04 scudi was paid out by the Apostolic Chamber, 140,000 of that in 1739 alone. But, as so often in the ancien regime, the energy and will for a sustained effort was lacking, unlike Tuscany where between 1780 and 1790 under Pietro Leopoldo the public debt was completely eliminated (albeit only to be restored in 1795 after the grand duke's departure).[29]

To complete the interest burden on the cameral balances, we still have to add the *uffici venali vacabili*, *vacabili* for short. There were three categories of them. The first two categories were usually filled by office holders who would vacate them on promotion or death. The third category consisted mainly of sinecures, whose title holders were grouped into colleges, of which the *collegio dei cavalieri di S. Pietro* was the largest. Although the venality of curial offices was started by Boniface IX

[29] Delumeau, *Vie économique et sociale de Rome*, 1:468–69; 2:822–23, 858–60; Petrocchi, *Roma nel Seicento*, 82; Caracciolo, *Lo Stato pontificio*, 452–53; Mario Tosi, *Il Sacro Monte di Pietà di Roma e le sue amministrazioni (1539–1874)*, (Rome, 1937), 150; Montesquieu, *Voyages. Oeuvres complètes*, 2:1100–1101, 1107–1108; Büchi, *Finanzen und Finanzpolitik Toskanas*, 337–43, 416–39; Cochrane, *Florence in the Forgotten Centuries*, 448; Diaz, *Gianni*, 218–24, 231–34; ASR, Camerale II, annona, discorsi e studi, busta 1; ASR, Famiglie diverse, Cavaletti, busta 1, vol. XII, no. XXII; busta 2, vol. XIII, nos. V and VII; ASR, Camerale II, conti dell'entrata e dett'uscita, busta 6, lib. 29.

(1387–1404), Julius II first exploited the system for the purpose of raising public credit by introducing the sinecures in 1509. But it was Sixtus V who would exhaust all possibilities in this area. At the close of his reign the capital invested in the 3,472 venal offices then in existence, of which 3,122 were sinecures, amounted to 4,880,725 silver scudi and the interest paid out for these offices required the annual sum of 483,930 scudi.

A century later the situation had improved slightly. In the period between 1667 and 1692/93 there were about 2,600 to 2,800 *uffici vacabili* for a capital value, in 1672, of 2,923,027 scudi. These *vacabili* yielded about 6 percent annually. So the papal authorities had to pay interest to the value of 155,382 scudi. Not all that sum was originally paid out by the Apostolic Chamber. Until about the middle of the seventeenth century it was only responsible for about two-thirds of the cost and in 1655 to 1657 it came to 58.7 percent. The difference was made up from the datary and other spiritual revenues, as well as non-recorded revenues such as fees taken in by many of the offices in the first two categories directly. With the decline of the spiritual revenues, however, the burden gradually fell more heavily on the cameral treasury.

Benedict XIV eventually undertook a drastic reduction in the number of *vacabili* by reimbursing 1,427 sinecures of the third category. It was not, however, until Napoleon in 1811 that this form of venality was abolished altogether. In the meantime, although the annual interest at 6 percent or 7 percent was still double that on the *luoghi di monte*, the *vacabili* became distinctly less attractive than the *monti* as a means of investment, because the latter were more easily transferable. Nevertheless, the *vacabili* still remained a burden upon the Apostolic Chamber, which had to pay out interest during the first three decades of the eighteenth century in the range of 173,000 to 177,914 scudi, that is, between 6 percent and 9 percent of the total expenditure. From 1746 on, as a consequence of Benedict's action, it settled down to roughly 4 percent of the total expenditure, only to rise a little in 1796. As such it was no longer a major factor in the budget, but in an overstrained financial situation it was felt more severely than the figures show.[30]

At this stage it is still difficult to discover the full extent of the papal public debt. All kinds of estimates have been put forward over time. Enzo Piscitelli in his *La riforma di Pio VI* suggested that the public debt of Rome in 1797 was around 85 million scudi, of which seven-ninths were held in *luoghi*. If we were to use this formula and work backwards, assuming that the interest represents 3 percent of the

[30] Reinhard, *Papstfinanz und Nepotismus unter Paul V*, 1:14–15, 20–21; Delumeau, *Vie économique et sociale de Rome*, 2:772–82; Stumpo, *Il capitale finanziario a Roma*, 173, 232, 304–305; Lutz, "Zur Papstfinanz von Klemens IX.," 79; Nina, *Le finanze pontifice sotto Clemente XI*, 62; Vicchi, *Vincenzo Monti (1778–1780)*, 219–21; Gorani, *Rom und seine Einwohner*, 78–79. Felloni estimated that the value of the *vacabili* stood at 3,500,000 scudi in 1723 and fell to 2 million scudi in 1786. Felloni, *Gli investimenti finanziari genovesi in Europa*, 166.

capital invested in the *monti*, we would arrive at the following sample figures (in scudi) based on Table 31 in this chapter:[31]

| | |
|---|---|
| 1706 | 53,437,369.84 |
| 1712 | 54,517,156.71 |
| 1729 | 54,764,557.13 |
| 1735 | 55,365,444.42 |
| 1740 | 57,599,999.13 |
| 1744 | 55,044,042.63 |
| 1750 | 54,230,702.13 |
| 1761 | 52,857,494.77 |
| 1770 | 53,915,705.77 |
| 1780 | 54,977,055.42 |
| 1790 | 55,845,432.00 |
| 1793 | 57,272,190.63 |
| 1796 | 59,545,291.69 |

These figures are great for a state whose annual balances hovered above the two million mark. In some respects they compare favorably with the finances of France. In 1714 the total French public debt, about 3 billion livres tournois (about 610,909,100 scudi), was equal to 30 times the ordinary revenue of the state, producing a debt burden per capita of roughly 33 scudi.[32] In the Papal States, on the other hand, the public debt in 1712 was only a little over 22 times the annual revenue of the Apostolic Chamber and even in 1793 it had only risen to 24.6 times. It came to something over 26 scudi per head in 1712. On the negative side, however, only 40 percent of the revenues in France were absorbed in interest payment on the public debt – and the French financial crisis at the time is only too well known to need repeating here – whereas that same year the burden of debt service on the Apostolic Chamber was 52 percent of its revenue, and that was a favorable year, the average over the century being around 56 percent. Contemporaries, not surprisingly, put the figure of the public debt even higher. Alessandro Verri claimed it was 60 million or a little more in 1781.[33]

Apart from interest payments, which formed by far the largest single item in the cameral budget, the heaviest regular expenses on the balance sheet were the military

[31] Enzo Piscitelli, *La riforma di Pio VI e gli scrittori economici romani* (Milan, 1958), 140–45.

[32] Herman van der Wee, "Monetary, Credit and Banking Systems," *The Cambridge Economic History of Europe* (Cambridge, 1977), 5:378.

[33] Revel, "Le grain de Rome," 275 n. 4; Giovanni Seregni (ed.), *Carteggio di Pietro e Alessandro Verri* (Milan, 1940), 11:302; Vicchi, *Vincenzo Monti (1778–1780)*, 106; Stumpo, *Il capitale finanziario a Roma*, 261. Felloni, using the archival records given in note 26, obtained slightly lower sums for the consolidated public debt of the Apostolic Chamber for the years he studied: 47,876,280 scudi in 1723, 51,026,033 scudi in 1744, 48,799,075 scudi in 1765, and 51,341,000 scudi in 1786. His interest payments, however, are higher. Felloni, *Gli investimenti finanziari genovesi in Europa*, 167.

Table 32

| Year | % of total expenditure | Year | % of total expenditure |
|---|---|---|---|
| 1706 | 10.61 | 1766–70 | 19.21 |
| 1712 | 15.43 | 1771–75 | 19.08 |
| 1716 | 15.72 | 1776–80 | 18.87 |
| 1735 | 16.37 | 1781–85 | 18.89 |
| 1739 | 15.51 | 1786–90 | 18.39 |
| 1744 | 18.57 | 1791 | 17.82 |
| 1746–50 | 19.01 | 1792 | 20.81 |
| 1751–55 | 18.76 | 1793 | 34.67 |
| 1756–60 | 18.98 | 1796 | 26.61 |
| 1761–65 | 19.06 | | |

expenses – and the broad category of the Apostolic Palace. The military expenditure, the larger of the two, is given in Table 32 as a percentage of the total budget (wherever possible as the annual average over a five-year period).

From the mid-1740s to the mid-1780s the military share of the cameral budget hovered around the 19 percent mark, almost a fifth of the total, which is a high proportion for a non-military state and a people who were incapable of engaging in serious war. This outlay may be looked upon as a waste of money. Would it not have been better to follow the example of Tuscany, where Pietro Leopoldo disbanded the grand ducal army in Florence and Pisa in 1780, rather than Naples, where the combined army and navy budget reached the enormous sum of 3,833,000 ducats (3,163,155 scudi) in 1788 and continued to rise to 10,023,000 (8,271,408 scudi) thereafter? In fact, even when the percentage of military spending began to fall after 1786, the papal expenditure in absolute terms of money did not decline, rather it rose. Alas, at that point the threat of the French Revolutionary campaigns moved the authorities to squander its money upon a totally abortive policy of rearmament.

The regular expenditure on the Apostolic Palace, if not as heavy as the military one, was also of dubious utility. After being between 3 and 5 percent of the total expenditure in the earlier part of the century, it then settled between 7 and 8.5 percent, and in the pontificate of the ostentatious Pius VI headed for 10 percent and even surpassed that figure, equalling the profligate court of Naples under Ferdinand IV (1759–1825). In actual money it more than tripled from 91,000 scudi in 1706 under Clement XI to 285,650.605 scudi in 1792. Even then, only part of the cost of the papal court came from the regular cameral allowance; much of it came under the heading of extraordinary expenses, including such capital outlay as building costs.

It is not possible to list all the individual items for which the Apostolic Chamber had to produce the sums needed for extraordinary expenses. In the forefront of these were the Vatican library and museum. Between 1756 and 1784, at least 361,640.555 scudi were spent on the new Vatican museum and another 32,398.32 scudi on the Vatican library, which included the building of the celebrated *stanza de' papiri* at a cost of 16,554.69 scudi. An expense sheet of the Chamber shows that in the decade between 1773 and 1783 the extraordinary expenses came to 1,518,639.07 scudi, a not inconsiderable sum. We know, of course, that some of this amount was covered by revenues from the lottery.

Yet it was only by 1782 that the really large expenses started to be felt. In a letter to his brother, Don Cesare, dated 1 September 1781, Vincenzo Monti declared, "Rome has need of money . . . The sacristy costs no less than one million; the Pontine marshes have already passed 300,000 scudi. Add to this a thousand other expenses, which together form a perennial expense . . ." The sacristy was the new sacristy of St. Peter's. Pius VI had laid the foundation stone on 22 September 1776. The cost of the project was originally estimated at 100,000 scudi. But it soon turned out that the overruns would be much higher so that the plan had to be pared down. But even then the available money proved insufficient. In June 1784, when the altar of the new sacristy was consecrated, the final cost came to about one and a half million scudi. By this time the financial difficulties had started to become acute.[34]

Those acquainted with Renaissance and Counter Reformation Rome may well ask at this point what happened to the large revenues the papacy once derived from its alum in the nearby Tolfa mountains. In its heyday, following the discovery of alum there in 1461, Rome exercised almost a monopoly in supplying Europe with this sought-after mineral, so much so that it not only obtained wealth, but diplomatic leverage from it. The apogee of production and exportation of the Tolfa alum was reached between 1553 and 1603 and within that half-century its maximum prosperity fell between 1553 and 1578, with an annual export average of 37,723 cantares (about 1,881 metric tons). In the course of the seventeenth century the alum mines suffered a progressive and slow decline caused by foreign competition, that of England and Liège and, from about 1680 on, of the Neapolitan mines at Lipari and Pozzuoli. Consequently the farmers of the alum could not export all they produced. By 1677 the amount of unsold alum stored at the warehouses at the port of Civitavecchia and in Tolfa reached 142,692.032 cantares (about 7,134 metric tons). Despite further reductions in output, the stock of alum at Civitavecchia and Tolfa in 1719 was still 116,180 cantares (about 5,809 metric tons). Production had to be reduced again and for the rest of the eighteenth century never exceeded an annual average of 15,000 cantares (about 750 tons).

At the close of the eighteenth century, the production and export of alum reached no more than half the level of 1660 and one-third of that of 1560. Between 1798 and

[34] ASR, Camerale II, camerlengato e tesorierato, busta 19; ASR, Camerale III, palazzi e ville, Vaticano, busta 2093, fasc. 2; ASR, Camerale II, camerlengato e tesorierato, progetti diversi, busta 18; Dal Pane, *Lo Stato Pontificio e il movimento riformatore*, 530; Pastor, *Geschichte der Päpste*, 16, pt 3:46–48; Diaz, *Gianni*, 303–4; Bianchini, *Della storia delle finanze del Regno*, 3:225, 244, 251, 254, 291–95.

1801 the establishment showed a deficit of 48,677.87 scudi. Hence the republic in 1798 decided to get rid of the liability and sold the enterprise to a company, which included the financiers Conte Domenico Lavaggi and Torlonia.[35]

Although a few of the more astute observers of the contemporary Roman scene had been acutely aware of the threatening bankruptcy of the papal treasury, the bulk of the Roman populace was blissfully ignorant of higher finance. After all, the Romans were largely cushioned from the burden of taxation, particularly since Clement XI failed to realize his *tassa del milione* by imposing a direct tax. But there was one element that brought home to them the reality of the situation in their everyday lives, and that was their coinage. Any treatment of Roman currency must take note of a complex, sometimes confusing interplay of foreign exchange, issues of minted coins, and paper notes.[36]

When looking at the budget, we have dealt only in money of account, but the ordinary Roman was more concerned with daily cash than with bookkeeping. The unit of currency in Rome was the scudo which was divided into ten paoli of ten baiocchi each. The baiocco was worth five quattrini. There were fourteen or more different kinds of Roman coins, gold, silver, copper, or composite, in circulation. In addition to these something like ninety different coins from foreign states, ranging from Naples to Germany, France, and Hungary, were legally circulated within the Papal States, causing no end of confusion and problems of exchange.[37]

The difficulties of the papal currency had their roots back in the sixteenth century. One was the problem of a bimetallic system with the constantly changing ratio between gold and silver. Between 1538 and 1542, there was a depreciation of silver and an excessive rise in the price of gold, which may be accounted for by the first great influx of American silver. After 1560 the rise in the bimetallic ratio took such an élan that the authorities had to abandon any effort at controlling it. The approximate ratio of gold to silver rose from 1:10.97 in 1530–39 to 1:12.76 in 1620–29. The fluctuations were to continue, causing monetary disturbance and affecting the economy. But gold and silver coins of large denominations were used only in bigger commercial transactions and international exchange, and only had an indirect impact on the common people.

What affected craftsmen and small folk in general was the quantitative increase and bad quality of coins of mixed metal. Always short of money, many countries multiplied small coins of little value, which did not cost them very much. In Rome, as elsewhere, these "mixed" coins became debased, with the authorities attributing to them an exchange value higher than their intrinsic value. On the eve of the Holy Year of 1600, Clement VIII had the courage to wipe out the evil by withdrawing the

35 Delumeau, *L'Alun de Rome*, 21, 128, 131, 136–39, 142, 161, 181–83, 315, 317, 397; Petrocchi, *Roma nel Seicento*, 53; ADP, busta 84.42.2; busta 87.42.1; ASR, Camerale II, camerlengato e tesorierato, busta 19; Lalande, *Voyage d'un françois en Italie*, 5:293.

36 La Marca, *Saggio di una ricerca storico-economica*, 31; ASR, Camerale II, zecca, busta 33.

37 Andrieux, *Daily Life in Papal Rome*, 71; Tournon, *Etudes statistiques sur Rome*, 2:27–29; Vicchi, *Vincenzo Monti (1778–1780)*, 209; ASR, Camerale II, zecca, busta 34, fasc. 103.

old "mixed" quattrini and replacing them with new coins of pure alloy. The problem was to rear its ugly head again in the eighteenth century.

The question of inferior money was related to the even more critical problem of the availability of petty cash so necessary in a period of urban demographic expansion. By the time of Clement VIII, Rome's period of prosperity and boom was clearly on the wane. One symptom of this decline was a fall in the emission of coins in Rome, which hit the smaller denominations particularly hard. Between 1615 and 1643 the farmers of the Roman mint, the *zecca*, were limited to an annual average issue of 30,000 scudi of silver in comparison to the annual average of 146,925 scudi between 1581 and 1615; this represents an 80 percent fall. While a moderate shortfall of cash is not an evil in itself, for it testifies to an active and growing economy where the money is quickly employed, a prolonged shortage indicates a decline in business and trade and is clearly a sign of an unbalanced and unhealthy economy.[38]

All three of the above elements reappeared in some form during the next two centuries. What we find is a continuous diminution of specie, which assumed crisis proportions from about 1730 on. The first symptom of this had already become apparent a few years after the turn of the century under Clement XI. In 1708 a printed appeal urged all citizens of the Papal States to bring in as much silver as possible to the *zecca*, because there was a shortage of primary metal for making coins. They were offered 21 scudi in the form of *luoghi di Monte Camerale* for a libbra of silver.[39]

At the same time the intrinsic content of gold and silver coins was continuously diminished. For instance, between 1684 and 1731 a giulio contained 2.8 grams of fine silver, but between 1731 and 1751 it sank to 2.55 grams and thereafter even fell to 2.45 grams. Part of this phenomenon was blamed on the changing ratio of gold to silver. One contemporary author suggested that in Asia it was 1:12, whereas in Europe it was more or less 1:15, which meant that the value of silver was higher in Asia, the reason being that by the middle of the eighteenth century the Brazilian gold mines were exhausted, but the newly opened silver mines in Mexico doubled the yield in the course of the century. The Turks, for their part, had a great abundance of gold, so that they preferred to pay in gold for their smaller purchases and be paid in silver. No effort was made in the Papal States to rectify the resultant imbalance in the gold–silver ratio. It led to a drain on the undervalued silver by foreign speculators, who bought it up cheaply.[40]

38 Delumeau, *Vie économique et sociale de Rome*, 2:660–61, 669–78, 685–88, 927 n. 4, 935.

39 ASR, Camerale II, zecce, busta 33.

40 Nuccio, "Precettistica economica di pascoli," 293–94; Lapauze, *Histoire de l'Académie de France à Rome*, 158; Anatole Montaiglon and Jules Guiffrey (eds.), *Correspondance des directeurs de l'Académie de France à Rome* (18 vols.; Paris, 1901–1908), 13:308; Lalande, *Voyage d'un françois en Italie*, 5:45–46; Wilhelm Abel, *Agrarkrisen und Agrarkonjunktur* (Hamburg and Berlin, 1966), 186; B. VALLICELL., ms. Z2, f. 173; Delumeau, *L'Alun de Rome*, 140 n. 3, 149 n. 3; ASR, Famiglie diverse, Cavaletti, busta 1, vol. XII, no. IV; Bianchini, *Storia delle finanze del Regno*, 3:430; Stumpo, *Il capitale finanziario a Roma*, 29–31.

By the end of 1732, the scarcity of liquid money in the city became really acute. The two public banking institutions, the Monte di Pietà and the Banco di Santo Spirito, which had taken the primary responsibility in procuring and importing precious metals for the mint and putting the coinage into circulation, were badly hit. Suddenly, at this point there broke on the Roman scene a very inferior type of money, the *giglietto* of Florence. Within ten or twelve years it destroyed the papal money. Rome stood by, helpless at the exodus of its own coins; silver left the state without hindrance and even the papal gold coins were cheerfully cornered by the Florentines, who reminted them into their own zecchini. To alleviate the situation new coinage to the value of 1, 2 and 4 baiocchi, composed of a silver and copper amalgam, was introduced in July 1735. The expectation was that the measure would remedy the lack of a common currency for small everyday transactions. The hope was dashed; the shortage of money was not eased.[41]

The chaos seemed complete: the flight of gold and silver currency abroad; a debased coinage aggravated by a growing shortage of small money at home, and bankruptcy staring the major banks in the face, not to speak of an unfavorable trade balance; and the financial damage incurred by the violation of the country's neutrality during the War of the Austrian Succession. Following the example of his predecessors in such critical moments of papal history, Benedict XIV set up a special congregation of the mint in 1741 for advice. Among its members were the bankers Girolamo Belloni and Clemente Argenvilliers. Belloni's advice centered very much on the reduction of the *monti* and the encouragement of trade in order to restore a favorable balance of payments, points which he was to publish ten years later in his treatise *Del commercio*.

After prolonged discussion, the new congregation reluctantly agreed upon a change in the gold–silver ratio in view of the fact that all the money markets in Europe had deviated from the old ratio. After careful examination, it was decided to adopt a ratio of 1 to 14.5 – which was closer, although not exactly equivalent to the true market ratio – and issue new scudo, half-scudo, and 20-baiocchi pieces with the value of silver content increased by 15.58 percent over those of 1700. At the same time the directors of the Monte di Pietà expanded the issue of minted money. This operation involved both banks, whose coffers were already almost empty, in further great losses. The new system, while meeting some of the immediate currency problems, was only to put ephemeral restraints on the chaotic state of the coinage.

Conditions in the first five years of Clement XIII's reign were very much as Benedict had left them. Then came the fateful year of 1764, when the shortage of grain and other calamities began to bring the brooding crisis right into the open. From that moment the popes had to order ever more frequently and in always larger quantities new issues of paper notes or cedole to meet the demands of the cameral

[41] Ermanno Ponti, *Il Banco di Santo Spirito e la sua funzione economica in Roma papale (1605–1870)*, (Rome, 1951), 91–93; ASR, Camerale II, zecca, buste 33 and 35, fasc. 106; A.Cap.R., no. 10. cred. VII, 158.

budget. Whereas these measures met the immediate emergency, they accumulated future difficulties, when the public would lose confidence in them. The Holy Year of 1775, which brought great crowds of foreigners with money to spend as well as an unusual abundance of food supply, also helped to ease temporarily the circulation of cash.[42]

But the money shortage and the outflow of gold and silver coins soon resumed. The government in conjunction with the banks continued to issue more and more paper money and for domestic purposes resorted to the so-called *moneta plateale*. The *moneta plateale*, a currency of convenience, was limited to small domestic transactions. Its value was assigned to it by the public authority and remained constant. It differed from the ordinary gold and silver coinage; known as *moneta di bontà*, which in principle was to correspond to the intrinsic value of its metal content and was subject to the fluctuations of exchange. Whereas the *moneta di bontà* still remained the instrument for major commercial transactions, especially with foreigners, the *moneta plateale*, together with the cedole, assumed an ever-greater role in the everyday life of the Romans. From about 1771 to 1782 roughly 20,000 scudi's worth of these inferior silver and copper coins were minted annually. At first they helped to ease the petty-cash shortage, but as yet were no major factor in the currency equation. But the true flood was only let loose in 1793, when the French were pouring into Italy. The treasurer general, Msgr. Della Porta, fearing a further depreciation of the paper cedole, tried to put a check to it by coining more than one million of this base alloy between 1794 and April 1796 alone. In the process the silver content of the alloy was constantly reduced.[43]

In spite of the increase in petty cash, the papal government relied most heavily on paper money or cedole to make up the financial shortage. It was to be eventually one of the principal contributors to its monetary crisis. With this unwholesome example, it pioneered the use of credit papers for purposes of general payment in the southern half of the peninsula; for it was not until 1794 that the Neapolitan government would follow in its footsteps by turning its certificate of deposit, the *fedi di credito*, into circulation. But in Rome the certificates of deposit, the original cedole, were already made transferable with the establishment of the new Banco di Santo Spirito in 1605 and so entered the commercial circulation. They enabled the parties to dispense with specie, which was to facilitate their future proliferation of these notes. The other bank, the Monte di Pietà, soon adopted the device. Although these bank notes had no standing beyond the borders of the Papal States, they were as good as gold within them. In fact, it was the complete confidence they enjoyed

[42] Venturi, *Settecento riformatore*, 1:107; Piscitelli, *La riforma di Pio VI*, 137–38; Claude Camille François d'Albon, *Discours sur l'histoire, le gouvernement, les usages, la literature et les arts, de plusieurs nations de l'Europe* (2 vols.; Geneva and Paris, 1782), 2:228–30; ASR, Camerale II, zecca, busta 3, fasc. 7, and busta 33 (Voto del Cardinale Pallotta); ASR, Famiglie diverse, Cavaletti, busta 1, vol XII, no. XXI, and busta 2, vol. XIII, no. XIV.

[43] ASR, Camerale II, zecca, buste 3 and 33; Clementi, *Il carnevale romano*, 2:217.

that first gave the Scottish financier John Law the idea for his ill-fated system. For what had once been an admirable device in Rome was discredited by Law in France during the first decades of the eighteenth century and would be abused a few years later in the papal capital itself.

Rome faced its first serious paper inflation of cedole after 1733–34. The bad harvest of 1737 and the calamities in the wake of the Spanish troops crossing through papal territory to put Charles VII on the Neapolitan throne left even less money and increased the diffusion of cedole. De Brosses, commenting on the situation, remarked: "They have manufactured an amount of notes that is much in excess of the money circulating as coinage in the state; which reduces the state to borrowing large loans and burdens it with enormous debts that are constantly multiplying, as is inevitable, and could end by bankrupting it." De Brosse's words were prophetic and the situation was to get worse.

By 1778 the two Roman banks would only exchange their own cedole for 5 percent of their face value in cash and the remaining 95 percent in new cedole. Still the number of cedole continued to mount. In 1780 Pius VI took some new measures to reduce the paper flood. The two banks were to put 50,000 scudi in circulation, converting the bullion they still held into scudo and half-scudo pieces. They were ordered to make all loans in ready cash. It does not seem to have made a dent in the huge volume of paper. Alessandro Verri, writing to his brother Pietro on 31 July 1782, told him that the cedole in circulation had reached the value of 11 million scudi, probably an exaggerated figure, since the pro-treasurer put it at 6,900,000 scudi in 1783. Verri complained that hard cash was scarce and it was difficult to defray small expenses.[44]

Until this point the cedole, true to their origin, had been handwritten notes. But the moment the cedole had become common currency, they became easy targets for falsification, forgery, and counterfeit. In November 1788, Pius VI ordered the Monte di Pietà to withdraw all manuscript cedole and replace them with printed ones. By failing to cooperate, the public rendered the order a dead letter and the handwritten copies continued to circulate without hindrance. Thereupon the treasurer Fabrizio Ruffo renewed the order in March 1789 for all handwritten cedole created up to 1782 to be handed in to the banks by 30 November, after which date they would no longer be accepted as legal tender. The deadline had to be extended twice to April 1790 and the cedole up to 1785 were then included. This brought the historical cycle of the handwritten cedole to a close. Each new printed cedola was now numbered and registered. By this time the value of the cedole greatly exceeded the available amount of hard cash, although no statistics on the ratio

[44] Delumeau, *Vie économique et sociale de Rome*, 2:936–37; Andrieux, *Daily Life in Papal Rome*, 71; Ponti, *Il Banco di Santo Spirito*, 94–96; De Brosses, *Lettres familières*, 2:28–29; Seregni (ed.), *Carteggio di Verri*, 10:124–25; 12:353; Enzo Piscitelli, "Fabrizio Ruffo e la riforma economica," 102–3, 105; ASR, Camerale II, zecca, busta 33; ASR, Camerale II, camerlengato e tesorierato, progetti diversi, busta 18; Bianchini, *Storia delle finanze del Regno*, 3:185–87.

exists. An anonymous treatise, *Discorso economico e politico sull'uso della moneta per ovviare alla di lei penuria in qualsiasi stato*, published in Bologna in 1786, claimed that a million or more cedole were already in circulation without backing.

To assist in the new papal enterprise the banks were saddled with an enormous debt of cedole issued without collateral, in addition to the burden of the *monti*, in order to make up the shortages of the Apostolic Chamber and the annona, and to supply the expenses of the drainage of the Pontine marshes and for the building of the sacristy of St. Peter's. On 20 December 1793, the Banco di Santo Spirito had 2,812,384 scudi's worth of printed cedole in circulation and we may surmise that the Monte di Pietà had double that sum, about 5,500,000 scudi. By 1797 the total amount may have reached as much as 14 million scudi, 11 million issued by the Monte di Pietà and 3 million by the Banco di Santo Spirito; one document put it even as high as 21 million.

While this enormous growth occurred, the value of the cedole fell. In 1794 they were exchanged at a discount rate of 3 or 4 percent for copper coinage and 5 or 6 percent for gold and silver. After February 1798 the discount had dropped to a minimum of 50 percent and a maximum of 80 percent. This rapid fall led to a run on the banks. Soldiers tried to disperse the crows. Nevertheless mobs managed to force the Banco di Santo Spirito and broke the glass windows.

The situation had become so bad that, in view of the rapidly rising prices and the loss of public confidence, the pope resorted to a desperate measure first mooted by Benedict XIV, and eventually resorted to by the revolutionaries in France when they printed their *assignats*: on 28 November 1797, Pius issued an edict using ecclesiastical lands to pay off the flood of cedole. He exacted a "loan" of a fifth of all the rural properties of the secular and regular clergy, of confraternities, and lay chapters in Rome and the Papal States, which were to be sold to amortize the paper money. Within a six months' period all cedole of 100 scudi or above were to be withdrawn from circulation by the purchase of these properties. Smaller denominations were to remain in circulation. Time, however, had run out for the papacy.[45]

How could the Papal States keep total bankruptcy at bay in view of the continuous depletion of their financial resources? This legitimate question finds at least a partial answer in the treasure laid up in the Castel Sant'Angelo by Sixtus V. The idea of a reserve treasure went back to Paul II (1464–71), if not earlier, but the real organizer of this major source of reserve was Sixtus V. At his accession in 1585, this pope found 351,500 gold scudi and 4,500 silver scudi in the coffers of the Castel

[45] Dal Pane, *Lo Stato Pontificio e il movimento riformatore*, 532; Piscitelli, "Fabrizio Ruffo e la riforma economica," 103; Piscitelli, *La riforma di Pio VI*, 140–45; Ponti, *Il Banco di Santo Spirito*, 146–49; ASR, Camerale II, zecca, busta 33; busta 34, fasc. 103, 104, 106; busta 43, fasc. 123, 125; ASR, Camerale II, camerlengato e tesorierato, progetti diversi, busta 18; ASR, Camerale II, arti e mestieri, busta 27; ASR, Camerale III, palazzi e ville, busta 2098, fasc. 1; B.N.Ro., Fondo Gesuitico, ms. 195, no. 4; A.Cap.R., no. 22, cred. XVIII.

Sant'Angelo. Within five years these sums had become respectively 3,000,000 gold scudi and 1,159,543.29 silver scudi. The gold reserve was particularly impressive since it was equal to three-quarters of the American gold that had arrived in Spain in the ten years between 1581 and 1590. Advantageous as such "iron reserves" may appear at first sight, they were achieved at the expense of the well-being of the Roman economy. The gold coins, which could have helped the economic revival of Rome and the provinces, were left idle in their strongboxes. In order to set up his treasury within such a short period and at the same time pay for his great public works, the pontiff was compelled to sell offices in enormous quantities and borrow at a rate hitherto unknown in Rome. But of this we have already spoken.

The treasure was divided into two parts. The silver scudi made up the "old treasure," which Sixtus V and his successors reserved the right to withdraw according to need. The gold scudi formed the *erario sanziore*, the "sacred treasure," which the pope could only touch in cases of the utmost emergency, such as the invasion of the Papal States or a plague or famine. In fact, the "old treasure" was almost wholly spent during the *sede vacante* following the death of Sixtus V and the famine of 1591. The *erario snaziore*, on the other hand, survived until the Treaty of Tolentino in 1797.[46]

In 1591 Gregory XIV took advantage of the "sacred treasure" to borrow money for food supply and the defense of Avignon. He was followed by Clement VIII and Urban VIII in the next century. The other large withdrawals had to await the start of the eighteenth century. In order to meet the expenses of the passage and billeting of foreign troops in 1708/09 in the Papal States, Clement XI withdrew 300,000 scudi, leaving 1,345,013.5 scudi. At his death, in March 1721, what remained unused of the 300,000 scudi, which came to 130,000 scudi's worth of gold, was returned. To repay another 110,000 scudi the government took a sum of money from the Apostolic Chamber for the purpose of continually reinvesting it and so forming what they termed a *moltiplico*, the proceeds from which were to be credited to the *erario sanziore*, until the debt was paid off. However, since 10,000 scudi annually were withdrawn from the yield of the *motiplico* to help the exiled James Stuart, the English Old Pretender, with his current expenses, the goal was never met. This shortfall was remedied when, as a result of the concordat between Benedict XIV and Spain, two million piasters sent to Rome by the Spanish crown were deposited at the Castel Sant'Angelo to refurbish its losses, but not for long.[47]

In 1763 a drought caused a bad harvest throughout Italy, especially in the southern half. Clement XIII was active in trying to lessen the suffering. But the unfavorable weather conditions persisted into 1764, so that work on the fields could not begin at the right time. Needy folks from everywhere streamed into Rome. It required a colossal effort to feed and shelter these masses. At the height of the crisis,

[46] Delumeau, *Vie économique et sociale de Rome*, 2:766–67; Nina, *Le finanze pontifice sotto Clemente XI*, 128–39; ASR, Camerale II, erario sanziore, busta 1, fasc. 1.

[47] Ibid., busta 1, fasc. 8; B.CORS., ms. 1173, ff. 418–19.

on 9 April, Clement authorized the withdrawal of half a million scudi; but a part of the curia objected, so that only about half the sum, 287,000 gold scudi, was released. To make up the loss, the *erario sanziore* was to be assigned the yield of a tax imposed on real estate and capital. As might be expected, the new tax provoked resistance in a city traditionally spared such everyday irritants.

Unfortunately, the 1764 shortage of food was to persist until 1766, so that the government had no alternative but to take out another 1,352,532.79 scudi, without any provision for repayment. The sum was prodigious, if you compare it with the Apostolic Chamber's ordinary expenditure for that year of 2,193, 243.66 scudi; the loan came to almost 62 percent of the cameral needs.

From that moment the treasure at the Castel Sant'Angelo was never to recover. As a result of the events of 1793, Pius VI withdrew another 547,192.23 scudi. Finally, on 28 June 1796, it was decided to remove secretly the money that still remained at the *erario sanziore* in the dead of night. It amounted to about 700,000 scudi, which was used as part of the payment imposed on the papal government by France. The money was exhausted, but the liability continued. As late as 1819 the general directory for the public debt dealt with matters associated with the *luoghi di monte* issued in connection with the "sacred treasure."[48]

The pace of the deteriorating financial situation in the Papal States was breathtaking during the last two decades before the establishment of the Jacobin republic by the French invaders. Leaving aside the legacy of the 1764–67 famines, the first indications of a strain on what remained of the state's financial resources came in late 1778. In a report in 1783 the accountant general of the Apostolic Chamber warned of the alarming deterioration of the financial condition since 1775. The extraordinary expenses between 1773 and 1782 had surpassed one and a half million scudi. Incomes from various sources had fallen by 16,000 scudi annually. It was almost possible to sell *luoghi di monte*, because of the excessive number of issues within a brief space of time. Between 1776 and 1786, 1,549,625 scudi's worth had come on the market, without counting those of individual communities and persons. Of this sum, 578,432.955 scudi were earmarked for draining the Pontine marshes, 460,285.17 for the building project at St. Peter's and 499,979.315 to prop up the ailing annona. Although the cameral treasury reported shortfalls, partly because some debtors were in default, it was not until 1789 that the ordinary deficit of its budget began its continuous upward curve. That year the papacy was deprived of its last revenues from France. At that point any withdrawal of the gold from the Castel Sant'Angelo had the effect of a drop of water in the sea of deficit.

[48] Nina, *Le finanze pontifice sotto Clemente XI*, 140 n. 3; 141 n. 3; De Brosses, *Lettres familières*, 2:85; Pastor, *Geschichte der Päpste*, 16 pt 1:461–62; ASR, Camerale II, erario sanziore, busta 1, fasc. 1, 5, 8; busta 2, fasc. 10, 13; busta 4; ASR, Camerale II, zecca, busta 34, fasc. 103; Franco Venturi, "1764–1767: Roma negli anni della fame," *Rivista storica italiana*, 85 (1973), fasc. 3, 527–30.

As with its Neapolitan neighbor to the south, emergency needs and expenditures simply piled up in Rome after 1790. The two public banks, their own credit already seriously impaired, had to extend loans to the value of 11,693,671.85 scudi in 1793. Then came the influx of French émigrés, who had to be supported by money out of the papal treasury. Pius VI was constrained to get rid of all the silver plate of the Apostolic Palace and some of the gold and silver of the churches. He also ordered the Chamber to sell the estates in its possession and cede the alum mines. As a last desperate measure he sent the banker Torlonia to Genoa in 1795 to obtain a loan in return for mortgaging part of his domain. The end came with Napoleon Bonaparte's entry into the Marches of Ancona in February 1797. On 19 February the Treaty of Tolentino was signed, which provided for the cession of the northern provinces and the payment of 32,700,000 francs. To meet this demand, the papal ruler not only had to withdraw the remaining treasure from the Castel Sant'Angelo, but he saddled the Monte di Pietà with interest-free loans of three million scudi within just over a month.[49]

It was now left to the Roman republic to find its way through the financial jungle. In October 1798 the total public debt of the whole state had swollen to 80,050,359 scudi, of which no less than 54,171,942 scudi (64.45 percent) were outstanding in *luoghi di monte*, 1,982,400 scudi (2.36 percent) in *uffici venali vacabili*, about 14 million (16.66 percent) in cedole, and 3,293,865 scudi (3.92 percent) was the amount of the debt of the Roman annona. One of the earliest acts of the new government, on 25 March 1798, was to pass a law to demonetize the cedole above 35 scudi in value. The cost was to be absorbed by the sale of national property. The old cedole were to be burned publicly; copper money was to be devalued by a quarter. However, confidence was not restored and speculators continued to exploit the evil. The financial morass only became deeper the longer the republic lasted.

Pius VII at his restoration inherited an imbalance in the papal currency estimated at ninety million scudi. The new pope took in hand the herculean task of rectifying the situation. He started by destroying the cedole and taking the debased coinage out of circulation. His economic and fiscal reforms brought in a favorable balance of four million scudi, from which two-fifths of the interest on the *luoghi di monte* were paid out. The remainder of the sum paid four-fifths of the interest on the *vacabili*, and 3 percent was given to the creditors who had provided precious objects to meet the indemnity exacted by the Treaty of Tolentino, the value of which was estimated at 881,850 scudi. But this policy was aborted in 1806, when the public revenue was absorbed in maintaining the French army, which Napoleon had

[49] Bianchini, *Storia delle finanze del Regno*, 3:212, 291–95; Montaiglon and Guiffrey (eds.), *Correspondance des directeurs de l'Académie de France*, 13:396; Seregni (ed.), *Carteggio di Verri*, 11:134; Alfonso Bertoldi (ed.), *Epistolario di Vincenzo Monti* (2 vols.; Florence, 1927), 148; Caracciolo, *Lo Stato pontificio*, 558–59; De Cupis, *Vicende dell'agricoltura nell'Agro Romano*, 344; Clementi, *Il carnevale romano*, 2:218; Ponti, *Il Banco di Santo Spirito*, 158; ASR, Camerale II, erario sanziore, buste 1 and 2, fasc. 9; ASR, Camerale II, zecca, busta 43, fasc. 125; ASR, Camerale II, camerlengato e tesorierato, progetti diversi, busta 18.

quartered in Ancona, Civitavecchia, and parts of the Marches. This army swallowed up all the assets of the treasury in one single year. Pius VII was obliged to suspend paying out on the national debt and had to impose on his subjects an anticipation of the property tax or a forced loan. This state of affairs continued until Napoleon drove out the pope in 1809.[50]

Napoleon was now left with the task of extinguishing the public debt. Pius VII, as part of his endeavour to improve the economic climate, had reduced the rate of interest on the *luoghi di monte* to 2 percent. The Romans forgave the reduction of the interest and even the occasional suspension of payment because of the difficulties the pope encountered. They felt these actions were temporary and their capital was safe. On 10 August 1810, the Napoleonic government set up a commission charged with reimbursing the debt and liquidating the *vacabili*. The commission recommended that the creditors be paid from land belonging to the national property. The other part of their decision was to be more disagreeable. While Pius VII had reduced the interest, he assured the holders of *luoghi* that their capital would not suffer any reduction. Now, however, the reimbursable capital was decreased, by using the interest, which in the case of the *monti* was only 2 percent, as the basis for calculating the new amount. The new capital would be twenty times the interest, that is, 40 percent of the original. Yet by a further convoluted operation which in 1812, the French prefect Tournon himself confessed not to understand, it was declared that 100,000 scudi would be reduced to 24,000 scudi with an annual revenue of 1,200 scudi. The reduction of the debt capital to such laughable sums was a hard blow to the investors, and even hit the smallest fortunes.[51]

The financial crisis of the ancien regime in Rome was not purely the consequence of its government's extravagance and mismanagement and, even less, the ineluctable experience shared by virtually all ancien-regime rulers. It was caused in part by the lack of a firm and coherent fiscal policy, coupled with the loss of most of the spiritual revenues from abroad, which had been partially responsible for supporting the temporal administration. But the crisis was aggravated by the prevalence of an archaic and stagnant economy, which we have seen in the last chapter contributed to an unfavorable balance of payments and trade.

Adding to the financial burden was the fact that the agricultural land surrounding the city, which should have relieved some of the expense of supplying the capital with food, was inadequately or, at least, uneconomically exploited.

[50] Felloni, *Investimenti finanziari genovesi in Europa*, 172; Albert Dufourcq, *Le régime Jacobin en Italie. Etude sur la République Romaine (1798–1799)* (Paris, 1900), 194–97.

[51] Madelin, *Rome de Napoléon*, 485–92; Ilario Rinieri, "La liquidazione napoleonica del debito pubblico di Roma (1810–11)," *Civiltà Cattolica*, 1347 (4 August 1906), 281–84.

# 6

# The Agro Romano

Perhaps no city of its size and importance was cut off from its neighbors by a more inhospitable region than Rome, arid in the north and marshy to the south and rendered hazardous by suffocating heat and malaria. Napoleon Bonaparte, disobeying the orders of the Directory in Paris to march on Rome, advanced as his excuse the mortal risk of crossing the Campagna during the summer heat. For the traveller who had ventured to cross the deserted countryside, the sight of Rome from atop Monte Mario appeared like a solitary unreal flower blossoming forth in the wilderness. On departing the experiences was reversed. Montesquieu, leaving Rome on 4 July 1729 at two o'clock in the morning by way of the Porta Pia and the Ponte Molle, was happy to have escaped the bad air when he reached Otricoli, six post stages from the city, at three in the afternoon. The air was fearfully bad; there was no water. He was unable to find anything to drink, not even some water to cool the axles of the wheels of his post-chaise. The wells were dried up in the summer. All the countryside was deserted. From Otricoli to Narni and on to Terni the air improved the further one moved away from Rome and entered the mountains.[1]

It may, therefore, appear paradoxical when the geographer Jules Sion spoke of the Roman Compagna more recently as "incapable of being mediocre, it is either very rich or very poor according to the amount of effort put in."[2] Due to its geological formation, much of the ground, with the exception of the tops of the hills

[1] Valsecchi, *Italia nel Settecento*, 446–57; Giuntella, *Roma nel Settecento*, 36–37; Montesquieu, *Voyages. Oeuvres complètes*, 2:1185–86, 1192. There is a problem of distinguishing between the terms 'Roman Campagna' and 'Agro Romano'. Werner Sombart used the designation interchangeably and identified the area with the administrative unit which in the late nineteenth century was under the municipal administration of Rome, lying between latitudes 41°25′ and 42°5′N and longitudes 29°30′ and 30°30′E, and covering an area of about 2,000 sq. km. It was bordered on the north by the Sabine hills, on the east by the Alban hills and on the southwest by the Tyrrhenian Sea. The Agro Romano was the more literary denomination, whereas the Campagna was the more vulgar description, which had its origin among the common people. Jean Delumeau, admitting that the terms were susceptible to many interpretations, defined the Campagna from the geographical point of view, much like Sombart. The administrative area, as distinct from the geographical region, was known as the *distretto*. It encompassed an area larger than the Agro Romano, including everything within a circumference of 55 to 75 km around Rome. Werner Sombart, *Die römische Campagna. Eine sozialökonomische Studie* (Leipzig, 1888), 8, 170–74; Delumeau, *Vie économique et sociale de Rome*, 2:521–25; Rossi, *L'Agro di Roma*, 83–86.

[2] Paul Vidal de la Blache and L. Gallois, *Géographie universelle*. Vol. 7, pt 2: *Italie et Pays Balkaniques*, by Jules Sion (Paris, 1934), 342.

where the rocks projected through the thick humus and loam and the gulleys that emerged at every step in a countryside which at first sight appeared so flat, was covered with a rich black and reddish soil. The plain of the Agro Romano was extended to the north and the south by the Maremma, marshlands which stretched along the seacoast to the Tuscan border on the one hand and Terracina near the limits of the old kingdom of Naples on the other. Moreover, the Agro is one of the regions of Italy best supplied with water. The Tiber is the recipient of 27 minor tributaries in the Campagna alone, of which the Aniene is the largest. Another twelve streams flow directly into the sea. But not only has the Agro an abundant supply of surface water, it possesses also constant and perennial underground reserves. The sources of these waters are the lakes of the surrounding hills, such as the Lago Bracciano and Lago Martignano in the north and Albano and Nemi to the east. They all lie several hundred meters above the plain and their waters filter with considerable pressure through the porous rock formations of the volcanic tufa down to the level of the lower-lying lands.[3]

In spite of Napoleon's fears, the average temperatures in the Campagna were mild, varying between a summer average of 23.59°C and a winter average of 7.4°C. The summers are dry, the last rain usually falling at the end of June, but storms, frequent from June to September, sometimes ravage the regions. After a drought in July and August, the first rains descend at the beginning of September and become intensive in November. The cold is never excessive. What is treacherous, however, is the sudden variation of temperature. While the burning sun is still setting on the horizon, night sets in and, with it, the damp and cold fog.

With such a soil and climate the flora of the Agro Romano was once rich and beneficent. The question, therefore, arises as to how it could have deteriorated to the state in which Montesquieu and other travellers found it in the eighteenth century. The answer lies in the history of the region.[4]

Although there had been instances of depopulation before, it was in the fifteenth century that for a variety of reasons about half the inhabited places disappeared from the map. Feudal strife accounted for many of these cases: the struggle for lordship over a particular territory by one or the other feudatory, the exodus of inhabitants tired of being subjected to different lords, and the accompanying brigandage. In just a few cases natural causes such as epidemics, fire, or earthquakes, and other factors, among them an inconvenient location off the main routes of communication, were responsible. Several more centers disappeared in Lazio in the sixteenth and seventeenth centuries. When such places became

[3] Delumeau, *Vie économique et sociale de Rome*, 2:522–26; Sombart, *Die römische Campagna*, 16–21; Giuseppe Tomassetti, *La Campagna romana. Antica, medioevale, e moderna* (4 vols.; Rome, 1910–26), 1:8, 13–14; Story, *Roba di Roma*, 163–64.

[4] Nicolai, *Memorie, leggi, ed osservazioni*, 3:50; Sombart, *Die römische Campagna*, 23; Tomassetti, *La Campagna romana*, 1:19–21; Madelin, *Rome de Napoléon*, 39; Delumeau, *Vie économique et sociale de Rome*, 2:526–28, 534–38, 566.

Map 2 Environs of Rome in 1755 according to a map by Cristoforo Maire and Ruggero Giuseppe Boscovich

uninhabited they usually left a trace behind them marked by a *casale*. Within the Campagna at least seventeen villages, which had a total population of 9,650 people in 1300, had disappeared by the nineteenth century. This depopulation, in fact, spread north beyond the border to Tuscany, where the inhabitants of the Maremma around Siena likewise were reduced to about one-seventh of their number within this time period.[5]

With the baronial wars responsible for initiating the major depopulation of the Agro, other factors accelerated the process once it had started, malaria being the chief one. Spread by the anopheles mosquito, which Hannibal is reputed to have brought with him, malaria, which had already raged in the Middle Ages, became particularly devastating in modern times. The Campagna, we know, was filled with marshy areas. Deforestation, hurried on by heedless thirst for gain, had profoundly modified the morphology and hydrography of the Agro; the climatic conditions had denuded the mountains of their layers of soil and silted up the valleys, which turned into marshes. Along the coastline of Lazio and beyond, these marshes were covered with shrubs and bushes, very densely interwoven and interspersed with trees. This vegetation, the so-called *macchia* (maquis) of the Mediterranean region, became an impediment to the free circulation of air and did not permit the moisture in the soil to evaporate. So it became a breeding ground for mosquitoes.

All kinds of causation for this fever were suggested at the time. The most common made the vapors or miasma rising from the marshy soil responsible for the scourge. It was not, of course, until 1886 that Tommasi-Crudele discovered the existence of the malaria-bearing soil under the microscope. He thereby confirmed what the ancient Roman agronomist Varro first asserted (in his *Res Rustica*, I, 12), when he tried to explain the Roman fever by the existence of an "animalia quaedam mimita." Since the bacillus was aerobic, it would multiply quickly in the atmosphere if three conditions were met: a temperature of at least 20°C, direct access to the oxygen in the air, a moderate, but continuous degree of humidity. Hence the danger of malaria was least in mid-summer, because of the absence of the necessary humidity, while the worst outbreak of fever occurred during the first autumn rains. But these conditions did not exist in the city where the soil had no direct access to the air in paved and built-up areas. This precise information was unknown to the eighteenth century.[6]

5 Ibid., 2:528; Leopoldina Luzio, "Contributo allo studio dei centri scomparsi o abbandonati del Lazio," *Rivista di geografia italiana*, 20 (1953), 136, 138, 157–59; Guido Pescosolido, *Terra e nobiltà. I Borghese* (Rome, 1979); Tomassetti, *La Campagna romana*, 1:298; Sombart, *Die römische Campagna*, 71, 89–90; Angelo Celli, *Storia della malaria nell'Agro Romano* (Città di Castello, 1925), 308–11; Cochrane, *Florence in the Forgotten Centuries*, 357.

6 Celli, *Storia della malaria*, 3–5, 295–97, 315–17; Giorgio Roster, *Climatologia dell'Italia nelle sue attinenze con l'igiene e con l'agricoltura* (Turin, 1909), 554; Delumeau, *Vie économique et sociale de Rome*, 2:529; Tomassetti, *La Campagna romana*, 1:167, 222; Andrieux, *Daily Life in Papal Rome*, 14; Sombart, *Die römische Campagna*, 25–26; David Young, *Rome in Winter and the Tuscan Hills in Summer. A Contribution to the Climate of Italy* (London, 1889), 103; Gorani, *Rom und seine Einwohner*, 75–77; Nicolai, *Memorie, leggi ed osservazioni*, 3:233–54.

In spite of the availability of quinine, indications are that the incidence of malaria continued its upward trend throughout the eighteenth century, at times reaching epidemic proportions. From 1700 to 1730 the scourge invested Rome itself, hitting areas until then regarded as healthy. After an interval, the infection resumed its march from about 1750 to 1780 causing new zones of depopulation. Yet whenever the endemic sickness was interrupted by periods of relative relief, new hope stirred up scattered efforts to improve the region.[7]

The efforts, however, did little to augment the small population of the Agro. In the old diocese of Ostia, the most depopulated in all the Agro, the resident population never rose above 200, with a population density of about 0.8 per sq. km. Although the population in the diocese of Albano, in the south of the Agro, was larger – it rose from 10,900 in 1683 to 17,047 in 1782, only to drop to 15,536 by 1811 – the increase was in hilly areas, whereas the number of residents in the flatlands remained unchanged. During the season, the local population was greatly augmented by casual and migrant labor. The ratio between the stable and the temporary population was then at least 1 to 3, in the Ardea it was probably as much as 1 to 7, and in some areas of the diocese of Ostia it reached as high as 1 to 10.[8]

Turning from the physical and human factors to the economic, we witnessed in the course of the sixteenth century a phenomenon common to most of Europe: the expulsion of the peasants from the land and the formation of extensive estates. In England this phenomenon resulted in enclosures, which marked the beginning of capitalistic agriculture. The removal of the labor force from the fields gave way to a process of urbanization and proletarization, which eventually would be exploited by industry. In the Agro Romano the expansion of the large estates, most often by papal families, started a process of "refeudalization" of land and the urbanization of those peasants who had survived earlier depopulations, but who without the prospect of industry would have to live a life condemned to poverty and charity.

The central government shared responsibility in this development for its failure to lay down a rational agricultural policy that would have increased production. After some intervention to promote tillage,[9] the authorities, taking note that they were unable to make any mark on productivity, from the middle of the sixteenth century on limited themselves to interventions almost exclusively aimed at regulating the consumption of agricultural products. The policy sprang from the conviction that the recurring famines were largely a function of the cereal export. So they did away with the free circulation of grain. Although this policy was often contradicted by issuing export permits (*tratte*), the fact remains that the producer,

[7] Young, *Rome in Winter*, 84; M. R. Caroselli, "Aspects of the Economic History of the Roman *Campagna* in the Modern and Contemporary World," *Journal of European Economic History*, 13 (1984), 593–94; Schiavoni and Sonnino, "Popolazione e territorio nel Lazio" 200–1.

[8] Rossi, *L'Agro di Roma*, 98–105. [9] Nicolai, *Memorie, leggi ed osservazioni*, 3:10.

uncertain about such exports, lacked incentives to expand production and preferred to devote himself to pasture.[10]

The *congregazione del Sollievo*, in 1701, basing itself on a cadastral register drawn up in 1660, gave the Agro Romano an area of 108,285 rubbia (200,327.25 ha). The land was divided into 80,000 rubbia (73.8 percent of the total) of tilled and cultivated land, 11,192 rubbia (10.34 percent) of untilled and unploughed soil, 5,251 rubbia (4.84 percent) of meadow, and 11,702 rubbia (10.81 percent) of rough and wild land. In addition there were still 844 rubbia (1,561 ha) of gardens, vineyards, and meadows within the walls of Rome, and another 4,829 rubbia (8,952.15 ha) of gardens, vineyards, and meadows just outside the walls before the tenute started. The high percentage of cultivated land appears rather surprising in the light of the history of the Agro, casting doubt on its accuracy.[11]

But we have to wait until the cadastral register of 1783 for greater details. Twenty years after Pompeo Neri's *censimento* in Lombardy and three weeks before the establishment of a commission to draw up a cadaster for Tuscany, on 15 December 1777, a decree ordering the formation of a new cadastral register for five of the principal provinces of the Papal States was issued. Unlike the Lombard cadaster, which took about twenty years, this work was completed six years later. The purpose of the cadaster, in the Agro at least, was not primarily to be a tool for taxation as in the case of the Tuscan one, but, like its Lombard predecessor, it was meant to promote agriculture, more precisely, to ensure the food supply for the Roman annona. It was to stimulate the proprietors to cultivating the land by fixing the amount to be worked. The cadaster was to lay down what land was best suited for fallow pasture and what for arable farming, and its provisions were to be strictly followed by the cultivators so that there would be little fluctuation in the amount of grain available. According to the cadaster, 55,521 rubbia (about 102,713.85 ha) out of an area of 111,794 (206,818.8 ha), that is, about 49.6 percent, was to be tilled and sown, which would produce 444,168 rubbia of grain (c. 1,307,630.59 hectoliters or 963,844 quintals), reckoned on an annual yield of eight rubbia of grain for each rubbio of land sown. The scheduled breakdown of the amount of land to be tilled according to the size of the holdings was to be followed.[12] From Table 33 we are able to gauge that the percentage of land scheduled to be tilled diminished the larger the area of the tenuta was. Even then, the quotas were not to be fulfilled. De Cupis, who admittedly calculated his figures on the basis of an area less than half the above size,

[10] Alberto Balzani, "Primi interventi di bonifica dello stato unitario nella Campagna romana," *Studi Romani*, 18 (1980), 50–52. [11] ASR, Congregazione del Sollievo, vol. 1.

[12] Alessandro D'Alessandro, "Le tenute dell'Agro Romano alla fine del secolo XVIII," *Economia e storia*, 16 (1969), 35–37. Nicolai, *Memorie, leggi ed osservazioni*, 1:306, gives a slightly smaller quantity of land to be sown according to the 1783 cadaster, 54,772 rubbia (101,328.2 ha). Since the sowing was to be divided over four- or three-year periods (70.83 percent over a four-year period), he came up with 23,140.2 rubbia (42,577.97 ha) to be sown annually. I prefer D'Alessandro's figures, because he had reworked the cadaster more thoroughly.

Table 33

| Category of holdings (in rubbia) | Total area in rubbia within this category | Land scheduled to be tilled | |
|---|---|---|---|
| | | in rubbia | % of total area |
| to 10 | 42 | 22 | 52.3 |
| 11–50 | 1,192 | 593 | 49.7 |
| 51–100 | 4,093 | 2,628 | 64.2 |
| 101–300 | 26,660 | 17,771 | 62.9 |
| 301–500 | 19,665 | 10,633 | 54.0 |
| 501–1,000 | 26,365 | 13,250 | 50.2 |
| 1,001–2,000 | 18,674 | 6,418 | 34.3 |
| 2,001–3,000 | 4,511 | 1,233 | 27.3 |
| above 3,000 | 10,592 | 2,973 | 28.0 |

tells us that between 1782 and 1797 only 13,726 rubbia of land (25,255.85 ha) were sown annually, which produced only 96,758 rubbia of grain (c. 222,543.4 hl or 209,964.86 quintals). That would be considerably less than the annual consumption of Rome between 1585 and 1595, which fluctuated between 322,000 and 414,000 hectoliters. The purpose of the cadaster was defeated, because the cultivators were discouraged by the minimal profits or even the losses they incurred in growing grain. On eight rubbia of grain they would make about 30 baiocchi profit, some of which went for rents, farm implements, and other overheads. If they had to break up the land for tillage, too, they would actually be losing money.[13]

From the point of view of landholding, the Agro Romano contained the greatest concentration of privileged landholders in Italy. The 111,794 rubbia of land (206,818.9 ha) were divided into 357 tenute, and of these 170 tenute, which made up about 54.6 percent of the land, belonged to 113 noble families, and a further 153 tenute, that is, 42.8 percent, were in the hands of ecclesiastical institutions. Even in the Bolognese plain, another stronghold of agrarian privilege, the concentration was slightly less. In 1789, 216 proprietors, that is, 9.16 percent of those registered, possessed 82 percent of the surface area; 46.3 percent of that belonged to nobles, 20.8 percent to ecclesiastical institutions, and 32.4 percent to bourgeois proprietors. In the Agro the process of engrossing the land in a few hands would continue.

13 De Cupis, *Vicende dell'agricolture nell'Agro Romano*, 333–41; Nicolai, *Memorie, leggi ed osservazioni*, 1:x–xiii, 306–11; 2:21; 3:148, 161; Tomassetti, *La Campagna romana*, 1:228–29; Delumeau, *Vie économique et sociale de Rome*, 1:122–23; Jean Coste, "Missione nell'Agro Romano nella primavera del 1703," *Ricerche per la storia religiosa di Roma*, 2 (1978), 168; Seregni (ed.), *Carteggio di Verri*, 12:26; Celli, *Storia della malaria*, 307; Büchi, *Finanzen und Finanzpolitik Toskanas*, 336, 367–416; Diaz, *Gianni*, 225–26; Woolf, *History of Italy, 1700–1860*, 98; Daniel M. Klang, *Tax Reform in Eighteenth Century Lombardy* (New York and Boulder, 1977). Note that a rubbio (pl. rubbia) could be both a measurement of surface area and of volume, usually of grain.

Table 34

| Categories of surface area (rubbia) | Tenute | | Total surface area | |
|---|---|---|---|---|
| | Number | % | Rubbia | % |
| to 10 | 7 | 2.2 | 42 | 0.03 |
| 11–50 | 39 | 10.9 | 1,192 | 1.07 |
| 51–100 | 54 | 15.1 | 4,093 | 3.67 |
| 101–300 | 149 | 41.6 | 26,660 | 23.84 |
| 301–500 | 50 | 14.0 | 19,665 | 17.59 |
| 501–1,000 | 40 | 11.2 | 26,365 | 23.58 |
| 1,001–2,000 | 13 | 3.6 | 18,674 | 16.71 |
| 2,001–3,000 | 2 | 0.6 | 4,511 | 4.04 |
| above 3,000 | 3 | 0.8 | 10,592 | 9.47 |

Between 1690 and 1803 the number of proprietors was reduced from 443 to 362, and by 1870 it had shrunk to 70. In 1910 only 21 families shared three-quarters of the Agro.[14]

To define a tenuta, or large holding resembling a latifundia, is difficult: each one varied. In general it was an indeterminate mixture of arable land, grass land, permanent pasture, wood and scrubland, a modest house for the master, more usually occupied by his bailiff or agent, often in the form of a small crenellated castle, some buildings for the handful of hired servants, such as cowherds and ostlers, charged with looking after the miles and miles of countryside, a stable, and a granary. There was never enough permanent shelter for the casual labor. The management of the tenuta centered in the *casale*. The larger tenute, those say above 500 hectares, had an administrator, known as a *ministro*, a skilled farmer from a better social milieu. In such a case, his chief, be he the proprietor or the tenant farmer, would only have to visit his estates occasionally. Medium-sized tenute, on the other hand, did not need such a *ministro*, but might have only a *fattore*, or steward. The possessor would then have to keep a constant eye on his estate.

The 1783 cadaster provides us with an overview of the size of the tenute (divided in Table 34 by categories).[15] The largest number of tenute were to be found in the category of 101 to 300 rubbia with 149 holdings, equal to 41.6 percent of all holdings, with a total surface area larger than that of any category, equivalent to 23.84 percent. But in the latter respect it was followed closely by the 501 to 1,000 rubbia

[14] Giancarlo Angelozzi, "Le strutture sociale," in Aldo Berselli (ed.), *Storia della Emilia Romagna* (2 vols.; Bologna, 1977), 2:138; Schiavoni and Sonnino, "Popolazione e territorio in Lazio," 199; Delumeau, *Vie économique et sociale de Rome*, 2:595.

[15] Alessandro D'Alessandro, "I proprietori delle tenute dell'Agro Romano nel 1783," *Rivista di storia dell'agricoltura*, 9 (1971), 363.

Table 35

| Area of tenute (in rubbia) | Noble | Ecclesiastical | Bourgeois | Mixed | Community |
|---|---|---|---|---|---|
| to 10 | 4 | 2 | 1 | — | — |
| 11–50 | 14 | 15 | 9 | 1 | — |
| 51–100 | 24 | 26 | 2 | 2 | — |
| 101–300 | 59 | 73 | 10 | 6 | 1 |
| 301–500 | 32 | 18 | — | — | — |
| 500–1,000 | 25 | 13 | 2 | — | — |
| 1,001–2,000 | 11 | 2 | — | — | — |
| 2,001–3,000 | 1 | 1 | — | — | — |
| above 3,000 | — | 3 | — | — | — |

category, which, with a total surface area of 26,365 rubbia, formed 23.58 percent of the total area.

Ecclesiastical bodies possessed all the three tenute with an area above 3,000 rubbia and one of the two estates in the 2,001 to 3,000 range. They were strongly represented in the tenute of the 101 to 300 rubbia category, owning about 49 percent of them. The nobility possessed eleven out of the thirteen tenute between 1,001 and 2,000 rubbia, and 64 percent of those between 301 and 500 rubbia. The bourgeois element, weak as it was in Rome, also had a small share in the land of the Agro with 6.7 percent of the tenute. It made its presence felt particularly in the 11 to 50 rubbia category (23 percent), and to a much lesser extent in the 101 to 300 rubbia group. Table 35 shows the breakdown of the number of tenute by surface area categories as held by the different classes of proprietors.[16]

Another cadaster in 1803 showed little difference in noble holdings, recording a slight increase of 1 percent, whereas the ecclesiastical holdings fell from 42.8 percent to 36.2 percent, the loss no doubt due to the confiscations before and during the Jacobin republic. On the right bank of the Tiber baronial and ecclesiastical power was about equally divided to start with. Some smaller monastic possessions were eventually absorbed by nobles and bourgeois. It is on the left bank that the bourgeoisie was to acquire its most numerous and extensive possessions. Many of the new bourgeois proprietors came from among the ranks of the old tenant farmers, the *mercanti di campagna*, who alone had the experience to manage these large estates. Names such as the Giorgi, the Valdrambini, the Franchi, and the Acquaroni appear now for the first time.[17]

Among the largest noble proprietors in the Agro Romano were those shown in Table 36 (with percentage of the total area of the Agro Romano they possessed);

[16] D'Alessandro, "Le tenute dell'Agro Romano," 34.

while Table 37 indicates the largest ecclesiastical landholders. In addition the Apostolic Chamber fell heir to about 2.03 percent of the Agro largely through defaulting debtors.[18]

By far the largest noble landholders in the Agro, then, were the Borghese. Sombart distinguished three types of aristocracy in Rome: The old feudal nobility, the papal nepotistic nobility, and the more recent financial nobility. The Borghese belonged to the second. At one time the old baronial families of the Orsini and Colonna owned almost the whole of the Campagna. But in the bloody struggles of the fourteenth and fifteenth centuries the victorious papacy tore away from them the dominion of these lands, which they had held for almost half a millennium. The popes then used the land to endow their nipoti. This was the story of the Borghese.

The nucleus of the Borghese estates dates back to the papacy of Paul V. With his accession the Borghese were determined to become the equal, if not the superior, to the other landowning noble houses in Lazio. From 1607 to 1737 there were about thirty acquisitions of rural and urban property by the Borghese clan. In 1779 their possessions in the Agro Romano alone amounted to over 11,503 rubbia (21,263 ha).[19]

In addition to the tenute, some fiefs had still survived. They were the relics of the old baronial possessions, sometimes going back to the eighth century. They were particularly strongly represented along the rim of the Agro. Starting from the Tyrrhenian coast, the belt of the fiefs described an ample arc through the areas of Cerveteri, Bracciano, and Monte Soratte, until it reached the Sabine hills, beyond which it continued into the zones of Preneste, Velletri, and the Latian hills. Within that belt baronial property sometimes surpassed 50 percent of the total area recorded in the cadaster. The political and military power of the Roman barons, as we know, had been practically annihilated before the start of the modern period by the victorious struggle of the papacy. But the jurisdictional prerogatives over their vassals were to remain intact for the time being, only receiving their death blow when Clement XI in 1704 extended the financial control of the Buon Governo over the baronial communities. He abolished the fiscal exemptions of the baronial properties. In the course of the century the judicial rights were progressively withdrawn, although they were not abolished until 1834. By that time the transformation of the Roman nobility into a court aristocracy had been completed.[20]

17 Woolf, *History of Italy, 1700–1860*, 45; Dal Pane, *Storia del lavoro*, 4:53 n. 55; Delumeau, *Vie économique et sociale de Rome*, 2:595; Tournon, *Etudes statistiques sur Rome*, 32–36; Tomassetti, *La Campagna romana*, 1:274; Sombart, *Die römische Campagna*, 88–90; D'Alessandro, "Le tenute dell'Agro Romano," 28, 32–34; Rossi, *L'Agro di Roma*, 89–91; Caroselli, "Aspects of the Economic History of the *Campagna*," 597.

18 D'Alessandro, "I proprietori delle tenute," 366–81. The De Pietro were actually a family of *mercanti di campagna*.

19 Pescosolido, *Terra e nobiltà*, 19–25, 41–42; Sombart, *Die römische Campagna*, 56–60. For the rise of the Borghese see Reinhard, *Papstfinanz und Nepotismus unter Paul V*.

20 Pescosolido, *Terra e nobiltà*, 48–50; Mistruzzi, "La nobiltà nello Stato pontificio," 208–9, 215, 219.

Table 36

| Proprietor | % of area | Proprietor | % of area | Proprietor | % of area |
|---|---|---|---|---|---|
| Borghese | 10.67 | Rospigliosi | 1.73 | Carpegna | 0.997 |
| Sforza Cesarini | 4.19 | Albani | 1.44 | Lepri | 0.97 |
| Patrizi | 2.8 | De Pietro | 1.4 | Serluppi | 0.93 |
| Chigi | 2.42 | Giraud | | Santacroce | 0.887 |
| Altieri | 2.26 | Salviati | 1.32 | Strozzi | 0.88 |
| Ruspoli | | Bracciano (duca di) | 1.24 | Mattei | 0.84 |
| Falconieri | 1.88 | Riccardi | 1.22 | Giustiniani | 0.78 |
| Del Nero | | Barberini | 1.2 | Lante | 0.63 |
| Doria Pamphilj | 1.74 | Torregiani | 1.15 | Caffarelli | 0.56 |

Table 37

| Proprietor | % of area | Proprietor | % of area | Proprietor | % of area |
|---|---|---|---|---|---|
| Chapter of St. Peter's | 12.4 | Chapter of St. John Lateran | 2.19 | Collegio Germanico | 1.18 |
| Hospital of Santo Spirito | 7.47 | Chapter of S. Maria Maggiore | 1.36 | Chapter of S. Lorenzo e Damaso | 0.36 |
| | | | | Chapter of S. Maria in Trastevere | |

An example of the economic importance of both types of holdings to a noble family is the fact that in 1763 the Borghese derived 97,000.54 scudi from their rural possessions, which was just above 90 percent of the total family revenue. Between 1763 and 1805 there was an increase in the income from land in the order of 27.9 percent. Among the reasons for the rise was a general and constant increase in prices, especially cereals, during the second half of the eighteenth century in the whole of Europe. Thus, income from rents in Germany almost tripled between 1731/40 and the start of the nineteenth century, while grain prices in northern Italy and Austria rose by 205 and 259 percent respectively during the same period. The Papal States were not to remain immune to the general trend. Their prices of cereal, including wheat which was the most widespread commodity for food in Lazio, also increased. There existed, in fact, during those years two grain prices, as we shall show in the next chapter, that fixed by decree and imposed by the annona and that established on the free market. The price of grain on the market rose by 202 percent in the four decades between 1762 and 1801. Consequently the higher revenue at the beginning of the nineteenth century was a long way from compensating the proprietors for the rise in prices. The gross income of all the Borghese estates, both in and outside the Agro, in 1805 came to 135,999.99 scudi, of which 124,146.32 scudi (91.3 percent of the total) was derived from their landed possessions, as opposed to only 3.4 percent from urban yields.[21]

The average price of a tenuta in the Campagna grew in value over time. At the end of the sixteenth century a rubbio of good land (1.84 ha or c. 18,000 sq. m) cost 90 or 100 scudi, almost as much as a *luogo di monte*, but it paid less than a *luogo*. Attached to the cadaster of 1783 was a rent evaluation (*estimo censuale piano*), which sought to adopt a fair criterion. It established a sliding scale of between 120 and 170 scudi a rubbio. But this evaluation could not be maintained in the face of the universal rising tide. So in 1797, for instance, the land of the Arco Travertino, a tenuta close to Rome and suitable for various types of cultivation, was sold at the rate of 228 scudi per rubbio.[22]

The Roman nobility, however, had no inclination for a rural existence. Even though the family might move into the country for a few months during the healthier times of spring and fall, it dragged all the attractions of urban life along with it; consequently, in the case of the Borghese, 93 percent of their holdings had been let out in tenancy in 1763. The average duration of a leasehold in Lazio was between nine and twelve years, shorter in ecclesiastical lands where canon law sometimes restricted the term to three years. This period was obviously not long enough to encourage the tenant to bring about any permanent improvement to the

21 Pescosolido, *Terra e nobiltà*, 36, 81, 134, 145–48; Abel, *Agrarkrisen und Agrarkonjunkturen*, 182–83, 198.

22 Tomassetti, *La Campagna romana*, 1:276; Stumpo, *Il capitale finanziario a Roma*, 40; Sombart, *Die römische Campagna*, 56–60; Silvagni, *La corte pontificia*, 1:74; Cochrane, *Florence in the Forgotten Centuries*, 399–400.

holding. Some contemporary writers, including Nicola Nicolai, advanced this practice as a reason for the poor state of the Agro. Many tenants, instead of devoting themselves more diligently to raising the yield of the soil, sublet the land for pasture and lived off the income. Nicolai advocated a heavy tax on the proprietors to discourage them letting out the land.

Parallel to the process of expanding the system of leaseholds in the second half of the eighteenth century occurred also a process of concentrating the land in the hands of fewer and fewer tenants. The Borghese tenute themselves provide an example of this consolidation of tenancies. Their number of leaseholders shrank from thirty to nineteen between 1763 and 1805, although the total area of land remained substantially the same.[23]

Consequently the future of the Agro Romano belonged not so much to the great landholders but to the large tenant farmers, many of them *mercanti di campagna*. Present since the sixteenth century on the economic scene of much of Lazio and Umbria, the group of *mercanti di campagna* constituted by the end of the eighteenth century one of the main pillars of the economic life of this region. Historiography has not always given a unanimous verdict on the role of the *mercante di campagna* within the agrarian system of Lazio, and particularly the Agro, sometimes seeing him as a purely parasitic element and at other times as the only dynamic and enterprising force within a static economy. The proprietors, with a few minor exceptions, preferred to hand their lands to these merchants rather than to other, more numerous, cultivators, because they had fewer administrative problems in this way and were assured payment; but, beyond this, the tenant almost always provided the owner with revenues which were close enough to what they could expect to have received had they run them themselves with the help of a *ministro* in each of their holdings. The *mercante di campagna*, in turn, took over one or more tenute in leasehold from a single or, sometimes, several proprietors and in part cultivated them directly, in part sublet them to a number of cultivators. He did not limit himself to being a leaseholder, however, but pursued other activities connected with the land, which provided him with further, and no less substantial, profits.[24]

The *mercanti di campagna*, as their name implies, were rural entrepreneurs. The evolution of a family of medium-sized *mercanti*, the Merolli, will illustrate the nature of their economic activities. Carlo Merolli left his home at Arpino in the southern Papal States to settle in a small *vigna* (vineyard) outside the Porta di S. Giovanni in Rome, which he rented from the Lateran chapter in 1695. His main income appears to have come from mining pozzolana for the building industry. His

[23] Pescosolido, *Terra e nobiltà*, 105–9, 113, 123; Nicolai, *Memorie, leggi ed osservazioni*, 3:150–51, 267–70; Petrocchi, *Roma nel Seicento*, 59; Story, *Roba di Roma*, 350–52; Dal Pane, *Storia del lavoro*, 4:234 n. 24. At the start of the nineteenth century, some Roman nobles, Marcantonio Borghese among them, began to take a direct interest in their lands. Bartoccini, *Roma nell'Ottocento*, 227–28.

[24] Rossi, *L'Agro di Roma*, 90–91; Dal Pane, *Storia del lavoro*, 4:53, 105 n. 25; Pescosolido, *Terra e nobiltà*, 83–85; Caroselli, "Aspects of the Economic History of the *Campagna*," 597; De Felice, *Aspetti e momenti della vita economica*, 191–98.

sons Lorenzo and Tommaso enlarged the family tenures, adding two portions of rented land. In the early eighteenth century the Merolli became agents of the Roman annona. They collected and delivered increasing quantities of grain and other cereals and forage which had been harvested on the properties of the Borghese, and the chapters of St. Peter's and St. John Lateran. In 1738 the then head of the Merolli family, Carlo, moved into the city to a three-story house in what is now the Via S. Giovanni in Laterano. This marks the formal transition of the Merolli into *mercanti di campagna*. Shortly after becoming urbanized the family acquired the tenancy of two tenute of 118 and 75 rubbia respectively. By 1772 the total family assets amounted to 41,253.29 scudi, 22,696 of which were in property. Thereafter, a particularly able offspring of the Merolli clan, Giuseppe, acquired four medium-sized tenute between 1793 and 1802. At that time he held 1,113.23 rubbia of land in the Agro as tenant. In order to exploit such a large terrain more effectively, Giuseppe resorted to subletting. But he was by no means among the giants of the *mercanti di campagna*. At the start of the nineteenth century Giovanni Battista Canori held 19 tenute with a total area of 6,664 rubbia, and the Truzzi family 7 tenute amounting to 6,393 rubbia.[25] Some of these *mercanti* also became exporters of grain and tax farmers.

Their numbers were few. In 1701 the *congregazione del Sollievo* estimated there were 70. At the beginning of the nineteenth century there were no more than 138. In spite of their name and the arena of their activities, their center of interest was not the countryside, but, as in the case of the Merolli, the city of Rome where they had their residence. They were merchants first and foremost and, as such, they formed the backbone of the small Roman bourgeoisie. Yet whatever important part they may have played in the local economy, they never enjoyed a correspondingly significant role in Rome's civic life.[26]

From the point of view of land utilization, we witness over time a diminution of the area devoted to cereal production, with a limited and qualified reversal in the second part of the eighteenth century. Even then, what happened in the Agro Romano cannot compare with the contemporary expansion in the area of cultivated land over most parts of Europe, where, in France, for instance, by dint of tax incentives the amount of tilled land increased by 25.8 percent between 1751/60 and 1781/90.

In the Agro a steady expansion of pasture had occurred in the sixteenth and seventeenth centuries. As the population of Rome grew its need for meat became greater. Animals were normally a better source of revenue than grain for the agricultural sector. They not only gave meat, but also tallow, hides, and dairy products. The barons and great landholders drew their conclusion and systemati-

[25] Enzo Piscitelli, "Una famiglia di mercanti di campagna: I Merolli," *Archivio della società romana di storia patria*, 81 (1958), 119–62; De Cupis, *Vicende dell'agricoltura nell'Agro Romano*, 384.

[26] ASR, Congregazione del Sollievo, vol. 1; Nicolai, *Memorie, leggi ed osservazioni*, 3:231–33; Sombart, *Die römische Campagna*, 67–68.

Table 38

| Period | Fallow land (maggesi) sown in Agro Romano (rubbia) | Arable land sown in Agro Romano (rubbia) | Fallow land (maggesi) sown in distretto (rubbia) | Arable land sown in distretto (rubbia) | Grain harvested in Agro Romano (rubbia) | Grain harvested in distretto (rubbia) | Total grain harvested in annona province | |
|---|---|---|---|---|---|---|---|---|
| | | | | | | | Rubbia | Index |
| 1731–50 | 8,456 | 1,749 | 21,130 | 2,477 | 69,417 | 154,964 | 224,381 | 100 |
| 1751–60 | 7,853 | 1,667 | 38,909 | 4,743 | 77,163 | 234,085 | 311,248 | 139 |
| 1761–70 | 8,692 | 1,699 | 37,709 | 3,883 | 86,193 | 244,223 | 330,416 | 147 |
| 1771–80 | 11,380 | 2,310 | 39,295 | 2,773 | 97,993 | 246,279 | 344,272 | 153 |
| 1781–90 | 11,237 | 2,195 | 33,444 | 2,154 | 102,615 | 208,111 | 310,727 | 138 |
| 1791–97 | 11,911 | 1,924 | 31,095 | 1,474 | 83,250 | 188,824 | 272,074 | 121 |

cally sabotaged every effort by the authorities to stop or curtail them turning their land into pasture. Hence the shrinkage of tillage continued into the first half of the eighteenth century.

In 1712, during the pontificate of Clement XI, measures were enacted to try and stem the decay. But these could only touch the fringe of the problem and were never able to reverse the trend. In fact, it was government policy that was to a great extent responsible for the falling productivity. For part of the grain crop in the Campagna had to be sold to the annona at the stipulated price. It was this competition of the annona with its artificially depressed prices that became ruinous to the cultivators.

The attempted revival of agriculture in the Papal States as a whole had its beginnings in the middle of the eighteenth century and coincided with the first concrete manifestations of the economic reform movement in the country. While the bad harvests of 1763 and thereafter may have added to its urgency, the actual start slightly predated the famine. The real motive was not any concern on the part of the government to increase production and agricultural income, but to secure the provisioning of Rome and other urban centers. At that time the system of nutritional autarky had entered a crisis, because of the increased demand and the protectionist policies in neighboring countries. Hence the need for raising cereal production and the demand for free trade occurred simultaneously. Unfortunately, increased production was not sought by technical progress in agriculture that would have rendered larger yields, an avenue impeded by the ignorance of the cultivators and the scarcity of available resources, but by the expansion of the cultivated surface area. The reformers started out with the conviction that the Agro was derelict solely because of the absence of inhabitants and cultivation, but was inherently fertile. Consequently the not very extensive expansion of cultivation realized in the Agro in the last decades of the eighteenth century was obtained by ploughing up new land only marginally fertile or by simply intensifying the rhythm of crop rotation. The encroachment upon existing pasture land was real, but limited in extent. The effect of the new approach on the average yield was always negative. In the absence of artificial fertilizers or new fodder, which would have maintained the level of livestock raising equal to the needs for animal manure, even the best soil, subjected to a too-rapid rotation by farmers anxious for profit, showed early signs of exhaustion by about 1775.

What actually occured were violent fluctuations of grain production in both the Agro and the wider distretto, starting as early as 1744, which contrasted with the firm stability of demand for grain consumption in Rome. The extremes of the series of grain production between 1744 and 1797 were a maximum of 454,191 rubbia (1,337,138.3 hectoliters or 985,594.47 quintals) of grain in 1776 and a minimum of 190,779 (561,653.38 hectoliters or 413,990.43 quintals) in 1781. The normal variations were between 250,000 rubbia (736,000 hectoliters or 542,500 quintals) and 400,000 (1,177,600 hectoliters or 868,000 quintals). Although the actual figures were not totally reliable, Table 38 gives the annual average grain production in the

Table 39

| Period | Rubbia of grain harvested per one rubbio of land sown | |
|---|---|---|
| | Agro Romano | distretto |
| 1731–50 | 6.80 | 6.56 |
| 1751–60 | 8.11 | 5.36 |
| 1761–70 | 8.29 | 5.87 |
| 1771–80 | 7.16 | 5.85 |
| 1781–90 | 7.64 | 5.85 |
| 1791–97 | 6.00 | 5.80 |

Agro Romano and the distretto.[27] The highest total for all the grain harvested in the territory of the annona was during the decade of 1771–80. This is mainly due to the productivity of the distretto; for in the smaller area of the Agro the maximum was reached in the following decade, by which time the output in the distretto had already decreased by close to 10 percent. Thereafter we notice a serious decline in productivity; the productive capacity of the soil had clearly been exhausted. This contrasted with a 24 percent increase in grain production in neighboring Tuscany between 1765 and 1792. The same trend can be traced, if not as plainly, in the yield of grain per rubbio. Table 39 indicates that the yield was highest in the decade of 1761–70, when the drive for expanding tillage first got under way, in other words, when much of the soil was still fresh. However, the yield in the Agro during the four decades from 1751 to 1790 was considerably higher than in the distretto. It is not easy to speculate on the reason; it may be due to the better soil of the plains in the Agro or the fact that its large landholders or their tenants were driven more by business motives than the peasants who still made up an important part of the distretto.[28]

We have referred to the backwardness of agriculture in Lazio. The papal government did almost nothing to modernize techniques and cultivation. Technical

[27] Nicolai, *Memorie, leggi ed osservazioni*, 3:142–45.

[28] Abel, *Agrarkrisen und Agrarkonjunkturen*, 192; Nicolai, *Memorie, leggi ed osservazioni*, 3:146, 162; Delumeau, *Vie économique et sociale de Rome*, 2:539–40, 566–67, 585; Petrocchi, *Roma nel Seicento*, 60; De Cupis, *Vicende dell'agricoltura nell'Agro Romano*, 292–94; Luigi Dal Pane, "Discussioni e leggi annonarie in Roma nel primo quarantennio del secolo XVIII," *Studi in onore di Armando Sapori* (Milan, 1957), 1206–1207; De Felice, *Aspetti e momenti della vita economica*, 13–16, 52–54; Pescosolido, *Terra e nobiltà*, 152, 154 n. 29, 161–63; Revel, "Le grain de Rome," 243, 277–80; ASR, Famiglie diverse, Ruffo, buste 3–10; Cochrane, *Florence in the Forgotten Centuries*, 400. The *maggesi* – which I translated fallow land – is really land cultivated with wheat on soil that had been left to rest for two or three years and was ploughed beforehand in six different directions, a relatively expensive process.

development was left to private initiative. If there were any efforts at transforming agriculture, they encountered the passive resistance of the peasants. While in some progressive regions of northern Italy crop rotation with a fallow year had completely disappeared, it continued to be standard practice in the Agro Romano. Nothing could have been ruder than the agricultural implements used by the Romans. They seemed to have made little progress since the time of Virgil's *Georgics*. Their primitive ploughs could cover at the most nine to ten rubbia of land during the season and only about seven if the soil had not been cultivated for a long time. The soil which had been used for pasture over a long period required about five or six operations for tearing up the ground in both directions between February and October, in view of the lightness of the plough.[29]

Despite its later unsuccessful attempt to halt the drift, the Roman government bore a great share of the responsibility for first turning much of the Campagna from cultivation to pasture. Under Boniface IX (1389–1404), the state took the decision to abandon large tracts of land extending from the gates of Rome to the borders of Tuscany and Umbria to pasture and set up the *dogana dei pastorizie*. The institution proved to be a financial boon to the papal treasury, for the *dogana dei pastorizie* was more lucrative than the export of grain. It collected a tax called *fida* – or security deposit – from flocks which entered within the bounds of its purview ostensibly to shield them from harassment by the local authorities or private individuals. In addition, the herders had to pay rent for the pasture to the Apostolic Chamber. Seeing its immediate interest, the papal government did everything to encourage owners of flocks and herds to send their animals into the Campagna; and by a number of measures tried to make their sojourn as smooth as possible. Their privileges were codified in 1646 and constantly reconfirmed until they resembled those of the Spanish Mesta. The herders enjoyed complete immunity from paying compensation for any damage they caused and exemption from transit tolls.

But these favors were not always sufficient for promoting animal husbandry in the Agro Romano, as might appear at first. Some considerable shortcomings existed. There was the chain of frequent zootic epidemics which struck the countryside during the last years of the seventeenth century and the first three decades of the eighteenth. The usual response on these occasions was to slaughter the animals prematurely, a device which interfered with the regular supply to the local consumers. Another hurdle for effective animal raising was the marked deterioration of spontaneous fodder production. Since artificial grazing land was almost unknown, natural pasture was still the general practice. Over time these would become marshy and covered with thick undergrowth. Stables for pasture

[29] De Felice, *Aspetti e momenti della vita economica*, 17–18, 26–27, 37–46; Dal Pane, *Storia del lavoro*, 4:27; Sombart, *Die römische Campagna*, 34–36; Story, *Roba di Roma*, 353–54; Caroselli, "Aspects of the Economic History of the *Campagna*," 593–94. Even in the agriculturally more advanced region of the Bolognese, there were no basic changes in the method of breaking up the soil. Dal Pane, *Economia e società a Bologna*, 76.

animals were still non-existent. As a consequence, though a steady expansion of pasture would occur it was not enough to offset its low quality. Moreover, the reversal of the trend in the second half of the eighteenth century with the development of tillage, however limited both in time and space it might have been, had the effect of reducing the area of pasture at a time when demand for meat rose. Thus, while on the Venetian mainland and also in Lombardy we note a revival in animal raising, no such increase can be detected in the Agro; the increased supply of sheep for the Roman market must be sought elsewhere. An indicator of the change is the fate of the *dogana dei pastorizie*. After 1770 it passed into entrepreneurial hands, which drew greater profits from the cultivation and commerce in grain than from pasture by way of the *fida* and animal husbandry.[30]

The shepherds of the Agro practiced transhumance. The animals only grazed for about nine months in the Campagna and spent the summer months on the mountain meadows. The flocks left the Campagna around the feast of St. John, 24 June, and started on their return trip usually on 24 September, but some shepherds waited for the first snowfall. They travelled in groups of 2,400 to 3,000 sheep, known as *masseria*, along the traditional routes, often taking as much as ten days. The breed of sheep which grazed in the Campagna originated in the mountains and was accustomed to staying in the open and wandering about. It is very doubtful if this improved the quality of the meat; certainly its wool was superior to its meat. Hence the young lambs, the *abbachi*, which were brought to the market at the age of 35–40 days, were most popular for consumption. Sheep milk was used exclusively for cheese, the *pecorino*, which was prepared on the spot, and the more sweetly tasting *ricotta* produced from what remained. Tournon in 1813 estimated that there were about 710,000 head of sheep in Lazio, about four sheep to every inhabitant. Of these about 300,000 were slaughtered annually, to which the Agro contributed about 70,000.[31]

The principal use of cattle was for haulage and draft animals. Milk cows played a subordinate role; the *vacca romana* produced rather good milk, but only a small quantity, usually 4 to 5 liters a day. On the estates close to Rome the milk was sold directly to local vendors. In the rest of the Campagna it was processed into an inferior kind of cheese. Calves were usually slaughtered very young to produce veal. On the other hand, it was almost impossible to find a really good piece of beef.

[30] Delumeau, *Vie économique et sociale de Rome*, 2:572–78; De Cupis, *Vicende dell'agricoltura*, 324–54; Maria D'Amelia, "La crisi di un mercato protetto: approvigionamente e consumo della carne a Roma nel XVIII secolo," *Mélanges de l'Ecole française de Rome. Moyen Age, Temps Modernes*, 87 (1975), 532–33.

[31] Jacques Revel, "Les privilèges d'un capitale: l'approvisionnement de Rome à l'époque moderne," *Annales, E.S.C.*, 30 (1975), Catherine Delano Smith, *Western Mediterranean Europe. A Historical Geography of Italy, Spain and Southern France since the Neolithic* (London and New York, 1979), 236; Petrocchi, *Roma nel Seicento*, 58; Sombart, *Die römische Campagna*, 45–48; De Cupis, *Vicende dell'agricoltura*, 364; De Felice, *Aspetti e momenti della vita economica*, 97–98.

Tournon estimated that there were around 100,000 head of cattle, including about 2,000 buffaloes, in Lazio in 1815, which would come to about one head of cattle to every six inhabitants or to every 2.7 hectares of arable land, among the highest figures in Europe at the time. About 12,000 head were slaughtered annually to supply the city of Rome. The consumption of pigs was also very high and the export, especially to Naples, important. It is estimated that 25,000 head were raised in the Agro and another 12,000 in the region around Velletri, of which the capital alone consumed about 14,000 annually.

As late as 1883, 20 percent of the whole surface area of the Agro Romano was still covered with woodland, compared to 13 percent for Italy as a whole. But a great deal of this consisted of impenetrable shrubs; other parts were still virgin forest, economically of little value, even if delightful to behold. In the course of the ancien regime the forestry industry had revived in Lazio. Not only were the products of the woodlands, timber for construction and heating, charcoal, resin, and chestnuts, sufficient for domestic needs, but they produced a noteworthy export. Severe laws regulated the cutting of trees and bushes to preserve this national asset, but in the face of rising domestic demand during the second half of the eighteenth century these regulations were disregarded. The foundries of Ronciglione, Bracciano, Tivoli, and Conca, the alum works, and the numerous other industrial workshops and lesser craftsmen absorbed great quantities of wood annually. All the while the good price offered on foreign markets made the export attractive. The Romans had about 70 kg per head available annually for fuel between 1774 and 1781. This quantity dropped somewhat precipitously to 56 kg between 1782 and 1791, only to recover in 1794 to about 81 kg. The supply of charcoal stayed steady at just above 100 kg per head a year.[32]

True orchards scarcely existed in the Campagna. The best quality fruit was grown in the gardens around Rome. Similarly olives were rare in the Agro Romano. The major areas of production in Lazio were Tivoli, Velletri, and the Sabina. For much of the century there was a contraction, in sharp contrast to the prosperity of the Neapolitan oil industry at that time. The proprietors, out for quick gain, were reluctant to plant new trees, because it took too long before the fruit could be harvested. So on the one side no new trees were planted, and on the other the existing stock diminished by the natural process of attrition and through inclement weather. The freeze of 1709 marked the beginning of a crisis in olive growing in Lazio. The government, assisted actively by provincial agricultural societies, responded by trying to encourage the growth of olives. The most important single measure was the order of Fabrizio Ruffo, on behalf of Pius VI, granting a prize of one paolo for each olive tree planted in various places, but very few of these were in

[32] Sombart, *Die römische Campagna*, 39–43; Delumeau, *Vie économique et sociale de Rome*, 2:528 n. 1, 568; Friz, *Consumi, tenore di vita e prezzi*, 110–11; De Felice, *Aspetti e momenti della vita economica*, 94–96, 101–2. The Romans used virtually no turf for fuel.

the Agro Romano. Despite this increase in the oil supply the country remained at a deficit, encouraging several unsuccessful attempts to find substitutes.[33]

Wine production, which had started to increase by the seventeenth century, continued to do so in some areas in the eighteenth century, being sufficient to supply the domestic needs, and since 1745 even led to periodical overproduction in Lazio, with a consequent drop in prices. In Rome the wines of Genzano and the Castelli Romani were the most sought after. As with olives the cultivation of vine was expensive and only became profitable after many years. Hence its development was tied to the whole question of land tenure. As long as the peasants only had leases of brief duration, the extent of viniculture remained almost stationary; once the land began to be changed to more permanent tenure, with the first of such grants at the start of the seventeenth century, vine growing spread noticeably.[34]

The city of Rome, too, was ringed with vineyards and parks. They formed a kind of suburb which penetrated the very walls of the city and dotted its more rustic districts, such as Trastevere. Here the nature of the vineyards was somewhat different. Whereas leasehold was most prominent in Lazio, in Trastevere it formed only a minute part. Of the 172 vineyards at the close of the seventeenth century in the two parishes of S. Maria in Trastevere and S. Cecilia only 4, that is 2.3 percent, were let out. With the exception of 7 (4.07 percent) the majority of the 172 were not in the hands of peasants, but were worked with hired labor. Even the contracts by which the few vineyards were let out gave all the advantages to the proprietor of the holding, who regulated the type of cultivation and the number of stocks planted, neither of which the tenant was able to alter. This state of affairs certainly had an influence on the system of work, so that by the end of the eighteenth century the growers still had not adopted modern and rational methods of cultivating vine.[35]

The Pontine marshes at the southern end of the Campagna had long been the object of drainage schemes, both by popes and private individuals, usually with little or no practical results. Boniface VIII, in the thirteenth century, made the first attempt. Leo X conceived of a vast project for draining the marshes. But the work on a canal was halted in 1516, because of local fears that it would cause malaria. Sixtus V not only took up the work of the Medici pope in the area of Terracina, but planned to carry out a drainage project much further in the interior at the foot of the mountains where the water had accumulated. But the rain deluge in the winter of 1589–90 partially destroyed the hopes set on this work by flooding the drained land. So at Sixtus' death the enterprise was abandoned.

[33] Ibid., 71–72, 85–88; Sombart, *Die römische Campagna*, 48; Petrocchi, *Roma nel Seicento*, 63; De Cupis, *Vicende dell'agricoltura*, 342; Chorley, *Oil, Silk and Enlightenment*, 81; ASR, Camerale II, arti e mestieri, busta 24, fasc. 54; ASR, Camerale II, commercio e industria, busta 11, fasc. 58.

[34] Giuliano Friz, "Produzione e commercio dei vini del Lazio nei secoli XVIII e XIX," *Annales cisalpines d'histoire sociale* 3 (1972), 223.

[35] Madelin, *Rome de Napoléon*, 37–38; De Felice, *Aspetti e momenti della vita economica*, 76–79, 91; Caroselli, "Aspects of the Economic History of the *Campagna*," 595; Sombart, *Die römische Campagna*, 27; Lepre, "Agricoltura e manifattura in un rione," 354–56.

A host of plans for draining the marshes and improving the climate of the area appeared in the following two centuries. But we have to wait for the period after the famines of 1763–67 for the next serious attempts at drainage. In 1766–67 the Jesuit engineer Leonardo Ximenes advocated bringing the Tuscan Maremma back to cultivation by building drainage canals and dikes. He received the support of the new grand duke, Pietro Leopoldo. His work was only partially successful. Nevertheless the Tuscan effort stirred plans for the Pontine marshes. When Pius VI was elected pope in 1775, various Lombard and French entrepreneurs offered to carry out the scheme. The pope turned them all down, wanting the task to be performed directly by the Apostolic Chamber. As director of the drainage scheme he chose Gaetano Rappini, an hydraulic engineer from Bologna. Rappini dug a canal along the Via Appia, into which all the water from the low-lying lands was to flow and then drain into the sea. Known as the Linea Pia, it was placed like a central axis among the marshy spots, with thousands of individual ditches entering it, forming a single network.

The work was not without its setbacks, however. On 14 February 1783, a day-long torrential rainfall flooded the area which had just been dried out. The first reaction was to abandon the thankless task, but it was resumed again in April. By the time it was completed 1,475 hectares of land that had been under water at the commencement of the enterprise in 1780 had been drained; 3,300 men were employed on the project, of whom the majority came from the kingdom of Naples. Consequently the money from their wages went out of the state. As it was, the cost reached 1,621,963 scudi, a sum far in excess of that projected by Rappini and one which drove the Apostolic Chamber, already financially strained, into ever greater debt.

Viewed from another angle, Pius VI's work was but one more evidence of the inability of the ancien-regime popes to face up to the fundamental problems of the Agro Romano to which reformers had been drawing attention for most of the century. By draining the Pontine marshes Pius avoided a grave confrontation with the nobles and great ecclesiastical landowners, which would have been the inevitable outcome of any attempt to reorganize the existing Agro. Nor did it bring about the economic and social transformation of the Campagna which he hoped for. The great landholders alone benefited. In 1791, the land which had been drained was assigned to thirty long-term tenants, of which the pope's nephew Principe Luigi Onesti-Braschi received the lion's share. The rent from these tenants was not enough for the upkeep of the drainage plant. The real task of draining the Pontine marshes had to await the Mussolini regime.[36]

[36] Delumeau, *Vie économique et sociale de Rome*, 2:579–82; B.CORS., ms. 2517, no. 1; De Cupis, *Vicende dell'agricoltura*, 345–47; Giuntella, *Roma nel Settecento*, 37–40; Story, *Roba di Roma*, 374; Dufourcq, *Le régime Jacobin en Italie*, 8; Cretoni, *Roma Giacobina*, 204; Venturi, "Enlightenment in the Papal States," 254; Franco Venturi, "Quattro anni di carestia in Toscana (1764–1767)," *Rivista storica italiana*, 88 (1976), 689–94; Cochrane, *Florence in the Forgotten Centuries*, 436–37; Seregni (ed.), *Carteggio di Verri*, 11:55–56, 106; Bertoldi (ed.), *Epistolaria di Vincenzo Monti*, 1:342; Montaiglon and Guiffrey (eds.), *Correspondance des directeurs de l'Académie de France*, 14:311, 319.

As every large city, Rome enjoyed a symbiotic relationship with its immediate environs. In spite of the sparsity of its population and its desolation the Agro Romano, once the city's breadbasket, was still the most important single factor in the food supply of the capital, even though it had failed to meet its basic needs since about 1720.[37] In an age when the threat of hunger was ever present, it continued to be an integral part both of the urban economy and the dietary regime of Rome, thus inevitably assuming an importance out of proportion to its condition.

[37] Nicolai, *Memorie, leggi ed osservazioni*, 3:146.

# 7

# Food supply

"This beautiful land of the Scipios is in constant dread of dying from hunger," wrote Alessandro Verri to his brother Pietro in May 1767, near the close of a prolonged period of famine. And he was not the only outsider in ancien-regime Rome to be struck by the fear of hunger which was so widespread among the populace, and the frequency with which the pope was appealed to to increase the bread supply and reduce its price. "In Rome, if the pope is to maintain himself on the throne, he has to pacify the people by keeping bread at a constant price and holding down taxes," noted the French geographer Gabriel-François Coyer with but a modicum of exaggeration. Yet only this state of mind can explain the great lengths to which the legislation went in its concern to protect the city from hunger.[1]

There is no doubt that the papal capital enjoyed certain dietary privileges in relation to the rest of the country, a position it shared with other capitals such as Paris, Naples, Milan, and, to a lesser extent, Florence. Rome's privileges were of a dual nature. On the one hand, the regularity and quality of its food supply was always assured at the expense of the rural consumer. On the other hand, the nutritional needs and dietary preferences of the urban population determined the profitability of production, especially in the large holdings of the Campagna and Lazio.

At the start of the seventeenth century, the system of the Roman annona was still able to ensure the provisioning of the city at the highest level, at least for the principal items of food. It guaranteed a more than adequate supply of wine and meat. But as the population became more numerous and its purchasing power diminished, the authorities were compelled to intervene in market conditions: to limit profits through price regulations, reduce the opportunities for exporting commodities, and, finally, to assume the role of economic partner, with the financial organs of the state providing the means. In "freezing" the market by giving priority to the annual regularity of the supply rather than the quantity of production, it assuredly contributed to the inertia in agricultural production which we saw in the previous chapter.[2]

1 Seregni (ed.), *Carteggio di Verri*, 1:375; Gabriel-François Coyer, *Voyage d'Italie e de Hollande* (2 vols.; Paris, 1775), 2:170; Giuntella, *Roma nel Settecento*, 30–31.

2 Revel, "Les privilèges d'une capitale," 564, 572; Büchi, *Finanzen und Finanzpolitik Toskanas*, 167; Chorley, *Oil, Silk and Enlightenment*, 60; Grab, "Politics of Subsistence," 197; Steven L. Kaplan,

In 1766 it was estimated that one person in Rome consumed on the average one rubbio of grain a year, that is, 2.944 hectoliters, as compared to 2.768 hl in Naples, c. 2.75 hl in Bologna, and 2.93 hl in Florence; that quantity included rye and other sorts of cereal, but consisted mainly of wheat. For since the triumph of the large estates in the late fourteenth century wheat had established its dominance over all other forms of grain. If we exclude oats, which was reserved for animals even in times of crisis, secondary cereals represented between 5 percent and 8 percent of the supplies for Rome and its immediate surroundings. Wheat's predominance was so well established in public taste that it blocked any significant production of rice and corn in the region until 1830. The wheat which was eaten in the form of bread was the soft and delicate kind, which provided a whiter meal and was easier to mill into flour, although it did not travel or store well. In contrast to Naples, where pasta represented 50 to 60 percent of the cereal food in the eighteenth century, the latter was still something of a luxury dish in Rome; vermicelli cost double the price of bread in 1700. Consumed on its own or accompanied with some other food or used to thicken the soup, bread was the staple item of food.[3]

In gathering statistics, the *congregazione del Sollievo* of 1701 put the annual consumption of milled grain at 132,000 rubbia (338,608 hl or 286,440 quintals). From July to the following June, being the year upon which figures of grain supply are based, the amount of grain entering the city in 1697/98 came to 130,283 rubbia and in 1698/99 to another 142,041.5 rubbia. That year, in retrospect, appears to have been a rather large one. The figure for grain that was actually milled in Rome itself, which is obviously more modest, hardly reached 120,000 rubbia. But it began to rise steadily, if unevenly, with the growing population, according to figures given by Nicolai. In 1735 the amount came to 129,869 rubbia, in 1745 to 136,341 rubbia, in 1751 to 141,118 rubbia, and in 1764, during the great famine, it reached the exceptional figure of 146,025 rubbia. The 1764 figure, which comes to 437,209 hl,

*Bread, Politics and Political Economy in the Reign of Louis XV* (2 vols; The Hague, 1976), 1:36. In Bologna, in contrast to Rome, the city had no fully organized annona, but the money necessary for obtaining grain was arranged by some members of the senate, who formed an ad hoc *assunteria di abbondanza*, through borrowing against their personal guarantee. Alberto Guenzi, "Sistema annonario e controllo sociale a Bologna nei secoli XVII e XVIII," in Ercole Sori (ed.), *Città e controllo sociale in Italia tra XVIII e XIX secolo* (Milan, 1982), 295–98; Dal Pane, *Economia e società a Bologna*, 37, 441.

3 The rubbio is a measure of capacity, not weight. It is therefore very difficult to convert into weight; according to an annona document of 1648, the lightest grain, that of Danzig, contained 570 libbre ($192\frac{1}{2}$ kg) to the rubbio and the heaviest grain, that from the area around Rome, weighed 700 libbre (237 kg) per rubbio. Tomassetti put the rubbio at 217 kg. Because of these discrepancies I shall refrain from giving weights unless my sources give them. However, there are also differences in giving the metric equivalents to capacity measures. Delumeau gave the rubbio 2.3 hl as an approximation, whereas the more common assumption is 2.944 hl. Delumeau, *Vie économique et sociale de Rome*, 1:122–23; Ronald Edward Zupko, *Italian Weights and Measures from the Middle Ages to the Nineteenth Century* (Philadelphia, 1981), 232, 291; Friz, *Consumi, tenore di vita e prezzi*, 57, 63–64; Franco Venturi, "Napoli nell'anno della fame," 395–96 n. 7; Guenzi, "Sistema annonario e controllo sociale a Bologna," 293–94; Carla Penuti, "Carestie ed epidemie," in Aldo Berselli (ed.), *Storia della Emilia Romagna* (Bologna, 1977), 195.

compares roughly to the Neapolitan grain supply of 1,106,000 hl in the late 1760s for a population more than double.[4] Yet in the decade between 1780 and 1790, when the effects of the 1783 cadaster to raise production should have been felt, the annual average only comes to 125,021 rubbia with a maximum of 137,083.065 rubbia in 1782/83. Obviously the great famine of 1764/67 had taken its toll.

In relation to the needs of the capital the production in the region around Rome subject to the annona appeared barely sufficient. This area, we pointed out in the last chapter, was divided between the Agro and the more extensive distretto. From the point of view of grain production, this distinction was based on the fact that the former was generally given to speculative exploitation, whereas the latter, forming a circle from Viterbo to the basin of the Rieti and the frontiers of Naples, was sprinkled with villages, which kept back a significant part for their own consumption. According to the records of the *Sollievo*, which must be treated with reserve, the Agro supplied 139,587 rubbia of grain for Rome in 1699 and 133,113 in 1700, which was its total output after subtracting what was needed for the following year's sowing. But there was clearly a progressive deterioration in the availability of wheat in the course of the century. Nevertheless, on the assumption that there was a total mobility of cereals from the Agro and the distretto to the city, a rough equilibrium between consumption and production existed as late as between 1743 and 1753, with a possible deficit of an insigificant 1,200 rubbia at times. This assumption does not take into consideration, however, private and public stockpiling, legal or illegal exportation, nor other losses. Surely with such a narrow safety margin, the peasants and the provincial communities would try to build up reserves of their own and the middlemen, at all levels, would forestall the grain in expectation of a price rise or wait for a market where they could multiply their gain. No wonder that in nine out of ten years between 1744/45 and 1752/53 the accounts of the Roman annona were to show that it had to bring in from outside of its jurisdiction, especially from the Marches, on the average more than 9,000 rubbia.[5]

The system of the annona, which handled the greater proportion of the grain supply for the papal capital, was one that Rome shared with most Italian and some other cities, although it was probably more highly organized and centralized than in most. At first the provisioning of the city had been a municipal function in the hands of the conservators, as was still the case in Naples, Florence, Bologna, and even Milan as late as the second half of the eighteenth century. But in Rome we note a progressive

[4] Nicolai, *Memorie, leggi ed osservazioni*, 3:142–45; Dal Pane, *Lo Stato Pontificio e il movimento riformatore*, 572; Tournon, *Etudes statistiques sur Rome*, 2:24.

[5] Revel, "Les privilèges d'une capitale," 565; Revel, "Le grain de Rome," 226–28, 254–56 n. 4; ASR, Congregazione del Sollievo, vol. 1; Alberto Caracciolo, *Le port-franc d'Ancône. Croissance et impasse d'un milieu marchand au XVIIIe siècle* (Paris, 1966), 183 n. 2; ASR, Camerale II, arti e mestieri, busta 40, fasc. 87; BAV, Cod. Barberini lat. 5056, relazione . . . annona, 1724; Dal Pane, "Discussioni e leggi annonarie in Roma," 1191–92; Dal Pane, *Lo Stato Pontificio e il movimento riformatore*, 559–61; De Cupis, *Vicende dell'agricoltura nell'Agro Romano*, 333.

elimination of all municipal magistrates in favor of papal functionaries under the authority of the cardinal camerlengo. In the fifteenth century the camerlengo devolved his responsibility for the capital's grain supply to a chierico of the Apostolic Chamber, who in 1512 took the title of prefect of the annona. In 1557, a directive of Paul IV gave the prefect sole responsibility for provisioning the city with wide powers to perform his duties. In theory, the full jurisdiction of the prefect extended only over the Agro Romano and the contiguous areas of the Patrimony of St. Peter, the Campagna, Marittima, and the Sabina. But in practice the prefect of the annona had from the beginning a qualified right of control and intervention in all matters of grain policy throughout the Papal States.

The links between the policy of the annona and the agricultural policy of the state were much more deeply and durably marked in Rome than elsewhere. Because of the retreat of cultivation in the Campagna in the face of pasture, the annona could not confine itself simply to counting and requisitioning the available supply; it had to legislate on production. The popes, anxious for administrative efficiency, but also increasingly concerned for the growing needs of Rome, provided the annona with the instruments which it needed. In 1572 the tribunal of the annona was established. At the side of the prefect, it was charged with applying the legislation, setting the official prices after the harvest and collecting quantitative data on the yield, while penalizing breaches of the law. Like the majority of the tribunals set up in Rome, it was both an organ of arbitration and an administrative machinery to help the prefect.[6]

The inventory and the mobilization at any given moment of disposable grain was the first, and oldest, function of the annona. To intervene effectively in the distribution, the state had to know with as much precision as possible existing quantities, so that it could tap them for the urban markets. Unlike Florence, where the annonary system was dismantled between the end of the famine in 1767 and 1783 because it subordinated unfairly the welfare of the Tuscan peasantry to the interests of the capital, in Rome the requisition continued to be strictly regulated until the end of the eighteenth century. Every grower of grain had to report to a fiscal or other government official how much grain he had sown. Immediately after threshing, the grower, furnished with a special document issued by the annona, the *assegna*, would have to take his grain to a specified locality, usually inside Rome, within a stipulated time, leaving behind only enough to feed his household for four months.[7]

Closely linked to the recording of available stocks was the organization of the distribution of grain in Rome. It was not enough to direct the cereal to Rome; it still needed the public authority to control the function of the urban market and to

[6] Revel, "Le grain de Rome," 201, 205–208, 281; Nicolai, *Memorie, leggi ed osservazioni*, 3: 63; Chorley, *Oil, Silk and Enlightenment*, 60; Büchi, *Finanzen und Finanzpolitik Toskanas*, 33; Grab, "Politics of Subsistence," 197; Delumeau, *Vie économique et sociale de Rome*, 2: 598–600; Lalande, *Voyage d'un françois en Italie*, 5: 22. [7] Nicolai, *Memorie, leggi ed osservazioni*, 3: 99.

secure its regularity independently of the variations of production, in order to minimize the effects of fluctuations on the consumers. To do this, the annona controlled the stocks, the prices, and the retail market.

For the purpose of controlling the stability of the bread market, the annona possessed two complementary means. The first was that of fixing the maximum price (*calmiere*) annually. That took place generally in September, based on the price current at the annona's official retail outlet for grain during the first eight or ten weeks of the harvest year. It was thus an arbitrary price, but also a reflection of the market at a point when one could reasonably evaluate the results of the season which had just ended. However, since the principal concern of the annona was always the urban consumer and his need for daily bread, the price was normally tilted in his favor. Such prices threatened to attenuate the profits which producers and middlemen were expecting. Hence the archives of the camerlengo and the publicistic literature are full of complaints from *mercanti di campagna* and bakers, who, with figures to support their case, evaluated the losses which they sustained from the action of the annona.

The second available means was that of stockpiling in Rome. As early as 1575 Gregory XIII built very large granaries at the Baths of Diocletian for public storage. For the same purpose he also constructed many warehouses at the ports. Urban VIII was to enlarge the depot at the Baths and Clement XI added another warehouse. But the grain would only keep for two years in these depots. Hence a congregation at the time of Benedict XIII limited the public reserves to 30,000 rubbia (88,320 hl or 65,100 quintals); but the measure had little effect.[8]

For the period of 1744 to 1785, excepting in moments of emergency during the great famine of 1762–67, the available reserves of grain of the annona were always greater than the annual needs. This flexibility reflects a certain effectiveness of the machinery of the annona. In an average year, it could secure supplies of between 150,000 and 190,000 rubbia (441,600 to 559,260 hl or 325,500 to 412,300 quintals), in which sum the remainder of the previous year is included. But, beginning from 1785, and especially after 1790, the cushion between consumption and reserves began to decline visibly.[9]

For its grain supply the annona counted in the first place upon its own countryside. There its powers were real and its network of representatives well established. Next it called upon the surplus from the rest of the Papal States, beginning with the rich grain lands of Montalto and Castro. But they were not an absolutely sure solution, since the lands were subject to the same climatic vagaries as the regions of the annona. Beyond these districts were a collection of impoverished

[8] Ibid., 2: no. 17, 3:102–103; Petrocchi, *Roma nel Seicento*, 33; De Cupis, *Vicende dell'agricoltura nell'Agro Romano*, 294; Revel, "Le grain de Rome," 217 n. 1.

[9] Revel, "Le grain de Rome," 208–22, 239–41, 246, 258–62; Revel, "Les privilèges d'une capitale," 565; Dal Pane, *Lo Stato Pontificio e il movimento riformatore*, 580–85; A.Cap.R., no. 7, cred. VII, editti e bandi, 123, 128; Lanciani, *Storia degli scavi*, 4:80.

lands, the northern Abruzzi, the upper Sabina, and Umbria, which themselves had regular deficits. They came between Rome and the productive provinces on the Adriatic coast. One of these, the Romagna, it is true, tended to look rather to Ferrara and Bologna, and even Venice, for its grain exports. But in a crisis it would help Rome with any excess. On the other hand, the Marches of Ancona made up an enormous area with almost always a surplus, in spite of a probable contraction of the area cultivated since the seventeenth century. The yield there was actually mediocre, four or five grains to one seed, but a fairly small population in relation to cultivation left an exportable surplus fluctuating between 30,000 and 70,000 rubbia according to the type of year. It was enough to make them the granary of a poor state.

Outside the provinces of the annona the mobilization of grain for the benefit of Rome posed difficult problems, a witness to the persistent tension between the capital and the periphery. In these cases the annona resorted to a special representative with farreaching powers, perhaps a great merchant. The demands of Rome were always an opportunity for intense speculation in these northern provinces. As soon as rumors of a bad harvest in the Roman Campagna reached them, the grain disappeared from sight and the price rose. The selfish concern for the food supply of Rome was enough to plunge the provinces into hunger. It must be admitted, however, that this preference for the welfare of the capital at the expense of the rural population was an inherent defect of the annonary system at large, which the Papal States shared with their neighbors in Naples and Tuscany.

Once loaded, the grain could be brought to Rome from the Marches either overland by way of the Tiber or by sea. The latter was much cheaper. The cost of transportation of a shipment by sea in 1754/55 came to 33.83 percent of the initial cost of the grain, whereas the transportation cost overland by carriage and by river down to Rome amounted to more than 116 percent of the initial cost of grain. Although the most convenient and cheapest form of transportation would, therefore, have been by sea, yet the most frequent route taken was that by way of land and river. Between 1720 and 1780, as against 127,000 rubbia (378,888 hl or 275,590 quintals) of grain imported to Rome by sea, more than 829,000 rubbia (2,444,576 hl or 1,798,930 quintals) were brought overland. Some of the reasons advanced for the preference of the land route in spite of the higher costs were such perils of maritime transportation as inclement weather, threats of corsairs, and the frequent seizures made by the authorities of the kingdom of Naples when they themselves were in periods of difficulty and for which they paid ridiculously small indemnities.[10]

The purchases of wheat from abroad made up only 10 percent of the total supply

[10] Revel, "Le grain de Rome," 228–32, 235 n. 1; Bertoldi (ed.), *Epistolario di Monti*, 354; Chorley, *Oil, Silk and Enlightenment*, 60; Büchi, *Finanzen und Finanzpolitik Toskanas*, 32–33; Mira, "Note sui trasporti fluviali nell'economia dello Stato Pontificio," 30–33; Nicolai, *Memorie, leggi ed osservazioni*, 3:147; Delumeau, *Vie économique et sociale de Rome*, 2:626, 630–31.

for the period of 1744–97. These, too, were made as close as possible to Rome, usually in the ports of the Tyrrhenian coast, particularly the Tuscan port of Livorno. Supplies from Sicily, once the granary of Italy, had dried up after 1605. Only as a last resort would the annona turn to buying grain from places abroad. It was a hazardous solution. Everything contributed to making a purchase abroad a perilous venture: the absence of commercial expertise in the Papal States, a defective knowledge of the European market, the inevitable recourse to the services of great merchants, whose operations were often not trustworthy, purchase on a sample of the merchandise. Rome, beside having little or nothing to offer in return, would be subjected to the laws of the suppliers who knew how to profit from its emergency. Without fail, these undertakings ended up in financial disaster and sometimes scandal. The most important consignment of grain from northern Europe, quantitatively speaking, was only a temporary measure. During the famine of 1766–68, the annona bought in London, Dunkirk, Amsterdam, and Brussels.[11]

While supervising the supply of grain, the annona was not its major dealer in normal times. From a commercial point of view the direct sales of grain by merchants represented the most important sector. In an average year they made up 70 to 80 percent of the grain transactions that took place in Rome. This proportion only diminished appreciably when a critical situation compelled the annona to intervene forcibly in the market by freeing a part of its own reserves. In short, the annona primarily used the grain from its own warehouses to stabilize the market.

As was customary in annonary systems elsewhere in Italy, a certain amount of these reserves was sold by the Roman annona at a fixed price to the bakers every year. Around 1750 this amount came to between 20,000 and 30,000 rubbia (between 58,880 hl or 43,400 quintals and 88,320 hl or 65,100 quintals), which compared favorably with the 110,000 to 120,000 tomoli (60,830 to 66,000 hl) reserved in Naples. The annona tried to keep the price unaffected by seasonal fluctuations. In the years 1754 to 1758 it succeeded in maintaining that price at around 7 scudi the rubbio, first fixed toward 1740 on the then real market value. Certainly this was a costly policy, but had the advantage of permitting a relative stabilization of the *pagnotta a baiocco*, the staple loaf for the masses, by removing the bakers from the movement of the market.

The guild of bakers, *università dei fornari*, retained the monopoly of making and selling bread. Its monopoly extended beyond bread to the sale of flour, only limited by the one retail outlet at the Campo dei Fiori run by the annona itself, accounting for about 6.86 percent of the total sales between 1754 and 1758. Belatedly organized as a guild and granted their statutes in 1552, the bakers were almost from the beginning enmeshed in a web of annonary regulations. In return for the privilege of supplying about three-quarters of the urban consumption, their making and selling of bread was strictly controlled. The quality, weight, and price of bread was

[11] Ibid., 2:637–39; Revel, "Le grain de Rome," 232–34, 240–41.

regulated by the *tariffa perpetua per li fornari di Roma*, instituted by Paul V in 1605. It was a kind of sliding scale intended to establish a fixed ratio between the price of grain on the market and the weight of the loaf (*pagnotta*) of common bread, while the unitary price of one baiocco for the *pagnotta* remained unchanged.[12]

Although the *tariffa* foresaw a wide variation in its sliding scale of both the grain price (4 to 20 scudi per rubbio) and the corresponding weight (from 15 to 3 oncie, that is, from 4.25 to 0.85 kg the *pagnotta*), the annona in the eighteenth century tried to avoid gambling with this possibility and clung as much as possible to the normal weight of 8 oncie (2.26 kg) for the *pagnotta*, which corresponded to a price of 7.50 scudi for a rubbio of wheat. The system of a sliding scale, however, was confined to the common or "brown" bread, which made up four-fifths of the total production of the bakeries; the luxury bread could be sold freely at the market price.

Whereas the 1766 estimate for the annual consumption of one rubbio of grain per person in Rome, mentioned at the start of the chapter, was a reasonable average, a more careful calculation made available to each mouth only close on 0.9 rubbio. These theoretical calculations, however, do not take into account the differences in the distribution of grain by socioeconomic groups.[13]

Rome experienced grain shortages intermittently during the earlier decades of the ancien regime whenever there were bad harvests, but the authorities were generally able to cope with the situation. There were famines in 1718, when hungry people crowded into the city from outside, and under Benedict XIV in 1747, and again in 1758–59. But none could compare to the serious situation that confronted Clement XIII in 1763/64, when a great drought hit all of Italy and especially the central and southern regions. It was this calamity that bared the defects of the whole agrarian structure, not only of Rome and the Papal States, but their neighbors in Naples and Tuscany, and was to test the traditional institution of the annona as far north as Lombardy.[14]

Actually, Rome, in contrast to the area immediately surrounding it, was able to weather the first crisis of 1763 fairly well. However, the city became the epicenter of the disaster in the early months of 1764. Outsiders crowded in to buy up available grain to take home and so prevented citizens from getting bread. For not only did papal subjects suffer, but by 1764 the first symptoms of insufficiency in the kingdom to the south and in Tuscany drove people to the papal capital. They rushed to the

[12] Nicolai, *Memorie, leggi ed osservazioni*, 2:57.

[13] Revel, "Le grain de Rome," 215–16, 251 n. 1; 262–63, 273; Revel, "Les privilèges d'une capitale," 566; Bianchini, *Storia delle finanze di Napoli*, 3:333–34; Dal Pane, *Lo Stato Pontificio et il movimento riformatore*, 585–86; De Cupis, *Vicende dell'agricoltura nell'Agro Romano*, 296; Seregni (ed.), *Carteggio di Verri*, 12:388; ASR, Camerale II, arti e mestieri, busta 16, ff. 183–89; ASR, Congregazione del Sollievo, vol. 1; Petrocchi, *Roma nel Seicento*, 31.

[14] Nicolai, *Memorie, leggi ed osservazioni*, 2:77, 3:100–1 (mistakenly numbered 200–1), 126; Giuntella, *Roma nel Settecento*, 4–5; Pastor, *Geschichte der Päpste*, 15:392; 16, pt 1:463; ASR, Camerale II, arti e mestieri, busta 16, f. 184; A.Cap.R., no. 95, cred. VII, 18; Corridore, *La popolazione dello Stato Romano*, 24–25.

granaries at the Baths of Diocletian to provide for themselves and fill the many Neapolitan lateen boats that had sailed up the Tiber. At first the authorities tried to stop this drain by raising prices. The measure was ineffective and the granaries had to be closed. Not only flour, but loaves of bread were taken out of the city. On 22 March the weight of the *pagnotta a baiocco* had to be reduced and the export of bread prohibited. At the end of the month a start was made with the rationing of bread; but the needed force and energy was wanting for it to be implemented properly. On 4 April, an inventory of grain, flour, and bread available in Rome established that the supplies were scarcely enough for a month, the more so that the number of "foreigners" may have increased to as many as 26,000 in spite of the growing surveillance at the city gates.

The papal authorities, only with the greatest reluctance, resolved to have recourse to the international market when it became clear that the internal process of supply and the mechanism of the annona had come to a halt. They now put the matter in the hands of wholesale merchants, often difficult to control. The conditions in the Mediterranean as a whole were reflected on the market. The papal commissioners charged to procure grain in Livorno, Genoa, Marseilles, Nice, and elsewhere soon confronted the violent rivalries and the commercial speculations rampant in such a year of shortages. Livorno became the center of growing competition for provisions, where Rome, Naples, and Tuscany all tried to appropriate for themselves grain, using all means, fair and foul, including commandeering ships and seizing cargo. From France Cardinal Secretary of State Torrigiani was informed that the papal request had come too late, all the available grain had already been assigned to Naples. This decision by the government in Paris was probably influenced by their opposition to what they viewed as the favorable policy of Clement XIII toward the Jesuits. A great sigh of relief was given when the Sardinian ruler, Charles Emmanuel III, agreed to export about 8,000 sacks from Piedmont. But there were difficulties with the Genoese in bringing the consignment to Civitavecchia. At last, at the end of April, there arrived when least expected a number of boats with grain, some commissioned, others at random. By 15 May, there were thirty ships in all. The international market had finally come to the pope's rescue. But the grain had to be paid for.

In the late spring and summer of 1764, a new famine occurred, which was no longer centered on Rome, but it brought a deluge of requests to the capital from the hungry local communities. Fortunately the year 1764–65 was less bad than feared. The areas of the annona produced almost 100,000 rubbia (294,000 hl or 217,000 quintals) of grain more than in the preceding year. Besides, a hitherto new and unexpected way of importing grain opened up from northern Europe: 33,117 rubbia of grain at the moderate price of 9 scudi were purchased in Brussels, followed by consignments obtained at the markets of London, Amsterdam, and Dunkirk; in the case of Amsterdam, the first since 1649. The debt continued to increase, but 1764–65 passed as a period of relative calm between two storms.

By July 1965 rumors of another bad harvest began to circulate insistently. The continuous rains, which fell all over central Italy and did not show any signs of abating even during the spring, produced floods and disasters everywhere. It was the start of the famine of 1765–67, which for the Papal States and Tuscany was worse than that of 1764. By the end of July 1766, the weight of bread had to be further reduced and the bakeries made it of such bad quality that a group of women at the Quirinal shouted protests at the pope. At the close of the summer, however, grain from Apulia, where the situation was not as serious as in Rome, and eventually from northern Europe began to arrive. Thanks once again to the international market, the year 1766–67 was not as bad as had been feared. But it was only in July 1767 that the gazettes could heave a sigh of relief; for the anniversary of Clement XIII's coronation a considerable increase in the weight of the loaf of bread was announced.

This was not to be the last crisis in ancien-regime Rome. In 1771–74 there were some food riots in the city. Alessandro Verri informed his brother that he was unable to obtain the most essential articles of consumption for himself. There was a 6-month drought in 1779, raising the price of wheat to 12 scudi. Another frightful famine occurred in 1779–83, and again in 1793 on the eve of the French Revolutionary threat to the very existence of the Papal States. But the 1763–67 crisis marked a turning point.[15]

If the annona was able to overcome the famines of the 1760s, albeit with difficulties, the price paid for this effort was clearly a growing one. Between 1765 and 1766 money became very scarce in the city and the foreign exchange rate had fallen unfavorably, while bankruptcies multiplied. In December 1765, Rome lost 3 percent on its commercial transactions with the kingdom of Naples, which itself had suffered greatly from the famine of 1764/65 and whose annona, too, was beginning to lose money.

What was even more unfortunate, following the catastrophe of the 1760s, Rome was organically incapable of carrying through, or lacked the energy to carry through, the needed reforms with any rigor. The crisis called the effectiveness of the annonary system in question. Physiocrats and some reforming ministers in Europe began to advocate lifting the old restrictions. In neighboring Tuscany, Grand Duke Pietro Leopoldo abolished the *abbondanza* in 1767, thereby doing away with the dietary primacy of Florence, after free trade in grain had already been introduced. The experience of the famine in Rome, however, produced the opposite response. The papal government, which as early as 1748, under Benedict XIV, had experimented with internal free trade and would do so again under Pius VI in areas

[15] Venturi, "Roma negli anni della fame," 514–26, 530–35; Venturi, "Quattro anni di carestia in Toscana," 649–50, 672–79; Venturi, "Napoli nell'anno della fame," 464–66; Revel, "Le grain de Rome," 243; Madelin, *Rome de Napoléon*, 105 n. 2; La Marca, *Saggio di una ricerca storico-economica*, 95; Bertoldi (ed.), *Epistolario di Monti*, 1:63, 66; B.CAS, ms. vol. 3815; Petrocchi, *Roma nel Seicento*, 33–34.

outside the jurisdiction of the annona, decided to maintain and further consolidate the annonary system, convinced that the true problem of the state was not one of grain production but of consumption, that is, of feeding Rome. Indeed, the motive for the cadaster of 1783 for the Agro Romano, treated in the previous chapter, only confirmed this preoccupation. In this respect the Roman attitude resembled that of Naples, where the chief minister Bernardo Tanucci, in the face of the views expressed by more enlightened writers, Antonio Genovesi among them, persisted in retaining the Neapolitan annona and resisted the introduction of free trade.[16]

A brief comparison with the Parisian experience is of some interest here. Like Rome, Paris enjoyed a privileged position in the competition for subsistence and for the same reason; but, in contrast to the papal capital, it possessed no special organ akin to the annona. Nonetheless the Parisian police under the paternal eye of the secretary of the royal household comprehended the surveillance of grain supply and bread prices under its overall charge of preserving public tranquillity. Only merchants accredited by the lieutenant-general of police could deliver grain to the urban market. Paris did not suffer a famine in 1764. However, in May 1763, the French government liberalized the grain trade. Although, like Rome, Paris was not covered by the legislation, the French capital by implication lost its special status. Fear of a breakdown of the traditional regulatory apparatus and familiar trading patterns emerged. Hence, behind the facade of a semi-private company, an official reserve of grain was maintained in the hope of improving the city's subsistence. The experiment would fail when eventually famine struck Paris in 1768. In November of that year the lieutenant general of police for the first time had to impose a price ceiling on bread, which the rapidly improving situation would fortunately make soon unnecessary. The effort to impose a permanent sliding scale of bread prices, one somewhat similar to Rome's, foundered on the resistance of the bakers. In 1770 the government capitulated and abandoned its experiment at liberalization.[17]

Paris, like Rome, persisted in the old ways, except that the more fearsome experience of Rome led its annona into increasing activities and interventions in the last third of the eighteenth century, which eventuated in a financial crisis. The annona's fiscal assets were ridiculously small, almost wholly invested in administration buildings and warehouses, with a small portfolio of quickly diminishing *luoghi di monte*, the whole amounting in 1745 to a fixed capital of 250,922 scudi. In

16 Venturi, "Roma negli anni della fame," 536–37, 540; Revel, "Le grain de Rome," 204–5, 209–10 n. 12; Venturi, "Enlightenment in the Papal States," 235–37; Venturi, "Quattro anni di carestia in Toscana," 699–707; Büchi, *Finanzen und Finanzpolitik Toskanas*, 148–67; Grab, "Politics of Subsistence," 185, 192–93; Venturi, "Napoli nell'anno della fame," 439–51; Venturi, *Settecento riformatore*, 1:108–9; Bianchini, *Della storia delle finanze di Napoli*, 331–41, 349, 541; Silvagni, *La corte pontificia*, 1:131, 332 n. 149; BAV, Cod. Barberini lat. 5056, relazione . . . annona, 1724; BL, Add. mss. 8467, Relazione sullo stato dell'annona, ff. 1, 2, 13; ASR, Camerale II, annona, discorsi e studi, busta 1: De Cupis, *Vicende dell'agricoltura nell'Agro Romano*, 299–301, 331–33, 344–45; Dal Pane, *Lo Stato Pontificio e il movimento riformatore*, 200–1.

17 Kaplan, *Bread, Politics and Political Economy*, 1; xxvi–xxviii, 6, 18–20, 33, 66–67, 300–1, 310–12, 329–38, 359, 406.

addition, it received revenues from some taxes. The imposts on the middlemen were increased during the second half of the century, and the Apostolic Chamber granted the annona a little from its own revenues. Its financial resources expanded thus from an annual average of 54,426 scudi in 1744–48 to 93,520 scudi in 1791–95. This doubling hardly measured up to the new demands. To meet the difference the logic of the system required that the annona cover deficits from the profits of the previous financial years. Yet it was precisely this equilibrium that was thrown out of gear in the 1760s. Until the crisis of 1763 the annona was successful in maintaining a surplus of about 400,000 scudi. From then on until the end of the century all its balance sheets were in the red. However, until 1779, in spite of the famine of 1772/73, when the annona intervened massively, the deficit remained stable, between 700,000 and 800,000 scudi. It was on the occasion of the five uninterrupted years of hardship from 1779 to 1783 that its financial shipwreck became pronounced, until it reached dizzying proportions by 1794. Between 1776 and 1782, 499,979.325 scudi derived from emergency issues of *luoghi di monte* were used to prop up the annona. Nevertheless the debt rose to 3,293,865.855 scudi by 1797. Almost certainly the paper inflation of 1792–97 contributed to swell that amount artificially. A document of 1805 announced that the arrears of the annona, by then abolished, had risen to more than 200,000 scudi in interest payments alone. Its financial autonomy had become no more than a fiction in the face of a bankruptcy that had engulfed the finances of the entire Roman state.

The financial disarray of the annona was accompanied by an administrative disorganization. The failure of the administration became evident after 1780, only to be complete in the 1790s. The arrears of debts to the suppliers accumulated, while the accounts of its commissioners showed enormous delays. Two, three, even four years would pass between the arrival of grain in the warehouses of the annona and the remittance of payment for these accounts. Certainly, the food supply continued to be sufficiently safeguarded as far as the quantities are concerned. But this security was dearly paid for, for the annona no longer had the technical means to oversee the modalities. In 1800, the old system of the annona was abandoned and, by a decree of 2 September was replaced by a new deputation of the annona. On the advice of the lawyers of the Apostolic Chamber, the old annona filed for bankruptcy in 1805. Its financial debacle may be explained by its effort to maintain a rigid and basically anti-economic system in the face of accelerated seasonal changes. But from a broader perspective the annona fell victim to the whole political and economic dissonance of the Papal States, the general financial dilemma, the inability to improve the economy permanently and the failure of the 1783 cadaster to increase grain production in the Agro.[18]

[18] Revel, "Le grain de Rome," 203, 238–39, 267, 271–76; Nicolai, *Memorie, leggi ed osservazioni*, 3: 130, 153, 156–67; ASR, Camerale II, zecca, busta 43, fasc. 125.

But the Romans did not live by bread alone. They also had a strong preference for fresh meat, just as they had for wheat bread; and that preference extended to all classes. The price the urban poor paid to consume fresh meat was to select their items carefully, whether it was that of old animals or less valuable parts, such as intestines, lungs, and feet, whose taste was redeemed by the way they prepared the dishes and the spices they added. Salted meat was consumed principally by the rural poor.

Although beef was the preferred kind of meat, usually constituting well over half of the available ration, in contrast to Bologna where pork was the favored meat,[19] the consumption of different types of meat by the Romans was ultimately determined, not so much by price or preference, but by the seasonal restrictions on slaughtering imposed by the grascia. From the feast of St. John (24 June) to the carnival of the following year, the slaughter of cattle was authorized. From November to Maundy Thursday hogs could be killed. Finally, from Easter to 23 June, the period was exclusively reserved for sheep. The result was that only from November to January could there be found two kinds of meat, beef and pork, on the market, while for the rest only one type of meat was offered. Due to the inadequacy of the available sheep after 1750, there was a tendency to enlarge the number of special permits granted for slaughtering beef during the so-called *stagione dell'agnellatura*.

The ideal the Roman authorities set themselves was to provide one libbra (0.339 kg) of meat daily per head. That would have come to about 84.75 kg annually, excluding fast days. This was the ration foreseen in prison. Of course, such a high target was out of reach. Nevertheless, with the available archival records it is possible for some groups of years, starting in the middle of the sixteenth century, to follow the number of animals killed annually in the slaughterhouses of Rome. The slaughterhouse tax, known as the *scannatura*, for which these records form the basis, was in theory imposed on the weight of the meat sold; however, since the start of the seventeenth century the custom was to assign to each type of animal a fixed median weight. But the butchers accused the grascia of deliberately and consistently overestimating this median weight for fiscal purposes.

The French historian Jacques Revel has worked out the average annual ration of meat available per head, using the raw data supplied by these fiscal documents. Since this procedure is rather rough, the figures should be regarded as no more than orders of magnitude (in kilograms):[20]

[19] Friz, *Consumi, tenore di vita e prezzi*, 66, 78–80; Dal Pane, *Economia e società a Bologna*, 41–44.

[20] Revel, "Les privilèges d'une capitale," 568–69; D'Amelia, "La crisi di un mercato protetto," 496, 503 n. 1. Friz gives a lower estimate for the annual availability of meat at 15 to 19 kg. Friz, *Consumi, tenore di vita e prezzi*, 76, 80. For the weekly lists of cattle and sheep brought to the Campo Vaccino and the animals slaughtered in Rome, taken from the lists of the *gabella di scannatura della dogana della grascia*, see ASR, Camerale II, grascia. For the list of prices see, among others, A.Cap.R., no. 94, armadio XXIV, libri delli prezzi delle carne.

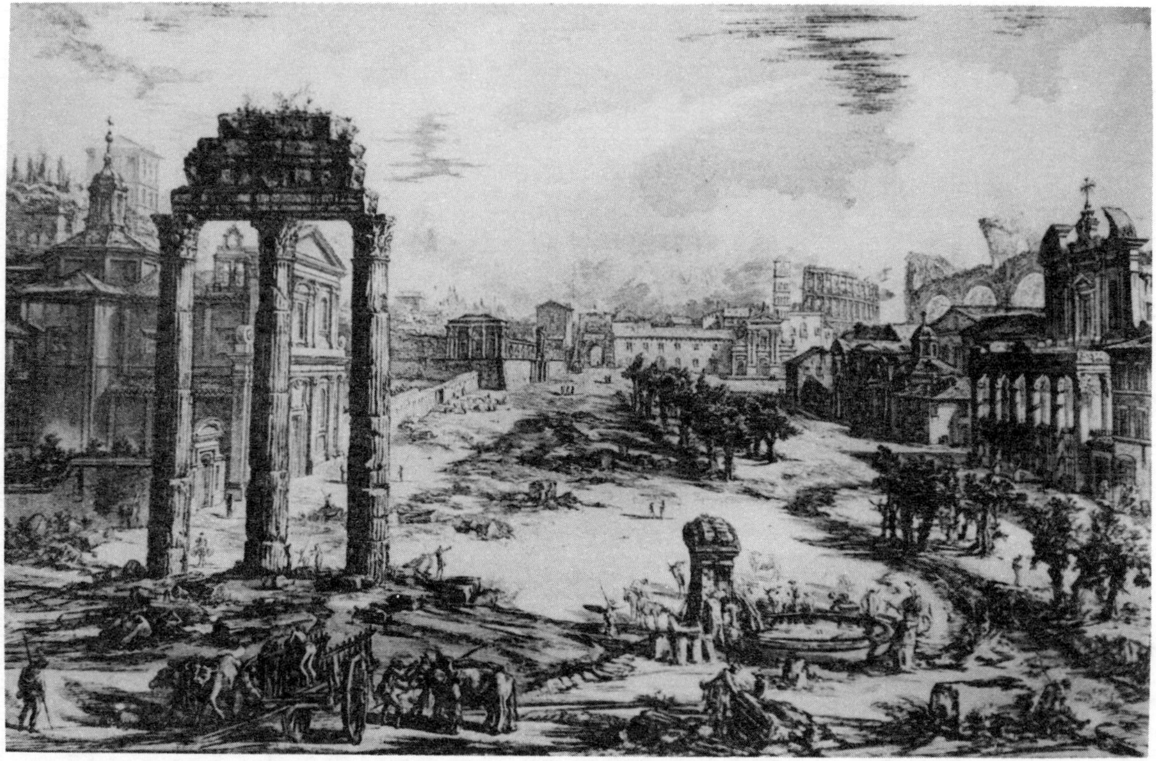

5 The Old Forum, Rome's cattle market, by Giovanni Battista Piranesi

| | |
|---|---|
| 1600–1605 | 38.3 |
| 1655–1660 | 31.4 |
| 1700–1704 | 29.4–32.3 |
| 1757–1762 | 24.4–28.1 |
| 1785–1789 | 21.5–24.7 |

Although far from ideal, the years of the seventeenth century appear to have marked the optimum in meat consumption. Delumeau has calculated that, at the close of the sixteenth century, each Roman consumed annually about three-quarters of a lamb, one-fifth of a sheep, one-fifth of a pig, one-seventh of a head of cattle, and one-seventh of a calf. Even if the animals may have been more scraggy than nowadays, the consumption of meat seems singularly large for the times.

We will note, however, a gradual recession in the dietary regime, which reached its lowest point in the middle of the nineteenth century. Between 1600 and 1800 the average ration of meat per head fell almost by half. Until the end of the sixteenth century the number of animals slaughtered had followed without difficulty the demographic growth of Rome. During the whole of the seventeenth century the supply stayed on the level it had reached, while the population of Rome grew by about 30 percent. However, as in the case of grain, it is a fact that the meat ration, which started off very generously, ended after a somewhat steep decline at a figure that was still exceptionally favorable in comparison to Italy as a whole. In 1700 the average Roman theoretically consumed almost half a sheep (which includes lamb), one-fourteenth of a head of cattle, one-sixteenth of a calf, a quarter of a goat, and one-eleventh of a pig. But during the eighteenth century a general crisis in animal husbandry would be felt.[21]

Meat and all its products were under the jurisdiction of the grascia, the counterpart of the annona. Established in 1620, it had sufficient time to define its role and competence. Its means were modest in comparison to the annona, with about sixteen officials at its disposal and an annual budget of around 3,000 scudi. Like the annona its authority was limited to the annonary provinces. Its principal functions included the collection of the *scannatura* and the stabilization of meat and oil prices, chiefly through the supervision of about 67 places of outlet. But its most important obligation was to ensure the supply of meat to the city. It performed this task by way of requisitioning (*precettazione*), through which it controlled 70 percent of the supply of the sheep and hog market, and 20 percent of the beef market. Some noble families and ecclesiastical and hospital establishments bypassed the grascia by making direct contributions.

Each year on the first of October, the president of the grascia required the owners of large flocks (*masseria*) within his jurisdiction to give a sworn statement of the

21 Delumeau, *Vie économique et sociale de Rome*, 1:123–25; D'Amelia, "La crisi di un mercato protetto," 517–19, 529–30; ASR, Camerale II, arti e mestieri, busta 22, fasc. 47; ASR, Camerale II, grascia, busta 1; ASR, Congregazione del Sollievo, vol. 1.

Table 40

| Years | Index of population growth | Index of animals slaughtered | | |
|---|---|---|---|---|
| | | Beef | Pork | Sheep |
| 1692–1700 | 100 | 100 | 100 | 100 |
| 1701–1710 | 100.4 | 100.2 | 94.3 | 99.1 |
| 1711–1720 | 100.8 | 89.4 | 93.2 | 100.1 |
| 1721–1730 | 106.7 | 105.2 | 97.2 | 102.0 |
| 1731–1740 | 111.0 | 99.1 | 89.0 | 100.4 |
| 1741–1750 | 112.0 | 100.8 | 91.4 | 113.7 |
| 1751–1760 | 115.1 | 100.1 | 93.5 | 106.3 |
| 1761–1770 | 118.5 | 95.3 | 101.1 | 115.9 |
| 1771–1780 | 120.7 | 96.2 | 106.4 | 125.4 |
| 1781–1790 | 121.9 | 93.1 | 81.7 | 140.1 |

quantity and quality of their sheep. The accuracy of their reports was checked by commissioners, who estimated what was needed for consumption in Rome. Not all the animals requisitioned on the list, therefore, were required by the grascia, but at the end of the Lent the owner had to bring the stipulated number to the Roman market. During Msgr. Camillo Cibo's term as president from March 1717 to February 1718, a total of 78,080 lambs were slaughtered to supply the city's appetite. A similar system of *precettazione* was instituted for hogs. The whole system was eventually abolished on 19 September 1789 by Pius VI, at the recommendation of Ruffo as part of a wider program to encourage internal trade, with the consequent hope for a growth in meat production. Yet the measure would do little to abate the fear of shortages.

For the eighteenth century marks a continuing decline in the availability of meat. There was an increasing difficulty to meet the needs of a growing population, whose demographic growth reached an annual median of about 0.25 percent. D'Amelia has worked out an index of animals slaughtered per decade in relation to the index of population growth with the years 1692–1700 as 100 (Table 40).[22] It shows a decline in the number of beef cattle, including calves, and hogs slaughtered in relation to the population. Only in the sheep sector do we see any growth. The decline was not too abrupt thanks to the protective policy of the grascia. Nevertheless the fact that the individual beef ration fell by 27 percent over the century when beef made up the

[22] D'Amelia, "La crisi di un mercato protetto," 505–8; the table is taken from p. 506. Friz, *Consumi, tenore di vita e prezzi*, 72–76.

greatest share of the meat supply (65 percent) meant a drastic cut. Added to this was a 22.2 percent loss in pork, which provided a little more than 10 percent of the meat.

The impending crisis, which gave its first signals around 1752 and became permanent after 1760, led the Roman authorities to change their policy. At the start of the eighteenth century Rome remained almost totally closed to meat production outside the Campagna, but now they tried to facilitate the import of cattle. In the 1750s about 60 percent of the cattle slaughtered in Rome came from the countryside around the city; those coming from Umbria made up no more than 20–25 percent. Thereafter the share of Umbrian cattle breeders was to grow. Since the grascia could not directly control the beef supply through *precettazione*, it wanted to ensure the city's provisioning by granting incentives to Umbrian cattlemen. This policy would ultimately founder on the rigidity of market prices in Rome. To enlarge the supply of mutton and lamb the grascia extended its net of sheepowners subject to its *precettazione* from 200 to 300, bringing in some of the smaller producers.

Other factors also came into play. There seems to have been a change of taste away from fatty meats. This meant that the meat of young animals, veal and lamb, of a few months old began to be favored. Consequently there was less need for pasture. Abetting this change were the rising grain prices and the official policy of reconverting pasture into cultivated land. The Roman *dogana dei pastorizie* registered a fall of about 20 percent in sheepholding. As the cost of sheep production grew, the owners decided to slaughter their animals at an earlier age. This, in turn, reduced the number of animals for breeding. Indeed, the restriction on pasture and the expansion of cultivation embodied in the 1783 cadaster would also have another effect. It would lead to a rise in prices of animal products. Between 1760 and 1800, the price of fresh mutton rose by 74 percent and of local beef by more than 14 percent; between 1763 and 1805 the cost of veal by 33.6 percent, the price of ricotta cheese by 41 percent and of butter by 18.7 percent.[23]

The Romans, according to Cibo, consumed annually on the average 100,000 libbre (33,900 kg) of cheese from cows' milk and 1,300,000 libbre (440,700 kg) of cheese from sheep milk. The difference in the quantity can be explained by the progressive displacement, between 1670 and 1720, of a breed of red cows, reputed to be better milkers, by white cows more suitable for fattening. The milk from the remaining red cows was largely used to make butter. So with the scarcity of cheese from cows' milk the *pecorino* (cheese from sheep milk), produced locally, consolidated its position. Its popularity may be gauged from the number of loaves of such cheese brought annually into the city:[24]

[23] D'Amelia, "La crisi di un mercato protetto," 497–500, 505–21, 524–26, 531; Piscitelli, "Fabrizio Ruffo e la riforma economica," 114–18; Pescosolido, *Terra e nobiltà*, 166.

[24] ASR, Camerale II, arti e mestieri, busta 33, fasc. 70. Friz, *Consumi, tenore di vita e prezzi*, 88–90. Friz estimated that in the years before the French Revolution an annual average of 4 kg was available to each inhabitant.

| | |
|---|---|
| 1701–10 (statistics available for 5 years) | 100,747.6 |
| 1711–20 (statistics for 2 years) | 134,095.5 |
| 1721–30 (statistics for 5 years) | 107,868.0 |
| 1731–40 | 92,528.9 |
| 1741–50 (statistics for 8 years) | 100,274.7 |
| 1751–60 (statistics for 8 years) | 91,392.0 |
| 1761–65 (5 years only) | 110,073.6 |

In order to supplement the declining cheese production from cows' milk, recourse was had to consuming *mozarella* made from buffalo milk and to importing Ligurian and Campanian (Neapolitan) cheese, such as *cavallo*, as well as Parmigiano.

Given fast days, the effective consumption of meat in Rome was reduced to no more than 210 days in the year. Hence, for a third of the year the dominant element was fish. A case could be made that the loss of animal proteins during the ancien regime was partially compensated for by fish. The figures for the years 1697–99 show an annual per capita consumption of almost 26 kg, in which fresh fish outweighed salted and cured fish. The former constituted an important addition to the protein balance. However, much of the supply of fresh fish was not susceptible to growth. The availability of fish in the Tiber and along the coast had been exhausted from overfishing; there was also conflict with the Neapolitan fishermen, who received energetic government support, over fishing in territorial waters. The main source of fresh fish came, therefore, from the local lakes, which were exploited by concessionaires for their own profit, and from imports of French and English cod. Hence there was little prospect of fish replacing meat when the price rose, especially since the price of fresh fish itself increased until a maximum was imposed in 1788.

In addition to fresh fish significant amounts of salted, pickled, and smoked fish were consumed. From September 1700 to February 1701, 1053 barrels (605.5 hl) of pickled tunny, 743 barrels (427 hl) of smoked herrings, 365 barrels (209 hl) of salted sardines, and 1,319 barrels (759.5 hl) of anchovy arrived at the port of the Ripa Grande. By the end of the century, the consumption of dried and salted fish had reached such proportions that the pamphleteer John Denham blamed it for the state's unfavorable trade balance. One of the reasons for this popularity of salted fish may have been the fact that the upward movement of prices in the second half of the century affected almost all food items with the exception of salt, of which there was an abundance and which kept the price of salted fish down, an important factor fo the urban workman.[25]

[25] B.N.Ro., Fondo Gesuitico, ms. 86; Revel, "Les privilèges d'une capitale," 569, 571–73; Mira, "Not sui trasporti fluviali nell'economia dello Stato Pontificio," 38–39; Montesquieu, *Voyages. Oeuvre complètes*, 2:1115; Lalande, *Voyage d'un françois en Italie*, 4:185, 523–24; ASR, Congregazione d Sollievo, vol. 1, especially p. 134; ASR, Camerale II, zecca, busta 33; ASR, Camerale II, commercio

Olive oil unquestionably dominated the fat element in the Roman diet, being present everywhere from the table of the wealthy to the ration of the wage earner, although its uses extended beyond those of nutrition. Cibo estimated, in 1717, that 14,000 *barili* (8,050 hl) were needed annually for human consumption, 10,000 barili (5,750 hl) for the use of lamps and another 10,000 for boiling soap and woollen making. So the minimum need for Rome was 34,000 barili (19,550 hl). But whenever the price fell, the consumption could go up to as much as 36,000 barili (20,700 hl). The poorer folk accounted for this increase in consumption. Given a stable rate of approximately 15,000 barili a year for dietary purposes, this figure would allow an annual ration of 5.77 liters in 1700 and 5.17 liters in 1794 per person. In spite of the proximity of some larger areas of olive production, the Roman demand could never be met locally; even with imports the authorities were never able to make up the chronic shortage of oil.

Fats, other than olive oil, took a minority role in the Roman diet. Lard, banned from the table of the more affluent, replaced oil for the frying of giblets or fish, so characteristic of the popular diet. Butter was a luxury food, which had virtually disappeared at the end of the seventeenth century with the red cattle. It reappeared hesitantly at about 1780 on the tables of seminaries and colleges, always in the forefront of the evolution of refined taste. But, until Italian unification, at least, it remained a vaguely exotic delicacy.

It appears that with the exception of milk, practically absent among the bulk of the population, the diet of Rome showed no large gaps. Fresh vegetable consumption, of salads, carrots, cabbage, chicory, onions, and artichoke was widespread; the average daily supply of dry legumes, beans, and lentils, a secondary source of proteins, came to about 47 grams per person, eggs were cheap, and each inhabitant had about 10 kg of citrus fruit. In a meat-eating Europe, the city looked to be in a good position, provided the individual had the necessary money available. With the maximum budget stipulated in Chapter 4,[26] a Roman would have 2,840 calories a day, of which about 328, that is, 82 grams, were proteins; with the minimum budget that would come to 2,515 calories, of which about 308, that is, 77 grams, were proteins. In Paris the average inhabitant was only provided with 1,669 calories, of which 208, that is, 52 grams, were proteins. (The average American consumes about 3,300 calories of which 12 percent come from proteins.) On first glance, therefore, the Roman diet was adequate and even slightly superior to that of Paris, although the proportional content of proteins was a little less, but well above the 30 grams that are considered physiologically essential for an adult. Yet the fall of the meat ration, in a way much more significant than that of grain, was an ominous sign that the food supply system had grown out of date. We have to wait, however,

industria, busta 12, fasc. 70; Friz, *Consumi, tenore di vita e prezzi*, 151 n. 1. Around 1790 the annual availability of salt per head came to $17\frac{1}{2}$ kg, whereas the need for human nutrition was calculated at 4 to 5 kg. Ibid., 150. [26] See pp. 113–15.

until the middle of the nineteenth century for the break to be really completed. This will be the time of bread and pasta, with its excess of carbohydrates.[27]

Included within those figures are calories supplied by alcohol. For Rome, wine was the principal supplier of alcohol. Urban demand had determined the formation of successive zones of wine production. There was the ancient sector, the vineyards of Rome, a broad belt that stretched around the city and produced wines of irregular quality, generally mediocre; a mass of small pieces of garden worked by individual families, who produced 40 percent to 60 percent of the output for their own consumption. This *vino romanesco*, which was usually left to ferment until about Halloween, was often drunk sour (*asciutto*). It was the wine of the poor and was abundant. The traditional sector of long-distance commerce comprised the *vini navigati*, which since the Middle Ages had come from Campania and, more recently, from Sicily, as well as Corsica and Languedoc. Those were the wines with high alcoholic and sugar content, which travelled and aged well. They were luxury products and were often drunk diluted with water. A more recent sector, whose development followed the demographic growth of Rome since the sixteenth and seventeenth centuries, was the vineyards of the Castelli Romani; its production best mirrors the fluctuations of the local markets. Worked by wage-earning labor, these vineyards produced the light white wines of medium quality that were relatively standardized.

A crisis in the suburban vineyards at the turn of the century and a fall in the availability of foreign wines, importation of which was henceforth limited, was in general compensated for by the wines of the Alban hills. Between 1630 and 1710 the vineyards of the Castelli doubled their output. The consumption, however, increased more rapidly than the population at that point. For 2 baiocchi a foglietta (0.456 liter) this wine acted as a sort of cheap calorific compensation for any decrease in the ration of grain and meat. From about 1760 to 1820 one notices, however, a creeping stagnation of the market. The reason for this must be sought in the food crises and the rise in food prices in the last third of the century. Bread and, to a lesser extent, meat had a prior claim on the purchasing power of the urban masses. As a consequence the Castelli wine region was saddled with overproduction, finding in 1770 an outlet for only two-thirds of what it had produced in 1710.

Whatever its long-term fluctuations, the annual average share of wine per head in Rome always stayed above 2 hl:

| | |
|---|---|
| 1630 | 2.10 |
| 1660 | 2.70 |
| 1708–09 | 2.80 |

[27] Friz, *Consumi, tenore di vita e prezzi*, 86–87, 90–91, 159 prosp. 8; Robert Philippe, "Une opération pilot: l'étude du ravitaillement de Paris au temps de Lavoisier," in Jean-Jacques Hémardinquer (ed.), *Pour une histoire de l'alimentation* (Paris, 1970), 60–65; Revel, "Les privilèges d'une capitale," 573.

| | |
|---|---|
| 1750 | 2.50 |
| 1790 | 2 |
| 1802 | 2.12[28] |

In addition to wine, about 3,500 bareli (2,012.5 hectoliters) of acquavita (gin) was consumed in 1700, which comes to about 1.35 liters per head. Chocolate, coffee, and, to a lesser extent, tea were the new beverages that started to take the public's fancy in the seventeenth century, but they spread slowly, mainly among the upper classes. By 1800 no more than 5 percent of the population consumed them.[29]

As with so much of Rome's experience in this epoch, the overall functioning of the food supply deteriorated in the course of the century. Although one can pinpoint the individual causes for these conditions, they simply become part of the overall malaise. The individual Roman was fortunate in feeling little of the effect. He enjoyed a quality of life that compared well to that of other urban dwellers, the Parisians among them, while blissfully unaware of the cost to his government and his rural neighbor. If he fell on evil days – and the precariousness of employment and low wages of those employed draw our attention to the ever-present possibility of such hardship – there was an adequate, almost generous, safety net. Rome was the home of charity and provided its people with a reasonably good health service.

[28] Ibid., 570–71; Andrieux, *Daily Life in Papal Rome*, 147; Story, *Roba di Roma*, 321; ASR, Congregazione del Sollievo, vol. 1; Friz, "Produzione e commercio dei vini del Lazio," 225.

[29] Friz, *Consumi, tenore di vita e prezzi*, 50 n. 2, 97; Delumeau, *Vie économique et sociale de Rome*, 1:372; ASR, Camerale II, arti e mestieri, busta 23, fasc. 48.

# 8

# Poor relief and health

Adequate nutrition was not the sole concern for the welfare of the Romans. We can only echo the words of Giuntella that Rome in the eighteenth century posed as the capital of charity, of charity raised to a principle of government, even quite apart from any religious motivation, although the latter element was never absent. It was the city of both public and private aid, a relief town. A sad society of individuals lived off the inexhaustible Roman charity. About twenty hospitals or hospices received the old and the orphans, numerous others rendered their services and care to the indigent, free shelter was given to the foundlings at Santo Spirito and San Michele. In numerous convents discreet refuges were organized for women who wanted to leave their gloomy past to start life anew. In addition to all these organized forms of assistance, which for good or ill tried to eliminate the phenomenon of poverty, there were the activities of small religious orders, of unknown ladies working away in seclusion, of confraternities who found their *raison d'être* in the exercise of charity. Consequently the most wretched citizen could never die of hunger and help was provided in every misfortune.

The network of official charity was supplemented by the confraternities and religious houses. The Counter Reformation devotion and spirituality had produced associative modes among the laity, which unlike the medieval ones were no longer penitential, but socially active and practical. This form of piety issued in the foundation of new lay confraternities in the last decades of the sixteenth century, the impetus for which did not come so much from the Council of Trent, which only fleetingly treated the question of confraternities in its twenty-second session in September 1562, as from the spirit of the new religious orders and from a growing awareness of the social duties of a Christian. The traditional marks of these associations of lay people – worship, prayers for their dead brothers, mutual help and assistance – were not abandoned, but others were added. They assumed a series of social tasks and religious reforms. These confraternities were then no longer closed communities seeking a monastic ideal of perfection. Instead, they became the chosen instruments for attracting the lay citizenry to Catholic reform. In short, they manifested the new presence of the church in the city by way of lay works.

During the ancien regime the religious fervor and the zeal for works of charity which had animated the first founders of many of the confraternities had perceptibly waned. The associations began to be reabsorbed in devotional spirituality, concentrating on ostentatious worship, and thereby attenuating their social influence. Nonetheless, however weakened and circumscribed in their activities they might have been, they were still there ready to relieve the hardships of the poor. Two brotherhoods, those of the Santissimi Apostoli and of the Pietà Divina, were devoted to the relief of hidden misery. They visited needy families, gave them the money they required and disappeared without identifying themselves. The confraternities of Sant'Ivo and San Girolamo acted as legal aid societies. The work of the Pietà dei Carcerati went far beyond their original prison visitation. The brotherhood of San Giovanni Battista, attached to the church of San Giovanni Decollata, prepared condemned criminals for a Christian death. More than one confraternity, among them the Orazione e delle Morte, were ready to bury the poor with dignity.

Within the limited sphere of their own membership the craft guilds also served philanthropic purposes. They extended help to their sick brothers. Orderlies went to comfort with good works those confined to bed and, where needed, brought money and material help, according to the resources of the guild. Some corporations maintained a physician who treated sick members free of charge: he was expected to pay them at least two visits a day. The wealthier guilds even supported their own hospitals. In a very limited number of *arti*, pensions were paid to members who had fallen on evil days, or those in old age, and to their widows and orphans.[1]

Then there was private charity. Rich and poor alike responded to the rule of charity. Some great families were often bountiful. Disdaining parsimony on the score of rank and tradition, they had to respond to countless calls for assistance made upon them, apart from what they gave to regular good works. The great patron Cardinal Benedetto Pamphilj, to take one example, was called upon innumerable times to become the godfather not only of the children of household servants, but of many a poor devil. He never lost sight of his spiritual children for the rest of their lives, generously supporting them with money, as much as 20 scudi a month, and clothing. Principe Giovanni Battista Pamphilj, between 1692 and 1702, donated the selling price of 12,500,000 libbre (4,237,400 kg) of sulphur and his annual revenue of 1,000 scudi from the abbey of Sant'Eufemia in Treviso to several charitable institutions, among them the girls' hostel at San Michele. A noble churchman, Cardinal Federigo Marcello Lante, in his will in 1773 left the annual interest on a capital of 36,000 scudi, amounting to 1,110 scudi, to the poor girls at

[1] Fiorani, *Rite, ceremonie, feste e vita del popolo*, 226–27; Vincenzo Paglia, "*La Pietà dei Carcerati.*" *Confraternite e società a Roma nei secoli XVI–XVIII* (Rome, 1980), xii, 61, 77–81, 86, 228; Delumeau, *Vie économique et sociale de Rome*, 1:392; Dal Pane, *Storia del lavoro*, 4:321; Carlo Luigi Morichini, *Degli istituti di pubblica carità e d'istruzione primaria in Roma* (Rome, 1835), 220; ASR, Camerale II, arti e mestieri, busta 13, fasc. 30; ASR, Camerale III, 114/II, busta 1968. For a perspective of the Italian problem of poverty see Mario Rosa, "Pauperismo e riforme nel Settecento italiano. Linee di ricerca," in Peter Brown *et al.*, *Povertàle carità dalla Roma tardo-antica al '700 italiano* (Padua, 1983), 91–125.

the Conservatorio di San Giovanni in Laterano, and to the old men and women and boys at San Michele a Ripa. Some families distributed small alms to individuals. In the case of the Orsini, for instance, the sums ranged from a mere 20 baiocchi to the maximum of 3 scudi. The total of such donations for one particular month (November 1773) came to 134.30 scudi.

Admittedly, with so much poverty around them, some people would consider these sums paltry. But even Morichini, the historian of Roman charity, writing in the 1830s, who was sympathetic to this form of social activity, complained that charity in Rome had exceeded the needs of the poor. Since alms provided a reasonable living, some preferred to stay without work, while others demanded higher wages before they would work. It led to vice and made Roman products uncompetitive in foreign markets.[2]

Rome had always been a refuge for foreign beggars. It was the international capital of the poor as well as the rich. In a memorandum to Innocent XII in 1694, the beggars claimed that in the capital of a religion which had elevated charity to a theological virtue, the poor and the beggars had the right of citizenship in a "common homeland." Even the poor pilgrim, weighing the toil of earning a living by the sweat of his brow against the ease of obtaining alms, chose to remain in Rome and made begging his profession. Hence the line of demarcation between beggars by fate and beggars by choice, the true "rogues," became very tenuous.

But Rome was not only the seat of a huge settled and permanent begging establishment formed by both true and false poor. As capital of a state it also had to make provisions for the periodic and seasonal poverty of the manual laborers, who, after they had completed their summer jobs in the great tenute in the Campagna, were struck down exhausted by toil and malaria, as well as the peasants who every winter, during the break in agricultural work came down from the hills to live off the city's charity.

Unlike the reflection in so much contemporary literature and so many measures in other parts of Europe, the attitude toward the poor in Rome did not start off with the presupposition that these unfortunates were a race of pagans to be converted. The myth of the vagrant belonging to a world of magical practices, of debaucheries, of heresy scarcely found an echo in Rome, where the population recognized in the poor person almost always the neighbor, the jobless, the old, the cripple of the quarter, and where the threshold of poverty was fairly constant, involving many people. The idea was to restore to the poor and those on the edge of society the social framework in which they had once been able to live as Christians.

To achieve this ideal would require a considerable material outlay. It is virtually impossible to calculate the amount of money and the various types of assistance supplied to the poor in relation to the general expenditure, and even less so in

[2] Montalto, *Un mecenate in Roma barocca*, 228; ADP, 88.6.4; ASR, Famiglie diverse, Lante-Della Rovere, busta 51; A.Cap.R., Orsini, serie 2, nos. 211–12; Andrieux, *Daily Life in Papal Rome*, 61; Morichini, *Degli istituti di pubblica carità*, xxxix–xl.

absolute terms during this period. But in the early nineteenth century (1836), Rome spent 764,271.84 scudi on the poor from all sources, which is roughly 530,000 scudi in eighteenth-century terms, against 10,500,000 francs (1,957,281.55 scudi at the 1785 exchange rate) in Paris; since Paris had nearly five times Rome's population, one can say that Rome spent about 25 percent more on charity than the French capital.

By looking at the expenses for poor pilgrims, however, one may infer that every pauper cost the administration and the city from 15 to 20 scudi a year in the sixteenth and seventeenth centuries. Although we do not know the exact figure of people in need of assistance in Rome, we may estimate it very conservatively at 10 percent, which would compare very favorably with 8 percent in Berlin in 1785, 10 percent in France in the 1790s, about 20 percent in Bologna in the 1730s, and possibly as much as 38 percent in Florence in 1765. By this calculation we would arrive at an absolute minimum of 200,000 scudi. Even this sum formed a significant part of the annual budget for the whole of the Papal States, even though almost half of that sum came from private sources.[3]

It has been cogently argued that this expense should not be regarded totally as a dead weight; for if it was employed properly, it would maintain the stability of property and the artisanal structure of the city. In that respect it was a kind of social security, paid out with special regard to the feebleness of the employment conditions in Rome. An illustration of this point is the massive amount of charitable dowries available to female orphans and other indigent girls, who through their marriages entered predominantly into the sector of those working in small trades and crafts. In the same sense must be viewed the committal of orphan boys to families to teach them a trade and become adoptive sons. It would, therefore, be fairer to count this burden of assistance as a form of reintegration into a conservative society, always providing, of course, that the charity was not more lavish than the need. The local vagrants, too, came most often from families of day laborers (*braccianti*) and tradesmen thrown out into the gutter by sickness, bereavement, and famine. Thus, wherever it performed its function properly Roman charity did not necessarily encourage idleness as its critics affirmed. The fact remained, however, that the system was greatly abused. There never was a total integration and vagrancy continued.

In the course of the seventeenth century, therefore, the distinction between "true" and "false" poor was clarified. An attitude of greater harshness developed toward the latter and a clear line was drawn between those who were entitled to assistance and the enjoyment of certain privileges and those who were not so entitled, at least in official circles. Parallel to this was an increasing propensity to

[3] Dal Pane, *Economia e società a Bologna*, 396; Giacomelli, "Carlo Grassi e le riforme bolognesi," 45; Antonio Rotondo, "Introduzione," in Cosimo Amidei, *Opere* (Turin, 1980), 121–22 n. 345; Mario Rosa *et al.*, "Poveri e marginati: un problema religioso," *Ricerche per la storia religiosa di Roma*, 21–23.

laicize assistance by the intervention of the state. This new approach found its clearest expression in France with the establishment of the *hôpitaux généraux*, the first of which was set up for 1,500 vagrants at Lyons in 1614. In 1662 a royal decree ordered a network of these institutions throughout the cities of the realm. Since the middle of the 1670s the Jesuits took a direct hand in running these *hôpitaux*. The purpose of this policy was to bring the beggars and vagrants under control and discipline them for work. This same attitude was adumbrated in a little work of 1693 inspired by the papal court, entitled *La mendicità provveduta nella città di Roma coll'ospizio pubblico fondato dalla pietà e dalla beneficenza del Nostro Signore Innocenzo XII P.M.* It was attributed to the French Jesuit Guévarre, who had accompanied Père Chaumand to Rome, when the latter was called to the papal capital in 1692 to establish a similar *hôpital général*. Guévarre wrote his work on the pope's orders to convince the Romans of the appropriateness of the hospice Innocent was establishing in the Lateran Palace and to reply to the many objections which were being raised.

When Innocent XII was elected pope on 12 July 1691, he brought with him a reputation for charity to the poor earned during his tenure as archbishop of Naples. Yet he was soon to reveal an unexpectedly coercive approach to poor relief. The prisons which had remained almost empty for at least a year were made ready to receive the idle, the vagrants, and the false beggars. For if left free, these would continue to beg, and begging itself was an occasion for sin and irreligiosity, especially if practiced in church. So after issuing in 1692 his bull against nepotism, Innocent was able to tackle the problem of his "true nipoti," as he was fond of calling the poor. On 2 October 1692, the first edict on the confinement of the poor was issued by the cardinal vicar. It ordered all beggars of both sexes to report within eighty days at the portico of S. Maria in Trastevere. Those considered truly needy and unable to work were to be given a distinctive sign and confined in a particular place, whereas the able-bodied men who could work were forbidden to beg.

The edict marked the start of an operation in grand style, which took account of the contemporary French experience. In November, Innocent XII presented his palace of the Lateran with the adjoining garden, on which the work of restoration and adaptation had already begun under the direction of Carlo Fontana, to the beggars. The men and women selected to be confined there had in the meantime been collected at the hospice of Trinità dei Pellegrini.

Although the papal authorities initially claimed the action to have been a success, it encountered enormous difficulties, both in principle and in practice, that would eventually prejudice its effectiveness. One of the difficulties of principle concerned the legitimacy, from the Catholic point of view, of the operation. It had become part of the mentality of the less well-to-do circles that private alms to the poor gained merit with God. Moreover, apart from the threatened liberty to live either by begging or working, which every Roman claimed as his birthright, the fear spread that with the prohibition of begging the traditional Roman charity toward the poor pilgrim and the poor peasant would be impaired. In practice, the measure came up against the reality of a pauperism that reproduced itself by geometrical progression, when the public hostels could not even cope with an arithmetrical progression, so that even the financial means, estimated at about 140,000 scudi a year, although huge, soon proved insufficient. Therefore, the objective of eliminating the crime of begging was never achieved. After February 1696 admission to the Lateran hospice was made on the basis of a voluntary request, as in all private hospices. By the following year the plan to eliminate begging can be said to have failed, even though there were sporadic attempts to take it up again, update it, and adapt it to new times.[4]

Thus, although Rome continued to trust in coercive measures for most of the eighteenth century to clean up the sores of begging and dissoluteness, and tried to confine vagrants and idlers in institutions such as San Michele a Ripa, or even use them as forced labor at low cost, beggars and parasites swarmed everywhere and came to be looked upon as a normal phenomenon of everyday life.

When a provisional census was taken of the whole of this unfortunate class at the close of the century, it was found that the number of those without work had reached the incredible figure of 70,000, or almost half of the Roman population. Yet we have to wait until the time of the French occupation for the first general provisions against unemployment to be made. In the interval the whole apparatus of Roman charity, official, religious, and private, tried to cope with this social problem as best as it could.[5]

Among the ranks of Rome's poor were the debtors. Civil debtors formed more than half of Rome's prison population. All those who incurred debts and were unable to repay them could be sued by their creditors and confined to prison. These debtors were usually persons whom we would comprehend under the term of working poor, the small craftsmen and merchants, those who had to resort to debts in order to live. The reasons for which they contracted debts were manifold, but fell mainly into three classes. The most frequent was for the failure to pay rent or for being unable to pay back money they borrowed for rent. The second class were those who borrowed to purchase materials or tools for their trade. The third group came under the heading of what we might call debtors for personal and family reasons – to live, to

[4] Fatica, "La reclusione dei poveri a Roma," 136–51, 156–58, 165, 168–70; Karl H. Metz, "Staatsraison und Menschenfreundlichkeit. Formen und Wandlungen der Armenpflege in Ancien Régime Frankreichs, Deutschlands und Grossbritanniens," *Vierteljahrschrift für Sozial- und Wirtschaftsgeschichte*, 72 (1885), 2–7, 12; Olwen H. Hufton, *The Poor of Eighteenth-Century France, 1750–1789* (Oxford, 1974), 132–33; Paglia, *"La Pietà dei Carcerati,"* 47, 54, 153–48; Pastor, *Geschichte der Päpste*, 14, pt 2:1085; Morichini, *Degli istituti di pubblica carità*, xxviii–xxxi, 110–12, appendix – third sheet.

[5] Rosa *et al.*, "Poveri e marginati," 26; Andrieux, *Daily Life in Papal Rome*, 59–61; Story, *Roba di Roma*, 57–59; Dal Pane, *Storia del laboro*, 4:317 n. 17; Fiorani, *Riti, ceremonie, feste e vita del popolo*, 226; Nicolai, *Memorie, leggi ed osservazioni*, 3:263.

eat, for medicines, for a daughter who married, or a son at school. From the social provenance and the trade exercised by these folk emerges with some clarity this particular facet of Roman poverty. It was a poverty different from that of the beggars and vagrants always without means of sustenance because they were not integrated in the social organism. These groups of working poor were integrated, while living on a precarious margin. They were not proletarians in the Marxist sense, for many managed their own workshops. The confraternity of the Pietà made such unfortunates its special concern. Frequently it acted as an intermediary between the imprisoned debtor and his creditors, trying to bring the parties to compose their differences. Whenever it set such a prisoner free, it made itself the guarantor with the creditors. Because of the great number of debtors involved and the money required, the confraternity was to find itself in great difficulty. But its story will be treated below.[6]

One of the other social problems the Roman authorities faced was that of the extremely high number of foundlings and abandoned children. In this respect Rome shared the experience of most cities in Italy. In Florence, of the 6,959 children baptized in 1785–86, 9.3 percent were foundlings. The registers of baptisms of abandoned children in Rome are kept in the Archivio del Vicariato. The books cover the years 1585 to 1896 (with a gap for 1801–17). Notwithstanding the importance of this source, which has not yet been fully exploited, it is neither complete nor fully trustworthy. In the register are noted only those abandoned children presented at the "wheel" (*ruota*) without baptismal certificates, but many other babies were entrusted to foundling hospitals with baptismal certificates in accordance with the exhortation of Gregory XIII in 1585, in which infants were to be baptized before being abandoned. The presence in the city of charitable institutions for foundlings and orphans in general was also an attraction for the rural areas, so that many abandoned children did not come from Rome at all.

Rome was the first city in Europe to have such a house for foundlings, the Pia Casa degli Esposti in Santo Spirito in Sassia. It was founded by Innocent III as far back as 1198 and enlarged by Benedict XIV in 1750. Near the entrance to the hospice was a round wheel, the *ruota*, with enough room to accommodate a three-month-old child on a mattress. A bell which rang at the very slightest turn of the wheel announced that a child had been placed there. A young watchman came immediately and carried the infant to a nurse.

The institution had a number of resident wetnurses. These were chosen in accordance with strict criteria and considerable care was taken for their physical well-being. They had to have a certificate from their curate stating the exact time of the birth and death of their own children and the fact that they were free from any sickness which would prevent them from nourishing a child. They were prohibited

[6] Paglia, "*La Pietà dei Carcerati,*" 60–67, 204–205.

Table 41

| Year | Roman population | Foundlings | 0/000 |
|---|---|---|---|
| 1700 | 149,447 | 962 | 6.44 |
| 1750 | 157,881 | 1,060 | 6.71 |
| 1790 | 162,982 | 1,765 | 10.83 |
| 1800 | 153,004 | 2,793 | 18.25 |

from leaving the hospice during their period of service, but were very well paid and fed. Each one had normally two, sometimes three, babies at the breast. The children were kept at the institution for the shortest possible time, before being sent out to private wetnurses either in the city or the countryside. The care of these wetnurses did not end with lactation, but continued until the seventh, eight, or even tenth year, when they returned the child to Santo Spirito. The number of foundlings in relation to the population of Rome is shown in Table 41.

However, it should be noted that a high percentage of the babies received at the Roman foundling hospital died within a few days of entry, so that the total number of foundlings actually fell considerably. Their mortality at the start of the nineteenth century touched 69 percent (although between 1727 and 1738 only 33.2 percent of the babies left at the *ruota* died before their second birthday). Nevertheless it was fewer than the 84 percent recorded for Paris in 1773–77 and the 82.3 percent for Florence in 1792–94. The death rate was in part a reflection on the trauma the newly born suffered on the way to Santo Spirito from distant places. But a proportion was due to the difficulty of adapting to the wetnurses or to the sicknesses contracted during this stage of lactation. For the wetnurses who nurtured these babies were almost always carriers of germs, since they suckled others whose health was already precarious. Moreover, although they lived in rooms apart, they did move through areas of the hospital where there were cases of influenza and other infectious diseases.

As in so much of Roman life abuses were rife in the system. It appears that parents who were themselves comfortably well off sent their infants to the hospital and wetnurses who had already received their wages put their foster children back through the *ruota* as if they were new foundlings.[7]

Lalande counted ten conservatories or centers for the care of orphans, children,

[7] Livi-Bacci, *A History of Italian Fertility*, 37 n. 22; Sergio Pagano, "Gli esposti dell'Ospedale di S. Spirito nel primo Ottocento," *Ricerche per la storia religiosa di Roma*, 3 (1979), 354–55, 357–59; Morichini, *Degli istituti di pubblica carità*, 87–91; ASR, Ospedale di S. Spirito, repertorio dei proietti, busta 1305; Dante Bolognesi and Carla Giovannini, "Gli esposti a Ravenna fra '700 e '800," in Ercole Sori (ed.), *Città e controllo sociale in Italia tra XVIII e XIX secolo* (Milan, 1982), 307–308, 317 n. 19.

and women in 1765. The largest and best run was the hospice at San Michele founded by Sixtus V and subsequently enlarged by Innocent XII in 1693, Clement XI in 1708, and Pius VI in 1790. In the decade of 1741–50, an average of 400 girls were living there. They wore black uniforms and had a school where they learned reading, writing, and arithmetic, as well as singing. The girls made uniforms for the papal soldiers and sewed for the papal household, and took on commissions for private merchants. In addition to this income, the institution received subsidies from public revenues, and the confraternity of the Santissima Annunziata gave them annually a sum of 800 scudi to be used for dowries. The problem of marrying off these orphan girls and foundlings, or persuading them to be nuns, weighed heavily on the authorities. Since the time of Innocent XI (1676–89), it was left to the master of the house to guide the girls in the direction they chose. It seems that many girls were forced into marriage and given husbands, which they resented. To prevent this abuse, an order was given in 1737 to explore the will of each marriageable girl individually. Whenever an opportunity to marry came, the oldest girl would always be given preference provided the match was mutually accepted. At marriage she was provided with a dowry of 100 scudi.

Paul III, on the advice of Ignatius Loyola, opened a shelter for orphan boys in S. Maria in Aquiro, and supplemented it with a house for orphan girls on the Tiber island. They were managed by the confraternity of the Visitazione di Maria Vergine degli Orfane and sheltered as many as three hundred individuals of both sexes. Cardinal Antonmaria Salviati, believing that among the poor children there were those with enough talent to receive an academic education, founded in 1591 a college that bore his name. The number of boys' orphanages and hospices was never as large as the girls', since, in the opinion of the public, the boys were less exposed to moral danger. But Santo Spirito, San Michele, and Sant'Aquiro, to name only three, trained boys in a trade.

Santo Spirito, too, under its broad umbrella of social work, provided a home for the aged, both men and women, where, if they chose, they could perform light tasks to earn pocket money. Other homeless had many shelters where they could live until they found lodgings. Aside from the lesser refuges numbered in the hundreds, where help was given to all, poor invalided priests could go to the Ospizio Ecclesiastico, impoverished women could spend the night at the Ospizio di San Luigi, and impoverished men in the Ospizio di San Gallo, founded by Marcantonio Odescalchi in 1650. These last three provided shelter for at least four hundred individuals, although they did not dispense food. Help at home for the sick was given by the Limosineria Apostolica, which dated back to the twelfth century.[8]

[8] Morichini, *Degli istituti di pubblica carità*, xvii–xxii, 91–93, 99–101, 112–119, appendix – sheet two; ASR, Ospedale di S. Spirito, repertorio dei proietti, busta 1304, ff. 89, 124; busta 1414; Lalande, *Voyage d'un françois en Italie*, 5:278–80; Andrieux, *Daily Life in Papal Rome*, 51, 64; Petrocchi, *Roma nel Seicento*, 118.

Indeed, the concern for health became an integral part of public welfare. Seen from that perspective, the eighteenth century was a satisfactory one for the city; none of the seasonal epidemics could be classed as a plague, although threats of malaria were not unknown. At the start of the century the Florentine ambassador in his correspondence repeatedly emphasized the danger of staying in Rome during the summer months. While Clement XI, in spite of warnings, persisted in remaining at the Vatican throughout the year, others having little faith in the healthfulness of some Roman districts, particularly in the neighborhood of the Colosseum, moved elsewhere for the summer or left Rome to join their families in what were considered more salubrious centers nearby, such as Tivoli and Frascati.

The literature of the eighteenth century pointed to better sanitary conditions, but a new recrudescence of malaria occurred in 1765 and especially after 1778, when the Roman physician Pietro Orlandi observed an extraordinary amount of pernicious fever, which he treated effectively with the bark of quinine. Another Roman physician, Vincenzo Ambrogi, noted in those years the spread of what he called a pseudo-pernicious fever because it bore a great resemblance to the ordinary malignant fever, but refused stubbornly to respond to quinine treatment. Instead, santonico, a plant similar to wormwood, was administered in the form of a tincture or extract with some success.

Roman sicknesses had their own annual cycle. They varied in kind and virulence according to the intensity of the weather that prevailed. Thus, during the cold and rough winters chest colds and catarrhs were widespread. Usually not of long duration, they could degenerate into violent and convulsive coughs and even pneumonia. In hospitals, where this wretched condition affected the weakest constitutions, gangrene and abscesses followed the inflammation in many cases. When the winter was dry, apoplexy, that is, strokes, and opthalmic inflammations abounded. By the middle of spring, such children's diseases as measles and chickenpox carried off many of them before vaccination was introduced. With adults acute fevers and hemorrhages broke out, which a physician such as Petit-Radel regarded as harmless, but which often turned serious as a result of bad treatment, especially if the sick were crammed with quinine. Summer brought some intermittent fevers, but more often the continuous pernicious kind, which was even more frequent toward the end of fall. Tertian fever raged as well as smallpox. As the season advanced toward autumn several other fevers characterized by skin eruptions developed among children. Toward the late season tuberculosis appeared among those who had neglected their chest complaints during the summer, in addition to colics, and bilious vomiting.

The bulk of medical practice in Rome, as in the rest of Italy, during the eighteenth as well as the nineteenth century, therefore, was made up of acute, rather than chronic, diseases. Among the great causes of death were such infectious

Table 42

| Year | Outbreak | Year | Outbreak |
|---|---|---|---|
| 1692 | Gangrene | 1775 | Pneumonia |
| 1695 | Apoplexy | 1778 | Intermittent fever |
| | Intermittent fever | 1779 | Pneumonia |
| | Typhus | 1780 | Intermittent fever |
| 1702 | Apoplexy | | |
| | Malignant fever | 1781 | Apoplexy |
| | Erysipelas | | Pneumonia |
| | (St. Anthony's Fire) | | Typhus |
| | Smallpox | 1782 | Apoplexy |
| 1703 | Apoplexy | | Influenza |
| | Skin eruptions | | Measles |
| | Smallpox | | Typhus |
| 1703 | Apoplexy | 1783 | Smallpox |
| | Skin eruptions | 1784 | Smallpox |
| | Smallpox | 1785 | Intermittent fever |
| 1704 | Malignant fever | | |
| 1706 | Apoplexy | 1786 | Apoplexy |
| 1707 | Measles | | Intermittent fever |
| | Pneumonia | | |
| | Smallpox | 1786 | Apoplexy |
| 1708 | Sudden death | | Intermittent fever |
| 1709 | Pneumonia | 1787 | Typhus |
| | Influenza | | Smallpox |
| 1713 | Pneumonia | 1790 | Angina |
| 1719 | Sudden death | | Apoplexy |
| 1720 | Pneumonia | | Pneumonia |
| 1730 | Influenza | 1796 | Intermittent fever |
| 1736 | Typhus | | |
| | Smallpox | 1803 | Typhus |
| 1737 | Measles | 1804 | Intermittent fever |
| 1743 | Smallpox | | |
| | Influenza | 1806 | Smallpox |
| 1753 | Polymorphous | 1807 | Spots |
| | Parotitis | | Opthalmia |
| 1754 | Pneumonia | 1808 | Intermittent fever |
| | Smallpox | | Measles |
| 1764 | Hospital fever | | Smallpox |
| 1766 | Intermittent fever | | |
| | | 1817 | Intermittent fever |
| 1772 | Sudden death | | Typhus |

diseases as typhoid, smallpox, which the Romans believed recurred in six-year cycles, whooping cough, and scarlet fever, which was first observed in the seventeenth century but spread rapidly toward the end of the eighteenth century (there was still some uncertainty about differentiating scarlet fever from measles), followed by acute infections of the digestive tract such as enteritis, dysentery, diarrhoea, and of the respiratory organs, including bronchitis. Apoplexy or cerebral congestion and chronic heart trouble also were significant killers. The medical literature of the time points to a widespread prevalence of gall and kidney stones among the Roman population.[9]

Alfonso Corradi has provided a chronology of the various epidemics – or shall we say outbreaks, since the Roman medical authorities were wont to exaggerate a little – which afflicted the city in the course of the ancient regime period (Table 42).[10] To treat these and other maladies, hospitals, some of them the legacy of Counter Reformation piety, were more freely available in Rome than anywhere else. They were well managed according to the standards of the day. The biggest was the Santo Spirito, which was situated in the Borgo. Innocent III had opened there in 1198 a hospital for the sick together with his shelter for foundlings. In 1471 Sixtus IV rebuilt the original structure which had fallen into decay while the popes had been away in Avignon. He constructed a large hall with three rows of beds. In 1601 it normally accommodated 150 beds, but could be extended to 400 beds. Under Alexander VII in 1665–67, another small hall was added. It was reserved for the sick who had undergone surgery. In time the infectious sick were separated.

In 1743 those suffering from infectious skin troubles, collectively comprehended under the term *rognosa*, were removed from the rather crowded conditions in Santo Spirito to the more spacious and airy location of San Gallicano in Trastevere, where they had better medical attention and where there was less danger of them infecting other patients or even the hospital staff. The improvement was marked by the fact that whereas out of every 4,500 or so patients who came for treatment with this complaint to Santo Spirito every year about 20 to 25 percent were cured and 12 to 13 percent died, in San Gallicano out of 4,200 patients, 80 to 90 percent were cured and only 6 to 7 percent died.

9 Celli, *Storia della malaria*, 312–13, 317–22; Andrieux, *Daily Life in Papal Rome*, 15; Young, *Rome in Winter*, 58, 63–64, 66, 82–83, 89; Krautheimer, *Rome, 312–1308*, 317; Arturo Castiglioni, *Storia della medicina* (new ed.; Milan, 1936), 556; Petit-Radel, *Voyage historique*, 538–41; Petit-Radel had been professor of surgery in Paris and surgeon to the king. Alfonso Corradi, *Annali delle epidemie occorso in Italia dalle prime memorie fino al 1850 compilati con varie note e dichiarazioni* (4 vols.; Bologna, n.d.), 2:149; Alessandro Canezza, *Gli arcispedali di Roma nella vita cittadina nella storia e nell'arte* (Rome, 1933), 139–40.

10 Corradi, *Annali delle epidemie*, 2:277–84, 293–95, 298–99, 325–26, 344–45, 363–67, 384–85, 398–408, 572, 575, 587, 619, 687, 709–10, 752, 758–59; 5:28–29, 403, 547–48; Montaiglon and Guiffrey (eds.), *Correspondance des directeurs de l'Académie de France*, 1:161–62, 377; Bertoldi (ed.), *Epistolario di Monti*, 1:136; Pastor, *Geschichte der Päpste*, 15:359; Johann Wolfgang Goethe, *Italian Journey*, translated by W. H. Auden and Eizabeth Mayer (London, 1962), 472; Del Panta and Livi-Bacci, "Le componenti naturali dell'evoluzione demografica," 120–21.

But since the population of Rome had doubled in the time between Sixtus IV and Benedict XIV, there were about one thousand sick who could not be accommodated in the hospital of Santo Spirito and had to be put up in barns nearby. Benedict XIV ordered an extension of the original Sistine building in 1742 in the direction of the Ponte Sant'Angelo. The new hall executed by the architect Ferdinando Fuga was completed twenty months later. Benedict also added new kitchens, dining halls, and an infirmary for the employees, as well as a fine anatomical theater, which Pius VI was to enlarge. This pope also authorized the addition of a new building, the Ospedale di San Carlo, placed in front of the older one and separated from it by a fine road.

In the files of the hospital at the Archivio di Stato di Roma are records of admissions, discharges, and deaths for just a few years during the eighteenth century. For the first half of the century we have five years (1717, 1723, 1733, 1735, and 1750), where the data are given per months and for the second half four years (1767, 1776, 1784, 1793), where the data are given according to medical categories. While there are some rather erratic fluctuations in numbers, it would be fair to say that on the average 9,000 to 10,000 cases were admitted to Santo Spirito annually. As to the distribution of admissions per months, the busiest season was in late summer and fall. The winter months of January to March were also very busy and very dangerous. The bulk of the patients in this hospital were afflicted with fevers of various types and this may account for the particular statistical configuration. The death rate in proportion to those admitted came to about 10.26 percent.

In the second half of the century we notice a striking increase in number of patients treated in the hospital during the last two decades of the century. The rate of discharges – presumably cured – was on the average about 86.85 percent, which appears very credible. Conversely, the death rate amounted to an average of 9.27 percent. Thus one had an almost nine to one chance to leave the hospital well on the way to recovery. Since Santo Spirito was the principal fever hospital, most of the cases, especially males, ended up there. The chances of discharge were better than average. Consumption (tuberculosis), which made up around 1 percent of the admissions, was a great killer with a death rate of 84.78 percent. There was no hope for the isolated cases of hydrophobia. Scorbutic diseases, such as scurvy, caused by nutritional deficiencies, could also be dangerous, with a death rate of about 41 percent, but one which fluctuated from year to year. The number of those sufferers made up about 1.5 percent of the patients. Wounds and surgical procedures were also precarious with a death rate of 20.5 percent; and so were stones, which usually involved some surgery, with 28.5 percent. But Santo Spirito, we know, was not the only hospital in Rome.[11]

Almost every district had a hospital. Trastevere, for instance, had two, Santa Maria della Consolazione and San Gallicano. The former, with about 150 beds,

[11] Morichini, *Degli istituti di pubblica carità*, 1–11; Canezza *Gli arcispedali di Roma*, 114–16; B.N.Ro., Fondo Gesuitico, ms. 202, no. O; ASR, Ospedale di S. Spirito, busta 1414.

admitted patients of both sexes in need of surgery for wounds and bruises sustained from cuts and stabbings with knives and daggers, a not very uncommon occurrence in Rome, or those suffering from fractures or burns. It operated not unlike a modern casualty department. San Gallicano, with 50 beds, was established in part from funds left by the renowned physician Lancisi for those suffering from skin diseases. Patients were treated with peroxide cream and sulphur ointment. In an adjoining ward infants with ringworms received topical treatment. No internal medication was dispensed to them. San Giacomo degli Incurabili on the Via del Corso admitted persons of both sexes with advanced venereal diseases and terminal cancerous afflictions. It was founded in the fourteenth century by the Colonna family.

But the true pride of Rome was its special institutions. The hospital of Trinità dei Pellegrini was founded by the Florentine Filippo Neri in 1549 with the primary intention of harboring pilgrims, especially during Holy Years. Between Holy Years the building was opened to those who had recovered from sickness and needed help during convalescence. By the middle of the eighteenth century the hospice of the confraternity was by statute obliged to receive all the convalescents discharged from the hospital of Santo Spirito. They were kept there three days, sometimes four, and given two good meals a day before they could go on their way. With it, Rome was far ahead of other European capitals in providing a general convalescent home for its sick.[12]

Childbirth in the time of the ancien regime took place mostly at home. Midwives presided not only over physical birth, but performed baptisms when the infant's life was in danger, procured abortions, permitted or carried out infanticide. Upon their expertise depended the survival of the woman in labor. Hence the ecclesiastical and medical authorities paid great attention to these practitioners. In 1699, the cardinal vicar ordered the priests to licence the midwives in their parish and to verify their moral and religious qualifications, as well as their competence. By all appearances the parish priests were either negligent or unable to control the competence of these midwives. Admittedly, it was very difficult for them to carry out their duties; because so often under pressure of economic conditions, many women came from other parishes to carry out the profession in order to augment the family income. A recent study of five parishes in the eighteenth century showed that 85 to 90 percent of these midwives worked in a parochial jurisdiction other than that in which their baptism was registered. Between 1785 and 1787, however, three practical courses in obstetrics were set up at the university, and at the hospitals of Santo Spirito and San

[12] Delumeau, *Vie économique et sociale de Rome*, 1:170–71, 408–11; Andrieux, *Daily Life in Papal Rome*, 61–63; Morichini, *Degli istituti di pubblica carità*, xi–xiv, 31–34, 68–74, appendix – first sheet; Canezza, *Gli arcispedali di Roma*, 187, 200–208, 213; Petit-Radel, *Voyage historique*, 232–35; ASR, Ospizio della Trinità dei Pellegrini e Convalescenti, atti relativi e ricoverati, busta 561; ASR, Camerale II, Ospizio della SS. Trinità dei Pellegrini, movimento giornaliero, busta 1271; Madelin, *Rome de Napoléon*, 103–4; ASR, Ospedale di San Gallicano, busta 14; B.N.Ro., Fondo Gesuitico, ms. 292, no. O.

Rocco. By a decree of the cardinal vicar would-be midwives had to attend and demonstrate a mastery of the rudiments of the art. Yet, as before, the responsibility was left to the parish priest, which made compliance very uncertain.

There was, however, a lying-in hospital in Rome. For those too poor to bear the expense of childbirth, as well as for those women anxious to conceal their pregnancy, the hospital of San Rocco offered a shelter and a hiding-place. This hospital, situated next to the Ripetta, was founded in the Jubilee year of 1500 to receive men suffering from fevers, but soon also admitted pregnant women. In 1770 Clement XIV limited the place solely to women in confinement. Apart from the one great ward of about fifty beds, each separated from the rest by curtains and screens, there were also other rooms for those women who wanted privacy. Any woman near her confinement, whether married or not, who presented herself, was received at once. Her name and condition were not asked and she was allowed to conceal her face if she so desired in order not to be recognized by anyone. On the register of the hospital each patient was distinguished by a number instead of a name. No outside persons were allowed admittance, be they parents, relatives, or strangers, save the medical staff, midwife, and female attendants. The woman who entered it was secure from molestation of any kind; and when she chose to leave, provision was made to enable her to depart in the most secret way and at the most opportune time.

The hospital of Santa Maria della Pietà de' Poveri Pazzi for the insane of both sexes was founded in 1548 at the Piazza Colonna. Benedict XIII moved it to a larger building in the Via Lungara in 1725. A report to Benedict XIV claimed that the number of inmates had doubled and the place was overcrowded, despite the fact that the more dangerous cases were kept in prison. What happened was that judges sent there indigent people, drunkards, sufferers from epilepsy or simply troubled and weakminded persons, not appropriate for the hospital. Certainly treatment at the Pietà de' Poveri Pazzi could not compare to the humane approach at the hospital of Bonifazio at Florence, which Vincenzo Chiarugi turned virtually into a psychiatric clinic in 1785.[13]

Physicians enjoyed a comparatively low status in the eighteenth century. Nobody really believed that they knew their business. Undoubtedly there were in Rome some physicians who were anything but contemptible, but in general the students of the Sapienza left the institution with a state of mind that limited their treatment to bleeding, purging and giving enemas. Almost all the sick exposed to their care had a purgative at breakfast and a bleeding at dinner, at a minimum. The Roman savant Cristoforo Amaduzzi tells us of a Conte Carlo Simonetti, who in 1762 was confined to bed for a fever for which he had fourteen bloodlettings a day! He was quickly cured of his fever, but not surprisingly continued to suffer the pain from the

[13] Fiocca, "Struttura urbane e controllo sociale," 391–97; Pastor, *Geschichte der Päpste*, 15:602; Story, *Roba di Roma*, 490–91; B.N.Ro., Fondo Gesuitico, ms. 206, no. 17; Lalande, *Voyage d'un françois en Italie*, 5:271–74.

phlebotomies.[14] These ignorant, pedantic doctors, administering kitchen Latin under the veil of remedies, were inferior in practical knowledge to the herbalists, who made the ointments for them. For next to purgation and bleeding, medical concoctions of bizarre ingredients enjoyed favor among both doctors and the public. Only toward the end of the eighteenth century did new medicines begin to make headway.

In their place the ordinary Roman had a whole pharmacopoeia of popular remedies in which he put his trust, with good reason. The Romans referred to popular medicines as the *rimedi simpatiche* and the art of healing was generally reserved to women. If some of these remedies appear strange and ridiculous to us, the answer lies in the Roman adage, "peggio nun è morto ma," (nothing is ever worse than death). For, however bizarre the potion, it could creditably compare with the remedies of some of the physicians of their own day. As late as 1759 a distinguished French physician asserted that human feces acted as a laxative and relieved digestive problems. It was prescribed for a sore throat, for epilepsy, and against intermittent fever. Dried, pulverized and mixed with honey it was applied to ulcerated carbuncles and was known as the golden plaster – *empiastro aureo.*

As for the Roman layman, fresh cow dung mixed with some vinegar into a paste formed a curative fermentation for scrofula, boils, swellings, and tumors. Chilblains were bathed in hot urine before one went to bed; although a paste of cooked mallow or sage, crushed garlic, or boiled honey, or chickpea meal reheated in suet or tallow would also do the job. Garlic was another favorite remedy believed to be able to prevent things from turning foul and very useful against biliousness. In order to purify the blood at the start of spring, the water in which endives or watercress had been boiled or the juice of crushed chicory was recommended for a forty-day cure.

Some remedies were less outrageous. The use of prunes as a natural laxative is still as commonplace nowadays as it was in the eighteenth century. Less attractive, on the other hand, was the recommendation for clean white teeth: they were to be washed in the morning and at night with warm urine. But Romans were given more acceptable alternatives: pounded charcoal, cigar ash, or bicarbonate powder.

The list of such cures could go on indefinitely; the principle, however, behind these home remedies was an amalgam of herbal cures, common sense, tradition, with an admixture of superstitition and pagan incantations that were given a Christian veneer. The danger of such an approach was not the effectiveness of some of the treatment, which might even have been superior to that of the physicians of their day, but that it cultivated an attitude that exposed the credulous Roman mob to exploitation. Dr. Dulcamara of Donizetti's *Elisir d'Amore* or variations of him were widespread in eighteenth-century Rome. In 1764, a Dr. Piccioni claimed to have discovered a "miracle drug," a potion that could cure epilepsy. Alessandro

[14] BAV, Cod. Ferraioli, ms. 415.

Verri himself was impressed with a charlatan by the name of Rosetti, who went about restoring people afflicted with incurable venereal infections within as short a period as one week. Then there were the miraculous cures performed in some religious houses, as allegedly happened in the monastery of S. Maria in Campo Marzio to those suffering from scrofula and malarial fevers.

If all else failed, there were the health springs of the Acqua Acetosa, on the banks of the Tiber, not far from Monte Parioli, and the baths of Albula, midway between Rome and Tivoli. In 1771, the physician Luca Massimi in his work *Dell'Acqua Acetosa a Ponte Molle* assured his readers from direct experience that the acid water of the spring was useful for headaches, neuralgic pain, chest diseases, and asthma; in skin diseases, such as scabs and mites, it cleared the skin of every scabrous ugliness, and it was a sure remedy for diarrhoea, dysentry, and cholera; not to speak of its effectiveness in diseases of the liver and the spleen, scurvy, dropsy, inflammation of the urinary tract, diabetes, stone, and even gonorrhea, if the last affliction had not advanced too far. In summer the area attracted great crowds, who either came to drink the waters with their diuretic qualities directly at the source and spend a quiet day in the country or fill up flasks to sell or keep at home.

The waters known to the ancient Romans as Aquae Albulae from their milky color contained large quantities of sulphurated hydrogen, as well as borax and sulphate of soda. The Romans flocked to it, chiefly in search of a cure for their skin afflictions.[15]

But death would come sooner or later. Whenever it was imminent the priest was called at once to hear final confession and give the last sacrament; from that moment it was his duty to stay with the dying person until he had drawn his last breath. The candles were lit, the friends left the chamber, and priest and penitent were left alone together. After extreme unction had been given, the friends were allowed to return; often they never came back, but left the dying person in the hands of the priest. Once death came, the body was entirely abandoned to the priests, who took possession of it, watched over it, and prepared it for burial, while the family found refuge elsewhere and stayed away a week. The Romans had such horror of death, they did not willingly return to a place where one of the family had died. The corpse was not ordinarily allowed to remain in the house for more than twelve hours, except on condition it was sealed up in lead or zinc.

At nightfall a sad procession of *becchini* – gravediggers – and friars took the body amid chants of the *Miserere* to church. Once there, the coffin was laid out on a large catafalque which stood before the altar in one of the chapels. A mass was celebrated

[15] Andrieux, *Daily Life in Papal Rome*, 56–57; Castiglioni, *Storia della medicina*, 563–64; Canezza, *Gli arcispedali di Roma*, 110, 112; Madelin, *Rome de Napoléon*, 87–88; B.CORS., ms. 1589, f. 90; B.N.Ro., Fondo Gesuitico, ms. 78; ms. 85, ff. 76–78; Cesare D'Onofrio, *Il Tevere e Roma* (Rome, 1970), 51–52; Tomassetti, *La Campagna romana*, 3:225; Young, *Rome in Winter*, 210; Cochrane, *Florence in the Forgotten Centuries*, 431–32. For a list of popular medicine and folk cures see Zanazzo, *Tradizioni popolari romane. Usi, costumi*, 7–86. Seregni (ed.), *Carteggio di Verri*, 10: 190–91; B.CAS., ms. vol. 3815; Mario Lizzani, "Una miscellanea romana del Settecento," *L'Urbe*, 4 (1939), no. 10, 14; Story, *Roba di Roma*, 100.

for the soul of the departed. This over, the corpse was left alone in the church in charge of a priest whose duty it was to watch over it. At midnight came the *becchini*, stripped off the velvet pall, and, placing the naked coffin on an ordinary cart, carried it off for burial. For those dead whose families were without means, the Confraternità della Morte e dell'Orazione, whose primary responsibility was to bury the bodies of those found dead in the Campagna, in common with other confraternities performed the final services without payment.

In Rome, as elsewhere at the time, the numerous cemeteries ranged around parish churches, convents, and hospitals, such as Santo Spirito. Unless a person was fortunate enough to possess sufficient money to buy himself the right of burial within the walls of a church or convent, which was done in evasion of a specific prohibition, he was simply thrown into a mass grave that could contain as many as a thousand corpses and was cleared out every seven or eight years. In general, there were no cemeteries outside the inhabited zones, except the Jewish one at the Porta Portese and, in the latter part of the eighteenth century, the Protestant one at the foot of the pyramid of Cestio. Although the municipal authorities decided as far back as 1591, at a moment when famine and epidemics raged in the city, to open a cemetery outside the inhabited quarters as a measure of hygiene, it was really only in the nineteenth century that the French founded the first large cemetery in the city, the Campo Verano, behind the basilica of San Lorenzo fuori le Mura.[16]

Both as far as social welfare and medical services are concerned, Rome inherited a foundation derived from the Counter Reformation zeal for charitable works that could have made her the envy of most cities in Europe. Nevertheless, even here we detect changes. The effort of Innocent XII to laicize the control of the poor, however unsuccessful, marks a new departure. Indeed the failure of Rome to solve its problems, while by no means unique to the papal capital, marks an end of the Tridentine goal of the Christian community taking care of its more unfortunate, a phenomenon we shall see illustrated in the following chapter by the decline in charitable giving of time and money for prisoners. On the other hand, there was still too much charity for the economic health of the city. The physical health was well enough cared for, but, before the end of the century, the medical profession, in spite of some fine teachers in the medical faculty of the Sapienza, lagged behind the advances in the science made in the north, among which the failure to adopt the practice of innoculation looms large.

[16] Ibid., 498–503, 506. Although Story wrote his account in the nineteenth century, there is good reason to believe that it holds true for the eighteenth century. Delumeau, *Vie économique et sociale de Rome*, 1:246; Fiorani, *Riti, ceremonie, feste e vita del popolo*, 243–44; Madelin, *Rome de Napoléon*, 543; Canezza, *Gli arcispedali di Roma*, 115.

9

# Law enforcement and criminal justice

The Roman, intolerant of any yoke, observed no laws, decrees, or regulations. And when he suffered wrong – or, at least, believed he did – he took the law into his own hands. His readiness to use the knife for the settlement of any issue has generally been attributed to the passionate impulse of his nature; but it probably arose from his entire distrust of the possibility of legal redress in the courts. Wherever law enforcement is lax and courts are ineffectual, public justice assumes the shape of private vengeance. So the system was in part responsible for its transgressions.[1]

The law enforcement agents were the sbirri, who were divided into detachments under the command of bargelli. Their total number came to about 168, of whom 50 served in two companies in the Campagna. Of the remainder, 96 were attached to the tribunal of the governor of Rome. The tribunals of the cardinal camerlengo, the cardinal vicar, the Apostolic Chamber, and the senator of Rome each had a handful of men who were expected to lend a hand to the bargello of the governor, if the need arose, as were the officers and soldiers of the garrison. Among the latter were the so-called *corsi*. Originally made up of Corsicans, the corps in the eighteenth century consisted mainly of papal subjects. Their number fluctuated between 215 in 1700 and 583 in 1792. Their character was more that of police than soldiers, as was that of the guard regiment of the reds, the *rossi*, with a complement of about four hundred. The ultimate responsibility for public order in the city rested with the governor, who normally carried out this function with a budget of around 15,000 scudi a year, which was roughly 0.6 percent of the cameral budget.[2]

The service, while not adequate, performed tolerably well, given the character of the personnel and funds available. Giuseppe Retti, writing at the time of Innocent XI, described the sbirri as the "vilest of the vile." This remark may be an exaggeration, but it would not be amiss to say that the origins of the sbirri were often

[1] Silvagni, *La corte pontificia*, 1:48; Zanazzo, *Tradizioni popolari romane. Usi, costumi*, 285–86; Story, *Roba di Roma*, 120.

[2] ASR, Camerale II, birri, memorie diverse, busta 1; birri, ruolo delle paghe delle compagnie, busta 2; ASR, Camerale II, camerlengato e tesorierato, progetti diversi, busta 19; ASR, Camerale II, conti dell'entrata e dell'uscita, busta 5, lib. 22; Da Mosto, *Milizie dello Stato romano*, 229–38, 242–44. Luigi Cajani estimated that the city was policed in the second half of the eighteenth century by about 1,500: for a population of about 160,000 inhabitants, a ratio of about 1 to 100. Paris, with a population of 524,000 permanent inhabitants and a floating one between 100,000 and 120,000 in 1789, had according to Neckar a similar proportion with a garrison of 7,000 men. Luigi Cajani, "Giustizia e criminalità nella Roma del Settecento," in Vittorio Emanuele Giuntella (ed.), *Ricerche sulla città del Settecento* (Rome, 1978), 266.

base and their morality nil. Badly dressed and badly paid, about 4.50 scudi a month for an ordinary sbirro, they scarcely gave the appearance of a disciplined organization. The corruption in the force seems not only to have been confined to the lowliest ranks. In 1778 the bargello of Rome, Michele Cicoli, was found guilty of malfeasance in office, pocketing money by keeping the force under official strength and selling the coveted positions of police spies for personal payment to known criminals.

It was no wonder that the worst insult to throw at an enemy was to call him a "figlio di sbirro." It became an article of popular faith that the officers of the law were everybody's enemy, and collaboration with them was frowned upon. Honor forbade not only the denunciation of a criminal, but even the giving of assistance in arresting him. Given the popular odium in which they were held, the sbirri, in contrast to the courts, were not inclined to mercy. If a patrol caught a criminal in the act, it was likely to carry out summary justice on the spot without trial, in defiance of a law of 1741 prohibiting such violence.

But in fairness to the sbirri, their work was hampered and frustrated by the fact that Rome was a city full of places of refuge, which criminals could easily reach, and the crowd was only too eager to help them. With a church every few steps, domestic chapels on all sides, and convents everywhere, the miscreant had no trouble finding a refuge.[3]

The word "sanctuary" was given the widest possible connotation. Since 1591, when Gregory XIV gave the local immunity of sacred palaces a broad interpretation, this right of asylum had tended to undermine the maintenance of public order not only in Rome, but in other Catholic states. The situation was exacerbated in Rome, because the ambassadors and the chief members of their staff enjoyed extensive diplomatic immunities, not only of their persons and their residence, but they frequently exercised autonomous jurisdiction over the piazzas and areas surrounding the embassies. Since the middle of the seventeenth century, however, many popes, beginning with Innocent XI, tried to reclaim their rights with varying success. In 1692 the congregation in charge of roads decided to reassert papal jurisdiction over all the squares in Rome. The right of ecclesiastical asylum was also moderated in practice when popes since Clement XI's time extradited clandestinely criminals hidden in churches. The normal procedure of a lay judge having to apply to an ecclesiastical judge for extradition was frequently waived. Nevertheless what remained of sanctuary was still an obstacle to effective law enforcement.[4]

[3] Tournon, *Etudes statistiques sur Rome*, 2:107; Andrieux, *Daily Life in Papal Rome*, 93, 97–101; Zanazzo, *Tradizioni popolari romane. Usi, costumi*, 237–38; Vicchi, *Vincenzo Monti (1778–1780)*, 120; Madelin, *Rome de Napoléon*, 67–68; Seregni (ed.), *Carteggio di Verri*, 10:130, 142–43; 11:100; Raffaelle Ajello, *Il problema della riforma giudiziaria e legislativa nel regno di Napoli durante la prima metà del secolo XVIII* (Naples, 1961–65), 1:26–31.

[4] Cajani, "Giustizia e criminalità nella Roma," 269–70; Michel, "Vie quotidienne au Palais Farnèse," 1:2:510; Morelli (ed.), *Lettere de Benedetto XIV*, 1:103; Cosimo Amidei, *Opere* (Turin, 1980), 197–200; Montaiglon and Guiffrey (eds.), *Correspondance des directeurs de l'Académie de France*, 3:387.

Giuseppe Retti in a memorandum to Innocent XI on the abuses of the sbirri put forward various points for a program of reform, which may be summed up as follows: careful and thorough choice of recruits after their moral and criminal past had been examined; the constitution of a special corps of police formed from professional military men to guarantee discipline; and integration of the various organs of law enforcement. His proposals were not heeded and it would take another century and a half before papal Rome would see a corps of efficient police operating at the service of the governor. When Cardinal Ignazio Busca was governor under Pius VI, he planned to introduce a police force into Rome such as he had observed as papal nuncio in Paris, Brussels, and other capitals, but he quickly met with such resistance that he gave up the project. In 1793, at the time of the French threat, the responsibility for maintaining public order had to be transferred to military patrols and the functions of the sbirri were largely limited to carrying out the orders of the courts.[5]

The other guardians of the law in Rome were the soldiers; or, at least, this was the intention. In 1729, a commission of cardinals appointed to recommend savings for the Apostolic Chamber advised against reducing the garrison in the city, because it was needed for the preservation of order, in particular for guarding burning buildings against looting. There was a hint of the prevalence of arson. But a great gulf separated the ideal from reality. The papal soldier turned out to be nothing else than a licentious fellow in garrison life. To meet one in a deserted place was as perilous as meeting a dangerous bandit. Women on the street were always in fear of becoming targets of their molestations. They were only too ready to perpetrate crimes for people in return for payment.

What was perhaps most offensive were the constant quarrels and brawls between the two "guardians of the law" in Rome, the soldiers and the sbirri, with patrols of armed soldiers, instead of maintaining peace, taking the side of their squabbling companions. The sbirri, for their part, passed by military officers and sentries with caps on their heads, refusing to salute them while uttering villanies and obscenities.

In addition to the sbirri and the soldiers, a host of police spies or informers were kept on the payroll. Although legally permitted to carry weapons, this extraordinary force was not meant to engage in criminal investigation. Its activities were confined to gathering data of an administrative or political nature. Consequently when a Roman resident applied for some place or benefice, the relevant authority did not need to undertake a fresh background check, but had the information already on file.[6]

[5] Giulio Pisano, "I 'birri' a Roma nel '600 ed un progetto di riforma del loro ordinamento sotto il pontificato d'Innocenzo XI," *Rivista di studi e di vita romana*, 10 (1932), 544–47, 551–55; Del Re, *Governatore di Roma*, 43–45; Gorani, *Rom und seine Einwohner*, 85; ASR, Camerale II, birri, memorie diverse, busta 1.

[6] B.N.Ro., Fondo Gesuitico, ms. 195, no. 1; Da Mosto, *Milizia dello Stato Romano*, 373–80; Seregni (ed.), *Carteggio di Verri*, 10:342; ASR, Camerale II, birri, memorie diverse, busta 1; ASR, Camerale III, teatri, giuochi, busta 2140, no. 26; Andrieux, *Daily Life in Papal Rome*, 97 n. 1.

We have already alluded to the fact that one of the weakest features of the papal administration was the judicial system. There was a hopeless tangle of law courts. Without taking into account the higher judicial instances in the Papal States, the courts in the city had multiplied so much because every authority in Rome was at one and the same time judge and every great department of state and congregation had individual tribunals for cases affecting its interests or its employees. This complexity meant that litigants might well look to more than one tribunal, resulting in endless bickering over competence. Indeed, the distribution of criminal competence was so entangled that a man might be hauled before several courts on the same charge, and there was nothing to prevent opposing verdicts being returned by different judges on the same question. The defendant stood in multiple jeopardy. The appeals courts could not supply any effective remedy, because their system had evolved along the same defective lines as the lower courts. In all fairness, Rome was not unique in this respect; the Neapolitan system also suffered from conflicts of jurisdiction and slowness of legal proceedings, while its lawyers were accused of ignorance, venality, and corruption. Similarly, efforts by Cosimo III to speed up Tuscan penal procedure in 1680 were aborted.

In Rome, criminal proceedings, at least the more serious ones, were carried on behind closed doors. The accused was given a defender, appointed and paid for by the government. He could also choose another lawyer, but the latter was not allowed to attend the proceedings in person; he could merely submit written memoranda. The judges, for their part, were not obligated to justify their verdicts.

This practice made the defendants' fate even more hazardous. For Rome, like other Italian states at the end of the seventeenth century, had no penal code. Criminal lawyers had to fall back on the authority of Prospero Farinacio (1554–1616), whose voluminous *Praxis et theoricae criminalis* (Venice, 1596–1607) provided them with a classified account of the material of criminal law. In conjunction with Farinacio, they also possessed a collection of *bandi*, or decrees, issued over the centuries by secretaries of state, governors of Rome, and other officeholders, which not infrequently contradicted one another. Only toward the middle of the eighteenth century, when a movement toward codification swept both the German and Italian lands, did Cardinal Silvio Valenti, Benedict XIV's foresighted secretary of state, put some order into the jumble with the constitution *Post diuturnas*, which dealt with criminal procedure. It listed felonies and misdemeanors with their corresponding penalties, and incorporated a law prohibiting the carrying of weapons of any kind without proper authorization. The selling or making of short pistols and rifles with cut-off barrels was forbidden under threat of life imprisonment and loss of property. Whether Valenti was directly inspired in his work by Muratori's *De' difetti della giurisprudenza*, published in 1742, whose principles provided the basis of new law codes in Tuscany and Modena, is not certain, although Muratori's essay was dedicated to Benedict XIV. It is a fact, however, that the minister's achievement lasted longer than the brief effort to reform the criminal system in Naples in the early years of Charles VII, which was compromised by budgetary difficulties, or Pompeo Neri's stymied attempt in Tuscany in 1745–48. Valenti's legislation remained in force until 1833.[7]

A new chapter in the history of Italian criminal justice opened with the anonymous publication of Cesare Beccaria's *Dei delitti e delle pene* in July of 1764 at Livorno. Not only did the work make a case for the abolition of torture and capital punishment, but under the influence of Enlightenment thought, especially Montesquieu, and the teachings of secular natural law, it proposed a radical laicization of the judicial process. The work postulated a divorce between the concept of sin and the concept of crime, a distinction between church and civil society more profound than any contemporary Italian legal writer would have dared to advocate until then. A mendicant from nearby Vallombrosa, Ferdinando Facchini, quickly recognized the threat Beccaria's book presented and, in early 1765, labelled him the "Rousseau degli italiani," affirming that his ideas were not only erroneous but blasphemous. Only in the fifth edition of 1766 did Beccaria shed his anonymity, but before its publication the work had been put *in toto* on the Index, without making allowance for any expurgations. Its fate in Rome was further sealed by the appearance of Cosimo Amidei's *La chiesa e la repubblica dentro i loro limiti* two years later, in which the author delimited the jurisdictional ambits between the spiritual and temporal powers, a concept of separation which, of course, was anathema to the papacy. In Rome the similarity between Beccaria's and Amidei's ideas and the danger they represented to the church were quickly recognized.

It is, therefore, not surprising that Beccaria had no influence on the actual practice of Roman courts. A Roman rejoinder to his views appeared in an anonymous work, *Apologia della giurisprudenza romana* (1784), now known to have been written by Antonio Giudici. Giudici condemned the abuses of torture, the death penalty, judicial discretion, and privileges, but he also rejected the idea that courts should be reduced to a simple instrument for the mechanical application of the law. At times he claimed torture might be useful, when the clearly guilty criminal persisted in silence, and the death penalty was necessary for crimes which attacked the basis of society or disturbed public or private security with premeditated malice. Giudici, however, defended his principles with restraint and moderation.

7 Ibid., 90–92, 99; Tournon, *Etudes statistiques sur Rome*, 2:105–7; Silvagni, *La corte pontificia*, 2:102–4; Pastor, *Geschichte der Päpste*, 15:739; Venturi, "Enlightenment in the Papal States," 238; Vincenzo Piano Mortari, "Tentativi di codificazione nel Granducato di Toscana nel secolo XVIII," *Rivista italiana per le scienze giuridiche*, 89 (1952–53), 305, 309, 315–37, 353; Diaz, *Gianni*, 273; Diaz, *Il Granducato di Toscana*, 497–99; Ajello, *Problema della riforma giudiziaria*, 6–9, 187–90, 267–70, 283–86; Petraccone, *Napoli dal '500 all '800*, 177; Eric W. Cochrane, *Tradition and Enlightenment in the Tuscan Academies, 1690–1800* (Chicago, 1961), 216–17; Cochrane, *Florence in the Forgotten Centuries*, 358–59; Eric W. Cochrane, "Muratori: The Vocation of a Historian," *Catholic Historical Review*, 51 (1965), 154–56; Cajani, "Giustizia e criminalità nella Roma," 270–72.

Shortly before the appearance of the Giudici book, Filippo Maria Renazzi (1742–1808), professor at the Sapienza, published his celebrated work on criminal law, the *Elementa juris criminalis* (4 vols.; Rome, 1773–81), a methodical work and perhaps the first one in that age to reduce the material of crimes and punishment to a scientific system. His aim was to cleanse the criminal law of the extraneous accretions with which he found it encumbered. He laid most of the blame for the shocking corruption of penal science on Farinacio. Some have described Renazzi's work as "a broader and more methodical development of the principles of Beccaria's work." It is true that Renazzi admired the writers of the school of natural law, praising Grotius, Pufendorf, and Montesquieu. He commended Beccaria and, like him, called for greater attention to the prevention of evil than to sharpening punishments. He condemned torture, but would not speak on the question of the death penalty. Renazzi is clearly seen in his work as one who understood his age; yet fearful of the outcome of unbridled innovations, he maintained a prudent reserve, marked by good judgment and dignity. In so doing he became Rome's counterpart to Naples' Gaetano Filangieri, whose *Scienza della legislazione* appeared in 1780. But like Filangieri in Naples, Renazzi never succeeded in breaking the cultural and political deadlock in Rome and his influence on penal legislation was slight.[8]

Only the drafting of a new criminal code would be able to break that deadlock and take the reform of the criminal system seriously in hand. In Prussia Frederick II and in Austria Maria Theresa had already embarked upon such enterprise. The first such piece of legislation in Italy was the *Codice Estense* in 1771. In 1776 a start was made on reforming the criminal law in Tuscany by Pietro Leopoldo, which eventuated in a new *Codice Leopoldino* in 1786. The code was an organic systematization of the country's penal system, that included the abolition of imprisonment for debtors and of the death penalty, as proposed by Beccaria. Encouraged by the new wave of activity, at the end of 1785 Pius VI ordered work on a new criminal code. The outbreak of the French Revolution would prevent the completion of the task. Nevertheless, a document of the commission entrusted with the work, which contains observations about the criminal justice system and the courts together with some recommendations, has survived. It complains of a surfeit of lawyers, ill trained and educated, who flee from the criminal to the civil courts in search of pecuniary gain. The public has become so mistrustful of judges and criminal lawyers that an honest craftsman was ashamed to walk beside a criminalist. This called for a change in public opinion, otherwise all reforms would be ineffective. All judicial officials were to be given a background check and an

[8] Carlo Calisse, *A History of Italian Law*, translated by Leighton B. Register (Boston, 1928), 354, 462–65; Franco Venturi, "Beccaria e la sua fortuna," in *Atti del convegno internazionale su Cesare Beccaria* (Turin, 1966), 9–14; Luigi Firpo, "Contributo alla bibliografia del Beccaria (Le edizione italiane settecentesche del 'Dei delitti e delle pene')," in *Atti del convegno internazionale su Cesare Beccaria* (Turin, 1966), 337, 363; B.CORS., ms. 1591, f. 97; Venturi, *Settecento riformatore*, 2:235–49; Rotondo, "Introduzione," 9–11, 85–88; Giulio Natali (ed.), *Storia letteraria d'Italia: Il Settecento* (2 vols.; Rome, 1929), 1:305; Clementi, *Il carnevale romano*, 2:2–3.

examination before being admitted to practice in criminal courts. No employee of the governor's tribunal was to hold a second job, which would distract him from his judicial duties.

For obvious reasons not many traces of Beccaria's ideas were to be found in these recommendations. The philosophy behind law enforcement, in the eyes of the commission, was deterrence rather than retribution, the most patent example of which was the death penalty. The certainty of the penalty and the speed of its execution rather than its severity, it was emphasized, contributed to public tranquility. The principle of certainty in judgment depended on the tribunals, which had to be able to pursue the criminal without let or hindrance wherever he happened to be in the Papal States. Another lengthy section treated criminal procedure and tried to lay down norms for preventing multiple trials for one offense committed by the same person.

Had these points been implemented, Roman criminal justice would have seen a genuine reform. As it was, however, too much vested interest in the old mismanagement and the patent lack of energy shown by the authorities frustrated such change.[9]

In one area there was a measure of improvement. Whereas the system of torture to extract confessions was only definitely abolished in Rome in 1831, apart from the short interval of the Jacobin republic, the governor of Rome issued an order in June 1735, at the moment when penal legislation was being stiffened with the papal decree *In supremo justitiae solio*, in which he did away with torture for obtaining confession in cases of heinous crimes, a rather large undefined category. The purpose was to prevent the abuse of the system; the result was to modify, both in spirit and practice, the judicial process. The groundwork of this striking action had already been well laid before the appearance of Beccaria's work in subtle changes in the law of evidence. Since the seventeenth century European courts had bypassed the old Roman canon law requirement of two eyewitnesses to a crime by implementing the legal concept of *poena extraordinaria* where full proof was lacking, but where sufficient and persuasive circumstantial evidence existed. So, under an ordinance of 1670, French courts could sentence an accused to punishment short of death, even when he had not confessed. The gubernatorial decision was simply an extension of this. Torture, when imposed, consisted of two forms, the *corda* or racking rope and the *veglia* or enforced wakefulness. In the *corda*, the victim's hands were tied behind him with a rope run on a pulley; he was then drawn seven to ten meters from the ground. Suspended from there, the rope was then released either gently or abruptly, depending on the severity of his tormentors. In the *veglia* the victim was put on a pointed stool for five to ten hours and tied in a precarious balance by several leather straps. Under the enormous physical pressures exerted

[9] B.VALLICELL., ms. Z7, ff. 160–61, 164–82, 204–6; Pastor, *Geschichte der Päpste*, 16 pt 2:34; Mortari, "Tentativi di codificazione," 311, 366–70, 376; Diaz, *Gianni*, 258–70; Cochrane, *Florence in the Forgotten Centuries*, 462–66.

by this position the tortured person frequently collapsed and suffered severe internal injuries.[10]

Turning to the actual practice in the Roman courts, we would have to start with the most important, and probably most efficient, of the criminal tribunals in the city, that of the governor, which sat at the palace of the Montecitorio. Since it possessed the authority to impose the death penalty, it handled the more serious cases. The fact that its written procedure did not favor eloquence impressed the French visitor Gabriel-François Coyer, who assumed somewhat disingenuously that it thereby eliminated chicanery.

The records of this tribunal, as indeed those of others, are enormous in bulk and would yield only to a very protracted examination. Just in one year, 1780, the tribunal dealt with 3,565 cases, in the following monthly distribution:

| | | | | | |
|---|---|---|---|---|---|
| January | 262 | May | 347 | September | 230 |
| February | 397 | June | 314 | October | 223 |
| March | 361 | July | 303 | November | 279 |
| April | 340 | August | 206 | December | 303 |

The numerical distribution does not indicate any special pattern, except that perhaps the inflated figures for February and March may be attributed to the general high spirits of carnival.

A glance through the tribunal's registers reflects much of the day-to-day life of the city. There are the usual cases of theft and petty pilfering. A number of complaints concerned young people playing in the street. The books abound with quarrels and brawls, a drunken brawl with knives after a card game, or one between coach drivers over the right to pass each other after a stage performance at the Teatro Argentina.

Conflicts within the family, such as mother-in-law quarrels, were also frequent. Suits involving prostitution and sex-related offenses made their appearance on the registers. There was a case of rape in the ghetto; or of a drunken husband who beat his wife and tried to force her to become a prostitute. A youth, seduced by a married woman, was set upon by her husband and his friends. In 1780/81 there was the notorious case of adultery of the wife of the noted painter Marco Benefial with a soldier from the Castel Sant'Angelo, met by a countercharge of wife beating.

An early form of medical malpractice suit was brought against Dr. Teodoro Angelucci, brother of the physician Liborio Angelucci, who would play a role in the early months of the Jacobin republic. He was accused by the husband of a certain Beatrice Angelini for failing to save her life; she died of a rabbit bite on her finger.[11]

10 Cajani, "Giustizie e criminalità nella Roma," 273–75, 289; John H. Langbein, *Torture and the Law of Proof. Europe and England in the Ancien Regime* (Chicago and London, 1977), 45–49, 61–68.

11 Cajani, "Giustizia e criminalità nella Roma," 265–66. The statistics were taken from ASR, Tribunale del governatore, serie processi, buste 1333–1357. The selected cases were taken from that series and ASR, Tribunale del governatore, miscell. artisti, busta 5.

As for killing, the knife was everything to the Romans, it was their life. It became the duel weapon of the mob, for homicide was rarely committed in cold blood or through treachery. Instead the victim was stabbed with a knife in a duel. In such a fight, the blows of the combattants continued until one of the two fell wounded. If the wounds did not produce death, the wounded extended his pardon and the matter was closed. But if death occurred, a vendetta by the relatives ensued.

Usually when a sbirro came on the scene no one knew anything and no one had seen anything, not even those who had helped the killer to flee. For he who did the killing was always in the right; the dead always deserved it. A proverb in the Roman dialect, in fact, said as much:

> Nun dite pover 'ômo a cchi mmôre ammazzato;
> Perchè si ha ffatto er danno l'ha ppagato!
>
> (Do not say that the poor man who died was killed;
> Because he who had done the injury has paid for it!)

The frequent inability of the police to seize the murderer and the subsequent failure of the administration of justice to punish him drove, and in a sense authorized, the family of the victim to seek its own justice sooner or later in the form of a vendetta.

In addition to murder with the knife, poisonings were not unknown in Rome, although for obvious reasons less public. They usually took place among relatives. The most notorious poison was Acqua Toffana, named after the infamous poison mixer who first concocted it in Naples. It was as clear as water and had no taste.

Given the fact that the Romans looked rather benevolently upon law breakers, we need not be surprised that there are no reliable statistics on murder for the city. Cacault, the French agent in Rome, reporting to his foreign minister, gave the number of killings from knife stabbings during the summer of 1797 at three to four persons a day. On the other hand, the criminal records during the eleven years of Clement XIII's pontificate (1758–69) claim that 4,000 murders were committed in Rome, which comes to one a day, probably too low an estimate. But murder did not always earn the death penalty. Giovanni Bugatti, the Roman executioner for 44 years, states that between 1796 and 1808 he put to death 105 people – less than nine a year – many of them for offenses that were no hanging matter at all. Offenses against the person were more readily pardoned in Rome than those against property.[12]

Indeed, this attitude would account for the frequency of personal crimes in the papal capital. A statistical inquiry in the law suits pending or conducted before the

[12] Silvagni, *La corta pontificia*, 1:4 285–86; Zanazzo, *Tradizioni popolari romane. Usi, costumi*, 201–203, 212–13; Carl Justi, *Winckelmann und seine Zeitgenossen* (3 vols.; Cologne, 1956), 2:23; ASR, Arcispedale di S. Giacomo degli Incurabili, ferite, busta 829; Pastor, *Geschichte der Päpste*, 16, pt 1:463; Montaiglon and Guiffrey (eds.), *Correspondance des directeurs de l'Académie de France*, 17:74; Madelin, *Rome de Napoléon*, 66–67; Goethe, *Italian Journey*, 461; Gorani, *Rom und seine Einwohner*, 61–64; Seregni (ed.), *Carteggio di Verri*, 12:71; Paglia, "*Pietà dei Carcerati*", 241 n. 84; B.N.Ro., Fondo Gesuitico, ms. 90, ff. 1–213; B.Lancisi., LXXV, 2 (137).

tribunal of the governor in 1780 showed 1,027 suits. Of these 534 (52.29 percent) were for crimes against the person, as against 278 (27.07 percent) involving offenses against property and 215 (20.9 percent) against public authority. The last lumps together such miscellaneous infractions as carrying arms, playing forbidden games, resisting an agent of justice, desertion, and violation of a sentence of exile. Among the 534 cases of offenses against persons only 39 concerned homicide. This distribution contrasts sharply with the experience of Paris. An inquiry of the four years of 1755, 1765, 1775, and 1785 showed that 92.7 percent of all crimes that were tried at the Châtelet were against property, 7.1 percent against persons and 0.2 percent against public authority. In the worst year, 1755, offenses against the person came to only 10.14 percent of the total, of which 13 cases (4.7 percent of the whole) involved homicide.[13]

Stealing may have been despicable in the eyes of the Roman mob and, unlike a fight, aroused its disdainful hostility, but it happened often enough. Such petty offenses were brought before the criminal tribunal of the senator of Rome, where the senator with the help of assessors judged the small suits of the people summarily and without appeal.[14] The criminal tribunal of the camerlengo and treasurer general quite appropriately dealt with questions of currency, such as the illegal export of coins, the hoarding of foreign currency, which was particularly rife among small craftsmen and petty merchants threatened by the flood of cedole, and the circulation of counterfeit and defective money. In addition, it exercised jurisdiction over the bullion trade, and archeological excavations and finds. The brisk export trade without permission of objects found in digs kept the court busy. But it was usually the small, somewhat naive, transgressor who was hauled before it, not the big entrepreneur. Family matters, testamentary affairs, cases involving parochial clergy and their servants, and a limited number of moral offenses, as well as most matters pertaining to the Jews in the ghetto were in the purview of the tribunal of the cardinal vicar.[15]

The Roman penal system compared favorably with the judicial system. In the history of penology under Roman law three periods can be distinguished, in each of which a different punitive system prevailed; from pecuniary penalties, much used in the earlier Middle Ages, we pass to corporal and capital punishment, and by the seventeenth century end up with detentive punishment. The last entered through

[13] Cajani, "Giustizia e criminalità nella Roma," 284–86; Porphyre Petrovitch, "Recherches sur la criminalité à Paris dans la seconde moitié du XVIIIe siècle," in *Crimes et criminalité en France sous l'Ancien Régime, 17e – 18e siècles* (Paris, 1971), 208.

[14] Vicchi, *Vincenzo Monti (1778–1780)*, 222–23; Andrieux, *Daily Life in Papal Rome*, 93; Coyer, *Voyage d'Italie*, 1:288. Cases before the tribunal are found in ASR, Tribunale del senatore, costituti, investigazioni, buste 436–556. They do not readily lend themselves to analytical study.

[15] ASR, Tribunale criminale del tesoriere e camerlengo, buste 338, 339, 449, and ASR, Tribunale criminale del tesoriere e camerlengo, antichità, buste 71–75; ASR, Tribunale del vicariato, ufficio criminale e civile, busta 325.

the tradition of canon law. The church, not accepting the principles of the Roman penal code, changed the entire penal system in the Middle Ages and at the outset of the modern period. It was constrained to exercise upon its undisciplined clergy the first rudimentary forms of sanctions. In this way the concept of prison as an aspect of punishment became enshrined in the canon law penal system almost from the start. The church had to have recourse to prison as a detentive penalty, since, while it disposed of criminal jurisdiction, it could not morally impose sentences of death. The penalty of life imprisonment was therefore equivalent to the civil authority's death penalty.

The prevalence of the ecclesiastic magistracy over the civil one at the end of the sixteenth century in Rome had its repercussions in the area of detentive imprisonment. In the canonical conception of punishment the principal purpose was the correction of the prisoner and prison was to serve this function. The rapport between prison and monastery was not lost on the ecclesiastical tradition, with the idea of repentance and reformation. In the writings of the seventeenth-century penologists a new spirit intruded, however. Punishment was regarded as a vindictive reaction to the misdeeds of the offender, which overtook the guilty individual in order to save society.

The highest authority over Roman prisons was the cardinal camerlengo, who had replaced the senator of Rome and the Capitoline magistracy. With the reform of the statutes by Gregory XIII in 1580, the camerlengo carried out this authority through the governor of Rome. One of the principal charges of the governor was the visitation of prisons and prisoners in the city. Earlier decrees by Clement VII, Paul III, and Pius IV had already set up a visitation committee. It was to inspect every Thursday morning the places of confinement, examine the inmates and listen to their complaints. Extraordinary visitations were to take place monthly and courtesy ones at Easter and Christmas. After having gathered the information, the visitors discussed collegially the position of each inmate and issued a general decree about the matters examined. It was a most effective device against extortion by the prison guards, and helped to eliminate many potential abuses.[16]

For there were plenty of loopholes for such abuses, given the way prisons were run in Rome. Anyone who had the misfortune of falling into the hands of the sbirri was brought to prison and entrusted to the "captain," also called *soldano*, who had the contract, or farm, for the prison services. The *soldano* was theoretically responsible to the president of prisons, a chierico of the Apostolic Chamber, who was in direct charge of running the prisons. Every prisoner had to provide the expenses of detention himself, keeping account with the *soldano*. Such a situation naturally lent itself to the abuse of authority by the *soldano* and the guards toward the prisoners. As for the poor prisoners who were unable to pay for their keep, they

[16] Paglia, "*La Pietà dei Carcerati*", 5–7, 11, 16–18, 20–24; Del Re, *Governatore di Roma*, 49 n. 119.

had to turn for help to public charity, either through the work of the confraternities or other compassionate visitors.

In the second half of the sixteenth century Rome had six prisons. The oldest was that of the Campidoglio, which was the prison of the tribunal of the senator, reserved for lay citizens, and the largest that of the Tordinona, directly subject to the governor. The prisons were generally places of communal habitation.

A new direction in the concept of a prison was given by Innocent X with the building of the Carceri Nuove between 1652 and 1655 for those arrested by order of the governor, the cardinal vicar, and the cameral auditor. The decision to create a new penal institution in the Via Giulia inspired by avant- garde ideas was an act of policy of farreaching consequences. By taking monastic architecture as his model, the pontiff transformed the prison into a school of collective re-education and redemption from sin, while anticipating the countries of Europe in realizing the first prison with cells. He thereby started an institution that qualitatively surpassed imprisonment as practiced hitherto.

The five-story building, whose external appearance gave the impression of a cut-off pyramid, was divided internally by two courtyards. On the ground floor were the offices of the prison service, including the kitchen and mess. The prison quarters were divided into *larghe*, large rooms which held numerous detainees and, on the two top floors, seventeen *segrete* for those accused of more serious crime. These latter were rather large rooms (8.30 × 5.10 m) that held at the most ten persons. Some were reserved for men, others for women. They were further subdivided for major and minor offenders. With the building of the Carceri Nuove ended a preliminary stage in the evolution of modern penal practice.

This phase found its culmination in Rome with the construction of a house of correction at the Ospizio di San Michele. In November 1703, Clement XI ordered its building alongside the older edifice on the Ripa Grande for youths of twenty and below who had been sentenced to prison for theft and other offences. The prison, designed by Carlo Fontana, was in the form of a rectangular block of cells, with sixty separate cells on three floors, grouped around a large central space, where there was an altar for celebrating mass. Beneath an open loggia was a large commodious room where the inmates were taught to work wool, silk, and cotton. San Michele, with its system of detention in cells, isolation at night, work during the day in silence, became one of the first European experiments in modern correctional prisons, although it failed as an economic venture. In 1735 Clement XII was to add a special prison for women to the house of correction.[17]

[17] Lalande, *Voyage d'un françois en Italie*, 4:41–42; Cajani, "Giustizia e criminalità nella Roma," 275–78; Petit-Radel, *Voyage historique*, 2:239; Paglia, "*La Pietà dei Carcerati*", 19–20, 24–8, 31–38; Andrieux, *Daily Life in Papal Rome*, 101; Morichini, *Degli istituti di pubblica carità*, 102–6, 108–9; Pastor, *Geschichte der Päpste*, 15:748; B.CORS., ms. 1173; ASR, Camerale II, carceri, affari diversi, busta 2, f. 421; B.CAS., ms. vol. 5336.

Table 43

| | | | | | |
|---|---|---|---|---|---|
| 1696–1700 | 302 | 1736–1740 | 306 | 1776–1780 | 389 |
| 1701–1705 | 339 | 1741–1745 | 359 | 1781–1785 | 430 |
| 1706–1710 | 298 | 1746–1750 | 305 | 1786–1790 | 532 |
| 1711–1715 | 254 | 1751–1755 | 327 | 1791–1795 | 570 |
| 1716–1720 | 282 | 1756–1760 | 293 | 1796–1800 | 635 |
| 1721–1725 | 218 | 1761–1765 | 324 | 1801–1805 | 681 |
| 1726–1730 | 185 | 1766–1770 | 372 | 1806–1808 | 882 |
| 1731–1735 | 257 | 1771–1775 | 384 | | |

In the *stati delle anime* the prisoners were registered under the respective parishes in which the prisons were located. The synoptic tables give the number of detainees in the prisons between about 1600 and 1765, apart from the decade of the 1720s, as around 300. Thereafter a steep climb occurred, reaching a thousand by 1806. This rise may perhaps be attributed to the deteriorating economic conditions following the famine of 1764–66, and the revolutionary conditions in the nineties.

The annual averages of prisoners (corrected to decimal point) over five-year periods are shown in Table 43. However, these numbers do not include all those imprisoned throughout the course of the year, but represent only those in jail at the moment of census taking. So, for example, the total number of prisoners for the whole of 1652 amounted to 6,533, whereas only 257 were given on the census. Similarly, the total number of prisoners for 1582 was 6,420. Perhaps it would not be too far off the mark if we multiply the census figure by a factor of 25 to arrive at the annual figure.[18]

In view of the type of prison administration in Rome, which required prisoners to fend for their keep and pay for their food, there was an urgent need for charity to step in and succor the poor and helpless. Three fraternities arose to fill the gap and help the prisoners; the Arciconfraternità di San Girolamo della Carità, which provided subsidies for prisoners and support for poor litigants, the Arciconfraternità della Pietà dei Carcerati, which extended aid, especially monetary, to prisoners, and the Confraternità di San Giovanni Decollata, which concentrated on those condemned to be executed. The Confraternità of San Girolamo della Carità had its origin with Cardinal Giulio de' Medici, later Clement VII, in 1519. It was charged with providing food and other necessities for prisoners. Many poor prisoners who were ready to be released had to remain in prison because they were unable to meet the cost of their confinement and food. In such cases the confraternity would always pay the bill either in full or in part. It helped the poor, friendless prisoner in criminal cases with prosecuting their law suits, especially with the cost of briefs, letters, and

[18] Paglia, "*La Pietà dei Carcerati*", 39–43; Delumeau, *Vie économique et sociale de Rome*, 1:497–98; Friz, *La popolazione di Roma*, 64–65.

commissions. Moreover, the confraternity had overall charge of the spiritual and physical welfare of the inmates. It appointed the chaplains to celebrate mass in the Carceri Nuove and was in charge of the prison infirmaries for all of Rome's jails.

The involvement of the confraternity went even further. Pius V transferred the contract for the prison of the Tordinona from a private *soldano* to the Carità. When the inmates were moved to the Carceri Nuove, the Carità retained its concession. With its new responsibilities the confraternity soon found itself in financial difficulties. In 1693 it was already 33,919 scudi in arrears. By 1711 it was decided that the Apostolic Chamber would pay the confraternity a subsidy of 1,000 scudi a year. The sum proved insufficient to pay off the debts and, in 1748, Benedict XIV had the Carità agree to let out the running of the refectory and the infirmary to a private contractor.[19]

The shortage of the Carità's funds may have been responsible in part for the foundation of the Confraternity of the Pietà dei Carcerati. It arose within the ecclesial renewal which in the second half of the sixteenth century had seen the rise of the new Society of Jesus. In fact, it was at the initiative of a young Jesuit of Norman birth in Rome, Jean Tellier, that it was founded. He had become the apostle to the prisoners in the city. He turned for recognition to Gregory XIII, who with the bull *Pii Patris* of 28 June 1759, approved the confraternity.

The primary function of the Pietà, as was that of the Carità, was to provide money and food to the detainees. Four of its deputies distributed bread directly to the prisoners. But its most distinctive work was with those imprisoned for debt. The confraternity became vital for their liberation. Frequently it acted as an intermediary between the imprisoned debtor and his creditors, trying to bring both parties to compose their differences. Whenever it set such a prisoner free, it made itself the guarantor with his creditors.

Between 1702 and 1712, 889 prisoners were released for civil debt, making an annual average of 87. This generous activity, however, brought the confraternity itself into debt for about 2,000 scudi.

Back in the sixteenth century, Sixtus V, wishing to free the brotherhood from this burden, granted it an annual income of 2,050 scudi to be used at Christmas and Easter for the debtors. Other donations were added later. But the fervor which had animated the first founders of the confraternity began to cool. In effect, since the end of the seventeenth century the Pietà underwent a gradual attenuation of its associative structure and a diminution of its charitable work. In the ten years between 1694 and 1703 its revenue came to a total of 22,930.61 scudi and its expenditure to 22,969.14 scudi. Most of this expenditure was the direct result of its liberating poor debtors.

In the course of the eighteenth century, there was a noticeable decrease in this work of compassion, accompanied by a waning in religious zeal. In part, these

19 B.CAS., ms. vol. 2367, pp. 237–40; ms. vol. 5028; ms. vol. 5336, ASR, Camerale II, carceri, affari diversi, busta 3.

conditions stemmed from the pervasive influence of the new ideas about the state's function in poor relief, which, as we have seen, had begun to supplant the older conception and, in part, from the passing of the Tridentine vision. These factors had their repercussions on the membership of the confraternity. Only one member was admitted in each of the years between 1756 and 1758, and then no more admissions were reported until 1775. The final blow to the Pietà dei Carcerati came with the suppression of the Jesuits and the subsequent ostracism it faced from the Roman curia, since the confraternity had been a byproduct of Jesuit activities. It was therefore difficult for the confraternity to disengage itself from the disgraced Society, even though in its later years there had been no Jesuit presence in its life.

Aware of all these problems, the framers of its new statutes in 1775 attempted to revitalize the association on a smaller scale both in the number of its members and its activity. The leaders in this new life of the confraternity were Roman nobles and ecclesiastics. The number of members was restricted to fourteen, now to be called deputies, no longer brothers. The communal dimension which had occupied such a prominent part in the previous centuries came to an end. The primary object of the deputies was directed almost wholly to the religious life and worship. In order to bring help to the prisoners a special "institute" consisting of a few "technically qualified" men was joined to the confraternity. There was also a drop in the number of prisoners set free. Between 1754 and 1764 the average had come to about 85 a year; by 1778 the total had fallen to 44 and subsequently to around 40. This decline must almost certainly be attributed to the precarious finances of the confraternity, following the loss of its devoted adherents.[20]

One of the privileges the Carità and the Pietà shared with other confraternities and guilds was to ask annually for the liberation of someone condemned to death. Capital punishment was not a rarity in the Roman statute books. Yet in actual practice the number of executions carried out in Rome were not too many. Between 1700 and 1799 there were 251 persons executed in Rome, that is, 2.5 annually. In the last thirty years of the century the number of executions actually fell dramatically; whereas there were 215 executions in the first seven decades, making an average of 3.1 a year, in the latter years, with a total of 36 executions, the annual toll came to 1.2. So, while the population increased, the number of executions actually fell. The reasons are not totally clear. The overall paucity of executions must be sought in the prevailing climate of indulgence in a state where the sovereign claimed to be the vicar of the forgiving Christ. But the same reason that caused the changed approach to torture could also be operative here. In the absence of full proof for a capital crime under Roman–canon law the judge could impose a *poenia extraordinaria* in cases where sufficient or persuasive circumstantial evidence existed, subject to the important limitation that the penalty was less severe than the one prescribed for full

[20] Paglia, "*La Pietà dei Carcerati*", 93–102, 191–201, 206–9, 217–27, 230–36; Delumeau, *Vie économique et sociale de Rome*, 149–501; ASR, Camerale III, 114/II, busta 1968; Vicchi, *Vincenzo Monti (1778–1780)*, 121.

proof under torture. Such limitation ruled out the death penalty. Finally the drop in the last three decades may have been an inverse reaction to Beccaria. Although overtly condemned, his ideas may have shamed the papal authorities into being no less merciful than its "atheistic" detractor.[21]

Capital punishment, whenever it was carried out, assumed an important role not only in the administration of justice but in the social life of the city and in the imagination of the citizenry. The execution of the offender by means of a terrifying spectacle was regarded as an act of redemption for the people. Presented as a public spectacle, it would so impress itself on the memory of the spectators as to become a deterrent for other criminal action. "Spectacularity," therefore, became an integral part of the punishment inflicted upon those condemned. Since 1488 executions were held at the Piazza del Ponte di Sant'Angelo, although in the eighteenth century it had also become customary to hang criminals at the Piazza del Popolo.

In capital cases, in contrast to the protracted civil cases, consummation of the sentence was carried through very rapidly, execution occurring usually on the same or the following day. Hanging was the most common form of execution. Out of the 251 cases of people being put to death, 163 (64.9 percent) were hanged and another 26 (10.36 percent) hanged and quartered, that is, their throats slit. Another mode of execution, more shocking in appearance than painful in reality, which was resorted to in 47 cases (18.73 percent of the total), was hitting with a mallet. The condemned being seated on a scaffold, the executioner struck him on the head with a mallet of special construction that deprived him at once of all sensation. When it was certain that the victim was dead, the executioner cut his throat with a large knife. The last part of the ceremony was thought to make a stronger impression on the minds of the spectators than the bloodless blow which took the life of the criminal. Whatever the method of execution, frequently the condemned would have to go through torments before being finally dispatched. The reason for this unintended agony was to be found in the ineptitude of the executioners, who were often chosen randomly from the dregs of Rome's rabble.[22]

The Confraternity of San Giovanni Decollata, also known as Misericordia, founded by Innocent VIII in 1488, helped those condemned to death by administering the last rites and assisting them with the disposition of all business, such as the last will. Once the victim was dead, the body was taken down solemnly and placed in a coffin, which was carried to the church of San Giovanni Decollata accompanied by the brothers. After prayers for the dead, the corpse was interred in the confraternity's cemetery. The work of the confraternity did not end with the burial, however. Apart from such spiritual ministrations as masses for the executed,

21 Cajani, "Giustizia e criminalità nella Roma," 278–81; Langbein, *Torture and the Law of Proof*, 46–49.

22 Alessandro Ademollo, "Le giustizie a Roma dal 1674 al 1739 e dal 1796 al 1840," *Archivio della società romana di storia patria*, 4 (1881) and 5 (1882), 4:433–38; 5:310–11; Paglia, "*La Pietà dei Carcerati*", 12; Vicchi, *Vincenzo Monti (1778–1780)*, 113–17; Moore, *A View of Society*, 1:475–76; A.Cap.R., no. 8, cred. VII, editti e bandi, 54.

it also provided consolation and limited aid to the dependents of the condemned, be they parents, wives, or children.[23]

More common than these poor devils who were put to death were the galley slaves. Usually those guilty of graver misdeeds were sent to the galleys after being paraded through the town for the benefit of decent citizens. But the galleys furnished a dangerous example of punishment that was no punishment. The *galeotti* never rowed a papal galley at sea, since the pope virtually possessed no fleet. They were not even cut off from ordinary life as similar convicts in other lands. They ate better than soldiers, had good beds, and were allowed to leave the house when they pleased. In Civitavecchia, where most of them were taken, they were always on the lookout for any opportunity to improve their lot. They looked for gain doing odd jobs, or they took service with private families. On the square by the docks they set up booths to sell food or articles which they had made. Benedict XIII had the piazza cleared in 1728, but this prohibition would only last a brief time. When the galley slaves worked for the governor or swept the streets of Rome they could earn as much as 20 baiocchi a day. The condition of the *galeotti*, therefore, created a disturbing paradox. If a convict grew tired of it all, escape was easy enough under these circumstances or he could obtain a remission of his sentence, simplified by the fact that a prison month was usually calculated as twenty days.[24]

Thefts and crimes which were not of a capital nature and for which the offender was not put into prison were often punished by the *corda*. For lesser offenses, the *cavaletto* and the pillory were set up in public places, such as the Piazza Navona, where large crowds were wont to gather. On the *cavaletto*, not far from the Pace and the Pallacorda theaters, as many as fifty lashes with a whip could be administered on the buttocks of a pilferer at the summary decision of the bargello, amid the groans of the delinquent and the cruel howls of the mob.[25]

Ancien-regime Rome could certainly boast of some enlightened penal institutions, even if its law enforcement, antiquated and inadequate, frequently clashed with the popular conception of personal justice and morality of the ordinary Romans. But the loss of the Tridentine spirit is perhaps more clearly and directly identifiable in this area than others. The financial breakdown of both confraternities which ran the prison system and performed the needed works of mercy is the consequence of the disappearance of the social responsibility that practical Counter Reformation piety

[23] Morichini, *Degli istituti di pubblica carità*, appendix – third sheet; Paglia, "*La Pietà dei Carcerati,*" 111–12; Moore, *A View of Society*, 1:476–82; Andrieux, *Daily Life in Papal Rome*, 103–4; Ademollo, "Le giustizie a Roma," 4:438; ASR Arciconfraternità di San Giovanni Decollata, lettere e carte diverse, busta 19, fasc. 39; miscellanea personale, busta 17, fasc. 36 and fasc. 37.

[24] Carlo Calisse, *Storia di Civitavecchia* (Florence, 1936), 561; Charles Victor de Bonstetten, *Voyage sur la scène des Six Derniers Livres de Enéide* (Geneva, 1805), 77–80; Andrieux, *Daily Life in Papal Rome*, 102; Zanazzo, *Tradizioni popolari romane. Usi, costumi*, 282–83.

[25] Moore, *A View of Society*, 1:474–75; Silvagni, *La corte pontificia*, 1:53; 2:145; Friedrich Noack, *Deutsches Leben in Rom, 1700 bis 1900* (Stuttgart and Berlin, 1907), 59–60.

had not only encouraged but demanded. Thus, however humane and charitable the existing institutional structure, in the absence of a complementary ethos, it failed to perform both effectively and in an enlightened manner. There are here some similarities between the system of criminal justice and that other institution of social control and public enlightenment, education.

# 10

# Education

As in the case of criminal justice, Rome possessed the potential for being a model among European cities in the field of both popular and higher education, but the reality fell far short. We may fairly say that on paper opportunities for learning were better in this city than anywhere else in Europe. In practice, however, the schools catered almost exclusively to middle-class boys. Lower-born children rarely attended them. Not that these children were excluded, but the parental example and incompetent and unattractive teaching discouraged them from attending. Besides, everybody, at home or at school, aimed primarily at the formation of pious people. Had not Sixtus V started life as a swineherd?

Rome was the first city in Europe to make universal primary education available. The *scuole regionarie*, scattered throughout the rioni, were the oldest places of elementary education in the city, although they were, strictly speaking, not primary schools, since in almost all of them Latin grammar and some humanities were being taught. The basic subjects, however, were writing, reading, and arithmetic. At the end of the eighteenth century the students in several of them were also given French lessons. It is difficult to determine the number of such schools since records for some parishes are missing or incomplete, but Giuntella calculated that in 1703 there were 126 masters for boys' schools, scattered over 53 parishes. These teachers were not paid a regular salary from the city, but collected a small fee from their charges. They were, however, appointed by the city, which had them examined by a commission composed of the professors of the Collegio Romano and other institutions. But this formality appeared to have been neglected in the second half of the century so that among the masters were men who lacked the needed qualifications for their task.

Somewhat more successful were the schools run by religious orders. They remained mainly at the service of the wage-earning and artisanal classes and were conducted in the vernacular. Among the reasons for the success of these schools were the generally free and assured good instruction by masters who had dedicated themselves to teaching as a religious vocation after having prepared themselves in appropriate schools. Hence these religious schools, outstanding among them those of the Piarists and the Brethren of the Christian Schools, attained a high pedagogical standard. This was not the case with the lay teachers, who often seemed to have taken up teaching as a means of livelihood after having cut short an unsuccessful clerical career, and after having failed to find better employment. Among women teachers this was even more evident. Many of them became teachers because they were widows or because they had to cope with poverty. There were, of course, honorable exceptions.

For the early part of the seventeenth century Rome was the center of the educational activities of the Spaniard, Giuseppe Calasanzio, a Roman by adoption, who started his work in 1597 in some small rooms near the church of Santa Dorotea in Trastevere. In 1600 he acquired the house at San Pantaleone. His pedagogical method was based on a system of emulation and competition, rather than coercion and punishment. In 1646, Innocent X formed Calasanzio's *scuole pie* into an order, the Piarists, for whom teaching remained the principal field of activity. During the eighteenth century, a new and much larger house at San Pantaleone became a teacher institute and a school for more than a thousand boys. A smaller one at San Lorenzo in Borgo served as an elementary school for 150 pupils.

The Fathers of the Christian Doctrine came from France via Nice to the Papal States in 1710. They first established schools and seminaries in the provinces. The convent of S. Maria in Monticelli, which was to become their headquarters, was given to the Doctrinaires by Clement XI in 1716. Their students there numbered around two hundred, with about a hundred more in a second house, Sant'Agata in Trastevere, which they acquired in 1747. The Brethren of the Christian Schools, also known under the name of *Ignoranti*, an order founded by Jean-Baptiste de la Salle in Rheims in 1674, came to Rome in 1702 and operated two schools, San Salvatore in Lauro and SS. Trinità dei Monti, aided by an annual subvention from the government.

Among the girls' schools the leading ones were perhaps those of the *maestre pie* at the Gesù, established in 1707, and at San Tomasso in Parione, which was set up in 1716. The institution was founded in Viterbo and brought to Rome under Clement XI by Rosa Venerini. Other girls' schools were those of the *maestre pie filippine* and of the *pie operarie*. Then there were the smaller schools of the Ursulines, started in 1688. These girls' schools in charge of religious orders normally taught reading, the catechism, and women's work, but no writing, much less arithmetic or languages as was the case in the boys' and public schools.

Given these circumstances, illiteracy was undoubtedly rife. There is no way to gauge the amount of it in a city the size of Rome. Among the domestics in the Orsini household we can gain a clue as to how many could sign their names, since they were obliged to acknowledge receipt of their wages on the page opposite their name. Most of the men, except stable employees and coachmen, were able to sign, although frequently with difficulty and with very child-like letters. Women and the lowest rank of servants often were unable to do so; occasionally wives were signed for by their husbands. But semiliteracy reached even the ranks of the master craftsmen, such as masons. It is no surprise, therefore, that public scriveners, who often hailed from the Marches or Umbria, made a brisk business and were able to return home to take up the life of a gentleman.[1]

In sum, it is reasonable to conclude that the elementary schools of Rome, lay and religious together, were not capable of carrying out their mission. The situation for the higher schools was somewhat better. The great Roman colleges attracted students from outside the state. The families who sent their sons to Rome to complete their studies may have thought more of the possibility of establishing them in the capital of the Catholic world than of giving them a better education, but the fact remains that the Roman colleges enjoyed a great reputation even after reform of studies and secularization had taken place elsewhere.

The best of the boarding colleges in Rome was the Collegio Clementino, simply known as the Clementina. Founded in 1596 by Clement VIII, it was entrusted to the fathers of the Congregation of the Jerusalemites, commonly known as the Somaschi fathers. Its student body was limited almost exclusively to the nobility. It numbered among them Prospero Lambertini, the future Benedict XIV, who entered it in 1689, a host of cardinals, a dozen doges of Genoa and one of Venice, a future prince-bishop of Bamberg in Germany and an elector of Mainz. The curriculum extended all the way from reading and writing to theology and jurisprudence. Attention was given to living languages. But like other ecclesiastical academies it did not confer degrees. In its theater students performed classical pieces.

The Collegio Nazareno, run by the Piarists, who competed with the Collegio Clementino in providing superior education, excelled from the literary point of view, with Alessandro Verri, Francesco Algarotti, and Paradisi as its graduates. Founded in 1618 by Cardinal Tonti, bishop of Cesenna, it inherited his residence in 1622 as its property. Aside from the regular curriculum, elocution, dancing, music, and fencing, the accomplishments of a truly polished gentlemen, were taught there. A colony of the Arcadians, commonly known under the name of the *Incolti*, prospered within its walls.

In 1704 Clement XI established the Ecclesiastical Academy. It was to receive young men, at least eighteen years of age, from the Papal States and abroad to study theology and jurisprudence in order to follow distinguished ecclesiastical careers. To be admitted you had to prove that you were of noble birth and declare your

[1] Giuntella, *Roma nel Settecento*, 119–22; Vittorio Emanuele Giuntella, "Documenti sull'istruzione popolare in Roma durante il settecento," *Studi Romani*, 9 (1961), 553–54; Andrieux, *Daily Life in Papal Life*, 54; Morichini, *Degli istituti di pubblica carità*, xxxi–xxvi, 227, appendix – third sheet; Petrocchi, *Roma nel Seicento*, 110–11, 117; B.CORS., ms. 2274; A.Cap.R., no. 7, cred. VII, editti e bandi, 1739; A.Cap.R., Archivio Orsini, serie 2, vol. 191, ruoli dei provisionati salariati; ASR, Camerale II, arti e mestieri, busta 4, fasc. 1; Zanazzo, *Tradizioni popolari romane. Usi, costumi*, 242–43; Filippo Maria Renazzi, *Storia dell'università degli studi di Roma detta communemente la Sapienza* (4 vols.; Rome, 1803–1806), 4:306–10; Brizzi, *Formazione della classe dirigente*, 23.

intention of embracing the clerical estate. Limited to twenty, the students were given a monthly allowance of 80.25 scudi, with which they had to maintain themselves.

Then there was the college of the Propaganda Fide for training youths from oriental lands for missionary work at home. Fallen on rather evil days under Pius VI, it was somewhat outside the mainstream of the educational activity in Rome. Its greatest glory was its printing press, which produced works in about eighteen or nineteen foreign languages, some with exotic alphabets.[2]

Before their suppression the Jesuits directed at least eight educational institutions in Rome, which included some "foreign" institutions whose objective was to educate individuals to propagate the Catholic religion and defend it against heresy. These comprised the Hungarian, Irish, Scottish, Greek, and Maronite colleges, as well as the German and English colleges. The last two were founded by Gregory XIII at the advice of Loyola to combat Protestantism. By 1778, 36 bishops in Germany and Hungary had been students at these colleges.

The Collegio Romano, also founded by Gregory XIII, became the leading educational institution of the city, contending for primacy in the field of higher education with the Sapienza, the university of Rome. The fields of instruction in this forerunner of the present-day Gregorian University ranged from the elements of grammar to theology. The Jesuits received the right to confer doctorates in theology and philosophy, but were never permitted a faculty of law. Its library was one of the most renowned in Italy, consisting of the collections of several prominent men who had entered the Society of Jesus, as well as those of certain other cardinals. The *Giornale dei Savanti d'Italia*, in 1712, gave the number of volumes as 60,000; it must have been much greater at the end of the eighteenth century. One of the rooms of the library was filled entirely with Latin, Greek, Arabic, and Hebrew manuscripts.

Although the college always had astronomical studies, its observatory was built only in 1789. In 1741, when Orazio Borgondio was rector, the young Roggero Boscovich, a former student of his and later his successor as professor of mathematics (1740–50 and 1752–60), began to show his extraordinary ability, which was to make him famous throughout Europe. He joined Borgondio in proposing the idea of an observatory. The death of Borgondio prevented the plan from being carried out immediately, although Benedict XIV favored it. When Boscovich returned to Rome in 1785 he took up his old project with the then professor of mathematics, Don Giuseppe Calandrelli. Pius VI agreed to provide astronomical instruments for the new observatory and Cardinal Zelada brought the enterprise to completion. Professor Calandrelli was entrusted with its direction.

At the time of the suppression of the Jesuits in November 1772, the Collegio

[2] B.CORS., ms. 2274, 16–22; Montesquieu, *Voyages, Oeuvres complètes*, 2:1112; Vicchi, *Vincenzo Monti (1778–1780)*, 132–33; Giuntella, *Roma nel Settecento*, 117–18, 122–24; Gorani, *Rom und seine Einwohner*, 132–34.

Romano received a new organization. It was placed under a special congregation of three cardinals and the direction was handed over to secular clergy. The Apostolic Chamber took charge of all the property and became responsible for the maintenance of both the Collegio Romano and its sister institution, the Seminario Romano, the nursery of the higher Roman clergy. The two were amalgamated. But the congregation had difficulty in finding qualified substitutes for the Jesuit professors. It was eventually driven to rehire quite a few of them.[3]

With a student body that had stabilized around two thousand and the right to grant doctorates (laureates) in some fields since 1553, the Collegio Romano outshone the archgymnasium of Rome, better known as the Sapienza, which was for all practical purposes the university of the city. Its foundation has been attributed to Boniface VIII in 1303, but it only received the right to bestow degrees from the time of John XXII, when he transferred the school to Avignon. On the return of the popes to Rome, Eugene IV assured it in 1431 of a regular income from the gabelle on wine and from imposts on other commodities bought in the city. At that time it also moved to the building in the rione of Sant'Eustachio, which would remain its seat until early this century. Alexander VII completed the building of the Sapienza. He founded its library and presented the university with a botanical garden on the Gianicolo. In comparison with the Collegio Romano the accommodation at the university was crowded, for the ground plan was only one-third that of the Jesuit institution. The pressure on space was aggravated in 1715, when the printer to the papal curia, Giovanni Maria Salvioni, was allowed by Clement XI to move his press into a corner of the building.

The academic structure of the university consisted of five faculties. Two of these faculties had an eminently scientific character, medicine and philosophy. Medicine, in addition to the regular medical subjects and anatomy, included also instruction in chemistry and botany. The faculty of philosophy and the arts taught, besides ethics, logic, and metaphysics, arithmetic, geometry, algebra, and physics. The other faculties were those of the sacred sciences, languages, and law. The languages in the curriculum were Greek, Latin, Hebrew, Syriac-Chaldean, and Arabic. The teaching of Greek shared the general fate that befell that language throughout most of Italy in the late seventeenth and early eighteenth century, when students hardly ever had direct contact with a classical text. In the law faculty there were chairs in civil law, criminal law, and ecclesiastical law.

Although in other universities the practice of setting prescribed books for the students to read and study in their courses had long been in vogue, at the Sapienza

[3] B.CORS., ms. 1533; ms. 2275, 13–15, 24–28, 114–16; B.N.Ro., Fondo Gesuitico, ms. 882; ms. 1363, fasc. 7, 8, 13; ms. 1565; Renazzi, *Storia dell'università*, 4:302–5; Paglia, *"Pietà dei Carcerati"*, 82; Petrocchi, *Roma nel Seicento*, 142, 237–38; Giuntella, *Roma nel Settecento*, 115–16, 121–22; Vicchi, *Vincenzo Monti (1778–1780)*, 134–37; Riccardo G. Villoslada, *Storia del Collegio Romano dal suo inizio (1551) alla soppressione della Compagnia di Gesù (1773)*, (Rome, 1954).

the antiquated routine of the professor dictating his lectures to the students continued to persist throughout the eighteenth century; he dictated a text or notes for the first half of class time and spent the next half explaining and elucidating the matter. The language in use was Latin.

At the close of the seventeenth century the university found itself in a state of serious decline. The sacred sciences had never enjoyed great popularity; after the pontificate of Alexander VII, some classes had only one or two students. The theological schools and colleges of the various regular orders, especially the Collegio Romano, were able to compete successfully for the brightest youths.

The school of philosophy was in a not much happier position. None of the professors at the time were distinguished either for their pedagogical skills or for their published works. Only the chair of mathematics did not reflect the general desolation. There, Vito Giordani was appointed to teach and many rushed to learn the subject at the hands of what for the times was a distinguished man.

In the school of law the professors of civil and canon law, never ready to give their lectures on the appointed day, so disgusted the students that they rarely attended lectures. Hence, professors, eager to supplement their meager annual stipends, which ranged from 60 scudi to 350 scudi, would either hold open school in their houses or wander from palace to palace to tutor the young offspring of noble houses in return for ample compensation. The instruction was based on the canons of the *mos italicus*, a survival of the old Bartolist method at its most mindless, which used Aristotelianism and scholasticism as a means to give an overall unity to legal studies. Apart from Vincenzo Gravina, the law professors at the Sapienza were unknowns until 1748.

Medicine suffered less from the vicissitudes of the Sapienza and remained strong and respectable, the reason being that Rome had no competing school of medicine and it was not easy to obtain private teachers. Busy physicians had neither the time nor inclination to occupy their leisure at home with giving theoretical instruction to students. So amid the desolation of the class rooms only medicine continued to attract sufficient students. The reputation of the professors and their published works, among them Lancisi, Giorgio Baglivi, a student of Malpighi, and the Perugian anatomist Alessandro Pascoli, contributed greatly to the faculty's well-being. Paradoxically, many of the practicing physicians in the city frequently did not reflect the distinction of the medical faculty in the treatment of their patients, as we noted in Chapter 8. The reason may be attributed to the existing gap between medical theory and therapeutic techniques.

Given the overall dismal condition, the learned scholar and scientist Giovanni Giustino Ciampini left a legacy to found an Athenaeum Romanum, whose curriculum, based on the study of science, music, sculpture, painting, and modern languages was to replace the more hidebound Tridentine one of the Sapienza. It never materialized. Another proposal to close the university and turn it over to the Scolopians for a school for poor children found a favorable reception with Innocent

XII. But the premier professor of law, Didaco d'Aghirre, got wind of the project and, enjoying influence with a number of cardinals, managed with the help of his colleagues to avert the realization of the plan.

So Innocent XII contented himself with some minor reforms, such as prohibiting law classes in private houses and raising the salaries of law professors. Clement XI would make the first coherent and serious attack on the confused and uncertain organizational structure and curriculum of the Roman university, but because it blatantly favored the law and medical faculties it encountered lively opposition. Although some isolated appointments of more modern and anti-scholastic scholars, such as Bottari in church history and Giustino Fontanini in Sacred Scripture were made, further attempts at reform had to wait until Benedict XIV.[4]

A new impetus for bringing the Sapienza more up-to-date would come from that other center of learning in the Papal States, Bologna. In the seventeenth and early eighteenth century the once distinguished University of Bologna, like its sister institution in Rome, fell on evil days. Total enrollment had dropped to around 400 students, half of whom attended the law faculty. While the size of the student population is not necessarily a sufficient indicator of the health of a university, a declining enrollment in an institution previously well attended is always a sign of crisis. The decline of Bologna can be largely attributed to the diminishing influx of foreign students, who had once flocked there to hear teachers with a universal reputation, whereas now, with a teaching body almost exclusively of local origin, they preferred to study at the newer universities at home. In part, the decline may also be attributed to the crisis following the condemnation of Galileo. The intellectual forces, joined by the political ones, failed to rally sufficiently around the Galilean program. In fact, the new experimental disciplines met the resistance of the hidebound Bolognese faculty.[5]

Change had to come from outside the university. In 1689 the grand chancellor of the university, the Archdeacon Antonio Felice Marsigli submitted a plan for reforming the institution, which found a sympathetic hearing in the city's senate, but was rejected by the academic community in alliance with the bourgeoisie, fearful of further reduction in their power. Certain of the more progressive elements

[4] Renazzi, *Storia dell'università*, 4:1–6, 26–28, 32–33, 38–39, 50, 85–92, 97–99, 230, 251, 392; B.CORS., ms. 2274, 6–11, 107–11; B.N.Ro., Fondo Vittorio Emanuele, ms. 414; Giuntella, *Roma nel Settecento*, 116–17; Brizzi, *Formazione della classe dirigente*, 223; Maria Rosa di Simone, *La "Sapienza" romana nel Settecento. Organizzazione universitario e insegnamento di diritto* (Rome, 1980), 18–19, 26–29, 43–45, 69–70, 78–79, 82–84, 110.

[5] Ibid., 15; Luigi Simeoni, *Storia della Università di Bologna* (2 vols.; Bologna, 1947), 2:89; Massimo Roatti, "La cultura scientifica tra conservazione e innovazione," in Aldo Berselli (ed.), *Storia della Emilia Romagna* (2 vols.; Bologna 1977), 2:405–6; Carlo Gentili, "Il modello epistemologico dell' *Institutum scientiarum et artium* di Bologna," in Università degli studi di Bologna (ed.), *I materiali dell'Istituto delle Scienze* (Bologna, 1979), 30–31; Marta Cavazza, "La *Casa di Salomone* realizzata?" in Università degli studi di Bologna (ed.), *I materiali dell'Istituto della Scienze* (Bologna, 1979). 44–45.

among the scholars, such as the astronomer and Newtonian Eustachio Manfredi, formed in response a private academy of scientists, the Accademia degli Inquieti, which was to take the place of the defunct Tuscan Accademia del Cimento and keep the Galilean tradition alive. Among its members was the nephew of the old archdeacon, Luigi Ferdinando Marsili, an amateur scientist and geographer, who had served as general in the imperial army. Like his uncle, he wrote a proposal for reforming and modernizing the university in 1709, in which he took the universities north of the Alps as his model. Among his suggestions was to replace the primacy of legal studies with that of the natural sciences and applied mathematics. His project fell on deaf ears.

Rebuffed, Marsili dedicated all his energy toward setting up a scientific academy, which would be the center for advanced scientific and experimental research and a place for the diffusion of the new ideas to the broader public. By 1711 he succeeded in establishing the Istituto della Scienze in Bologna as an outgrowth of the Inquieti. The activities of the academicians were rationally organized into five disciplines – astronomy, chemistry, natural history, military architecture, and physics – without, however, any ruinous barriers between them. The institute was to exchange knowledge with the leading academies in Europe, the Royal Society of London among them. Its purpose was not only to complement the work of the university, but, as Marsili hoped, to produce a new generation of teachers, who in time would positively influence the curriculum of the university and initiate a process of renewal. In partial realization of his hopes, a chair of chemistry was established at the university in 1737, and later on members of the Institute would double as university faculty in their respective fields.[6]

Prospero Lambertini, the future Pope Benedict XIV, was deeply interested in the Institute from the time of its inception. A scholar and a native of the Bolognese, and later its archbishop, he was early on chancellor of the institution and would remain an intelligent patron and loyal interpreter of Marsili's project. When, in 1726, a conflict of views arose between Marsili and the Bolognese authorities, Msgr. Lambertini was appointed arbitrator by the papal curia and decided the issues in favor of Marsili. As pope, in the 1740s and 1750s, he provided the Institute with new buildings and facilities for research and demonstration purposes and presented it with machines and instruments, mainly imported from Holland, for its physics laboratory. He also raised the salaries of the academicians and their assistants. It was

[6] Ibid., 44–50; Gian Paolo Brizzi, "Le istituzione educative e culturali: università e collegi," in Aldo Berselli (ed.), *Storia della Emilia Romagna* (2 vols.; Bologna, 1977), 2:456–57; Giacomelli, "Carlo Grassi e le riforme bolognesi," 32–33; Gentili, "Il modello epistemologico dell' *Institutum*," 22, 30–32; Ettore Bortolotti, "La fondazione dell'Istituto e la riforma dello 'Studio' di Bologna," in R. Accademia delle Scienze dell'Istituto di Bologna (ed.), *Memorie intorno a Luigi Ferdinando Marsili, pubblicate nel secondo centenario della morte* (Bologna, 1930), 385–419, 423–35; Roatti, "La cultura scientifica," 411–12; Simeoni, *Storia della Università di Bologna*, 2:81, 110–12, 116; Maurizio Matteuzzi, "La matematica a Bologna nel secolo XVIII," in Università degli studi di Bologna (ed.), *I materiali dell'Istituto delle Scienze* (Bologna, 1979), 75–76.

6 Msgr. Prospero Lambertini, later Pope Benedict XIV, by Pier Leone Ghezzi

therefore expected that when he became pope in 1740, Lambertini would bring his experience and predilections to bear on the problems of the Roman university.[7]

There is no doubt that Benedict XIV favored reform. Yet the high hopes that had been put in him were not to be fully realized. In the field of university politics his efforts culminated in a reorganization that consolidated rather than transformed the existing condition. His intervention in rationalizing the chaotic situation at the

[7] Giacomelli, "Carlo Grassi e le riforme bolognesi," 33; Bortolotti, "La fondazione dell'Istituto," 437; Vincenzo Pallotti, "Per una storia dell'Istituto delle Scienze," in Università degli studi di Bologna (ed.), *I materiali dell'Istituto delle Scienze* (Bologna, 1979), 58–59; Giorgio Dragoni and Vincenzo Pallotti, "Strumenti, didattica e ricerca: la fisica sperimentale nell'Istituto delle Scienze," in Università degli studi di Bologna (ed.), *I materiali dell'Istituto delle Scienze* (Bologna, 1979), 218; Cavazza, "La *Casa di Salomone* realizzata?" 53.

Sapienza did not contribute to improving the level of scholarship and finished by assuming a conservative character. In 1744, he issued new statutes for the Sapienza, which laid down the terms for choosing professors, although his effort to recruit faculty by open competition (*concorso*) rather than by selection at the hands of the administrative bodies (in law, the consistorial advocates) was aborted by the refusal of the latter to surrender their prerogatives. A commission headed by the rector, Msgr. Clemente Argenvilliers, worked out some internal reforms, which it submitted to Benedict for review and approval. It drew up the academic calendar, set the teaching load for the instructors, and formulated a salary scale, which, although it brought up the range to a height of 1,800 scudi, still remained one of the lowest in Europe. But the principal defect of these reforms was that they deprived the professors of any hope of improving their condition, which, in turn, contributed to a degree of demoralization.

More significant for the progress of the Sapienza than these ambivalent reforms was the change of personalities in the oversight of the university. Annoyed at the fact that Msgr. Argenvilliers had arrogated to himself too much of the cardinal's power over the school, Cardinal Annibale Albani, in high dudgeon, resigned his office of cardinal camerlengo at the beginning of 1747. Benedict XIV put in charge of the university his confidant and friend Cardinal Silvio Valenti Gonzaga, a man with a great fund of learning and intelligence and a former student of the Neapolitan Celestine monk Celestino Galiani, who had made Rome the center of Newtonian scholarship in the early eighteenth century. Valenti had a sincere interest in improving and modernizing the Sapienza.[8]

Although the university had a chair for mathematics, its incumbent concentrated for the most part on teaching the elements of geometry. There was no professor until the time of Benedict who specifically taught the more abstruse branches of the mathematical sciences, although these flourished in other universities. Similarly the study of chemistry, which had become the fashionable science of the day and was making surprising progress, was not pursued in Rome. Cardinal Valenti persuaded Benedict to establish two chairs and provide for the expenses incurred in chemical experiments. So, in 1748, almost at the same time that the pope signed the university reform decree, he founded a chair for higher mathematics, including astronomy, and another for chemistry. Thomas Lesueur, a distinguished French minim from the monastery of SS. Trinità dei Monti, was named the first holder of the chair of higher mathematics. He was succeeded by a Piarist, Francesco Maria Gaudio, who enjoyed a reputation as an able hydrostatic engineer. The appointment of the first professor of chemistry, the Ferrarese Filippo Giraldi, appears to have been a less happy choice.

Prior to this, Benedict had already made provisions for the professorship of physics. The chair until then had been held as an appendage to the secretaryship of

[8] Di Simone, *La "Sapienza" romana*, 117–30, 133, 154–61; Venturi, *Settecento riformatore*, 1:112–14.

the congregation of the Index. As a consequence of this arrangement, instruction was still based on the old-fashioned Aristotelian philosophy, ignoring the great advances made in this field in the interval. In 1746, when the incumbent Orsi, later to become a cardinal, vacated the post, Benedict called Lesueur's fellow minim, François Jacquier, the respected editor of Newton's *Principia mathematica* to occupy the position, whom he entrusted with the teaching of modern experimental physics. Jacquier was succeeded by the Venetian Piarist, Girolamo Fonda, from the Collegio Nazareno, who had published a treatise on lightning and under whose direction lightning rods were installed on the corners of the Sapienza building.

In conjunction with all these innovations a new physics theater on the upper floor and a chemistry laboratory on the ground floor, with the necessary apparatus, some imported from abroad, were set up. However, critics still regarded science teaching as inadequate.

In 1660 Alexander VII had opened a botanical garden for the university on the Gianicolo. In 1678 the Bolognese Giovanni Battista Trionfetti assumed the post of director of the gardens and four years later began to teach botany at the Sapienza. Under Trionfetti the botanical gardens became so famous that it was Rome's boast to have created one of the finest gardens of its kind in Europe with more than 3,000 species of plants. Trionfetti died in 1708 and his death was a disaster for the gardens, because the directors who came after him were good physicians but not really botanists, who regarded their post as a mere stepping stone to be abandoned for the next vacant chair in medicine. Benedict XIV, in an effort to restore the botanical gardens to their pristine state and give an impetus to botanical studies, established two chairs of botany: theoretical botany was taught at the Sapienza together with mineralogy, and practical botany was given at the botanical gardens by its director. The Roman Francesco Maratti, abbot of Vallombrosa, and expert on the flora of Lazio, was the first incumbent of the chair of practical botany, which he held for thirty years. Under him the botanical gardens regained their reputation.[9]

The new reforms in the sciences were introduced at the expense of the legal studies. The number of law courses was reduced to six to make room for the new science courses. In that respect Rome followed the trend in the rest of Europe. As for the content of the law curriculum, while the legal reforms of many Italian rulers in the second half of the century were followed up by reforms in the teaching of law with the introduction of such fields as public and natural law in the universities, there was no change at the Sapienza. Even after the curricular reorganization of 1788 the traditional combination of Roman–canon law and statutary law remained the basis. A slight concession to modernity was the order given to the professor of moral philosophy to lecture on the principles of natural law and international law.

[9] Renazzi, *Storia dell'università*, 4:12–13, 30–31, 204–11, 214–17, 235–38, 247–49, 260–62, 268–69; Enrico Carano, "La botanica in Roma e nel Lazio," in Federico Millosevich (ed.), *Le scienze fisiche e biologiche in Roma e nel Lazio* (Rome, 1933), 201–4; B.CORS., ms. 2275, 124–26; P. J. S. Whitmore, *The Order of Minims in Seventeenth-Century France* (The Hague, 1967), 236–37.

This does not mean, of course, that the law faculty had no distinguished scholars in its ranks. We have earlier referred to Filippo Maria Renazzi, who in 1769 at the ripe age of 27 was appointed to the chair of criminal law, in which he would make the fundamental lines of Beccaria's thought his own, while careful not to offend Catholic orthodoxy. Emanuele Duni, generally recognized to have been first to apply the principles of Vico's thought to jurisprudence, lectured on the Pandects from 1754. His use and exaltation of the historical method constituted a break with the *mos italicus*, which was still very much alive at the Sapienza.[10]

The reforms do not appear to have had the desired effect. The enrollment at the Sapienza continued to be small. In 1753/54 the student body amounted to 140, of which 101 attended courses in law, 21 in medicine, and 18 in other fields. The figure did not change a great deal for the next twenty years. In 1773/74 the student total came to 180, with 125 studying law and 19 medicine. The faculty of law continued, as in the past, to be the best enrolled. The lure for place seekers in the papal administration was still strong. On the other hand, the university failed to attract an appreciable increase in enrollment in the sciences, which had been Benedict XIV's goal. With the expulsion of the Jesuits from the Collegio Romano, the number of students in the faculty of philosophy slowly quadrupled from 10 to 39, and from 1788 the number of medical students almost tripled from an average of 24 to 73.[11]

The attempted reforms and improvements in Roman higher education, begun somewhat conservatively by Benedict XIV and carried on, after an interval, by Pius VI, were but a response to the changing conditions in both the intellectual climate and the university curriculum north of the Alps, which filtered down into the Papal States by way of Bologna. The efforts did not bear the hoped-for fruit. As in so many other spheres they were mired in the uncertain spirit of the time, the abandonment of the Tridentine world view and the inability or lack of energy to come to terms with the new rational outlook. For the actual encounter with the scientific and rationalist outlook we cannot look to the universities. Indeed, with the possible exception of Germany, Scotland, and, in a specific sense, Cambridge, the Enlightenment took hold in intellectual circles outside academe. Rome was no exception. Such intellectual ferment as there was was confined to vigorous but small groups, usually organized into academies.

10 Di Simone, *La "Sapienza" romana*, 132–33, 176–86, 193–94, 198–202, 208–17. Around 1740 matters affecting natural and international law were discussed privately in Rome in the circle around the lawyer Gaetano Forti, a friend of Benedict XIV. Venturi, *Settecento riformatore*, 1:114–15.

11 Di Simone, *La "Sapienza" romana*, 146, 295.

PART II

# Aspects of Rome's intellectual and cultural life

11

# Intellectual life

One of the first impressions a student of ancien-regime Rome gains is the distance, or rather fracture, between the intellectual and cultural life of the city and the reality of its material and institutional conditions. The learned world appears to have created a hiatus between society and culture. Yet, while it is often difficult to establish direct causal relationships between these two areas, the same tell-tale signs of entropy following the Tridentine period gradually emerge.

Roman intellectual life was borne by an elite, as is the case almost everywhere, but an elite of individuals, the majority of whom were of non-Roman origin and were attracted to the city because it was still the seat of Catholicism and, as such, it offered opportunities and influence. The need to improve their fortunes engendered in them a love of work and study. Their diligence gave them a decided advantage over the less energetic natives.

Most of Rome's social life, above the popular level, was played out in gatherings known as *conversazioni*. These were usually assemblies for the exchange of light gossip and frivolous amusements. Parallel to these, but very different in nature, were the learned *conversazioni*. Their heyday was at the end of the seventeenth and beginning of the eighteenth century. They were almost the only social relaxation for the more serious-minded scholars, after having worked with their heads and eyes all day; but they also served as the media for learned exchanges in the absence of other public forms of communication. The older scholars obtained much of their information there; the younger strove to gain entry into the circle of savants. One example of these were the late seventeenth-century medical *conversazioni* at the house of the learned physician Girolamo Brasavoli, where some of his medical confrères and other scholars used to gather an hour after Ave Maria to discuss the healing art.[1]

Beyond these learned *conversazioni* there were also more formal, if unofficial, local groups or learned societies which met together to serve some specific purpose. These academies, which abounded throughout Italy, had their roots in the Renaissance. They would either concern themselves with literary activities, promoting certain linguistic aims, or they could be of a more scientific character. It

[1] Renazzi, *Storia dell'università*, 4:159–60; Moore, *A View of Society*, 1:381–84; Justi, *Winckelmann und seine Zeitgenossen*, 2:147–49; B.CORS., ms. 2274, 1–3; Giuntella, *Roma nel Settecento*, xiv, 99–100, 135–37.

is within the matrix of these societies that the intellectual life of Rome would flourish. At the same time the need for such academies reflect the sad state of the Italian universities of the day.[2]

Rome had once been in the forefront of this development. In 1603 a group of young people eager to pursue natural history alongside mathematics and belles lettres formed the Accademia dei Lincei, one of the earliest and most important scientific academies in Italy. It would inspire similar societies north of the Alps. On 26 March 1616, Galileo, who only eight days before had received orders from Cardinal Bellarmine to abandon his teaching on the movement of the earth, was inscribed among its members. This act of courage was its eventual undoing. For following the death in 1630 of Federico Cesi, its moving spirit, the Lincei succumbed to financial hardship in the wake of the Galilean reaction. The academy would only be revived in 1745, and then in Rimini, not Rome. It did not return to the capital until 1795, under the patronage of Francesco Caetani, duke of Sermoneta, who welcomed it to his palace in the Via delle Botteghe Oscure and provided it with room for its physical laboratory.

The dissolution of the Lincei, however, did not mark the end of scientific inquiry in Rome. The interest in cosmological questions never wholly disappeared. The very cosmopolitanism of Rome's scholars, not to speak of the church's role in the conflict of ideas, made it inevitable for the city to be drawn into the ferment. The fact that Rome enjoyed an unexpected degree of freedom of speech, if not of the press, assured some response from among its educated circle. Galileo's work, although condemned by the Inquisition, continued to find admirers even in Rome, despite the fact that its advocacy of the empirical and experimental method was an insidious assault on the Aristotelian-scholastic foundation on which the church and its learning were built. The Chigi Pope Alexander VII (1655–67) had been one of the admirers of Galileanism, and by the dawn of the eighteenth century the eminent Roman doctor Giovanni Maria Lancisi, personal physician to several popes and distinguished professor of anatomy and medicine at the Sapienza, firmly planted and tended the philosophy of Galileo in the very gardens of the Vatican. So the Galilean drama, far from shutting off the widespread debate on cosmological questions that went back to the time of Copernicus, simply had the effect of restricting the debate to a smaller circle of scholars.

Thus, in the second half of the seventeenth century, Rome once more became the center of scientific interest. The Rospigliosi Pope Clement IX was sympathetic to the exponents of the new methodology. Under his successor Clement X, various experiments were carried out in the Chigi family palace under the direction of the Neapolitan Luca Antonio Porzio. But, more importantly, three years later Msgr Giovanni Giustino Ciampini founded the Accademia Fiscico-matematica in his house, where some very high level scientific experiments were conducted, the

[2] Robert J. W. Evans, "Learned Societies in Germany in the Seventeenth Century," *European Studies Review*, 7 (1977), 129.

results of which were communicated to its members through the presentation of papers. Within a brief time Ciampini's Academy became the best informed center of scientific inquiry in Italy. Because of its reputation and its fruitful contacts the institution was able to attract some of the finest minds of the day irrespective of their ideological direction. It was able, therefore, to foster the symbiosis of men such as the mathematician Alfonso Borelli and the anatomist Giorgio Baglivi, who were openly Galileans and receptive to the new scientific theories, with implacable anti-Galileans, such as Francesco Eschinardi. The activities in the Academy were both another sign of the waning of the Tridentine spirit and an attempt by the papacy to confront the new ideas which were circulating in Europe. Its ultimate purpose was to neutralize modern thought or transform it to its own ends. Such an operation, it will soon become evident, would be difficult to control. Another facet of this same endeavor was the launching of the Roman *Giornale dei Letterati* in 1668, the first Italian journal explicitly modelled on the French *Journal des savants*, which gave the students in the peninsula a relatively easy access to the great scientific findings all over Europe.[3]

The *Giornale dei Letterati* ceased publication in 1683 and Ciampini died in 1698. With his passing, the Accademia Fisico-matematica closed, and for a time the great experimental tradition, which had become a characteristic element of Roman scientific learning, had no longer a seat in which to develop and maintain its contact with other European academies. In the meantime, a cultural revival had swept Naples in the second half of the seventeenth century as a consequence of the political realignment of the time. Spain, to which Naples was still tied, drew closer to England, the United Provinces, and the German princes. Neapolitan savants were able to follow the scholarly literature and learned journals of those countries and become informed of developments in France. About the same time a new office-holding class of lawyers, the *ceto civile*, emerged. The loyalty of this new class was first and foremost to the state and they became the champions of the right of the crown against the claims of the church and the papacy. This brought them into conflict with the Jesuits, whose intellectual armory was a form of Aristotelian scholasticism and an array of metaphysical arguments. Consequently, the lawyers found their ammunition in the new anti-Aristotelian ideas, with which they countered the entrenched philosophy.

The first rallying point in the struggle against Aristotelians was atomism. Some humanists in the late Renaissance and the early seventeenth century had already looked for an alternative to the Peripatetic world view. Among the new conceptions of the world and humanity they had arrived at the atomistic philosophy, by way of reconstructing fragments of such pre-Aristotelian philosophers as Leucippus and Democritus, and through Lucretius' poem *De rerum natura*. Camillo Colonna

[3] Gabriel Maugain, *Etude sur l'évolution intellectuelle de l'Italie de 1657 à 1759 environ* (Paris, 1909), 76–77; Renazzi, *Storia dell'università*, 4:151, 185–88; Vincenzo Ferrone, *Scienza Natura Religione. Mondo newtoniano e cultura italiana nel primo Settecento* (Naples, 1982), 11–17, 35.

became the initiator of this classical form of atomism in the academy that met at his home.

Meanwhile, at Aix-en-Provence, the priest Pierre Gassendi worked out a corpuscular theory of matter, carefully purged of all its atheistic overtones. In 1647 he published his *De vita et moribus Epicuri* in Lyons, in which he restored the Renaissance image of Epicurus as a pre-Christian saint. In this effort to create a Christian form of the corpuscular theory he was joined by the English chemist Robert Boyle. The latter, in his work *The Christian Virtuoso* (1690), held that not Lucretian change but the divine will was at the origin of the universe and, contrary to what René Descartes propounded, continued to preside over the movement of matter after the initial phase.[4]

The corpuscular theory as advanced by Gassendi and Boyle would become intertwined with the new science of Galileo, especially in Rome. So it was not by chance that the Neapolitan physician and mathematician Tommaso Cornelio picked up these concepts in the course of a journey through Italy and fused them into an advanced philosophic synthesis, which became the ideology of the Neapolitan Accademia degli Investiganti, of which he was a founder. Atomism not only presented the new science with a general hypothesis for the ultimate structure of matter, a useful framework for new discoveries, but it introduced the mind to a dynamic and mechanistic vision of life. One of the best examples of this new direction was Alfonso Borelli, who after teaching mathematics in Pisa ended his life in 1678 in Rome as a protégé of Queen Christina and a valued member of Ciampini's academy. In his *De motu animalium*, published posthumously, he depicted the body of the animal as a kind of hydraulic machine by reducing physiology to geometry and mechanics.

Borelli's devoted student Alessandro Marchetti, who taught mathematics in Pisa, started translating Lucretius' poem in 1664. By 1669 he had it ready for printing, but Cardinal Leopoldo de' Medici prohibited its publication unless Marchetti suppressed everything in the manuscript that would be injurious to the Christian faith and submit it for approval by the Holy Office in Rome. The translator believed that to correct Lucretius would be to distort him. So by the end of the seventeenth century the work was simply circulated in a mass of manuscript copies. It is believed that at least one such copy was read by a prelate at the papal court.

During the pontificate of Innocent XI, Gassendi's teaching had progressed so much that some traditional scholars aimed at having his work condemned, but through the efforts of Cardinal d'Estrée, who then represented the affairs of France at the papal court, it was saved for the time being only to be attacked again and put on trial in 1693. This time the opponents were partially successful, but failed to wipe out atomistic thought in Rome, as the popularity of Marchetti's translation testified. The elegance of its language was so greatly admired that Giovanni Maria

4 I. Bernard Cohen, *Franklin and Newton. An Inquiry into Speculative Newtonian Experimental Science* (Philadelphia, 1956), 93–103.

Crescimbeni, the first head of the Arcadia, who was a priest loyal to the curial line, inserted a long passage from it in one of his pastorals in 1711. In it he attested the enthusiasm of a great number of fellow Arcadians for the translation. Marchetti died in 1714. Only then did the congregation of the Index decide to put his work on its list. By that date, however, the fashionable phase of atomism had already given way to other ideas.[5]

Descartes was appreciated more for his critical stance, as a symbol of free research, than his exact method. The same Tommaso Cornelio, who had introduced Gassendi to Naples, is also credited with bringing Cartesianism to that city in 1663. Among the earliest Cartesians was the Neapolitan Gregorio Caloprese, the teacher of Pietro Metastasio, Rome's own literary pride and joy, who does not seem to have separated Descartes completely from Lucretius in his own mind. Gian Vincenzo Gravina, the distinguished natural law author, literary theorist, and adoptive father of Metastasio, also championed a Cartesianism, which, however, was modified by Platonic influences.

Cartesianism outlived the earlier atomism on the Italian scene. Around the turn of the century its loyal followers tried to show that Cartesian ideas, far from being opposed to the principles of Christianity, were a truly providential restorer of Catholicism, a line of thought that was supported by the adhesion of the French Oratorian Nicolas Malebranche. The Piarist priests were in the forefront of introducing Cartesianism into their educational curriculum, as they were in so many innovations. Descartes could be used to deny the notion of individual free will. In this respect he appealed to Italian Jansenists in their struggle against Aristotelian scholasticism and the Jesuits. Hence this broader Cartesian influence would outlive the vogue of Cartesian philosophy in the more precise sense, when the latter was replaced by Newtonianism. For Cartesianism, not in its orthodox version, which was never studied in its organic entirety, but in the version filtered through Malebranche, signified for a whole generation until the time of Muratori clear and distinct ideas, methodological doubt, and a persuasive foundation for modern science to counteract Aristotelianism.[6]

5 Ferrone, *Scienza Natura Religione*, 17–18, 29; Natali (ed.), *Storia letteraria: Il Settecento*, 1:205, 213; Gasperoni, *Settecento italiano*. 1: *Amaduzzi*, 84–85; Maugain, *Etude sur l'évolution intellectuelle*, 13–43, 130; Cochrane, *Tradition and Enlightenment*, 114, 120–21, 248; Cochrane, *Florence in the Forgotten Centuries*, 243–44, 321–22; Salvo Mastellone, *Pensiero politico e vita culturale a Napoli nella seconda metà del Seicento* (Florence and Messina, 1965), 19–23, 30, 85–88, 91–100, 146–67; Eugenio Garin, *Storia della filosofia italiana* (3 vols.; Turin, 1966), 2:838–39, 855–60, 871–72; Nino Cortese, *Cultura e politica a Napoli dal Cinque al Settecento* (Naples, 1965), 100–2, 129–33; Tullio Gregori, "Studi sull'atomismo del Seicento," *Giornale critico della filosofia italiana*, 43 (1964), 38–45, 64; Diaz, *Il Granducato di Toscana*, 505–6, 507 n. 7; Ajello, *Problema della riforma giudiziaria*, 297.

6 Natali (ed.), *Storia letteraria: Il Settecento*, 1:43, 193, 527; Maugain, *Etude sur l'évolution intellectuelle*, 132, 167 n. 7, 187–88 n. 4, 324–27; Marcus Landau, *Geschichte der italienischen Litteratur im achtzehnten Jahrhundert* (Berlin, 1899), 17–18; Justi, *Winckelmann und seine Zeitgenossen* 2:171; Bertoldi (ed.), *Epistolario di Monti*, 117, Mastellone, *Pensiero politico e vita culturale*, 29, 40–42; Cortese, *Cultura e politica a Napoli*, 137–40, 144–45, 151–53, 159; Eugenio Garin, "Cartesio e l'Italia," *Giornale critico della filosofia italiana*, 29 (1950), 394–99, 404; Garin,

Having lost the intellectual initiative to Naples after the death of Ciampini, Rome would once again recapture it for a while by exploiting the misfortunes of the Neapolitan scholars. In 1688 some members of the Accademia degli Investiganti were hauled before the Inquisition in Naples, accused of atheism. The trial dragged on for nine long years. Although the accused were not the most prominent members of the Academy, their fate was immediately seen as an attack on the principle of freedom of thought. Indeed, the prefect of the Jesuit schools, Giovan Battista De Benedictis, openly charged the Investiganti with being a vehicle for atheism, despite their denials that a confrontation between Christianity and modern science exists. The consequences of these events reduced the area of free scientific research in Naples and opened the way for the reception of Newtonianism in Rome.

Italian scientists were probably first alerted to Isaac Newton's work through reading Christian Pfaultz's long review in the *Acta eruditorum* of Leipzig in 1688. But the crucial moment in the history of Newtonianism in Italy would actually occur in Rome at the cloister of the Celestines at Sant'Eusebio, then a peaceful oasis of retreat on the edge of the city. The Neapolitan Celestino Galiani, who was the central figure in the establishment and spread of the new anti-Cartesian and anti-metaphysical learning in early eighteenth-century Italy, moved in there in 1706. He gathered a group of scholars around him, among them Cardinal Lorenzo Imperiali, Francesco Landi, Joseph Roma, Gaspare Cerati, Francesco Bianchini, Giustino Fontanini, and, during his intermittent Roman stays, Antonio Niccolini. In their meetings they would carry out sophisticated experiments and comment on Newtonian and Cartesian texts. Above all, they planned future action for reviving Italian sciences. They also made intelligent use of the international contacts of the Holy See in order to be informed promptly of new scientific research conducted throughout Europe.

Among these contacts was the British minister in Florence, Sir Henry Newton, who enjoyed the friendship of the Roman cultural circles and had been admitted to the Arcadia. Thanks to him the Roman scientists would come to know the works of Isaac Newton directly. In 1706 they begged him for a copy of the *Principia mathematica*. Such a request was not the fruit of an isolated interest, but the expression of a need, felt in ecclesiastical circles, to evaluate through the original text a cosmology which had first been demonstrated to the Royal Society in April of 1686. But the bookseller to whom Sir Henry turned sent the recent Latin edition of Newton's *Opticks*, translated by Samuel Clarke, instead of the *Principia*. Newton's experimental approach to light rays, which he explained under the concept of corpuscules, stirred the enthusiasm of Galiani, who was entrusted with the difficult task of replicating the experiments and explaining the Newtonian theories to his

*Storia della filosofia italiana*, 2:864–67, 875–78, 901; Romano Palozzi, "Mons. Giovanni Bottari e il circolo dei giansenisti romani," *Annali della Scuola Normale Superiore di Pisa. Lettere, storia, e filosofia*, 2nd series, 10 (1941), 85–86; B.CORS., ms. 1891, pt 1, f. 20; Ferrone, *Scienza Natura Religione*, 150–51.

7 Celestino Galiani, by Pier Leone Ghezzi

colleagues. Galiani made the most important of these experiments in 1707/8 in some rooms at the Quirinal palace under the patronage of Alessandro Albani, Clement XI's nephew. They were certainly among the first, if not the absolute first, performed on the continent to verify the Newtonian optical theories. Although it happened by accident, the reading of Newton's *Opticks*, full of experimental results that could be verified, favored the subsequent benevolent reception of the celestial mechanics of the *Principia* on the part of the Roman scholars. How much this first positive judgment would influence the future attitude of the Holy See toward Newtonian science appears evident from the fact that, unlike the Cartesian works which were put on the Index in 1663, those of Newton and the Newtonians were never subject to the same censure. Only Francesco Algarotti's poem *Newtonianismo per le dame* was included in 1744, and that only because the author proposed a cultural model which connected Newtonian physics with the banned empiricism of John Locke and because of his avowed freemasonry.[7]

[7] Ibid., 6–10, 22–37; Francesca Sofia, Review: "Vincenzo Ferrone, *Scienza Natura Religione*," *Clio*, 19 (1983), 314–15; Cohen, *Franklin and Newton*, 67–68, 153–63, 177–84; Mauro de Zan, "La messa all'Indice del *Newtonianismo per le dame* di Francesco Algarotti," in Renzo Cremante and Walter Tega (eds.), *Scienza e letteratura nella cultura italiana del Settecento* (Bologna, 1984), 140.

Two events occurred that would further help to promote Newtonianism among Catholic scientists in Rome and beyond. The first centered around Francesco Bianchini, who with Celestino Galiani was the leader of the small scientific community in Rome. As a young man Bianchini, a native of Verona, had entered the service of Pope Alexander VIII and, while attending Ciampini's Academy, wrote, in 1687, a treatise on the Cartesian theory of vortices. In 1701, Bianchini in conjunction with the Parisian astronomer Jacques-Philippe Meraldi constructed an astronomical gnomon in the church of S. Maria degli Angeli. This effort was part of a commission by Clement XI to reform the Gregorian calender, for which the pope appointed a congregation with Cardinal Enrico Noris as president and Bianchini as secretary. His position enabled Bianchini to intensify his contacts with Protestant savants such as Leibniz and the distinguished English astronomer John Flamsteed, while retaining the trust of the pontiff. In 1713 Clement sent him on a diplomatic mission to France, which would include presenting the cardinal's hat to Armand de Rohan and renewing contacts with the Catholic minority in England. Bianchini used the opportunity to attend meetings at the French Académie des sciences and the Royal Society in London, and to visit Oxford University. The highlight of his tour, however, was his three long discussions with Isaac Newton.

On Bianchini's return, Cardinal Filippo Antonio Gualtieri, who had been papal nuncio in France in 1700, where he came to admire European scholarship and formed a close friendship with Malebranche and Mabillon, started a scientific academy at his residence, with Bianchini and Galiani as its principal members. It held its first official meeting on 5 May 1714, in which Bianchini explained the theories of Gassendi on light and Galiani those of Descartes and Newton. The cardinal's purpose in setting up his academy was to join the various scientific centers scattered throughout Italy in a common program of scientific research, much the same goal we shall see as the Roman Academy of Arcadia tried in the field of literature. But he tended to relegate the more general work of renewing scholarship to a secondary role. Galiani, however, considered the latter function as indispensible. Since the task of coordinating the sending out of reports on the experiments made in the new academy was left in his hands he was able to put his plan, based on spreading the theories of Newton, into action. It started with his unpublished commentary on the *Principia*, copies of which had in the interval reached Rome. Thanks to these privately distributed *Osservazioni sopra il libro del Newton*, the fundamental aspects of Newtonian thought became known among the local community of scientists. Thereafter he turned to Italy as a whole. He launched his campaign with a brief treatise against the Cartesian theses on gravity and the vortices. The work, originally destined for publication in the *Giornale de' Letterati d'Italia*, had its beginnings in the discussions at the Gualtieri academy. On the suggestions of Gian Vincenzo Gravina it was directed publicly against Gregorio Caloprese, one of the most authoritative of the Italian Cartesians.

For his part, Bianchini contributed personally by establishing ties with scholars in Pisa and with the Institute in Bologna, in particular with Eustachio Manfredi, who, like Bianchini, was closely linked to the curia. Two of Galiani's students in Rome, Bernardo Andrea Lama and Joseph Roma, spread Newtonianism to Piedmont. In short, the Gualtieri Academy represented the first serious attempt on the part of a group of Catholic intellectuals to restore the dialogue between modern science and Catholic learning, which had been so precipitously interrupted by the clamorous trial of the "atheists" in Naples. Appropriately enough this delicate operation started in Rome with the cautious sympathy of members of the hierarchy.[8]

Cardinal Gualtieri died in 1728 and Galiani, who had held the chair of church history at the Sapienza, returned to Naples in 1731. By that time the meetings at the Gualtieri Academy had become more infrequent until they ceased altogether. The great goal of bringing about a harmony between Catholic teaching and experimental science would elude Galiani and, under the less sympathetic successors of Clement XI, Rome missed its one opportunity to lead the quest. Not that the interest in Newtonianism died out. Galiani, starting from his Newtonian premise, had tried to unify methodologically the fields of scholarship and history with that of the exact sciences. His efforts would not be totally in vain, as we shall see below. In the meantime the principles of scientific observation were applied to studies beyond that of physical nature. Antonio Leprotti, with Galiani's encouragement, used this methodology to study the characters at the Roman court and the passions which dominated there, so attempting to demonstrate the acquired usefulness of Newtonian science in the field of moral psychology. By adapting Galiani's argument, Leprotti claimed that one could construct a system of attraction vis-à-vis repulsion of moral forces to explain the behavior of people. Francesco Maria Zanotti, a prominent member of the Bolognese Institute, was so totally enamored with the Newtonian laws of attraction that he wrote an essay *Della forza attrattiva delle idee*, in which he expounded one of the most complex aspects of the life of the mind, the mechanism of association. He claimed that reciprocal attraction allowed us to understand why one memory recalled another and why mature persons had greater memory than young people; the bodies by long use were more highly charged with electricity.

But these were individual endeavors, no longer a concerted effort to confront the new challenges. What would be more disconcerting is that Newtonianism tended to degenerate into a fashion fad, just one more aspect of the anglomania that was sweeping segments of the Italian population at the time. An honorable exception to

[8] Ferrone, *Scienza Natura Religione*, 42, 45–85, 99–101; Marina Caffiero, "Scienza e politica a Roma in un carteggio di Celestino Galiani (1714–1732)," *Archivio della società romana di storia patria*, 101 (1978), 311–21; Lalande, *Voyage d'un françois en Italie*, 3:385–88; Renazzi, *Storia dell'università*, 4:152–57; C. Pighetti, "Per la storia del newtonianismo in Italia," *Rivista critica di storia della filosofia*, 26 (1961), 426–30, 433; Cortese, *Cultura e politica a Napoli*, 134; Garin, *Storia della filosofia italiana*, 3:962–63; Natali (ed.), *Storia letteraria: Il Settecento*, 1:225–26.

this trend was the scholarly four-volume *Commentaire sur Newton* by the two learned Franciscan minims who resided at the French monastery atop SS. Trinità dei Monti, François Jacquier and Thomas Lesueur.[9]

These two are proof that scientific learning and curiosity had not died out completely in Rome. François Jacquier, whom Cardinal Valenti Gonzaga was successful in bringing to Rome, had already published works on mathematics and physics in Geneva in 1739 and had visited Voltaire in Cirey in 1744. After holding a chair in Turin and a short stay in Parma he came to the papal capital where he continued to be intimately associated with the cosmopolitan culture of his age, while teaching at the Sapienza. He died in 1788. As collaborator and successor he chose his fellow minim Thomas Lesueur. The two created a veritable meeting place for scientists and scholars on the Pincio to which many distinguished visitors resorted, Goethe among them. Aside from being one of the more significant mathematicians of his century and a commentator on Newton, Jacquier combined his expertise with a wide interest and knowledge of natural history, chemistry, and the arts.[10]

A similar example is that of the Jesuit mathematician Ruggero Giuseppe Boscovich, a native of Dubrovnik and one of the great scientific lights of the century. His arrival in Rome to teach mathematics at the Collegio Romano in 1740 appeared to awaken the Roman scientific circles from the torpor into which they had fallen since the death of Bianchini and the departure of Galiani. While in the city he developed his molecular theory of matter, better known as dynamic atomism, in which he tried to assume an intermediary position between Leibniz and Newton, all within the limits of scientific investigation. His ideas were first enunciated in his *De viribus vivis* in 1745 and perfected in his *Philosophiae naturalis theoria* (Rome, 1758). From Leibniz he borrowed the concept that the primary or ultimate elements were invisible points, which had neither length nor breadth, nor groups of particles. From Newton he obtained the notion that these points were centers of force, the distance between which determined whether the force attracts or repels. His theory antedated by a century the birth of the modern atomic theory. Both Immanuel Kant and Michael Faraday were to accept his formulation. In mathematics, and particularly in the application of probability to the theory of errors, he became the precursor of Pierre Simon Laplace, who repeatedly used his method. In his teaching at the Collegio Romano, Boscovich fearlessly attacked the Cartesian teaching on vortices in defiance of his Jesuit brothers who still held to it. From 1745

[9] Giuntella, *Roma nel Settecento*, 126; Landau, *Geschichte der italienischen Litteratur*, 282–83; Maugain, *Etude sur l'évolution intellectuelle*, 329–31; De Brosses, *Lettres familières*, 2:39–40; Silvagni, *La corte pontificia*, 1:345.

[10] Maurice vicomte de Boutry, *Choiseul à Rome. Lettres et memoires inedites, 1754–1757*. Introduction by André Hallays (Paris, 1895), 296–97; Casanova, *Histoire de ma vie*, 1:295 n. 2; Petit-Radel, *Voyage historique*, 2:33; Venturi, *Settecento riformatore*, 1:113 n. 5, 229–30; Vicchi, *Vincenzo Monti (1778–1780)*, 330–32; Seregni (ed.), *Carteggio di Verri*, 11:139–40; 12:274, 278, 337–38; Goethe *Italian Journey*, 155; Gorani, *Rom und seine Einwohner*, 215–19; BAV, Cod. Ferraioli, ms. 514, f. 29v Natali (ed.), *Storia letteraria: Il Settecento*, 1:212.

he and others made known in Rome the most up-to-date scientific debates on the Newtonian theories through the pages of the *Giornale de' Letterati*. This journal, bearing the same name as the earlier one published by Ciampini, was founded through the patronage of Valenti to reflect the latest cultural trends, and appeared between 1742 and 1754. Despite his achievements and world-wide renown Boscovich only underlines Rome's inability to regain the scientific initiative. He remained more or less an isolated alien implant. Honored as his teaching might have been in words, it failed to take root in the city and become assimilated as part of its life and culture.[11]

There was also an active astronomical interest in the city. The famous comet of 1680, for example, was observed by Joseph Dionysius Ponthaus, the secretary of Ciampini's Accademia Fisico-matematica, together with other scholars, from his private observatory at S. Maria in Vallicella. His observations were valuable enough for Newton to use in his *Principia* to determine the orbit of this comet. Bianchini had his own observatory on the slopes of the Quirinal. Other small observatories existed scattered throughout the city.

A great deal of this type of scientific activity, however, never rose above the level of dilettantism. The Caetani family, noble offspring of an ancient papal clan, are an illustration. Onorato Caetani was an alumnus of the Collegio Nazareno, where he studied between 1751 and 1762 and acquired a love of foreign languages, which later bore fruit in a wide reading of works by Malebranche, Christian Wolff, Voltaire, Bayle, Helvetius, Pope, and Robertson in the original. Entering a career in the church, he joined the rest of his family, including his older brother Francesco, duke of Sermoneta, when they moved into the new family palace in the Via delle Botteghe Oscure in 1775. There he would indulge his taste for physical experiments. Electricity became one of his fads. Remembering a public demonstration of the electric globe and chain performed by Johann Winkler of the University of Leipzig in Rome in 1746, Onorato some decades later conducted similar experiments. They were good enough for the physicist Giambattista Beccaria of Turin to commend him for his work.

Onorato Caetani was also an active supporter of the astronomical observatory which his brother set up in 1778 in the family residence. With the help of the Dominican Giovanni Battista Audiffredi, librarian of the Biblioteca Casanatense, who had published observations on the planet Mercury, and the advice of Boscovich, the brothers provided the technical and scientific equipment, among them a mercury seismograph, perhaps the first one in Rome. At his own expense the duke sent a promising youth, Luigi De Cesaris, to Pisa to study with the eminent

[11] Lalande, *Voyage d'un françois en Italie*, 3:388; Garin, *Storia della filosofia italiana*, 3:966; Natali (ed.), *Storia letteraria: Il Settecento*, 1:225–27; Roberto Marcolongo, "Le scienze fisiche e matematiche in Roma," in Federico Millosevich (ed.), *Le scienze fisiche e biologiche in Roma e nel Lazio* (Rome, 1933), 364–66; Villoslada, *Storia del Collegio Romano*, 240–43; Pastor, *Geschichte der Päpste*, 16, pt 1:135; Ferrone, *Scienza Natura Religione*, 644.

astronomer Giuseppe Antonio Slop de Cadenberg for three years before putting him in charge of the observatory. De Cesaris was succeeded in 1784 by the Carmelite Attanagio Cavalli, who taught physics at the Collegio Romano after the suppression of the Jesuits. From 1785 a daily record was kept at the observatory of wind, precipitation, temperature, and pressure. In this, it paralleled the official observatory at the Collegio Romano, where barometric observations were begun in 1782.[12]

By now serious science had become trivialized. With the passing of the institutionalized pursuit of science in Rome, learning became almost a private matter. What elsewhere had become a profession or occupation for life could only be pursued as a form of dilettantism. This was in sharp contrast to other countries where by then the whole body of knowledge was enlarged and passed on by a special coterie of paid specialists, who were strictly divided by their fields. What the sociologist Joseph Ben-David suggested for Italy as a whole is particularly apt for Rome. Whereas in other parts of Europe, he claimed, the defense of science was assumed by classes that had everything to gain from a change in the social order, in Italy science was espoused only by an intellectual clique that was trying to displace the official university philosophers and modernize the intellectual outlook of the Catholic church. Science, therefore, remained dependent on that narrow group that already ruled the country and church and had some interest in learning. As long as those circles were convinced that natural science was important and worthwhile enough for them, they gave their blessing to the endeavor. But when it failed to produce the needed synthesis between faith and modern science, and thought became threatening, they withdrew public recognition.[13]

At that point, the curial authorities reverted to an adversary relationship. About the time that Galiani and Bianchini launched their campaign to spread Newton's experimental concepts in Italy, John Locke's empirical ideas began to penetrate some of the same learned circles. Sometime before 1713 the Paduan Antonio Conti found Locke's *Essay Concerning Human Understanding* at a bookstore in Venice and read it with delight, but not without some suspicion. Soon Locke's ideas found resonance among groups from Naples to Turin, Rome included. His empiricism

[12] Filippo Eredia, "Il clima di Roma," in Federico Millosevich (ed.), *Le scienze fisiche e biologiche in Roma e nel Lazio* (Rome, 1933), 21; Pio Emanuelli, "L'astronomia in Roma," in Federico Millosevich (ed.), *Le scienze fisiche e biologiche in Roma e nel Lazio* (Rome, 1933), 312–18; Renazzi, *Storia dell'università*, 4:299–301; Giovanni Agamennone, "La seismologia a Roma e nel Lazio," in Federico Millosevich (ed.), *Le scienze fisiche e biologiche in Roma e nel Lazio* (Rome, 1933), 338; Giuntella, *Roma nel Settecento*, 110; Krautheimer, *Rome, 312–1308*, 159; Villoslada, *Storia del Collegio Romano*, 187–88; Luigi Fiorani, *Onorato Caetani. Un erudito romano del Settecento* (Rome, 1969), 15–20, 85–89; B.CORS., ms. 1589, f. 213.

[13] Seregni (ed.), *Carteggio di Verri*, 12: 107 n. 1; Ludwig Schudt, *Italienreisen im 17. und 18. Jahrhundert* (Vienna and Munich, 1959), 110–11; Joseph Ben-David, *The Scientist's Role in Society. A Comparative Study* (Englewood Cliffs, N.J., 1971), 59–65; Gentili, "Il modello epistomologico dell' *Institutum*," 33–34.

proved more difficult to assimilate than Newton's ideas, because of its threatening implications for religious beliefs. Although Zanotti saw no necessary tie between Lockeism and unbelief and claimed that in Bologna you could appreciate Locke without being thought an unbeliever, Clement XII banned the book in 1734. At that point Lockian ideas had spread too far already and, between 1732 and 1748, a growing number of opponents were to challenge them. The first to jump into the lists was Muratori with his *Filosofia morale esposita e proposita ai giovani* (Verona, 1735), on the issue of the influence of the physical on the moral. Without, however, accepting innate ideas in the fullest sense, Muratori insisted that at birth we bring with us the power of discovering proportions, some attributes of causality, and, above all, the ability to discern between the just and the unjust.

But Muratori's efforts were not successful. So, in 1747, the man who has sometimes been called the greatest apologist of Catholic Christianity in the eighteenth century, the Savoyard Giacinto Sigismondo Gerdil, a learned Barnabite monk, came to the rescue with his first two works, *L'immortalité de l'âme demontrée contre M. Locke* (1747) and the *Defense du sentiment du M. Malebranche sur la nature et l'origine des idées contre l'examen de M. Locke* (1748). Gerdil was a convinced Cartesian who had to watch how the ecclesiastics themselves, who ought to have recognized an ally in Descartes – or, at least, Malebranche's version of Descartes – unmercifully persecuted him. He had no illusions, however, about the result of his attempts; he did not expect to increase the number of Malebranche's partisans nor diminish those that gathered around Locke.[14]

The official condemnation of Locke in 1734 during the pontificate of Clement XII would be followed by that of freemasonry in 1738. The earliest record of a lodge in Rome is that of the "Noble Order of the Gormogons" in 1724. It probably was no masonic lodge at all, but simply a fraternity behind which the followers of the Stuart Pretender, who had lived in Rome since 1718, concealed themselves. But it aroused suspicion because its founder was Philip Wharton, who had been president of the Hell Fire Club (an infamous association of unrepentent libertines and drunkards) and grand master of the great lodge of London, from which he was expelled for his open Jacobite indiscretions. This society did not long survive its founder, who ended his young days in Spain, worn out by alcohol and dissipation. On its ruins was founded in 1735 a Jacobite lodge, consisting exclusively of Catholic and Protestant Englishmen with the exception of one, Conte Soderini. They met in taverns in the area of the Corso and attempted to bring masonic rites in line with rituals of the Catholic church. Despite some contributions its members made to the Stuart and Catholic cause, the lodge was unexpectedly suppressed by the governor of Rome in 1737, probably because some Hanoverian double agents had infiltrated its ranks. A

[14] Woolf, *History of Italy, 1700–1860*, 79–80; Maugain, *Etude sur l'évolution intellectuelle*, 224–27; Garin, *Storia della filosofia italiana*, 2:899; 3:958–60; Natali (ed.), *Storia letteraria: Il Settecento*, 1:198–99; Caffiero, "Scienza e politica a Roma," 330; Renazzi, *Storia dell'università*, 4:328–30; Gorani, *Rom und seine Einwohner*, 135–36.

little earlier, some time in 1731 or 1732, however, a group of Englishmen residing in Florence established a masonic lodge there. Around this English nucleus clustered a group of Florentine nobles and intellectuals, about sixty in number, intent upon carrying on the struggle for cultural reform in Tuscany. These Florentine masons, among whose number were some libertines and atheists, as well as followers of Gassendi and Newton, fought against prejudice, religious intolerance and for greater intellectual freedom. Unlike the Stuart lodge in Rome it had no definite political goal. Yet this lodge presented enough of a danger to the ecclesiastic establishment for Clement XII to condemn freemasonry by the bull *In eminenti* in 1738.[15]

There is no indication of another masonic lodge in Rome during the next years. But around 1750 Benedict XIV began to wrestle seriously with the problem of irreligion, materialism, and atheism, and his concern to put restraints on these dangerous trends found a ready echo in the curia. As archbishop of Bologna, Lambertini had shown a certain degree of familiarity with the spokesmen of freethinking and masonic learning, as well as with the leaders of Bolognese jurisdictionalism. His goal was really to make Bologna a test for reform. But as freemasonry and irreligion in general spread in Bologna during the years of the War of the Austrian Succession, Benedict XIV himself became suspect, hence his concern. As early as 1744 he asked Cardinal Tencin to intervene with Louis XV to suppress masonry in southern France, because it infected Avignon. By 1749 we have reports of lodges in Naples headed by great nobles, such as the Principe di Sansevero, whose interests tended more to the occult than the rationalistic. Apprehension arose when in 1746 an anonymous book entitled *Les Francs-Maçons écrasés* appeared in Paris, which claimed Oliver Cromwell as the founder of the movement. Cromwell had become in the period of the ancien regime the symbol of political and social revolution, whose aim was to destroy both the Catholic religion and the power and authority of absolute rulers, and to set up republics. Adding extra urgency was a rumor that the pope was about to revoke Clement XII's bull. So to allay any malicious gossip, Benedict XIV issued the bull *Providas Romanorum Pontificum* in May 1751, which, while reiterating the wording of the bull promulgated thirteen years previously, emphasized the dangers of secret societies both to the Catholic religion and the state.[16]

Following this bull freemasonry was suppressed in Naples, only to triumph again by 1782. Rome, however, remained untouched. When the Danish archeologist Friedrich Münter visited the papal capital in February 1785, he founded a small lodge of the Austrian *Illuminati* type, of which Goethe's friend Wilhelm Tischbein became the overseer, but it had no Italian members. He was to be more successful in

[15] Carlo Francovich, *Storia della massoneria in Italia dalle origini alla rivoluzione francese* (Florence, 1974), 39–40, 43–49; B.CORS., ms. 1589, f. 111; ms. 2459, f. 154.

[16] Giacomelli, "Carlo Grassi e le riforme bolognesi," 55, 63; Morelli (ed.), *Lettere di Benedetto XIV*, 1:159; 2:388, 390; Francovich, *Storia della massoneria*, 94, 103–5, 114–24.

Naples where the faith in the gradual controlled change espoused by the official masonic lodges was being slowly eroded by the egalitarian, communistic propaganda of the more militant *Illuminati*. This would keep Rome in a state of alert lest these groups appear within the threshold of the city itself.[17]

Having acted against the threat of freemasonry, Benedict XIV turned his attention to the works of the French philosophes, starting with Montesquieu and Voltaire. The latter's works were put on the Index between 1753 and 1757. But events did not move so smoothly and rapidly in the case of Montesquieu and his *Esprit des Lois*. During his two visits to Rome in 1728/29, where he intended to study the goverment of the Papal States at first hand, the French philosophe made the acquaintance of Antonio Niccolini and Gaspare Cerati, both belonging to the first generation of reformers who were attempting to bring about moderate changes in the church to meet the challenges of the new age of Enlightenment. The two men were close to the circle of the Archetto, which met at the Palazzo Corsini and whose head was Msgr. Bottari. It does not seem that Montesquieu ever met Bottari in person. Within a few months of the *Esprit de Lois* appearing in Geneva in 1748 some copies reached Italy. By 1749 many learned Italians knew of the work and even Bartolomeo Corsini, Clement XII's nephew, had read it. The following year there was already talk of putting the *Esprit des Lois* on the Index. But the initiative ran into the opposition of Cardinals Angelo Maria Quirini and Domenico Passionei, both of whom were openly sympathetic to the new ideas coming from France. Their intervention, as well as the fear of arousing complications with France, where Montesquieu enjoyed official esteem, account for the earnest effort to evade a negative decision on the *Esprit des Lois*. Passionei sent a copy of the work to Bottari, then librarian in the Corsini household, for an evaluation of the book. Bottari, freshly exposed to French rationalist thought, probably failed to grasp the full import of the work. He published a very critical review in the Roman journal *Novelle Letterarie Oltramontane*, but sent a much less critical and more sober report to Passionei. The latter then asked Bottari to defend Montesquieu before the congregation of the Index, a task he accomplished so well that the matter was temporarily deferred. Not until an Italian version of the *Esprit des Lois* with notes by Antonio Genovesi was published in Naples in 1752 was the book put ultimately on the Index. Even then it was treated gently. The condemnation did not mention the name of the author and the comments which Bottari had sent to Passionei were appended to the bull, drawing out much of the sting.

Consequently Montesquieu's influence never wholly disappeared from the Roman scene. Writers on the Roman economy, for instance, were attracted by his relativistic approach. Girolamo Belloni, in his *Dissertazione sopra il Commercio*, applied Montesquieu's principles of trade in the ancient world to his treatment of currency and of the distinction between active and passive trade. Giovanni

[17] Ibid., 189–93, 398.

Cristoforo Amaduzzi, the foremost champion of the second generation of Catholic reformers in Rome, nurtured an excessive admiration for Montesquieu, whom he considered much superior to Voltaire, the Encyclopedists, and Rousseau. Before the end of the century, Montesquieu would even end up in the service of the fierce papal protagonist Francesco Antonio Zaccaria and the conservative *Giornale ecclesistico romano.*[18]

The idea of a social contract, which spread rapidly in France after the publication of Rousseau's work in 1762, did not generally find a good press in Italy before the Revolution. With the exception of Beccaria, who made use of it to justify the right to punish, most better-known Italian writers either did not touch upon it directly or subjected it to severe criticism. This holds true for Rome, where, apart from citations in the *Annali di Roma*, only some feeble traces of his can be found, foremost among them the reading of the *Nouvelle Héloise* in the salon of the Marchesa Gentili Boccupaduli, where a portrait of Rousseau quite openly graced the walls. Even after the coming of the French Revolution, evidence of direct penetration of Rousseau's thought among the Roman Jacobins is minimal.

But there is one significant exception and it was in the field of political thought. Nicola Spedalieri (1740–95), a Sicilian who had taught moral philosophy at the seminary of Monreale before moving to Rome in 1774, was to produce a work in 1791 that incorporated Rousseau's idea of the social contract. Spedalieri, a fervent Catholic thinker with an acute intellect, had already established his reputation as a polemicist against the innovators with a fat volume against Nicole Frèret – or whoever passed for Nicole Frèret – in 1778 on the proofs of Christianity, and a two-volume rebuttal of Edward Gibbon's *Decline and Fall of the Roman Empire* in 1784. Now he tried to realize a desire of Pius VI to integrate the new philosophy with religion. The result was his *Dei diritti dell'uomo libri VI*, which appeared in 1791 while France was already in the throes of revolutionary convulsions. Its ostensible twin purpose was to defend human rights against every kind of tyranny and to demonstrate that the Catholic religion was the best safeguard against every kind of oppression. The target of his attack was the Catholic absolute rulers, who were challenging the papal prerogatives. To this end he advocated an alliance of the pope with the people; he became a democrat in order to make democracy popish. While he rejected Rousseau's state of nature, Spedalieri affirmed that in human society the social contract which united men into a civil state was formed directly and immediately by the people themselves; they, not God, were the primary cause. The sole duty of the sovereign was to look after the common good. If the ruler acted contrary to it, he violated the contract and the people had the right to depose him. In

[18] Mario Rosa, "Sulla condanna dell'*Esprit des Lois* e sulla fortuna di Montesquieu in Italia," *Rivista di storia della chiesa in Italia*, 14 (1960), 412–17; Paola Berselli Ambri, *L'opera di Montesquieu nel Settecento italiano* (Florence, 1960), 3–8, 13, 20–25, 29–38, 58–62, 73–74; Natali (ed.), *Storia letteraria: Il Settecento*, 1:393–94; Pastor, *Geschichte der Päpste*, 16, pt 1:263; B.CORS., ms. 1484, ff. 141–226; ms. 1659, ff. 341–42.

his view the Christian religion was the surest guardian of the social contract and the rights of man in society and, what is more, the only one capable of bringing them about. Accordingly every state must have its established religion and refuse to tolerate any other. Without intolerance no society can exist. The true faith, of course, was Catholicism.

This intersection of politics and religion earned Spedalieri the opposition of both the supporters of the ancien regime, who were alarmed at his acceptance of what in 1791 could be regarded as the inevitable work of the Revolution, and of the Jacobins, to whom the ultimate goal of reconciling the political achievements of the French Constituent Assembly with the principles of the Catholic religion could not but appear reactionary. The severest onslaught came from Jansenist circles. Spedalieri had not only accused Jansenism of leading people into atheism and skepticism, but he tried to insert a wedge between the Jansenists and the Catholic absolute rulers who supported them, by claiming that Jansenism stirs up anarchy and the democratic spirit. Pietro Tamburini responded on behalf of the Jansenists. He rejected the concept that society, morality, and laws originated in a social contract and countered by upholding the divine right of Catholic monarchs.[19] However, this last attempt at reconciling Enlightenment thought and the authority of the papacy was already obsolete, for the French Revolution was about to alter the face of Europe.

Rome's experience in the field of critical historical and philological studies ran a course similar to that in the area of scientific inquiry. In fact, in the early stages many of the same persons were engaged in both. The learned circles in Rome probably shared a greater interest in the former than the latter, for they believed that to build the Christian faith on secure historical foundations would form an even better bulwark against the new challenges. The first necessity, therefore, was to examine the historical sources more critically. This involved a mastery of numerous ancillary disciplines, not the least of which was the command of philology.

The movement actually started in France. The political and religious debates of the seventeenth century had discredited the work of historians. Bias was found everywhere. A new skepticism pervaded the air. In 1668 Felix de La Mothe Le Vayer was to formulate this sentiment into what became known as historical

[19] Giuntella, *Roma nel Settecento*, 124–25; Natali (ed.), *Storia letteraria: Il Settecento*, 1:205, 213; Gasperoni, *Settecento italiano.* 1: *Amaduzzi*, 84–85; Maugain, *Etude sur l'évolution intellectuelle*, 130, 134–43; Bruno Brunello, *Il pensiero politico italiano del Settecento* (Milan, 1942), 175–83, 186–96; Alfonso Prandi, *Il Cristianismo offeso e difeso* (Bologna, 1975), 349; Arnaldo Momigliano, "Edward Gibbon fuori e dentro la cultura italiana," in *Sesto contributo alla storia degli studi classici e del mondo antico* (2 vols.; Rome, 1980), 1:239–41; Furio Diaz, "Rivoluzione e controrivoluzione," in Luigi Firpo (ed.), *Storia delle idee politiche, economiche e sociale*: Vol. 4: *L'età moderna* (Turin, 1975), 2:718–19; Giovanni Giraldi, "La sovranità popolare nella polemica Spedalieri-Tamburini," *Rivista internazionale di filosofia del diritto*, 32 (1955), 297–314; Roberto Mazzetti, *Pietro Tamburini, la mente del Giansenismo italiano* (Messina and Ferrara, 1948), 199–200.

Pyrrhonism in his essay *Du peu di certitude qu'il y a dans l'histoire*. But it was Pierre Bayle who in his *Critique général de l'histoire du Calvinisme* related this form of Pyrrhonism more specifically to the history of dogma and beliefs.

Historical Pyrrhonism, therefore, was undermining both traditional historical studies and traditional religious beliefs. It was only natural then that members of religious congregations should make the best contributions toward resolving the doubts in historical studies. At the Benedictine monastery of St. Maur new norms for archival research and paleography were developed in the quest for establishing certainty in ecclesiastical history. With his *De re diplomatica* (1681) and *Traité des Etudes Monastiques* (1691), Jean Mabillon founded the new science of diplomatics. In the process he affirmed the right of criticism, based on archival evidence, in judging tradition, both sacred and profane, and demanded that human facts should be submitted to criteria of rational sense. He was convinced that the times imposed on learned Catholics this duty to demonstrate and make alive their own faith. At the same time he put an internal limit to such research by subjecting the work of a scholar to the realm of the conscience and the laws of good and evil. His fellow Maurist Bernard de Montfaucon in his *Palaeographia graeca* in 1707 not only developed paleography to embrace Greek manuscripts but showed in an unprecedented way how to collect and classify archaeological evidence. The learned Italian public was informed early on of these new methodological studies north of the Alps, but the critical change came when Mabillon toured Italy in 1685/86, followed by Montfaucon in 1698–1701. It was Mabillon, even more than Montfaucon, who would leave behind a group of followers headed by the Benedictine Benedetto Bacchini of Monte Cassino, who believed that the work of Mabillon appropriately continued the plan of Cardinal Cesare Baronio. Bacchini was enthusiastically supported by the bibliophile Antonio Magliabechi, librarian to the Grand Duke Ferdinando of Tuscany. The work and the personality of Bacchini were to exercise a decisive influence on the intellectual development of his students, who included Scipione Maffei and Ludovico Muratori.[20]

Francesco Bianchini heard Mabillon expound his methodology before Ciampini's Accademia Fisico-matematica. Through him Rome would add to the new Maurist approach its own tradition of antiquarian studies and archeology. Although this study of antiquities left much to be desired by our standards, the scholars were able to begin to redefine the nature of historical sources in order to

20 Arnaldo Momigliano, "Ancient History and the Antiquarians," in *Contributo alla storia degli studi classici* (Rome, 1955), 79–81, 90; Arnaldo Momigliano, "Gli studi classici di Scipione Maffei," in *Secondo contributo alla storia degli studi classici* (Rome, 1960), 257–62, 267; Landau, *Geschichte der italienischen Litteratur*, 5, 335; Ezio Raimondi, "I Padri Maurini e l'opera del Muratori," *Giornale storico della letteratura italiana*, 128 (1951), 433–42, 447–57; Woolf, *History of Italy, 1700–1860*, 76; Cochrane, "Muratori: The Vocation of a Historian," 161; Alberto Caracciolo, *Domenico Passionei tra Roma e la repubblica delle lettere* (Rome, 1968), 42–43; Mastellone, *Pensiero politico e vita culturale*, 115–18; Ezio Raimondo, "Scienza e letteratura," in Università degli studi di Bologna (ed.), *I materiali dell'Istituto delle Scienze* (Bologna, 1979), 13–16; Johns, "Art Patronage of Pope Clement XI Albani," 62–65.

adapt them to the needs of historiography. Bianchini would be the pioneer of this combination of critical method with archeological evidence in his *Storia universale provata con monumenti e figurata con simboli degli antichi* (Rome, 1697). Insisting, like Galileo, whose experimental method he adopted for himself, on the importance of facts and empirical proofs, he went beyond archeological evidence to search for documentary references to eclipses and other astronomical phenomena so as to help him construct a credible chronology. Although Bianchini in his book tried to defend the correctness of the chronology found in the Bible against the heretical pre-Adamite thesis of Isaac de Lapeyrère, he showed no inhibiting fear to submit the sacred text to the discipline of historical research.

Just as in the field of scientific investigation, Bianchini did not work in isolation. Apart from his Accademia Fisico-matematica, Ciampini had also been active in the establishment of an Accademia de' Concilj in 1671, located in the Collegio De Propaganda Fide, which was to form a framework for the study of broad biblical and theological questions. Even before starting on his work on Newton, Celestino Galiani, on his arrival in Rome in 1706, plunged avidly into the study of biblical and church history, learning Hebrew and perfecting his knowledge of Greek and Latin. He also began cultivating the friendship of other scholars beside Bianchini, Domenico Bencini, Giustino Fontanini, and Biagio Garofalo. The intellectual atmosphere in Rome, we have noted, was very stimulating, with Clement XI willing to exploit every opportunity within the Catholic structure to bring about a renaissance of Catholic scholarship. Among these was the reform in 1708 of the Academy of Councils, which had stagnated for years. Its direction was entrusted to Domenico Bencini, with Giustino Fontanini assisting him, and the young Cardinal Annibale Albani, nephew of Clement XI, as president. The role of the latter stressed the desire by the curia to keep direct control over the academy. However, many of its leading members were also members of the Circolo del Tamburo – those who "beat the drum" for awakening Catholic scholarship – that met in Cardinal Passionei's house, where the seeds of Roman Jansenism were to be sown. Hence, although the outlook of individual members differed, that of the Tamburo was frequently reflected there.

The rules for the Academy drawn up by Bencini emphasized the absolute precedence of the Maurist historical-philological analysis. Bencini himself tried to steer the Academy into forming answers to the heresies of his day, the deism of Herbert of Cherbury, the religion of state of Hobbes and the criticism of the Mosaic authorship of the Pentateuch by Spinoza, so as to help Catholics confute those teachings. Often, instead of following the more traditional lines of research, the members would introduce new elements of comparative religious scholarship, beyond the Judeo-Christian confines. They discussed the religious phenomenon in the history of humanity in general, the political significance of the religions in the ancient world, the origin of pagan religions, and the role of heroes in antiquity.

Such diversions were to open the way to dangerous departures from Catholic orthodoxy. Even Galiani was not to be unaffected. Although in his teaching duties both to the monks at Sant'Eusebio and, since 1718, at the Sapienza, he maintained a steely orthodoxy, in his little cell he repudiated his ostentatious conformism and accepted the critical-philological method of Spinoza and Richard Simon. To meet the problems of reconstructing Christianity on a rational basis Galiani was forced from the safe harbor of Catholic orthodoxy. To doubt the truth of the Bible, to demystify the sacrality of the Hebrews and reconstruct the historical reality of the early Christians threatened the very foundation of the edifice on which western society was built. Hence there was born in him a conception of a culture intrinsic of doubt, different from the Tridentine model of certainty and absolute truth.

Of course, Galiani did not pioneer this critical approach. He inherited it from his colleague at the academy Biagio Garofalo, who in 1707 dedicated his book *Considerazioni intorno alla poesia degli ebrei e dei greci* to him. The work of an esteemed Hebrew scholar, it was the first book in eighteenth-century Italy to be inspired by Spinoza's *Tractatus theologico-politicus* and influenced by Richard Simon's *Histoire critique du Vieux Testament*. In it Garofalo put the sacred text under critical-philological analysis as a purely human document, albeit an important record of history. Despite the *imprimatur* this work received from Giustino Fontanini and the protection the author enjoyed from his fellow members of the Tamburo, it was inevitably put on the Index in 1718. Freedom of inquiry had gone too far to aid the cause of Catholicism in the nascent age of rationalism.[21]

If the Accademia de' Concilj came to an end, the Circolo del Tamburo continued to carry on the Maurist approach. Behind their historiographical achievement was a deeper motivation. Its adherents were all proponents of Catholic reform, in sympathy with Jansenist aims, if not actually Jansenists. Already in the 1690s Muratori, along with other scholars, began to realize the utility of history for reforming Catholicism. He had been attracted by the Augustinianism of Cardinal Enrico Noris and looked around for some historical foundation upon which to ground his cause. With the publication of Mabillon's *De cultu sanctorum ignotorum* he discovered that the free pursuit of historical truth based on archival documents provided Catholicism with the best defense against its opponents on both fronts, the Protestant polemicists and those who sought to raise the more dubious aspects of popular piety to the level of Catholic dogma. Rejecting the more radical course of critical scholars like Garofalo, the Roman group was to build on the Muratorian foundation. For them history became a weapon of war. The religious history of the church was a way of bringing it back to the primitive evangelical simplicity, of restoring the purity of manners, of combatting the wealth of the clergy, by saving it from worldliness and corruption. Bottari, who had an impressive record of archeological and philological works to his credit, and his colleagues maintained

[21] Maugain, *Etude sur l'évolution intellectuelle*, 91–92; Renazzi, *Storia dell'università*, 4:151, 185–88; Ferrone, *Scienza Natura Religione*, 367–94, 418; Sofia, Review: "Ferrone, *Scienza Natura Religione*," 315–16.

close ties to the Benedictines of St. Maur thanks to the latter's representatives in Rome, Claude Estreimont de la Serre and Guillaume Laparre. Apart from books there was an exchange of editorial information, erudite notes, and philological problems. The Circolo del Tamburo appropriated the Maurist method of direct documentary evidence and its demand for intelligent criticism. In the process Bottari's closest collaborator Pier Francesco Foggini would transform the writing of church history into a defense of the Augustinian school. Between 1754 and 1771 he concentrated mainly on the publication of works by the early fathers, reinforcing a tradition that went back at least two centuries and which found renewed interest at the time of Innocent XII.

But not all authors involved in the theological controversies of their time had learned their lesson quite as thoroughly. The Florentine Dominican Giuseppe Agostino Orsi, who became secretary of the Index in 1740, started on a twenty-volume *Storia ecclesiastica*, which began to appear in 1747. This work was designed to counteract the Jansenist *Histoire écclesiastique* by abbé Fleury, which had only recently been translated into Italian. Given its purpose the history obviously lacked impartiality and had been criticized for the absence of thorough research. Yet under the influence of Giovanni Lami, Orsi gradually came to realize that doctrine could be formulated only on the basis of verifiable historical documents; he accordingly modified his radical position on papal infallibility when the documents failed to support him.[22]

In the tradition of Clement XI, Benedict XIV was convinced of the need for educated Catholics to fortify and enlighten themselves with rigorous scholarly learning so that they could persuasively face their adversaries. A scholar himself, it was clear to him that Catholics themselves were responsible for the intellectual crisis of the post-Tridentine period by their inadequate assumptions. Accordingly, the pope shortly after his accession in 1740 aimed at mobilizing the considerable intellectual talent available in Rome by establishing four academies. As we already know, learned *conversazioni* were the best means to assemble outstanding minds in the papal capital and stimulate them to produce fine work of scholarship. Only this time the Academies not only had the official blessing as at the time of Clement XI, they were set up in a much more formal manner, each with its own seat and select membership. Three embraced sacred learning, one each for the study of church

22 Pastor, *Geschichte der Päpste*, 15:365–66; Arnaldo Momigliano, "Eighteenth Century Prelude to Mr. Gibbon," in *Sesto contributo alla storia degli studi classici e del mondo antico* (2 vols.; Rome, 1980), 1:251–54; Momigliani, "Studi classici di Maffei," 256–59, 264, 271; Momigliano, "Ancient History and Antiquarians," 85–86; Cochrane, *Tradition and Enlightenment*, 101–2, 161, 172–73; Cochrane, *Florence in the Forgotten Centuries*, 265, 381; Cochrane, "Muratori: The Vocation of a Historian," 166–67; Romano Palozzi, "Mons. Bottari e il circolo dei giansenisti romani," 86–87; Raffaello Morghen, "La visione storica di L. A. Muratori," in *Miscellanea di Studi Muratoriani* (Modena, 1951), 296–97; Landau, *Geschichte der italienische Litteratur*, 83; Mario Rosa, "Atteggiamenti culturali e religiosi di Giovanni Lami nelle *Novelle Letterarie*," *Annali della Scuola Normale Superiore di Pisa. Lettere, storia e filosofia*, 2nd series, 25 (1956), 310–12; Rosa, "Sulla condanna dell'*Esprit des Lois*," 414–17.

councils, church history, and sacred rites (liturgy). In essence they were a revival of Clement XI's Accademia de' Concilj. The fourth one, devoted to secular learning, was the academy of ancient history and profane antiquity. It was to recall a similar Roman academy which the Renaissance humanist Pomponio Leta had founded in his garden on the Quirinal and which closed in 1533. Appropriately the Campidoglio became its seat and Livy's history formed the basis for the antiquarian discussions held there. Muratori enthusiastically welcomed the announcement of the establishment of the academies, but again appealed for scholarly independence, especially in the ecclesiastical field.

With the end of the pontificate of Benedict, the academies fell upon unfavorable times. In the words of Renazzi, they became more theaters than learned academies. Indeed, with the failure of earlier efforts to bring Roman scholarship in line with that of the rest of Europe, it appeared that a pall descended upon learning in the city. The savants wanted to play safe; hence, except for a few dilettanti who dabbled in innocuous science, especially astronomy, the majority were theologians or writers of sacred history. Anyone who aspired to the least bit of learning wrote a large dissertation on archeology, since knowledge in this field caused little offense, with an occasional treatise on philology.[23]

Most works of this kind were weighed down with two flaws: the first was a literary style without taste, heavy, affected, confused. The sterility of ideas, as Joseph Gorani critically remarked when visiting the city, was replaced by a surfeit of expressions that flattered the ear, but did not speak to the mind. The other flaw was erudition. Gorani attended the salon of Maria Pizzelli, a highly intelligent and learned lady, whose apartment in the Palazzo Bolognetti became a true academy where Italian and foreign artists and men of letters would meet. It dominated much of the latter part of the eighteenth century. Jacquier, Boscovich and Renazzi, among other distinguished names, had frequented it at one time or another. There, to Gorani's disappointment, he discovered that the Romans knew exactly where Hannibal had pitched his tent, the spot where one of the Gracchi brothers had been assassinated, and they had little difficulty in analyzing the verses of Virgil or Juvenal. Their misfortune was not that they knew these trivial things to perfection, but that they could not go beyond them to arrive at a global or synthetic vision of the whole problem. This inability to go beyond superficial knowledge without being bogged down in details dominated every field. Thus the old vibrancy that pervaded Roman learning at the start of the eighteenth century had, except in isolated cases, been dissipated. At the time when myopic erudition was replaced in favor of a broad

[23] Pastor, *Geschichte der Päpste*, 16, pt 1:136–38; Woolf, *History of Italy, 1700–1860*, 112; B.CORS., ms. 1615, ff. 9–27; ms. 2054, ff. 2–4, 40; ms. 2461, ff. 38–49; Renazzi, *Storia dell'università*, 4:149–50, 277–80, 335; Caracciolo, *Passionei tra Roma e la repubblica delle lettere*, 38–39; Fredegard Callaey, "La critique historique e le courant pro-Jansenite à Rome au XVIIIe siècle," *Analecta Gregoriana*, 71 (1954), 189–90; Caracciolo, *Lo Stato* pontificio, 486–87; Cochrane, *Tradition and Enlightenment*, 51–62.

philosophic vision of history and the discussion of the ideas of the French and Scottish philosophes and of Vico stirred scholars in other parts of the peninsula, their colleagues in Rome reversed the trend and sank back into the swamp of learning for its own sake.[24]

Not without significance, some of the same people who had been active in the earlier part of the eighteenth century in the endeavor to bring Catholicism in line with current ideas in science and scholarship, particularly within the Circolo del Tamburo, would also be at the heart of the reformist current that agitated Catholic intellectual controversies of the time. This reformist current received some of its intellectual impetus from the wide range of developments in France, as we have already noted in this chapter. Yet what became known as Roman Jansenism was more than a mere reflection of what happened abroad. It had its own character, that was in part a reaction to the local circumstances, the excesses and superstitions which accompanied the popular piety of the Roman masses and, even more so, it was an extension of the native reformist tradition nurtured by such minds as Ludovico Muratori and Giovanni Lami.

[24] Giuntella, *Roma nel Settecento*, xiv, 99–100, 135–37; Caracciolo, *Lo Stato pontificio*, 487; Lalande, *Voyage d'un françois en Italie*, 5:56; Madelin, *Rome de Napoléon*, 88; B.CORS., ms. 2274, ff.1–3; Gorani, *Rom und seine Einwohner*, 176–80, 386–92; Di Simone, *La "Sapienza" romana*, 186; Woolf, *History of Italy, 1700–1860*, 122. In the case of Vico, who enjoyed the esteem of Cardinal Neri Corsini and Bottari, his principles were applied by the law professor at the Sapienza, Emanuele Duni, in his legal history of ancient Rome, *Origine e progressi del cittadino romano e progressi del governo civile di Roma* (Rome, 1763–64), Natale (ed.), *Storia letteraria: Il Settecento*, 1:398–99; Maugain, *Etude sur l'évolution intellectuelle*, 205; Luigi Rava, *Un salotto romano del Settecento "Maria Pizzelli,"* (Rome, 1926), 35–36.

12

# Jansenism as a Roman phenomenon

A great deal of what happened in Rome during the ancien regime can only be explained in terms of the Jansenist controversy. Even areas beyond the strict confines of theology were shaped by events and thought patterns that on the surface had little to do with the confrontation of Jansenists and Jesuits, but which were still couched in those terms. To that extent the subject may be viewed as an extension of the intellectual activity in the papal capital, involving many of the same people prominent in the previous chapter.

The usually perceptive De Brosses, although no theologian, assures us that the Jansenism of Rome scarcely resembled that of France. He declared:

> The Roman clergy has its Jansenists, they are even among the cardinals, but they are a different sort from ours. The Jansenism of Italy does not revolve around the question of the fact of the rightness of the Five Propositions nor the jargon of efficacious or sufficient grace, but of knowing whether a decision of the pope, *ex cathedra*, was fallible or not.[1]

De Brosses may not have had his finer theological points correct, but he surmised properly that Roman Jansenism, while by no means isolated from the movement elsewhere, was *sui generis*. In part, this distinction must be attributed to the fact that the movement was both an intellectual and devotional response to local conditions. The ethos of popular Catholicism in Rome contributed perhaps as much to the shaping of Roman Jansenism as the influences from more distant France and nearby Tuscany and Naples. The attitudes of reigning popes, too, was a significant factor.

The broader Roman milieu in which Jansenism existed can best be relegated to the sphere of popular piety. The people's religion in the ancien-regime city once again bore the character it used to have before the Reformation. Dupaty, in 1785, described the temperature of the Romans' faith as "mild as their own skies." "Good Catholics and bad Christians," could be said of them, which is to say their external comportment did not correspond to their personal morality. All their spiritual experience seemed exhausted in outward manifestations which in the course of the century assumed exuberant dimensions. While the practice of religion was a habit that was deeply engrained in the inmost soul of the people, they lived through their

[1] De Brosses, *Lettres familières*, 2:52, 136.

senses and an etherealized faith meant nothing to them. They had to hear and see and touch religion. Therein lurked the danger. A process of externalization, progressively more disintegrating, enveloped all dimensions of religious life. The faith of the people at times transformed itself into a tissue of beliefs consisting of superstitious dross and unbridled emotions.

The Romans, for example, thought of all heavenly powers as having bodies and faces, and discarded any theological concept they could not picture in corporeal form, the Holy Ghost for example. Their great popular devotion was directed to Mary the Mother of God, who was worshipped in a frenzy of tenderness. In the popular faith she was the chief power in heaven; she had made the world. She replaced the god Hermes of ancient times. No work was done, no enterprise or business launched without sheltering under the image of Mary. She was the repository of the city's collective memory and the rallying point of the Roman masses.[2]

To the extent that it became harder for these people of little education and religious sophistication to share in rites from which they had been progressively estranged, the need arose for new structures and associations which would give them more immediate direction for religious expression. It was in the bosom of the confraternities that these spiritual aspirations had full play; here a Roman could find religion again as a lively reality more compatible with his daily life. Much of the religious experience of so many Romans in the previous century, therefore, was conditioned by these confraternities. But, alas, as we know, even they entered a period of distinct decline in the eighteenth centuury.

So the regular cure of souls fell amost wholly to the lot of the parish clergy. Even in the absence of a detailed prosopographical study of the Roman priesthood, we know from general reports that they were ill-prepared for the task of restraining the misdirected zeal of their parishioners and educating them in the rudiments of their faith and its observance. Montesquieu was probably not exaggerating by much when he declared a parish priest to be in a status below a man servant in the Papal States.[3] The upshot was that the Romans were on a footing of greatest ease and intimacy with their priests and the needed respect was lacking. A report on the state of the Roman parishes by the vicariate in 1766 speaks of priests who "were unable to read, and stumbled over almost all their words while celebrating mass; and not to lose time, they did not even bother to correct themselves, although they knew that they had made mistakes, because all their thought was on getting the dreaded act over."

In the mass the secular priests failed to live according to the provisions of the

[2] Palozzi, "Mons. Giovanni Bottari," 71; Giuntella, *Roma nel Settecento*, 140–43; Fiorani, *Rite, ceremonie, feste e vita de popolo*, 229–30; Zanazzo, *Tradizioni popolari romane. Usi, costumi*, 176–77, 270–72, 424–25; Andrieux, *Daily Life in Papal Rome*, 118–21; Story, *Roba di Roma*, 55, 82, 319–20; A.S.Vic., t. 81, f. 250; A.Cap.R., no. 33, cred. XIII, 164; Nussdorfer, *City Politics in Baroque Rome*, 208. [3] Montesquieu, *Voyages, Oeuvres complètes*, 2:1191.

canons and the councils. A long series of injunctions tried to bring them back to ecclesiastical discipline. In 1677 an edict forbad priests to live outside their residences, but by the end of the century there were numerous instances of priests dwelling in private houses, who had fallen into temptation by living too close to women. Innocent XII reimposed the duty of clerical residence in 1692 and ordered priests to wear canonical vestments. But it was an uphill struggle and not very successful, as an 1775 *Editto circa la vita e honestà degli ecclesiastici* over the signature of the cardinal vicar showed. In it, the clergy were exhorted to observe the sacred canons on the dignity and the devotion of processions, the singing of divine offices, and the sacrifice of the mass, the celebration of which was to last no less than one-third of an hour and was permitted only to priests in possession of the requisite licence. Hidden amid other prescriptions, the edict stressed what was still one of the most serious evils. It prohibited priests every type of fashionable dress which was unbecoming a person of the sanctuary. It also ordered all of them to wear their hair short with tonsure, where appropriate, and without wigs or powder. They were not to linger long in coffee houses, where gossip and idle chatter were exchanged, nor play cards, nor proffer their arms to ladies in the theater. An earlier attempt by Clement XIII in 1759 to ban priests completely from the theater had been abandoned because it proved impossible to enforce. If the cardinal vicar was prepared to put these and other stern warnings in a widely published edict, it is reasonable to suppose that the laxity among the secular clergy had reached scandalous proportions.[4]

Indeed, a document of this period set forth proposals which in the view of the drafter would help to eliminate some of these very abuses among the lower clergy in the city.[5] The clerics in minor orders, he urged, should spend six months in a mission school before becoming priests, as Benedict XIII had foreseen in the statues of his Council of Rome; or, at least, a period of three months, as had been the practice prior to that council, instead of the perfunctory twenty days they were going through at the time of writing. Many priests had found it beyond their means to live in a house of their own and could lodge for less expense in other households, with lay people among whom were usually women, sometimes young women. Inevitably, they became familiar with them over the years to their own undoing and that of the poor young women. The remedy for this evil would be to provide a proper living for these ecclesiastics so that ordained priests could live a life suited to their station. Another failing, almost wholly confined to Rome, the document pointed out, was that many careers and positions of employment fit for secular priests had become the monopoly of religious orders, among them the professorial chairs at the college of the Propaganda Fide and the Sapienza. These posts were

[4] B.N.Ro., Fondo Vittorio Emanuele, ms. 603, ff. 12–14; A.Cap.R., no. 33, cred. XIII, 36; Clementi, *Il carnevale romano*, 2:142; Petrocchi, *Roma nel Seicento*, 103–5; Giuntella, *Roma nel Settecento*, 154; Pastor, *Geschichte der Päpste*, 14 pt 2:1129–30: B.CORS., ms. 1876, ff. 40r–42r.

[5] A. S.Vic., t. 81, ff. 250–54.

moderately lucrative and could have maintained many a secular priest with dignity. If these and similar employment had been conferred on worthy secular priests, many of them would have found a serious incentive to devote themselves to studies useful for the public. Seculars should also have been employed as consultors to the many papal congregations in Rome, which ordinarily only had places for the regulars. People complain that the priests do not study, yet all roads to using their knowledge have been blocked to them. In short, the paper suggested that the absence of incentives was responsible for the low morale among the secular priests, who made up the majority of the parish clergy.

As one of the last suggestions, the writer proposed that the parish priests in Rome should be chosen by competition (*concorso*), and, whenever possible, native Roman priests, who had the necessary experience, were to carry out the ministry. This point is revealing. In July 1781, Alessandro Verri told his brother that Rome used to be flooded with Calabrian, Apulian, and Abruzzese priests, all in wretched condition and celebrating masses which had been endowed by the infinite number of pious bequests and foundations. As a result of the stiffer regulations for admission to the priesthood laid down by the king of Naples, this cheap supply had begun to dry up and there was a shortage of priests. Too many ignorant and demoralized priests or too few, the Romans were certainly without adequate spiritual guidance or leaders whom they could respect.[6]

To bring the masses back to a more realistic Christian consciousness, the church resorted to missions and special Lenten preparation. The office of the cardinal vicar, among others, set up special courses in some of the most important churches in the city, usually lasting from the fourth Sunday in Lent to Easter, in order to awaken sinners to their vices and prepare the souls so close to Easter to receive the sacraments of penance and the eucharist. It appears – but it is still open to investigation – that the Lenten instruction with its serious approach and careful organization won the favor of large segments of the Roman populace and constituted a call for a more genuine Christian life, which did not always go unheeded. Within the orbit of Lenten preaching, although not always limited to a particular season, came the revival of popular preaching, which found its typical expression in the great oratorical cycles of the mission.[7]

Missions, which had almost disappeared among the Italians during the fourteenth century, were revived with new vigor by Padre Paolo Segneri the Elder (died 1694), with the support of his nephew and disciple Paolo Segneri the Younger (1673–1713); the latter, in turn, inspired the ardent Ligurian Leonardo da Porto

[6] Seregni (ed.), *Carteggio di Verri*, 12:27–28.

[7] Zanazzo, *Tradizioni popolari romane. Usi, costume*, 221; Fiorani, *Riti, ceremonie, feste e vita del popolo*, 232–39; Giuntella, *Roma nel Settecento*, 170–73. For a recent treatment of the Spanish missions, and their differences from the Roman counterparts, see Charles C. Noel, "Missionary Preachers in Spain: Teaching Social Virtues in the Eighteenth Century," *The American Historical Review*, 90 (1985), 866–92.

Maurizio (1676–1751). And there was San Paolo della Croce (1694–1775), founder of the Passionist fathers, an order specializing in missions, which received the approval of Benedict XIV in 1741. Under the two Segneri and Leonardo the program of mission preaching among the Catholic populace assumed a definite form and character. The preaching was often modelled on the old hackneyed Spanish sermon, but the Italian friars put even greater zeal into it to excite the crowd. The tone and some of the gestures of Leonardo's preaching would strike us today as theatrical and choreographed. The missioners went out of their way to address the senses of the audience. They would bring with them crowns of thorns, scourges, crosses. Their voices ran the gamut from bass to falsetto, while they paced up and down their pulpits like pendulums. Some rent their beards, beat their hands, and uttered frightful groans. At more solemn moments, the missioner would scourge himself mercilessly with a whip, while the crowd looked on in horrified silence. However disconcerting the format might have been, it sprang not so much from a desire to impress the faithful as to arouse in them a spirit of penitence.

Benedict XIV, concerned for the evangelization of the massses, encouraged and supported the work of the missions. To Leonardo da Porto Maurizio he entrusted the preaching in the city, while the young Paolo della Croce was first assigned the preaching in the Campagna and the Maremma and only after Leonardo's death in 1751 did the pope let him come to Rome. Paolo, like Leonardo, came before his crowds with a crown of thorns pressed so deeply into his forehead that drops of blood ran down his face. With a criminal's rope around his neck and an iron chain to beat his back, he would beseech sinners to repent. In the Holy Year of 1775, he died an old man, leaving behind his foundation, the Passionists, to continue his work.[8]

However sincere such missioners may have been, their histrionic appeal to the emotions cannot but have stirred up the Roman mob to religious frenzy and passions which went beyond the reasonable limits of their message. A direct outcome of this excited state of mind was the case of Benoît Joseph Labre. The story of this extraordinary French vagrant tells us a great deal about the nature of Roman religiosity. Born in 1748 to a well-to-do peasant family in Artois, Labre turned into a pilgrim and vagrant, after his repeated attempts at becoming a Trappist or Carthusian monk were frustrated. After having visited numerous shrines throughout Europe, he finally decided in 1777 to remain in Rome, which he had already visited five times previously. There where the memory of Leonardo da Porto Maurizio and Paolo della Croce was still very much alive, Labre spent the nights beneath the arches of the Colosseum to pray. During the day he could be seen in contemplation and even ecstasy in the foremost churches of Rome. On Wednesday

[8] Gustavo Cantini, *S. Leonardo da Porto Maurizio e la sua predicazione* (Rome, 1936), 15–16, 29, 62–68, 72–85, 91–94, 104, 1124–23; Gustavo Brigante Colonna, "Il santo ligure che impiantò la *Via Crucis* nel Colosseo," *L'Urbe*, 8 (1943), fasc. 11–12, 8–12; Adamo Pierrotti, "Alcune aspetti della strategia religioso-apostolica di S. Leonardo," *Studi francescani*, series 3, 24 (1952), 117; BAV, Cod. Ferraioli, ms. 415, 54r.

or Thursday of Holy Week 1783, by now very sick and emaciated, he attended mass at Madonna dei Monti. Feeling unwell, he collapsed on the steps on his way out. By nightfall his life had expired, just one of thousands of Roman vagrants.

Yet this was really only the beginning. The dawn after Labre's death the streets were crammed with children shouting, "The saint is dead." Urchins, who had been insulting the beggar the day before at Trajan's forum, were transformed into heralds of sanctity. Devotees broke into the death chamber. Toward the evening his wasted corpse was taken to the church of the Madonna dei Monti. The whole neighborhood cheered and clapped as if in a theater, "Il santo . . . Ecco, il santo!" From the evening of Maundy Thursday until Easter Sunday, when he was laid out in church, it seemed the whole town rose to honor Benoît Labre. There had been nothing like it since the death of Filippo Neri. His body was handled, kissed, and pulled apart by unrestrained devotion, that often came close to hysteria and violence. He died in April and in June it was still necessary to regulate the flow of visitors and avoid disorder in the church. More than a hundred types of images and memorabilia of the people's saint circulated in Rome.

But there were more sinister implications on the horizon. To Cardinal de Bernis the hubbub around Labre was embarrassing. Had the man been an Italian, he would merely have smiled over the affair. But Benoît was French. To Bernis the whole matter exuded bad taste and, worse, fanaticism. As ambassador of France it was his job to see that no shadow of ridicule touched the honor of his country and his king. In a report to Comte de Vergennes, then French foreign minister, on 30 April, the cardinal declared the event to have been a Jesuit intrigue. This suspicion was further underlined by the fact that Labre had felt a peculiar veneration for the Sacred Heart, a cult which was known to be the special object of the Society of Jesus' protection.

By 29 July Bernis had changed his tune. There had been a decrease in fervor and the French envoy gave as a reason that Benoît was known not only to have read himself the sermons of Père Le Jeune, an intimate friend of the well-known Jansenist Père Quesnel, but had made his parents read them, too. This taint of Jansenism had dampened the enthusiasm of the pro-Jesuit party. Friends of the Jesuits and of the Jansenists were now fighting to patronize Benoît Labre and the beggar had become the plaything of the factions.[9]

It was in this type of milieu that Roman Jansenism grew up. And, although the movement was not solely a reaction to the propensity by the Roman populace and its abettors to create their own emotional piety, verging frequently on the superstitious

[9] Agnès de la Gorce, *Un pauvre qui trouva la joie* (Paris, 1954), 5–103, 111–44, 154–59, 171–208; André Dhôtel, *Saint Benoît Joseph Labre* (Paris, 1957), 136–270; Francesco Dante, "Una fonte per lo studio della religiosità romana nel '700," *Clio*, 16 (1980), 210–12, 219–20; Sir Marcus Cheke, *The Cardinal de Bernis* (London, 1958), 236, 245; Giuntella, *Roma nel Settecento*, 173–74; Montaiglon and Guiffrey (eds.), *Correspondence des directeurs de l'Académie de France*, 14:321–22, 324–25, 328, 333–34, 337, 339, 352–53, 402; Natali (ed.), *Storia letteraria: Il Settecento*, 1:65.

and the ignorant, these circumstances certainly encouraged the growth of a more austere and intellectual response, and gave a special poignancy to its ideas. From this perspective, Roman Jansenism may be considered an attempt at religious renewal. Yet, at the same time, you cannot speak truly of a wholly native Jansenism with an autonomous life and separate traditions. Its theological concepts were mainly imported. Those members of the Archetto group (see p.280) known for their Jansenist sympathies were mostly Tuscan educated and in close contact with the Tuscan intellectual world. On the other hand, almost all the major exponents of the Italian Jansenist movement passed some period of their lives in Rome, nearly always in their formative youth, where they took part in the discussions on learning, philosophy, morals, and religion in the circle of Roman Jansenists. There they acquired those fundamental notions which would guide their future conduct.

Since 1643, when the first Roman edition of Jansen's *Augustinus* had appeared, Roman theologians, with the echoes of the bitter controversy between grace and free will of Bañez and Molina still in their ears, began to take note. With the condemnation of the work by a papal bull the same year, Jansenism became a Roman problem. In fact, on the heel of two missions by the abbé de Pontchateau, who carried a letter from the bishop of Alet, Nicholas Pavillon, to the pope in 1677, a Jansenist agency was active on behalf of the French Jansenists in the papal capital, but it was mainly composed of French churchmen and did not produce a local movement.

The Roman movement had other roots, one of which was the school of strict Augustinian thought which had been revived by Cardinal Enrico Noris and was carried on by his fellow Augustinians Fulgenzio Bellelli and Gianlorenzo Berti. Its following was never large and was almost wholly recruited from among the Augustinians. But its practical importance was much greater for the development of Jansenism in Italy, because, recognized as orthodox by the pope, it served as a refuge for all those whose sympathies lay with Jansenism. It differed only slightly from Jansen on the question of grace. In fact, Noris and, after him, Bellelli and Berti, had to defend themselves constantly against charges of being Jansenist.[10]

There was also a more centrist current. Its disparate adherents had certain characteristics in common. For the most part they had studied with the Oratorians and, therefore, shared a neo-Platonic outlook, mediated through Augustinianism and the spirituality of Bérulle. They maintained friendship with the Jansenists, occasionally had family ties with them and yet admired the Counter Reformation saint, Carlo Borromeo. Without being great theologians, they all had a solid education and their interest revolved around questions of morality. They were eager for the education of the clergy and the faithful. They were stern with themselves and viewed laxity with horror. Yet, despite their severity, there was a human warmth about those prelates. In Italy, this third party, which was active

[10] Morelli (ed.), *Lettere di Benedetto XIV*, 2:241, 381–82.

even before the publication of the bull *Unigenitus* that condemned Jansenism in 1713, included such names as Magliabecchi, Muratori, and Lambertini. Together with Jansenism they fought the same enemy. While the two movements took roughly the same theological stance in the struggle, they differed in their inspiration, their tone, and their ultimate aim. The moderates eschewed rigorism, intransigence, and dogmaticism, and demonstrated some social concerns.[11]

At the start of the eighteenth century Giustino Fontanini, the librarian to Cardinal Imperiali, became the Jansenist protagonist in Rome. He was to point the way for the young Domenico Passionei and exercised a direct influence on Bottari. Fontanini, we know, was active in the Tamburo circle, which met at the house of Passionei. Beside the scientific and literary interests of which we spoke in the last chapter, the Jansenist question was their principal subject of discussion. Fontanini continued the meetings after Passionei's departure from Rome in 1706. During the latter's stay in France the group's ties of friendship to Mabillon and Montfaucon were reinforced. Fontanini died in 1736, two years before Passionei returned to Rome from western Europe as cardinal. But his work survived.[12]

In July 1762, Cristoforo Amaduzzi wrote to his correspondent, the physician Giambattista Bianchi in Rimini, that he went to the Villa Corsini "to pay [his] respects to Msgr. Bottari . . . where also all the anti-Jesuits meet, of whom he has become the head, so that he is of little or no esteem in the Sacred Palace." Giovanni Gaetano Bottari was regarded as the center of that group of individuals in Rome who shared similar views on issues of ecclesiastical reform and opposition to the Jesuits and who had become collectively identified as the Roman Jansenists.[13]

Born in 1689, Bottari had acquired a great reputation in his native Tuscany for his astonishingly vast erudition. After four years' study of theology with the Dominicans of San Marco in Florence, he devoted himself to mastering non-Aristotelian systems of philosophy, mathematics, and the natural sciences. After his ordination as priest, he was made director of the grand ducal press and, what is more important, the Florentine Accademia della Crusca entrusted him with the new edition of its renowned *Vocabolario della Lingua Italiana*, a task of distinction which he completed between 1729 and 1737.

A few months after the Tuscan Lorenzo Corsini was elected pope as Clement XII in 1730, he summoned Bottari to Rome. Henceforth, Bottari would owe his patronage to the Corsini family, and especially the pope's nephew, the newly created Cardinal Neri Corsini. At Rome he took up residence at Neri's palace in the Lungara, and soon rendered himself indispensible to the cardinal. He became his

[11] Francesco Margiotta Broglio, "Estremisti e moderati nelle lotte dottrinale," *Rivista di storia della chiesa in Italia*, 16 (1962), 291–94.

[12] Enrico Dammig, *Il movimento giansenista a Roma nella seconda metà del secolo XVIII* (Vatican City, 1945), 16–21, 39–41; Mazzetti, *Pietro Tamburini, le mente del Giansenismo italiano*, 25–26; Cochrane, "Muratori: The Vocation of a Historian," 156; Palozzi, "Mons. Bottari e il circolo dei giansenisti romani," 70, 72–73; Renazzi, *Storia dell'università*, 4:172–73.

[13] BAV, Cod. Ferraioli, ms. 415 (Amaduzzi to Bianchi, 21 July 1762).

adviser on all important matters and prepared the cardinal's opinions for the sessions of the Holy Office. He was also busy with organizing and enlarging the Corsini library and shared in the education of the younger members of the Corsini family. For a short while, until 1738, he held the chair of church history at the Sapienza in succession to Galiani, which he then resigned at the request of Neri Corsini to become a custodian of the Vatican library. In 1735 he was also appointed private chaplain to Clement XII, a position he was to hold under three subsequent popes. When Cardinal Prospero Lambertini was elected pope in 1740, Bottari's influence continued to rise. He was already bound to Lambertini in friendship over many years, probably going back to Bottari's first stay in Rome in 1725/26. Since that time an intimate and friendly correspondence had been maintained between the two. As Benedict XIV, Lambertini valued Bottari for his erudition in the fields of literature, history, archeology, and theology. He recognized his scholarly achievements by naming him in 1740/41 to three of his recently founded academies, and later also made him consultor to the congregation of the Index and qualificator of the Holy Office (1751). But with those appointments his public career reached its pinnacle. His influence, however, was to remain until the death of Benedict XIV.

Bottari appeared to have received his earliest Jansenist notions in Rome. Among his friends in the city, who were later to become respected figures in Italian Jansenism, were Antonio Niccolini, with whom Bottari had carried on a correspondence since 1722, and Gaspare Cerati, an Oratorian in Rome, who in 1733 became director general of the University of Pisa. Both of these men had been in contact with Fontanini, and Bottari himself had made the acquaintance of Fontanini during his first brief visit to Rome, when his interest in Jansenism was visibly aroused. Subsequently he would assume a more decisive anti-Jesuit position in dogma and morals. He laid the responsibility for the decline in morality and conduct on the shoulders of the Society, while he happily embraced the theology of Berti, the champion of strict Augustinianism. But all during this first half of the century Bottari's intellectual development evolved quietly and he refrained from entering into open controversy.

When Bottari came into closer relationship with Cardinal Passionei, his life took a decisive turn from that of a savant to a participant in an active struggle. Although there may have been occasional meetings of no consequence before, it was only in 1749 that the two men established contact and the occasion, we have noted, was the threat to put Montesquieu's *Esprit des Lois* on the Index. Passionei was not a theologian, still less a moralist. His long stay in France and the Netherlands, where he became papal observer at the peace negotiations at Utrecht and Baden, as well as his stint as nuncio to the Swiss cantons, had brought him into direct contact with the new currents of thought and free inquiry, including the interpretation of texts as practiced by the school of Mabillon. Throughout his life he would carry on correspondence with some of the luminaries of the Enlightenment in Europe, among them Voltaire, for whom he publicly showed his admiration. Not being a profound mind, he may never have fully comprehended the ramifications of the new thought, but saw it as a natural continuation of the literary currents in which he himself was formed. His ties with the French circles close to Jansenism and Port Royal are clear; but they were more of a cultural nature than anything else. Passionei never really shared in the teachings of Jansen, Arnauld, and Quesnel, despite some appearances to the contrary. He lacked too many of the qualities of a Jansenist: the deep faith and, above all, the moral rigor. For him the problem of the salvation of the soul was essentially secondary. Instead he was a man with a broad outlook, fond of free speech and a quiet life.

Nevertheless, given his position as cardinal and secretary of Latin briefs, it is certain that by the favor he extended to Jansenist sympathizers and by his contacts with the French Jansenists he contributed much to the development of a local pro-Jansenist circle. Therefore, the letter to Bottari in which Passionei described Bottari and himself as heads of the Roman Jansenists ("I calumniatori al solito non sanno, che il Priore e Fra Giovanni sono capi de' Giansenisti a Roma . . ."), while it should be taken in a humorous sense, was not without a grain of truth.[14]

The most important of Bottari's co-workers was Pier Francesco Foggini. The son of the sculptor Giovanni Battista Foggini, like Bottari, was a Florentine, who obtained his doctorate of theology in Pisa in 1735, where the teaching of strict Augustinianism propounded by Noris prevailed in theology and Enlightenment ideas were widely circulated. He was a pupil and close friend of Giovanni Lami, who founded the *Novelle Letterarie* of Florence in 1745. Their collaboration lasted for about thirty years. Lami offered in place of the existing piety of prodigies, flagellation, and even self-mutilation, that of St. Augustine and the fifteenth-century bishop of Florence, St. Antonino, whose *Summa moralis* he helped to edit in 1741. It was the piety of the moderate Augustinians which promoted morality by imitation rather than by way of casuistry. It also looked forward to substantial changes in the structure and practices of the ecclesiastical institutions. The chief weapon in the struggle was to be history pursued in the critical spirit of the Maurist tradition.[15] In his Florentine years, Foggini, therefore, occupied himself mainly with questions of church history, producing several myth-destroying dissertations on Florentine saints.[16]

[14] Caracciolo, *Passionei tra Roma e la repubblica delle lettere*, 15–27, 31–37, 50–51, 57–62, 67–121, 124–52, 170–73, 179–84; Salvatore Rotta, "Una lettera inedita di Domenico Passionei al Voltaire," *Rassegna della letteratura italiana* (May–August, 1959), 264–66, 268 n.4; Eugène Bouvy, *Voltaire et l'Italie* (Paris, 1898), 301–2; Berselli Ambri, *L'opera di Montesquieu*, 35–36.

[15] Mario Rosa, "Atteggiamenti culturali e religiosi di Giovanni Lami nella *Novelle Letterarie*," 297–99; Cochrane, *Florence in the Forgotten Centuries*, 339–40, 374, 380.

[16] Dammig, *Il movimento giansenista a Roma*, vii–viii, 48–60, 63–115, 124–36, 228–36, 308–11; Woolf, *History of Italy, 1700–1860*, 75, 113; Giuntella, *Roma nel Settecento*, 167; Girolamo Amati (ed.), *Alcune lettere dell'abate Antonio Niccolini a Monsignore Giovanni Bottari*, 7–13, 39–41, 43–44; Justi, *Winckelmann und seine Zeitgenossen*, 3:28–29, 118, 125–26; Palozzi, "Mons. Bottari e il circolo dei giansenisti romani," 70, 73–74; Pastor, *Geschichte der Päpste*, 15:682, 744; B.CORS., ms. 1588, ff. 136, 214; ms. 1590, ff. 45, 172; ms. 1591, f. 70; ms. 1615; ms. 1891, pt 1, ff. 12r, 20, 22, 129, 155–59, 163–69; ms. 2054, ff. 5, 19–112; ms. 2460, ff. 3, 7, 11–13, 25; B. CAS., ms. vol. 3177, f. 101.

Their writings apart, Bottari and Foggini used as their vehicle the informal gatherings known as the Archetto at the Palazzo Corsini, which brought together an assortment of enlightened Catholics, Augustinians, Jansenists, and anti-curialists. What held the group together was its hostility to Jesuit influence and its belief in reform within the structure of the church. The group enjoyed the protection of some eminent cardinals with Neri Corsini at the head. The latter attended the meetings of the Archetto regularly and was totally under the influence of Bottari. Neri's nephew, Andrea Corsini, who later became a cardinal and distinguished himself by his special zeal at the time of the suppression of the Jesuits, grew up in the spirit of the Archetto. Among other cardinals, who were in the anti-Jesuit camp and to varying degrees patronized Bottari and his circle, were Gaetano Fantuzzi, a friend of the Corsini, Mario Marefoschi, Giuseppe Spinelli, the skillful theologian Antonio Andrea Galli, and, at some distance, the Dominican Giuseppe Agostino Orsi, theologian at the Biblioteca Casanatense and later master of the Sacred Palace.

Behind the meetings of the Archetto hovered the shadow of Muratori. In 1747, he published his classic manifesto of the new piety, *Della regolata devozione*. It was based on the proposition taken from St. Augustine, and which he had advocated earlier, that incredulity is less damaging than superstition. He distinguished between the beliefs of the Apostles and the Fathers and those introduced subsequently. The latter might be considered admissible or even commendable as long as they did not detract from the first, but they were in no way binding. He consciously returned to the inspiration of Erasmus and even to Ignatius Loyola personally in demanding a greater emphasis on the sanctification of the laity and a more prudent vigilance over clerical vocations.[17]

Considering then the various influences brought to bear upon this group at the Palazzo Corsini, we may describe the Roman Jansenists as belonging to the transitional phase between the first generation of Italian Jansenists and the rebels of the second half of the eighteenth century. They were tenacious foes of the Jesuits, both at the point of their theology and their moral teaching. They admired the solitaries of Port Royal, who became to them the symbol of a pure religious life, austere and in intimate contact with God. They did not reject the bull *Unigenitus*, but would not accept it as dogma and deplored the damage it had done to the teachings of both St. Augustine and St. Thomas Aquinas. Bottari claimed that the Council of Rome in 1725, during the pontificate of Benedict XIII, was wrong in investing the bull with the character of a rule of faith. Rigorists in their polemic against licence, luxury, and debauchery in Rome, the Archetto group called for a purification of worship, the active participation of the people in the liturgical life and a struggle against superstition, in particular the cult of the Virgin. They desired not only a moral, but also an intellectual regeneration, which would raise standards both among clergy and laity.

[17] Cochrane, "Muratori: The Vocation of a Historian," 168.

Ecclesiologically they were Catholic and faithful to the pope and the unity of the church. They distinguished, however, between the spiritual and the temporal power. Rather than being open adversaries of the latter, they made it clear that they did not consider it a vital concern of the papacy and, instead, were preoccupied with saving its moral authority. Setting out from this very principle of guaranteeing the exclusively spiritual character of the power of Rome, they became the enemies of clerical wealth and the temporal power, going as far as upholding the authority of the bishops in the individual national churches.

To achieve their goal they aimed at controlling education in the colleges of the city in order to instill the proper notions in the future clergy. Their effort promised success, because a goodly number of them taught at these colleges. They had their greatest influence undoubtedly in the Collegio Nazareno, where men such as the Piarist theologians Martino Natali and Giambattista Molinelli propounded Jansenist views. Several members taught at the Sapienza. The attempts in this direction were particularly intense after the suppression of the Jesuits. With great zeal they championed a reform of studies at the time. Foggini put the colleges sequestered from the Society into the hands of the secular clergy, an effort in which he was successful thanks to the help of Cardinal Marefoschi. But they failed to reach all their goals before the premature death of Clement XIV put an end to their hopes and aspirations.

What the Enlightenment and the philosophes were to the Paris of the eighteenth century, Jansenism and its adherents or sympathizers were to Rome, *mutatis mutandis*. For some of the finest energies, especially among the religious orders, were drawn to the papal capital from all parts of Italy. These fresh forces infused the intellectual life of the city with new impulses and gradually broadened its parochial outlook beyond the confines of the city, as becomes the center of a world-wide church.

At the outset of the reign of Benedict XIV, Jansenist activities would assume visible forms in Rome. From his earliest days Prospero Lambertini had been particularly close to Celestino Galiani and his circle. When he became archbishop of Bologna he showed the same pro-Jansenist proclivities as Bottari and the Corsini did in Rome, although they were more of a reforming and political nature than of a specific theological character; hence there was always an element of ambiguity in his attitude. With his own preference for canon law, he had a great aversion to the subtler arguments of the scholastics and claimed that the only duty of the pontiff was to defend dogma and, where this was not in question, the various schools were to be given the widest latitude to propound their views. In the polemic over probabilism he assured his correspondent Cardinal Tencin that he was not inclined to one side or another. But he had to admit that Christian morality was in a sad plight because of the penetration of laxist ideas.[18] He was also reputed to have said

[18] Giacomelli, "Carlo Grassi e le riforme bolognesi," 1:42–43; Morelli (ed.), *Lettere di Benedetto XIV*, 1:12.

that the Jansenist sect was an invention of the Jesuits and that they had extorted the bull *Unigenitus*.

Taking advantage of the pope's attitude, the group around the Archetto began work, which at first had a Muratorian tinge and only later occupied itself with strict Jansenist principles. Its activity grew, generally under the banner of simple Augustinianism, until it had rallied many sympathizers by the end of the reign. Nevertheless there were disappointments; Benedict XIV did not turn out to be the hero many would-be reformers, including Muratori, thought him to be. After 1750, fearing the spread of irreligiosity, materialism, and atheism, the pope and the curia, we have seen, tried to put reins on the diffusion of dangerous currents. His interest in eliminating superstition waned. Given his support of the work of Leonardo da Porto Maurizio, he may be accused of even encouraging it.

While Benedict XIV lived, the struggle for ecclesiastical reform by Bottari and the others remained within the church and largely on the intellectual plane. Its standardbearers gave no more than sympathetic support to the wider jurisdictional claims of the Catholic sovereigns over the church within their states. But the more pro-Jesuit policy of the new pope, Clement XIII, and his secretary of state, Cardinal Torrigiani, dashed their hopes of an internal reform. Increasingly the church reformers and Jansenists in Rome turned abroad and to the Italian princes in search of allies. Contacts were strengthened with Jansenists in France and schismatics in Utrecht. One of their principal intermediaries was the abbé Augustine Jean Charles Clément, canon of Auxerre, who had visited Italy twice and there joined Bottari's circle. Bottari strove hard for a reconciliation between Rome and the schismatic church of Utrecht. He also contributed to the *Nouvellès ecclésiastiques*, the French Jansenist organ.[19]

A new epoch of hope began under Clement XIV, who from the outset not only prepared the decisive stroke against the Society of Jesus, but also a full rehabilitation of the Jansenist circles in Rome. But, alas, their expectations remained unfulfilled and the premature death of the pope destroyed their last illusions. This period also ushered in the last, and most radical phase of Roman Jansenism represented by a group around Pietro Tamburini, which had grown out of the Bottari circle. With the suppression of the Jesuits, the Jansenists believed they had entered their golden age. Tamburini and Giuseppe Zola, already well known for their views, came to Rome in 1772 after they had been dismissed from their professorial posts at the seminary at Brescia by the local bishop for their radical Jansenist teachings. Cardinal Marefoschi obtained the position of prefect of study at the Irish College for Tamburini and at the Collegio Fuccioli for Zola, in place of

[19] Woolf, *History of Italy, 1700–1860*, 114; Broglio, "Estremisti e moderati nelle lotte dottrinale," 295–97; Dammig, *Il movimento giansenista a Roma*, viii–ix, 269–74, 320–23, 359–78, 382–89; Cochrane, *Florence in the Forgotten Centuries*, 385, 393; Cochrane, "Muratori: The Vocation of a Historian," 168; Palozzi, "Mons. Bottari e il circolo dei giansenisti romani," 71–72, 75–80, 89; Rosa, "Sulla condanna dell'*Esprit des Lois*," 413–14; B.CORS., ms. 1590, f. 45; ms. 2461, ff. 96–97.

the expelled Jesuits. They held their own meetings, usually in the Marefoschi library, where they chose the apologists of the early centuries, Ignatius, Tertullian, Origen, and Justin, for their topic of discussion. But the suppression did not bring them the satisfaction that they had hoped for. Zola, therefore, decided to leave Rome for a chair in Pavia in 1774 and Tamburini, who remained behind, found his literary activity met with the disapproval of Pius VI. Fortunately for him, he was invited to Venice in 1778, just in time to avoid an expulsion from Rome.

The advent of Pius VI in 1775 showed the Jansenists that there was no room for new initiatives. The failure of the plan to have a *Synopsis dogmatum*, an entire treatise of the Port Royal type written with the help of Tamburini, printed in Rome, and the spontaneous break-up of the Tamburini circle were clear indications. Perhaps the biggest disappointment was that the Jansenists gained little advantage from the suppression of the Jesuits because of the subsequent defection of the Dominicans. Toward 1760, when Roman Jansenism entered its critical phase, it became evident that beneath the common struggle against the Jesuits there lurked some serious differences between Jansenists and Dominicans. When Cardinal Orsi, the most eminent figure among eighteenth-century Dominicans, died in 1761, his successor as Master of the Sacred Palace, Tommaso Mamachi, and other Dominicans left the Jansenist company. Little by little their recriminations became more bitter. With the suppression of the Jesuits the Dominicans replaced them as theological foes. Mamachi and the former Jesuit Francesco Antonio Zaccaria became the most vociferous defenders of papal authority and the most dogged enemies of Jansenism. In response, we have the most significant men of the movement leave the city. Those who remained in Rome were the least radical elements, who, realizing after 1788 that they had obtained the maximum from the Holy See with the suppression of the Jesuits and could no longer hope for further church reform, kept a prudent silence.[20]

In the interval, the center of Jansenism and, with it, the attack on papal primacy shifted from the city to neighboring Tuscany, where, during his visit in 1774, the great propagandist of French Jansenism, the abbé de Bellegarde, had forged some strong links. In 1780, Grand Duke Pietro Leopoldo nominated Scipione de' Ricci as bishop of Pistoia. While a student in the Jesuit Collegio Romano in 1757, the sixteen-year-old Ricci frequently attended the Archetto, since Foggini was a close personal friend of his family in Florence. After Ricci left Rome, Foggini continued to keep in touch with him. On the occasion of Ricci's consecration in Rome he stayed with Foggini, where he met some of the younger pro-Jansenists, including Giovanni Cristoforo Amaduzzi; the latter had helped Clement XIV draw up the bull suppressing the Jesuits. Although Ricci would introduce certain reforms in line with Jansenist thinking right from the start of his tenure, the climax came with the

20 Dammig, *Il movimento giansenista a Roma*, ix–x, 22, 176–83, 358–59; Broglio, "Estremisti e moderati nelle lotte dottrinale," 300–1; Giuseppe Pignatelli, *Aspetti della Propaganda Cattolica a Roma da Pio VI a Leone XII* (Rome, 1974), 20–25; A.S.Vic., Misc. arm. VII, vol. 82, ff. 2–7.

meeting of the Synod of Pistoia from 18 to 28 September 1786, in which Pietro Tamburini played a leading role. The decisions pushed through at the synod were so radical that the publication of the acts of the synod was cautiously delayed by the grand duke until October 1788. A commission appointed in Rome to examine the acts at the time apparently was divided on whether they contained anything contrary to Catholic dogma. Its members were probably anxious not to precipitate a break between Tuscany and the Holy See, such as had occurred earlier with other Catholic powers; Pietro Leopoldo had already expelled the nuncio and recalled his minister in Rome at the time. The decisions taken at Pistoia were therefore only condemned by a papal bull in 1794, well after Ricci had resigned his see in 1790 under pressure of local rioting. Although the authorship of the bull of condemnation is uncertain, some saw it as the work of Cuccagni, Marchetti, and Zaccaria, the champions of papal primacy in Rome. Not surprisingly, the bull was banned by the governments of Austria, Tuscany, Naples, Savoy, Venice, Milan, Spain, and Portugal, all Catholic powers that no longer acceded to papal claims.[21]

Thus by 1784 the direction of ecclesiastical interest in Rome changed in order to counter the new Jansenist offensive outside Rome, launched through the works of Pietro Tamburini, the actions of Scipione de' Ricci, and the pages of the *Annali ecclesiastici* of Florence. The person in Rome who was most aware of the need for a propaganda counter-offensive was Tommaso Maria Mamachi, now also secretary of the Index, a loyal servant of the papacy, always ready with an intransigent defense of the interest of the clergy and the hierarchy. The response was the new *Giornale ecclesiastico di Roma*, which was born in April 1785. It was the first periodical which acted, at least semi-officially, as the mouthpiece of the Roman curia by adhering faithfully to its directive for the thirteen years of its existence. The enterprise was started by a group of only seven, of which Luigi Cuccagni was director. Cuccagni, who had been in touch with the pro-Jansenist circles of Msgr. Foggini and Cardinal Marefoschi, never abandoned the Augustinian line on doctrine, but he opposed the anti-curial strain that marked some Jansenist circles in Italy and beyond the Alps and the ecclesiological innovations propounded by the Gallicanists and Emperor Joseph II.

Hence the journal, in substantial agreement with the curia, saw the danger of Jansenism not in its Augustinian doctrine, but in the support it lent to the enlightened despots in their claims on the Catholic church in their countries. Here was the target of its propaganda and it would continue into the early years of the French Revolution. The battle against the Revolution was simply viewed as a natural extension of the period of reform. The real culprits were the Catholic sovereigns of Europe. At first the journal preferred to demonstrate the small importance of theological disputes among the various schools in the face of the truth

[21] Charles A. Bolton, *Church Reform in 18th Century Italy (The Synod of Pistoia, 1786)*, (The Hague, 1969), 1–4, 9–22, 37–38, 56, 61–113, 125–28, 137.

proclaimed by the church, and to show itself the champion, without partisanship, of the Augustinian school. In short, it tried to deprive the Jansenists and the Catholic advocates of royal power over the church throughout Europe of the basis of any doctrinal claims and simply accused them of discrediting the Holy See by introducing discord into the church. For tactical reasons, it was extremely critical of the theological and moral teachings of the suppressed Society of Jesus.

The radicalization of the battle after the Council of Pistoia had the effect of weakening the moderate line espoused by Cuccagni. Without dismissing Cuccagni, a change in the editorial balance in favor of a line violently opposed to Scipione de' Ricci became noticeable. All the while, the *Giornale ecclesiastico* could not ignore the fact that some of the former Jesuits, such as Zaccaria, had become the most prolific authors in defense of papal primacy and the curia itself had started to use their pens. With some hesitation and even dissimulation it began to admit their works for review.[22]

The attempt at reform and renewal in both the Roman church and among Rome's laity, which local Jansenism represented, at least in its more moderate or Muratorian form, failed to take hold in the Eternal City. With the Tridentine age of religious zeal having passed, the papacy found itself in retreat on every front politically. Even a pope such as Benedict XIV, who from his background in Bologna might have been supportive of the effort, was more concerned with holding on to what the papacy still possessed. In a moment of weakness change, even for the better, looked like surrender. Ironically, Roman Jansenism, which might conceivably have recovered some of the energy dissipated in this post-Tridentine era in the capital, would now be exported to other parts of the peninsula, where it would be turned against the papacy, further undermining its foundation and throwing it on the defensive.

Just as Rome struggled in vain on the intellectual and religious plane to meet the new challenges following the end of the baroque, despite bold but inadequately organized and supported efforts to confront the problems, it would have the same difficulties in the realm of literature and art, where a revived classicism gradually began to replace an enfeebled baroque. The process began in the field of literature to be closely followed by the plastic arts.

22 Pignatelli, *Aspetti della Propaganda Cattolica*, 8–9, 37–43, 47–58, 63–66, 89–90, 100–2, 109–16, 165, 173, 193–94, 199–203; Carlo Capra, "Il giornalismo nell'età rivoluzionaria e napoleonica," in Valerio Castronovo *et al.* (eds.), *La stampa italiana dal Cinquecento al Ottocento* (Rome and Bari, 1976), 386–87.

13

# Literature

The course of Rome's literary experience bears resemblance to its intellectual history. For a brief moment during the early part of the ancien regime Rome was the capital of a new republic of letters whose dominion reached the far borders of the Italian peninsula and occasionally beyond. The Roman elite always had a more or less educated interest in literary subjects, which became the principal topic at many of its more serious *conversazioni.* Cardinal Benedetto Pamphilj, grandnephew of Innocent X, held one such literary salon at his palace at the Via del Corso during the first two decades of the eighteenth century, which was wholly confined to poetry. The cardinal, who had himself developed a gift for poetry, turned his house into a kind of domestic school of poetry, where young poets could read and critique their works. Another *conversazione* was held at the Cancelleria; there Cardinal Pietro Ottoboni, undoubtedly the most energetic patron of all the arts of his time, frequently had the works of contemporary poets set to music. The largest gatherings for a literary *conversazione*, however, were in the house of Msgr. Marcello Severoli, who made it a point to favor and further members of the Arcadia. More humble and not so numerous were the meetings at the house of the lawyer Felice Zappi and Canon Giuseppe Paolucci, both founders and luminaries of the Accademia degli Arcadi, who entertained their fellow Arcadians. But the real work was accomplished not in conversazioni but in the celebrated academy itself, which arose in the city in 1690 and lasted, with varying fortunes, more than a century. Its sway marked the Italian literary landscape between the age of Tasso and Marini on the one hand and of Parini, Alfieri, and Monti on the other.[1]

Characteristic of the authors during the first three quarters of the seventeenth century had been their attempt to astonish the reading – or, in the case of drama, the viewing – public with works full of marvels and prodigies, and to seduce their senses with lascivious coarseness. This period has been identified under the name of *marinismo*, after the capricious Giovanni Battista Marini (1569–1625), whose idylls and nuptial songs are credited with having begun that verbose and bombastic school which characterized so much of the seventeenth century. German literary critics equated this *marinismo* with the Italian baroque.[2]

[1] Renazzi, *Storia dell'università*, 4:160–63.

[2] Walter Binni, *Classicismo e neoclassicismo nella letteratura del Settecento* (Florence, 1963), 13; Ranieri Schippisi, "L'Arcadia," in *Letteratura italiana. Le correnti* (Milan, 1956), 508–9; Michel, "Vie

It was now necessary to revive good literary taste and liberate it from the abuses and licence of the baroque. This revision demanded both a new look at the writers of the past, those of the Greek, Latin, and Italian classics, as well as a confrontation with contemporary foreign literature. The first halting steps were taken by Queen Christina when she formed a private academy at her palace in Rome in 1656. Important personalities among the prelates and laity became members, including Cardinal Giovan Francesco Albani, subsequently Pope Clement XI. At about the same time the lawyer Vincenzo Leonio, a great admirer of Petrarch, planned to put a barrier to the bad taste of the century. He and a number of young men associated with him used to meet together in the evening hours in solitary places to recite some of their compositions. As their reputation spread, Christina invited these peripatetic men of letters to assemble in her palace and read their works in her presence. The poet Alessandro Guidi led the proceedings. The death of the queen in October 1689 broke up the meetings. A year later the Accademia degli Arcadi was born.

The inspiration for Arcadia came from the pastoral romance *Arcadia* by the fifteenth-century Neapolitan poet Jacopo Sannazaro, whom the Italians considered the greatest bucolic poet after Virgil and Theocritus. The people of Arcadia had always been regarded as the true expression of the pastoral life. The character of the place recalled the classical Golden Age. Hence each member of the new academy, known as a shepherd, was given a pastoral name and a plot of mythical land in Arcadia, the name of which he added to his Arcadian title. The assembly usually – but not always – met in the open in the Bosco Parrasio, where the members read their compositions. The location of the Bosco Parrasio changed fairly often in the early years until, in 1726, King John V of Portugal gave them 4,000 scudi with which they bought themselves a plot of land on the Gianicolo, where they built an amphitheater and established their archive.[3]

The pressure of legal practice did not allow Leonio to assume the direction of the new Arcadia, which he left to his friend Crescimbeni. Giammaria Crescimbeni of Macerata, a canon of S. Maria in Cosmedin at Rome, became thus the first custodian general of Arcadia, an office he held until his death in 1728. At the insistence of Leonio he laid down the principles for Arcadia, which he incorporated in two works. The first of these was his *Istoria della volgar poesia* (first edition, 1698), sometimes dismissed as a catalogue of facts and citations without originality or critical sense, and the other his *Della bellezza della volgar poesia* (Rome, 1712). In them he outlined a program that was distinctly anti-Marinistic. Against the ingenuity, the games with fanciful ideas, the excessive display of imagery with the exclusive aim at dazzling the readers, the Arcadians proclaimed the need to return to the classics, without any pretentious illusions of surpassing the ancients; they

quotidienne au Palais Farnèse," 2:551; Emilio Bigi, "La critica letteraria nella seconda metà del Settecento," in *Nuove idee e nuova arte nel '700 italiano* (Rome, 1977), 9–10.

3 Barone Emanuele Portal, *L'Arcadia* (Rome, 1922), 15–19, 37–45; Giuntella, *Roma nel Settecento*, 131–32; Maugain, *Etude sur l'évolution intellectuelle*, 232.

became the heralds of a sort of new poetic humanism. The Arcadians understood and vigorously emphasized that a renaissance of poetry to be truly effective and to count in the annals of literary history could only arise from resuming the interrupted dialogue with the Latin classics – and also with the Greeks who together with the Latins had become the honorary citizens of the national Parnassus – and with the Italian poets considered authoritatively "classical," from Petrarch to the *cinquecentisti*.

Arcadia, however, far from being an anti-historical movement of classical reaction, was actually tied to that part of the seventeenth-century literary production which had remained for the most part immune from the verbal fireworks of the Marinists and had not broken the bridges with the classicism of the age-old Italian poetics. It is a classicism not without its own pomposity and bombast, which was often only an excuse for lofty declamation and ambitious oratory, a vehicle for authors of solemn *canzoni*, of sonorous hymns, and grandiloquent odes. Yet it cannot be denied that there was another current that flowed into Arcadia. It is to be found in the works of Gabriello Chiabrera (1552–1638). To justify the enthusiasm the Arcadians expressed for him, we must look to his Anacreontic and short songs of various meters with their facile and graceful melodies. These demonstrated a remarkable musical fusion of rhythm and rhyme achieved through his arrangements of words in conformity with sound. In this regard he became the forerunner of Pietro Metastasio.

On closer examination, therefore, there were really two underlying streams in Arcadia. Crescimbeni, in his plan to restore all genre and all forms of poetry, was certainly concerned with the various shades of grand poetry. But, in spite of his will for an Arcadia for all, his choice ultimately came down on the side of the Petrarchist-Anacreontic sonnets and *canzonette* of the type of Chiabrera. In short, he seconded the evolution toward pleasing and melodramatic sentimentality, toward more grace and charm.[4]

So the sonnet and the *canzonetta* triumphed over the formal and complex *canzone*, the long poem. In fact, the Anacreontic *canzonetta*, a short humorous song, which resumed the Italian lyrical tradition begun with the ballads of the fourteenth and fifteenth centuries, interrupted in the sixteenth century, was the unique and true glory of Arcadia. With time the melodic elements pervaded the lyric poetry more and more; and with the arias of the opera and the idyllic *canzonette* flourished the secular cantata and the carnival song.

Poets worthy of the name are a rare sight among men; the odd one inspired with the true poetic genius usually arises from among a cluster of versifiers and

[4] Walter Binni, "Sviluppo della poesia arcadica nel primo Settecento," *Rassegna della letteratura italiana*, 58 (1958), 325–28; Renazzi, *Storia dell'università*, 4:111–13, 122–23; Natali (ed.), *Storia letteraria: Il Settecento*, 1:370–71, 654–55; Schippisi, "L'Arcadia," 510–11; Max Fehr, *Apostolo Zeno (1668–1750) und seine Reform des Operntextes* (Zurich, 1912), 8; Bruno Maier, *Faustina Maratta Zappi. Donna e rimatrice d'Arcadia* (Rome, 1954), 3–9, 17; Casanova, *Histoire de ma vie* 12:247 n. 9.

poetasters.[5] The latter were innumerable in the Arcadian age. The principle of imitation, rigidly applied in Arcadia to their "classical" model, gave to the poetic productions of this period the character of monotonous uniformity. While the academic gatherings spread the taste for making poetry, the use of anthologies of verses to celebrate special events, such as births, taking the veil, weddings, graduations, and deaths, had their only value as pleasing entertainment. We are confronted for the most part – between 1716 and 1720 when the first eight volumes of the *Rime degli Arcadi* appeared – with pseudo-poetry, pleasing, clear in facile verses and rhymes, or in dignified blank verse; in part erotic and amatory, which however remained on the level of elegant society; in part facetious and at once satirical; or veiling scientific knowledge and moral disquisitions in didactic poetry, a convention derived from Virgil's *Georgics*; or, finally, geared to celebrate the special occasions in the course of human life. The fact cannot be gainsaid that Arcadia did not create poetry nor did it produce a poet who could be called great for his power and complexity. The eventual sterility of true poetry and the abundance of verses applied to non-poetic ends became the limits of Arcadia.

Yet throughout the century of Arcadia a few more or less strong poetic accents were heard. Standing out among these were Giambattista Felice Zappi from Imola and his wife Faustina Maratta, daughter of the distinguished Roman painter. Felice Zappi came to Rome, where he made a brilliant career in a short time, distinguished himself simultaneously by his fluent eloquence at the law courts and by his limited, but genuine and sincere vein of poetry in the assemblies of the Arcadia.

If he was graceful, his wife was the stronger poet, especially in her sonnets which described maternal affections. The position of literary women in Arcadia was exceptional. There were 74 women members among a total of 2,619 members, that is, 2.8 percent. Yet in the *Rime*, the official publication of Arcadian verse, from among 237 authors selected to have their compositions included 20 were women, which is equal to 8 percent of all the authors, making up 27 percent of all the Arcadian shepherdesses. It was a deliberate strategy to hold them up as models for both intellectual and social fashion.[6]

Surpassing all the women was Faustina Maratta, the Aglamo Cidonia of Arcadia. She became the exemplar par excellence of the *donna* who was able to take part in her own right at the attempted restoration of a society and a literature which once more gave great importance to the presence of women as an essential pole in the vital literary tension, after their exclusion in the baroque era. Born around 1679, the natural daughter of Carlo Maratta, she probably received her poetic baptism through Alessandro Guidi, who, it is believed, taught her the art of the sonnet. In

[5] Helmut Koenigsberger argued that it is historically very rare indeed to have real artists, let alone geniuses, without a rich background of artistic craftsmen and, usually, quite a long tradition of the particular art. Helmut G. Koenigsberger, *Politicians and Virtuosi. Essays in Early Modern History* (London and Ronceverte, 1986), xiii, 259–61.

[6] Amadeo Quondam, "L'istituzione Arcadia. Sociologia e ideologia d'un accademia," *Quaderni Storici*, 23 (1973), 412–13.

8 Faustina Maratta Zappi, by Pier Leone Ghezzi

1704 she was admitted to Arcadia, where she quickly became known for the strength of her verses no less than the exceptional charm of her personality. The following year she married Zappi. But a little before these events something happened to Faustina that made her the center of one of Rome's causes célèbres. In May 1703, Giangiorgio Sforza Cesarini attempted to rape the poetess. While, from a strictly legal point of view, she obtained full satisfaction, Faustina experienced a mental trauma, which was only exacerbated by the slanderous rumors circulating about her. All this won her the sympathy of large circles in Rome and gave her a hearing for her work.

The lessons of Petrarch held an important place in the work of Faustina, who derived not only an impressive repertoire of words, imagery, and stylistic devices from the master of Italian national verse, but also some individual themes. Yet the Petrarchism of Faustina was not without some baroque echoes and those of the seventeenth century in general.[7]

From the very beginning the two currents in Arcadia were in conflict: those poets who simply wanted to uphold its more lyrical side, of whom the Zappis were examples, and the others who wanted to harmonize poetry and philosophical principles, the more classical or rationalist type. The decisive moment for the development of Arcadian poetry in the first years of the eighteenth century was the clash between the two personalities of Gian Vincenzo Gravina and Crescimbeni and the effective victory of the latter. The defeat of Gravina could be represented as a check to the more serious endeavor. Henceforth, the line which was to prevail in Arcadia was that based on the poetics and expressive exercises of Leonio and the Roman sonnet writers and on the proposals of Crescimbeni, which, in their more academic fashion, were substantially accepted and codified.

Gravina, a native of Cosenza, who became professor of law at the Sapienza, was, like Celestino Galiani, one of the points of contact between the dynamic Neapolitan culture and Rome. He is perhaps most widely known for adopting the young Pietro Metastasio. A fine Latinist and a devoted student of Greek literature, he made his name with a work on the history of civil law (1701–08), which earned him the respect of scholars throughout Europe and the approbation of Montesquieu in his *Esprit des Lois*. He was the first to study law as the product and expression of a particular culture. In this respect, Gravina anticipated Vico, who in his autobiography remembered him with affection.[8]

But it is in the field of literary criticism that he made his most immediate impact on Roman life. In 1708 he published in Rome his *Ragion poetica*, which has been described with some hyperbole as the true codification of neoclassicism. Certainly both Gottsched and Winckelmann valued the work, and Vincenzo Monti would recommend it later. It was Gravina's contention that poetry – and this includes both epic and dramatic – should reproduce reality and aim at instructing by images and allegories. Its purpose was to give art a seriousness that had been lacking for too long a time. The ends of poetry in Gravina's scheme were both delight and utility. The poets were the first civilizers of the world; with their fables they awoke the truth dressed in popular guise. Hence Gravina gave Homer an honored place among poets. To appreciate Gravina's esthetics you have to put it in its historical perspective as a reaction to Marinism, a return to that simplicity and naturalness,

[7] Calogero Colicchi, *Le polemiche contro l'Arcadia* (Messina, 1972), 14–16; Maugain, *Etude sur l'évolution intellectuelle*, 320–23; Eugenio Donadoni, *A History of Italian Literature*, translated by Richard Monges (2 vols.; New York and London, 1969), 1:312–14; Benedetto Croce," L'Arcadia e la poesia del Settecento." In *La letteratura italiana del Settecento* (Bari, 1949), 7–18; Natali (ed.), *Storia letteraria: Il Settecento*, 1:154; 2:674, 677; Maier, *Faustina Maratta Zappi*, 18–19, 23–24, 41–57, 64–68; Binni, "Sviluppo della poesia arcadica," 331–32, 335–36.

[8] Giambattista Vico, *Autobiography*, translated by Max Harold Fisch and Thomas Goddard Bergin (Ithaca, N.Y., 1944), 154.

9 Gian Vincenzo Gravina, by Pier Leone Ghezzi

the very components of *classicità* which are the color of the true and the heart of real eloquence, of which the Greeks and Romans were the masters. For Gravina poetry was imitation, but not of Pindar or Petrarch as earlier Arcadians propounded it, but of the real, historical, and natural truth. His fundamental canon was verisimilitude.

When it came to putting his lessons into practice Gravina was a failure. Apart from some mediocre eclogues, Gravina wrote five very bad tragedies, which were published in Naples in 1712. They display a poverty of inventive faculty, a lack of action, an absence of vitality in the characters, and flaccid verse, all violations of the very rules which he himself had postulated. More Grecian in style, as if they had been written by Sophocles, each of them was a series of small dissertations. Beside their programmatic significance in the struggle against the operatic libretto and against theatrical sensationalism, which aligned him with the general demands for the Arcadian reform of the theater, the tragedies were interesting as efforts in promoting a new anti-Jesuit and rationalist learning in the theater.

That introduces another underlying, if not openly expressed, ideological reason for the breach. Crescimbeni was a man of exemplary piety and an almost naive credulity, even for his age, in such matters as relics. It has been rumored that there was some Jesuit influence, particularly of a Jesuit by the name of Carlo d'Aquino, Crescimbeni's teacher, behind the foundation of Arcadia. Gravina, as is not surprising from someone nurtured in the Neapolitan intellectual climate, had as early as 1691 written under a pseudonym a fierce attack on the lax morality of Jesuit casuists with the title of *Hydra mystica*. The essay was more blunt than Pascal's *Lettres provinciales*, although not as elegantly written. When eventually the authorship of the work became known he made many enemies and was even charged with atheism. Thereafter discretion led him to abandon the topic. Nevertheless the conflict in Arcadia in 1711 became just one more facet, albeit one of the earlier and a rather subdued one, of the rift between the pro-Jesuit and anti-Jesuit factions that seemed to affect the most unsuspected corner of life in the eighteenth century. To that degree it, too, marks the end of the Tridentine culture.[9]

Looked at from a broader perspective, Arcadia sprang from a widespread aspiration among the best men of letters in Italy. Among their number was Muratori, who in 1703 launched the idea of a *repubblica letteraria italiana*, in which he proposed to unite into one academy the scholars in all the Italian cities scattered among the local and provincial academies, and outlined a program for that academy, which was to act as moderator for scholarship in all the peninsula. He put his plan in writing in the introduction to the *Reflessioni sopra il buon gusto*. In some respects Arcadia had already anticipated Muratori. For, once having established itself in Rome in 1690, it followed the example of ancient Rome by planting its pastoral colonies through the various regions of Italy and by merging the many literary academies which already existed throughout the peninsula, thereby scattering its influence everywhere and spreading its style of writing. Between 1690 and 1699 about six new colonies were founded. By 1761 the custodian Michele Morei reported 56 colonies through the length and breadth of Italy and at least one foreign branch in Portugal, all dependent on the Arcadia in Rome. Arcadia thus became one national cultural movement with its seat in the papal capital.

At least in its initial stages each colony was totally subordinate to its Roman headquarters. It could not carry on an independent cultural policy and could not

[9] Portal, *L'Arcadia*, 11–12, 31–33; Caffiero, "Scienza e politica a Roma," 317–18; Binni, "Sviluppo della poesia arcadica," 323–24; Natali (ed.), *Storia letteraria: Il Settecento*, 1:368–70, 494–96; 2:643–47, 948–49; Landau, *Geschichte der italienischen Litteratur*, 42–46, 222; Renazzi, *Storia dell'università*, 4:80–83; Vincenzo Gravina, *Della Ragion Poetica Libri Due* (Rome, 1708), 1:15–16, 34–35, 64–65, 82–86; 2:177–98; Donadoni, *A History of Italian Literature*, 1:317–18; Charles Burney, *Memoires of the Life and Writings of the Abate Metastasio* (3 vols.; London, 1796), 1:13–14; Maugain, *Etude sur l'évolution intellectuelle*, 350; Bertoldi (ed.), *Epistolario di Monti*, 376.

entertain contacts with other colonies on the periphery. All had to pass through Rome, which decided the admission of new members to the individual colonies and the publishing enterprises of its branch academies; at the same time it formed the only bridge of communication between the colonies. Consequently, until 1711 when the printed catalogue with the names of the respective members of the Arcadian colonies was published, one colony did not know the members of the other. The same centralization was to be found in the exhaustive publications of the academy. Between 1708 and 1727, the first five volumes of the *Vite degli Arcadi illustri*, the first eight volumes of the *Rime degli Arcadi*, and three volumes of the *Prose degli Arcadi* appeared. This vast amount of material reflected the ideology of Arcadia. For it excluded from its official corpus those texts and those shepherds who were not truly representative of the institution and who were not authentic witnesses to its cultural attachment.[10]

By the middle of the eighteenth century the heyday of Arcadia had passed. The coronation of two *improvvisatori* as poets laureate on the Campidoglio, the first since Petrarch in 1341, did not contribute to enhancing its reputation. Arcadia coincided with the age of the improvisers. It appears that the Italians had a special gift for extemporary versifying, which went back at least to the fourteenth century. Thanks to the favor shown it by the Arcadians it flourished in the eighteenth century, when improvised lyric poetry at times took the place of the moribund improvised comedy. To compose in verse without first having to think about it, without having to change one's mind, or to correct oneself, on topics usually proposed by others, in the required meter and rhyme, in the presence of the public, that was the sign of true mastery. The new esthetic put this skill at the head of its list, beside and above taste and genius, and insisted that this concept was proper to poetry and the arts. On this misunderstanding rested the dignity attributed to the *improvvisatori* and the admiration they received.

The prince of the *improvvisatori* of his time was Bernardino Perfetti (1681–1747), a law professor from Siena, whom Goldoni, who had heard him improvise at Siena in 1742, likened to Pindar. Although Metastasio thought him little better than mediocre, his talent seemed so marvellous to the Romans that by order of Benedict XIII he was solemnly crowned with laurels on the Campidoglio on 13 May 1725. A profoundly religious man, Perfetti believed his poetic faculty to have been a supernatural gift communicated to him every time he had to improvise.[11]

[10] Quondam, "L'istituzione Arcadia. Sociologia e ideologia," 392–95, 400–41, 417–19: Renazzi, *Storia dell'università*, 4:117–21; Portal, *L'Arcadia*, 50–51; Maugain, *Etude sur l'évolution intellectuelle*, 264; Mario Fubini, "Arcadia," in *Arcadia e illuminismo* (Milan, 1950), 9–10; Caracciolo, *Passionei tra Roma e la repubblica delle lettere*, 49.

[11] Croce, "L'Arcadia e la poesia del Settecento," 13–14; Benedetto Croce, "Gl'improvvisatori," in *La letteratura italiana del Settecento* (Bari, 1949), 299–305; Walter Binni, "Il Metastasio," in *L'Arcadia e il Metastasio* (Florence, 1963), 285; Pastor, *Geschichte der Päpste*, 15:506; Natali (ed.), *Storia letteraria: Il Settecento*, 1:98–101; Alessandro Ademollo, *Corilla Olimpica* (Florence, 1887), xiv–xvii.

More damaging was to be the coronation of Maria Maddelena Morelli-Fernandez, better known under her Arcadian name of Corilla Olimpica, in 1776. She was the most famous female *improvvisatore* of the eighteenth century. A native of Pistoia, separated from her husband, a Spanish dignitary, and indifferent to her only son, mistress of princes and abati, Corilla wandered from court to court, and was expelled from many cities without ever losing her composure. Her triumphs compensated her for her misfortunes. When she improvised, with her hair flowing, with her matronly beauty, with her voice modulated, she charmed her public, stirring it into ecstasy. The fashionable world flocked to her *conversazioni* in Rome, Naples, and Florence.

Unbeknown to her, a proposal to crown her laureate would serve as a pretext for a struggle of ascendancy over the newly elected Pius VI's mind on the Jesuit question, which despite the suppression of the Society was still brooding beneath the surface. While Corilla was away in Florence on a brief visit, two sides among the cardinals and Arcadians began to be drawn up. Eventually the anti-Jesuit party, which supported the plan for her coronation, prevailed and Pius VI ordered arrangements to be made for the ceremony. The coronation took place on the evening of 31 August in the palace of the conservators. On her return trip in the golden carriage of the senator of Rome, a large crowd gathered, but instead of applause she received a salvo of hisses, probably organized by the opposition party. The hisses were followed by satires and pasquinades against Corilla, Arcadia, the senator, and finally the pope himself. Pius VI, regretting that he had been party to this farce, ordered Corilla to leave the city immediately. The academy had once more been caught in the crossfire of the aftermath of the Jansenist–Jesuit controversy, but by this time the debacle seemed to have put the final nail into the coffin of the original Arcadia, which found it difficult thereafter to continue as a serious literary institution.[12]

The roots of Arcadia's eclipse, however, went back to the 1720s, when the operatic verse of Pietro Metastasio and his cohorts started to win widespread popularity and adherence. In the course of the subsequent years an anti-Arcadian polemic was growing in volume and vehemence, reaching strident proportions by mid-century. In his *Lettere virgiliane*, published in 1757, the Jesuit Saverio Bettinelli expressed the view that the flood of poetry which had drowned Italy was solely the result of imitation, which allowed everyone to improvise for himself and regard himself as a poet. He repudiated Arcadian poetry as cold and bloodless. At the conclusion of his tract he made the following proposal: "Let Arcadia be closed to everyone for fifty years, and not send out colonies and grant diplomas for another

[12] Andrieux, *Daily Life in Papal Rome*, 168–70; Pastor, *Geschichte der Päpste*, 16, pt 3:38–39 n. 8; Ademollo, *Corilla Olimpica*, xviii, 56–73, 149–237, 244–321; Silvagni, *La corte pontificia*, 1:236–38; Charles Burney, *Musical Tour or the Present State of Music in France and Italy* (London, 1771), 250–51; Clementi, *Il carnevale romano*, 2:174–75; Mario Dell'Arco, *Pasquino e le pasquinate* (Milan, 1957), 221–24; Luigi Morandi, "Pasquino e pasquinate," *Nuova Antologia di Scienza, Lettere ed Arti*, 3rd series, 19 (1889), fasc. 4, 772.

fifty. Meanwhile let it join with the Crusca in a needed rest for both to recover their fame and vigor."

More severe were the restrictions of Giuseppe Baretti in his *Frustra letteraria* in 1763, in which he heaped abuse and exaggerated criticism on the institution of Arcadia, in conjunction with most of the existing Italian literary tradition. He accused the members of the academy of being nothing more than a multitude of idlers, who wasted their time writing pastoral yarns. Both Bettinelli and Baretti were convinced that Arcadia was most directly responsible for the degeneration of the national poetic production into a useless flood of verses with scarcely any esthetic value.[13]

These reproaches did not appear to have fallen on totally deaf ears. A change in direction became noticeable. Gioacchino Pizzi, pro-custodian of Arcadia since 1766, devoted himself to the question of the tragic theater, which at the time was regarded as the most distinguished and the most difficult genre of poetry. It was probably through his personal initiative that in 1770 the second day of the annual "Olympic games" organized by Arcadia was devoted to tragic and comic poetry.

Pizzi used the occasion to read his *Ragionamente sulla tragica e comica poesia*. In it he set out to examine and resolve one of the most hotly debated literary questions of the century, the appropriateness of Italian authors imitating the French tragic theater. Conscious of the impracticability of a position that cut off Arcadia from the new trends in taste that the enormous spread of French literary works brought to maturity in Italy, he advocated a moderate receptive imitation, equidistant from the excesses of a narrow, prejudiced nationalism and an equally pernicious, uncritical, and indiscriminate xenophilia. While acknowledging the great qualities of the dramatic works of Corneille and Racine, he maintained that they could still be improved upon. Pizzi's program represented a worthy effort to place the Roman academy into the mainstream of contemporary national literature and so brought the Arcadians face to face with the deeply felt need of almost all the intellectuals of the time, the creation of an autochthonous dramatic literature. The theoretical initiative of Pizzi, however, was almost completely nullified by the nearly total inability of the Arcadians to support their programmatic efforts with poetic results of any value.

Gradually the realization began to dawn that in order to experience a genuine tragic theater it was first of all necessary to abandon definitely the mode of composing operatic libretti. This idea was first advanced in Arcadia, albeit in a rather discreet manner, by the abate Gaetano Golt, one of the first and most convinced champions of the need to renew Arcadian poetry, at a time when the admiration for the work of Metastasio was still unchallenged. In the course of the preface to his translation of Addison's *Cato in Utica* (1776), Golt took the opportunity to stress the incompatibility of the compositional and expressive

[13] Colicchi, *Le polemiche contro l'Arcadia*, 29–33, 43–44.

patterns of operatic libretto with tragedy. Without taking explicit sides for one or the other form, he let it be understood that his preference was for the second.

The decisive change in direction came with the ode *Sulla tragedia* by abate Luigi Godard in 1780. Since the coronation of Corilla Olimpica, Godard had unequivocally called for the abandonment of operatic patterns and their replacement with more profound dramatic forms. In his ode he joined those who, like Bettinelli, maintained that to bring about an effective restoration of the dramatic literature in Italy it was necessary to realize a powerful, weighty, and stern tragedy in the Greek mold. He proposed to gather under the cultural patronage of the Roman Arcadia all the various forms of tragic theater, from the Jesuit compositions of Varano and Granelli to the tragedies of Alfieri and the two Pindemonte, a goal which Bettinelli had already anticipated. All this was obviously a mere illusion. Nevertheless, at least in the first moments, the operation which Godard was able to conduct with undoubted skillful strategy, extending its scope beyond the tragic theater even, appeared to achieve some success and proved itself very advantageous for the cultural reputation of the Roman Arcadia.

If, on the one hand, the formulation of Godard's theory had the positive effect of assuring the academy important adhesions such as that of Alfieri, the two Pindemonte, Giovanni and Ippolito, and Melchiorre Cesarotti, who, at least on the surface, seemed to restore its waning prestige, on the other hand it introduced a further element of confusion into a situation that was already extremely chaotic. For, paradoxically, to the degree that admission into Arcadia was made easier for persons, however famous, who did not share in the cultural traditions of the academy – one need only to think of Alfieri – so it finished by losing any credibility it had left. By the same token it forfeited all its pristine ideals of restoring the great classical and Renaissance tradition of Italian verse.[14]

During the time that the leaders of Arcadia tried to win the tragic stage with their new dramatic concepts, the Roman stage was dominated by one man, Pietro Metastasio. Even Baretti, who was otherwise critical of so much poetic production, bestowed the highest accolade on this Roman native, affirming that "Metastasio has . . . many other excellent qualities, which make him a poet on many counts and one of the greatest in the world."[15] Another contemporary, the Jesuit Stefano Arteaga in his massive work, *La rivoluzione del teatro musicale italiano* (Venice, 1785), rated Metastasio higher than Ariosto, calling him the first philosophical poet of his nation. But there was also another side to Metastasio's genius. In his person we have the confluence of the Arcadian tradition at its most original with the deeply rooted popular Roman tradition of public entertainment and the people's theater. His

[14] Giandomenico Falcone, "L'aspirazione al teatro tragico nell'Arcadia romana degli anni 1770–1780," *Studi Romani*, 26 (1978), 503–21; Portal, *L'Arcadia*, 87–90; Renazzi, *Storia dell'università*, 4:375; Bertoldi (ed.) *Epistolario di Monti*, 1:62.

[15] Giuseppe Baretti, *Opere scelte*, ed. by B. Maier (Turin, 1972), 1:127–28.

libretti for the opera, the general art form of his day, sprang less from programmatic intellectual necessity than that they were prompted by sentiment and human experience, frequently that of his fellow Romans, even if cloaked in heroic or Arcadian garb.[16] For the Romans had a strong propensity for the popular theater. To understand Metastasio and the almost unrivalled esteem that he enjoyed, it is, therefore, not enough to look for his literary and Arcadian inspiration, but we must also trace his autochthonous Roman roots.

The Romans found their entertainment throughout the city. Like Paris, the city provided popular entertainment for all classes and groups of inhabitants. This form of entertainment changed little over the centuries. It was the substratum of everyday life, which allowed people of all ranks, occupation, wealth, age, and sex to mingle freely, thus becoming a means of social integration. Much of this life was played out in the streets and the open air. It ranged from the ballad singers (*cantastoria*), who, reciting stories taken from ancient Rome or medieval legends in a monotonous rhythm accompanied by guitar, haunted the squares of Rome, the Piazza Barberini in particular, to the high wire artists and magic lantern shows at the Piazza Navona. The last, indeed, resembled the culture of the Pont-Neuf and later the Place Royal in Paris.[17]

But the Romans were most enamored with the theater, whether it was outdoors or, more often, indoors, but preferably accompanied by music. They were seized with a positive craze for the puppet theater or *burattini*. Many of the puppeteers, among them the well-known brothers Antonio and Sebastiano Faldi, would give their performances at the Piazza Navona and in Trastevere. Others were held in private houses or haylofts, and eventually reached some of the wooden theaters such as the Pallacorda, the Teatro dei Granari, the Teatro della Valle, and even the Capranica. The most famous was probably the one located in the Palazzo Fiano, which had enjoyed the patronage of Cardinal Pietro Ottoboni and for which the distinguished architect Filippo Juvara had once carved puppets. These puppet shows usually played genuine Italian theater, occasionally heroic and tragic pieces, but more often they openly mocked authority and their humor was plainly salacious. But papal censorship left them alone, conscious that they provided a safety valve through which popular criticism of the government could be aired. As such they were full of satire and social commentary.[18]

Not all Rome's theatrical entertainment, however, was performed by wooden

[16] Schippisi, "L'Arcadia," 543, 546.

[17] Emilio Calvi, "Il teatro popolare romanesco nel Settecento," *L'Italia Moderna*, 6, vol. I (1908), 600; ASR, Camerale III, teatri, busta 2140, nos. 5, 6, 12, 16, 17, 19, 21, 24, 26, 27, 34, 37, 43, 47, 51; ASR, Tribunale del governatore, miscell. artisti, fasc. 452, busta 5; Robert M. Isherwood, *Farce and Fantasy. Popular Entertainment in Eighteenth-Century Paris* (New York and Oxford, 1986), 3–4, 217–25, 252–53.

[18] Calvi, "Il teatro popolare romanesco nel Settecento," 600; Silvagni, *La corte pontificia*, 2:128–29; Lalande, *Voyage d'un françois en Italie*, 5:11; Anton Giulio Bragaglia, *Storia del teatro popolare romano* (Rome, 1958), 303, 308; Andrieux, *Daily Life in Papal Rome*, 32, 159–60; ASR, Camerale III, teatri, busta 2140, nos. 3, 4, 5, 7, 8, 9, 10, 11, 13, 14, 15, 20, 22, 25, 26, 27, 28, 31, 32, 48.

actors. There were young amateur actors who put on plays and farces in rented halls around the city. Their enterprising managers had to ask permission from the papal governor of the city, who, being responsible for public order, supervised all theatrical offerings. But to understand Roman popular theater we have to look at the *commedia dell'arte*. An Italian invention of the sixteenth century, it stood for improvisation, the recurrence of masked characters, and professional players. Horseplay and extempore wit were standard ingredients of all popular drama, but it remained for the Italian stage to take the decisive step toward farce. The *burla*, something between a comic turn and a regular subplot, became the unit of farce construction and was structurally incorporated into the *commedia*. The other distinctive feature of this genre was the typed characters who became fixed as masks. The audience recognized them by their special make-up. For all, except lovers, wore masks or some correspondingly comic make-up. Their success depended on their immediate recognition as types. These masked actors made no attempt to show the development of individual characteristics. Rather, a mask represented a collection of individuals.[19]

The *commedia dell'arte* appeared in Rome around 1565 or even a little earlier and found its foothold in a small theater in the Via Giulia close to where the Carceri Nuove later stood. The art form received a boost in the papal capital when Tiberio Fiorelli, the creator of the mask of Scaramuccia, who contributed so much to the introduction of Italian comedic drama into France, visited Rome four times between 1651 and 1669, the last time performing at the residence of Queen Christina before an audience of cardinals and nobles. In the course of the seventeenth century, however, the *commedia dell'arte* underwent a transformation in Rome. Having once resembled the somewhat vulgar and obscene street theaters of Paris, the *parades*, a genre now evolved that was not wholly identical with the real improvised comedy. Its performance was not always extempore and the prologues very often contained personal attacks and acted out libels. On the other hand, the dialogue was uniformly as excessively vulgar as elsewhere. Consequently two kinds of *teatro dell'arte* came into being in the city: the traditional improvised comedy, which was played exclusively by professional actors, and the comedy partly improvised and partly not, performed by some dilettanti or amateurs, not always with money in mind. The best examples of the latter were the theaters of Salvator Rosa and Gian Lorenzo Bernini. To the traditional commedia dell'arte the Romans, in addition to the standard repertoire of masks, would add also their own, in which they reflected their vices, defects, and virtues; Rugentino, the growler, dressed as a

[19] ASR, Camerale III, teatri privati, busta 2139, nos. 30, 31, 32; Bragaglia, *Teatro popolare romano*, 296; Emilio Calvi, "Il teatro popolare romanesco nel Cinquecento," *L'Italia Moderna*, 6, vol. I (1908), 60–62; Emilio Calvi, "Il teatro popolare romanesco nel Seicento," *L'Italia Moderna*, 6, vol. I (1908), 356–57; Clementi, *Il carnevale romano*, 2:50–51; Katherine Marguerite Lee, *Italian Popular Comedy. A Study in the Commedia dell'Arte, 1560–1620, with Special Reference to the English Stage* (2 vols.; New York, 1962), 1:3–4, 17–22, 25–35, 41–66, 71–84, 89–101, 129–31, 167–69; Story, *Roba di Roma*, 263; De Brosses, *Lettres familières*, 2:342–43.

sbirro, who, although frequently receiving a thrashing from the Roman mob and always complaining of his fate, nevertheless bore any amount of oppression with patience, and Cassandrino, pretentious and boastful, who thought all women were in love with him and constantly vaunted of exploits that had no existence outside his imagination. But by the eighteenth century the *commedia dell'arte*, sometimes performed in the local *romanesco* dialect, had passed its heyday.[20]

To some degree it would be replaced by what we now know as the legitimate theater, primarily – but by no means exclusively – operatic theater. The eighteenth century was for the musical theater in Rome what the days of Michelangelo and Raphael had been for the plastic arts. Of the four centers in Italy – Venice, Rome, Naples, and Bologna – where you were able to hear on the average four or more different operas a year, Rome, without having music schools, even without artists of its own, claimed primacy. It was a primacy of wise judgment, fine appreciation, and sober eclecticism, notwithstanding a great deal of exaggeration, and some strong partisan feelings. The operatic theater at the time played the same social function which films assumed later and which is increasingly performed nowadays by television. A broad cross-section of the population spent as many free evenings as possible – in Rome usually only for the limited period between Christmas and Lent – in the theater. Because of its wide appeal, the theater became the medium for diffusing the Italian literary and artistic tradition, admittedly often in a watered-down version.

In spite of all the enthusiasm of the populace and the social importance of the theater, it was only tolerated not protected in Rome. While theatrical performances were given in the city before princes, cardinals, and very occasionally even a pope, such entertainment for the public was viewed almost as a forbidden fruit. In fact, the theaters of the time often were encased in a structure that did not give them the appearance of a theater. One went in with difficulty, through small entrances which had no sign or facade. In 1697, Innocent XII, for instance, ordered the destruction of the Tordinona theater on grounds of public morality. It was not, in fact, until 1800 that Pius VII tempered the old austerity of Rome by permitting greater frequency of performances and more ornamentation for the theaters.[21]

Thus, although the Romans adored the theater, at the start of the eighteenth century the city possessed no playhouse to seat a large audience for drama or opera

20 Calvi, "Il teatro popolare romanesco nel Seicento," 355–60; Calvi, "Il teatro popolare romanesco nel Settecento," 592–94; Bragaglia, *Teatro popolare romano*, 16–17, 20, 25–29, 55–57, 69, 305–6; Francesco Sabatini, "Rugentino," *Il Volgo di Roma*, 3 (1901), 250–52; Story, *Roba di Roma*, 263–64; Isherwood, *Farce and Fantasy*, 30–32.

21 Giulia De Dominicis, "Roma centro musicale nel Settecento." *Rivista musicale italiana*, 30 (1923), 511–16; Roberti, "La musica in Italia nel secolo XVIII secondo le impressioni di viaggiatori stranieri," 539; Alberto De Angelis, *Il Teatro Alibert o delle Dame nelle Roma papale* (Tivoli, 1951), 20, 38; Reinhard Strohm, *Die italienische Oper im 18. Jahrhundert* (Wilhelmshaven, 1979), 11–15; Burney, 382–83; Rinaldi, *Due secoli di musica al Teatro Argentina*, 1:xviii, 69–70, 186–87; Silvagni, *La corte pontificia*, 2:125–27; Coyer, *Voyage d'Italie*, 1:259; Emilio Calvi, "Il teatro popolare romanesco dal 1800 al 1849," *L'Italia Moderna*, 9 (1908), 751.

in the comfort and elegance that one might expect. Dramatic, as well as musical, recitals were staged privately in the residences of princes and ambassadors. The greatest of these private patrons was Queen Christina of Sweden. The tradition set by her was carried on in a number of Roman households, outstanding among them being those of Cardinals Benedetto Pamphilj and Pietro Ottoboni, and Principe Francesco Maria Ruspoli. In addition to these great patrons of theater, there was Queen Maria Casimira of Poland, widow of John II Sobieski, who was as eager as she was unsuited to carry on the tradition of the inimitable Christina. Between 1710 and 1714 she maintained a private theater at the Palazzo Zuccari.[22]

But the days of the great patrons and the domestic theaters restricted to a select audience were numbered. What we are about to witness in Rome is something that would develop in Paris only in the latter part of the century, the convergence of popular and elite entertainment by the opening of permanent public theaters. The first of these was the Tordinona, which owed its inception in 1669 to Jacques D'Alibert, a native of Orleans, who had been in the service of Queen Christina. It would open its doors for opera in 1671. By 1689 the Tordinona received a rival when Alexander VIII gave permission to Pompeo Capranica to enlarge his private theater, built twelve years earlier in his own palace at S. Maria in Aquiro, and open it to the public. To compete, D'Alibert was driven to rebuild the Tordinona and engage Carlo Fontana for the task. Two years later, however, in a papal campaign against obscene and corrupting spectacles it had to be torn down, not to be rebuilt until 1733, all in wood. In the meantime, Rome had acquired two other theaters of the first order – the Capranica and the Teatro delle Dame, popularly known as the Alibert, because it was founded by Antonio D'Alibert, Jacques' son – and three or four of the second order. The last of Rome's major theaters was the Argentina, constructed at the initiative of Duca Giuseppe Cesarini Sforza in the hope of recouping some of his family's financial fortunes. It became the aristocratic theater par excellence and even managed to attract a certain official blessing, since the governor of Rome often attended first nights and acted as master of ceremonies.[23]

In the auditorium of these theaters, which were almost wholly constructed of timber, society occupied the boxes and the middling and lower orders the benches in the pit. But the history of the theater was written in the pits. And there, among the multitude of abati and serving folk, Metastasio was the hero.

22 Alberto Cametti, *Il teatro di Tordinona poi di Apollo* (2 vols.; Tivoli, 1938), 1:6–8, 15; Montalto, *Un mecenate in Roma barocca*, 311–38; Howard E. Smithers, *A History of Oratorio*. 1: *The Oratorio in the Baroque Era* (Chapel Hill, N.C., 1977), 261, 264–74, 356–59; Hans Joachim Marx, "Die Musik am Hofe Pietro Kardinal Ottobonis unter Arcangelo Corelli," *Studien zur italienisch-deutschen Musikgeschichte 5*, *Analecta musicologica*, 5 (1968), 104–16; De Brosses, *Lettres familières*, 2:121–22; Roberto Zanetti, *La musica italiana nel Settecento* (3 vols.; Busto Arsizio, 1978), 1:223–25; Ralph Kirkpatrick, *Domenico Scarlatti* (Princeton, N.J., 1953), 35–39; Körte, *Der Palazzo Zuccari*, 48–52.

23 Isherwood, *Farce and Fantasy*, 230–31, 250–51; Cametti, *Il teatro di Tordinona*, 1:17–27, 31–99, 105–27, 134–36, 140, 145–88, 196–97; 2:378–84, 392–413; Rinaldi, *Due secoli di musica al Teatro Argentina*, 1:xix, 3–4, 8–23, 96–99, 119, 128–41, 148–49, 205, 232, 251–52, 300, 310–11; Zanetti, *La musica italiana nel Settecento*, 1:100–1; Clementi, *Il carnevale romano*, 2:58–59, 187; ASR, Camerale III, teatri, busta 2126, fasc. 44–45, 52, 64; busta 2127; busta 2128, fasc. 3, 4; busta 2131, fasc. 1.

Pietro Trapasso, the second son of Felice Trapasso of Assisi, was born in Rome on 6 January 1698. His father had enlisted in the regiment of the *corsi* and, having saved some money, became a partner in a grocery store. The young Pietro exercised his remarkable talent as an *improvvisatore* after school hours, when great crowds used to assemble in the streets to hear him. He was also gifted with a fine voice. On one occasion the learned Gravina passed by by chance and was so struck by the boy's gifts that he offered to adopt him informally and become his teacher. Since the child was to remain in Rome, his parents accepted. Gravina changed the boys' name to the more dignified Metastasio. He set the youth to studying law and made him learn Cartesian philosophy. At the age of fourteen, during an early period of indulgence, Metastasio produced a tragedy, *Giustino*, conforming to the rigor of all the rules of the ancient Greek dramatic writers which his preceptor had instilled in him. After this Gravina seems not only to have tolerated, but encouraged his pupil's adoration of the muses; at eighteen he took him to Naples to sing extempore with the most celebrated *improvvisatori* of the time. He became the idol of all who saw and heard him. In 1718, Gravina died leaving Metastasio as his heir. The latter dissipated the inheritance within two years, during which period he wrote sonnets, *canzonette*, and secular cantatas. He then went to work for an outstanding lawyer, Paglietti, who despised music and literature as being incompatible with the law. But Naples was the country of music and song, and Metastasio's specialities were nuptial songs. So Metastasio became the poet of noble weddings. His first theatrical productions, such as *Galatea* and *Endimione*, followed along these lines.

On the birthday of Empress Elizabeth, the Austrian viceroy commissioned him to write a cantata – a name generally given to a one-act musical drama involving mythological persons – entitled the *Orti esperidi*, which was set to music by Nicola Porpora. The work so pleased the famous singer Marianna Bulgarelli, popularly known as *La Romanina* because of her Roman birth, who took the role of Venus, that she fell in love with the author, took him to her home, and introduced him to the mysteries of the theater. He now had an opportunity to study music with the Neapolitan maestro Porpora. This knowledge enabled him to form the poetic-musical unity of the opera. In fact, his libretti, until 1730, the year he received his permanent employment in Vienna, were always created from the start in close cooperation with the musicians and singers on whom their success depended. It may be said that Rome had made an Arcadian of Metastasio and Naples a poet with a sense of musicality. The disciple of Gravina henceforth forgot Descartes in order to become a successor to Tasso.

His *Didone abbandonata*, written under the inspiration and guidance of Bulgarelli, in which she sang the title role, was a resounding success. It decided Metastasio's reputation, and he now took his place beside the Venetian Apostolo Zeno as the premier poet of libretti. The work was soon performed in that other operatic center, Venice, and in the carnival of 1726, set to music by Leo Vinci, was received amid great acclaim in his native Rome. In 1727, Bulgarelli persuaded

Metastasio to move with her and her husband back to Rome. There he conceived the idea of raising opera to the dignity and status of tragedy with his *Catone in Utica*. He chose the subject deliberately to please the Romans by displaying the tragic virtue of one of their heroes. It became the prototype of the Metastasian heroic drama. But it did not meet the taste of the audience of his day and was a failure. The action of the play finished gloomily with the stage stained with the blood of the dead hero before the eyes of the public. Since the viewers refused to tolerate such horrible catastrophes, he rewrote the third act, letting a character simply narrate the death of the principal figure. The attempt at tragedy having failed in his home town – he would renew it only very much later – Metastasio, following the taste of his century, gave preference to the happy ending, and turned to intrigue and conspiracy as more powerful for stirring up popular interest.

In 1729 he received a letter from the inspector of the imperial theater in Vienna offering him the appointment of imperial poet laureate in succession to Apostolo Zeno, who had held the post since 1718 and wanted to retire. Metastasio accepted. He was allowed to complete the two dramas which he had contracted with the managers of Roman theaters, and eventually arrived in the imperial capital in early 1731. When Marianna Bulgarelli died in 1734, Metastasio's personal contact with Rome virtually ended. In 1754 Marchese Patrizi extended to him an invitation on behalf of the pontiff to return, but Metastasio declined by reason of his age.

In Vienna Metastasio would make the European reputation that earned him the approbation of De Brosses and the admiration of Voltaire. Rousseau described him as "the only poet of the heart." Even Alessandro Verri, for whom Italian opera was poison, to use his words, conceded that "if the poetry is not by Metastasio, I have to flee during the first act." No poet was so popular in his time, none had penetrated so intimately the spirit of the masses. For the Romans the departure of Metastasio produced disappointment for a while, but the successes which the poet enjoyed everywhere stirred new pride and enthusiasm among his compatriots. Until his death in 1782 and beyond, the plays of Metastasio drove the Roman masses to the point of fanaticism and the theaters where they were given were so crowded, the demand for tickets so intense, that it became a matter of who arrived there first.[24]

[24] Walter Binni, "Poetica e poesia nel Settecento italiano," in *L'Arcadia e il Metastasio* (Florence, 1963), xxii–xxv; Grout, *A Short History of Opera*, 185–86; Natali (ed.), *Storia letteraria: Il Settecento*, 2:327–28, 783, 786–89, 801–4; Francesco De Sanctis, *Storia della letteratura italiana* (Lanciano, 1950), 359–68, 377–78; Donadoni, *History of Italian Literature*, 1:314–15; Burney, *Memoires of Metastasio*, 1:1–12, 14, 18–75, 97–103; Binni, "Il Metastasio," 251, 297, 345; Clementi, *Il carnevale romano*, 2:33–37, Fehr, *Apostolo Zeno*, 29, 120–23; Strohm, *Die italienische Oper im 18. Jahrhundert*, 176; Mario Fubini, "Metastasio," in *Arcadia e illuminismo* (Milan, 1950), 151–53; Jole Maria Baroni, "La lirica musicale di Pietro Metastasio," *Rivista musicale italiana*, 12 (1905), 393–98; De Angelis, *Il Teatro Alibert o delle Dame*, 67; Luigi Ronga, "L'Opera Metastasiana," in Mario Fubini (ed.), *Pietro Metastasio. Opera* (Milan and Naples, n.d.), ix–xii; Mario Dell'Arco, *Pasquino e le pasquinate* (Milan, 1957), 195; De Brosses, *Lettres familières*, 2:327–30; Mario Fubini, "Introduzione a Metastasio," in *Pietro Metastasio. Opere* (Milan and Naples, n.d.), 11; Seregni (ed.), *Carteggio di Verri*, 10:179.

On 18 August 1782, the abate Giuseppe Antonio Taruffi held a memorial eulogy for Metastasio. At the conclusion of his oration he extended high praise to Alfieri, whose *Antigone* had been staged a little time before.[25] His remarks are indicative of a significant change. Arcadia and Metastasio were Rome's direct contribution to Italian literature in the eighteenth century. But when it came to spoken drama, tragedy in particular, Rome merely shared the experience with the rest of Italy. We have already described the rather futile, if not self-destructive effort of Arcadia in between 1770 and 1780 to revive its effectiveness by emphasizing the tragic drama. But the problem of Italian tragedy dated back to the end of the sixteenth century. Italian men of letters in the eighteenth century saw many reasons for the "lento progresso della tragedia in Italia." The passion for musical opera was almost unanimously cited as one of the most baleful; Muratori and Maffei and many others until Alfieri repeated the same line and foreigners from Burney to Voltaire and Lalande echoed their lament.

To look for an active spoken theater in Rome at the start of the eighteenth century we have to turn to the colleges. The Jesuits had composed tragedies for the use of their students in Latin, partly as a pedagogical tool and partly to turn the stage into a pulpit against Luther and Calvin. By the eighteenth century they had adopted the vernacular. With this change the Jesuit theater lost its original character of religious theater – *argumentum sacrum sit ac pium*, as laid down in the *Ratio studiorum* – and became, as much as possible, identical both in subject matter and form to the secular theater. Several tragedies by Corneille, Racine, and Voltaire in translation entered the theaters of the Society, which started them on the road to classicism. In Rome, where the Jesuit-controlled Collegio Romano led the way with the performance of classical and French tragedies, the Collegio Nazareno and the Collegio Clementino were to follow suit, abandoning the comedies of Plautus and Terence, which had been their staple, and replacing them with works by Corneille, Racine, and, especially after 1737, the date of the first translation of his *Zaïre* into Italian, Voltaire.[26]

Although the French influence was embraced by many prominent Italian men of letters throughout the century, there was some opposition to it. Muratori at the very start of the century found the influence of French manners repugnant and Scipione Maffei tried to ridicule the gallomania of the Italians in his comedy *Raguet*.

In fact, Maffei was so concerned about the glory of Italian literature and scholarship that he decided to do something about it, and in the process became one

[25] Ibid., 12:359 (17 August 1782).

[26] Emilio Bertana, "Il teatro tragico italiano del secolo XVIII prima Alfieri," *Giornale storico della letteratura italiana*, supplement 4 (Turin, 1901), 2–5, 13–16, 42–48, 109–13, 116, 121, 126, 143; Natali (ed.), *Storia letteraria: Il Settecento*, 1:521; 2:941, 960–62; Burney, *Present State of Music*, 2–3, 199–201; Calvi, "Il teatro popolare romanesco nel Settecento," 599; Bragaglia, *Teatro popolare romano*, 292; Clementi, *Il carnevale romano*, 2:8, 30, 38, 62; Justi, *Winckelmann und seine Zeitgenossen*, 2:410–11; Bouvy, *Voltaire et l'Italie*, 231–33.

of the first and most significant reformers of the Italian tragic stage. After his effort to replace the French tragedies with Italian tragedies of the sixteenth century with the help of the distinguished actor-manager Luigi Riccoboni failed, Maffei, although no poet by nature, completed his five-act drama *Merope* within two months. The subject matter, taken from classical mythology, had been an important theme in the Italian theater. The premiere of the play at Modena in 1713 aroused a great stir. It then made the rounds of the Italian stages, and won the plaudits of the Roman masses. With simplicity of line and language Maffei composed a tragedy in blank verse on maternal love, which even today cannot be read without some emotion. At the same time he created a work that met the different requirements of the various currents within Arcadia, a tragedy that united literary style, comprehensibility, and theatricality, to make it both recitable and performable on stage, a work capable of competing with opera and of meeting the interest and taste of a large and educated audience.

Maffei's *Merope* was to stand alone until the rise of Italy's greatest tragic playwright Vittorio Alfieri later in the century. It is symbolic of the new era that Alfieri during his stay in Rome in 1782 was not only to read and study Maffei's drama as the work which represented, in the common view of contemporary men of letters, the best product of Italian tragic theater, and which he would have to confront to prove his own theatrical technique, but he also proceeded to rework it in accordance with his own basic principles.[27]

Alfieri came to Rome five times in the period between the spring of 1767 and the spring of 1783. The last time he followed his beloved Luisa, Countess of Albany, who had fled her husband, the debauched Young Pretender to the British throne, in December 1780. Alfieri arrived in the city on 12 May. At first he stayed for a short while in the Piazza Rondanini and then moved to the Villa Strozzi in the Via Viminale. There the poet spent a great part of the day immersed in his favorite activity. His productivity was staggering. He turned seven tragedies into verse in ten months, planned and wrote two new ones; altogether he finalized and corrected fourteen, not to speak of his completing the narrative poem *L'Etruria vendicata*, with its anti-Medicean, that is anti-tyrannical, theme and anti-clerical tone; and composed five odes exalting America's struggle for liberty. Besides, Alfieri often read his tragedies in various meetings, in his own house or in the Roman salons, particularly that of Maria Pizzelli, where he recited his *Virginia*, which would stir Vincenzo Monti to imitate him. When his *Antigone*, in which Alfieri himself took the part of Creon, was performed in the winter of 1782 at the palace of the Duca Grimaldi, the Spanish ambassador, the journal *Effemeridi letterarie* of 4 December

[27] Bertana, "Il teatro tragico italiano," 51–61; Landau, *Geschichte der italienischen Litteratur*, 9–10, 375–76; Maugain, *Etude sur l'évolution intellectuelle*, 269–70, 273–76, 352–53; Walter Binni, "Il periodo romano dell'Alfieri e la *Merope*," in *Saggio Alfieriani* (Florence, 1969), 57–60: Natali (ed.), *Storia letteraria: Il Settecento*, 2:945–55; Zanetti, *La musica italiana nel Settecento*, 1:28 n. 47; Strohm, *Die italienische Oper im 18. Jahrhundert*, 236–37; Donadoni, *History of Italian Literature*, 1:313; Silvagni, *La corte pontificia*, 2:136–37; Bouvy, *Voltaire et l'Italie*, 196.

hailed its performance with the same enthusiasm as the *Giornale dei letterati* of Venice had that of Maffei's *Merope* at the beginning of the century. Buoyed with pride at the success of the play, Alfieri was persuaded for the first time to have his plays printed.

The conditions that favored his emotional and poetic life in Rome, upon which he would look back later with nostalgia in his *Vita*, certainly imposed upon Alfieri a bitter abdication of his personal pride and his disdainful attitude to court life, compelling him to a painful dissimulation about the real nature of his relationship with the Countess of Albany, so contrary to his true character. The dissimulation went so far as a compulsion to pay a visit to Pius VI and offer the dedication of his *Saul* to the pontiff, who, however, declined it. But Alfieri was to read his tragedy in the presence of a great number of monsignori and abati in the Arcadia, which enrolled him in the ranks of its shepherds.

With his *Saul*, one of the great works in the world's tragic repertoire, Alfieri reached the high point of his last stay in Rome. By April 1783, the Cardinal Duke of York indicated to his sister-in-law that the meetings with Alfieri in her house had to stop. The matter had stirred up such a great excitement in Rome that, it is said, the pope intimated that Alfieri should remove himself from the scene. In order to avoid a greater scandal the poet left immediately and arrived on 4 May 1783, in Siena. For a parting shot he published his sonnet *Vuota, insalubre region*, in which he denigrated Rome and all the Papal States as the seat of every vice and of slavery. Yet it was not until 1790 that the papal authorities banned the performance of Alfieri's plays, at a time when the author was living in Revolutionary Paris.[28]

It took Vincenzo Monti to restore the muse of tragedy to the city for a while. He was born in Fusignano in the Romagna in 1754, the ninth son of a large landholder. After overcoming the resistance of his father, who wanted him to study law, he devoted himself to literature, particularly poetry. The Bible and Virgil exercised the strongest influence on him during his formative years and at the age of twenty-two he published his ode *Visione d'Ezechiello*. It attracted wide attention and won him the patronage of the legate of Ferrara, Cardinal Borghese. After his arrival in Rome in 1778 he was admitted into the ranks of the Arcadians and the literary circle which met in the house of Baldassare Odescalchi, duke of Ceri, in spite of the fact that he held a very low opinion of Roman poets and of the state of Arcadia as a whole.[29] On the occasion of the discovery of a bust of Pericles near Tivoli, he composed, at the instigation of the antiquary Ennio Quirino Visconti, the *Prosopopeia di Pericle*, a

[28] Donadoni, *History of Italian Literature*, 1:349–58; Binni, "Il periodo romano dell'Alfieri," 41–57, 60–61; Natali (ed.), *Storia letteraria: Il Settecento*, 2:978–79, 1004, 1009; Silvagni, *La corte pontificia*, 1:240–43, 343–44; De Sanctis, *Storia della letteratura italiana*, 2:411–13; Vittorio Alfieri, *La Vita* (Turin, 1920), 58–59, 181–86, 195–208; Rinaldi, *Due secoli di musica al Teatro Argentina*, 1:223, 238–39, 319–20; Bragaglia, *Teatro popolare romano*, 325; De Angelis, *Il Teatro Alibert o delle Dame*, 82–86; Pastor, *Geschichte der Päpste*, 16, pt 3:504; Cretoni, *Roma Giacobina*, 180–81.

[29] Walter Binni, *Monti. Poeta del consenso* (Florence, 1981), 67–76.

work overladen with fawning flattery for Pius VI. The marriage of Luigi Braschi, the pope's nephew, to the beautiful Costanza Falconieri furnished the material for the *Bellezza dell'universo*. These poems not only won him acclaim, but, in October 1781, the position of secretary to the princely Braschi family. Six years later he would fall in love with his master's wife and it appears the mutual attraction was more than simply Platonic. Whatever may have happened, this relationship found an end in 1791 when Monti took the 22-year-old Teresa Pickler, daughter of a distinguished engraver, as his wife, with whom he lived for many years in an apparently happy marriage.

During the first seven years of his stay in Rome Monti was, in fact, the poet laureate of the house of Braschi. Only with the appearance of Alfieri was he stirred up to try his hand at drama. In 1783, Monti, having heard Alfieri read his *Virginia* in the salon of Maria Pizzelli, set to work on his first tragedy *Aristodemo*, which he reworked fitfully until the final version was ready about the start of 1786. Before sending it to be printed by Bodoni in Parma, he recited it privately. On one occasion Goethe heard it and was favourably impressed. It won a prize at Parma and had its Roman premiere at the Teatro della Valle on 14 January 1787. The reception which the *Aristodemo* received there could not have been more triumphal. Yet Monti had no real talent for tragedy. The dignified grace of his verse sounded well to the ears of a public that was getting slowly satiated with the sentimentality of Metastasio, but was not yet ready for the harsh tragedies of Alfieri. Even before the *Aristodemo* had been put on stage Monti sat down to write a second drama, *Galeotto Manfredi, Signore di Faenza*, a domestic tragedy taken from Machiavelli's *History*. It was performed a year after the *Aristodemo* on the same stage. It, too, was well received, but not as enthusiastically as the first. Some critics believed to see in the piece a satire of courts and courtiers in general and of the government of Pius VI in particular. If the latter were the case, it was a presentiment of the author's future conduct.

Monti wrote under the influence of Shakespeare. Although not the first, he was clearly the Italian author who owed most to the English bard, whose works he read in Le Tourneur's French translation (Paris, 1776–82). Shakespeare's contribution to the dramatic stock-in-trade of the time consisted of three elements – the use of ghosts, the introduction of the people as a speaking character, and the funeral orations in *Julius Caesar*. All of these had been hallowed on the European continent by Voltaire's imitations and they all find a place in Monti's tragedies. There is Dirce's ghost in *Aristodemo*, more material than those of Shakespeare, who can drag Aristodemo around the stage, and the borrowings from *Henry VIII*, *Othello*, and *Julius Caesar* in his *Galeotto Manfredi*.

In January 1793 the representative of the French revolutionaries in Rome, Hugon de Bassville, was murdered. This event occasioned Monti's writing of the *Bassvilliana*, perhaps his best lyrical epic, the four cantos of which he wrote in the summer of 1793. In them he imagined that Bassville, who deserved the punishment of hell for his unbelief, had repented at his death and, pardoned by God, his soul was led by an angel through France in order to witness all the horrors and brutality committed during the Revolution with his connivance. He watches the execution of Louis XVI, which followed Bassville's own death by a week, and the torments of hell suffered by the unbelieving philosophes and demagogues. It is obvious that at this point Monti was impelled to the work by outward circumstances, for the firm anti-revolutionary sentiment which is expressed in the poem no longer corresponded fully to Monti's own conviction. He had had friendly contacts with the assassinated Bassville, borrowed some banned books from him, and may even have been secretly a freemason. Other friends of Bassville were fleeing Rome, feeling no longer safe after his murder; Monti may have had similar thoughts at first, but decided to stay. He used his *Bassvilliana* to protest his correct anti-republican views and his respect for the pope and the church. Yet Monti felt increasingly uncomfortable in Rome, where he published little more worth mentioning. When Colonel Marmont arrived in the city in February 1797, sent on the orders of General Bonaparte after the Peace of Tolentino, Monti made his acquaintance and gladly accepted his invitation to accompany him to Florence. He stole away without taking leave and, after various ups and downs, the new republican landed in Milan, the capital of the Cisalpine republic, where he wrote ultra-revolutionary and anti-religious poems, and repudiated his *Bassvilliana*.[30]

With Monti we note the first literary traces of neoclassicism. Although his ode *Prosopopeia de Pericle* of 1779 was an attempt at handling a neoclassic topic, particularly suited to the Roman archeological climate of his day, Monti failed at that point to attain the pure neoclassical style, based on the principles laid down by Winckelmann, of "nobile calma e tranquilla grandezza." The first real neoclassical motifs and themes appear in his poem *Musogonia*, written in 1792/93. But it was only just before his hasty departure from Rome that Monti would achieve the noble simplicity and lofty tranquillity that bore the hallmark of neoclassicism in his narrative poem *Ferionade*, which celebrated the draining of the Pontine marshes. That work and the start of his translation of the *Iliad*, which albeit would not be completed until the Napoleonic age, brought Rome's literature abreast with the developments in archeology and art.[31] It was in those spheres where the classical

[30] Bertoldi (ed.), *Epistolario di Monti*, 49–51, 60–61, 157, 159, 168–69, 203, 251, 255–56, 280–81, 286–87, 290, 298–99, 314, 317, 356–57, 373–75, 398–402, 436, 442–43, 455–56, 460–62; 2:2, 4–7, 10; Landau, *Geschichte der italienischen Litteratur*, 10, 678–82; Donadoni, *History of Italian Literature*, 2:365–66; Vicchi, *Vincenzo Monti (1778–1780)*, 306–8, 324–25; Goethe, *Italian Journey*, 130–31, 149; Gasperoni, *Settecento italiano* 1: *Amaduzzi*, 102–4; Dal Pane, *Lo Stato Pontificio e il movimento riformatore*, 528–37; De Sanctis, *Storia della letteratura italiana*, 2:420; Lacy Collison-Morley, *Shakespeare in Italy* (New York, 1916), 69–71: Clementi, *Il carnevale romano*, 2:200–1; Binni, *Monti*, 84, 111–15.

[31] Ibid., 77, 130; Binni, *Classicismo e neoclassicismo*, 93–95; Donadoni, *History of Italian Literature*, 2:370, 374.

renewal, which failed to mature in the formal literature of the Arcadia, was to find its most visible expression. For both Arcadia and neoclassicism were cultural movements that spread their influences beyond the confines of the particular art in which they were born.[32]

[32] Vittorio Moschini, "Giaquinto artista rappresentativo della pittura barocca tarda a Roma," *L'Arte* (1924), 105; Schippisi, "L'Arcadia," 517; Pinto, *Trevi Fountain*, 224–49. For the influence of Arcadia on Nicola Salvi in the iconography of the Trevi fountain, see chapter 1, p.29.

14

# Antiquarianism and neoclassicism

Antiquarian art was almost the only topic which would attract the sluggish attention of the ordinary Roman. For antiquities were the egalitarian element in Roman culture, and anyone who understood anything about them, whatever his station, could eagerly participate in the discussions. The eminent editor Giovanni Ludovico Bianconi could, with some justification, boast that "for twenty centuries at least, Rome had been destined to lay down the laws . . . It is to us, not to others, that France, Spain, Lusitania send their youth with the hope that we would initiate it into the fine arts which could be said to be ours. The new Semiramis of the North and this Alexander . . . entrust their children to us." During the period of the ancien regime, the city more than ever became the magnet for antiquarian activities.[1]

With the start of the eighteenth century Rome saw the emergence of a group of scholars who made the study of antiquity one of their principal concerns. Outstanding among their number were Francesco Bianchini, Ridolfo Venuti, and Ennio Quirino Visconti. Bianchini we have already come across as a leading light, together with Celestino Galiani, in the early efforts to bring Roman thought in line with the latest scientific and scholarly trends. After 1705 he directed the excavations in the Palatine gardens, which revealed the remains of the palace of the Caesars. His account of the findings was published posthumously in 1738. But eleven years before, a work of his, *Camera ed iscrizioni sepolcrali de' liberti, servi, ed ufficiali della casa di Augusto*, appeared. Late in 1725, a smallholder with property along the Appian Way outside Rome had been persuaded to form a partnership in a commercial speculation, sharing the cost of digging up some promising bumps in his vineyard and the profit on the sale of any discovery. The excavators were lucky enough to strike into a large communal tomb dating from the early first century A.D., which was used for the ashes of the freedmen and slaves of the household of the Empress Livia, wife of Augustus. Although the burial chamber was not as rich in valuable works as the partners had hoped, there was quite a good haul of antiquities. Bianchini, as papal commissioner for antiquities at the time, left us an account of the layout of the discovery as well as the history of the persons buried.

[1] Hautecoeur, *Rome et le renaissance de l'antiquité*, 55; Giuntella, *Roma nel Settecento*, 104–5; Delumeau, *Vie économique et sociale de Rome*, 1:155; Lanciani, *Storia degli scavi*, 4:197–207; Petrocchi, *Roma nel Seicento*, 205.

The abate Ridolfo Venuti, a patrician from Verona who made his home in Rome, devoted himself to describing the ancient monuments of the city. For his many achievements he was elected member of the Royal Society of Antiquaries of London. He died, however, in 1763 before he saw the publication of his principal work, *Accurate, e succinte descrizione topografica delle antichità di Roma.*

Preeminent among his fellow archeologists – and philologists as well – was Ennio Quirino Visconti, perhaps the greatest native mind the city produced in the eighteenth century. Born in 1751, the son of Giambattista Visconti, himself a brilliant archeologist, Ennio Quirino was so precocious that when he was only ten he amazed observers with his knowledge of history and at thirteen was able to translate Euripides' *Hecuba* without any help. At the age of twenty he was appointed librarian of the Vatican, where he continued to pursue his philological and literary studies, which reached their high point with his *Discorso sullo stato attuale della letteratura romana*, which dates from 1785 (but was not published until 1841). It reveals Visconti as a keen literary critic. But his real greatness lay in archeology. With Winckelmann's death the office of commissioner for antiquities fell to Giambattista Visconti, who in 1778 was asked by Pius VI to make illustrations of the pieces in the Museo Clementino. The father called in his son, who, having grown up amid the statues of the Vatican, labored tirelessly on the project. The work was immediately hailed as a classic, unique in its genre. This masterpiece of Italian archeological scholarship, the first volume of which bears the name of Giambattista Visconti, was published in Rome in eight folio volumes between 1782 and 1800. It was, in truth, the achievement of Ennio, who had inherited his father's post when the latter died. When the Roman republic was proclaimed in February 1793, Ennio Quirino Visconti was made head of the ministry of the interior. This was a natural development on his part. For like most of his contemporary men of letters, he was imbued with those Enlightenment ideas that he identified with the virtues of classical antiquity. He had welcomed the pontificate of Pius VI only insofar as the pontiff was the restorer of the revered antiquity; and with no less enthusiasm he now hailed the resurrected Roman republic.

To Visconti goes the credit for having established the foundations for the hermeneutics of ancient monuments. In many respects he incarnated the ideal of the archeologist. "Archeological science," he wrote, "is the fruit of a judicious reading of the classics, of a diligent comparison of monuments, of a sure taste for the fine arts, a deep knowledge of the customs, laws, religion, and the character of the ancient peoples, a knowledge which is not distinct from philosophy."[2]

To be honest, however, in spite of a few impressive works, notably in the field of

[2] Noack, *Deutsches Leben in Rom*, 39; Scott, *Piranesi*, 107–8, 307 n. 5; Renazzi, *Storia dell'università*, 4:157–58, 352–53; Natali (ed.), *Storia letteraria: Il Settecento*, 1:418–19; Hautecoeur, *Rome et la renaissance de l'antiquité*, 69; Landau, *Geschichte der italienischen Litteratur*, 344–46; Silvagni, *La corte pontificia*, 1:239; Rava, *Un salotto romano del Settecento*, 31–34; BAV, Cod. Ferraioli, ms. 415, f. 25v.

Christian antiquities, on which we have already commented, the archeological fever of the time consisted of no more than making shallow digs without prior plans from which statues, bas-reliefs, and fragments of all sorts were pilfered to be put in a gallery. The century's real mania was for collecting. The popes considered it their duty to bring the glorious past to light and enclose it within a museum. The cardinals showed similar enthusiasm. Rich foreigners on their Roman tour all longed to discover, on a site or at some dealer's, some classical object to take home as a memento of their travels. All this investigation enriched the galleries, but, with an occasional exception, did little else. The investigators delved into the ruins and took away their treasure with no thought of any light these might shed upon the original structure of the building. Only under Pius VI did archeology start to divorce itself from its intimate connection with art. It began to assert its autonomy, gradually overcoming the common existence it still shared methodologically with sculpture and architecture under the two earlier commissioners for antiquity, Ridolfo Venuti and Winckelmann. The call of Visconti, who succeeded Winckelmann, for guardianship of antiquities involving historical values beyond the simple esthetic ones was to prove a turning point. But change was slow.

One of the prime examples of the neglect surrounding systematic topographical excavations is the Roman forum. In the eighteenth century the forum was still covered with several layers of soil, goats sought pasture in the shade of a few elm trees, and the cattle market was held there. Between 1774 and 1780 desultory excavations were carried out on the spot by gangs of convicts. Not surprisingly the results were meager. The first planned excavation of the forum had to await the initiative of the French under Napoleon I, who put his prefect Tournon to work in 1803.[3]

So we must accept the fact that classical archeology was still a science in the process of birth. Even when Pius VI initiated a period of great activity of excavation, he was moved largely by motives other than pure scholarship. The pope saw a double gain in the enterprise: it would attract foreigners eager to purchase ancient Roman relics and it would help fill the Vatican museum started by his predecessor. Alessandro Verri was clearly aware of these motives in 1778 when referring to the English antiquary Jenkins.

There is a certain Signor Thomas Jenkins, an Englishman who came to Rome with five paoli, who then became a servant. This man at present has a hundred thousand zecchini in property and a coach, a beautiful house and all the emoluments, all through antiques. Consequently the Apostolic Chamber noticed that there was some advantage behind this and for this reason excavations were undertaken in various parts of the Roman Campagna and

[3] Noack, *Deutsches Leben in Rom*, 2–3; Andrieux, *Daily Life in Papal Rome*, 170–73; Werner Oechslin, "L'intérêt archéologique et l'expérience architecturale avant et après Piranèse," in Georges Brunel (ed.), *Piranèse et les Français. Colloque tenue à la Villa Médicis* (Rome, 1978), 399–400; Scott, *Piranesi*, 107; Carlo Pietrangeli, *Scavi e scoperte di antichità sotto il pontificato di Pio VI* (Rome, 1958), 53, 61–62; Madelin, *Rome de Napoléon*, 536–40; Sandro Pinto, "La promozione delle arti negli stati italiani dall'età delle riforme all'Unità," in *Storia dell'arte italiana* (Turin, 1982), part 2, vol. 2, 2:890; Bartoccini, *Roma nell'Ottocento*, 102–3.

elsewhere, and one can confidently say that the number of all the beautiful statues in Rome will be doubled within a few years. Hence you can understand very well that since the country lacked all other sources of revenue, had it no statues and did it not preserve the sacred ruins of ancient monuments, it would not have as much as one foreigner.[4]

One of the most important excavations outside the city in the eighteenth century was in the ruins of the villa which the Emperor Hadrian had built for himself near the modern town of Tivoli. These had been known since the fifteenth century and occasional excavations had brought statues to light. It was not, however, until 1550, that Cardinal Ippolito d'Este, governor of Tivoli, began to pursue the digging in earnest in order to decorate his own beautiful Villa d'Este, while his antiquary, Pirro Ligoro, wrote various treatises about the villa, which spread its fame in the world of scholarship. During the seventeenth century excavations continued sporadically, but as the property was divided among some forty-five separate owners, little could be done on a systematic scale. In 1724, however, an amateur dealer, Conte Fede, began buying up as much of the estate as he was able; when he had accumulated a substantial portion he beautified it by planting great cypresses and undertook more thorough investigations than had hitherto been possible. In this, he was followed by the other principal landowners on the site, the Jesuits and the Bulgarini family, who, however, rather rashly sold their rights to the ambitious and erudite Msgr. Furietti. A series of spectacular discoveries followed in quick succession. Among the earliest must have been the full-length *Antinous*, which Cardinal Albani sold to the pope in 1733. Some years after this transaction the cardinal acquired possession of a bas-relief of Hadrian's favorite. Both of these representations of Antinous were quickly ranked with the most famous works of antiquity to have survived. In 1736 the *Faun in Rosso Antico* was dug up, and in the same year Furietti excavated the two *Centaurs*, and, shortly thereafter, a mosaic which aroused great interest; in 1744 the *Flora* came to light. All these were much publicized and copied in engravings after only a short delay. Thus, within a little more than a decade almost half-a-dozen statues of world-wide fame had been added to the stock of those which had attracted universal attention. Indeed, from the 1730s on, the lure of Hadrian's Villa was a potent one for art lovers and speculators of all kinds. Nothing could compete with this excavation for popular appeal.[5]

The remains of the Domus Aurea, which then went by the name of the Baths of Titus, were already well-known by the artists of the Renaissance. In 1774 a new excavation undertaken by the picture dealer Ludovico Mirri exposed an important group of five large chambers whose walls were adorned with well-preserved pictures. Mirri was not satisfied with simply lighting up and opening the rooms to the public; he also sponsored a magnificent publication with sixty tables which reproduced the fresh discoveries. The pictures were engraved by Marco Carloni.

[4] Seregni (ed.), *Carteggio di Verri*, 10:58–59.

[5] Francis Haskell and Nicholas Penny, *Taste and the Antique. The Lure of Classical Sculpture, 1500–1900* (New Haven and London, 1981), 64–65.

The same artist also etched and colored twelve reproductions of pictures found in 1780 under the Rospigliosi palace among the remains of buildings antedating the Baths of Constantine. The originals were taken out and preserved in the palace. Some other wall paintings depicting scenes from Greek mythology, still fresh and radiant, were discovered in 1777 in a house dating from imperial times within the Villa Negroni between the Viminale and Esquiline hills. On the Esquiline, too, beneath the palace of the duke of Sermoneta was found the mosaic with Medusa which was restored by the mosaist Alessandro Cocchi and laid into the floor of the Sala delle Muse in the Vatican.

In 1776 Pius VI started the foundations for the new sacristy of St. Peter's. While digging some interesting finds were made. They included two marble heads, some coins, a sarcophagus with a bacchanalian scene, and two marble fragments of the Acts of the Arvali brothers from the time of the Emperor Heliogabolus, with a prayer or chant recited by them in very ancient Latin, perhaps from the time of Romulus, founder of the college of those priests. Another large and impressive haul was harvested by Giovanni Pietro Campana, inspector general of the Monti di Pietà in 1779–1780 in the orchard of the Sancta Sanctorum behind the pharmacy of the Lateran hospital. These excavations are but a sample of the hectic archeological activity of the latter part of the century. There were 130 digs in Rome alone in the first five years of Pius VI's reign. The Roman nobles, too, shared in this feverish activity. Both the pope and professionals such as Gavin Hamilton were tireless on their own behalf. The latter excavated at Tor Colombano, Albano, Genzano, near Città Lavinia, at Ostia, Romavecchia, Castel Gondolfo, Tivoli, and elsewhere.[6]

And what happened to the crop of all these excavations? Montesquieu put it most succinctly. "Rome nouvelle vend pièce à pièce l'ancienne."[7] The art market had become the true datary of Rome in the eighteenth century; with the only difference that instead of despoiling other lands to raise its needed finance, it now sold off its own treasures. The vogue for the Antique – although it reestablished Rome as the artistic center of Europe and attracted painters, noblemen, and even crowned heads – stripped her in the end of a large part of her artistic inheritance.

Since the Byzantine emperors had begun to plunder her, Rome had been despoiled at intervals over the centuries. Although the modern transfer of works of art reached back to the fifteenth century, no pillage was more thorough than that which the city suffered at the hands of foreigners in the eighteenth century. The English, we have noted, were the greediest of all. They came to take home what their houses lacked most, works of art. Italy, and particularly Rome, was the natural

[6] Pietrangeli, *Scavi e scoperti di antichità*, 24–30, 43–44, 51–52, 68–70, 80–82, 115–17; Kurt Gerstenberg, *Johann Joachim Winckelmann und Anton Raphael Mengs* (Halle an der Saale, 1929), 31–32; Andrieux, *Daily Life in Papal Rome*, 72; Pastor, *Geschichte der Päpste*, 15:368–69; 16 pt 3:53; Montaiglon and Guiffrey (eds.), *Correspondance des directeurs de l'Académie de France*, 13:314–15; Hautecoeur, *Rome et la renaissance de l'antiquité*, 73–74; Anna Ottani Cavina, "Il Settecento e l'antico," in *Storia dell'arte italiana* (Turin, 1982), part 2, vol. 2, 2:615.

[7] Montesquieu, *Voyages, Oeuvres complètes*, 2:1139.

hunting-ground for such collectors as Lord Shelburne for Lansdowne House, William Weddel for Newby, Henry Blundell for Ince, Charles Townley for his London town house, and Lord Palmerston for Broadlands.[8] The English example was followed by Gustavus III of Sweden who wanted to create a museum of sculpture in Stockholm which he filled with Roman works through the good offices of his consul Francesco Piranesi, son of the engraver. Catherine the Great of Russia in the same way secured the help of the sculptor Cavaceppi in adding to her gallery of antiquities. The French normally stayed on the sidelines.

With such great demand, Rome had become one huge craftsmen's studio. There was undoubtedly a great deal of sham and artificial art produced. Lalande, for instance, warns of counterfeit medallions and coins of ancient popes being hawked about. Deceit and fraud went far beyond the bounds of the world of commerce to that of the connoisseur and artist. Gorani urged would-be purchasers to select an enlightened connoisseur with insight who would make it a point of honor to help strangers with their advice and counsel. Outright forgeries were the greatest problem. A few craftsmen made pseudo-antique works from scratch and supplied them with an artificially rough surface. Others made it easier for themselves; they took some kind of mediocre old fragment and embellished it with ornamentation copied from genuine antiques. Others still bought for a few baiocchi works of Renaissance sculptors who had aped the ancients and simply removed such latter-day accoutrements as weapons, cherubims, and crosses. Genuine artists and Roman and German gem cutters of the first rank were guilty of such practices while working in the pay of the dealers in the Piazza Navona.[9]

More problematic was the question of restoration. Since incomplete statues fetched lower prices, British dealers brought in artists to doctor their finds and restore missing limbs. As the collectors desired the antiques less to satisfy their curiosity than to decorate their palaces, the statues had to be in a condition in which they could be set up in a noble fashion. Sometimes sculptors of renown abandoned their art for this more remunerative work. Since the 1520s it had become standard practice to restore the better antique statues. It is true that one or two of the best statues were never restored because Michelangelo felt unequal to the task, but Cellini was acting in a more typical manner when, confronted in the 1540s with the broken statue of a boy, he told Duke Cosimo that he admired the work so much that, despite his contempt for the bunglers usually employed to patch up such things, he

8 Oehler, "Das Zustandekommen einiger englishchen Antikensammlungen," 301–2; Seymour Howard, "Bartolomeo Cavaceppi and the Origins of Neo-classic Sculpture," *The Art Quarterly*, 33 (1970), 120,126.

9 Seregni (ed.), *Carteggio di Verri*, 12:212; Delumeau, *Vie économique et sociale de Rome*, 1:130–31; Lesley Lewis, *Connoisseurs and Secret Agents in Eighteenth Century Rome* (London, 1961), 21; Lalande, *Voyage d'un françois en Italie*, 5:36–37; Andrieux, *Daily Life in Papal Rome*, 79, 172–73; Gorani, *Rom und seine Einwohner*, 306–9; Justi, *Winckelmann und seine Zeitgenossen*, 2:94–102; 383–84; Haskell and Penny, *Taste and the Antique*, 68, 93–94, 102–3; Hautecoeur, *Rome et la renaissance de l'antiquité*, 58–59.

would feel honored to "restore" it as a Ganymede, which he promptly did by repairing the extremities and adding an eagle. Stories have often been told of how a great sculptor's restoration surpassed the original.

By the middle of the eighteenth century, when the neoclassic style came into vogue, a certain theoretical ambivalence about artistic restoration arose. Winckelmann was not opposed to restoration in general, but only to inexact restoration. What disturbed him was the uncritical acceptance of these works by the scholars. He had no trouble in detecting the great number of mistakes these restorers committed. Indeed, it was the minute care with which he scrutinized the state of even the most famous statues that ultimately led to a dramatic loss in the reputation of many, among them the *Farnese Bull*, the *Dying Seneca*, and the *Curtius*. But it was Bartolomeo Cavaceppi, perhaps the most eminent restorer of his day, who in 1786 laid down the rules for restoring. To restore well, he observed dogmatically, it was first of all necessary to know the subject of the sculpture well, not only from the studies of scholars, but through one's own experience, in order to restore the parts in each detail. For Cavaceppi restoration was not a function of preservation, but essentially one of education, so that one might learn from them.[10]

A quite new development occurred in Rome in the 1780s with the commercial production of a wide range of small bronze copies of classical statuary at a price attractive to the average gentleman traveller. In this business Francesco Righetti was the leading figure, but he had a close competitor in Giovanni Zoffoli. Before his death in 1785 the Roman goldsmith Luigi Valadier introduced lavish desserts consisting of miniature reproductions of antique statues and temples. In the same year Giovanni Volpato, a prominent engraver and friend of Hamilton, Canova, and Angelika Kauffman, opened a factory in the Via Pudenziana. He specialized in biscuit porcelain reproductions in the same size and in many cases of the same subjects as the statuettes sold by Righetti and Zoffoli. But these ventures were only spin-offs of the real trade in antiquities.[11]

When foreigners came for a tour of the city, they needed somebody to introduce them to the most important sights and monuments. To meet this need a profession of guides to antiquities in Rome had emerged at the beginning of the eighteenth century. These *ciceroni* usually were people with some education, such as abati, secretaries, and agents of noble patrons of antiquities, sometimes even real scholars of distinction, among them Bianchini, Gori, Ficoroni, Venuti, Bracci, and Winckelmann himself. There was a reciprocal advantage in this activity. For these scholars acting as *ciceroni* profited in their turn by being compelled to extend their knowledge to meet the questions set them; and many of them were subsequently

[10] Bartolomeo Cavaceppi, *Raccolta d'antiche statue, busti, bassirilievi ed altre sculture restaurate da B.C. sculture romano* (3 vols.; Rome, 1786); Cagiano de Azevedo, *Il gusto nel restauro*, 42–51, 68–70.

[11] Hugh Honour, "Statuettes after the Antique. Volpato's Roman Porcelain Factory," *Apollo*, N.S. 63 (1967), 371–73.

10 Baron Philipp von Stosch, by Pier Leone Ghezzi

encouraged to write for the tourists, as Ficoroni confessed in the preface to his *Vestigia di Roma antica*. Among the number of the *ciceroni* there were also, of course, loud-mouthed, ignorant swindlers, and pseudo-antiquaries.[12]

Since Rome had become the most important European market for trade in antiquities and ancient works of art, some of these *ciceroni* were only too eager to meet the demands of customers, generally Englishmen. At the beginning the agents were almost all Italians, such as Francesco de' Ficoroni, or Italianized expatriates, such as Peter Grand from the Scottish College. But soon this lucrative occupation

[12] Noack, *Deutsches Leben in Rom*, 54; Justi, *Winckelmann und seine Zeitgenossen*, 3:48, 79; Hautecoeur, *Rome et la renaissance de l'antiquité*, 19–20; Pastor, *Geschichte der Päpste*, 16 pt 3:62–63; Scott, *Piranesi*, 317 n. 15; Moore, *A View of Society*, 487; Goethe, *Italian Journey*, 419–20.

attracted foreigners.[13] In the earlier part of the century the best known of these people was Baron von Stosch, highly esteemed and consulted on all disputed questions of ancient art, but otherwise an infamous and debauched character. Offspring of an old Silesian noble family whose title had not been claimed for several generations because of their poverty, Stosch arrived in Rome in 1714, after a checkered career which had carried him to Holland, France, and England. Bernard de Montfaucon had recommended him to Giustino Fontanini, through whom he presumably came to know Clement XI. The pope received him warmly as a fellow scholar, and gave him a pension which continued until the pontiff's death in 1721. Although resisting the pope's efforts at converting him to Catholicism, Stosch remained on close and affectionate terms with him. He left Rome after a two-years' stay, summoned home by his father to attend to family matters. On his way he made long stopovers in Florence and Vienna. In the imperial capital his assistance with the emperor's and Prince Eugene of Savoy's collection of antiquities laid the foundation for considerable patronage from the Habsburg court.

In 1721 the greffier of Holland, Franz Fagel, a passionate amateur antiquary, gave Stosch a commission to go to Italy to add to his collection. The commission, however, was a cloak for the far more important secret assignment which he received at the same time from the British government and was to hold for the rest of his life. He was appointed to live in Rome and report to Lord Carteret, the secretary of state, on the doings of the exiled Stuarts and their adherents, and on British travellers in general. The income from this source enabled Stosch to settle down in Rome, work on his gem collection, converse with antiquarians and scholars about excavations in the city of Rome, and offer advice on artistic and scholarly subjects to any who would listen. In 1724 his great work on ancient gems, *Gemmae antiquae caelatae*, appeared in Amsterdam. The book established Stosch as the greatest authority of his day on the subject of ancient gems, which were then highly valued collectors' items. His ability to detect forgeries and imitations was doubtless very useful to his friends who were collectors. But Stosch may also have used his talents for a somewhat more questionable purpose. It is not impossible that he himself had a hand in the profitable business of counterfeiting. The majority of his contemporaries seem never to have accused him of this, but rumors began to circulate and Francesco de' Ficoroni thought him an arch imposter. In January 1731, Stosch departed hastily from Rome for Florence under unexplained circumstances.[14]

[13] Oehler, "Das Zustandekommen einiger englischen Antikensammlungen," 307.

[14] Montesquieu, *Voyages. Oeuvres complétes*, 2:1112; John Fleming, *Robert Adam and his Circle in Edinburgh and Rome* (Cambridge, Mass., 1962), 341; Justi, *Winckelmann und seine Zeitgenossen*, 2:279–81, 329–31; D. H. Quynn, "Philipp von Stosch," *Catholic Historical Review*, 27 (1941), 332–44; Lewis, *Connoisseurs and Secret Agents*, 49–57, 85–88, 90; Pastor, *Geschichte der Päpste*, 15:366; Thomas Hollis, *Memoires of Thomas Hollis, Esq., F.R. and A.SS.* (2 vols.; London, 1780), 2:804; Noack, *Deutsches Leben in Rom*, 39–42; Lesley Lewis, "Philipp von Stosch," *Apollo*, N.S. 63 (1967), 320–27; Peter Zazoff, "Von Gemmensammeln zur Glyptikforschung." In H. Beck *et al.* (eds.), *Antikensammlungen im 18. Jahrhundert* (Berlin, 1981), 367.

Stosch was perhaps the most notorious example of a foreigner who profited from Europe's greed for the treasures of ancient Rome by dubious means. But his misfortune, if we may call it such, was that he lived in the first half of the eighteenth century. For only in the last third of that century, when English art dealers such as Gavin Hamilton were themselves conducting excavations within papal territory, did it become possible to spirit abroad whole sculptures acknowledged to be of the highest quality. These dealers acted very much like mineral prospecting companies nowadays, which would negotiate the lease and mining rights over promising sites. The pope would give his permission for this kind of enterprise upon certain conditions. When an excavation was made, the antiquities discovered were divided into four shares. The first went to the pope, the second to the Apostolic Chamber, the third belonged to the owner of the ground, and the last was the right of the adventurer. But numerous times all the shares were bought up by the contractor even before the ground was opened up. The most prominent of these art dealers-cum-excavators were the two Britons Gavin Hamilton and Thomas Jenkins.

Hamilton, a native of Murdoston in Lanarkshire, was both painter and art dealer. In the 1740s he stayed in Rome to study painting under Masucci. He returned to the city in 1756 where he was to play a significant role in the evolution of the neoclassical movement. On canvas he showed early on his enthusiasm for classical antiquity, and particularly for Greek subjects. First in the 1760s and later in the 1780s he painted two series of pictures based on the Homeric incidents. The first of his paintings to be completed in 1761, *Andromache Bewailing the Death of Hector*, was of sufficient importance to merit a long comment by Winckelmann in a letter to Stosch, in spite of its still bearing traces of an earlier style. While painting himself, Hamilton acted as picture dealer. Through his business acumen many churches and collectors were to part with altarpieces and canvases to adorn English country houses. His most sensational acquisition was Leonardo's *Virgin of the Rocks* for the National Gallery in London in 1785.

But Hamilton was also very active in archeological excavations of his own. His work at Hadrian's villa between 1769 and 1771 was particularly fruitful. Many of his finds at this site were added to the papal collection and that of Catherine II of Russia, and some were to find their way to his English clients. But this was only a start. His other excavations from 1771 at Tor Colombano – where he unearthed a copy of the *Belvedere Antinous*, now known as *Hermes* – Castel Guido, Romavecchia, and Ostia, also earned him a rich harvest, much of which ended up in Britain. Unlike many of his fellow dealers Hamilton maintained a reputation for honesty, as a man who did not tamper with the antiquities that passed through his hands.[15]

The other prominent dealer was Thomas Jenkins. He was actually born in Rome in 1722. But as a youth he studied with the English portrait painter Thomas Hudson, before returning to his native city in 1753 to study historical painting.

15 David Irwin, "Gavin Hamilton: Archaeologist, Painter, and Art Dealer," *The Art Bulletin*, 44 (1962), 87–95, 98–102.

Realizing he would never make a career as an artist, Jenkins transferred his attention to antique dealing. In 1761 he had the distinction of being elected to the Accademia di San Luca. Soon connoisseurs like Cardinal Alessandro Albani, Mengs, and Winckelmann, who made his acquaintance in 1763, valued him as a trusted adviser, and Msgr. Braschi, shortly to become Pius VI, bought a group of a *Satyr and Nymph* from him in the early 1770s. Around that time he also became British agent in Rome, a position corresponding to that of an informal ambassador, which he held until 1797. This status formed the springboard for his interests in banking and commerce. The gains from his lucrative banking venture and his art transactions enabled Jenkins to vie with the Roman nobility in splendor and made it possible for him to entertain sumptuously in his villa at Castel Gondolfo that had once belonged to the Jesuit general.[16]

The period between 1780 and 1790 was a particularly fortunate one for both Jenkins and Hamilton, for it was then that the finest English galleries were formed, those of Shelburne, Townley, his friend Henry Blundell, who built a rotunda in imitation of the Pantheon, and of Thomas Hope. But it was not only to these two compatriots that the owners of English country houses owed their antique treasure. One of the most useful services which Alessandro Albani performed for English collectors such as Lord Leicester at Holkham was helping them get home to England the works of art he had sold them in the first place or which he was instrumental in finding for them, thereby bypassing the papal prohibitions on their export. A combination of expertise, influence, and sheer ingenuity was required, not to speak of bribery, and although Albani was not the only practitioner he was certainly one of the most successful, and to him must be attributed many choice items in English collections, among them those of George III.[17]

In sharp contrast to the passionate acquisitiveness of the affluent English nobility, the exhaustion of their wealth forced old Roman families to alienate, piece by piece, their ancient legacy. The Giustiniani had to part with a share of their marbles. Then, in 1724, the Odescalchi yielded to Spain those of Christina of Sweden. Ficoroni served as intermediary between the Chigi and the Elector of Saxony, to whom Alessandro Albani sold thirty statues before passing the remainder to the pope. After 1740, several more collections were dispersed, those of the Barberini, the Ottoboni, the Mattei, and the Albani. But the soil of Rome seemed inexhaustible. The number of applications for export licences in the archives for the second half of the century appears staggering. Rome was in the process of being

[16] Thomas Ashby, "Thomas Jenkins in Rome," *Papers of the British School in Rome*, 6, no. 8 (1913), 488–99.

[17] Fleming, *Robert Adam*, 230, 342; Lewis, *Connoisseurs and Secret Agents*, 154–69, 184–85; Haskell and Penny, *Taste and the Antique*, 67–68; Scott, *Piranesi*, 241–42, 316 n. 12; Justi, *Winckelmann und seine Zeitgenossen*, 2:396–97; Pietrangeli, *Scavi e scoperti di antichità*, 74, 85, 89, 91–96, 111–14, 139–40; Giuntella, *Roma nel Settecento*, 106–7; Hautecoeur, *Rome et la renaissance de l'antiquité*, 72; Gorani, *Rom und seine Einwohner*, 31–34.

despoiled of its patrimony, or at least the best pieces of it. Antiquities may have been the city's best export, but the permanent loss was irreplaceable and the spiritual impoverishment injurious. As early as 1534, the papacy recognized the danger and, desirous of exercising some surveillance, created a Delegato sopra la conservazione delle antichità di Roma, entrusted with implementing the legislation. In the course of the seventeenth century several edicts had been published requiring a papal licence for every excavation. In 1701 Clement XI forbad the export of statues, bronzes, gems, and pictures. Three years later he was compelled to issue a new edict which reiterated the earlier one and extended it to include mosaics, inscriptions, manuscripts, and documents. He tried to prevent this exodus and preserve the splendor of Rome. But in vain. His successors from time to time renewed the measures against the export of antiquities with no more success. The sack continued. The only way the popes could intervene and rescue all the statues and remains that came on the market, let alone those that were being dug up every day, was to place them into official museums. That was a tall order, but at least a worthy start was made.[18]

The first record of a public museum to preserve some of Rome's treasures only dates from the time of Sixtus IV (1471–84). A few months after his accession this pontiff donated to the palace of the conservators on the Campidoglio a number of ancient bronzes. Among them were works which were to retain their authority over the centuries, such as the *Wolf*, the *Camillus*, and the *Spinario*. At the end of the fifteenth century these and a few others, which were added not long afterwards, made up by far the most impressive group of antique sculpture to be seen anywhere in Rome. The prestige that they acquired must have played its part in stimulating the creation of a rival museum in the Vatican by his nephew Julius II, who started in the Belvedere court a collection of classical pieces that became the sanctuary of art and school of good taste for almost three centuries; or, as Lalande put it, "the most remarkable place there is for the arts in all Italy, yea, in the entire world."

But it was only in the eighteenth century that these two official permanent and public collections were to receive any further notable increase. At the start of the century the concept that cultural institutions should be accessible to the public began to take hold. It was first implemented with libraries, such as the Biblioteca Casanatense in 1698, but twenty years later abbé Du Bos in his *Réflexions critiques sur la poésie et la peinture* staked out for the general public an important role in evaluating art. Clement XI was to turn this program into practice, when he not only added newly acquired statuary to the Campidoglio collection, but, in 1719, had a new portico built in the Capitoline palace, on a design by Alessandro Specchi, to house these treasures. However, the full realization of the ideal had to await the Corsini pope. In 1733, Clement XII bought all the Albani antiquities and made

[18] Hautecoeur, *Rome et la renaissance de l'antiquité*, 56–61; Giuntella, *Roma nel Settecento*, 105–6; ASR, Camerale II, antichità e belle arti, esportazioni, busta 11, fasc. 280, to busta 12, fasc. 294; busta 3, fasc. 125.

them the nucleus of a new museum on the Campidoglio. The Albani had managed to acquire from various sources a few sculptures which had once been famous, although they had been neglected in more recent years; they included the *Della Valle Satyr* and the *Cesi Juno*. The real attraction of this collection, however, was a statue of *Antinous*, excavated at Hadrian's Villa, and a very large group of ambitiously identified portrait busts, whose interest depended more on their historical than their esthetic distinction. This new Capitoline museum was now set up under the direction of the Marchese Alessandro Gregorio Capponi in the third of the Capitoline palaces and opened to the public, the first art museum to do so. Under Benedict XIV, whose personal attitude to archeology was rather ambivalent, the museum was further developed and diversified. He added an Egyptian collection and a picture gallery which appropriately abounded with works from the Bolognese Renaissance and classicism.[19]

Little had changed at the Vatican since the completion of the Belvedere statue court. Benedict XIV took the first step by planning, in 1756, a Christian museum in a place adjoining the library. But the impetus for the Vatican museum would come from elsewhere. In about 1769 Grand Duke Pietro Leopoldo of Tuscany inaugurated a long campaign to rationalize the Medici collection which had been left to Florence, during the course of which he decided, on the advice of Mengs, to bring back to his capital the most famous works of art that were scattered throughout Tuscany and elsewhere. Although Cosimo III had already removed some of the principal pieces to Florence in 1677, among the works of art that still remained in the Villa Medici were the *Niobe* group, the *Apollino*, and the *Lion*, which had been among the chief sights of Rome. Clement XIV protested vigorously against their removal, but not only was there nothing he could do, but worse was to follow. Some 422 pieces of the Farnese collection from the Palazzo Farnese, the Farnesina, and the Villa Madama had already been transferred to Naples in 1741, in the wake of Charles VII, son of Elizabeth Farnese, where they formed the nucleus of the present Museo Archeologico Nazionale. But, between 1787 and 1800, the rest of the Farnese marbles were removed. Their loss included the celebrated *Farnese Bull*, unearthed in 1545 at the Baths of Caraccala and later identified as the statue of Dirce and her step-sons, and the huge decapitated *Hercules*, found in the same area. Paradoxically, these antiquities left at a moment when, more than ever, young artists arrived to learn directly from these ancient remains.[20]

Indeed, in resisting these actions, it had been Clement's XIV's contention that Rome was the capital of art, the study center of artists from all of Europe. With the city facing the loss of its antique treasure, the pope decided on drastic action.

[19] Liebenwein, "Der Portikus Clemens' XI. und sein Statuenschmuck," 74–79, 101; Morelli (ed.), *Lettere di Benedetto XIV*, 2:51; Haskell and Penny, *Taste and the Antique*, 2, 6, 8–12, 15, 63–66.

[20] Insolera, *Roma*, 299; Olivier Michel, "L'*Accademia*." In Ecole française de Rome, *Le Palais Farnèse* (2 vols.; Rome, 1981), 1 pt 2:604–5.

Almost simultaneously he began to buy whatever became available, such as the *Meleager*, and build a new museum behind the Vatican palace to house the acquisitions he had already made and those he was planning to make on an ever-increasing scale. The arrangements and the extensive campaign of restoration and of purchases, which required the cooperation of every dealer in Rome, were in the hands of the antiquary Giambattista Visconti and his son. With the help of the treasurer general, Gianangelo Braschi, they bought, among others, the most beautiful statuary of the Mattei collection and several pieces of the Barberini.

Clement XIV's museum was extended by the addition of two new tracts, which were closed with an atrium, by his successor Braschi, when he became Pius VI. Under the direction of the architect Simonetti, one can almost imagine the new museum as a sort of applied textbook on ancient architecture, which followed Vitruvius' rules for the appropriate use of orders. To decorate the buildings he resorted to antique remains: mosaics from Tusculum, from Otricoli, from Tivoli, and the Esquiline served as pavements. Hadrian's Villa supplied two cariatides, Pius VI the collected works scattered throughout Rome's official buildings, the Cancelleria, Castel Sant'Angelo, the Lateran, and others. Not to let any masterpiece escape him, he arrogated to himself the right of preemption on all discoveries; he bought many and rarely drew back at great expenses. More than three hundred marbles entered the Vatican during his pontificate. In his eagerness he had excavations carried out under state auspices in all the Papal States and special squads explored the subsoil of the streets, squares, and orchards of Rome, all at a time when Rome's finances were running short. Hence the enormous expense of the excavations, acquisitions, and restorations fell largely upon the funds derived from the proceeds of the lottery. The Vatican, from a small museum grouped around an octagonal courtyard, became the most extraordinary collection of antiquities in the world.[21]

But the popes were not the only collectors. By the first half of the seventeenth century it had become common practice for the pope's nephews and close family to devote a large portion of their resources to building, patronage, and collecting after the pattern set originally by the Farnese. The Borghese, who amassed antiquities as well as lands, and the Ludovisi were exceptional only as regards the taste and lavishness with which they made use of their good fortune. The villas they built

[21] Haskell and Penny, *Taste and the Antique*, 70–73, 76; Justi, *Winckelmann und seine Zeitgenossen*, 2:29–33, 53–54, 175–77, 180; Pastor, *Geschichte der Päpste*, 15:369–70, 745–46; 16, pt 3:43; Hautecoeur, *Rome et la renaissance de l'antiquité*, 9–11, 64–68; Lanciani, *Storia degli scavi*, 1:2, 17, 154–55; Pietrangeli, *Scavi e scoperti di antichità*, 3–5; Noack, *Deutsches Leben in Rom*, 63; Renazzi, *Storia dell'università*, 4:181–83; Madelin, *Rome de Napoléon*, 541; Goethe, *Italian Journey*, 150, 342–43, 358; Venturi, *Settecento riformatore*, 1:115; De Brosses, *Lettres familières*, 2:207; Lalande, *Voyage d'un françois en Italie*, 3:183–89; Scott, *Piranesi*, 316 n. 14; Pinto, "La promozione delle arti," 894–95; Steuben, "Das Museo Pio-Clementino," 152, 157; ASR, Camerale II, antichità e belle arti, busta 5, fasc. 159.

came to house statues of almost equal splendor to those that were to be found in the Vatican, the Farnese palace, and the Villa Medici.[22]

In the eighteenth century Alessandro Albani, whose activities and predilections were probably of greater seminal importance in precipitating the vogue for classical taste than those of any other single person in the Rome of his day, followed the example of these earlier papal families. Born in Urbino in 1692, he was the third and youngest son of Orazio Albani, brother of Clement XI. On Clement's election the whole family moved to Rome to enjoy the advantages of relatives of the reigning pope. Being highly cultured himself, his uncle fostered similar tastes in his two nephews, Annibale and Alessandro. In 1714 Alessandro acquired from Clement XI Cassiano dal Posso's famous collection of drawings of antique remains. Three years later he initiated simultaneous excavations in Tivoli, Cività Lavinia, and Nettuno. Soon he would be digging throughout the whole of the Campagna. It netted him the most complete series of emperor busts which had been accumulated up to that time. His cabinet of coins was extremely valuable. But the young cardinal had managed his affairs recklessly and had to start selling. In 1738 the Elector of Saxony acquired 32 pieces from his collection, including the *Dresden Venus*, for which Albani received a mere 2,000 scudi. The rest of his collection was bought by the pope for 66,000 scudi and given to the Capitoline museum.

No sooner had Alessandro Albani got rid of one magnificent collection than he began to fill again his empty rooms at the Palazzo Albani on the Quattro Fontane. Although the first collection could not be replaced, it only formed a prelude to the achievements of the second museum. How the cardinal acquired the pieces for the new collection, where they were found, and what he paid for them, has remained for the most part a secret. Some of the best pieces came from Hadrian's Villa and the new Villa d'Este at Tivoli; Albani was related to the owners, the dukes of Modena. Others were from the ruins of the theater in Porto d'Anzio.

To house his new collection Albani started to build a suburban villa near the Porta Salaria in 1746 in the tradition of the Borghese, Ludovisi, and other papal families. The architect was Carlo Marchionni (1702–86). The villa, which cost 400,000 scudi, was a departure from the standard type of suburban villa. It was planned first of all with the cardinal's collection in mind. Displayed in the buildings and hedges of the garden in this necropolis of antiquities was the most important collection in Rome after the pope's. Following Albani's own antiquarian taste, Marchionni couched the villa in classical forms under an eighteenth-century disguise. On the ceiling of the principal room Anton Raphael Mengs painted his *Parnasso* in 1760/61, according to an iconography that reflected Winckelmann's thought, making it a programmatic manifesto of neoclassicism. Although purists

[22] Haskell and Penny, *Taste and the Antique*, 25–26, 28; Hautecoeur, *Rome et la renaissance de l'antiquité*, 70–71; Golzio, *Palazzi romani dalla rinascita*, 68–70; Montesquieu, *Voyages, Oeuvres complètes*, 2:1101–2.

would reject the claim, the Villa Albani became the symbolic, if not the stylistic, announcement of the arrival of neoclassicism in Rome.[23]

Eighteenth-century Rome was the birthplace of neoclassicism in its esthetic and academic form. However, to assume a causal relationship between the city's antiquarian interests and activities and neoclassicism would be too simplistic. The Roman cult of antiquity must be regarded as a catalyst rather than the driving force behind this new style. For neoclassicism really rests on roots that are non-Roman and alien to its recent cultural development. Paradoxically, therefore, neoclassicism, instead of enhancing Rome's cultural and artistic life over the long haul, would eventually extinguish the feeble traces of whatever original genius and ethos still remained and destroy its importance as a magnet for artists.

From the outset we must distinguish neoclassicism from the classic trends that preceded it. Neoclassicism, as we understand it, is identified with Johann Joachim Winckelmann, who, shortly after his arrival in Rome in 1755, became librarian and protégé of Cardinal Alessandro Albani. Winckelmann and his friend, the painter Anton Raphael Mengs, were not the first ones to think of the idea of linking up the art of their age with that of antiquity; they only brought the problem of classicism, with which generations before them had grappled, to a new resolution. For a hundred years or more all the various strands of imitative classicism had converged upon Rome, because the particular conditions of taste and culture prevailing in the city, already announced by the program of Arcadia and especially its Gravina wing, made it the ideal city. But this classicism was by and large "a free interpretation of principles developed by antiquity and the Renaissance," as the art historian Germain Bazin put it.[24]

Therefore it was not the "return to antiquity" as such that was new. In Rome itself such demand could trace a continuous line going back to the late sixteenth century with artists of the caliber of Annibale Caracci and Domenichino, and continued by Poussin and Carlo Maratta. It found its elaboration in the writings of seventeenth-century theorists, the Bolognese Giovanni Battista Agucchi (1570–1632), and Giovanni Pietro Bellori (1615–96) in his *Vite de' pittori, scultori, ed architetti moderni* (Rome, 1672). Classicism, it has by now been recognized, was an important component of baroque art and, particularly in Rome, was always present, even in the most exuberant baroque compositions. Many of its values

[23] Howard, "Cavaceppi and the Origins of Neo-classic Sculpture," 125–26; Justi, *Winckelmann und seine Zeitgenossen*, 2:38, 353–54, 359–67; Haskell and Penny, *Taste and the Antique*, 28, 62, 65–66; Lewis, *Connoisseurs and Secret Agents*, 38–48; Hautecoeur, *Rome et la renaissance de l'antiquité* 62–63; Golzio, *Palazzi romani dalla rinascita*, 23–26; Scott, *Piranesi*, 152, 309 n. 6; Pastor, *Geschichte der Päpste*, 16, pt 1:468–69; Fleming, *Robert Adam*, 164–65; Gorani, *Rom und seine Einwohner*, 204–11; Andrieux, *Daily Life in Papal Rome*, 175; Cavina, "Il Settecento e l'antico," 623, 629–33.

[24] Germain Bazin, *The Baroque. Principles, Styles, Modes, Themes* (New York, 1978), 131; Cavina, "Il Settecento e l'antico," part 2, vol. 2, 2:600–1; Giovanni Previteli, "La periodizzazione della storia dell'arte italiana," in *Storia dell'arte italiana* (Turin, 1979), pt 1, vol. 1:88.

enjoyed the patronage of eighteenth-century popes. Bottari, Neri Corsini's protégé, made this clear in his treatise on the fine arts, *Dialoghi sulle arti del disegno* (Rome, 1754). Since 1719 Roman artists had a large reservoir of classical iconography readily available to them, with extensive illustrated compilations of ancient ruins, in such publications as Montfaucon's six-volume *L'antiquité expliquée et représentée en figures* (Paris, 1719), which they did not hesitate to consult.[25]

Although we shall note isolated intimations of neoclassicism before the middle of the century among some painters, neoclassicism did not arise from simply looking back on Roman antiquity. Neoclassicism arose in Rome – and given the circumstances of the time, probably could only have been perfected in Rome – but it was not of Rome.

The change occurred at about the time of the Peace of Aix-la-Chapelle in 1748, which ended the War of the Austrian Succession. At that point the old Vitruvian view of the cultural continuum between Greece and Rome was being questioned. Greece and Rome were now seen as alternative sources. The former was being recognized as the fountain of European culture, one more archaic and for that reason more in harmony with the intellectual requirements of modern culture. The impetus for this shift occurred actually in the neighboring kingdom of Naples. Usually the discovery of Herculaneum in 1738 (the Duc d'Elboeuf had stumbled upon the first finds in 1711 already) and the start of the excavations at Pompeii in 1748 are quoted as the catalyst for the change. But these were Roman remains and were primarily used as instruments of propaganda by Charles VII, the new Bourbon ruler, intent upon acquiring status and credibility in the eyes of European courts.

We must rather look at the Doric temples at Paestum, the ancient Greek Poseidonia. Although not unknown in the sixteenth century, these remains aroused not much more than local interest. They only began to attract more widespread attention with Count Gazzola between 1745 and 1750. He planned to have a series of drawings made which would provide a complete documentation of Paestum. While he failed to have these illustrations published himself, they were to provide the basic material for the first French and English publications on the Paestum monuments. By then visitors made the difficult journey. As early as 1750 the young M. de Vaudières, brother of Madame de Pompadour, on his visit to Naples, made an unscheduled detour to Paestum. Soufflot, one of his entourage, made drawings of the temples, which were soon brought to the attention of antiquaries and travellers. From then on, Paestum became an essential goal for artists, lovers of antiquity, and men of letters, Winckelmann and Goethe among them.[26]

25 Pinto, *Trevi Fountain*, 226, 250–51.

26 Giulio Carlo Argan, "Preface" to Joselita Raspi Serra (ed.), *Paestum and the Doric Revival, 1750–1830* (Florence, 1986), 12; Cavina, "Il Settecento e l'antico," part 2, vol. 2, 2:605; Elvira Chiosi, Laura Mascoli, Georges Vallet, "The Discovery of Paestum," in Serra (ed.), *Paestum*, 41–43; Angela Pontrandolfo, "Paestum and its Archeological History," in Serra (ed.), ibid., 51; Giuliano Briganti, "Paestum and View Painting in the Eighteenth Century," in Serra (ed.), ibid., 57; Joselita Raspi Serra, "Introduction" to *Paestum and the Doric Revival*, 15.

The new enthusiasm for Greek remains would not stay confined to southern Italy. In 1748 Gavin Hamilton made an expedition on foot from Rome to Naples in the company of two other Britons, James Stuart and Nicholas Revett. It was probably during this journey that a visit to Greece, then under Ottoman rule, to study antiquities *in situ* was first proposed. The idea seems to have originated with Hamilton and Revett; but the former for unknown reasons would never participate. Stuart and Revett left Rome in March 1750. Harassed by hardships, plague, and civil unrest, the two took leave from Turkey in 1753 and eventually returned to England early in 1755. The first volume encompassing their harvest, *The Antiquities of Athens*, was not published until 1762, having had to wait for a subvention from the Society of Dilettanti. In the interval the French challenged the English initiative. Supported by royal patronage and private interests, Le Roy made a journey from Rome to Athens in 1753 and was able to bring out an account of his researches much sooner. By 1759, an illustrated English translation of his work was already on the market.[27]

In this atmosphere of "Greek gusto," the neoclassical doctrine of style arose. Although shattering prevailing Roman concepts of art as an evolutionary ascent from Egypt through Greece to Rome, it ironically found in Rome one of its birthplaces. This inherent contradiction must be sought in the ambivalent nature of the man who, more than any other individual, was responsible for articulating the academic rules of neoclassicism, Johann Joachim Winckelmann. Born in 1717, the son of a poor Prussian cobbler, Winckelmann seemed to have arrived at the concept of Greek art from the perfection of Greek literature. In 1755, shortly before leaving for Rome, he published in Dresden a brief essay, *Gedanken über die Nachahmung der Griechischen Monumente in Malerei und Bildhauerkunst*, which became the first programmatic statement in which he betrayed his passionate enthusiasm for Greek sculpture.

Winckelmann came with this feeling to Rome. Strangely, this admiration was not tempered or attenuated while he remained in the city, but, on the contrary, it conditioned his view on everything new and admirable that he encountered. He saw in the Mediterranean life of the city and its surroundings a reflection of ancient Greek life. The same happened with art. Whatever was beautiful was Greek. And since he was able to show on the basis of literature that the Romans had imported many works from Greece and that many Greek artists were active in Rome, it was not difficult to reconcile his emotional attachment with his knowledge as a scholar. Hence it was an indisputable fact to him that his favorite piece, the *Belvedere Apollo*, was a Greek work, although his friend Mengs had already recognized it as a Roman copy. He regarded the *Laocoön* and the *Belvedere Torso* in the same light.[28]

When Winckelmann came to Rome his original intention was to work on Greek manuscripts in the Vatican library, but within a few weeks the young Mengs

[27] Irwin, "Gavin Hamilton," 89; Cust and Colvin, *Society of Dilettanti*, 74–81.

[28] Hellmut Sichtermann, *Winckelmann e Roma (nel secondo centenario della morte)* (Rome, 1969), 6, 9.

befriended and steered him back to working on good taste in art. Mengs had already thought deeply and extensively about art; his opinions led to two publications, the *Reflessioni sulla bellezza* of 1762 and the *Sogni sulla belleza*, which appeared posthumously in 1787. In these he propounded a Platonic view of beauty. Beauty depended on the conformity of the object with the idea which we have of it. It must satisfy reason and not the senses; hence it is universal. Since the role of reason was that of reducing multiplicity to unity, beauty was also simple.

The two appear to have hatched a plan to write a joint treatise on the style of Greek artists. It was never carried to fruition. Instead Winckelmann was to find employment with Alessandro Albani in 1758, who offered him a position in his palace to run his library, advise him with his antiquarian hobbies, and, in general, pursue his own scholarly work in complete freedom. The nine years he spent in the Albani household were the most productive, during which he completed the writings that were to establish his authority throughout Europe as founder of the scholarly history of ancient art. The most influential of his books, his magnum opus, was the *Geschichte der Kunst des Altertums* of 1764. In it, he produced a thorough, comprehensive, and lucid account of all antique art, chiefly sculpture, from that of the Egyptians and the Etruscans through the Greeks and Romans. Although there had been previous attempts at the history of art, no one had ever presented it with such breadth and detailed learning. Winckelmann came to the conclusion that the concept of a Roman style in ancient art was an illusion. The Romans, he claimed, had first imitated the Etruscans and then the Greeks. If they ought to be commended for anything, it was only for the fact that they imitated so well.[29]

We have arrived at the curious point where a German scholar, whose love and devotion to the city of Rome were second to none, and whose expertise and feel for Roman archeology was unrivalled, as his *Monumenti antichi inediti*, written in Italian the year before his tragic murder in 1768, testify, denied the existence of an autonomous Roman art, and that in Rome itself.

But Winckelmann had a broader goal. In the preface to his *Geschichte der Kunst des Altertums* he declared his intention to present not only a history but a system of art. Consequently he set out to extrapolate an esthetic from his observation of the ancient works. Then he measured these works against this esthetic. Although a rationalist approach to esthetics had grown up, Winckelmann, not being of a philosophical bent, refused to found his esthetics on any metaphysical doctrine. He set up a simple theory, which had the advantage of being both fashionable and of justifying the growing admiration for the antiquities. Because "beauty cannot be

[29] Justi, *Winckelmann und seine Zeitgenossen*, 2:15–19, 24–50, 66–79, 122, 132–43, 251–53; Noack, *Deutsches Leben in Rom*, 76–81; Hautecoeur, *Rome et la renaissance de l'antiquité*, 26, 32–33; Gerstenberg, *Winckelmann und Mengs*, 7, 10–11; Haskell and Penny, *Taste and the Antique*, 106; Robert Rosenblum, *Transformations in Late Eighteenth Century Art* (Princeton, 1967), 10 n. 23; Cavina, "Il Settecento e l'antico," 633; Sichtermann, *Winckelmann e Roma*, 9–11.

compared to anything higher than itself" we cannot define it. We can nevertheless know its attributes, which are simplicity and unity.

One consequence for the artist of Winckelmann's theory was that beauty was not achieved by dimensions or wealth of ornamentation, but by proportions; the other was the superiority of the form, which is intelligible, over color, which is perceptible to feeling, and at best only sets off or improves form. But among the array of forms it was necessary to choose the simplest; linear unity was found above all in young forms, where the muscles are still not developed. The artist had to choose the most beautiful parts to constitute the ideal beauty.[30]

This conception of ideal beauty derived its roots from Greek sources, not Roman ones, but it was not new in Roman cultural circles. This *greca felicità* had already been propounded in its literary form by Gianvincenzo Gravina at the start of the Roman Arcadia. But in Winckelmann it reached its highest expression. Consequently neoclassicism was born as a reflection of archeology amid the Hellenistic statuary of eighteenth-century Rome.[31]

The philhellenic argument did not go unchallenged in Rome. The distinguished engraver Giovanni Battista Piranesi took up the cudgels on behalf of Rome in his work *Della Magnificenza e Architettura de' Romani*, which appeared in 1761, in reply to the rationalism of such French theorists as the Comte de Caylus, who asserted the superiority of Greek art over Roman. Piranesi, who felt threatened, both culturally and nationally, contrasted the severity of Etruscan architecture and, what he claimed its survival in the utilitarian achievements of Rome with the vain pettiness (*vana leggiadria*) of the Greeks. But his attack was meant to reach a further target, whom he did not mention by name, Winckelmann. The latter pointedly ignored Piranesi. However, over time, Piranesi himself began to modify his position and gradually approached the view of the German antiquary, acknowledging the decorativeness of Etruscan architecture and, in his *Parere su l'architettura* of 1765, following a visit to Paestum, expressed a new awareness of the beauty of simple forms. It is almost as if Winckelmann had won a deathbed convert.[32]

30 Justi, *Winckelmann und seine Zeitgenossen*, 3:92–93; Hautecoeur, *Rome et la renaissance de l'antiquité*, 27–32, 37, 40, 190, 207; Luigi Grassi, *Costruzione della critica d'arte* (Rome, 1955), 117–18; Haskell and Penny, *Taste and the Antique*, 100–2; Portoghesi, *Roma barocca*, 1:129; Ferdinando Bologna, "I metodi di studio dell'arte italiana e il problema metodologico oggi" in *Storia dell'arte italiana* (Turin, 1979), part 1, vol. 1:206–7.

31 The Grecian argument was much broader than can be treated here. It was developed in France by Comte de Caylus, who published the seven volumes of his *Recueil d'Antiquités égyptiennes, étrusques, grecques, romains, et gauloises* between 1752 and 1767. In them, he claimed that in Greece the arts, based on the achievements of the Egyptians and Etruscans, attained their greatest perfection. Roman art, derived from Greece, marked an anti-climax and decline. Rudolf Wittkower, "Piranesi's Architectural Creed," in *Studies in the Italian Baroque* (London, 1975), 236–37. However, Winckelmann's influence on Rome and its artistic reputation was more baneful for the city.

32 John Wilton-Ely, "Vision and Design: Piranesi's *Fantasia* and the Graeco-Roman Controversy," in Georges Brunel (ed.), *Piranèse et les Français. Colloque tenu à la Villa Médicis. 12–14 mai 1976* (Rome, 1978), 534–37; Wittkower, "Piranesi's Architectural Creed," 238–40.

The triumph of Winckelmann's neoclassical doctrine would affect the arts of Rome. Its consequences are but one more symptom of that loss of energy, that entropy, that afflicted the papal capital. Sprung out of Rome's archeological activity, it diminished the importance of the one function in which Rome boasted to be still supreme. When Rome was still under the influence of the Tridentine spirit, the archeology of Christian antiquity aroused most interest. Beginning gradually with Alexander VII, but particularly under Clement XI, pagan archeological or antiquarian art was emphasized to attract tourism and trade. By the time of Clement XIV and Pius VI it was officially state-sponsored. In boosting itself, however, Rome almost unwittingly drew attention to Athens, which, as it had been in the days of the ancient empire, would once more be its cultural nemesis on its own soil. The rise of neoclassicism contributed to the ultimate disappearance of Rome as the center of west European art, a proud claim that now would definitely pass to Paris. But this loss did not come totally unexpectedly; it came at the close of almost a century of changes in art.[33]

[33] Bartoccini, *Roma nell'Ottocento*, 247.

# 15

# Painting and sculpture

The supremacy of Roman art was a rooted conception among Italians ever since the days of the Renaissance art historian Giorgio Vasari. But this view was to change in the course of the eighteenth century. When Gabriel-François Coyer visited the city in 1764, he wrote that "the Roman school of painting and sculpture had lost its glory . . . But Rome will always have the advantage of being the School of the World, because of the originals it possesses."[1] His words express the dilemma and paradox of Roman art during the period of the ancien regime. On the one hand Rome was still important. It was a sort of museum, in which the relics of classical antiquity, whether of Hellenistic or genuine Roman origin, and the monuments of the High Renaissance, were preserved. It was a center in which artists met, as neighbors, as collaborators, in the making of works of art, as fellow members of confraternities and academies. They could visit each other's studios and influence each other. Rome was important too as a source of imagery. This is especially, although not exclusively, true for landscape and *vedute* painters.[2]

On the other hand, the deep crisis of Italian society as a whole and, still more, the weakness of the Roman court in the context of European power politics and the fading of the Tridentine ideology prevented the artistic paradigm to impose itself as it had done in the not too distant past, when the artistic prestige of Rome, as capital of the Catholic world, had assured its world-wide success. This success was not to repeat itself again, except in certain restricted genres such as that of the *vedutisti*, who took advantage of the growth of tourism. During the first thirty or forty years of the century, before neoclassicism and its forerunners had appeared on the scene, there was still a limited capacity for art in Rome to show some vitality of its own, but even then it was mainly a case of Italian artists working in Rome rather than the creation of a genuine autochthonous art. For, with the death of Bernini in 1682, the baroque, that peculiarly native Roman art form still associated with Counter Reformation zeal – although it also produced a secular or aristocratic version – would first become diluted into a complex of new stylistic endeavors, perhaps best grouped together under the name of late baroque classicism[3] and, after exhausting

1 Wittkower, "Piranesi's Architectural Creed," 238; Coyer, *Voyage d'Italie*, 1:276.

2 Philip J. Barlow, *Ideal and Classical Landscape. Exhibition, 6 February – 3 April 1960* (Cardiff, 1960), 5; Anthony M. Clark, "Sebastiano Conca and the Roman Rococo," *Apollo*, N.S. 63 (1967), 328.

3 Moschini, "Giaquinto artista rappresentativo della pittura barocca tarda," 105–7; Roberta Chyurlia, "Pompeo Batoni o del classicismo settecentesco," *Emporium* 117 (1953), 63–65.

itself completely, give way after the middle of the century to the International Style that eventuated in neoclassicism.[4]

Part of the reason for the Roman dilemma was that after the death of Alexander VII in 1667 official patronage declined precipitously, although it did not disappear at once. The overall economic and financial situation of the state and of the most promising private patrons, cardinals and princes, was largely although not totally responsible. Innocent XII's abolition of nepotism contributed its share. The great spending sprees of cardinal nipoti was now gone for ever. With it went not all, but a good part of the large-scale, extravagant art projects that great wealth made possible. Old families would less often commission sculpture for embellishment of churches. But even here, there were significant exceptions to the trend: Tommaso Antamoro, a Roman patrician, erected a chapel to Filippo Neri in the church of S. Girolamo della Carità with statuary by Pierre Le Gros, and Scipione Lancellotti, a wealthy Neapolitan landowner, was responsible for the lavish chapel in honor of S. Luigi Gonzaga at S. Ignazio. All were surpassed by the most generous patron of the arts in the early eighteenth century, Pietro Ottoboni, grand nephew of Alexander VIII, who, in addition to being the liberal sponsor of writers, composers, and musicians, also patronized painters and architects, Baciccio, Francesco Trevisani, Sebastiano Conca, and Filippo Juvara among them. Of course, the Borghese could still afford to keep some prominent painters employed toward the end of the century. Some old papal families continued to commission tombs for their papal ancestors. But, in general, the Roman nobles who formed the papal entourage still thought of themselves far more as Florentines, Venetians, and Bolognese and turned to painters of distinction from their native provinces rather than from Rome, if they could afford it.

Some popes still tried to act as patrons. Clement XI sponsored the marble statues of the Twelve Apostles at the basilica of St. John Lateran. He was also responsible for the tomb of Queen Christina at St. Peter's, the series of statues along the top of the straight arm of the colonnade of St. Peter's Square, and the new portico with statues for S. Maria in Trastevere. There were always commissions for special occasions; Benedict XIV ordered Conca to paint a picture of the Virgin with St. Francis de Sales and Vincent de Paul for the beatification of Jeanne-Françoise de Chautel. Religious orders, too, such as the Jesuits, Dominicans, and Carmelites, could still afford a limited patronage. These isolated cases, however, could not hide the general shrinkage in patronage.

One of the consequences of this development was a certain reversal in the trend. During the heyday of papal patronage, under the Barberini pope Urban VIII, few foreign potentates had much chance of success in competing with the popes for the services of artists. Now many painters and sculptors became aware that there were

[4] Previtali, "La periodizzazione della storia dell'arte," 81–83; Enrico Castelnuovo and Carlo Ginsburg, "Centro e periferia," in *Storia dell'arte italiana* (Turin, 1979), part 1, vol. 1:248–49; Pinto, *Trevi Fountain*, 238.

greater opportunities for them abroad. This ironic situation is in part responsible for Rome's wide-ranging cultural influence, discussed in the Introduction. The Liechtenstein family in Vienna and the Schönborn family in Pommersfelden (Franconia) could readily commission works from such prominent artists in Rome as Carlo Maratta, Benedetto Luti, and Francesco Trevisani.[5]

By the start of the eighteenth century Roman artistic life had become more complex and intricate than it had been in the previous centuries, both because of the numerous and continuous foreign influences and also because it was conditioned by a society which had come to prefer clear designs and simple compositions, accompanied by a finesse of expression, but which was still not freed from the weight of both its baroque and earlier classical tradition.[6]

Much of the tone of artistic life in Rome during this period was set by the Accademia di San Luca. Founded in 1577 with a papal charter, and a cardinal as its protector, the academy marked the appearance among artists of a consciousness of their enhanced position in the new order of society. With it we have in the papal capital the first school of painting in modern times to be governed by "academic" standards. Hence, an artist's success depended to a large extent upon "official" recognition.[7]

With the passing of time the position of the Accademia di San Luca was further enhanced. By the statutes which Clement XI confirmed in 1715, membership of the academy was simply no longer regarded as an abstract recognition. It was in the spirit of the ancien regime a privilege, which exempted the holders from all burdens and taxes to which non-academicians were subject and which gave them the right to teach the young, to hold public schools, to use nude models. They alone were allowed to carry out public commissions. In return each academician was obligated to uphold the prestige of his privilege by not working in retail stores selling works of art and by not finishing works of art started by non-academicians. To fall foul of the academy could spell one's ruin.

Nevertheless, some hardy spirits did not hesitate to criticize what they considered the severe regime of the Accademia di San Luca, even before the promulgation of the new statutes. In 1704 the little-known painter and art historian Ludovico David, a product of the Lombard school of art who had resided in Rome since 1686, launched an attack on the academy in a small work, *L'Amore dell'Arte*, in which he called for a change in the esthetic propounded by San Luca. More

5 Haskell, *Patrons and Painters*, 4, 127–28, 164–66, 194, 199; Morelli (ed.), *Lettere di Benedetto XIV*, 2:419 (29 September 1751); Enggass, *Early Eighteenth-Century Sculpture*, 1:9, 19–24; John A. Pinto, "Nicola Michetti and ephemeral design in eighteenth-century Rome," in Henry A. Millon (ed.), *Studies in Italian Art and Architecture. Fifteenth through Eighteenth Centuries* (Cambridge, Mass. and London, 1980), 291–92.

6 Giancarlo Sestieri, "Contributi a Sebastiano Conca," *Commentari*, 20 (1969) and 21 (1970), 20:328.

7 Ellis Waterhouse, *Roman Baroque Painting. A List of the Principal Painters and their Works in and around Rome* (London, 1976), 4.

significant was the revolt of Marco Benefial, a native Roman whose style has been linked to Bolognese classicism. An impetuous nonconformist by nature, he led the artists who had been excluded by the statutes of 1715 against the narrow-minded corporative restrictions of the academy, an act of foolhardiness which cost him a thirty years' delay in being admitted to San Luca. After some further conflict, which dragged on to 1720, non-members were relieved of some of the disabilities; but the academicians still retained their privileged status.[8]

In 1750 Cardinal Valenti established a school for nude drawing at the Campidoglio, where students of the Accademia di San Luca were taught gratis by academicians, who rotated their duties. Rome had no other public institution with the right to pose nude male models until that date, except at the French academy. Another significant date was 1771, when Anton Raphael Mengs became prince of the academy. Using his chair at the academy as a pulpit, he expounded his thoughts on beauty and taste in painting. They did not take deep root instantly, but survived in the bosom of the Accademia di San Luca, where they would help to form a young generation of painters.

But Mengs' was by no means the first outside, non-Italian influence on Roman art or on the Accademia di San Luca. The Romans had always welcomed foreign artists; the more there were the better they liked it. Many European artists of note made their Roman pilgrimage and some stayed on. They were honorably received and could live in contact with the great works there displayed. The single most active element on this cosmopolitan scene was the Académie de France à Rome. Established in February 1666 by Jean-Baptiste Colbert, in conjunction with the Académie royale de peinture et de sculpture in Paris, it served as the pinnacle of a highly structured system of art education to produce artists at the disposal of Louis XIV. The academy in Paris was to provide art students with suitable training in painting and sculpture. Its prize-winning students were then given travel grants and bursaries to Rome for at least four years. In the mind of the founders, aided by the official genius of Charles Le Brun, these students were to learn the rudiments of their craft from the classical and Renaissance models surrounding them in order to contribute to the artistic grandeur of the French realm. The French academy in Rome fell on bad days at the close of the reign of Louis XIV, when the marquis (later duc) d'Autin became director-general of buildings for the king, but he found sufficient subsidies to save Colbert's valuable foundation. From that moment the

[8] Arnaud, *L'Académie de Saint-Luc à Rome*, 4–12, 21–34, 61–62, 69–71; Haskell and Penny, *Taste and the Antique*, 17; Ferdinando Arisi, *Gian Paolo Panini* (Piacenza, 1961), 48; *Settecento a Roma*, 60; Italo Faldi, "Gli inizi del neoclassicismo in pittura nella prima metà del Settecento," in *Nuove idee e nuova arte nel '700 italiano* (Rome, 1977), 496–97; Nicholas Turner, "An attack on the Accademia di S. Luca: Ludovico David's *L'Amore dell'Arte*," in *British Museum Yearbook*, 1 (1976), 157–59, 163–70; Marisa Volpi, "Corrado Giaquinto e alcuni aspetti della cultura figurativa del '700 in Italia," *Bollettino d'arte*, 43–44 (1958), 267; Mattia Loret, "I pittori napoletani a Roma nel Settecento," *Capitolium* (1934), 548.

French academy embarked upon a brilliant career, not without setbacks but without any failures, until the turmoils of the French Revolution.[9]

The French academy in Rome accounted for the presence of many French artists in Rome, but not for their success with the Romans, who had convinced themselves of the cultural inferiority of the French, as Bernini concluded during his stay in France in 1665. Throughout most of the second half of the seventeenth century and into the first part of the eighteenth, however, France was considered the richest and most powerful of European powers and the court of Louis XIV the most brilliant. And grandeur, in the sense of splendour, was a quality the Romans adored. During most of the seventeenth century the popes had provided it in abundant supply, but from 1685, in particular, that supply was exhausted. France now stepped into the gap and thereby raised its cultural influence.

The Accademia di San Luca was so impressed with French grandeur that they made Charles Erard, the first director-general of the Académie de France à Rome, their own *principe* in 1672, in place of Nicolas Poussin who, unanimously elected to the post, was unable to assume the charge. In 1676 the two academies were joined, but only nominally. Charles Le Brun, director of the Académie royale in Paris, was elected *principe in absentia* of San Luca in Rome. This practice was on occasions repeated in the eighteenth century. No Italian, however, was ever named director of the Académie de France à Rome, although Panini would teach there.

An indication of the indirect influence the French academy exerted on the world of Roman art is the papal brief of 1703 with which Clement XI set aside special Capitoline revenues for the Accademia di San Luca in order to award prizes to the most deserving artists in an annual competition. The *prix de Rome* of the French academic system certainly inspired this institution, even though the Capitoline prize was more honorific and carried no bursary with it. The first competition was won, certainly not by chance, by the French sculptor Pierre Le Gros.[10] This exchange of ideas and inspiration between the principal academies in Rome would give Roman art a cosmopolitan flavor; but before the century was out it would also deprive it of its native tradition and roots, resulting in the loss of its cultural primacy to Paris.

Although every artistic style created in Italy since antiquity has been based on ancient classical models, baroque art was the first style which was created on the soil of Rome and its immediate neighborhood. By about 1710, however, baroque painting in the city came to an end. The turn of the century was still marked with

[9] Lapauze, *Histoire de l'Académie de France à Rome*, 153; Noack, *Deutsches Leben in Rom*, 13–14, 55; Hautecoeur, *Rome et la renaissance de l'antiquité*, 42–43, 51; Montaiglon and Guiffrey (eds.), *Correspondance des directeurs de l'Académie de France*, 11:235–36; De Rinaldis, *L'arte in Roma*, 177; Enggass, *Early Eighteenth-Century Sculpture*, 1:26.

[10] Ibid., 1:26–27; Santangelo, "La scultura," in *Il Settecento a Roma*, 33.

the last traces of the high baroque as cultivated by Bernini and the Jesuits. Giovanni Gaulli, generally known as Baciccio, a native of Genoa, became the perfecter of the second baroque style. When he arrived in Rome in 1657, not yet twenty years old, he came under the decisive influence of Bernini and Pietro da Cortona. Distinguished by the decorative illusionism of his frescoes, Baciccio began the great work of his life. Bernini had recommended him to the Jesuit general Giovanni Paolo Oliva to paint the frescoes and decorations of the church of the Gesù, a task which occupied him for fourteen years. He would leave a permanent impress on the church. His ceiling of the nave still represents the pure Roman, or Jesuit, style.

The only other figure of serious importance in the same vein was the Jesuit Fratel Andrea Pozzo, a native of Trent, who appropriately enough was the continuator of the Jesuit tradition already found in Baciccio. Soon after the death of Bernini, Oliva summoned Pozzo to Rome, when he was already a formed artist. His Roman work was associated with his order, climaxing in 1691 to 1694 in what was probably the most important work of the decade, the nave ceiling of the church of Sant'Ignazio, which was a logical continuation of Baciccio's ceiling in the Gesù. With it we also witness the conclusion of the whole thesis of baroque illusionism.[11]

With Baciccio and Pozzo, pictorial baroque painting came to a brilliant end. While Baciccio was busy at the Gesù, Carlo Maratta painted the ceiling of the great hall in the Altieri palace across the street. At the death of Bernini, Maratta had succeeded him as the principal intellectual force among Roman artists. His influence, and in part his direct teaching, was the most powerful factor in painting in Rome during the last decades of the seventeenth and the first of the eighteenth century. As a student of Andrea Sacchi, he opposed the movement started by Pietro da Cortona and the current of Baciccio. By way of Sacchi, Maratta tried to recapture the Roman artistic tradition that boasted a noble origin in Raphael and had found its best expression in Annibale Caracci.

The latter, when called to Rome by Cardinal Odoardo Farnese in 1595 from his home in Bologna to paint the gallery in the family palace, had created a work that in the eyes of the Romans, Bernini among them, could take its place at the side of Michelangelo's Sistine chapel and Raphael's Vatican stanzas. Breaking with the mannerism in Roman art, Caracci brought with him the Bolognese technique of making use of wide expanses of perspective in decorating palaces, known as *quadratura*, which he used to illustrate the theme of Profane Love in Antiquity. In so doing he was able to sum up the results of the Renaissance and establish for the

[11] Hermann Voss, *Die Malerei des Barock in Rom* (Berlin, 1924), 579–80, 583–84, 591–92; Fokker, *Roman Baroque Art*, 1:15–18, 328; Waterhouse, *Roman Baroque Painting*, 32–38; Emilio Lavagnino, "La pittura," in *Il Settecento a Roma*, 24; *Il Settecento a Roma*, 109; Oreste Ferrari, "Painting in Naples under the Austrian Viceregency (1707–1734)," in *The Golden Age of Naples. Art and Civilization under the Bourbons, 1734–1804* (2 vols.; Detroit and Chicago, 1981), 1:48; Portoghesi, *Roma barocca*, 2:559–65; Haskell, *Patrons and Painters*, 160–61.

first time the canons for an academic style that could be readily passed on to competent pupils; it would last about two hundred years.[12]

With his great fresco *Trionfo della clemenza* on the ceiling of the great hall of the remodelled Altieri palace, which dates from about 1673, Maratta reached the high point of his painting. It was the masterpiece of the founder of a movement which was to serve his followers as a practical lesson. The fresco, flat on the ceiling and fully contained within a frame without any suggestion of illusionism, was the first example of the "grand style," the style which was to be for almost a century the idiom of the cultured court art in Europe. Although Roman in origin, it proved to be an artistic language, easily appreciated by princes and the general public alike and transmitted without difficulty from master to pupil, admirably fitted for allegorical utterances of a political or ecclesiastical nature, and in contrast to the vigor of the high baroque, lacking any strong personal or national color. A Frenchman such as Charles-André van Loo could easily pick it up second-hand during his stay in Rome and carry it back to Paris in 1734, where he acquired a large clientele.[13]

The appearance of Maratta marked the last time that a natural Italian artistic style was developed in Rome, even though it would be internationalized. Although he was not a revolutionary, his paintings were certainly tied to a preceding pictorial tradition. The heavy hand of Marattism, however, would continue to weigh on Roman art after his death in 1713, so much so that the activities of his imitators and followers gave the impression of a mood of crisis and exhaustion that boded ill for the autochthonous school of painting. The most they could muster was to animate their pictures with new touches of light and color. Giuseppe Chiari, a native of Rome born of Florentine parents, who had studied with Maratta since the age of twelve, was probably the most faithful among the pupils of Maratta. Although regarded by some as the best painter in Italy in the early part of the eighteenth century, only a slight tendency toward the rococo distinguishes him from his master. But more closely verging on the rococo was the most pronounced personality among the successor of Maratta, Benedetto Luti. Born in Florence, where he was trained in a Tuscan version of the style of Pietro da Cortona, he moved to Rome in 1690 under the patronage of the Grand Duke, who fostered an academy in the Medici palace. There he formed an association with the French academy, whose conception of art influenced him greatly. The last of the successors, and reputed pupil of Maratta, was Agostino Masucci. With him the Marattist school in

[12] Charles Dempsey, "Annibale Carrache au Palais Farnèse," in Ecole française de Rome, *Le Palais Farnèse* (Rome, 1981), vol. 1:1:270–72, 284, 301, 308; Olivier Michel, "L'*Accademia*," 2:568–70; Waterhouse, *Roman Baroque Painting*, 7–9; Bazin, *The Baroque*, 103–4.

[13] Waterhouse, *Roman Baroque Painting*, 34–35; *Settecento a Roma*, 143, 146; Haskell, *Patrons and Painters*, 165; Voss, *Die Malerei des Barock*, 592–95, 603–11; Lalande, *Voyage d'un françois en Italie*, 3:95–99; Ruscus, "Centenari di artisti minori: Carlo Maratta," *Emporium* (1925), 182–86; De Rinaldis, *L'arte in Roma*, 159–61, 169–70; Arnaud, *L'Académie de Saint-Luc*, 55–56.

Rome came to a close. As an early teacher of Mengs, Masucci became the link between the academism of Maratta and early neoclassicism.[14]

During the time when Maratta's influence pervaded over Roman art, two other hives of artistic activities, not counting the French academy, existed in the city, bringing stylistic innovations from outside. The more important of these was the Farnese palace with its Caracci gallery. In 1626, at the death of Cardinal Odoardo Farnese, the palace ceased to be the residence of the Farnese family and became the embassy first of Parma and Piacenza and later of the kingdom of Naples. Toward the end of the seventeenth century, the last dukes of Parma, exhausted after almost a century of wars and unsuccessful diplomacy, resumed an artistic tradition which had once created the splendor of the Farnese palace, but of which their new ambitions could be but a reflection of their enfeebled power. The vastness of the building was able without difficulty to shelter artists under their patronage, the young in need of lodgings and the acknowledged masters of studios.

The main wave of these protégés consisted of northerners from Emilia, or from Parma and Bologna, all linked artistically. Their sojourn in Rome gave them an opportunity to perfect their art, but, above all, it held out the chance of a less provincial career. In Rome they found employment as stage designers and theater architects. The first of these was Sebastiano Ricci, a native of Belluna, who came by way of Venice to Bologna to complete his apprenticeship, an essential stage for entering the service of the dukes of Parma. He arrived in Rome in 1691 and three years later replaced Francesco Bibienna as stage designer for Cardinal Ottoboni at the Cancelleria, thus initiating the bond between the Palazzo Farnese and that other center of artistic activity.[15]

In 1704 Bonaventura Lamberti, a Modenese who had been trained by Bolognese artists, moved into the palace. Already fifty years of age, he was a painter of renown and a champion of the Caracci tradition, the right subject for Farnese patronage. Among his pupils was the young and brilliant Marco Benefial. Lamberti was followed by a series of young protégés of the house of Parma, the best known of whom was Pompeo Aldrovandini. He was joined in 1719 by Aureliano Milani, who arrived in Rome from the north. Since infancy Milani had been an admirer of Caracci and it was his ambition not only to recover the spirit, but to reproduce the very forms of this artist. Milani and Aldrovandini, in the evening of their lives, were able to collaborate in the gallery of mirrors at the Pamphilj palace, where they realized their mature dream of planting the Bolognese style in the heart of Rome.[16]

But the fascination of the Palazzo Farnese was not limited to Emilian artists. The

[14] Moschini, "Giaquinto artista rappresentativo della pittura barocca tarda," 104–5; Lavagnino, "La pittura," 24–25; *Settecento a Roma*, 82, 143–44, 148; Waterhouse, *Roman Baroque Painting*, 65, 88–89; Tornézy, *Bergeret et Fragonard*, 254; Pastor, *Geschichte der Päpste*, 15:373; Golzio, *Palazzi romani dalla rinascita*, 30; Mariani, *Le chiese di Roma dal XVII al XVIII secolo*, 217; Lorenza Cocchetti, "Pompeo Batoni e il neoclassicismo a Roma," *Commentari* (1952), no. 4, 274–75.

[15] Geneviève Michel, "Vie quotidienne au Palais Farnèse," 2:520; Olivier Michel, "L'*Accademia*," 2:567, 570–72, 578, 582–83.

[16] Ibid., 2:579–82, 587–90; *Settecento a Roma*, 145.

directors of the Académie de France à Rome ceaselessly pleaded for access to the paintings for their students, to both the Raphael loggia in the Farnesina and the Caracci frescoes. The dynastic connection between the Bourbons and the Farnese favored the young French painters. In 1693 at least seven a day came to draw and copy and this practice would continue on and off until 1775. Many of these budding artists have left their graffiti behind them. One French artist, albeit a sculptor, actually took up residence. Pierre Le Gros, deprived of his scholarship at the French academy for accepting a commission for the altar of St. Ignatius at the Gesù without asking permission, rented a studio in the corner of the palace. There he enjoyed an outstanding success with Italians, while continuing to receive the patronage of the French. His approach to sculpture, however, did not rest upon the elements of Italian style. It lacked that substratum of classicism which had characterized Italian art since the Renaissance, even that of Bernini. This did not prevent Le Gros from surrounding himself with friends and students. Indeed, his studio became a cosmopolitan meeting place for artists, including Romans (such as Gaetano Pace), as well as Liègeois, French, German, Piedmontese, and others. Through his second marriage he became the uncle of Gian Paolo Panini and of Nicolas Wheughels, director of the French academy between 1725 and 1737 and one of the most successful intermediaries between that institution and the Roman artistic milieu of the early eighteenth century.[17]

In 1734 the administration of the Farnese palace changed from Parmesan to Neapolitan sovereignty, when Charles VII became king of Naples. The transfer took place smoothly enough, accompanied by a shift from Emilian to Neapolitan artists among its population. Neapolitan art was formed in the early seventeenth century by the fusion of influences from Annibale Caracci and Caravaggio, with the latter gaining the upper hand. This art assumed its own character by the close of the century, thanks to the indefatigable industry of Luca Giordano, an instinctive and fertile assimilator of all Italian styles and schools, and to the most important of his many pupils, Francesco Solimena, who joined a scrupulous care for drawing, a clarity of arranging masses and an intensity of coloring to the decorative vein of his master. As far as we know Giordano stayed in Rome twice, in 1654 and 1702, but Solimena never worked in Rome; some of his followers, however, Onofrio Avellino (who came to Rome in 1715) among them, left their mark on the Roman artistic scene.[18]

Among the students of Solimena, Sebastiano Conca would exert the greatest influence on Roman painting, while preserving a great deal of the ardor and the alertness of the Neapolitan master. Coming to Rome at almost thirty years of age in 1707, after having produced successful canvases for a chapel at the abbey of Montecassino, Conca is said to have been so impressed by the Roman school that he

[17] Olivier Michel, "L'*Accademia*," 2:572–76, 579, 586; Enggass, *Early Eighteenth-Century Sculpture*, 1:42–43, 124–31; *Settecento a Roma*, 225.

[18] Loret, "I pittori napoletani a Roma," 542–43, 547–48.

did little else than draw.[19] Pierre Le Gros eventually persuaded him to take up the brush again. One of his first patrons was Cardinal Pietro Ottoboni, near whose palace he found lodgings in a house at the Campo de' Fiori, which was peopled by artists, mainly painters and engravers. It appears that there he started a school in his studio which, before the arrival of Mengs in Rome, attracted German and Spanish art students. Around 1714, when the work of restoring the basilica of S. Clemente drew to an end, Conca, together with other artists, was given the task of painting the frescoes in the central nave. His fresco, *Miracolo della fonte*, showed the chromatic influences of Maratta and his school. The same was reflected in his great work on the nave ceiling of S. Cecilia in Trastevere, completed between 1721 and 1724, although he translated there the somewhat exhausted Roman tradition into fertile and up-to-date terms.

Cardinal Francesco Acquaviva, the titular of the church and ambassador of Spain, sent a sketch of this fresco to Duke Francesco Maria of Parma, who thereupon gave Conca apartments for his studio and his school in the Farnese, and later put him in charge of the Neapolitan and Spanish students in Rome. Thus, Conca, as protégé of the last of the Farnese and subject of the new Bourbon sovereign of Naples, assured the smooth transition between the two patrons. In his new abode the painter continued his academy. With its reputation and its permanence, this school rivalled that of the French academy at a time when the Accademia di San Luca failed in its appointed task of training young artists from the various nations who came to Rome. It is therefore no coincidence that we have to wait until the departure of Conca in 1752 before Benedict XIV, at the suggestion of Panini, built a room in the Campidoglio to house an academy for the study of the nude. Conca also assembled around him young fellow countrymen from the south. In this way his studio came to prefigure in an informal fashion the Neapolitan academy which Charles VII set up officially in Naples in 1752. It was symptomatic of the migration of artists from Naples, for whom Rome was the nearest major artistic center.[20]

On two occasions, between 1729 and 1732, and again in 1739/40, Conca became the *principe* of the Accademia di San Luca, with the reputation as one of the best administrators the academy ever had. He was anxious to shake the assembly out of its torpor. Through his initiative a kind of artistic code to serve as directive for the young was drawn up. It provides us with an idea of the esthetic concepts of the generation of painters between 1730 and 1750. The document insisted on an in-

[19] One recently discovered painting, *Adorazione dei Magi*, of 1707, now in Tours, still shows strong traces of Solimenism, although there are signs of a superficial assimilation of the drawing style which prevailed in the Roman environment at the time. Sestieri, "Contributi a Conca," 1:317–18.

[20] Olivier Michel, "L'*Accademia*," 2:590–97, 602; Loret, "I pittori napoletani a Roma," 545–47; Clark, "Sebastiano Conca," 330–32; Sestieri, "Contributi a Conca," 1:330–31, 317; Geneviève Michel, "Vie quotidienne au Palais Farnèse," 2:528; Waterhouse, *Roman Baroque Painting*, 68; Geneviève and Olivier Michel, "Recherches biographiques sur Paolo Anesi," in *Studi offerti a Giovanni Incisa della Rocchetta* (Rome, 1973), 333.

depth study of the antique and not just blind imitation or copy. In general, the attention was on nature as an inexhaustible well-spring to which the artist should always revert. These postulates were to be expressed sixteen years later by Benefial with so much passion that they resulted in his expulsion from the academy. Despite his teachings, few of these precepts penetrated Conca's work. Indeed, responding to numerous requests, he painted in rather melodramatic fashion subjects inspired not only by poetry, but also by history and mythology, some of them reflecting closely the treatment which Metastasio had given them in his operatic libretti.[21]

Through his large circle of friends and fellow artists, Conca maintained connections with other popular artists. Among these was, of course, the engraver Giuseppe Vasi, who also received an apartment in the Farnese palace in 1749, where he remained until his death in 1782. Vasi, who may himself have attended Conca's classes, carried on the tradition of Le Gros and Conca of making his studio a gathering place for the international set of young art students. The landscape painter Paolo Anesi may have been another one of those influenced by Conca, as the latter was godfather of his eldest daughter. A contact of a very different style was the Parmesan painter Michele Rocca. More of a rococo artist, he was more popular than Conca with the French clientele, to whose taste he had a closer affinity.[22]

Even more representative of the Neapolitan invasion than Conca, who had adapted himself to a modified Marattism, was Corrado Giaquinto. A product of the school of Solimena, he arrived in Rome in 1723, where he quickly made his reputation. His first large commission was in 1731 in the church of S. Nicola dei Lorensi, which he executed in a revived baroque form. He left for Turin thereafter and worked together with Conca in the royal palace. In that city of Juvara, the meeting point of artists of various cultural origins, Giaquinto appears to have acquired the decorative and graceful lightness of the rococo which marks his next work, that of decorating the vault of the Ruffo chapel, designed by Salvi, in the church of S. Lorenzo in Damaso in 1735. It turned out to be one of the jewels of eighteenth-century Roman paintings, perhaps the most elegant expression of the rococo taste in the papal capital. Giaquinto's new style, however, failed to take root among the Romans.[23]

Going from one studio to another was very frequent and the influence of the Farnese palace was indissolubly mixed with that other center of artistic patronage in the first part of the eighteenth century, the Cancelleria, where Pietro Ottoboni, the most adventurous patron of painters and musicians in his time, held sway. We have

21 Loret, "I pittori napoletani a Roma," 547; Clark, "Sebastiano Conca," 328–29; *Settecento a Roma*, 84; Sestieri, "Contributi a Conca," 2:126.

22 Olivier Michel, "L'*Accademia*," 2:597–600; Michel and Michel, "Recherches biographiques sur Paolo Anesi," 327; Sestieri, "Contributi a Conda," 1:324; Hermann Voss, "Michele Rocca, ein vergessener italienischer Rokoko-Maler," *Zeitschrift für bildende Kunst*, (1921), 69–75.

23 Moschini, "Giaqinto artista rappresentativo della pittura barocca tarda," 107, 111; Volpi, "Corrado Giaquinto," 265–71, 275; Loret, "I pittori napoletani a Roma," 550–54; Lavagnino, "La pittura," 27.

already noted that Conca enjoyed the cardinal's patronage when he first arrived in Rome, before moving into the Farnese palace. Although Ottoboni could be eclectic in his choice of style, as an offspring of a Venetian noble house he naturally showed some preference for Venetian artists. At the turn of the century this current in Rome was represented by Sebastiano Ricci and Francesco Trevisani. The latter, in particular, became the protégé of Cardinal Ottoboni, more so than the younger Conca. A native of Capodistria, Trevisani arrived in Rome in 1681 and soon found quarters in the palace of the Cancelleria, Ottoboni's residence, with an allowance of 50 scudi monthly. The Roman ambience and the influence of Carlo Maratta, whom Trevisani eventually succeeded as the leading Roman painter, were, however, too powerful to be withstood. His general contribution to Roman painting was that of developing the graceful, the elegant, and the alluring element in both conception and technical treatment. Like Conca's at the Farnese palace, Trevisani's studio at the Cancelleria was freely open and art students, many of them of Roman birth, attended both, which led to a mixing of styles that preserved a tenuous artistic unity – if we except the French academy – within the city.[24]

Not all the painters of this period belonged to the circles at the Palazzo Farnese or the Cancelleria. Two of those who did not had their works deeply rooted in the social life of Rome to a degree that cannot be said of the majority of painters in the eighteenth century. Pier Leone Ghezzi, the son of Giuseppe Ghezzi, a mediocre painter of church pictures, who became a central figure in the Roman art world as secretary of the Accademia di San Luca from 1678 to 1719 and artistic adviser to Christina of Sweden and the Albani family, learned painting from his father and between 1708 and 1747 was official painter to the Apostolic Chamber. In this capacity he carried out decorations in various Roman churches, largely in the Marattist manner. As painter his reputation rests mainly upon his frescoes in the Villa Falconieri at Frascati, which were inspired by contemporary life. But it is as caricaturist and social critic in the eight volumes of his *Il mondo nuovo* that he is best known to posterity. With these caricatures we enter a world in which the famous and the unknown of eighteenth-century Rome, who form the human substratum of the city, pass before our eyes. Ghezzi shows himself thoroughly at home in this society which he rendered with subtle objectivity. These were achievements particularly gratifying in a country where the freedom of the pencil was thought a desirable addition to the license of the tongue. Ghezzi is cruel to his sitters in endowing them rather uniformly with strange lips, peculiarly thick and beak-like. By way of contrast, the notes that accompany his portraits often appear sympathetic to the person so harshly represented. But his style, which at first was so vital and

[24] Ibid., 25–26; Haskell, *Patrons and Painters*, 164–65; Clark, "Sebastiano Conca," 329; Olivier Michel, "l'*Accademia*," 2:595; Voss, *Die Malerei des Barock*, 614–16, 619–25, 634–36; Waterhouse, *Roman Baroque Painting*, 39.

spontaneous, began to show signs of fatigue; after about 1720 he tended to acquire a routine, which ended up in turning him into a mere jobber.[25]

The other artist was Antonio Amorosi, a fellow countryman of Giuseppe Ghezzi from the Abruzzi. Educated for a learned profession, he forsook it in Rome to learn painting with the elder Ghezzi. He specialized as a genre painter, depicting peasants, children, old people, rustic festivals, drinking scenes, and the like. In comparison to Pier Leone Ghezzi, whose interests were more bourgeois, Amorosi was primitive and popular. His preference was for the life of the humble folk of the Campagna.

The middle period of the eighteenth century in Rome was dominated by three painters, who are difficult to categorize or associate within a larger social or topographical group. The first of these was the Roman Marco Benefial, whom we have already encountered as an opponent of the monopoly of the Accademia di San Luca. As one might expect, he was a free spirit, independent, who reacted against the production of the followers of Maratta and of those of Trevisani alike. His opposition to the academy resulted in a shortage of commissions and domestic problems, which compelled him on two occasions to join with an inferior artist in a kind of partnership in which the work generally fell upon his shoulders and the recognition went to his partner. Although Benefial was partially successful in his campaign of having the privileges of San Luca revoked by 1723, it was not until 1741 that the academicians admitted him into their ranks, and allowed him to conduct their nude classes. Among his pupils was the young German Anton Raphael Mengs. Despite his opposition to existing trends, it would be an exaggeration to call Benefial a reformer of Roman painting; he lacked the requisite characteristics of a reformer, consistency and originality. He looked back rather to the seventeenth century to Guercino and Caravaggio. In him we find the vein of an exceptional storyteller, a poet in paint.

Another unattached figure was Pierre Subleyras from Languedoc. After winning a scholarship to the French academy in Rome in 1726, he spent the rest of his life in the city, married a Roman pastel artist, and became more organically assimilated into the Roman tradition than any of his countrymen. Praised for the grandeur of his artistic conceptions, he became known as the "Guido Reni of the eighteenth century," and enjoyed the patronage of Cardinal Valenti Gonzaga, from whom he received commissions for St. Peter's.[26]

25 Benisovich, "Ghezzi and the French Artists in Rome," 340–41, 347; Margherita Abbruzzese, "Note su Pier Leone Ghezzi (1674–1755)," *Commentari*, 6 (1955), 303–8; Lavagnino, "La pittura," 28–29; *Settecento a Roma*, 44–51; Waterhouse, *Roman Baroque Painting*, 81; Natali (ed.), *Storia letteraria: Il Settecento*, 1:87; Mariani, *Le chiese di Roma dal XVII al XVIII secolo*, 179.

26 Lavagnino, "La pittura," 27; Noack, *Deutsches Leben in Rom*, 65–67, 358; Noack, *Deutschtum in Rom*, 1:319–20; Friedrich Noack, "Marco Benefial. Ein Bahnbrecher des Klassizismus," *Monatshefte für Kunstwissenschaft*, 12 (1919), nos. 5/6, 125–29; Hautecoeur, *Rome et la renaissance de l'antiquité*, 145; De Rinaldis, *L'arte in Roma*, 173; Mariani, *Le chiese di Roma dal XVII al XVIII secolo*, 204; Ceschi, *Le chiese di Roma dagli inizi del neoclassico*, 15–16; *Settecento a Roma*, 205–6.

The third, and probably greatest, of this triumvirate of painters who were not dominated either by Marattism or the group at the Farnese palace was Pompeo Batoni, who also reached the height of his career during the pontificate of Benedict XIV. When he first arrived from his native Lucca in 1728, it was suggested to him that he take lessons with Conca and Masucci. But Batoni soon rejected their teaching and turned to the ancient statuary at the Belvedere and the works of Raphael and Caracci for classical inspiration. His adviser and, in a limited sense, his teacher was the gifted and independent painter Francesco Fernandi, who had strong British and German connections.[27] Fernandi opened a few doors for Batoni, who eventually became a protégé of Cardinal Angelo Maria Quirini. Although, unlike his mentor, Batoni would become an academician of San Luca, he remained very inactive within the institution, preferring a life of peace and quiet. In his style Batoni veered toward a more severe classicism than the latter-day followers of Maratta, with a determination to overcome the last traces of the baroque, so much so that his contemporaries, whether British or Roman, thought him still in the grand Roman tradition of Raphael and Caracci. Some went even further and saw in him an early exponent of neoclassicism. But, as the art historian Anthony Clark put it, Batoni simply is not a good candidate for an originator of the neoclassical, in spite of the fact that in his old age he would try to ride the crest of neoclassicism by praising the works of Jacques-Louis David and Antonio Canova. Batoni did not reject Bernini outright, as the strict esthetic of Winckelmann would have demanded. Instead, by the style he created, by his natural gift, and by the generation he belonged to, Batoni is the epitome of that artistic language of the middle of the eighteenth century, which formed an unnamed hiatus between late baroque classicism and its brief rococo aftermath on the one hand and actual neoclassicism on the other. It cannot be confused with the latter intellectualism of foreign import.[28]

With Batoni the last important master of what may still be called Roman art drew to a close. Of course, the baroque in its fullness, symbolic of the Tridentine spirit of the Counter Reformation, and in many ways the only truly autochthonous art form of the city in modern times, had been much diluted in the course of the eighteenth century. Other artistic styles, be they Emilian, Venetian, Neapolitan, or even French, had found their exponents in the city. But overall the spirit of Maratta and his disciples, more acceptable to the international community of artists though fundamentally still Roman, continued to weigh heavily on the majority of painters

[27] See Introduction, p. 4.

[28] Cocchetti, "Pompeo Batoni e il neoclassicismo," 277–81; Ernst Emmerling, *Pompeo Batoni. Sein Leben und Werke* (Cologne, 1932), 7–32, 38–43, 47–52, 83–86, 89; Voss, *Die Malerie des Barock*, 644–47; De Rinaldis, *L'arte in Roma*, 173–74; Clark, "Batoni's professional career," 323–36; Chyurlia, "Pompeo Batoni o del classicismo settecentesco," 62, 66; Emilio Lavagnino, "Roma nel Settecento," In *Il Settecento a Roma. Mostra a Roma, 19 marzo – 31 maggio, 1959* (Rome, 1959), 21–22; *Settecento a Roma*, 49–50; Ceschi, *Le chiese di Roma dagli inizi del neoclassico*, 17–18; Seregni (ed.), *Carteggio di Verri*, 10:250; 11:166; 12:28; BAV, Cod. Ferraioli, ms. 417, f. 30r.

after their arrival in Rome. And if it was not Marattism, then it was Raphael and Annibale Caracci who became the ideals directly. Despite their differences, there was still this tenuous bond among the artists.

But from around 1760 Roman art became so hydra-headed that any attempt to attack it from a single perspective runs the risk of oversimplification. The principal element contributing to this complexity was the emergence of neoclassicism, which, as codified by Winckelmann, was not programmatic of Rome at all, as we have already seen, but would become the preoccupation of nationals from everywhere. Nevertheless the new style was to characterize the artistic scene in what remained, if somewhat precariously, the capital of the arts until the onset of the French Revolution.

This change in style was also accompanied by a topographical shift. The new location of the artists moved from the Farnese palace and the Cancelleria to the area around the Spanish Steps, which had already become the favorite quarters of foreign visitors. The hub of this new activity was the Zuccari palace, which filled a triangular site on the slope of the Pincio at the juncture of Via Gregoriana and Via Sistina, close to the church of SS. Trinità de' Monti. Federico Zuccari had built the residence in 1597, taking advantage of Sixtus V's provision that granted tax exemption and freedom from guild dues for artists in order to encourage settlement in the *monti*. He also became a founder of the Accademia di San Luca. His move marked the beginning of the migration of artists to the area. At the start of the eighteenth century much of the palace was occupied by Queen Maria Casimira, who vainly strove to turn it into an aristocratic center of the arts, in imitation of Queen Christina. Thereafter, the palace was, in effect, converted into a boarding house for aspiring artists. When Winckelmann found lodgings there in 1755 the house was fully occupied by them up to the roof. Others, among them Piranesi and Mengs, took accommodations close by. Later on David would live in the house. It thus became the boarding school of neoclassicism, harboring an international set of artists, among whom the Germans formed a significant contingent.[29]

Although David's *Serment des Horaces*, painted in 1785, has been commonly accepted as the manifesto of neoclassicism, the style has a long prehistory. More than fifty years before the cultural pressures of the archeological discoveries and the writings of the theoreticians which fused into the programmatic neoclassic movement, one comes across some surprising premonitions of the more rigorous later manifestation. In 1724 Giacomo Zoboli produced in Rome a pair of paintings representing the *Death of Pompey* and the *Death of Caesar*, which, with their correct historical environment and careful choice of archaeological furnishings, revealed a state of mind created by the unexpected impact his confrontation with the culture of Roman antiquity had produced. He was followed in the 1740s by other proto-

[29] Lavagnino, "Roma nel Settecento," 21; Lavagnino, "La pittura," 29–30; Santangelo. "La scultura," 38–39; Körte, *Der Palazzo Zuccari*, 13–14, 20, 48, 54–56.

neoclassicists, among them his fellow Lombard Giuseppe Bottani and the Lucchese Gian Domenico Campigli. For the next two decades or so an ambiguity of style continued to prevail. Examples of this were the ceilings executed in the apartments of the Borghese between 1768 and 1774, one of the last acts of lavish private patronage in Rome. There, in the most public and prestigious room of the apartments, the drawing room, one has a formal discourse celebrating the dynastic mythology, painted by Ermenegildo Constantini, which represents the swan song of the Roman baroque. Relegated to the marginal rooms for private family use were episodes of the nascent neoclassicism, favored by the cultured master of the house, Marcantonio Borghese. The most important of these was the *Marriage of Cupid and Psyche* by the Lyonnais Laurent Pécheux, who had moved into the Palazzo Zuccari to be in close proximity to his master, Mengs.[30]

Mengs' reputation as a painter has been hurt by the fact that his name has hardly ever been mentioned except in connection with Winckelmann, and that his art has never been valued as something that he formed as an individual with a certain theory of art in mind. He may have had the will or desire to renew painting, but it was never accompanied by a corresponding productive capacity. Whatever his theoretical convictions might have been, at the outset his artistic style persisted fundamentally along the general line of Roman painting in the age of Benefial and Batoni.

The first change in style only occurred in 1758. It may have been provoked by his contact with the discoveries at Herculaneum; on the occasion of his visiting Naples to carry out a commission in the chapel of the new royal palace at Caserta, he visited the museum at Portici and viewed the frescoes recovered by the excavation. At that time Mengs had already been commissioned by Cardinal Alessandro Albani to paint a ceiling in his recently completed villa. The subject matter and general composition of the picture was inspired by Raphael's stanzas at the Vatican; it was *Parnasso*, Apollo among the muses. Completed in 1761, the fresco made the artist a household name. The archetype for the muses he obtained from ancient frescoes. Although this seminal work became a point of reference for all artists of the neoclassical school, it was flawed; for Mengs lacked a clear conception of ancient art, particularly Greek art, in its totality. Nor, as his later work in the stanza dei papiri at the Vatican library showed, had he been able to throw off all traces of late baroque illusionism. Nevertheless his contemporaries did not seem to notice and greeted his *Parnasso* as an example of revived antiquity.[31]

[30] Faldi, "Gli inizio del neoclassicismo in pittura," 497, 504, 507, 511–13, 518–19; Körte, *Der Palazzo Zuccari*, 54.

[31] Rosenblum, *Transformations in Late Eighteenth Century Art*, viii; Ceschi, *Le chiese di Roma dagli inizi del neoclassico*, 18–19; Gerstenberg, *Winckelmann und Mengs*, 14–20, 25–31; Voss, *Die Malerei des Barock*, 652–54, 660–61; Noack, *Deutsches Leben in Rom*, 67–75, 85–88; Hautecoeur, *Rome et la renaissance de l'antiquité*, 148–51; De Rinaldis, *L'arte in Roma*, 174–75; Noack, "Marco Benefial," 125; Justi, *Winckelmann und seine Zeitgenossen*, 2:401–3; Rinaldi, *Due secoli di musica al Teatro Argentina*, 188, 221; Seregni (ed.), *Carteggio di Verri*, 10:341.

Among those who were under the direct personal influence of Mengs were some lesser known Italians, one of whom, Giovanni Battista Casanova, who, as director of the academy at Dresden, transplanted this trend to Germany. Two artists from German-speaking lands, however, were to continue his tradition in Rome. The Viennese Anton Maron, who had married Mengs' daughter Theresa, worked on the ceilings of the Villa Borghese in 1784/85, at which time he was elected *principe* of San Luca. His most valued collaborator and pupil was the Tyrolese Christoph Unterberger, who painted alongside his master at the stanza dei papiri.[32]

The Palazzo Zuccari, however, was not only the residence of German followers of Mengs and, in his first years in Rome, of Winckelmann himself. The influx of Englishmen was just as important. Several of these were to found the Royal Academy in London. Chief among them was Sir Joshua Reynolds, in 1768 the first president of this artistic institution, who stayed there in 1752/53, while copying in the Sistine chapel. With him was the sculptor Joseph Wilton, who became conservator of the Royal Academy, and the architect Matthew Brett the younger. Later some of Reynolds' pupils appear to have followed his advice and lodged in the Casa Zuccari during their Roman sojourn.

But, from the Roman perspective, the most important and influential Briton associated with Mengs, Winckelmann, and the Zuccari circle, although he did not reside there, was Gavin Hamilton. Despite some early works on themes from Homer, completed between 1762 and 1765, which were to stir the admiration of Winckelmann, Hamilton confined himself mainly to paintings from non-classical sources taken from Scottish history and from Milton. From the middle of the 1770s on there occurred a marked change in taste toward classicism, which reached its climax in the eight paintings on the theme of Paris and Helen in the Stanze d'Elena in the Villa Borghese, executed between 1782 and 1784. Although Hamilton's concept of ideal beauty was formed from the works at the Belvedere, as was Winckelmann's, and from those he himself had excavated, he failed to experience the severity of pure Greek art at first hand. To that extent his paintings did not fully meet the austere demands of academic neoclassicism. As a younger neoclassicist, the Swiss Heinrich Füssli, put it in 1805: "Though he was familiar with the antique, the forms of Hamilton have neither its correctness nor characteristic purity."[33] Nonetheless he brought the process of neoclassic art a great deal further. And by taking the young Canova under his wings after his arrival in Rome would contribute to its ultimate triumph.[34]

In the interval some changes took place at the Académie de France à Rome, which would advance the ideal of the theoretician of neoclassicism. In 1751 Charles-Joseph Natoire became director of the institution. As a student in Rome he had tried

[32] Noack, *Deutschtum in Rom*, 1:324–26. [33] Quoted from Irwin, "Gavin Hamilton," 102.

[34] Ibid., 87–88, 95–96; Voss, *Die Malerei des Barock*, 661–62; Ceschi, *Le chiese di Roma dagli inizi del neoclassico*, 19; *Settecento a Roma*, 125; Körte, *Der Palazzo Zuccari*, 54; Eugenio Riccòmini, "La scultura del Settecento e gli inizi del Canova," in *Nuove idee e nuova arte nel '700 italiano* (Rome, 1977), 66.

to harmonize the style of Maratta and Luti with that of François Boucher. But now he began to share the interests of Panini: his love for the ancient ruins set amidst the Roman countryside. During his tenure, French painting was also attracted by subjects of traditional classical mythology, inspired by the "Pompeian" vogue. In 1756 Winckelmann's *Gedanken über die Nachahmung der Griechen* was translated into French, and in conjunction with the efforts of Caylus soon began to pay off. The French painter Greuze was one of the first to apply some of Winckelmann's precepts, in his *Severus and Caraccala*, which he submitted to the French academy in Rome as part of his application for admission in 1769.

A key moment, however, occurred in 1775 with the arrival of Joseph-Marie Vien, himself a former pupil of Natoire, as director. Under him the French academy became a true center of classical taste. More importantly Vien transmitted his taste to his star pupil Jacques-Louis David.[35]

In the eyes of many of his contemporaries the Parisian David was to realize the highest expression of neoclassicism. Originally a pupil of Boucher, from whom he picked up a purely naturalistic conception of inspiration, he was converted by Vien to a preference for the classical Italian taste. Apparently David never really liked Rome, but for some as yet unknown reason, when in Rome, antiquity conquered David. The crisis appears to have occurred during a month's tour in Naples in 1779 in the company of the young sculptor and antiquary Quatremère de Quincy. Not yet sure of his mastery, however, David left for Paris.

Some years later David returned to the Eternal City to follow his favorite pupil and disciple Jean-Germain Drouais, where the latter expected to receive a stipend for study at the French academy. Perhaps not by chance he took up lodgings at the Palazzo Zuccari, where Winckelmann had earlier started the work that would usher in the neoclassic era and where Hamilton and the younger disciples of Winckelmann were still active. Locking himself up in a studio close to the Piazza del Popolo he worked on what was to be the most memorable accomplishment in Roman painting in the second half of the eighteenth century.

When David exhibited his *Serment des Horaces* at his studio in August 1785, it took Rome by storm. The work was greeted as an authentic manifestation of the Roman spirit and the most glorious expression of the classical revival. No doubt an exaggerated infatuation. For in all honesty the painting did not conform to Winckelmann's standard of *Nachahmung*, emulation and self-perfection through imitation. David did not imitate, he copied and copied blatantly. The whole composition was taken from Beaufort's *Serment de Brutus*, in itself a French version

[35] Jean-Marie Pérouse de Montclos, "Piranèse, les français et le classicisme international," in Georges Brunel (ed.), *Piranèse et les Français. Colloque tenu à la Villa Médicis, 12–14 mai 1976* (Rome, 1978), 419–20; Lapauze, *Histoire de l'Acadèmie de France à Rome*, 1: vii, xi–xiv, 1–2, 7, 124–25, 135–36, 175–80, 184, 203, 208–9, 219–22, 248–50, 265–66, 380–83, 386; De Brosses, *Lettres familières*, 53, 153–55, 186–88; Rosenblum, *Transformations in Late Eighteenth Century Art*, 3–6, 56–57; Volpi, "Corrado Giaquinto," 275; *Settecento a Roma*, 222; Arisi, *G. B. Panini*, 67–70.

of Hamilton's of 1763/64; individual parts, such as the old woman and the grief-stricken Camilla, were derived from various works by Poussin.[36]

Whatever the criticism and shortcomings of this work may have been, symbolically it marked the arrival of full-blown neoclassic painting in Rome. There can be no doubt that this style is a strange phenomenon. Based on postulates drawn from ancient Greek, or at least Hellenistic, art by a German expatriate and executed by a French painter, the pupil of French painters, who at best entertained a love–hate relationship with Rome, the work was born in the papal capital. In one sense it marked perhaps the highest achievement of painting in Rome during the ancien regime, yet it was an alien implant, signalizing the nadir of Roman art. Perhaps more clearly than any other aspect of Roman life painting reflects that loss of direction and energy that hung like a heavy pall over the city, gradually depriving it of cohesion and originality, a long way from the buoyancy of the Counter Reformation ethos.

The baroque age was an era of hierarchies, even among the artistic genres. Historical paintings took precedence over all others, because of the belief that art was concerned with action and emotion. Figure painters ranked lower, and the painters of landscapes took a humble station, frequently struggling to be admitted into the academies; although their position would improve later, when landscapes were enlivened with small figures which even figure painters did not disdain to paint in.

Landscape painting and its cousin, *vedute* painting, can be said to be a Roman creation, yet it was not usually Roman painters who practiced it. In the sixteenth century it was better left to Flemings who were proficient at it. The Roman school of landscape painting can be said to have been started by Annibale Caracci, who derived elements of the style from Venetian masters such as Veronese and Tintoretto. But it was left to the Bolognese Domenichino, who had worked under Annibale, to establish what may be called classical landscape as a genre worthy of academic respect. He combined grandeur with the evocation of a pastoral spirit, thus enabling landscape to rise above the status of a merely decorative art.[37]

Domenichino influenced Nicolas Poussin and Claude Lorrain, two of the four masters who in the Rome of the seventeenth century would determine the

[36] Maurice Andrieux, *Les Français à Rome* (Paris, 1968), 190–92; Gerstenberg, *Winckelmann und Mengs*, 22–24; Anita Brookner, *Jacques-Louis David* (London, 1980), 23, 68–79; Arlette Serullaz *et al.* (eds.), *David e Roma: Mostra, dicembre 1981 – febbraio 1982* (Rome, 1982), 9–13, 18; Edgar Wind, "The Sources of David's *Horaces*," *Journal of the Warburg and Courtauld Institutes*, 4 (1940–41), 124, 128–30; Hautecoeur, *Rome et la renaissance de l'antiquité*, 152, 156–61; Rosenblum, *Transformations in Late Eighteenth Century Art*, 9, 19–20, 68–72, 90–91, 102–3; Körte, *Der Palazzo Zuccari*, 56–57; Lapauze, *Histoire de l'Académie de France*, 363–71, 410; Voss, *Die Malerei des Barock*, 56; Ceschi, *Le chiese di Roma dagli inizi del neoclassico*, 31; Montaiglon and Guiffrey (eds.), *Correspondance des directeurs de l'Académie de France*, 14: 19–20.

[37] Waterhouse, *Painting in Britain*, 207; Arisi, *G. B. Panini*, 46; Waterhouse, *Roman Baroque Painting*, 9; Barlow, *Ideal and Classical Landscape*, 5–6, 18–19; Rezio Buscaroli, *La pittura di paesaggio in Italia* (Bologna, 1935), 74–75.

international landscape painting of the late baroque, by fusing the Italian feeling for form with the northern sense of nature. The other two were Gaspard Dughet and Salvator Rosa. The Norman Poussin's landscapes are mostly the work of his later years, after he had abandoned the Venetian lyricism of his earlier years. Like all his later works they are classical in the most extreme sense, so austere that they could not be fully appreciated at the time. Claude Gellée, called Lorrain by the Italians, was probably the more eminent landscape painter at this time. His landscapes are truly Virgilian. He was a classical artist in the use of Greek mythology and of Roman architecture, but unlike Poussin he made no attempt at archeological accuracy. His architecture is of all periods and, although he went out to make pencil sketches in the Roman Campagna, his gentle views present a world set in an indeterminate landscape.[38]

To the Neapolitan Salvator Rosa, poet, musician, and actor as well as painter, who stayed in Rome between 1635 and 1639, we owe the introduction of the more savage aspects of nature, melodramatic crags, overcast skies, broken tree trunks. He was responsible for initiating the new landscape genre which British theorists labelled the "Sublime," in contrast to the "Beautiful" of Claude Lorrain. But despite his realism Rosa also introduced the fictitious landscape with the architectural perspective of the ancient ruins, which would wed together the art of the landscapist and the vedutist. The Roman-born Gaspard Dughet, also called Gaspard Poussin because he married Poussin's sister, was first influenced by Rosa and later by Poussin and Lorrain. From them he was able to develop his own original style, inspired directly by his study of wild nature in the Campagna. A very productive artist, he exercised a considerable influence on his contemporaries all over Europe and on successive developments in romantic landscape painting.[39]

In the last two decades of the seventeenth century Roman landscape painting was joined to a type of topographical view or *veduta*, characterized by its documentary precision and by a choice of vistas and viewpoints that was to enjoy great popularity. It was particularly suited as a genre for fostering the new antiquarian interests that accompanied the fashion of the Grand Tour. The principal painter associated with this new development was the Romanized Dutchman Gaspard van Wittel, father of the architect Luigi Vanvitelli. He became the bridge between the Roman landscape painters and the older Dutch vedutisti. As a landscape painter, like his Dutch fellow-countrymen in Rome, who were collectively nicknamed the "Bent-Veughels," he was influenced by Lorrain.[40]

[38] Ibid., 81–82; Richard Eisen, *Die deutsche Landschaftsmalerei des Spätbarock* (Leipzig, 1936), 18–20; Rudolf Wittkower, "The Role of Classical Models in Bernini's and Poussin's Preparatory Work," in *Studies in the Italian Baroque* (London, 1975), 112–14; Fokker, *Roman Baroque Art*, 1:18; Barlow, *Ideal and Classical Landscape*, 6–8, 15, 25.

[39] Ibid., 27; Buscaroli, *La pittura di paesaggio*, 83, 313–15; Nolfo di Carpegna (ed.), *Paesisti e vedutisti a Roma nel '600 e nel '700* (Rome, 1956), 18, 30; Waterhouse, *Roman Baroque Painting*, 74–75.

[40] Briganti, "Paestum and View Painting," 56; Buscaroli, *La pittura di paesaggio*, 88; Barlow, *Ideal and Classical Landscape*, 8; *Settecento a Roma*, 232; Noack, *Deutschtum in Rom*, 1:212–13.

The Romano-Dutch tradition of landscapes of the Campagna with inns, ruins, and animals was carried on by Pieter van Bloemen. He, in turn, was surpassed by his namesake Jan Frans van Bloemen, nicknamed Orizzonte, who became the great disseminator of a type of classical landscape of Arcadian and pastoral taste, which had its greatest vogue between the end of the seventeenth and the first decades of the eighteenth century. Unlike Van Wittel, Orizzonte no longer sought out his views up the distant Tiber valley or on the Alban hills, but stopped at the edge of the city, the outline of which was henceforth almost always in the background of the picture.[41]

Among the earlier eighteenth-century landscape painters in the city there were only two native Romans. Andrea Locatelli combined in his classical subjects and his country scenes influences derived of various origins, from Rosa to the Bolognese, in an elegant style which evolved over time from the more classicist and conventional character of his earlier landscapes to the picturesque and scenographic of his more mature period.[42]

The other Roman contemporary of Locatelli was Paolo Anesi, son of a Venetian silkworker, who had come to Rome under Clement XI. He shared many characteristics with Locatelli. Although there is no documented contact between the two, it is difficult to imagine that they did not know one another among the group of artists who worked for Cardinal Ottoboni. While residing in the Palazzo Farnese, Anesi was also a neighbor to Panini, who had his workshop next door in the palace. Through his wife he became the son-in-law of the distinguished architect Giuseppe Sardi. Anesi worked in two elements, as a painter and an etcher, alternating his activities as a pure landscapist with that of a vedutist. As engraver, Anesi offers us the natural aspect of Rome rendered with immediacy, with no monuments to clutter the scene, except such ancient ruins as were integral to the landscape itself. Many of his works are known to have ended up in English private collections. Indeed, by 1756, Anesi moved from the area of the Palazzo Farnese to the Via del Corso where the foreigners congregated, to be nearer to his clientele.[43]

Anesi and Locatelli had some lesser successors among Italian landscapists – as distinct from vedutisti – such as Paolo Monaldi, whose work was popular among the princely houses in Rome; but landscape painting now became the specialty of the French. They had the inspiration of Claude Lorrain, as well as Salvator Rosa and Van Wittel. The earliest of these was the Lyonnais Adrien Manglard, who spent the greater part of his life in Rome, where he died in 1760. Both in his paintings and etchings of seascapes and landscapes he showed the influence of Van

[41] Buscaroli, *La pittura di paesaggio*, 87; Barlow, *Ideal and Classical Landscape*, 8, 12; *Settecento a Roma*, 63; Carpegna (ed.), *Paesisti e vedutisti a Roma*, 10–11. Lavagnino, "Roma nel Settecento," 19; Lavagnino, "La pittura," 27–28.

[42] Fokker, *Roman Baroque Art*, 1:329; Buscaroli, *La pittura di paesaggio*, 336–37; Carpegna (ed.), *Paesisti e vedutisti a Roma*, 23; Barlow, *Ideal and Classical Landscape*, 23.

[43] Michel and Michel, "Recherches biographiques sur Paolo Anesi," 323–28, 333–36; Maria Catelli Isola, "L'incisione a Roma nel '700." In *Settecento a Roma. Mostra, 19 marzo–31 maggio 1959* (Rome, 1959), 381; *Settecento a Roma*, 44, 382.

Wittel. One of his pupils was the Avignonese Claude-Joseph Vernet. While in Rome Vernet spent five years, between 1748 and 1753 at the Palazzo Zuccari, where he was able to jettison as much as possible the scenographic residues that still adhered to the Italian vedutisti and landscape painters, in order to achieve something more realistic from the point of view of aerial perspective and light. In 1745 he married the daughter of an English naval captain, which opened up a market for his works among her compatriots.[44]

An exhibition at the Louvre in 1753 of Vernet's work cast the spell of the Roman landscape over the young Parisian Hubert Robert. Having already studied in Paris in the studio of the sculptor Michelangelo Slodtz, who had once worked with Panini in Rome, Robert sought the advice of Panini when he arrived in the Eternal City. Under the influence of the Italian master the love for landscape would give way to that of Roman ruins and architecture, in effect putting an end to the French phase of Italian landscapists.[45]

The taste for paintings of classical architecture in France was confirmed by the favor extended to the Italian Gian Paolo Panini, when he was unanimously elected to the Académie royale of Paris in 1732. A native of Piacenza, who had started his education in his home town, where the prince of perspective in stage design, Ferdinando Galli-Bibbiena, held sway in the service of the Farnese dukes of Parma from 1695 to 1715, Panini moved to Rome at the invitation of some fellow Piacentines to study figure painting with Benedetto Luti. Around 1718 he seems to have discovered the works of Rosa, which he freely interpreted in his use of color and light. Like Rosa, whose influence was still very much alive, Panini preferred to be considered a painter of figures, of "stories." Two years later, however, we begin to find the first real *vedute* alongside his "stories." The type of *vedute* he preferred were the so-called *prospettivi* or *capricci*. In fact, it was Panini who made them popular. A *capriccio* is a work in which the artist, instead of painting particular ruins in isolation, took his models from different places and grouped them together in an invented setting without regard to their actual distances. Nonetheless, Panini reconstructed the actual remains of both the ancient and the sacred city with extreme faithfulness and precision. A contemporary of the early Roman Arcadia, Panini did show some affinities to the literary movement. The landscape in which his classical remains are set reflect some of the longings for the fanciful and ideal Arcadian world peopled by the humble and rustic.[46]

44 *Settecento a Roma*, 146, 152, 220, 387; Michel and Michel, "Recherches biographiques sur Paolo Anesi," 328; Buscaroli, *La pittura di paesaggio*, 88–89; Körte, *Der Palazzo Zuccari*, 57 n. 15; Tristan Leclere, *Hubert Robert et les paysagistes français du XVIIIe siècle* (Paris, 1913), 35–39.

45 Pierre de Nolhac, *Peintres français en Italie* (Paris, 1934), 57–93; Leclere, *Robert et les paysagistes français*, 62; Arisi, *G. B. Panini*, 67–70; *Settecento a Roma*, 193; Carpegna (ed.), *Paesisti e vedutisti a Roma*, 29.

46 Adolfo Venturi, "I grandi pittori di rovine, Pannini e Piranesi," *Roma* (1925), 207; Leclere, *Robert et les paysagistes français*, 60; Leandro Ozzòla, *Gian Paolo Pannini, pittore. Cinquanta tavole con introduzione* (Turin, 1921), 5–12; Arisi, *G. B. Panini*, 17–21, 45–54, 58; Lavagino, "La pittura," 28; Voss, *Die Malerei des Barock*, 626–38; De Rinaldis, *L'arte in Roma*, 171–72.

The art of the *vedute*, views of Rome, both ancient and modern, as separate from the landscape was to reach its zenith, not among painters but in the etchings of the copperplate engravers. In eighteenth-century Rome the preeminent exponents of the art were Giuseppe Vasi and Giovanni Battista Piranesi. *Vedute* owe their ancestry to a marriage between the works of the landscape artists and the prints which had spread throughout Europe a knowledge of the most famous and beautiful of Rome's antiquities as far back as the High Renaissance. Most of those early prints were published as individual plates and could be assembled by the purchasers into anthologies. The first illustrated volume to be deliberately restricted to the finest antique sculpture was not published until 1638. It was the work of the French artist François Perrier. In 1704 the Roman publisher Domenico de' Rossi produced a large and lavishly illustrated volume of ancient Roman statues, with a few modern works by Bernini and others thrown in. In his endeavor to set up qualitative standards his book was the most authoritative that had appeared up to that time. Other collections of etchings edited by such notable scholars as Bottari, Winckelmann, and Visconti were to appear throughout the eighteenth century as new archeological finds were added.[47]

But it was Giuseppe Vasi who raised the reproduction of the Roman ruins in prints to a high art. A Sicilian by birth, his beginnings as engraver coincided with the accession of Charles VII of Naples. Thus, when he came to Rome at the age of 26, he already enjoyed royal patronage and was duly installed in the Farnese palace, in return for which he was to exalt the Roman presence of the Neapolitan monarchy by recording ceremonial events. But his purpose in coming to Rome was to refine his taste, widen the horizon of his knowledge, and find friends who would facilitate his career. At the palace he found a friend in Sebastiano Conca. In Rome was born the idea of his *Delle Magnificenze di Roma Antica e Moderna*, the publication of which, according to a plan which only slowly and methodically matured, was begun in 1747 and completed in 1761. But before he embarked upon this large enterprise he learned and improved his technique.

During his first four years in the city, Vasi became acquainted with contemporary architects and stage designers, and acquired a good knowledge of the magnificent collection of prints in the possession of Cardinal Neri Corsini. But, above all, he came in close contact with Canaletto and other Venetian etchers, whose silvery tone would somewhat modify the grimy sootiness of his provincial training. By 1744 the first edition of *Vedute sul Tevere* had appeared and preparation for the *Magnificenze* was also under way, though perhaps not in the format it was to have in its final stage. For it was only in 1747 that Vasi published the first book of his great work. It dealt with the gates of Rome. After an interval the second book, illustrating the principal piazze, followed in 1750. The tenth and last volume with views of gardens and villas appeared in 1761. But there is no need to think that the two hundred or so

[47] Haskell, and Penny, *Taste and the Antique*, 17–23.

illustrations of this work were all engraved in order of publication. The artist carried them out as inspiration and opportunity dictated and waited until he could insert them in the appropriate volume.[48]

At the Farnese palace Vasi carried on the fine tradition of Pierre Le Gros and Conca. His studio became the resort of young artists from all nations, including Florentines and Frenchmen from the academy, one of whom, Nicholas-Henri Jardin, became his pupil. But his most renowned student, Giovanni Battista Piranesi, would also become his bitter rival. Piranesi, who came from the Venetian mainland, arrived in Rome in 1740, with his imagination about ancient Rome as told in the histories of Livy already fired. Having been in the city for two years, he approached Vasi to teach him the art of etching with a single cut. This was at a time when Vasi was already at work on plates for his *Magnificenze*. Within six weeks he had learned all that Vasi could teach him, but that did not satisfy Piranesi. The story has it that he attacked his teacher in a fit of fury because he thought Vasi was hiding from him the true secret of using etching acid. Vasi promptly dismissed him. On leaving the shop, Piranesi may have taken some of Vasi's plates with him. In any case Piranesi was able to bring out his *Varie vedute* in 1745 to capture the market before the publication of Vasi's *Magnificenze* in 1747.[49]

In the long run the rivalry of these two artists would turn to the glory of Rome, as each exalted the city in his own way. But in the interval Piranesi visited Venice and spent a period in the studio of the greatest painter of his time, G. B. Tiepolo, who happened to be just then engaged in some fine etching. As a result of his experience with Tiepolo, Piranesi's later sketches became much lighter and freer in contrast to his rather rigid earlier drawings.

On his return from Venice to Rome, an act of desertion which lost him all respect in his homeland, Piranesi settled on the Corso opposite the Académie de France and turned to etching views of Rome at the rate of one a day. At this point he was unlikely to have had much choice in the selection of the sights his publisher Fausto Amidei would order him to etch, views the publisher thought would sell to the tourists, mainly those of Renaissance and baroque palaces. But once given free rein to produce the ruins of antiquity, his style altered immediately and his plates came to life. The firstfruits of this series of ruins were the 25 views of what became later known as *Alcune vedute di archi trionfali ed altri monumenti*, published in 1748 and dedicated to Giovanni Bottari. By then Piranesi had preserved for us eighteenth-century Rome in a long series of *vedute*, 133 in all, which were to establish his reputation and capture for him the influence over the French academy once exercised by Vasi.

48 Alfredo Petrucci, "I primi venticinque anni del Vasi a Roma," *L'Urbe*, 6 (1941), 11–20; Hautecoeur, *Rome et la renaissance de l'antiquité*, 8–9, 76–78; Justi, *Winckelmann und seine Zeitgenossen*, 2:145; Isola, "L'incisione a Roma," 381; Olivier Michel, "L'*Accademia*," 2:599–601.

49 Scott, *Piranesi*, 7–18, 25–29, 45; Petrucci, "I primi venticinque anni del Vasi," 18–19; Henry Millon, "Vasi-Piranesi-Juvarra," in Georges Brunel (ed.), *Piranèse et les Français. Colloque tenu à la Villa Médicis. 12–14 mai 1976* (Rome, 1978), 346–54.

In 1755 Piranesi decided upon a full coverage of the *Antichità romane* in four volumes. The publication of the *Antichità* was something of an international event. The monuments of Rome still held a preeminent position in European taste despite the incipient controversy with the champions of Greece. Piranesi was thus able to draw reflected glory from his subject matter. The *Antichità* was indeed a remarkable work; its very size, four heavy volumes with about 250 illustrations and maps, distinguished it from the average antiquarian tome. But since Piranesi lacked the ability to organize the enormous mass of available material it was not so much a systematic treatise as an anthology of whatever seized the author's imagination as the work progressed.

Piranesi earned his living by producing *vedute*, but such work did not give his fertile imagination enough scope. It was to find its expression in two groups of *capricci* etchings, the *Grotteschi* and the *Carceri*. The mythological allusion and rustic settings of the *Grotteschi*, with their enigmatic and elegiac subjects, may have been inspired by the nature of the Arcadian meetings, of which institution Piranesi had become a member in 1750. It was not until the Romantic Movement of the nineteenth century that the *Carceri* really came into their own. In them, Piranesi followed a whole convention of prison sets on stage which had grown up since the start of the century, beginning with Ferdinando Galli-Bibbiena, the most prominent of stage designers.[50]

Piranesi's output of etchings was in the region of one thousand plates. When he died, his sons Francesco and Pietro carried on the family business. But by now the *vedute* under the influence of the Italian masters in Rome had more in common with stage design than with landscape, in contrast to Venice where it continued to adhere to a more realistic and free observation of nature, while retaining some of the romantic tradition of Rosa.[51]

With the Romans abandoning the Roman landscape (it would only be revived after 1870 with Nino Costa and his school) for *vedute*, the northerners took over the tradition. It was probably Vernet, during his residence at the Palazzo Zuccari, who, in 1752, persuaded the Welshman Richard Wilson to abandon portraiture and turn to landscape art. He became the first British landscape painter of renown in Rome. Living off commissions from Englishmen on the Grand Tour, such as the second Earl of Dartmouth, Wilson used the years spent in Rome as an experimental stage in his artistic development, painting landscapes in the manner of Claude Lorrain and Salvator Rosa. In the best of these he abandoned the influences of scenography and

[50] Elena Bassi, "Il Piranesi tra Venezia e Roma," in *Nuove idee e nuova arte nel '700 italiano* (Rome, 1977), 451; Pastor, *Geschichte der Päpste*, 16, pt 1: 107–8; 16, pt 3: 49–50; Justi, *Winckelmann und seine Zeitgenossen*, 2: 435–37; Fleming, *Robert Adam*, 165–67, 207; Scott, *Piranesi*, 50–59, 109–11, 117–27, 149–57, 224–29, 247–54, 293–94, 299, 314 n. 12, 318 n. 26; Andrieux, *Daily Life in Papal Rome*, 177, 188; Ceschi, *Le chiese di Roma dagli inizi del neoclassico*, 21–22; Hautecoeur, *Rome et la renaissance de l'antiquité*, 102–5; Thomas J. McCormick, "Piranesi and Clérisseau's Vision of Classical Antiquity," in Georges Brunel (ed.), *Piranèse et les Français. Colloque tenu à la Villa Médicis. 12–14 mai 1976* (Rome, 1978), 308–10. [51] Buscard Li, *La pittura di paesaggio*, 62, 85, 334–35.

ruins completely for naturalness and light. On his return to London, he became one of the founders of the Royal Academy and used the numerous drawings he made during his Roman sojourn as the basis for his series of "Italian landscapes." Among the other British landscapists in Rome during the latter part of the century were the two Scots, the watercolorist Richard Cooper and the popular Jacob Moore. The latter became a protégé of Marcantonio Borghese.[52]

German painters had always concentrated more on landscape and still life than Italians had. There may have been as many as 1,500 of them at one time or other in Rome. At the end of the eighteenth century landscape painting, both in the form of *vedute* and classical landscapes, in oils, water color, or etchings, was carried on predominantly by Germans. Many of the view painters, however, in search of more archeological objectivity in the wake of the rise of neoclassicism, preferred Naples to Rome, where they were close to Paestum and Herculaneum. The earliest of these was probably Jakob Philipp Hackert, who after visiting Naples relocated there from Rome in 1786. He was followed by Frenchmen and Englishmen. But the more conventional German landscape painters and etchers returned to a preference for nature in the footsteps of Anesi. They etched and painted the environs of Rome, the Castelli, the cascades of Tivoli. Alexander Trippel, who settled in Rome in 1768 and opened a studio in the Via San Basilio, became the center of a circle of such German and Dutch artists, among them Franz I. J. Kobell, Wilhelm F. Gmelin, and Jean Grandjean.[53]

Roman landscape painting, therefore, while it played a principal role in carrying the glory of the city all over Europe in the eighteenth century, was in fact much less rooted in the Roman milieu than the other genres were. Apart from the work of Locatelli, Anesi, and, in a qualified sense, Panini, Vasi, and Piranesi, it was the pursuit of non-Italians, mainly Dutch, French and German. Because of this fact, the history of the genre is much less indicative of the general pattern of spiritual exhaustion we noted in the other sectors. Nevertheless, in one respect it shared the general fate when, with the rediscovery of interest in Paestum, Rome lost its primacy as a source for classical models to Naples.

As in the case of painting, by the end of the seventeenth century the feeling had arisen that with the work of Bernini the apogee of Roman baroque sculpture had been reached. He and his followers held the field almost uncontested until his death in 1682. He was active almost until the end and had taken most of the able sculptors in Rome into his studio to carry out his commissions. The last belated followers, not of Bernini himself, but of Berninism, tended to become enfeebled and to reduce the

52 Ibid., 88–89; Constable, *Richard Wilson*, 15–29; *Settecento a Roma*, 86, 153, 229–30; Bartoccini, *Roma nell'Ottocento*, 695.

53 Noack, *Deutschtum in Rom*, 1:212–13, 358–59, 376; Isola, "L'incisione a Roma," 381–82; Briganti, "Paestum and View Painting," 57; Körte, *Der Palazzo Zuccari*, 57; *Settecento a Roma*, 120, 124, 133, 188, 216, 390.

great fantastic impulses of the baroque to simplistic illustrative schemes, relying on unrealistic polychromatic effects, mixing marbles of different colors with granite and porphyry, and even gilded bronze.[54]

The year 1695 marks the watershed in Roman sculpture. That year the altar of St. Ignatius at the church of the Gesù, a vast project involving a dozen or more sculptors, was started. From an iconographical standpoint, the altar characterizes a final phase in the history of the triumphant church, a theme that belonged to the previous era, but none of the sculptors who worked on it, except the aged Lorenzo Ottoni, can be said to belong to Bernini's school. Those who received the largest commissions were not even Italian; they were French. Pierre Le Gros, that rallying point of the French at the Farnese palace, received the commission for the statuary group to the right of the altar and the silver statue in the center; and Jean-Baptiste Théodon, who tended to be more classical than Le Gros, the statuary group to the left. They and other French masters, such as Pierre-Etienne Monnot, although not jettisoning the Roman models, clearly worked in their own style. Working alongside these, but separate from the French artists, was the Genoese Angelo De' Rossi, who also had his studio at the Farnese palace.[55]

The Jesuits must have been pleased with Pierre Le Gros' work on the altar, for they commissioned him to do a statue of St. Stanislas Kostka for their novitiate at S. Andrea al Quirinale. The work, carried out in 1702/3, was something unexpected for Rome. Within the limits possible with marble it attempts to reproduce realistic polychromy, something for which the Roman sculptural tradition had not prepared us.[56]

When Clement XI assumed the chair of St. Peter in 1700, the nave of the basilica of St. John Lateran appeared much as Innocent X had left it after Francesco Borromini's renovation for the Holy Year of 1650. The colored marble niches set rhythmically in the spaces between the pilasters had failed to receive the statues they were intended to frame, namely the Twelve Apostles. Clement's predecessor Innocent XII, at the prompting of the Lateran archpriest Cardinal Benedetto Pamphilj, had set aside some money. So the new pope appointed a congregation to oversee what would be one of the last large-scale papal artistic undertakings. As artistic directors, two non-sculptors, the painter Carlo Maratta and the architect Carlo Fontana were named, of whom Maratta played the more significant role. By 1703 he had outlined the preliminary designs for the figures. Fontana's part was only to see that the statues fitted the architecture. It would appear that Maratta's influence was considerable; he conceived the pose, the contours and the arrangement of the drapery for the sculptures. The artists who were commissioned for the work were both Frenchmen, such as Le Gros, and Italians; the most

[54] Enggass, *Early Eighteenth-Century Sculpture*, 1:29; Santangelo, "La scultura," 33.

[55] Enggass, *Early Eighteenth-Century Sculpture*, 1:ix, 4, 18, 15; Fokker, *Roman Baroque Art*, 1:18; Olivier Michel, "L'*Accademia*," 2:576–78.

[56] Enggass, *Early Eighteenth-Century Sculpture*, 1:43.

11 The nave of St. John Lateran with the statues of the twelve Apostles

important among these was the Milanese Camillo Rusconi. He was given the task of modelling and sculpturing in succession the statues of St. Andrew, St. John, St. Matthew, and St. James the Greater, between 1708 and 1718.

Rusconi's work signalized a change of style toward greater severity and a rejection of pictorial decorativeness. The artist never worked in colored marble or stone. His spiritual formation developed alongside that of his close friend Giuseppe Chiari under the guidance of Maratta, of which his Lateran apostles bear ample testimony. Not only did Rusconi transpose the Marattan fashion into sculpture, but he passed its elements on to his numerous distinguished pupils, Giovanni Battista Maini, Pietro Bracci, Filippo della Valle and his namesake, the Ticinese Giuseppe Rusconi, best known for the *Four Virtues* he executed for the Corsini mortuary chapel at St. John Lateran. The list forms an honor roll of Italian sculptors in Rome in the first part of the eighteenth century.[57]

[57] Michael Conforti, "Planning the Lateran Apostles," in Henry A. Millon (ed.), *Studies in Italian Art and Architecture. Fifteenth through Eighteenth Centuries* (Cambridge, Mass., and London, 1980), 243–50; Frederick Den Broeder, "The Lateran Apostles. The Major Sculpture Commission in Eighteenth-Century Rome," *Apollo*, N.S., 63 (1967), 360–65; Enggass, *Early Eighteenth-Century Sculpture*, 1:39–40; 55–56, 89–94; Santangelo, "La scultura," 31; Sandor Baumgarten, "Les oeuvres de Camillo Rusconi à Rome," *Revue de l'art ancien et modern*, 70 (1936), 233–38; Johns, "Art Patronage of Pope Clement XI Albani," 166–73.

Another major commission was the series of monumental marble statues for the founders of religious orders in St. Peter's. The first of these was Pierre Le Gros' statue of St. Domenic. Giuseppe Rusconi completed, some time after 1728, the statue of St. Ignatius. It shows the saint trampling a large allegorical figure representing Heresy. This rather belated symbol of the Counter Reformation may be attributed to the fact that the Jesuits were a society already under siege, in particular because of the unconventional rites they had introduced in China, and therefore aimed at vindicating their orthodoxy. Another statue in the series, that of St. Elijah for the Carmelites, was carried out by Agostino Cornacchini. A Florentine, he naturally became the protégé of Clement XII and the Corsini family. He is perhaps best remembered for his attempted restoration of the *Laocoön* and for the statue of the *Equestrian Charlemagne*, which stands in the portico of St. Peter's opposite Bernini's *Equestrian Constantine*.[58]

From the third and fourth decade on, and more clearly after the middle of the century, works more evocative of ancient forms began to make their appearance. The French artists, mistrusting the more ostentatious Roman sculpture, were the exponents of this fashion. Their style was really determined by the French tradition of classicism, a "reasonable" classicism, which, unlike the later neoclassicism, involved no conscious severance from existing traditions, but sought to hold a balance between antiquity, history, and nature. Edme Bouchardon, who stayed in Rome between 1723 and 1732, was an early example. His bust of Baron von Stosch in the fashion of antiquity was one of the first of its kind. Michelangelo Slodtz held a special place in their ranks. His Roman masterpiece was the statue of St. Bruno, founder of the Carthusian order, in the series of St. Peter's, which he executed in 1744. The saint is shown in the act of refusing the mitre. In it the influence of Bernini is still noticeable, with the artist twisting the figure of the saint in a wavy line. Just before leaving Rome, Slodtz carried out the funeral monument for Alessandro Gregorio Capponi at the church of San Giovanni de' Fiorentini. Here the female figure in the act of meditating has a posture and drapery that would not be unknown in the neoclassical period and, given the different circumstances, could bear comparison with that in Canova's funeral monument for Clement XIV.[59]

The French sculptors only represented an interlude in Roman sculpture. The center stage was held by the pupils of Camillo Rusconi. The rather ponderous Milanese Giovanni Battista Maini was outshone by Pietro Bracci and Filippo della Valle. The Roman Bracci, son of a wood sculptor, who was one of the early artists to take up residence and work in the Palazzo Zuccari in 1724, had much in common with his master, although he was superior to Rusconi in the conception of his work.

[58] Enggass, *Early Eighteenth-Century Sculpture*, 1:22, 44–45, 193–200.

[59] Riccòmini, "La scultura del Settecento e gli inizi del Canova," 65–66; Hautecoeur, *Rome et la renaissance de l'antiquité*, 180–82, 184–86; Ceschi, *Le chiese di Roma dagli inizi del neoclassico*, 15–16; Golzio, "Le opere romane di Michelangelo Slodtz," 388–91; Schudt, *Italienreisen*, 330–32.

There is no doubt, however, that Bracci was trained in baroque classicism and that this style inspired the major part of his designs.

Like many of his contemporary sculptors, Bracci found his special gift in creating funeral monuments. Indeed, they were virtually the only avenues for important commissions left in Rome. One of the earliest of these was the tomb of Fabrizio Paolucci in the church of San Marcello on the Corso in 1726. But his crowning achievement was the monument to Benedict XIV in St. Peter's, executed in 1759. There is no great novelty about the architecture of the monument as a whole. The basic prototype, by then well established, had been created by Bernini, but had an ancestry that went back through Guglielmo della Porta's tomb of Paul III in St. Peter's and to Michelangelo's tombs in the Medici chapel in Florence. In the form established by Bernini, the effigy of the pope rests on a high podium in the center of a niche or above a door. In his tomb of Urban VIII the pontiff is enthroned with one hand raised in blessing. Below is the sarcophagus. What was new in Bracci's tomb was the position of Benedict XIV, depicted in the act of rising from his seat to bless. In it Bracci showed himself the portraitist par excellence.

Bracci's art was by no means confined to funereal sculpture, however. Commissioned to create sculptures for the Trevi fountain, he will be remembered for his Neptune. He lived through eight popes, from Innocent XII to Clement XIV, but it was the Corsini pope, Clement XII, who best recognized his ability. Having earlier contributed to the adornment of the Corsini chapel, Bracci was given in 1736 the highest honor to which a sculptor could aspire in his time. Clement XII asked him to create his statue, which was to be erected on the Campidoglio by the Roman authorities in appreciation of his generosity to the Capitoline museum.[60]

One of the most attractive and poetical sculptors of the eighteenth century and Bracci's great competitor was Filippo della Valle. Born in Florence, where he started his training in the studio of his uncle Giovanni Battista Foggini, Della Valle moved in 1725 to Rome, where he joined the studio of Rusconi shortly before the master's death. Thus he was never quite as beholden to Rusconi as Bracci.

For some 40 years Bracci and Della Valle were to work side by side as rivals, often contributing to the same project. Bracci was probably the better portraitist. In their larger works Filippo Della Valle reveals a greater tenderness and sensitivity, Bracci a greater force. But these are differences of personality rather than style. For the two artists were closer than they seem. Both sacrificed the grandeurs and sprightliness of the high baroque to a demand for charm, restraint, and elegance, and they carried on Camillo Rusconi's work of converting the papal tomb from a hieratic image of the vicar of Christ attended by allegories to an intimate

[60] Hugh Honour, "Filippo Della Valle," *The Connoisseur* (1959), 174; Gradara, *Bracci*, 9–21, 27, 38–42, 45–49, 55–74, 81–83, 91; *Settecento a Roma*, 145; Körte, *Der Palazzo Zuccari*, 53; Ceschi, *Le chiese di Roma dagli inizi del neoclassico*, 16–17; Escher, *Barock und Klassizismus*, 109[s]10; Enggass, *Early Eighteenth-Century Sculpture*, 1:52; De Rinaldis, *L'arte in Roma*, 100–3; Carl Ludwig Fernow, *Römische Studien. Erster Theil* (Zurich, 1806), 14–15.

conversation piece between the pope and two Roman ladies purporting to be the Virtues.

As a Florentine, Della Valle enjoyed the patronage of Clement XII and Cardinal Neri Corsini, who acted as his artistic adviser. He seemed to have had a special affinity for the Florentine architect Alessandro Galilei. Under his architectural direction he produced one of his youthful masterpieces, the statue of *Temperance* in the Corsini chapel at the Lateran and the relief of *The Preaching of the Baptist*, together with the statue of *Charity*, for the new facade of S. Giovanni de' Fiorentini. For the other Florentine architect in Rome, Ferdinando Fuga, he provided the statue of *S. Nicola Albergate* and the relief of the *Holy Spirit* on the balcony of blessing of the new facade of S. Maria Maggiore.

In the 1750s patronage dwindled and during the last eighteen years of his life Della Valle appears to have fulfilled only two important commissions, the statue of St. Theresa in St. Peter's and the two allegories of *Fertility* and *Health* for the Trevi fountain. These works are indicative of his inspirational and artistic fatigue. But there is no reason to suppose that Della Valle's chisel lay idle during much of the 1750s and 1760s. As we know, the most profitable source of patronage for all artists in Rome was provided not by the pope and the patrician families but by the tourists, especially the English. For this market he is known to have carved at least five statues and a bust; the most famous was his copy of an antique statue, the figure of *Pudicity*, for the monument of Lady Walpole at Westminster Abbey.[61]

With Bracci and Della Valle setting the example, the restoration and copying of ancient statuary became fully respectable in Rome. Indeed, as we have already remarked, it became a major industry and a source of revenue in the latter part of the century. Italian artists of the caliber of Bartolomeo Cavaceppi, the friend of Mengs and Winckelmann, and Agostino Penna made their living from restoring and copying. When the state under Pius VI took a more direct control over the archeological enterprise, the new generation of sculptor-restorers, Pietro Pierantonio, Filippo Albercini, and Vincenzo Pacetti, became more rigorous in their approach to restoration. In their own work, however, these sculptors remained faithful to variants of late baroque classicism, although Pierantonio's production was already permeated by a neoclassical sense in the way he polished the marble and modelled the nude body of the youthful *Genius*.[62]

It took the young Antonio Canova to do for sculpture what Jacques-Louis David had done for painting. Born on the Venetian Terra Ferma, Canova studied under the artist Bernardo Torretti, who mainly worked in the decorative tradition of the

61 Vittorio Moschini, "Filippo Della Valle," *L'Arte* (1925), 177–88; Honour, "Filippo Della Valle," 172–74.

62 Ibid., 173; Gradara, *Bracci*, 30, 34–37, 52–53; Fernow, *Römische Studien*, 16–17; Riccòmini, "La scultura del Settecento e gli inizi del Canova," 67; Hautecoeur, *Rome et la renaissance de l'antiquté*, 74–75, 191–92, 202; Ceschi, *Le chiese di Roma dagli inizi del neoclassico*, 32; Pinto, "La promozione della arti," 891.

seventeenth century. Had he continued along this path he would have remained a baroque sculptor and contributed nothing new. It is true that his group of *Daedalus and Icarus* of 1779 bears testimony to an interesting enlargement of Canova's cultural horizon in the direction of French art. But had he taken this route he would have never progressed beyond what Slodtz and his followers, including Jean Houdon, had achieved. Only in Rome would Canova come in direct contact with ancient art and truly assimilate its spirit.[63]

With the money earned from his *Daedalus and Icarus*, Canova, only 22 years old, took the road to Rome in November 1779. In the wake of all young artists who first arrived in the Eternal City, he immediately paid a visit to the Belvedere statuary. By the end of December, Canova seems to have familiarized himself with the leading figures in the Roman art world and on the 28th attended a dinner party given by the senator of Rome, Don Abbondio Rezzonico, himself a Venetian, where he met Gavin Hamilton for the first time.

The two became friends at once and an association was started that continued for more than a decade. As a consequence of Hamilton's favorable judgment, the Venetian ambassador, Girolamo Zulian, offered Canova a stipend with board and lodging at the Palazzo Venezia to continue his studies in Rome. Canova accepted and, before going back to settle his affairs in Venice, he made the mandatory tour to Naples to view the Portici museum and the temples of Paestum.

On his return to Rome at the end of 1780, Canova repeated his daily observations of the ancient Hellenistic and Roman masterpieces and cultivated the study of the Greek and Latin classics. But it was Gavin Hamilton who persuaded him to throw off the Venetian rococo and to "observe nature, but not to overlook the works of the ancients."[64] He loaded Canova's mind with the literary precepts of a stubborn classicist, which were merely popularizations of Winckelmann's ideas. Thus, between 1781 and 1785, Canova's classicism was born in Rome. It was a gradual process. In his first work, *Theseus slaying the Minotaur*, of 1781/82, he may have taken Gavin Hamilton's advice too literally. His figure of Theseus appears to have been directly derived from a classical original, the *Mars* in repose, from the Ludovisi collection.

The following year Canova was given his first major commission, the tomb of Pope Clement XIV Ganganelli in the church of SS. Apostoli. By the first half of April, 1786, the monument was opened to public view, almost two years after David's *Serment des Horaces*. The work signaled the end of baroque and rococo classicism in Roman sculpture and affirmed the new neoclassical style. Albeit it differed from David's concept of the style, who would tie his reform to the use of revolutionary ends. Canova's conception of art, on the other hand, was that of art as

[63] Riccòmini, "La scultura del Settecento e gli inizi del Canova," 67–68.

[64] Irwin, "Gavin Hamilton," 87–88; Riccòmini, "La scultura del Settecento e gli inizi del Canova," 67–68; Hugh Honour, "Antonio Canova and the Anglo-Romans," *The Connoisseur* (May and December 1959), May: 241–45; December: 225–30.

12 Tomb of Pope Clement XIV, by Antonio Canova

an activity detached from all contingent happenings, an idealization of the past without any apparent connection to the present. Such an esthetic view can often be applied to conservative subjects.[65]

And, indeed, the monument was at once both conservative and startlingly original. It was conservative in that it retained the principal features of all the papal monuments which had been erected since the early seventeenth century, a figure of the pope on a sarcophagus flanked by two allegories. But when the Ganganelli monument is compared to its immediate predecessor, Bracci's still baroque tomb of Benedict XIV in 1759, the originality of the work becomes apparent. Bracci's monument is light and animated, where Canova's is solemn and static; Benedict

[65] Riccòmini, "La scultura del Settecento e gli inizi del Canova," 68–69.

XIV is portrayed as if he were in the act of rising to his feet and the allegories beneath him appear to be engaged in a spirited conversation, while Clement XIV is enthroned for eternity and his attendant allegories reflect the silence of the tomb. Yet if at first sight Bracci's monument may appear to be more naturalistic, Canova's solemn figures reveal a deeper understanding of the human form, which is no longer concealed behind a billowy cloak, and a more subtle perception of human emotions.

Although Canova showed himself less classical in the tomb that he sculpted for the Rezzonico pope, Clement XIII, in St. Peter's between 1787 and 1791 than in Ganganelli's, the victory of Canova's form of neoclassicism was assured. His principal competitor was the Roman Giuseppe Angelini, a student of Cavaceppi and a continuator of the existing late baroque classicism, best known for his statue of Piranesi clad in a Roman toga at the church of S. Maria del Priorato. Angelini lost a public contest with Canova arranged by Don Abbondio Rezzonico by a unanimous decision in 1781. The field was now left to Canova, who would dominate Italian sculpture from his workshop in Rome.[66]

But the esthetic of Canova spread beyond the confines of Rome and Italy. Among the foreigners drawn to neoclassicism were the Irishman Christopher Hewetson and the English sculptor John Flaxman. Hewetson's monument for Cardinal Rezzonico, on which he worked for three years, was unveiled in 1787 in the small church of San Nicola in Carcere; it was a simple sarcophagus copied from the urn of Agrippa.

The person of greatest importance among the artists contemporary and immediately following Canova was the Dane Bertel Thorvaldsen, a student of Hans Wiedewelt, who in turn had been a close associate of Winckelmann during his Roman sojourn. Thorvaldsen came to Rome in 1797, amid the enthusiasm stirred up by the work of Canova. Although initially subjected to the influence of the great sculptor, Thorvaldsen's stern nordic education and the independent formation of his artistic vision would not allow him to submit to Canova's ideal in every work. Starting with the example of Canova, from whom he drew his earlier models, he suddenly arrived, with his statue of *Jason*, sculpted in 1802, at a personal posture, initiating a sort of unwilling polemic for a more rigid interpretation of the canons of Winckelmann.[67]

In comparison with painting, where the introduction of neoclassicism marked the definite loss of Rome's preeminence as the artistic center of the western world, the process in sculpture was more gradual. Canova, a Romanized Venetian, would

66 Santangelo, "La scultura," 37–38; *Settecento a Roma*, 46; Antonio Muñoz, *Antonio Canova. Le opere* (Rome, 1957), 7–36, 39–40, 45–47, 53–54, 60–65; Fernow, *Römische Studien*, 76–79, 84–103. Hautecoeur, *Rome et la renaissance de l'antiquité*, 186, 192–95, 198–202; De Rinaldis, *L'arte in Roma*, 108–110; Ceschi, *Le chiese di Roma dagli inizi del neoclassico*, 32–34, 39–40; Mariani, *Le chiese di Roma dal XVII al XVIII secolo*, 177–78; Natali (ed.), *Storia letteraria. Il Settecento*, 1:84; Justi, *Winckelmann und seine Zeitgenossen*, 2:102–6; Silvagni, *La corte pontificia*, 2:322–31.

67 Riccòmini, "La scultura del Settecento e gli inizi del Canova," 67; Jørgen Birkedal Hartmann, *Bertel Thorvaldsen. Scultore danese, romano d'adozione* (Rome, 1971), 7–17; tav. II.

uphold the city's reputation. But it was only a delaying action. Neoclassicism in sculpture would eventually become the property of northerners as it had already done in genre and landscape paintings. Nevertheless, however alien the roots of neoclassicism might have been to Rome's own artistic heritage, and however pagan in origin, it sprouted in the city. Winckelmann, Hamilton, David, and Canova, by their own confession, could have only created it in Rome. In that respect it was one of the random cultural elements broken off in the course of the entropic process that would be picked up abroad and enhance Rome's influence in Europe, while at the same time it was indicative of the loss of energy and direction at home.[68]

We have now traversed the whole spectrum from the vigor of the Tridentine baroque age, with Rome as its center, to the city simply becoming the depositary of antiquity's treasures and lore which attracted foreigners avid to exploit its cultural resources, both inspirational and material. In the process, its religious symbolism was reduced virtually to nil, even in the eyes of the Catholic monarchies.

But there was still life left in the city. It took the forcible intervention of a revolutionary power to extinguish it temporarily. Although a foreign imposition, with limited local support, the Jacobin republic of 1798/99 was in an exaggerated sense symptomatic of the advancing secularization and paganization of the papal capital.

[68] See Introduction, pp. 10–11.

# Epilogue

If certainly not static during the period of the ancien regime, Roman life, whether social, political or cultural, moved at a slow and leisurely pace. But with the emergence of the French Revolution in 1789 that tempo speeded up incrementally.

When the first storms of revolution broke out in Paris, they were ignored. Not that Rome was kept in ignorance. The *Notizie politiche*, a periodical founded in 1788, appeared twice a week and devoted a large amount of space to news from Paris. But the papal government was too preoccupied with the doings of the Catholic monarchs and the Romans with the public works of Pius VI.

In the meantime French emigrés had begun to pour into the city. However, these nobles and courtiers expected to wait only until the cloudburst would pass to return to Paris. Or so they thought. Not all Frenchmen were welcome; among the flood of those who flocked to Rome were some infected with revolutionary fever and suspected of spreading dangerous ideas. The old police laws for strangers lodging in Roman hostelries were revived. Frenchmen were stoned in the streets.

Soon, however, both papacy and the Roman populace began to feel the effects of the Revolution. The papal treasury suffered from the nationalization of ecclesiastical property in France and the cessation of payments to the curia. The rejection of the civil constitution of the clergy by Pius VI in March 1791, followed by the formal French annexation of Avignon in September led to the *de facto* breach of diplomatic relations between Rome and Paris.[1]

The French Republic was proclaimed on 22 September 1792. When Pius VI refused to recognize it the National Convention began taking threatening action. In view of the weak military situation of the Papal States, the inability of its allies to resist the French, and the dispatch of a French naval force against Naples, resulting in the recognition of the French Republic by that country, the papal government was left with no option but to moderate its policy toward France.

The arrival of Hugon de Bassville, secretary to the French envoy at Naples, in Rome, where he lodged with the French banker Etienne Mout at the Palazzo Palombara, led to further complications. Through Mout, Bassville made contact

[1] Madelin, *Rome de Napoléon*, 115, 121; Pastor, *Geschichte der Päpste*, 16, pt 2: 505–7; Andrieux, *Daily Life in Papal Rome*, 201–2; Giuntella, *Roma nel Settecento*, 182 n. 1, 184–86; Rinaldi, *Due secoli di musica al Teatro Argentina*, 1:272, 282–83, 290; Lapauze, *Histoire de l'Académie de France à Rome*, 424–25, 440–41; Cheke, *Cardinal de Bernis*, 285–86, 291–96.

with Giovanni Torlonia, who in turn was intimate with the Borghese, themselves favorably inclined toward the new ideas emanating from France, and the poet Vincenzo Monti. The order to replace the fleur-de-lys escutcheon with the republican coat of arms over the entrance to the French academy and the French consulates stirred the Roman populace to such a fever pitch that Bassville was assassinated during a provocative Sunday afternoon carriage ride along the Via del Corso. Thereafter the mob continued to vent its fury against the Palazzo Palombara, the French post office, and the Académie de France à Rome, as well as shops and houses of Frenchmen and their sympathizers. The Convention did not react to the incidents. Officially the generals of the Army of Italy were ordered to exact vengeance and unofficially were told to ignore the orders. For three years France remained passive.[2]

The Francophobe psychosis of both the Roman authorities and the people was never really justified. The contagion of revolutionary ideas in Rome was largely restricted to some professional men, offended at being excluded from participating in the public affairs of the Papal States, and to a few younger sons of noble families ruined by the system of entails, who were joined by a few disgruntled clerics. The Jacobin party in Rome was very small; as late as February 1797, one of their number, Nicola Corona, claimed that even if he were able to find 700 patriots, only 68 of these were actively working for the ruin of the papal tyranny.

Small though the number of genuine revolutionary activists was, the papal government remained apprehensive. It tried to avert their threat directly by bringing suspicious characters to trial and indirectly by playing on the superstitious passions of the Roman populace. The year 1794 was one of trials of alleged conspirators. But, in reality, the repressive activity of the Roman authorities was never severe; it was disorganized and incoherent, tolerant and arbitrary at the same time.[3]

The religiosity of the Roman masses tended naturally toward the superstitious, to which the period of the French Revolution only added a state of heightened excitement and expectation. As the French armies began cutting their way into the Papal States, a state of agitation akin to the "Great Fear" in France in 1789 was created. Starting with a flood of popular sonnets appealing to Roman patriotism and inciting the populace against freemasonry, the French Revolution, and the Jews, which cannot all have been the spontaneous expression of the popular will, this state

[2] B.N.Ro., Fondo Vittorio Emanuele, busta 245, massonaria, ff. 552–55; Natali (ed.), *Storia letteraria: Il Settecento*, 1:304; Carmelo Trasselli, "Processi politici romani dal 1792 al 1798." *Rassegna storica del Risorgimento*, 25 (1938), 1625–26; Mario Rossi, "L'occupazione napoletana di Roma (1799–1801)," *Rassegna storica del Risorgimento*, 19 (1932), 705; Lapauze, *Histoire de l'Académie de France à Rome*, 422–24, 446–51, 460; Pastor, *Geschichte der Päpste*, 16, pt 3: 503–4, 511 n. 6, 513–15, 518–23; Dufourcq, *Le régime Jacobin en Italie*, 32–35; Silvagni, *La corte pontificia*, 1:269–74, 278; Giuntella, *Roma nel Settecento*, 191–95; Clementi, *Il carnevale romano*, 2:213–17.

[3] Trasselli, "Processi politici romani," 1495–97, 1502–24, 1613–25; Tommasio Pedio, *Giacobini e Sanfedisti in Italia meridonale. Terra d'Otranto nelle chronache del 1799* (2 vols.; Bari, 1974), 1:7–8; Giuntella, *Roma nel Settecento*, 204.

of agitation reached a pitch of superheated excitement in 1796. A wave of alleged miracles radiating from Ancona swept the papal city by June. It appears that the government tried to channel the excitement into the area of popular devotion under the control of the priests and so keep the people in line. For the miracles were to continue with diminished frequency until January 1797, when they gave place to a period of passive prayers and resignation.[4]

These changes in the mood of the Romans coincided with the movements of the French army. Having set up the Cisalpine Republic in occupied Piedmont and Lombardy, the French army commanded by Napoleon Bonaparte, under the pretext of the murder of Bassville and of an invitation by the Italian Jacobins, invaded the papal provinces of the Romagna and the Marches in June 1795. It occupied Ferrara and Bologna, advancing as far south as Rimini. An armistice was concluded on 23 June, which stipulated a peace conference to be held in Paris. The negotiations, however, broke down because of the heavy demands made by the French. Thereupon Bonaparte denounced the armistice on 1 February 1797, occupied Ancona and encamped at Foligno, within three days' march from Rome. But Bonaparte, unwilling to offend the Catholics he might need one day, was not prepared to enter the Eternal City. For its part, Rome could not contemplate a defense to the utmost. So on 19 February, at Bonaparte's headquarters at Tolentino, a treaty was signed. As the price of peace, the papacy had to pay an indemnity of the thirty million livres tournois (about 5,600,000 scudi) to France, cede Avignon and the three legations of Bologna, Ferrara, and Ravenna, and surrender a hundred works of art and five hundred manuscripts, to be selected by a French commissioner. By ceding the papal provinces Pius VI violated the moral basis of the temporal power of the church.[5]

Napoleon Bonaparte left Italy in November on what was to be his illfated Egyptian campaign. On 20 January 1798, a French army setting out from Ancona marched on Rome and the general in command had orders to set up a republic. Within less than two months the political situation had been radically transformed. Responsible for this change was the insurrection of 28 December 1797, which ended with the shooting of General Matthieu-Léonard Duphot, a young and ardent republican, attached to the staff of Joseph Bonaparte, the new ambassador of the

[4] Renzo de Felice, "L'Italia nel periodo rivoluzionario," in *Italia Giacobina* (Naples, 1965), 14–15; Renzo de Felice, "Paura e religiosità popolare nello Stato della Chiesa alla fine del XVIII secolo," in *Italia Giacobina* (Naples, 1965), 291–302, 306–12; Dal Pane, *Lo Stato Pontificio e il movimento riformatore*, 513–17, 533–34; Bertoldi (ed.), *Epistolario di Monti*, 440; Trasselli, "Processi politici romani," 1616–17; Pignatelli, *Aspetti della Propaganda Cattolica*, 186–87; B.N.Ro., Fondo Gesuitico, ms. 1488, fasc. 10; B.N.Ro., Fondo Vittorio Emanuele, ms. 27.

[5] Bertoldi (ed.), *Epistolario di Monti*, 371–72; De Felice, "L'Italia nel periodo rivoluzionario," 16–21; Woolf, *History of Italy, 1700–1860*, 157, 163–64; Da Mosto, *Milizia dell Stato Romano*, 547–61; Giuntella, *Roma nel Settecento*, 198–204; Dufourcq, *Le régime Jacobin en Italie*, 39–47; Pasquale Sarli, "La politica del Direttorio e la Repubblica Napoletana in un *memoire* del Generale Lacroix," *Rassegna storica del Risorgimento*, 69 (1982), 142–44; Mario Rossi, "L'occupazione napoletana di Roma," 693; B.N.Ro., Fondo Gesuitico, ms. 195, nos. 19, 21.

French Republic who had taken up residence at the Palazzo Corsini. The death of Duphot was the unintended consequence of Jacobin unrest in Rome, stirred up deliberately by French agitators in conjunction with the local republicans.[6]

This event decided the Directory in Paris to bring about the fall of the pope. On 11 January 1798, it ordered General Alexander Berthier, who had replaced Napoleon Bonaparte, to march in all haste on Rome with instructions to use all his influence to organize a Roman Republic, while avoiding the appearance that the French government was behind the planning.

On the evening of 9 February, the French vanguard under General Giovan Battista Cervoni, a Corsican who had received his education at the Collegio Romano, had occupied the heights of Monte Mario. The next day the papal garrison surrendered the Castel Sant'Angelo. With the possession of the castle the French were, in fact, masters of the city.

It was not, however, until the following Sunday morning, the 11th, that, after Berthier had further humiliated the papal government by imposing several more demeaning conditions, the French army made its grand entrance into Rome and immediately occupied the most strategic places. There was no sign of reaction on the part of the fiery Roman population, only curiosity and a kind of gloomy stupor.

Even the champions of the new ideas in Rome watched the entrance of their French friends in silence at first. But when they saw all Rome occupied they gave free rein to their enthusiasm. Berthier, however, who did not trust the sporadic manifestations of a few patriots, ordered the symbols of the Revolution to be taken down and all assemblies that could disturb public order to be dispersed. Instead, he planned to organize a popular movement that would ask him for their freedom.

The anniversary of the accession of Pius VI fell on 15 February. At the very time that a little group of cardinals chanted the *Te Deum* at the Vatican, perhaps four to five hundred patriots met at the old forum to listen to a discourse delivered by Nicola Corona extolling liberty. They then proceeded to the Campidoglio, where they planted a huge tree of liberty, which had been prepared the day before with the help of Duca Francesco Maria Sforza. After a lengthy patriotic demonstration, there followed the solemn moment, the proclamation of the *Atto del Popolo Sovrano*, drawn up by three notaries under the eye of Cervoni. Eight delegates from this meeting were dispatched to announce the decision of the people to Berthier. He deferred to their request and entered Rome for the first time at the head of his staff to give the Roman people their liberty. Like a triumphant Roman he went to the Capitol, where, wreathed in laurels, he gave one of those flamboyant speeches for which all the revolutionaries had such a happy talent.[7]

[6] Montaiglon and Guiffrey (eds.), *Correspondance des directeurs de l'Académie de France à Rome*, 17:8–9, 26, 50–51, 71; Giuntella, *Roma nel Settecento*, 201–3; Woolf, *History of Italy, 1700–1860*, 164–65; Dufourcq, *Le régime Jacobin en Italie*, 48–62; ADP, 87.38.1.

[7] Cretoni, *Roma Giacobina*, 11–17, 23–38, 45–52; Dufourcq, *Le régime Jacobin en Italie*, 58–66, 73–106; Silvagni, *La corte pontificia*, 1:287–93; Hautecoeur, *Rome et la renaissance de l'antiquité*, 71–72; B.VALLICELL., ms. Z12, ff. 7–28.

With this act Berthier lowered the final curtain over the Rome of the ancien regime. Although progressively enfeebled by a loss of energy and direction in the absence of a galvanizing and unifying ideology, the papal capital was still capable of disparate bursts of reform and inspiration. It could have survived, were it not for an external *force majeur* that put an end to it. The Rome that would arise with the reforming Pius VII, while in many respects it looked like a continuation of that of Pius VI after the forcible hiatus of the Jacobin republic and the Napoleonic occupation, already marked the start of another epoch.

# Bibliography

## ABBREVIATIONS FOR MANUSCRIPT SOURCES

ROME

| | |
|---|---|
| A.Cap.R. | Archivio Capitolino di Roma |
| ADP | Archivio Doria-Pamphilj |
| ASR | Archivio di Stato di Roma |
| A.S.Vic. | Archivio Segreto del Vicariato |
| BAV | Biblioteca Apostolica Vaticana |
| B. CAS. | Biblioteca Casanatense |
| B. CORS. | Biblioteca Corsiniana |
| B. Lancisi. | Biblioteca Lancisiana (Arcispedale di Santo Spirito) |
| B.N.Ro. | Biblioteca Nazionale, Roma |
| B. VALLICELL. | Biblioteca Vallicelliana |

LONDON

| | |
|---|---|
| BL | British Library, Reference Division |

## SECONDARY SOURCES

Authors whose names are prefixed (de la, De etc.) are listed under their principal names.

Abbruzzese, Margherita. "Note su Pier Leone Ghezzi (1674–1755)," *Commentari*, 6 (1955), 303–9.

Abel, Wilhelm. *Agrarkrisen und Agrarkonjunkturen*. Hamburg and Berlin, 1966.

Ademollo, Alessandro. *Corilla Olimpica*. Florence, 1887.

"Le giustizie a Roma dal 1674 al 1739 e dal 1796 al 1840," *Archivio della società romana di storia patria*, 4 (1881), 429–534; 5 (1882), 305–364.

Agamennone, Giovanni. "La sismologia a Roma e nel Lazio," in Federico Millosevich (ed.), *Le scienze fisiche e biologiche in Roma e nel Lazio*. Rome, 1933.

Agnati, Archille (ed.). "Ricerche di cinematica storica. Il movimento dei prezzi nello Stato della Chiesa dal 1740 al 1800," *Il Giornale degli economista e Annali di economia* (1968), 727–57.

Ajello, Raffaelle. *Il problema della riforma giudiziaria e legislativa nel regno di Napoli durante la prima metà del secolo XVIII*. 2 vols., Naples, 1961–65.

Albon, Claude Camille François, comte d'. *Discours sur l'histoire, le gouvernement, les usages, la litterature et les arts, de plusieurs nations de l'Europe*. 2 vols., Geneva and Paris, 1782.

Alessandro, Alessandro D'. "I proprietari delle tenute dell'Agro Romano nel 1783," *Rivista di storia dell'agricoltura*, 9 (1971), 363–81.

"Le tenute dell'Agro Romano alla fine del secolo XVIII," *Economia e storia*, 16 (1969), 27–37.

Alfieri, Vittorio. *La Vita*. Introduction and notes by Luigi Negri. Turin, 1920.

Amati, Girolamo (ed.). *Alcune lettere dell'abate Antonio Niccolini a Monsignore Giovanni Bottari intorno la corte di Roma, 1724–1761*. Bologna, 1867.

Amelia, Marina D'. "La crisi di un mercato protetto: approvigionamente e consumo della carne a Roma nel XVIII secolo," *Mélanges de l'Ecole française de Rome. Moyen Age, Temps Modernes*, 87 (1975), 495–534.

"'Intrapredenti, lavoranti e Camera Apostolica': Potere e protesta in una fabbrica del '700," *Movimento operaio e socialista*, 11 (1979), no. 4, 315–66.

Amidei, Cosimo. *Opere*. Introduction, text and critical note by Antonio Rontondo. Turin, 1980.

Ancarani, Giovanni. "A proposito del movimento culturale riformatore settecentesco nello Stato Pontificio," *Jus*, N.S., 13 (1962), fasc. 3–4, 470–78.

Andrieux, Maurice. *Daily Life in Papal Rome in the Eighteenth Century*. Translated by Mary Fitton. London, 1968.

*Les Français à Rome*. Paris, 1968.

Angelis, Alberto De. *Il Teatro Alibert o delle Dame nelle Roma papale*. Tivoli, 1951.

Angelis d'Ossat, Gioacchino De. "Materiali da costruzione in Roma e nel Lazio," in Federico Millosevich (ed.), *Le scienze fisiche e biologiche in Roma e nel Lazio*. Rome, 1933.

Angelozzi, Giancarlo. "Le strutture sociale," in Aldo Berselli (ed.), *Storia della Emilia Romagna*. 2 vols., Bologna, 1977. Vol. 2, 131–52.

Aquarone, Alberto. "La restaurazione nello Stato Pontificio ed i suoi indirizzi legislativi," *Archivio della società romana di storia patria*, 78 (1955), 119–88.

Arco, Mario Dell'. *Pasquino e le pasquinate*. Milan, 1957.

Argan, Giulio Carlo. "Preface" to Joselita Raspi Serra (ed.), *Paestum and the Doric Revival, 1750–1830*. Florence, 1986. Pp. 11–13.

Arisi, Ferdinando. *Gian Paolo Panini*. Piacenza, 1961.

Arizzi-Clementel, Pierre. "Charles Percier et la salle Egyptienne de Villa Borghèse," in Georges Brunel (ed.), *Piranèse et les Français. Colloque tenu à la Villa Médicis, 12–14 mai 1976*. Rome, 1978. Pp. 1–32.

Arnaud, Jean. *L'Académie de Saint-Luc à Rome. Considérations historiques depuis son origine jusq'à nos jours*. Rome, 1886.

Arnheim, Rudolf. *Entropy and Art. An Essay on Disorder and Order*. Berkeley, Los Angeles and London, 1971.

Ashby, Thomas. "Thomas Jenkins in Rome," *Papers of the British School in Rome*, 6, no. 8 (1913), 487–511.

Baldelli, Franca. "Lo Studio bolognese tra Sei e Settecento," in Renzo Cremante and Walter Tega (eds.), *Scienza e letteratura nella cultura italiana del Settecento*. Bologna, 1984. Pp. 255–69.

Balzani, Alberto. "Primi interventi di bonifica dello stato unitario nella Campagna romana," *Studi Romani*, 28 (1980), 47–67.

Bandini, Carlo. *Roma nel Settecento*. 2 vols., Rome, 1930.

Baratta, Mario. *I terremoti d'Italia*. Turin, 1901.
Barbagli, Marzio. *Sotto lo stesso tetto. Mutamenti della famiglia in Italia dal XV al XX secolo*. Bologna, 1984.
Baretti, Giuseppe. *Opere scelte*, edited by B. Maier. Turin, 1972.
Barghiglioni, Publio. "Feste e canti della plebe romana," *Il Volgo di Roma*, collection of Francesco Sabatini, 3 (1901), 201–38.
Barlow, Philip J. (ed.). *Ideal and Classical Landscape. Exhibition, 6 February–3 April 1960*. Cardiff, 1960.
Baroni, Jole Maria. "La lirica musicale di Pietro Metastasio," *Rivista musicale italiana*, 12 (1905), 383–406.
Bartoccini, Fiorella. *Roma nell'Ottocento. Il tramonte della "città santa." Nascità di una capitale*. Bologna, 1985.
Bassi, Elena. "Il Piranesi tra Venezia e Roma," in *Nuove idee e nuova arte nel '700 italiano. Convegno internazionale, 19 – 23 maggio 1975*. Rome, 1977. 427–51.
Bassotti, Arturo. *La magistratura capitolina dal secolo XIV al secolo XIX, con speciale riferimento al senatore di Roma*. Rome, 1955.
Battaglini, Mario. "La soppressione dei conventi nella Repubblica romana giacobina," *Palatino*, 1–3 (1965), 13–23.
Baumgarten, Sandor. "Les oeuvres de Camillo Rusconi à Rome," *Revue de l'art ancien et moderne*, 70 (1936), 233–38.
Bazin, Germain. *The Baroque. Principles, Styles, Modes, Themes*. New York, 1978.
Bellettini, Athos. "L'evoluzione demografica dell'Italia nel quadro europeo del Settecento. Analogie e particularità," in Società italiana di demografia storica. *La popolazione italiana nel Settecento*. Bologna, 1979. Pp. 13–70.
*La popolazione di Bologna dal secolo XV all'unificazione italiana*. Bologna, 1961.
Belloni, Girolamo. "Dissertazione su commercio," in *Scrittori classici italiani di economia politica. Parte moderna*. Vol. 1. Milan, 1802. Pp. 3–153.
Bellori, Giovanni Pietro. *Le vite de' pittori, scultori ed architetti moderni. Parte prima*. Introduction by Eugenio Battisti. Reprint of the 1672 edition. Genoa, n.d.
Beloch, Karl Julius. *Bevölkerungsgeschichte Italiens*. Vol. 2: *Die Bevölkerung des Kirchenstaates, Toskanas und der Herzogtümer am Po*. 2nd ed.; Berlin, 1965.
Ben-David, Joseph. *The Scientist's Role in Society. A Comparative Study*. Englewood Cliffs, N.J., 1971.
Benisovich, Michel N. "Ghezzi and the French Artists in Rome," *Apollo*, N.S., 63 (1967), 340–47.
Berliner, Rudolf. "Zeichnungen von Carlo und Filippo Marchionni," *Münchner Jahrbuch der Bildenden Kunst* (1958–59), 267–396.
Bernardini, Bernardino. *Descrizione del nuovo ripartimento de' rioni di Roma fatto per ordine di N.S. Papa Benedetto XIV*. Rome, 1744.
Berselli Ambri, Paola. *L'opera di Montesquieu nel Settecento italiano*. Florence, 1960.
Bertana, Emilio. "Il teatro tragico italiano del secolo XVIII prima Alfieri," *Il Giornale storico della letteratura italiana*, supplement 4. Turin, 1901.
Bertoldi, Alfonso (ed.). *Epistolario di Vincenzo Monti*. Vol. 2: *1797–1805*. Florence, 1927.
Bianchini, Ludovico. *Storia delle finanze del Regno delle Due Sicilie*. Edited by Luigi de Rosa. 3 vols., Naples, 1971.
Bigi, Emilio. "La critica letteraria nella seconda metà del Settecento," in *Nuove idee e nuova*

*arte nel '700 italiano. Convegno internazionale, Roma, 19–23 maggio 1975*. Rome, 1977. Pp. 7–33.

Binni, Walter. *Classicismo e neoclassicismo nella letteratura del Settecento*. Florence, 1963.

"Il Metastasio," in *L'Arcadia e il Metastasio*. Florence, 1963. Pp. 247–424.

*Monti. Poeta del consenso*. Florence, 1981.

"Il periodo romano dell'Alfieri e la *Merope*," in *Saggio Alfieriano*. Florence, 1969. Pp. 41–70.

"Poetica e poesia nel Settecento italiano," in *L'Arcadia e il Metastasio*. Florence, 1963. Pp. ix–xliii.

'Sviluppo della poesia arcadica nel primo Settecento," *Rassegna della letteratura italiana*, 58 (1958), 323–44.

"Il teatro comico di Girolamo Gigli," in *L'Arcadia e il Metastasio*. Florence, 1963. Pp. 176–206.

Blunt, Anthony. "Architecture," in *The Golden Age of Naples. Art and Civilization under the Bourbons, 1734–1805*. 2 vols., Detroit and Chicago, 1981. Vol. 1, 23–45.

Bologna, Ferdinando. "I metodi di studio dell'arte italiana e il problema metodologico oggi," in *Storia dell'arte italiana*. Turin, 1979. Part 1: vol. 1, 165–282.

Bolognesi, Dante and Giovannini, Carla. "Gli esposti a Ravenna fra '700 e '800," in Ercole Sori (ed.), *Città a controllo sociale in Italia tra XVIII e XIX secolo*. Milan, 1982. Pp. 307–28.

Bolton, Charles, A. *Church Reform in 18th Century Italy (The Synod of Pistoia, 1786)*. The Hague, 1969.

Bonstetten, Charles Victor de. *Voyage sur la scène des Six Derniers Livres de Enéide*. Lausanne, 1971 (first published in Geneva, 1805).

Bortolotti, Ettore. "La fondazione dell'Istituto e la riforma dello 'Studio' di Bologna," in R. Accademia delle Scienze dell'Istituto di Bologna. *Memorie intorno a Luigi Ferdinando Marsili, pubblicate nel secondo centenario della morte per cura del Comitato Marsiliano*. Bologna, 1930. Pp. 383–471.

Boutry, Maurice vicomte de. *Choiseul à Rome. Lettres et memoires inedites, 1754–1757*. Introduction by André Hallays. Paris, 1895.

Bouvy, Eugène. *Voltaire et l'Italie*. Paris, 1898.

Bragaglia, Anton Giulio. *Storia del teatro popolare romano*. Rome, 1958.

Briganti, Giuliano. "Paestum and View Painting in the Eighteenth Century," in Joselita Raspi Serra (ed.), *Paestum and the Doric Revival, 1750–1830*. Florence, 1986. Pp. 56–58.

Brizzi, Gian Paolo. *La formazione della classe dirigente nel Sei-Settecento. I seminaria nobilium nell'Italia centro-settentrionale*. Bologna, 1976.

"Le istituzione educative e culturali: università e collegi," in Aldo Berselli (ed.), *Storia della Emilia Romagna*. Bologna, 1977. Vol. 2, 443–61.

Broglio, Francesco Margiotta. "Estremisti e moderati nelle lotte dottrinale," *Rivista di storia della chiesa in Italia*, 16 (1962), 275–310.

Brookner, Anita. *Jacques-Louis David*. London, 1980.

Brosses, Charles de. *Le Président De Brosses en Italie. Lettres familières écrites d'Italie en 1739 et 1740*. 2nd edition annotated, with an essay on the author's life and works by M. R. Colomb. Paris, 1861.

Brunel, Georges. "Recherches sur les debuts de Piranèse à Rome; les frères Pagliarini et Nicola Giobbe," in Georges Brunel (ed.), *Piranèse et les Français. Colloque tenu à la*

*Villa Médicis, 12–14 mai 1976*. Rome, 1978. Pp. 77–146.
Brunello, Bruno. *Il pensiero politico italiano del Settecento*. Milan, 1942.
Büchi, Hermann. *Finanzen und Finanzpolitik Toskanas im Zeitalter der Aufklärung, 1737–1790*. Berlin, 1915.
Burney, Charles. *Memoirs of the Life and Writings of Abate Metastasio*. 3 vols., London, 1796.
*Musical Tour or the Present State of Music in France and Italy*. London, 1771.
Buscaroli, Rezio. *La pittura di paesaggio in Italia*. Bologna, 1935.
Busk, Rachel Harriet. *The Folk-Lore of Rome Collected by Word of Mouth from the People*. London, 1874.
Caffiero, Marina. "Scienza e politica a Roma in un carteggio di Celestino Galiani (1714–1732)," *Archivio della società romana di storia patria*, 101 (1978), 311–44.
Cagiano de Azevedo, Michelangelo. *Il gusto nel restauro delle opere d'arte antiche*. Rome, 1948.
Cajani, Luigi. "Giustizia e criminalità nella Roma del Settecento," in Vittorio Emanuele Giuntella (ed.), *Ricerche sulla città del Settecento*, Rome, 1978. Pp. 263–312.
Calisse, Carlo. *A History of Italian Law*. Translated by Leighton B. Register. Boston, 1928.
*Storia di Civitavecchia*. Florence, 1936.
Callaey, Fredegand. "La critique historique et le courant pro-Janseniste à Rome au XVIIIe siècle," *Analecta Gregoriana*, 71 (1954), 185–95.
Calvi, Emilio. "Il teatro popolare romanesco nel Cinquecento," *L'Italia Moderna*, 6, vol. 1 (1908).
"Il teatro popolare romanesco nel Seicento," *L'Italia Moderna*, 6, vol. 1 (1908).
"Il teatro popolare romanesco nel Settecento," *L'Italia Moderna*, 6, vol. 1 (1908), Pp. 582–600.
Cametti, Alberto. "Critiche e satire teatrali romane del Settecento. Due stagioni musicali al Teatro Argentina (1761–1764)," *Rivista musicale italiana*, 9 (1902), 1–35.
*Il teatro di Tordinona poi di Apollo*. 2 vols. Tivoli, 1938.
Canaletti-Gaudenti, Alberto. *Delle corporazioni artigiane nella storia economica di Roma del secolo XVIII*. Rome, 1914.
Canezza, Alessandro. *Gli arcispedali di Roma nella vita cittadina nella storia e nell'arte*. Rome, 1933.
Cantimori, Delio. *Utopisti e riformatori italiani, 1794–1847. Ricerche storiche*. Florence, 1943.
Cantini, Gustavo. *S. Leonardo da Porto Maurizio e la sua predicazione. Uno scelto operaio nella messe*. Rome, 1936.
Capra, Carlo. "Alcuni aspetti del riordinamento tributario in Lombardia nell'età teresiana," in Ecole française de Rome (ed.), *La fiscalité et ses implications sociales en Italie et en France aux XVIIe et XVIIIe siècles*. Rome, 1980. Pp. 3–16.
"Il giornalismo nell'età rivoluzionaria e napoleonica," in Valerio Castronovo; Giuseppe Ricuperati; and Carlo Capra (eds.), *La stampa italiana dal Cinquecento all'Ottocento*. Rome and Bari, 1976. Pp. 373–537.
Caracciolo, Alberto. *L'albero dei Belloni. Un dinastia di mercanti del Settecento*. Bologna, 1982.
"I bilanci dello Stato ecclesiastico fra XVI e XVIII secolo. Una fonte e alcune considerazioni," in *Méthodologie de l'histoire et des sciences humaines. Mélanges en l'honneur de Fernand Braudel*. Toulouse, 1973. Pp. 99–104.
*Domenico Passionei tra Roma e la repubblica delle lettere*. Rome, 1968.

*Le port-franc d'Ancône. Croissance et impasse d'un milieu marchand au XVIIIe siècle*. Paris, 1966.

Carano, Enrico. "La botanica in Roma e nel Lazio," in Federico Millosevich (ed.), *Le scienze fisiche e biologiche in Roma e nel Lazio*. Rome, 1933.

Caravale, Mario and Caracciolo, Alberto. *Lo Stato pontificio da Martino V a Pio IX*. Turin, 1978.

Carcani, Michele. *Il Tevere e le sue inondazioni dall'origine di Roma fino ai giorni nostri. Descrizione geografica e storica*. Rome, 1875.

Carcopino, Jérôme. *Daily Life in Ancient Rome*. Translated by E. O. Lorimer. New Haven and London, 1960.

Caroselli, M. R. "Aspects of the Economic History of the Roman *Campagna* in the Modern and Contemporary World," *Journal of European Economic History*, 13 (1984), 591–98.

Carpegna, Nolfo di (ed.). *Paesisti e vedutisti a Roma nel '600 e nel '700. Mostra al Palazzo Barberini, marzo – aprile 1956*. Rome, 1956.

Casagrandi, Oddo. *La popolazione, le nascite, le morti negli ultimi due secoli a Roma (Studio demografico-statistico)*. Rome, 1903.

Casanova, Cesarina. *Le mediazioni del privilegio. Economia a potere nelle legazioni pontificie del '700*. Bologna, 1984.

Casanova de Seingalt, Jacques. *Histoire de ma vie*. 6 vols., Wiesbaden and Paris, 1960–62.

Cassinelli, Bruno. *Cagliostro dinazi al Sant'Ufficio*. Rome, 1930.

Castelnuovo, Enrico and Ginsburg, Carlo. "Centro e periferia," in *Storia dell'arte italiana*. Turin, 1979. Part 1: vol. 1, 285–352.

Castiglioni, Arturo. *Storia della medicina*. New revised edition. Milan, 1936.

Cavazza, Marta. "La *Casa di Salomone* realizzata?" in Università degli studi di Bologna (eds.), *I materiali dell'Istituto delle Scienze*. Bologna, 1979. Pp. 42–54.

Cavina, Anna Ottani. "Il Settecento e l'antico," in *Storia dell'arte italiana*. Turin, 1982. Part 2: vol. 2(2), 599–660.

Caylus, Anne Calude Philippe comte de. *Voyage d'Italie, 1714–1715*. 1st edition, annotated, with an essay on the author by Anulda A. Pons. Paris, 1914.

Celli, Angelo. *Storia della malaria nell'Agro Romano*. Città di Castello, 1925.

Ceschi, Carlo. *Le chiese di Roma dagli inizi del neoclassico al 1961*. Bologna, 1963.

Chaney, Edward P. de G. "Giudizi inglesi su ospedali italiani, 1545–1789," in Giorgio Politi, Mario Rosa, and Franco Della Peruta (eds.), *Timore e Carità. I poveri nell'Italia moderna*. Cremona, 1982.

Cheke, Sir Marcus. *The Cardinal de Bernis*. London, 1958.

Chiosi, Elvira, Mascoli, Laura, and Vallet, Georges. "The Discovery of Paestum," in Joselita Raspi Serra (ed.), *Paestum and the Doric Revival, 1750–1830*. Florence, 1986. Pp. 41–45.

Chorley, Patrick. *Oil, Silk and Enlightenment. Economic Problems in XVIIIth Century Naples*. Naples, 1965.

Chyurlia, Roberta. "Pompeo Batoni o del classicismo settecentesco." *Emporium*, 117 (1953), 56–67.

Cipolla, Carlo M. *Before the Industrial Revolution. European Society and Economy, 1000–1700*. New York, 1976.

"The Economic Decline of Italy," in Brian Pullan (ed.), *Crisis and Change in the Venetian Economy in the Sixteenth and Seventeenth Centuries*. London, 1968. Pp. 127–45.

"The Italian 'Failure,'" in Frederick Krantz and Paul M. Hohenberg (eds.), *Failed*

*Transitions to Modern Industrial Society. Renaissance Italy and Seventeenth Century Holland.* Montreal, 1975. Pp. 8–10.
Clark, Anthony M. "Batoni's Professional Career and Style," in Henry A. Millon (ed.), *Studies in Italian Art and Architecture. Fifteenth through Eighteenth Centuries.* Cambridge, Mass. and London, 1980. Pp. 323–37.
"Sebastiano Conca and the Roman Rococo." *Apollo*, N.S., 63 (1967), 328–35.
Clementi, Filippo. *Il carnevale romano nelle cronache contemporanee dalle origini al secolo XVIII.* 2 vols., Città di Castello, 1939.
Clerici, Enrico. "Geologia e la paleontologia in Roma e nel Lazio," in Federico Millosevich (ed.), *Le scienze fisiche e biologiche in Roma e nel Lazio.* Rome, 1933. Pp. 77–111.
Cocchetti, Lorenza. "Pompeo Batoni e il neoclassicismo a Roma," *Commentari* (1952), no. 4, 274–89.
Cochrane, Eric W. *Florence in the Forgotten Centuries, 1527–1800.* Chicago, 1973.
"Muratori: The Vocation of a Historian" *Catholic Historical Review*, 51 (1965), 153–72.
*Tradition and Enlightenment in the Tuscan Academies, 1690–1800.* Chicago, 1961.
Cohen, I. Bernard. *Franklin and Newton. An Inquiry into Speculative Newtonian Experimental Science and Franklin's Work in Electricity as an Example Thereof.* Philadelphia, 1956.
Colicchi, Calogero. *Le polemiche contro l'Arcadia.* Messina, 1972.
Collison-Morley, Lacy. *Shakespeare in Italy.* New York, 1916.
Colliva, Paolo. "Bologna dal XIV al XVIII secolo: 'governo misto' o signoria senatoria?" in Aldo Berselli (ed.), *Storia della Emilia Romagna.* 2 vols., Bologna, 1977. Vol. 13–34.
Colonna, Gustavo Brigante. "Il santo ligure che impiantò la *Via Crucis* nel Colosseo," *L'Urbe*, 8 (1943), fasc. 11–12, 7–14.
Conforti, Michael. "Planning the Lateran Apostles," in Henry A. Millon (ed.), *Studies in Italian Art and Architecture. Fifteenth through Eighteenth Centuries.* Cambridge, Mass. and London, 1980. Pp. 243–60.
Constable, W. G. *Richard Wilson.* Cambridge, Mass., 1953.
Corradi, Alfonso. *Annali delle epidemie occorso in Italia dalle prime memorie fino al 1850 compilati con varie note e dichiarazioni.* 4 vols., Bologna, n.d.
Corridore, Francesco. *La popolazione dello Stato Romano.* Rome, 1906.
Cortese, Nino. *Cultura e politica a Napoli dal Cinque al Settecento.* Naples, 1965.
Coste, Jean. "Missioni nell'Agro Romano nella primavera del 1703," *Ricerche per la storia religiosa di Roma*, 2 (1978), 165–223.
Coyer, Gabriel-François. *Voyage d'Italie et de Hollande.* 2 vols. Paris, 1775.
Cretoni, Antonio. *Roma Giacobina. Storia della Repubblica Romana del 1798–99.* Rome, 1971.
Crisafulli, Maria Caterina. "Il Cardinale Boncompagni e la bonifica in Emilia-Romagna," *Clio* (1985), 395–419.
Cristoferi, Maria Valeria. "Fiere e mercati," in Aldo Berselli (ed.), *Storia della Emilia Romagna.* 2 vols., Bologna, 1977. Vol. 2, 153–87.
Croce, Benedetto. "L'Arcadia e la poesia del Settecento," in *La letteratura italiana nel Settecento.* Bari, 1949. Pp. 1–18.
"Gl'improvvisatori," in *La letteratura italiana del Settecento.* Bari, 1949. Pp. 299–311.
Csáky- Loebenstein, Eva-Marie. "Studien zur Kavalierstour österreichischer Adeliger im 17. Jahrhundert." *Mitteilungen des Instituts für österreichische Geschichtsforschung*, 79 (1971), 408–34.

Cupis, Cesare De. *Le vicende dell'agricoltura e della pastorizia nell'Agro Romano. L'annona.* Rome, 1911.
Curione, Alessandro. *Sulla studio del greco in Italia nei secoli XVII e XVIII.* Rome, 1941.
Cust, Lionel and Colvin, Sir Sidney. *History of the Society of Dilettanti.* 2nd enlarged edition. London, 1914.
Dammig, Enrico. *Il movimento giansenista a Roma nella seconda metà del secolo XVIII.* Città del Vaticano, 1945.
Da Mosto, Andrea. *Milizia dello Stato Romano.* Città di Castello, 1914.
Dante, Francesco. "Una fonte per lo studio della religiosità romana nel '700: I processi di R. Venerini, G. B. de Rossi, B. J. Labre." *Clio*, 16 (1980), 198–221.
Delumeau, Jean. *L'Alun de Rome, XVe–XIXe Siècles.* Paris, 1962.
*Vie économique et sociale de Rome dans la seconde moitié du XVIe siècle.* 2 vols., Paris, 1957–59.
Dempsey, Charles. "Annibale Carrache au Palais Farnèse," in Ecole française de Rome, *Le Palais Farnèse.* Rome, 1981. Vol. 1(1), 269–311.
Den Broeder, Frederick. "The Lateran Apostles. The Major Sculpture Commission in Eighteenth-Century Rome." *Apollo*, N.S., 63 (1967), 360–65.
Dhotel, André. *Saint Benoît Joseph Labre.* Paris, 1957.
Diaz, Furio. *Francesco Maria Gianni dalla burocrazia alla political sotton Pietro Leopoldo di Toscana.* Milan, 1966.
*Il Granducato di Toscana. I Medici.* Turin, 1976.
"Rivoluzione e controrivoluzione," in Luigi Firpo (ed.), *Storia delle idee politiche, economiche e sociale.* Vol. 4: *L'età moderna.* Turin, 1975. Pp. 597–743.
Dini, Stefano. "Nuove ricerche intorno all'abolizione delle gabelle di transito nello Stato della Chiesa." *Rassegna storica del Risorgimento*, 72 (1985), 267–95.
Dominicis, Giulia De. "Roma centro musicale nel Settecento," *Rivista musicale italiana*, 30 (1923), 511–26.
Donadoni, Eugenio. *A History of Italian Literature.* Translated by Richard Monges. 2 vols., New York and London, 1969.
Dragoni, Giorgio and Pallotti, Vincenzo. "Strumenti, didattica e ricerca: la fisica sperimentale nell'Istituto delle Scienze," in Università degli studi di Bologna. *I materiali dell'Istituto delle Scienze.* Bologna, 1979. Pp. 217–38.
Dufourcq, Albert. *Le régime Jacobin en Italie. Etude sur la République Romaine (1798–1799).* Paris, 1900.
Dupâquier, Jacques. "Il problema della crescita demografica nel XVIII secolo. Lo stato della ricerca in Francia," in Società italiana di demografia storica. *La popolazione italiana nel Settecento.* Bologna, 1979. Pp. 141–50.
Eisen, Richard. *Die deutsche Landschaftsmalerei des Spätbarock.* Leipzig, 1936.
Emanuelli, Pio. "L'astronomia in Roma," in Federico Millosevich (ed.), *Le scienze fisiche e biologiche in Roma e nel Lazio.* Rome, 1933. Pp. 293–326.
Emmerling, Ernst. *Pompeo Batoni. Sein Leben und Werke.* Cologne, 1932.
Enggass, Robert. *Early Eighteenth-Century Sculpture in Rome.* 2 vols., University Park, Pa. and London, 1976.
Eredia, Filippo. "Il clima di Roma," in Federico Millosevich (ed.). *Le scienze fisiche e biologiche in Roma e nel Lazio.* Rome, 1933.

Escher, Konrad. *Barock und Klassizismus. Studien zur Geschichte der Architektur Roms.* Leipzig, 1910.

Evans, Robert J. W. "Learned Societies in Germany in the Seventeenth Century," *European Studies Review*, 7 (1977), 129–51.

Faccioli, Clemente. "Gio. Battista Nolli (1701–1756) e la sua gran *Pianta di Roma* del 1748," *Studi Romani*, 14 (1966), 415–42.

Falcone, Giandomenico. "L'aspirazione al teatro tragico nell'Arcadia romana degli anni 1770–1780," *Studi Romani*, 26 (1978), 503–21.

Faldi, Italo. "Gli inizi del neoclassicismo in pittura nella prima metà del Settecento," in *Nuove idee e nuova arte nel '700 italiano. Convegno internazionale, Roma, 19–23 maggio 1975*. Rome, 1977. Pp. 495–523.

Fatica, Michele. "La reclusione dei poveri a Roma durante il pontificato di Innocenzo XII (1692–1700)," *Ricerche per la storia religiosa di Roma*, 3 (1979), 133–79.

Fehr, Max. *Apostolo Zeno (1668–1750) und seine Reform des Operntextes.* Zurich, 1912.

Felice, Renzo De. *Aspetti e momenti della vita economica di Roma e del Lazio nei secoli XVIII e XIX*. Rome, 1965.

"Gli ebrei nella Repubblica romana del 1798–99," *Rassegna storica del Risorgimento*, 11 (1953), 327–56.

"Giuseppe Ceracchi," in *Italia Giacobina*. Naples, 1965. Pp. 61–130.

"Paura e religiosità popolare nello Stato della Chiesa alla fine del XVIII secolo," in *Italia Giacobina*. Naples, 1965. Pp. 291–316.

"Il problema ebreico in Italia," *Rassegna storica del Risorgimento* 40 (1953), 342–51.

Felloni, Giuseppe. *Gli investimenti finanziari genovesi in Europa tra il Seicento e la Restaurazione*. Milan, 1971.

Fernow, Carl Ludwig. *Römische Studien. Erster Theil.* Zurich, 1806.

Ferrari, Oreste. "Painting in Naples under the Austrian Viceregency (1707–1734)," in *The Golden Age of Naples. Art and Civilization under the Bourbons, 1734–1804*. 2 vols., Detroit and Chicago, 1981. Vol. 1, 47–54.

Ferrone, Vincenzo. *Scienza Natura Religione. Mondo newtoniano e cultura italiana nel primo Settecento*. Naples, 1982.

Fiocca, Giorgio. "Struttura urbana e controllo sociale a Roma nel '700 e nel primo '800: mobilità sociale, paesaggio urbano ed enti di sorveglianza pontifici," in Ercole Sori (ed.), *Città e controllo sociale in Italia tra XVIII e XIX secolo*. Milan, 1982. Pp. 381–99.

Fiorani, Luigi. *Il Concilio Romano del 1725*. Rome, 1977.

*Onorato Caetani. Un erudito romano del Settecento*. Rome, 1969.

"Il secolo XVIII," in Fiorani; Mantova; Pecchiae; *et al. Riti, ceremonie, feste e vita del popolo nella Roma dei papi*. Bologna, 1970. Pp. 217–57.

Firpo, Luigi. "Contributo alla bibliografia del Beccaria (Le edizioni italiane settecentesche del 'Dei delitti e delle pene.')," in *Atti del convegno internazionale su Cesare Beccaria, promosso dall'Accademia delle Scienze di Torino nel secondo centenario dell'opera "Dei delitti e delle pene."* Turin, 1966. Pp. 329–453.

Fleming, John. *Robert Adam and His Circle in Edinburgh and Rome*. Cambridge, Mass., 1962.

Fokker, Timon H. *Roman Baroque Art. The History of a Style*. 2 vols., London, 1938.

Francovich, Carlo. *Storia della massoneria in Italia dalle origini alla rivoluzione francese*. Florence, 1974.

Friz, Giuliano. *Consumi, tenore di vita e prezzi a Roma dal 1700 al 1900*. Rome, 1980.
*La popolazione di Roma dal 1770 al 1900*. Rome, 1974.
"Produzione e commercio dei vini del Lazio nei secoli XVIII e XIX," in *Annales cisalpines d'histoire sociale*, 3 (1972), 207–28.
Frommel, Christoph Luitpold. "Papal Policy: The Planning of Rome during the Renaissance." *The Journal of Interdisciplinary History*, 17 (1986), 339–65.
Frutaz, Amato Pietro (ed.). *Le piante di Roma*. 3 vols., Rome, 1962.
Fubini, Mario. "Arcadia," in *Arcadia e illuminismo*. Milan, 1950. Pp. 1–11.
"Introduzione a Metastasio," in *Pietro Metastasio. Opere*. Milan and Naples, n.d. Pp. 3–34.
"Metastasio," in *Arcadia e illuminismo*. Milan, 1950. Pp. 136–212.
Gabetti, Roberto. "Architettura italiana del Settecento," in *Storia dell'arte italiana*. Turin, 1982. Part 2: vol. 2(2), 670–721.
Garin, Eugenio. "Cartesio e l'Italia." *Giornale critico della filosofia italiana*, 29 (1950), 385–405.
*Storia della filosofia italiana*. 3 vols., Turin, 1966.
Gasperoni, Gaetano. *Settecento italiano. Contributo alla storia della cultura*. 1: *L'abate Giovanni Cristoforo Amaduzzi*. Padua, 1941.
Gentili, Carlo. "Il modello epistemologico dell'*Institutum scientiarium et artium* di Bologna," in Università degli studi di Bologna, *I materiali dell'Istituto delle Scienze*. Bologna, 1979. Pp. 22–41.
Georgescu-Roegen, Nicholas. *The Entropy Law and the Economic Process*. Cambridge, Mass., 1971.
Gerstenberg, Kurt. *Johann Joachim Winckelmann und Anton Raphael Mengs*. Halle an der Saale, 1929.
Giacomelli, Alfeo. "Carlo Grassi e le riforme bolognesi del Settecento. 1: L'età lambertiniana," *Quaderni culturali bolognesi*, 3 (1979), no. 19, 3–87.
Giovannoni, Gustavo. "Il Settecento." In Ferdinando Castagnoli; Carlo Cecchelli, Gustavo Giovannoni, and Mario Zocca (eds.), *Topografia e urbanistica di Roma*. Bologna, 1958. Pp. 455–70.
Giraldi, Giovanni. "La sovranità popolare nella polemica Spedalieri-Tamburini," *Rivista internazionale di filosofia del diretto*, 32 (1955), 297–317.
Giuntella, Vittorio Emanuele. "Documenti sull'istruzione popolare in Roma durante il settecento," *Studi Romani*, 9 (1961), 553–60.
*Roma nel Settecento*. Bologna, 1971.
"Roma nel Settecento. La capitale e i problemi dello stato," *Studi Romani*, 14 (1966), 269–91.
"Scuole e cultura nella Roma settecentesca," *Studi Romani*, 11 (1963), 528–41.
Goethe, Johann Wolfgang. *Italian Journey*. Translated by W. H. Auden and Elizabeth Mayer. London, 1962.
Golzio, Vincenzo. "Le opere romane di Michelangelo Slodtz," *Dedalo* (1930–31), 383–91.
*Palazzi romani dalla rinascita al neoclassico*. Bologna, 1971.
Gonzalez-Palacios, Alvar. "I mani del Piranesi-Valadier padre e figlio," in *Nuove idee e nuova arte nel '700 italiano. Convegno internazionale, Roma, 19–23 maggio 1975*. Rome, 1977. Pp. 47–63.

Gorani, Joseph. *Rom und seine Einwohner am Ende des XVIII. Jahrhunderts.* Riga, 1794.
Gorce, Agnès de la. *Un pauvre qui trouva la joie.* Paris, 1954.
Grab, Alexander. "The Politics of Subsistence. The Liberalization of Grain Commerce in Austrian Lombardy under Enlightenment Despotism," *Journal of Modern History*, 57 (1985), 185–210.
Gradara, Costanza. *Pietro Bracci, scultore romano, 1700–1773.* Milan, 1920.
Grassi, Luigi. *Costruzione della critica d'arte.* Rome, 1955.
Gravina, Vincenzo. *Della Ragion Poetica Libri Due.* Rome, 1708.
Gregori, Tullio. "Studi sull'atomismo del Seicento." *Giornale critico della filosofia italiana*, 43 (1964), 38–65.
Guenzi, Alberto. "Sistema annonario e controllo sociale a Bologna nei secoli XVII e XVIII," in Ercole Sori (ed.), *Città e controllo sociale in Italia tra XVIII e XIX secolo.* Milan, 1982. Pp. 293–306.
Hartmann, Jørgen Birkedal. *Bertel Thorvaldsen. Scultore danese, romano d'adozione.* Rome, 1971.
Haskell, Francis. *Patrons and Painters. A Study in the Relations between Italian Art and Society in the Age of the Baroque.* London, 1963.
Haskell, Francis and Penny, Nicholas. *Taste and the Antique. The Lure of Classical Sculpture, 1500–1900.* New Haven and London, 1981.
Hautecoeur, Louis. *Rome et la renaissance de l'antiquité à la fin du XVIIIe siècle.* Paris, 1912.
Heres, Gerald. "Der Neuaufbau des Berliner Antikenkabinetts im Jahre 1703," in H. Beck, P. C. Bol, W. Prinz, *et al.* (eds.), *Antikensammlungen im 18. Jahrhundert.* Berlin, 1981. Pp. 187–98.
Hershey, Daniel and Hsuan-Hsien Wang. *A New Age-Scale for Humans.* Lexington, Mass. and Toronto, 1980.
Hibbert, Christopher. *The Grand Tour.* New York, 1969.
Hollis, Thomas. *Memoires of Thomas Hollis, Esq., F.R. and A.SS.* 2 vols. London, 1780.
Honour, Hugh. "Antonio Canova and the Anglo-Romans," *The Connoisseur* (May, 1959), 241–45; (December 1959), 225–31.
"Filippo Della Valle," *The Connoisseur* (1959), 172–79.
*Neoclassicism.* Harmondsworth, 1969.
"Statuettes after the Antique. Volpato's Roman Porcelain Factory," *Apollo*, N.S., 63 (1967), 371–73.
Howard, Seymour. "Bartolomeo Cavaceppi and the Origins of Neo-classic Sculpture," *The Art Quarterly*, 33 (1970), 120–33.
Hughes, Steven Charles. "Police, Public Order and Risorgimento." Unpublished Dissertation. University of Michigan, 1984.
Insolera, Italo. *Roma. Immagini e realtà dal X al XX secolo.* Rome and Bari, 1980.
Irwin, David. "Gavin Hamilton: Archaeologist, Painter, and Art Dealer," *The Art Bulletin*, 44 (June 1962), 87–102.
Isherwood, Robert M. *Farce and Fantasy. Popular Entertainment in Eighteenth-Century Paris.* New York and Oxford, 1986.
Isola, Maria Catelli. "L'incisione a Roma nel '700," in *Il Settecento a Roma. Mostra, 19 marzo – 31 maggio 1959.* Rome, 1959. Pp. 381–82.
Johns, Christopher M. S. "The Art Patronage of Pope Clement XI Albani and the

Paleochristian Revival in Early Eighteenth Century Rome". Unpublished Dissertation. University of Delaware, 1985.

Justi, Carl. *Winckelmann und seine Zeitgenossen*. 5th edition. 3 vols., Cologne, 1956.

Kaplan, Steven L. *Bread, Politics and Political Economy in the Reign of Louis XV*. 2 vols., The Hague, 1976.

*Provisioning Paris. Merchants and Millers in the Grain and Flour Trade during the Eighteenth Century*. Ithaca and London, 1984.

Kirkpatrick, Ralph. *Domenico Scarletti*. Princeton, N.J., 1953.

Klang, Daniel M. *Tax Reform in Eighteenth Century Lombardy*. New York and Boulder, 1977.

Koenigsberger, Helmut G. *Politicians and Virtuosi. Essays in Early Modern History*. London and Ronceverte, W.V., 1986.

Körte, Werner. *Der Palazzo Zuccari in Rom. Sein Freskenschmuck und seine Geschichte*. Leipzig, 1935.

Krautheimer, Richard. *Roma Alessandrina. The Remapping of Rome under Alexander VII, 1655–1667*. Poughkeepsie, N.Y., 1982.

*Rome, Profile of a City, 312–1308*. Princeton, N.J., 1980.

Lalande, Joseph Jérôme de. *Voyage d'un françois en Italie, fait dans les années 1765 et 1766*. 2nd enlarged edition. 8 vols., Paris, 1786.

La Marca, Nicola. "La manifattura statale delle Terme di Diocleziano da Clemente XIV e Pio VI al prefetto de Tournon," *Capitolium*, 44 (1969), nos. 10–12, 19–33.

*Saggio di una ricerca storico-economica sull'industria e l'artigianato a Roma dal 1750 al 1849*. Padua, 1969.

Lanciani, Rodolfo. *Storia degli scavi di Roma e notizie intorno le collezioni romane di antichità*. 4 vols., Rome, 1902–12.

Landau, Marcus. *Geschichte der italienischen Litteratur im achtzehnten Jahrhundert*. Berlin, 1899.

Langbein, John H. *Torture and the Law of Proof. Europe and England in the Ancien Regime*. Chicago and London, 1977.

Lapauze, Henri. *Histoire de l'Académie de France à Rome*. Vol. 1 (1666–1801). Paris, 1924.

Lavagnino, Emilio. "La pittura," in *Il Settecento a Roma. Mostra, 19 marzo – 31 maggio, 1959*. Rome, 1959. Pp. 24–30.

"Roma nel Settecento," in *Il Settecento a Roma. Mostra, 19 marzo – 31 maggio, 1959*. Rome, 1959. Pp. 17–23.

Leclere, Tristan. *Hubert Robert et les paysagistes français du XVIIIe siècle*. Paris, 1913.

Lee, Katherine Marguerite. *Italian Popular Comedy. A Study in the Commedia dell'Arte, 1560–1620, with Special Reference to the English Stage*. 2 vols., New York, 1962.

Lepre, Anna. "Agricoltura e manifattura in un rione di Roma nel seicento e nel settecento," *Studi Romani*, 25 (1977), 353–70.

Lewis, Lesley. *Connoisseurs and Secret Agents in Eighteenth Century Rome*. London, 1961.

"Philipp von Stosch." *Apollo*, N.S., 63 (1967), 320–27.

Liebenwein, Wolfgang. "Der Portikus Clemens' XI. und sein Statuenschmuck. Antikenrezeption und Kapitolsidee im frühen 18. Jahrhundert," in H. Beck, P. C. Bol, W. Prinz, *et al.* (eds.), *Antikensammlungen in 18. Jahrhundert*. Berlin, 1981. Pp. 73–105.

Livi-Bacci, Massimo. *A History of Italian Fertility during the Last Two Centuries*. Princeton, N.J., 1977.

Lizzani, Mario. "Una miscellanea romana del Settecento," *L'Urbe*, 4 (1939), no. 10.
Loret, Mattia. "Attività ignota di Filippo Juvara a Roma," *Critica d'Arte*, (1936), 198–201.
"I pittori napoletani a Roma nel Settecento," *Capitolium* (1934), 541–55.
Lutz, Georg. "Zur Papstfinanz von Klemens IX. bis Alexander VIII. (1667–1691)," *Römische Quartalschrift für christliche Altertumskunde und Kirchengeschichte*, 74 (1979), 32–90.
Luzio, Leopoldina. "Contributo allo studio dei centri scomparsi o abbandonati del Lazio," *Rivista di geografia italiana*, 20 (1953), 134ff.
McCarthy, Michael. "New Light on Thomas Major's *Paestum* and Later English Drawings of Paestum," in Joselita Raspi Serra (ed.), *Paestum and the Doric Revival, 1750–1830*. Florence, 1986. Pp. 47–50.
McCormick, Thomas J. "Piranesi and Clérisseau's Vision of Classical Antiquity," in Georges Brunel (ed.). *Piranèse et les Français. Colloque tenu à la Villa Médicis, 12–14 mai 1976*. Rome, 1978. Pp. 303–10.
Madelin, Louis. *La Rome de Napoléon. La domination française à Rome de 1809 à 1814*. 2nd edition. Paris, 1906.
Maier, Bruno. *Faustina Maratta Zappi. Donna e rimatrice d'Arcadia*. Rome, 1954.
Maravall, José Antonio. *Culture of the Baroque. Analysis of a Historical Structure*. Translated by Terry Cochran. Minneapolis, 1986.
Marchetti, G. *Del denaro straniero che viene a Roma, e che se ne va per cause ecclesiastiche, calcolo ragionato*. Rome, 1800.
Marcolongo, Roberto. "Le scienze fisiche e matematiche in Roma," in Federico Millosevich (ed.), *Le scienze fisiche e biologiche in Roma e nel Lazio*. Rome, 1933. Pp. 351–72.
Mariani, Valerio. *Le chiese di Roma dal XVII al XVIII secolo*. Bologna, 1963.
Marucchi, Orazio. *Le vicende edilizie di Roma a traverso i secoli*. Albano Laziale, 1926.
Marx, Hans Joachim. "Die Musik am Hofe Pietro Kardinal Ottobonis unter Arcangelo Corelli," *Studien zur italienisch-deutschen Musikgeschichte 5, Analecta musicologica*, 5 (1968), 104–16.
Mastellone, Salvo. *Pensiero politico e vita culturale a Napoli nella seconda metà del Seicento*. Florence and Messina, 1965.
Matteucci, Anna Maria. *Carlo Francesco Dotti e l'architettura bolognese del Settecento*. Bologna, 1969.
Matteuzzi, Maurizio. "La matematica a Bologna nel secolo XVIII," in Università degli studi di Bologna (ed.), *I materiali dell'Istituto delle Scienze*. Bologna, 1979. Pp. 75–77.
Maugain, Gabriel. *Etude sur l'évolution intellectuelle de l'Italie de 1657 à 1759 environ*. Paris, 1909.
Mazzetti, Roberto. *Pietro Tamburini, la mente del Giansenismo italiano*. Messina and Ferrara, 1948.
Metz, Karl H. "Staatsraison und Menschenfreundlichkeit. Formen und Wandlungen der Armenpflege im Ancien Régime Frankreichs, Deutschlands und Grossbritanniens," *Vierteljahrschrift für Sozial- und Wirtschaftsgeschichte*, 72 (1985), 1–26.
Michel, Geneviève. "Vie quotidienne au Palais Farnèse (XVIIe – XVIIIe siècle)," in Ecole française de Rome (ed.), *Le Palais Farnèse*. 2 vols., Rome, 1981. Vol. 1 (2), 509–65.
Michel, Geneviève and Olivier. "Recherches biographiques sur Paolo Anesi," in *Studi offerti a Giovanni Incisa della Rocchetta*. Rome, 1973. Pp. 323–36.
Michel, Olivier. "L'*Accademia*," in Ecole française de Rome (ed.), *Le Palais Farnèse*. 2 vols.,

Rome, 1981. Vol. 1 (2), 2, 567–609.

Milano, Attilio. "L'*Editto sopra gli Ebrei* di Pio VI e le mene riccattatorie di un letterato," *La Rassegna mensile di Israel*, 19 (1953), 65–80, 118–25.

*Ricerche sulle condizioni economiche degli ebrei a Roma durante la clausura nel ghetto (1555–1838)* (Città di Castello, 1931).

Millon, Henry. "Vasi-Piranesi-Juvarra," in Georges Brunel (ed.), *Piranèse et les Français. Colloque tenu à la Villa Médicis, 12–14 mai 1976*. Rome, 1978. Pp. 345–62.

Mira, Giuseppe. "Note sui trasporti fluviali nell'economia dello Stato Pontificio nel XVIII secolo," *Archivio della società romana di storia patria*, 77 (1954).

Mirri, Mario. *La lotta politica in Toscana intorno alle "riforme annonarie" (1764–1775)*. Pisa, 1972.

Mistruzzi, Carlo. "La nobiltà nello Stato pontificio," *Rassegna degli archivi di stato*, 23 (1963), 206–44.

Momigliano, Arnaldo. "Ancient History and the Antiquarians," in *Contributo alla storia degli studi classici*. Rome, 1955. Pp. 67–106.

"Edward Gibbon fuori e dentro la cultura italiana," in *Sesto contributo alla storia degli studi classici e del mondo antico*. 2 vols., Rome, 1980. Vol. 1, 231–48.

"Eighteenth Century Prelude to Mr. Gibbon," in *Sesto contributo alla storia degli studi classici e del mondo antico*. Rome, 1980. Vol. 1, 249–68.

"La Nuova Storia Romana de G. B. Vico," in *Sesto Contributo alla storia degli studi classici e del mondo antico*. Rome, 1980. Vol. 1, 191–210.

"Gli studi classici di Scipione Maffei," in *Secondo contributo alla storia degli studi classici*. Rome, 1960. Pp. 255–71.

"Two English Books on Vico," in *Sesto Contributo alla storia degli studi classici e del mondo antico*. Rome, 1980. Vol. 1, 211–30.

Montaiglon, Anatole and Guiffrey, Jules (eds.). *Correspondance des directeurs de l'Académie de France à Rome*. Vols. 1–18. Paris, 1901–1908.

Montalto, Lina. *Un mecenate in Roma barocca*. Florence, 1955.

Montesquieu, Jean-Baptiste de Secondat, Baron. *Voyages*: VII, *Rome* and IX, *Rome (second séjour)*, in *Oeuvres complètes de Montesquieu*, under the direction of M. André Masson. Vol. 2. Paris, 1950. Pp. 1092–192.

Moore, John. *A View of Society and Manners in Italy*. 2 vols., London, 1781.

Morandi, Luigi. "Pasquino e pasquinate," *Nuova Antologia di Scienza, Lettere ed Arte*. 3rd series, 19 (1889), fasc. 4, 755–82.

Morelli, Emilia. "Benedetto XIV. Uomo e pontifice," in *Tre Profili*, Rome, 1955. Pp. 3–45.

(ed.). *Le lettere di Benedetto XIV al Card. de Tencin dai testi originali*. Vols. 1–2. Rome, 1955–65.

Morelli, Gonippo. *Le corporazioni romane di arti e mestieri dal XIII al XIX secolo*. Rome, 1937.

Morghen, Raffaello. "La visione storica di L. A. Muratori," in *Miscellanea di Studi Muratoriani*. Modena, 1951. Pp. 292–99.

Morichini, Carlo Luigi. *Degli istituti di pubblica carità e d'istruzione primaria in Roma*. Rome, 1835.

Moroni, Alessandro. "Vite, voci e viandanti della vecchia Roma," *La Nuova Rassegna*, 2 (March–May, 1894), nos. 12–19, 376–80, 407–10, 437–40, 475–77, 506–10, 539–41, 574–76, 597–99.

Mortari, Vincenzo Piano. "Tentativi di codificazione nel Granducato di Toscana nel secolo XVIII," *Rivista italiana per le scienze giuridiche*, 89 (1952–53), 285–387.

Moschini, Vittorio. "Filippo Della Valle," *L'Arte* (1925), 177–90.

"Giaquinto artista rappresentativo della pittura barocca tarda a Roma." *L'Arte* (1924), 104–23.

Muñoz, Antonio. *Antonio Canova. Le opere.* Rome, 1957.

Nardi, Carla. "La campagna nella città. L'opera dei Maestri Giustizieri (secc. XV–XVIII)," *Storia della città*, 29 (1984), 51–60.

Natali, Giulio (ed.). *Storia letteraria d'Italia: Il Settecento.* 2 vols., Rome, 1929.

Nicolai, Nicola Maria. *Memorie, leggi, ed osservazioni sulle campagne e sull'annona di Roma.* 3 vols., Rome, 1803.

Nicoll, Allardyce. *The World of Harlequin. A Critical Study of the Commedia dell'Arte.* Cambridge, 1963.

Nina, Luigi. *Le finanze pontifice sotto Clemente XI (Tassa di milione).* Milan, 1927.

Noack, Friedrich. *Deutsches Leben in Rom, 1700 bis 1900.* Stuttgart and Berlin, 1907.

*Das Deutschtum in Rom seit dem Ausgang des Mittelalters.* 2 vols., Berlin and Leipzig, 1927.

"Marco Benefial. Ein Bahnbrecher des Klassizismus." *Monatshefte für Kunstwissenschaft*, 12 (1919), nos. 5/6, 125–29.

Noel, Charles C. "Missionary Preachers in Spain: Teaching Social Virtues in the Eighteenth Century," *The American Historical Journal*, 90 (1985), 866–92.

Nolhac, Pierre de. *Peintres français en Italie.* Paris, 1934.

Nuccio, Oscar. "La precettistica economica di Leone Pascoli (1674–1744)," *Studi Romani*, 27 (1979), 282–301.

Nussdorfer, Laurie. "City Politics in Baroque Rome, 1623–1644." Unpublished Dissertation. Princeton University, 1985.

Oechslin, Werner. "L'intérêt archéologique et l'expérience architecturale avant et après Piranèse," in Georges Brunel (ed.). *Piranèse et les Français. Colloque tenu à la Villa Médicis, 12–14 mai 1976.* Rome, 1978. Pp. 395–410.

Oehler, Hansgeorg. "Das Zustandekommen einiger englischen Antikensammlungen im 18. Jahrhundert," in H. Beck, P. C. Bol, W. Prinz, *et al.*, *Antikensammlungen im 18. Jahrhundert.* Berlin, 1981. Pp. 295–316.

Onofrio, Cesare D'. *Il Tevere e Roma.* Rome, 1970.

Ozzòla, Landro. *Gian Paolo Pannini, pittore. Cinquanta tavole con introduzione.* Turin, 1921.

Pagano, Sergio. "Gli esposti dell'Ospedale di S. Spirito nel primo Ottocento," *Ricerche per la storia religiosa di Roma*, 3 (1979), 353–92.

Paglia, Vincenzo. *"La Pietà dei Carcerati." Confraternite e società a Roma nei secoli XVI–XVIII.* Rome, 1980.

Pallotti, Vincenzo. "Per una storia dell'Istituto delle Scienze," in Università degli studi di Bologna (ed.), *I materiali dell'Istituto delle Scienze.* Bologna, 1979. Pp. 55–62.

Palozzi, Romano. "Mons. Giovanni Bottari e il circolo dei giansenisti romani," *Annali della Scuola Normale Superiore di Pisa. Lettere, storia, e filosofia.* 2nd series, 10 (1941), fasc. 1–2, 70–90.

Pane, Luigi Dal. "Discussioni e leggi annonarie in Roma nel primo quarantennio del secolo XVIII," in *Studi in onore di Armando Sapori.* Milan, 1957. Pp. 1187–215.

*Economia e società a Bologna nell'età del Risorgimento. Introduzione alla ricerca.* Bologna, 1969.

*La finanza toscana dagli inizi del secolo XVIII alla caduta del Granducato*. Milan, 1965.
*Lo Stato Pontificio e il movimento riformatore del Settecento*. Milan, 1959.
*Storia del lavoro in Italia dagli inizi del secolo XVIII al 1815*. (Vol. 4 of *Storia del lavoro in Italia*, edited under the direction of Amintore Fanfani.) 2nd edition. Milan, 1958.
Panta, Lorenzo del and Livi-Bacci, Massimo. "Le componenti naturali dell'evoluzione demografica nell'Italia del Settecento," in Società italiana di demografia storica, *La popolazione italiana nel Settecento*. Bologna, 1979. Pp. 71–139.
Parlasca, Klaus. "Die Potsdamer Antikensammlung im 18. Jahrhundert," in H. Beck, P. C. Bol, W. Prinz, *et al.*, *Antikensammlungen im 18. Jahrhundert*. Berlin, 1981. Pp. 211–29.
Partner, Peter. "Papal financial policy in the Renaissance and Counter Reformation," *Past and Present*, 78 (1980), 18–62.
Pastor, Ludwig Freiherr von. *Geschichte der Päpste seit dem Ausgang des Mittelalters*. Vol. 14, pt 2 to vol. 16, pt 3. Freiburg im Breisgau, 1930–33.
Pastura, M. G. Ruggiero. *La Reverenda Camera Apostolica e i suoi archivi (secoli XV–XVIII)*. Rome. 1984.
Penuti, Carla. "Carestie ed epidemie," in Aldo Berselli (ed.), *Storia della Emilia Romagna*. 2 vols., Bologna, 1977. Vol. 2, 189–207.
Pérouse de Montclos, Jean-Marie. "Piranèse, les français et le classicisme international," in Georges Brunel (ed.), *Piranèse et les Français. Colloque tenu à la Villa Médicis, 12–14 mai 1976*. Rome, 1978. Pp. 419–22.
Pescosolido, Guido. *Terra e nobiltà. I Borghese*. Rome, 1979.
Petit-Radel, Philippe. *Voyage historique, chorographique, et philosophique dans les principales villes d'Italie en 1811 et 1812*. 2 vols., Paris, 1815.
Petraccone, Claudia. *Napoli dal '500 all '800. Problemi di storia demografica e sociale*. Naples, 1974.
Petrocchi, Massimo. *La restaurazione romana, 1815–1823*. Florence, 1941.
*Roma nel Seicento*. Bologna, 1970.
Petrovitch, Porphyre. "Recherches sur la criminalité à Paris dans la seconde moitié du XVIIIe siècle," in *Crimes et criminalité en France sous l'Ancien Régime, 17e–18e siècles*. Paris, 1971. Pp. 187–261.
Petrucci, Alfred. "La giovanezza di Giuseppe Vasi," *L'Urbe*, 5 (1940).
"I primi venticinque anni del Vasi a Roma," *L'Urbe*, 6 (1941), 11–12.
Philippe, Robert. "Une opération pilote: l'étude du ravitaillement de Paris au temps de Lavoisier," in Jean-Jacques Hémardinquer (ed.), *Pour une histoire de l'alimentation*. Paris, 1970. Pp. 60–67.
Pierrotti, Adamo. "Alcune aspetti della strategia religioso-apostolica di S. Leonardo," *Studi francescani*, 3rd series, 24 (1952), nos. 1–4.
Pietrangeli, Carlo. *Scavi e scoperte di antichità sotto il pontificato di Pio VI*. Rome, 1958.
Pighetti, C. "Per la storia del newtonianismo in Italia," *Rivista critica di storia della filosofia*, 26 (1961), fasc. 4, 425–34.
Pignatelli, Giuseppe. *Aspetti della Propaganda Cattolica a Roma da Pio VI a Leone XII*. Rome, 1974.
Pinto, John A. "Nicola Michetti and ephemeral design in eighteenth-century Rome," in Henry A. Millon (ed.), *Studies in Italian Art and Architecture. Fifteenth through Eighteenth Centuries*. Cambridge, Mass. and London, 1980. Pp. 289–322.
*The Trevi Fountain*. New Haven, Conn. and London, 1986.

Pinto, Sandra. "La promozione delle arti negli stati italiani dall'età delle riforme all'Unità," in *Storia dell'arte italiana*. Turin, 1982. Part 2: vol. 2(2) 793–1060.
Pisano, Giulio. "I 'birri' a Roma nel '600 ed un progetto di riforma del loro ordinamento sotto il pontificato d'Innocenzo XI," in *Rivista di studi e di vita romana*, 10 (1932), 543–56.
Piscitelli, Enzo. "Fabrizio Ruffo e la riforma economica dello Stato Pontificio," *Archivio della società romana di storia patria*, 74 (1951), 69–148.
"Una famiglia di mercanti di campagna: I Merolli," *Archivio della società romana di storia patria*, 81 (1958), 119–73.
*La riforma di Pio VI e gli scrittori economici romani*. Milan, 1958.
Poliakov, Léon. *Les banquiers juifs et la Saint-Siège du XIIIe au XVIIe siècle*. Paris, 1967.
Ponti, Ermanno. *Il Banco di Santo Spirito e la sua funzione economica in Roma papale (1605–1870)*. Rome, 1951.
Pontrandolfo, Angela. "Paestum and its Archeological History," in Joselita Raspi Serra (ed.), *Paestum and the Doric Revival, 1750–1830*. Florence, 1986. Pp. 51–55.
Portal, Emanuele barone. *L'Arcadia*. Rome, 1922.
Portoghesi, Paolo. *Roma barocca*. 2 vols., Bari, 1973.
Prandi, Alfonso. *Il Christianismo offeso e difeso*. Bologna, 1975.
Previtali, Giovanni. "Bottari, Maffei, Muratori e la riscoperta del medioevo artistico italiano," *Paragone*, 113 (1959), 3–32.
"La periodizzazione della storia dell'arte italiana," in *Storia dell'arte italiana*. Turin, 1979. Part 1: vol. 1, 5–96.
Prodi, Paolo. *Il sovrano pontifice. Un corpo e due anime: la monarchia papale nella prima età moderna*. Bologna, 1982.
Pucci, Luigi. "La diffusione delle idee economiche e sociale nel XVIII secolo," in Aldo Berselli (ed.), *Storia della Emilia Romagna*. 2 vols., Bologna, 1977. Vol. 2, 479–500.
Quarré, Pierre. "J.-B. Lallemand, paysagiste du XVIIIe siécle," *La Revue des Arts*, 4 (1954), 241–44.
Quondam, Amadeo. "L'istituzione Arcadia. Sociologia e ideologia d'un accademia," *Quaderni storici*, 23 (1973), 389–438.
Quynn, D. H. "Philipp von Stosch," *Catholic Historical Review*, 27 (1941), 332–44.
Raimondi, Ezio. "I Padri Maurini e l'opera del Muratori," *Giornale storico della letteratura italiana*, 128 (1951), 429–71.
"Scienza e letteratura," in Università degli studi di Bologna (ed.), *I materiali dell'Istituto delle Scienze*. Bologna, 1979. Pp. 13–17.
Rava, Luigi. *Un salotto romano del Settecento "Maria Pizzelli."* Rome, 1926.
Re, Niccolò Del. *Monsignor Governatore di Roma*. Rome, 1972.
Reinhard, Wolfgang. *Papstfinanz und Nepotismus unter Paul V (1605–1621)*. 2 vols., Stuttgart, 1974.
Renazzi, Filippo Maria. *Storia dell'università degli studi di Roma detta comunemente la Sapienza*. 4 vols., Rome, 1803–1806.
Revel, Jacques. "Le grain de Rome et la crise de l'annone dans la seconde moitié du XVIIIe siècle," *Mélanges de l'Ecole française de Rome. Moyen Age, temps modernes* (1972), 201–82.
"Les privilèges d'une capitale: l'approvisionnement de Rome à l'époque moderne," *Annales, E.S.C.*, 30 (1975), 563–74.
Ricci, Giovanni. *Bologna*. Rome and Bari, 1980.

Riccòmini, Eugenio. "La scultura del Settecento e gli inizi del Canova," in *Nuove idee e nuova arte nel '700 italiano. Convegno internazionale, Roma, 19–23 maggio 1975*. Rome, 1977. Pp. 63–69.

Ricuperati, Giuseppe. "L'epistolario dei fratelli Verri," in *Nuove idee e nuova arte nel '700 italiano. Convegno internazionale, Roma, 19–23 maggio 1975*. Rome, 1977. Pp. 239–81.

Rifkin, Jeremy. *Entropy. A New World View*. New York, 1980.

Rinaldi, Mario. *Due secoli di musica al Teatro Argentina*. Vol. 1. Florence, 1978.

Rinaldis, Aldo De. *L'arte in Roma dal Seicento al Novecento*. Bologna, 1948.

Rinieri, Ilario. "La liquidazione napoleonica del debito pubblico di Roma (1810–11)," *Civiltà Cattolica*, quaderno 1347 (4 August 1906), 247–88.

Roatti, Massimo. "La cultura scientifica tra conservazione e innovazione," in Aldo Berselli (ed.), *Storia della Emilia Romagna*. Bologna, 1977. Vol. 2, 397–414.

Roberti, Giuseppe. "La musica in Italia nel secolo XVIII secondo le impressioni di viaggiatori stranieri," *Rivista musicale italiana*, 7 (1900), 698–729, and 8 (1901), 519–59.

Rodocanachi, Emmanuel Pierre. *Les corporations ouvrières à Rome depuis la chute de l'Empire romain*. Paris, 1894.

*Les Institutions communales de Rome sous la papauté*. Paris, 1901.

*Le Saint Siège et les Juifs. Le ghetto à Rome*. Paris, 1891.

Romano, Pietro. *Pasquino in Settecento*. Rome, 1934.

Ronga, Luigi. "L'Opera Metastasiana," in Mario Fubini (ed.), *Pietro Metastasio. Opere*. Milan and Naples, n.d. Pp. vii–xxxiii.

Rosa, Luigi de. *Studi sugli arrendamenti del Regno di Napoli. Aspe : della ricchezza mobiliare nel mezzogiorno continentale (1649–1806)*. Naples, 1958.

Rosa, Mario. "Atteggiamenti culturali e religiosi di Giovanni Lami nelle *Novelle Letterarie*," *Annali della Scuola Normale Superiore di Pisa. Lettere, storia e filosofia*. 2nd series, 25 (1956), 260–333.

(ed.). *Cattolicismo e Lumi nel Settecento italiano*. Rome, 1981.

"Sulla condanna dell'*Esprit des Lois* e sulla fortuna di Montesquieu in Italia," *Rivista di storia della chiesa in Italia*, 14 (1960), 411–28.

Rosa, Mario, Monticone, Alberto, Giuntella, Vittorio E., and Stella, Pietro. "Poveri e marginati; un problema religioso," *Ricerche per la storia religiosa di Roma*, 3 (1979), 11–41.

Rosenblum, Robert. *Transformations in Late Eighteenth Century Art*. Princeton, 1967.

Rossi, Giorgio. *L'Agro di Roma tra '500 e '800. Condizioni di vita e lavoro*. Rome, 1985.

Rossi, Mario. "L'occupazione napoletano di Roma (1799–1801)," *Rassegna storica del Risorgimento*, 19 (1932), 693–732.

Rossodivita, Ida. "Appunti per una storia della popolazione di Trastevere nel Settecento," *Studi Romani*, 23 (1975), 153–63.

Roster, Giorgio. *Climatologia dell'Italia nelle sue attinenze con l'igiene e con l'agricoltura*. Turin, 1909.

Rotili, Mario. *Filippo Raguzzini e il rococo romano*. Rome, 1951.

Rotondo, Antonio. "Introduzione," to Cosimo Amidei. *Opere*. Turin, 1980. Pp. 9–147.

Rotta, Salvatore. "Una lettera inedita di Domenico Passionei al Voltaire," *Rassegna della letteratura italiana* (1959), 265–74.

"Montesquieu nel Settecento italiano: note e ricerche," in *Materiale per una storia della cultura giuridica*. 2 vols., Bologna, 1971.

Ruscus. "Centenari di artisti minori: Carlo Maratta," *Emporium*, 1925, 182–86.
Sabatini, Francesco. "Rugentino," *Il Volgo di Roma*, 3 (1901).
Sanctis, Francesco De. *Storia della letteratura italiana*. Lanciano, 1950.
Santangelo, Antonino. "La scultura," in *Il Settecento a Roma. Mostra, 19 marzo – 31 maggio, 1959*. Rome, 1959. Pp. 31–39.
Sbrana, Carla, Traina, Rosa, and Sonnino, Eugenio. *Gli "stati delle anime" a Roma dalle origini al secolo XVII. Origini, consistènze, contenuti*. Rome, 1977.
Scavizzi, C. Paolo. "Le condizioni per lo sviluppo dell'attività edilizia a Roma nel sec. XVII: la legislazione," *Studi Romani*, 17 (1969), 160–71.
Schiavoni, Claudio and Sonnino, Eugenio. "Popolazione e territorio nel Lazio, 1701–1811," in Società italiana di demografia storica (ed.), *La popolazione italiana nel Settecento*. Bologna, 1979. Pp. 191–216.
Schippisi, Ranieri. "L'Arcadia," in *Letteratura italiana. Le correnti*. Milan, 1956. Pp. 505–56.
Schudt, Ludwig. *Italienreisen im 17. und 18. Jahrhundert*. Vienna and Munich, 1959.
Scioscioli, Donato. *La vita e le opere di Francesco Antonio Zaccaria erudito del secolo XVIII*. Brescia, 1925.
Scott, Jonathan. *Piranesi*. New York, 1975.
Seregni, Giovanni (ed.). *Carteggio di Pietro e Alessandro Verri*. Milan, 1940.
Serra, Joselita Raspi (ed.). *Paestum and the Doric Revival, 1750–1830. Essential Outlines of an Approach*. Florence, 1986.
Serullaz, Arlette, Sandt, Udolpho van De, and Regis, Michel. *David e Roma. Mostra, dicembre 1981 – febbraio 1982*. Rome, 1982.
Sestieri, Giancarlo. "Contributi a Sebastiano Conca," *Commentari*, 20 (1969), 317–41, and 21 (1970), 122–38.
*Settecento a Roma, Mostra, 19 marzo–31 maggio 1959* (Rome, 1959).
Sharp, Samuel. *Letters from Italy describing the Customs and Manners of That Country in the Years 1765 and 1766*. 3rd revised edition. London, 1767.
Sichtermann, Hellmut. *Winckelmann e Roma (nel secondo centenario della morte)*. Rome, 1969.
Silvagni, David. *La corte pontificia e la società romana nei secoli XVIII e XIX*. 4 vols., Rome, 1971.
Simeoni, Luigi. *Storia della Università di Bologna*. Vol. 2: *L'età moderna (1500–1888)*. Bologna, 1947.
Simoncelli. Paolo. "Note sul sistema assistenziale a Roma nel XVI secolo," in Giorgio Politi, Mario Rosa, and Franco Della Peruta. *Timore e Carità. I poveri nell'Italia moderna*. Cremona, 1982.
Simone, Maria Rosa di. *La "Sapienza" romana nel Settecento. Organizzazione universitario e insegnemento di diritto*. Rome, 1980.
Smith, Catherine Delano. *Western Mediterranean Europe. A Historical Geography of Italy, Spain and Southern France since the Neolithic*. London and New York, 1979.
Smither, Howard E. *A History of Oratorio*. Vol. 1: *The Oratorio in the Baroque Era*. Chapel Hill, N.C., 1977.
Sofia, Francesca. Review: "Vincenzo Ferrone. *Scienza Natura Religione*." Naples, 1982. In *Clio*, 19 (1983), 313–17.
Sombart, Werner. *Die römische Campagna. Eine sozialökonomische Studie*. Leipzig, 1888.

Spinosa, Nicola. "Neapolitan Painting under Charles and Ferdinand Bourbon: Continuity and Crisis within a Tradition," in *The Golden Age of Naples. Art and Civilization under the Bourbons, 1734–1805*. Detroit and Chicago, 1981. Vol. 1, 55–71.

Steuben, Hans von. "Das Museo Pio-Clementino," in H. Beck, P. C. Bol, W. Prinz, *et al.* (eds.), *Antikensammlungen im 18. Jahrhundert*. Berlin, 1981. Pp. 149–65.

Story, William Witmore. *Roba di Roma*. London, 1871.

Strazzullo, Franco. *Edilizia e urbanistica a Napoli dal '500 al '700*. Naples, 1968.

Strohm, Reinhard. *Die italienische Oper im 18. Jahrhundert*. Wilhelmshaven, 1979.

Stumpo, Enrico. *Il capitale finanziario a Roma fra cinque e seicento. Contributo alla storia della fiscalità pontificia in età moderna (1570–1660)*. Milan, 1985.

Tomassetti, Giuseppe. *La Campagna romana. Antica, medioevale, e moderna*. 4 vols., Rome, 1910–26.

Tornézy, M. Albert. *Bergeret et Fragonard. Journal inedit d'un voyage en Italie, 1773–1774*. Paris, 1895.

Toscani, Xenio. *Il clero lombardo dall'ancien regime alla restaurazione*. Bologna, 1979.

Tosi, Mario. *Il Sacro Monte di Pietà di Roma e le sue amministrazioni (1539–1874)*. Rome, 1937.

Tournon-Simiane, Philippe comte de. *Etudes statistiques sur Rome et la partie occidentale des Etats Romains*. 2nd edition. 2 vols., Paris, 1855.

Trasselli, Carmelo. "Processi politici romani dal 1792 al 1798," *Rassegna storica del Risorgimento*, 25 (1938), 1495–524, 1613–54.

Trease, Geoffrey. *The Grand Tour*. London, 1967.

Turner, Nicholas. "An attack on the Accademia di S. Luca: Ludovico David's *L'Amore dell'Arte*," in *British Museum Yearbook*, 1 (1976), 157–86.

Valsecchi, Franco. *L'Italia nel Settecento dal 1714 al 1788*. Milan, 1959.

Venturi, Adolfo. "I grandi pittori di rovine, Pannini e Piranesi," *Roma* (1925), 206–12.

Venturi, Franco. "Beccaria e la sua fortuna," in *Atti del convegno internazionale su Cesare Beccaria, promosso dall'Accademia delle Scienze di Torino nel secondo centenario dell'opera "Dei delitti e delle pene."* Turin, 1966. Pp. 3–17.

"The Enlightenment in the Papal States," in *Italy and the Enlightenment. Studies in a Cosmopolitan Century*. Translated by Susan Corsi. London, 1972. Pp. 225–64.

"Napoli nell'anno della fame," *Rivista storica italiana*, 85 (1973), 394–472.

"Quattro anni di carestia in Toscana (1764–1767)," *Rivista storica italiana*, 88 (1976), 649–707.

*Settecento riformatore*. Vol. 1: *Da Muratori a Beccaria*. Turin, 1969.

*Settecento riformatore*. Vol. 2: *La chiesa e la repubblica dentro i loro limiti, 1758–1774*. Turin, 1976.

"1764–1767: Roma negli anni della fame," *Rivista storica italiana*, 85 (1973), 514–43.

Vicchi, Leone. *Vincenzo Monti. Le lettere e la politica in Italia dal 1750 al 1820 (Trienno 1778–1780)*. Fusignano, 1885.

Vico, Giambattista. *Autobiography*. Translated by Max Harold Fisch and Thomas Goddard Bergin. Ithaca, N.Y., 1944.

Vidal de la Blache, Paul and Gallois, L. *Géographie universelle*. Vol. 7, part 2: *Italie et Pays Balkaniques*, by Jules Sion. Paris, 1934.

Villani, Pasquale. "Ricerche sulla proprietà e sul regime fondario nel Lazio," *Annuario dell'istituto storico italiano per l'età moderna e contemporanea*, 12 (1960), 172–96.

Villoslada, Riccardo, G. *Storia del Collegio Romano dal suo inizio (1551) alla soppressione della Compagnia di Gesù (1773)*. Rome, 1954.

Volli, Gemma. "Papa Benedetto XIV e gli ebrei," *La Rassegna mensile di Israel*, 22 (1956), 215–26.

Volpi, Marisa. "Corrado Giaquinto e alcuni aspetti della cultura figurativa del '700 in Italia," *Bollettino d'arte*, 43–44 (1958), 267–82.

Voss, Hermann. *Die Malerei des Barock in Rom*. Berlin, 1924.

"Michele Rocca, ein vergessener italienischer Rokoko-Maler," *Zeitschrift für bildende Kunst* (1921), 69–75.

Waquet, Jean-Claude. "Aux marges de l'impôt. Fraudeurs et contrebandiers dans la Toscana du XVIIIe siècle," in Ecole française de Rome (ed.), *La fiscalité et ses implications sociales en Italie et en France aux XVIIe et XVIIIe siècles*. Rome, 1980. Pp. 75–95.

Waterhouse, Ellis K. *Baroque Painting in Rome. The Seventeenth Century*. London, 1937.

*Painting in Britain, 1530 to 1790*. Baltimore, Md., 1953.

*Roman Baroque Painting. A List of the Principal Painters and their Works in and around Rome*. London, 1976.

Wee, Herman van der. "Monetary, Credit and Banking Systems," in *The Cambridge Modern History of Europe*. Vol. 5: *The Economic Organization of Early Modern Europe*. Cambridge, 1977. Pp. 290–392.

Weintraub, Karl J. *The Age of the Baroque* (The Crossely Lectures, St. Olaf College, 11–13 March 1985). Northfield, Minn., 1985.

Whitmore, P. J. S. *The Order of Minims in Seventeenth-Century France*. The Hague, 1967.

Wilton-Ely, John. "Vision and Design: Piranesi's *Fantasia* and the Graeco-Roman Controversy," in Georges Brunel (ed.), *Piranèse et les Français. Colloque tenu à la Villa Médicis, 12–14 mai 1976*. Rome, 1978. Pp. 529–52.

Wind, Edgar, "The Sources of David's *Horaces*," *Journal of the Warburg and Courtauld Institutes*, 4 (1940–41), 124–38.

Wittkower, Rudolf. "Documenti sui modelli per la sacrestia di San Pietro," *Bolletino della società piemontese di archeologia e belle arti*, 3 (1949), 158–59.

"Piranesi's Architectural Creed," in Rudolf Wittkower, *Studies in the Italian Baroque*. London, 1975. Pp. 235–46.

"The Role of Classical Models in Bernini's and Poussin's Preparatory Work," in Rudolf Wittkower, *Studies in the Italian Baroque*. London, 1975. Pp. 103–14.

Woolf, Stuart. *A History of Italy, 1700–1860. The Social Constraints of Political Change*. London, 1979.

Young, David. *Rome in Winter and the Tuscan Hills in Summer. A Contribution to the Climate of Italy*. London, 1889.

Zan, Mauro de. "La messa all'Indice del *Newtonianismo per le dame* di Francesco Algarotti," in Renzo Cremante and Walter Tega (eds.), *Scienza e letteratura nella cultura italiana del Settecento*. Bologna, 1984. Pp. 133–47.

Zanazzo, Giggi. *Tradizioni popolari romane. Canti popolari romani con un saggio dei canti del Lazio*. Turin and Rome, 1907.

*Tradizioni popolari romane. Usi, costumi, e pregiudizi del popolo di Roma*. Turin and Rome, 1907–10.

Zanetti, Roberto. *La musica italiana nel Settecento*. 3 vols., Busto Arsizio, 1978.

Zazoff, Peter. "Vom Gemmensammeln zur Glyptikforschung," in H. Beck, P. C. Bol, W. Prinz, *et al.* (eds.), *Antikensammlungen im 18. Jahrhundert*. Berlin, 1981. Pp. 363–78.
Zupko, Ronald Edward. *Italian Weights and Measures from the Middle Ages to the Nineteenth Century*. Philadelphia, 1981.

# Index

abati, 48, 301, 306
*abbachi*, 170, 191
*abbondanza* (Florentine), 184
abolition of: duties and tolls, 100, 102, 105, 125; torture and capital punishment, 218–20
abortion, 209
Abruzzi, 66, 180, 273, 343
absolutism, 41, 42
Académie de France à Rome, 5, 334, 335, 339, 347, 348, 354, 367
Académie des sciences, 254
academies 247–48; established by Benedict XIV, 267, 268; in Mannheim, 7
  Accademia degli Arcadi (Arcadia), 251, 252, 254, 286–97, 304, 305, 306, 309, 325, 329
  Accademia degli Inquieti, 239
  Accademia degli Investiganti, 250, 252
  Accademia de' Concilj, 265, 266, 268
  Accademia dei Lincei, 248
  Accademia della Crusca, 277, 296
  Accademia del Cimento, 239
  Accademia di San Luca, 4, 6, 320, 333–35, 340, 343, 344, 345
  Accademia Fisico-matematica, 6, 248–59, 250, 257, 264, 265
Acqua Acetosa, 212
Acqua Mariana, 96
Acqua Toffana, 222
Acqua Vergine, 28, 29, 136
Acquae Albulae, 212
Acquaroni family, 110, 160
acquavita, 127, 195
Acquaviva, Cardinal Francesco, 340
*Acta Eruditorum*, 252
Adam, Robert, 2
Addison, Joseph, 296
age distribution, 81, 83–84
aged, the, 198, 204
Agro Romano, 101, 152–72, 173, 174, 177, 178, 185
agronomic propaganda, 103–4
Agucchi, Giovanni Battista, 325
Aix-la-Chapelle, Peace of (1748), 326
Albani, Cardinal Alessandro, 6, 45, 253, 320, 324, 325, 328, 346
Albani, Cardinal Annibale, 241, 265, 313, 324
Albani family, 49, 320, 342
Albano, 153, 156, 314
Albercini, Filippo, 361
Alberti, Leon Battista, 17, 28
alcohol, 194–95
Aldrovandi, Pompeo, 338
Alexander VII, Fabio Chigi, 10, 20, 21, 22, 33, 130, 134, 207, 236, 242, 258, 330, 332
Alexander VIII, Pietro Ottoboni, 9, 254, 301, 332
Alfieri, Vittorio, 286, 297, 304, 305–6, 307
Algarotti, Francesco, 234, 253
Alibert, Antonio d', 301
Alibert, Jacques d', 301
alms, 198
altar of St. Ignatius, 357
alum, 94, 141–42, 150, 171
Amaduzzi, Giovanni Cristoforo, 210, 261–62, 277, 283
Ambrogi, Vincenzo, 205
Amelia, Marina d', 190
Amidei, Cosimo, 218
Amorosi, Antonio, 343
*Amplificatio Jurisdictionis*, 20
Amsterdam, 181, 183, 318
anacreontic verse, 288
Ancona, 105, 151, 368
Anesi, Paolo, 341, 351, 356
Angelini, Giuseppe, 364
Angelucci, Teodoro, 221
anglomania, 255
Aniene, 36, 153
animal husbandry, 169–71, 189; *see also* livestock
annona, 47, 91, 102, 105, 127, 149, 150, 157, 165, 167, 175, 177–89, 189; financial state of, 185–86
anti-arcadian polemic, 295–96
anticurialism, 40

# Index

antiquities, 129, 310, 316, 346, 365; export of, 320–22; loss of, 315
Antonino Pierozzi, bishop of Florence, 279
apartments, rental, 20, 37, 71
Apostolic Chamber, 37, 46–47, 85, 95, 96, 99, 101, 107, 108, 109, 110, 112, 116–41, 148–49, 150, 169, 173, 186, 216, 227, 236, 319, 342
apostolic palace, 116, 140–41, 147, 150, 161, 178
*appalti* (grants to tax farmers), 119, 126, 127–28
Apulia, 84, 273
Aquino, Carlo d', 293
Arcadians, 234, 286, 287, 288, 291, 292, 294, 352
Archconfraternity of San Girolamo della Carità, 226, 227, 228
archeological excavations, 310, 311–15, 319
archeology, 264–65, 268, 278, 308, 311, 312, 329, 345
Archetto, 261, 276, 280, 282, 283
Archivo di Stato di Roma, 135
Archivio Segreto del Vicariato, 202
Arco Travertino, 163
Ardea, 156
Argelli, Giuseppe, 98
Argenvilliers, Clemente, 111, 144, 241
Ariosto, Ludovico, 297
aristocracy, Roman, 48–51; privileges in the papal provinces, 51 n.37
Aristotelianism, 242, 249, 251, 277
army, papal, 42
Arnauld, Antoine, 279
Arteaga, Stefano, 297
artisans, 90, 96, 113, 199; proletariete of, 92; *see also* trades
art: esthetic of, 328–29, 333; forgenies of, 3, 315, 318; French hostility to, 5; loss of, 315; patronage of, 332, 357
art dealers, 2, 318–20, 323
art restoration, 315–16
artists, 1, 81, 112, 268, 345, 361
Arundel, Earl of, 2
*assegna*, 178
*assignats*, 147
astronomical observations, 235, 257–58
Athenaeum Romanum, 237
Athens, 327, 330
atomism, 249–50, 251, 256
*Atto del Popolo Sovrano* (15 February 1798), 369
Auber, François, 96
Audifreddi, Giovanni Battista, 257
Augustinianism, 266, 267, 276, 279, 284
Aurelian wall, 15, 39, 55
Avellino, Onofrio, 339
Avignon, 40, 55, 91, 104, 148, 207, 236, 260, 366, 368

Bacchini, Benedetto, 264
Baciccio (Giovanni Gaulli), 3, 332
Baglivi, Giorgio, 237, 249
Baiocco, 142, 144
balances, annual, 117–23, 139
Bamberg, 234
Banco di Santo Spirito, 137, 144, 145, 147, 150
Bañez, Domingo, 276
bankruptcy, 111, 119, 142, 144, 147
Baretti, Giuseppe, 296, 297
bargello, 214, 215, 230
Baronio, Cardinal Cesare, 264
baroque: art, 325, 331, 335, 336, 344, 346, 349–50, 356; Roman, 8–9, 335–36; in Rome, 18–20, 262, 365
Basi, Raimondo, 85
Bassville, Hugon de, 307–8, 366, 367, 368
Baths of Diocletian, 98, 108, 112, 179, 183
Batoni, Pompeo, 3, 112, 344, 346
Bayle, Pierre, 257, 264
Bazin, Germain, 325
Beccaria, Cesare, 218, 219, 220, 229, 243, 262
Beccaria, Giambattista, 257
*becchini* (gravediggers), 212–13
beggars, 100, 198, 200, 202
Bellarmine, Cardinal Roberto, 248
Bellelli, Fulgenzio, 276
Belli and Lazzari, 108
Belloni, Girolamo, 49, 103, 111, 126, 144, 261
Bellori, Giovanni Pietro, 325
Belvedere statue court, 33, 321, 322, 344, 347
Bencini, Domenico, 265
Ben-David, Joseph, 258
Benedict XIII, Pier Francesco Orsini, 25, 44, 118, 135, 179, 210, 230, 272, 280, 294
Benedict XIV, Prospero Lambertini, 29, 31–32, 40, 41–42, 43, 46, 102–3, 104, 111, 117, 118, 127, 136, 138, 144, 147, 148, 182, 184, 208, 210, 217, 234, 235, 239–243, 260, 261, 267, 268, 274, 277, 2778, 281, 285, 322, 340, 344, 360, 363–64
Benedictis, Giovan Battista de, 252
Benefial, Marco, 6, 221, 334, 338, 341, 343, 346
Benevento, 25, 40, 119
Bergeret de Grancourt, 15
Berlin, 199
Bernini, Gian Lorenzo, 5, 9, 10, 21–22, 27, 299, 331, 333, 336, 344, 353, 356, 359, 360
Bernis, Cardinal François-Joaquim de Pierre de, 275

Berthier, Alexander, 369, 370
Berti, Gianlorenzo, 276, 277
Bérulle, Pierre de, 276
Bettinelli, Saverio, 295, 296, 297
Bianchi, Giambattista, 277
Bianchini, Francesco, 6, 252, 254–55, 256, 257, 258, 264, 265, 310, 316
Bianconi, Giovanni Ludovico, 310
Biblioteca Casanatense, 257, 280, 321
birth rate, 59, 61–62
bishops, 44, 56, 130, 281
blanket making, 107
Bloemen, Jan Frans (Orizzonte), 351
Bloemen, Pieter van, 351
Blundell, Henry, 315, 320
Boccupaduli, Marchesa Gentili, 262
Bologna, 21, 40–41, 49, 59–60, 61, 62, 68, 88–89, 105, 107, 113, 116, 118, 129, 136, 137, 173, 176, 177, 180, 187, 199, 243, 259, 260, 281, 285, 300, 336, 338, 368; university of, 238, 239
Bolognese, 40, 158
Bonaparte, Joseph, 368–69
Bonaparte, Napoleon (Napoleon I), 150–51, 152, 153, 308, 312, 368, 369
Boniface VIII, 137, 172, 236
Boniface IX, 169
Borel, Ferdinand, 109
Borelli, Alfonso, 249, 250
Borghese, Marcantonio, 346, 356
Borghese family, 48–49, 161–63, 323, 332, 367
Borgo, 19, 207
Borgondio, Orazio, 235
Borromeo, Carlo, 276
Borromini, Francesco, 30, 357
Bosco Parrasio, 287
Boscovich, Roggero Guiseppe, 235, 256–57, 268
botanical garden, 236, 242
Bottani, Giuseppe, 346
Bottari, Giovanni Gaetano, 238, 261, 266, 267, 277–82, 326, 353, 354
Bouchardon, Edme, 359
Boucher, François, 348
Bourbons, 43, 117, 339, 340
bourgeoisie, 90, 160, 165
Boyle, Robert, 250
Bracci, Pietro, 29, 316, 358, 359–60, 361, 363, 364
Bracciano, 171
*braccianti* (day laborers), 199
Bramante, Donato, 18, 22, 34
Brasavoli, Girolamo, 247
Braschi, Msgr. Giovanni Angelo, *see* Pius VI
bread, 176, 179, 181–2, 183, 184, 194; rationing of, 183
Breschia, 282
Brethren of the Christian Schools (*Ignoranti*), 232, 233
Brettingham, Matthew, Jr, 3
brigandage, 88
Brussels, 183
budgets, papal, 116–41
Bugatti, Giovanni, 222
building: boom, 20; construction, norms for, 19; industry, 36, 94; secular program of, 22–29
building materials; lime, 36–37; marble, 36; tiles, 36
Bulgarelli, Marianna (*La Romanina*), 302, 303
Buon Governo, 45, 105, 161
bureaucracy, papal, 47–48
Burgundians, 81
burial, 212–13, 229
Burney, Charles, 304
Busca, Cardinal Ignazio, 216
Bussani, Giuseppe Giacinto, 107

Cacault, François, 222
cadaster (1783), 103, 111, 157, 158, 163, 185, 186, 191
Caetani, Francesco, duke of Sermoneta, 248, 257
Caetani, Onorato, 111, 257
Calabria, 273
*calancà* (calico), 108
Calandrelli, Don Giuseppe, 235
Calasanzio, Giuseppe, 233
*calmiere* (fixed maximum price), 179
Caloprese, Gregorio, 251, 254
Cambridge, 243
Camerlengo, Cardinal, 45–46, 53, 91, 178, 179, 224
Campagna, Giovanni Pietro, 314
Campagna, Roman, 97, 153, 155, 163, 169, 170, 171, 172, 173, 175, 178, 180, 191, 198, 214, 274, 343, 350
Campania, 81, 194
Campidoglio, 17, 18, 25, 51, 52–53, 56, 102, 116, 128, 268, 294, 321, 322, 340, 360, 369
Campigli, Gian Domenico, 346
Campo dei Fiori, 17, 181, 340
Campo Verano, 213
Camporesi, Giuseppe, 33
Canale, Francesco and Antonio, 108
canon law, 41, 130
Canova, Antonio, 316, 347, 359, 361–65
capital and credit, 88, 89, 90, 101, 102, 111
Capitoline Chamber, 116
Capitoline: museum, 129, 321, 322, 324, 360; tribunals, 53

*caporioni*, 51
Capponi, Marchese Alessandro Gregorio, 322, 359
Capranica, Pompeo, 301
*capriccio*, 352, 355
Caracci, Annibale, 3, 325, 336–37, 338, 339, 344, 345, 349
Caravale, Mario, 40
Carceri Nuove, 225, 227
cardinal secretary of state, 46, 53
cardinal vicar, 54, 56, 85, 209–10, 225
Cardinals, Sacred College of, 42, 44–45
Carloni, Marco, 313–14
Carrara, 36
carriages, 21, 127
Carteret, Lord John, 318
Cartesianism, 250, 251, 253, 254, 256, 259, 302
*casale*, 155, 159
Casanova, Giovanni Battista, 347
Caserta, 346
Cassiano del Posso, 324
Castel Gondolfo, 314, 320
*Castelli Romani*, 41, 172, 194, 356
Castel Sant'Angelo, 70, 107, 147, 148–49, 323, 369
Castro, 179
Catherine II of Russia, 315, 319
Catholic sovereigns, 282, 284, 365, 366
Cavaceppi, Bartolomeo, 315, 316, 361, 364
*cavaletto*, 230
Cavalli, Attanagio, 258
*cavallo*, 192
Caylus, Anne Calude Philippe comte de, 348
*cedole*, 38, 144, 145–47, 150
celibacy, 59
Cellini, Benvenuto, 315–16
cemetries, 213
censorship, 100
census, 55, 59
Cerati, Gaspare, 252, 261, 278
cereal: prices, 163; production, 167–68, 183, 186
cereals: oats, 176; rye, 176; wheat, 178
Cerveteri, 161
Cervoni, Giovan Battista, 369
Cesarini Sforza, Duca Giuseppe, 301
Cesarotti, Melchiorre, 297
Cesi, Federico, 248
*ceto civile*, 249
charcoal, 171
charity: private, 196, 197, 198, 199; public, 196, 204
Charles II of Spain, 42
Charles VII of Naples (Charles III of Spain), 131, 218, 322, 339, 340, 353
Charles Emmanuel III of Sardinia, 183
Chautel, Jeanne-Françoise de, 332
chemistry, 241
Cherbury, Herbert of, 265
Chiabrera, Gabriello, 288
Chiari, Giuseppe, 337, 358
Chiarugi, Vincenzo, 210
chierici of the Apostolic Chamber, 46–47, 48, 52, 178, 224
Chiesa Nuova, 21
Chigi family, 49, 248, 320
Christina of Sweden, 21, 35, 250, 287, 299, 301, 342
Ciampini, Giovanni Giustino, 6, 237, 248, 252, 264, 265
Cibo, Msgr. Camillo, 190, 191, 193
*ciceroni*, 316–17
Cicoli, Michele, 215
Circolo del Tamburo, 265, 266, 267, 269, 277
Cisalpine republic, 308, 368
citizenship, Roman, 52–53
city, ethos and character of a, 1, 7; modern planning in, 21–22; Tridentine planning, 18
civic: magistracy of Rome, 51–53, 116; nobility, 53
civil constitution of the clergy, French, 366
Civitavecchia, 89, 96, 105, 110, 141, 151, 183, 230
Clarke, Samuel, 252
classicism, late baroque, 28, 331, 344, 360, 361, 364
Claude Lorrain (Claude Gellée), 4, 19, 349, 350, 351, 355
Clement VII, Giulio de' Medici, 17, 127, 131, 224, 226, 321
Clement VIII, Ippolito Aldobrandini, 142, 143, 148, 234
Clement IX, Giulio Rospigliosi, 134, 248
Clement X, Emilio Altieri, 118, 128, 134, 248
Clement XI, Gianfrancesco Albani, 10, 23–25, 42, 44, 59, 62, 95, 96, 99, 101, 104, 110, 118, 127, 135, 136, 142, 143, 148, 161, 167, 179, 204, 205, 215, 225, 233, 236, 238, 253, 254, 267, 268, 287, 318, 321, 324, 330, 332, 333, 335, 357
Clement XII, Lorenzo Corsini, 28, 30, 34, 35, 39, 40, 42, 44, 93, 95, 117, 128, 135, 136, 225, 259, 277, 278, 359, 360, 361
Clement XIII, Carlo Rezzonico, 29, 33, 43, 44, 93, 95, 105, 118, 136, 144, 148, 182, 183, 184, 222, 272, 282, 364
Clement XIV, Giovanni Vincenzo Antonio Ganganelli, 10, 33, 44, 86, 93, 98, 136, 210, 281, 282, 283, 322, 323, 330, 359, 360, 362–64

Clément, Augustine Jean Charles, 282
clergy, regular male, 69, 147, 272; secular, 67, 69, 147, 236, 272–73, 281
clerical population, decline of, 67–70
climate, 153, 155; drought, 148–49
Cochin, Charles-Nicolas, 5
*Codice Estense* (1771), 219
*Codicillo del Testamento Politico*, 102
coinage, 142–45; debasement of, 88, 145, 150; mixed metal, 142–43, 144; *see also* cedole, scudo
Coke, Thomas, 3
Colbert, Jean-Baptiste, 103, 334
colleges, 234–36
  Collegio Clementino (Clementina), 48, 234, 304
  Collegio dei cavalieri di S. Pietro, 137
  Collegio de Propaganda Fide, 235, 265, 272
  Collegio Nazareno, 234, 242, 281, 304
  Collegio Romano, 235–36, 242, 256, 257, 258, 283, 304, 369
Colonna, Camillo, 249–50
Colonna family, 49, 161
colosseum 24, 205, 274
*Commedia dell'arte*, 299–300
communities (municipalities), 41, 45, 149, 183
*Computisteria*, 46
Comtat Venaissin, 40
Conca, Sebastiano, 6, 332, 339–42, 344, 353
concordats, 43, 131, 148
*concorso*, 241, 273
confraternities, religious, 91, 93, 147, 196, 197, 270
  Orazione e delle Morte, 197, 213
  Pietà dei Carcerati, 197, 202, 226, 227, 228
  Pietà Divina, 197
  San Giovanni Decollata, 197, 226, 229–30
  Sant'Ivo, 197
  Santissima Annunziata, 204
  Santissimi Apostoli, 197
  Visitazione di Maria Vergine degli Orfane, 204
congregations, papal, 45, 102, 116, 273
Congregazione dei Virtuosi, 10
Congresso accadèmico di agricolture, manifattura e commercio, 107
Conservatorio di San Giovanni in Laterano, 198
Conservatorio Pio, 95
conservators of Rome, 51, 52, 177
conspirators, 369
Constantini, Ermenegildo, 346
Consulta, 45–46, 129; Palace of the, 28
Conti, Antonio, 258
*conti dell'entrata e dell'uscita*, 117
convalescence, 209
convents, 21
*conversazioni*, 247, 267, 286, 295
conversion, 85
convicts, 109
Cooper, Richard, 356
*corda*, 220, 230
Corilla Olimpica (Maria Maddelena Morelli-Fernandez), 295, 296
Cornacchini, Agostino, 359
Corneille, Pierre, 296, 304
Cornelio, Tommaso, 250, 251
Corneto, 89
Corona, Nicola, 108, 367, 369
Corradi, Alfonso, 207
Correggio, 3
corsairs, 108
*corsi*, 214, 302
Corsica, 194
Corsini, Cardinal Neri, 35, 277, 280, 326, 353, 361
Cortona, Pietro da, 21, 22, 336, 337
Cosimo I, duke of Tuscany, 315
Cosimo III, grand duke of Tuscany, 217, 322
cost of living, 111–15
Costa, Nino, 355
cotton, 97–98, 108–11; cultivation of, 110
Council (provincial synod) of Rome, 44–45, 272, 280
Counter Reformation, 90, 94, 196, 276, 331, 344, 349, 359
Coyer, Gabriel-François, 175, 221, 331
credit papers, *see cedole*
Crescimbeni, Giovanni Maria, 250, 287, 291, 293
crimes against persons, 223
criminal: lawyers, 217, 219; procedure, 217–20, 221
Cromwell, Oliver, 260
crop rotation, 167, 169
Cuccagni, Luigi, 284, 285
curia, 43, 116, 228, 239, 282, 284
*curia graziosa*, 130

Dalmatia, 136
Danzig (Gdansk), 101
datary, 129–31, 138
David, Jacques-Louis, 345, 348, 362, 365
David, Ludovico, 331
*De Aedificis*, 20
De Brosses, Charles, 146, 270, 303
debtors, 161, 201–2, 219, 227
De Carolis palace, 35
De Cesaris, Luigi, 257
De Cupis, Cesare, 157

deficit, trade and payment, 88, 144, 151
deforestation, 155
Della Porta, Guglielmo, 360
Della Porta, Msgr., 145
Della Valle, Filippo, 29, 358, 359, 360–61
Delumeau, Jean, 40, 94, 134
Democritus, 249
demographic growth and balance, 58–59, 63, 66
Denham, John, 192
depopulation in the Agro Romano, 153–56
*depositaria generale*, 46, 117
De Sanctis, Francesco, 24–25
Descartes, René, 250, 251, 254, 259, 302
*Diario ecomomico di agricoltura, manifattura, e commercio*, 103–4
diet, 114–15, 174; Roman, 193–94; *see also* food
Dilettanti, Society of, 2, 4, 327
diplomatic immunity, 215
Directory, French, 152, 369
diseases: apoplexy, 205, 206, 207; bronchitis, 207; catarrhs, 205, 206; chicken pox, 205, 206; cholera, 212; dysentery, 207; fevers, 205, 206; gangrene, 205, 206; insanity, 210; kidney stones, 207; malaria, 152, 155–56, 172, 198, 205; measles, 205, 206, 207; scarlet fever, 207; scorbutic, 208; smallpox, 205, 206, 207; tuberculosis, 205, 208; typhoid, 206, 207; VD, 209, 212
*Dissertazione sopra il commercio*, 103, 144, 261
*distretto* of Rome, 119, 124, 125, 168, 177
*dogana dei pastorizie*, 169, 170, 191
*dogana di mare*, 23
*dogana di terra*, 23
*dogana generale*, 103, 125–26
Domenichino, 325, 349
Dominicans, 277, 283, 332
Domus Aurea, 313
Doria Pamphilj, Principe Andrea IV, 49
Doria Pamphilj, Giovanni Andrea, 89
Doria Pamphilj family, 37–38, 49
Drouais, Jean-Germain, 348
duelling with knife, 222
Dughet, Gaspard, 4, 350
Duni, Emanuele, 243
Dunkirk, 181, 183
Dupaquier, Jacques, 57
Duphot, Matthieu-Léonard, 368
Dutch fashion of clothmaking, 108
dyeing, 96, 108

Ecclesiastical Academy, 234–35
ecclesiastical: construction, 29–33; wealth, 89, 147
Economica, 45–46, 93–94
*Editto circa la vita e honestà degli ecclesiastici* (1775), 272
education: girls', 232; primary, 232–33
*Effemeridi Letterarie*, 305
Egypt, 36, 327, 328
electricity, 257
émigrés, French, 150, 366
Emilia, 338
encyclopedists, 262
England and Wales, 59, 89, 106, 114, 126, 141, 318
entertainment, popular, 298–300
entropy in enlightenment Rome, 10–11, 247, 349, 365
Epicurus, 250
epidemics, 205, 206; zootic, 169; *see also* diseases
Erard, Charles, 335
Erasmus, 280
Eschinardi, Francesco, 249
espionage, 318
*esprit des lois*, 261, 278, 291
Este, Cardinal Ippolito d', 313
*estimo*, 102
*estimo censuale piano*, 163
Estreimont de la Serre, Claude, 267
*Etats de la France*, 102
etching, 353–54
Etruscans, 328, 329
Eugene IV, Gabriele Condulmer, 53, 236
Eugene of Savoy, Prince, 318
executions, 228–29
Exeter, fifth Earl of, 2–3
expenditure of Apostolic Chamber, 131–36

Facchini, Ferdinando, 218
Fagel, Franz, 318
Falconieri, Costanza, 307
Faldi, Antonio and Sebastiano, 298
fallow, 157, 169
families, nuclear, 71–75
famines, 182, 184; (1763–66), 62, 167, 175, 181, 182–84
Fantuzzi, Cardinal Gaetano, 280
Faraday, Michael, 256
Farinacio, Prospero, 217, 219
Farnese, Cardinal Odoardo, 336, 338
Farnese palace, 35–36, 112, 322, 323, 338–44, 345, 351, 353, 354, 357
Farnesina, 322, 339
Fathers of the Christian Doctrine (Doctrinairs), 233
*fedi di credito*, 145
Ferdinand IV of Naples, 140, 273
Fernandi, Francesco, 4, 344
*Ferragusta* (Feast of Assumption), 113
Ferrara, 40, 105, 113, 116, 136, 137, 180, 368
fertilizer, 167

Ficoroni, Francesco de', 3, 316–17, 318
*fida*, 169, 170
fiefs, baronial, 41, 161
Filangieri, Gaetano, 219
Fiumicino, 89
Flamsteed, John, 254
Flaxman, John, 364
Flemings, 349
Florence, 41, 55, 60, 62, 81, 91, 94–95, 96, 97, 101, 117, 140, 175, 176, 177, 178, 199, 202, 203, 252, 260, 277, 295, 308, 318, 322, 337, 360
Florentine patriciate, 60–61, 77
flour, 127, 183
flying shuttle, 96
Foggini, Giovanni Battista, 279, 360
Foggini, Pier Francesco, 267, 279, 280, 283, 284
Foligno, 368
Fonda, Girolamo, 242
Fontana, Carlo, 22, 200, 225, 301, 367
Fontana, Domenico, 19
Fontana, Francesco, 29–30
Fontanini, Giustino, 252, 265, 266, 277, 278, 318
food: beef, 187, 189, 190–91; bread, 176, 179, 181–82, 183, 184, 194; butter, 191, 193; cheese, 170, 191–92; chestnuts, 171; fish, 192; lard, 193; olive oil, 193; pasta, 176, 194; pork, 187, 189, 191; salted meat, 187; veal, 191; vegetables, 193; vermicelli, 176
food budget, family, 114–15
food riots, 184
foreigners, 19
forum, 15, 312
foundlings, 196, 202, 203, 207; death rate of, 203
France, 5, 93, 101, 104, 114, 126, 127, 131, 139, 142, 149, 165, 199, 200, 233, 250, 254, 261, 262, 263, 269, 270, 275, 277, 278, 299, 308, 310, 318, 335, 367
Francesco Stefano, grand duke of Tuscany, 106, 117, 128
Frangipani, Mario, 52
Frascati, 205, 342
Frederick II of Prussia, 219
free market, 101
freedom of: speech, 248; trade, 100, 102, 104–105, 111, 167, 184
freemasonry, 253, 259–61, 367; Stuart lodge, 260
French Revolution, 1, 44, 61, 63–64, 68–69, 131, 140, 184, 219, 262, 263, 284, 308, 335, 345, 366–70
Freret, Nicole, 262
Friz, Giuliano, 64
Frosinone, 113
Fuga, Ferdinando, 23, 28, 31–32, 35, 208, 261
fulling mills, 96
Füssli, Heinrich, 347

*Gabella dello studio*, 116, 236
Galiani, Celestino, 241, 252, 253, 254, 255, 256, 258, 265, 266, 281, 291, 310
Galileanism, 248, 249, 250
Galilei, Alessandro, 27, 28, 30–31, 32, 361
Galilei, Galileo, 238, 248
galley slaves, 230
Galli, Cardinal Antonio Andrea, 280
Galli-Bibbiena, Ferdinando, 338, 353, 355
Gallicanism, 284
Garofalo, Biagio, 265, 266
Gassendi, Pierre, 250, 251, 254, 260
Gaudio, Francesco Maria, 241
Geneva, 256, 261
Genoa, 89, 128, 150, 183, 234, 336
Genoese financiers, 136–37
Genovesi, Antonio, 185, 261
Genzano, 172, 314
George III of Great Britain, 4, 320
Gerdil, Giacinto Sigismondo, 259
Germans, 81
Germany and Austria, 59, 97, 104, 142, 163, 235, 243
Gesù, 21, 233, 336, 337
ghetto, 84, 85–86
Ghezzi, Giuseppe, 342, 343
Ghezzi, Pier Leone, 242–43
Gian Gastone de'Medici, grand duke of Tuscany, 91
Gianicolo, 35, 236, 242, 287
Gianni, Francesco Maria, 104, 128
Giaquinto, Corrado, 341
Gibbon, Edward, 262
*Giglietto*, 144
Giordani, Vito, 237
Giordano, Luca, 339
*Giornale dei letterati* (1668–1683), 249
*Giornale de'letterati* (1742–1754), 257
*Giornale de' letterati d'Italia*, 254
*Giornale ecclesiastico di Roma*, 262, 284–85
Giudici, Antonio, 218
Giuntella, Vittorio Emanuele, 196, 232
Godard, Luigi, 297
Goethe, Johann Wolfgang, 256, 307, 326
gold, Brazilian, 143
gold–silver ratio, 88, 103, 142–43
Goldoni, Carlo, 294
Golt, Gaetano, 296–97
Gonzaga, Cardinal Silvio Valenti, 217, 241, 256, 257, 334, 343
Gorani, Joseph, 268, 315

Gottsched, Johann Christoph, 291
governor of Rome, 45, 53–54, 91, 214, 225, 230, 259
grain, 113, 167, 176–77, 178–81, 183; consumption of, 158, 176–77, 182; export of, 156, 177; stockpiling of, 179; yields, 167, 180
Grand, Peter, 317
"grand style", 4, 337
grand tour, 2, 64, 355
grapes, 113
Grascia, 47, 91, 102, 105, 187–91
Gravina, Gian Vincenzo, 237, 251, 291, 302, 325, 329
"Great Fear" (1789), 367
Great Schism, 1, 91
Greece, 36, 326, 327, 355
Greek art and literature, 236, 265, 286, 291, 327, 328, 346, 347, 362
Gregorini, Domenico, 32
Gregory I, 55
Gregory XIII, Ugo Boncompagni, 18, 19, 20, 51, 179, 202, 224, 235
Gregory XIV, Niccolo Sfondrato, 148
Grimaldi, Claudio Filippo, 6
Grotius, Hugo, 219
Gualtieri, Cardinal Filippo Antonio, 254, 255
Guercino, 3, 343
Guévarre, Père, 200
Guglielmo, Gregorio, 6
Guidi, Alessandro, 287, 289
guilds (*università*), 91, 127, 197, 228; suppression of, 93–94
Guttin, Julien, 107–8
Guynet, Henri, 109
gypsies, 99

Habsburgs, 43, 135, 318
Hackert, Jakob Philipp, 356
Hadrian's villa, 313, 319, 322, 323, 324
Hamilton, Gavin, 314, 319, 327, 347, 348, 349, 362, 365
Hannibal, 155, 268
harbors, 89
hay and straw, 127, 165, 167
health, 205–12; *see also* diseases
Hebrew, 236, 265
Helvétius, Claude-Adrien, 257
Herculaneum, 326, 346
heresy, 198, 265, 359
Hermes, 271
Hewetson, Christopher, 364
Historical Pyrrhonism, 264
historical studies, 263–68
Hoare, William, 4
Hobbes, Thomas, 265
Holland (United Provinces), 101, 114, 239, 249, 278, 318
Holy Years (Jubilees), 57, 64, 69, 142, 145, 209, 274, 357
Homer, 291, 319, 347
Hôpitauz généraux, 200
hospices, 196, 200, 201, 204
hospitals, 207–10; admissions and discharges, 208
house, one-family, 20, 36, 37, 71
household: children in, 75; density, 67; heads of, 77–81; non-relatives in, 75; one-person, 77–79; size of, 71
households, 66–67, 71
Howard, Henry, Earl of Carlisle, 3
Hudson, Thomas, 319
Hungary, 142, 235

*Illuminati*, 260–61
immigrants, 60, 64, 81–82
immigration and emigration, 64–66
Imperiali, Cardinal Lorenzo, 252, 277
import duties, 104
*improvvisatori*, 294–95, 302
index of forbidden books, 218, 241–42, 251, 253, 261, 266, 278, 284
industrial mismanagement, 109–10
Industrial Revolution, 96
industry: diversification of, 106–8; incentives for improving, 95; woollen, 94–96, 107, 112
*In eminenti* (1738), 260
infanticide, 209
inflation, 146, 186
Innocent II, 51
Innocent III, 207
Innocent VIII, Gian Battista Cybo, 229
Innocent X, Giovanni Battista Pamphilj, 18, 225, 286, 357
Innocent XI, Benedetto Odescalchi, 9, 134, 135, 204, 214, 215, 216, 250
Innocent XII, Antonio Pignatelli, 9, 22, 23–24, 44, 95, 135, 200, 204, 213, 237–38, 267, 272, 300, 332, 357, 360
Innocent XIII, Michelangelo Ponti, 102, 135
innoculation, 213
Inquisition (Holy Office), 248, 250, 252, 278
*In Supremo Justitiae Solio* (1735), 220
interest rates, 134–35
international style, 332, 345
Isham, Thomas, 2
Istituto delle scienze in Bologna, 239, 255
*Istoria della volgar poesia* (1698), 287
Italy, 130, 148, 171, 254, 258, 262, 281, 293, 297, 364

Jacobin republic, 49–51, 61, 62, 63, 64, 71, 81, 142, 149, 150, 160, 311, 365, 368–70
Jacobins, Roman, 262, 263, 367, 368–70
Jacobites, 259
Jacquier, François, 242, 256, 268
Jansen, Cornelius, 276, 279
Jansenism, 43, 251, 263, 265, 266, 269, 270, 275–85, 295
Jardin, Nicholas-Henri, 354
Jenkins, Thomas, 312–13, 319, 320
Jesuits, 10, 43–44, 183, 200, 227, 228, 235, 243, 251, 256, 258, 270, 275, 277, 278, 280, 281, 282, 283, 284, 293, 295, 297, 304, 313, 332, 336, 357, 359
Jewish community, bankruptcy of, 86; property of, 86–87
Jews, 54, 84–87, 108, 116, 223, 367
John V of Portugal, 287
John XXII, 236
Jones, Inigo, 2
Jones, Thomas, 5
Joseph II, emperor, 284
*Journal des savants*, 249
journeymen, 92–93
Julius II, Giuliano, della Rovere, 18, 40, 138, 321
jurisdiction, 41, 45, 48, 53, 161, 217, 223
jurisdictional disputes, 92, 98
jurisprudence, 234, 235
Juvara, Filippo, 32, 298, 332
Juvenal, 268

Kant, Immanuel, 256
Kauffman, Angelika, 316
Kent, William, 3, 4
Khevenhüller, Count Franz Anton, 6
Khevenhüller, Franz-Christoph, 6

labor, 102, 109; female, 100, 12; seasonal, 66, 100, 156, 159, 173, 198; unskilled, 90, 112
Labre, Benoît Joseph, 274–75
Lago Bracciano, 153
Lago Martignano, 153
Lalande, Joseph Jérôme de, 304, 315, 321
Lama, Bernardo Andrea, 225
Lamberti, Bonaventura, 338
Lambertini, Prospero, *see* Benedict XIV
Lami, Giovanni, 267, 268, 279
La Mothe le Vayer, Felix, 263
Lancisi, Giovanni Maria, 237, 248
land: leasehold, 163–64, 172; "refeudalization" of, 156; utilization in the Agro Romano, 164–72
Landi, Francesco, 252
Landri, François, 96
Lante, Cardinal Federigo Marcello, 45
Laparre, Guillaume, 267
Lapeyrère, Isaac de, 265
Laplace, Pierre Simon, 256
*Larghe*, 225
Lassels, Richard, 2
Lateran palace, 18, 200, 201, 323
Latin classics, 287, 288, 362
Lavaggi, Conte Domenico, 142
Law, John, 101, 145
law: enforcement, 42, 214–23; faculty, 233, 242–43
lawyers, 48
Lazio, 40, 61, 94, 97, 110, 153, 155, 161, 163, 164, 168, 170, 171, 172, 175
leather, 94, 98
Le Brun, Charles, 334, 335
legations, 40–41
Le Gros, Pierre, 332, 335, 339, 340, 341, 354, 357
Leibniz, Gottfried Wilhelm, 6, 254, 256
Leicester, Lord, 320
Lenten preaching, 273
Leo X, Giovanni de' Medici, 17, 172
Leonardo da Porto Maurizio, 47, 273–74, 282
Leonio, Vincenzo, 287
Leopold I, Emperor, 43
Leprotti, Antonio, 255
*Les Francs-Maçons écrasés*, 260
Lesueur, Thomas, 241, 242, 256
Leto, Pomponio, 268
library, 235, 236, 278
Libri, Leonardo, 101
Liechtenstein family, 6, 333
Liège, 141
Ligoro, Pirri, 313
Limosineria Apostolica, 204
Linea Pia, 173
linen manufacture, 97
Lipari, 141
literacy, 233–34
literary criticism, 291, 311
literature, 278, 286–309
livestock: buffaloes, 171; calves, 170; cattle, 89, 170–71, 191; hogs, 190; sheep, 187, 189, 191
Livia, wife of Augustus Caesar, 310
Livorno, 60, 181, 183, 218
Livy, 268
loans, 95, 107–10, 150
Locatelli, Andrea, 351, 356
Locke, John, 253, 258–59
Lombardy, 103, 105, 119, 135, 157, 170, 182, 368
London, 60, 181, 183, 356
looms, weaving, 96

lotto (lottery), 128–29
Louis XIV of France, 5, 7, 41, 135, 334
Louis XV of France, 260
Louis XVI of France, 308
Loyola, Ignatius, 204, 235, 280
Lucca, 97, 344
Lucretius, 249, 250
Luisa, Countess of Albany, 305, 306
Lungaretta, 27
*luoghi di monte*, 89, 90, 101, 130, 131–37, 149, 150, 151, 185, 186
Luti, Benedetto, 4, 333, 337, 348, 352
Lyons, 89, 108, 200

Mabillon, Jean, 254, 264, 266, 277, 278
*macchia* (maquis), 155
*macinato*, 127
Madelin, Louis, 42
Maderno, Carlo, 30
Madonna dei Monti, 275
*maestre pie*, 233
*maestre pie filippine*, 233
Maffei, Scipione, 264, 304–305, 306
magistracies: papal, 47; municipal, papal dominance over, 18, 22, 23
Magliabechi, Antonio, 264, 277
Maini, Giovanni Battista, 29, 358, 359
Mainz, 234
Malebranche, Nicolas, 251, 254, 257, 259
Mamachi, Tommaso Maria, 283
Manfredi, Eustachio, 239
Manglard, Adrien, 351–52
Maratta, Carlo, 3, 4, 289, 325, 333, 336–37, 340, 342, 344, 348, 357, 358
Maratta, Faustina, 289–91
Maratti, Francesco, 242
Maravall, José Antonio, 9
Marches of Ancona, 40, 81, 119, 123–24, 150, 151, 177, 180, 234, 368
Marchetti, Alessandro, 250, 251
Marchetti, G., 284
Marchionni, Carlo, 33–34, 324
Marefoschi, Cardinal Mario, 280, 281, 282–83, 284
Maremma, 153, 155, 173, 274
Maria Casimira, queen of Poland, 301, 345
Maria Theresa, Empress, 106, 219
Marini, Giovanni Battista, 286
*marinismo*, 286, 291
Marittima, 40, 178
Marmont, August Frédéric Louis Viesse de, 308
Maron, Anton, 347
marriages, 63–64
Marseilles, 183
Marsigli, Archdeacon Antonio Felice, 238
Marsili, Luigi Ferdinando, 239
*masseria*, 189
Massimi, Luca, 212
Masucci, Agostino, 319, 337–38, 344
mathematics, 236, 237, 241, 256, 277
Mattei collection, 320, 323
Maurist historical–philological methodology, 264–67, 279
meat: consumption, 187–89; supply, 165, 170–71, 187–91, 193
medical faculty, 237, 243
Medici, Cardinal Leopoldo de', 250
medicines: popular, 211; quinine, 156, 205
mendicants, religious, 134
Mengs, Anton Raphael, 320, 322, 324, 327–28, 334, 338, 343, 345, 346, 347, 361
Meraldi, Jacques-Philippe, 254
*mercanti di campagna*, 160, 164–65, 179
mercantilists, 101, 102, 103, 111
Merolli family, 164–65
Mesta, Spanish, 169
Metastasio, Pietro, 29, 251, 291, 294, 295, 296, 297–98, 301–4, 307, 341
Michelangelo Buonarotti, 4, 30, 34, 315
midwives, 209–10
Milan, 55, 61, 91, 128, 175, 177, 284, 308; state of, 63, 68, 126
Milanese patriciate, 60, 77
Milani, Aureliano, 338
military expenditure, 140
Miller, Giovanni Cristiano de, 105, 106–7
Milton, John, 347
mineral: springs, 212; wealth, 89
miniature reproductions, 316
*Ministro*, 159, 164
miracles, 368; cures, 211–12
Mirri, Ludovico, 313
missions, 273–74
Modena, 217, 305, 324
Molina, Luis de, 276
Molinelli, Giambattista, 281
*Moltiplico*, 148
Monaldi, Paolo, 351
monasteries, 21
*moneta di bontà*, 145
*moneta plateale*, 145
money of account, 118, 142
money lending, 86, 92
Monnot, Pierre-Etienne, 357
Montalto, 89, 107, 179
*Monte Camerale*, 143
Monte Cavallo, 19
Montecitorio, 22
*Monte Dataria*, 130

Monte di Pietà, 99, 137, 144, 145, 146, 147, 150, 314
Monti di San Pietro, 135
Montefiasco, 107
Monte Mario, 152, 369
Monte Sorette, 161
Montesquieu, Jean-Baptiste de Secondat, baron, 5, 25, 42, 95, 152, 153, 218, 261, 262, 278, 291, 314
Montfaucon, Bernard de, 264, 277, 318, 326
*monti*, 19, 100, 131–38, 139, 144, 148, 151; repeopling of, 19
Monti, Cesare, 111, 141
Monti, Vincenzo, 111, 141, 286, 305–8, 367
Moore, Jacob, 356
Morei, Michele, 293
Morichini, Carlo Luigi, 198
mortality, 59, 62–63
Mosca, Simone, 31
*mos italicus*, 237
Mout, Etienne, 366
Münter, Friedrich, 260
Muratori, Ludovico Antonio, 128, 217, 251, 259, 264, 266, 268, 269, 277, 280, 282, 293, 304
Museo Pio-Clementino, 10, 33, 129, 141, 311, 312, 323
musical instruments, 98–99
Mussolini, Benito, 173

Naples, city of, 55, 59, 60, 61, 62, 63, 97, 98, 99, 175, 176, 177, 249, 251, 252, 258, 260, 261, 292, 295, 300, 302, 322, 327, 340, 346, 356, 362
Naples and Sicily, kingdom of, 43, 60, 68, 81, 104, 117, 126, 131, 140, 142, 150, 153, 171, 173, 177, 180, 181, 182, 183, 184, 185, 218, 270, 284, 326, 338, 339, 348
Napoleonic rule, 61, 62, 63, 64, 86, 97, 138, 151, 370
Narni, 152
Natali, Martino, 281
Natoire, Joseph, 347–48
natural law, 218, 219, 242
Nemi, 153
neoclassicism, 33, 34, 308–309, 316, 324–30, 331, 332, 344, 345–49, 356, 362–65
Neri, Filippo, 209, 275, 332
Neri, Pompeo, 117, 157, 218
Neuchâtel, 109
Newton, Sir Henry, 252
Newton, Sir Isaac, 242, 252, 254, 256, 257, 259, 260, 265
Newtonianism, 241, 251, 252, 253, 254, 255, 256
*Newtonianismo per le dame*, 253
Niccolini, Antonio, 252, 261, 278
Nice, 183, 233
Nicholas V, Tommaso Parentucelli, 17, 18
Nicolai, Nicola, 164, 176
*nipoti*, 44, 130, 161, 322
nobles, disaffection of, 49–51
Noris, Cardinal Enrico, 254, 266, 276, 279
*Novelle letterarie*, 279

Odescalchi, Baldassare, duke of Ceri, 306
Odescalchi, Marcantonio, 204
Odescalchi, Tommaso, 23
oil of vitriol, 107
Oliva, Giovanni Paolo, 336
olives, 171–72, 193
Onesti-Braschi, Principe Luigi, 35, 173, 307
opera, 300–3, 304
operatic libretto, 292, 297, 302, 341
Oppio, 20
*Opticks* (Isaac Newton), 252, 253
Oratorians, 276, 278
orchards, 171, 323
Orlandi, Pietro, 205
orphans, 199, 202, 203, 204; asylum for, 23
Orsi, Cardinal Giuseppe Agostino, 242, 267, 280, 283
Orsini, Cardinal, 112, 198
Orsini household, 161
Ospizio Apostolico di San Michele a Ripa, 23, 95, 96, 196, 197, 198, 201, 204, 225
Ospizio di San Gallo, 204
Ospizio di San Luigi, 204
Ospizio ecclesiastico, 204
Ostia, 43, 156, 314, 319
Otricoli, 152, 323
Ottoboni, Cardinal Pietro, 286, 298, 301, 332, 338, 340, 341, 342, 352
Ottoni, Lorenzo, 357
Oxford University, 254

Pacetti, Vincenzo, 361
Paestum (Poseidonia), 326, 329, 356, 362
*pagnotta a baiocco*, 181–83
painting, 331, 335–49; landscape, 331, 349–56; *vedute*, 331, 349, 350, 352–55, 356
Palace of the Conservators, 18
palaces, family, 34–35
  Palazzo Albani, 324
  Palazzo Altieri, 337
  Palazzo Bolognetti, 268
  Palazzo Borghese, 24, 346
  Palazzo Braschi, 35
  Palazzo Corsini, 35, 261, 277, 280, 369
  Palazzo dei senatori, 51

palaces (*cont.*)
Palazzo dei tribunali, 22
Palazzo della Cancellaria, 286, 323, 338, 340, 341, 342, 344
Palazzo Fiano, 298
Palazzo Medici, 337
Palazzo Pamphilj, 338
Palazzo Riario, 35, *see also* Palazzo Corsini
Palazzo Rospigliosi, 314
Palazzo Sermoneta, 314
Palazzo Venezia, 362
Palazzo Zuccari, 301, 345, 346, 347, 348, 352, 355, 359
Palestrina, 36
Palladian style, 2, 32
Pallotta, Guglielmo, 105, 106
Palmerstone, Lord (Henry Temple), 3, 315
*palombino*, 36
Pamphilj, Cardinal Benedetto, 30, 197, 286, 301, 357
Pamphilj, Prince Giovanni Battista, 197
pamphleteering, economic, 100–4
Panini, Gian Paolo, 335, 339, 340, 348, 351, 352, 356
Panini, Giuseppe, 29
Paolo della Croce, 47, 274
Paolucci, Giuseppe, 286
Papal States, 40–51, 102, 106, 108, 113, 130, 139, 142, 147, 163, 178, 180, 182, 184, 186, 199, 235, 243, 261, 323, 366, 367
Parini, Giuseppe, 286
Paris, 1, 5, 15, 51, 63, 175, 185, 193, 199, 203, 223, 281, 298, 301, 306, 330, 337, 366, 369
parishes, 55–57, 67, 209
parish priest, 56–57, 67, 69, 209, 212, 213, 223, 271–73
Park, Robert Ezra, 1
Parma, 256, 307, 338, 352
Parmigiano, 192
Pascal, Blaise, 293
Pascoli, Alessandro, 237
Pascoli, Leone, 101–3, 128, 130
Pasquinades, 295
Passalacque, Pietro, 32
Passionei, Domenico, 261, 265, 277, 278–79
Passionist fathers, 274
pasture, 157, 164–67, 169–70, 191
*patria mundi, 64*
patrimony of St. Peter, 178
Paul II, Pietro Barbo, 147
Paul III, Alessandro Farnese, 18, 204, 224, 360
Paul IV, Gian Pietro Carafa, 127, 178
Pavia, 283
Pavillon, Nicholas, bishop of Alet, 276
Pécheux, Laurent, 346
*pecorino*, 170, 191
*Pellari*, 98
penal system, 223–30; Tuscan, 217
Penna, Agostino, 361
*peperino*, 36
Perfetti, Bernardino, 294
perfumery, 94
Pericles, bust of, 306
Perrier, François, 353
Perugia, 101
Petrarch, Francesco, 287, 291, 292, 294
Pfaultz, Christian, 252
pharmacists, 92
Philip V of Spain (Philip of Anjou), 42
philology, 263, 265, 268, 311
philosophy, 235, 237, 242, 243, 277
physicians, 39, 112, 113, 210–11, 237
physics laboratory, 239, 242
physiocrats, 101, 104, 108, 111, 185
Pia Casa degli Esposti in Santo Spirito in Sassia, 202, 203
Piarists, 95, 232, 233, 251, 281
Piazza Barberini, 20, 298
Piazza Colonna, 21, 210
Piazza del Ponte di Sant'Angelo, 229
Piazza del Popolo, 17–18, 21, 25, 229, 348
Piazza di Napoli, 98
Piazza Navona, 315
Piazza di San Lorenzo in Lucina, 38
Piazza di Spagna, 15, 19
Piazza San Marco, 21
Pica-Tofanini and Company, 98–99
Piedmont, 183, 368
Pietro Leopoldo, grand duke of Tuscany, 93, 128, 135, 140, 173, 184, 219, 283, 284, 322
piety, popular, 269, 270–71, 273–75
pigs, 171
pilgrims, 64, 145, 199, 209
Pincio, 19, 256, 274, 345
Pindar, 292, 294
Pindemonte, Giovanni, 297
Pindemonte, Ippolito, 297
Piranesi, Francesco, 315, 355
Piranesi, Giovanni Battista, 32–33, 329, 345, 353–55, 356, 364
Piranesi, Pietro, 355
Pisa, 60, 140, 255, 278, 279
Piscatelli, Enzo, 138
Pistoia, 295; Synod of (1786), 284, 285
Pius IV, Giovanni Angelo de' Medici di Marignano, 224
Pius V, Antonio Ghislieri, 54, 56, 94, 97
Pius VI, Giovanni Angelo Braschi, 6, 33–34, 39, 44, 93, 94, 103, 105, 111, 119, 126, 136, 140, 141, 146, 147, 149, 150, 171,

173, 184–85, 190, 204, 208, 216, 219, 235, 243, 262, 283, 295, 306, 307, 311, 312, 314, 320, 323, 330, 361, 366, 368, 369, 370
Pius VII, Barnaba Chiaramonti, 93–94, 104, 150, 151, 300, 370
Pizzelli, Maria, 268, 305, 307
Pizzi, Gioacchino, 296
Plautus, 304
ploughing, 167, 169
Po, 101
*poena extraordinaria*, 220, 228
poisoning, 222
police spies, 215, 216
policy, papal, 42
Pompeii, 326
Ponte Cavour, 24
Pontecorvo, 40,
Ponte Molle, 152
Ponte Sant'Angelo, 18
Ponte Sisto, 18, 27
Ponthaus, Joseph Dionysius, 257
Pontine marshes, 136, 141, 147, 149, 172–73, 308
poor, the, 56, 91, 100, 126, 187, 197, 198; confinement of, 200–1; cost of relief of, 198–99, 201
Pope, Alexander, 257
Popolo Romano, 51, 52, 53, 116
population, 55–86; density, 37; male–female ratio, 60–61
porphyry, 36
Porpora, Nicola, 302
Porta di San Giovanni, 164
Porta Pia, 152
Porta Portese, 213
Porto d'Anzio, 89, 324
Port Royal, 279, 280, 283
Portugal, 130, 284, 293
Porzio, Luca Antonio, 248
*Post diuturnas*, 217
Post-Tridentine Syndrome, 11–12, 111, 213, 227–28, 230, 243, 266, 267, 285, 330, 331, 370
Poussin, Nicolas, 19, 325, 335, 349, 350
Pozzo, Fratel Andrea, 336
Pozzolana, 37, 164
Pozzuoli, 141
*precettazione* (requisitioning of meat, 189–91
prefect of the annona, 178
Preneste, 161
*Present State of Great Britain*, 102
price tariff, 91, 167, 178
primacy, papal, 283–85
*Principia mathematica philosophiae naturalis*, 252, 253, 254, 257
prisoners, number of, 226
prisons, 224–28; visitation, 197, 224; women's 23, 28, 129, 225
Private Council (Consiglio segreto), 52–53
*Privativa*, 90, 107
privilege of the city, 7–8, 173
*Prix de Rome*, 335
Procaccini, Andrea, 96
Procopius, 5
Prodi, Paolo, 40, 42
proprietors, landed, 157, 158–61, 164
prostitutes, 221
Protectionism, 95, 102, 104, 167
protoindustrialization, 88
proto-neoclassicists, 345–46
*Providas Romanorum Pontificum* (1751), 260
provinces, papal, 40–41, 60, 117, 119, 124, 150, 157, 179–80, 233
provisioning of Rome, 167, 175–95
Public Council (Consiglio pubblico), 52
public debt, 135, 136, 17, 139, 150, 151, 173; liquidation of, 151
Pufendorf, Samuel, 219
puppet theater (*burattini*), 298
pyramid of Cesto, 213

Quatremère de Quincy, 348
Quattrini, 142
*quattrino della carne*, 116, 127
Quesnel, père, Pasquier, 275, 279
Quirinal, 19, 20, 28, 184, 253, 257, 268
Quirini, Cardinal Angelo Maria, 261, 344
*Quo Die* (1748), 105

Racine, Jean, 296, 304
*Ragion Poetica* (1708), 291
Raguzzini, Filippo, 25, 27
Ramsay, Allan, 4
Raphael, 4, 336, 344, 345, 346
Rappini, Gaetano, 173
*Ratio Studiorum*, Jesuit, 47, 304
Ravenna, 101, 368
*reclusori*, 106
regulation of food consumption, 156
remuneration in kind, 112
Renaissance Rome, 17–18, 247, 250, 268, 313, 331
Renazzi, Filippo Maria, 219, 243, 268
rents, 37–38
*Repubblica letteraria italiana*, 293
residential mobility, 38–39
resin, 171
Restoration (Pius VII), 85
Retti, Giuseppe, 24, 216
Revel, Jacques, 187

Revett, Nicholas, 327
Reynolds, Sir Joshua, 4, 112, 347
Rezzonico, Don Abbondo, 362, 364
Rezzonico, Giambattista, 32
Ricci, Scipione de', bishop of Pistoia, 283–84, 285
Ricci, Sebastiano, 338, 342
Riccoboni, Luigi, 305
Riccòmanni, Luigi, 103–104
*ricotta*, 170, 191
Rieti, 177
*rigattieri*, 92
Righetti, Francesco, 316
Rimini, 248, 277, 368
Ripa Grande, 23, 99, 192, 225
Ripetta, Porto di, 23–24, 27, 99, 210
*Rituale Romano* (1614), 55
Robert, Hubert, 352
Robertson, William, 257
Rocca, Michele, 341
rococo, Roman, 27, 337, 344, 362
*rognosa* (skin infections), 207
Roma, Joseph, 252, 255
Romagna, 40, 81, 119, 123–24, 180, 306, 368
Roman influence on Britain: on art collectors, 2–3; on artists, 3–5
Roman influence in Germany, 6–7
*romanesco* dialect, 300
*Romanum decet pontificem* (1692), 44
Romavecchia, 314, 319
Romulus, 314
Ronciglione, 171
Rosa, Salvator, 299, 350, 351, 352, 355
*rossi*, 214
Rossi, Angelo de', 357
Rota, tribunal of the, 48, 101
Rousseau, Jean-Jacques, 262, 303
Royal Academy, 4, 347, 356
Royal Society of London, 239
Rubens, Peter Paul, 19
Ruffo, Fabrizio, 96, 106, 108, 113, 146, 171, 190
*ruota*, 202, 203
Rusconi, Camillo, 358, 359, 360
Rusconi, Giuseppe, 358, 359
Ruspoli, Principe Francesco Maria, 301

Sabina, 103, 171, 178, 180
Sacchi, Andrea, 336
Sacred Heart, veneration of the, 275
sacred treasure (*erario sanziore*) of Castel Sant'Angelo, 146–49, 150
sacristy of St. Peter's, 33–34, 136, 141, 147, 149, 314
St. John Lateran basilica, 18, 332, 357–58, 361; facade of, 28, 30, 31–32, 129
St. Peter's basilica, 332, 343, 359, 360, 361, 364
St. Peter's Square, 18, 21–22, 332
salaries, professional, 238, 241
Salita de Marforio, 37, 38
Salvi, Nicola, 10, 28–29, 341
Salviati, Cardinal Antonmaria, 204
Salvioni, Giovanni Maria, 236
Sampieri, Cavaliere, 89
San Carlo, ospidale de, 208
Sancta Sanctorum, 314
sanctuary, ecclesiastical, 215
San Gallicano in Trastevere, ospidale di, 25–27, 207
San Giacomo degli incurabili, 209
San Giovanni de'Fiorentini, 30–31, 129, 259, 361
San Girolamo degli Schiavoni, 24
S. Lorenzo in Damaso, 341
San Marcello, 360
S. Nicola dei Lorensi, 341
S. Nicola in Carcere, 364
S. Pantaleone, 233
S. Pietro in Montorio, 97
S. Rocco (maternity hospital), 210
S. Salvator ai Monti, parish of, 70–84
S. Salvatore a Ponto Rotto, 37
Sannazaro, Jacopo, 287
Santa Cecilia, 172, 340
Santacroce, Francesco, 49–51
S. Croce in Gerusalemme, 19, 25; facade of, 32
S. Maria degli Angeli, 254
S. Maria del Priorato, 32–33, 364
S. Maria della Pietà de' poveri pazzi, ospedale di, 210
S. Maria in Aquiro, 204, 301
S. Maria in Montecelli, 38
S. Maria in Traspontina, parish of, 38–39, 70–84
S. Maria in Trastevere, 172, 332
S. Maria in Vallicella, 257
S. Maria Maggiore basilica, 18, 19, 361
Sant'Andrea della Valle, 21
Sant'Eufemia in Treviso, 197
Sant'Ignazio, 27, 30, 332, 336
SS. Apostoli, parish of, 70–84; restoration of, 29–30
SS. Trinità dei Monti, 18–19, 241, 345
Santo Spirito (hospital and hospice), 39, 95, 136, 196, 204, 207, 208, 213
Sapienza, 116, 210, 213, 235, 236–43, 248, 255, 256, 272, 278, 281, 291
Sardi, Giuseppe, 351
Sardinia, 43
Savelli, Cardinal Vicar Giacomo, 56
Sbirri, 38, 54, 214–16, 222, 224
*scannatura*, 187, 189

scholarship, 268–69, 312
scientific research, 252–58
Scolopian fathers, 237
Scotland, 59, 243
Scottoni, Gianfrancesco, 103
scudo, 118, 142, 144
sculpture, 312, 331, 356–65
*scuole regionarie*, 232
Secretariat of Briefs, 130
secularization, indications of, 9–10, 61, 365
*sede vacante*, 46, 148
Segneri, Paolo the Elder, 273
Segneri, Paolo the Younger, 273
Seminario Romano, 236
senator of Rome, 51–52, 295
*sensali*, 99
servants, household, 75–77, 99, 112, 197
Severoli, Marcello, 286
Sforza Cesarini, Francesco Maria, 51
Shakespeare, William, influence on Italian literature, 307
sharecroppers, 100
Shelburne, Lord, 315, 320
Sicily, 181, 194
Siena, 155, 294, 306
silk, French, 97
silk industry, 89, 97, 107
silver, 143, 144, 150; American, 142
Simon, Richard, 266
Simonet, Jean, 96
Simonetti, Francesco, 105
Simonetti, Michelangelo, 33, 323
sinecures, 134, 137, 138
Sion, Jules, 152
Sistine chapel, 336, 347
Sixtus IV, Francesco della Rovere, 17, 18, 19, 207–8, 321
Sixtus V, Felice Peretti, 18, 19, 45, 94, 118, 138, 147, 148, 172, 204, 227, 232, 345
Slodtz, Michelangelo, 252, 359, 362
Slop de Cadenberg, Giuseppe Antonio, 258
smuggling, 117
social contract, 262–63
soil of the Agro Romano, 152–53, 155, 167, 169
*soldano*, 224, 227
Solimena, Francesco, 339, 341
*Sollievo, congregazione del*, 101, 157, 165, 176, 177
Somaschi fathers, 109, 234
Sombert, Werner, 161
Sora, diocese of, 66
Soufflot, Jacques Germain, 5, 326
Spada, Principe Giuseppe, 49
Spain, 59, 85, 101, 130, 131, 148, 249, 259, 284, 310
Spanish Steps, 24–25, 345
Specchi, Alessandro, 23–24, 321
specie, shortage of, 143, 144, 145, 146
Spedalieri, Nicola, 262–63
Spiller, Xaver, 108
Spinelli, Cardinal Giuseppe, 280
spinning, 107
Spinoza, Baruch, 265, 266
spiritualities, 129–31, 138
*spogli*, 129, 130
Stanza de' papiri, 141, 346, 347
*stati delle anime*, 55–84, 226
statuary: funerary, 359, 360, 362–64; "Twelve Apostles", 332, 357–58
stock exchange, 102
Stockholm, 315
Stosch, Baron Philipp von, 318–19, 359
Strada Clementina, 24
*strade e acque*, administration of, 116
strike, 110
Stuart, James, English Old Pretender, 148
Stuart, James, 327
Suburra, 20, 24
Subleyras, Pierre, 343
Sulmona, diocese of, 66
surgery, 207, 208
Swiss, 81, 109–10, 278

tallow, 92, 165
Talbot, Bruno, 3
Tamburini, Pietro, 263, 282–83, 284
tanning, 91, 94
Tanucci, Bernardo, 185
tapestry, workshop for, 23, 96
tariff, customs, 105, 126
*tariffa perpetua per li fornari di Roma*, 182
Taruffi, Giuseppe Antonio, 304
*tassa del milione*, 127, 142
Tasso, Torquato, 286, 302
taxes, indirect, 124, 126–27, 128
tax exemption, 90, 142
tax farming, 103, 117, 119, 128
Teatro Alibert or Delle Dame, 301
Teatro Argentina, 301
Teatro Capranica, 298, 301
Teatro dei Granarim 298
Teatro della Valle, 298, 307
Teatro Pace, 230
Teatro Pallacorda, 230, 298
Teatro Tordinona, 300, 301
Tellier, Jean, 227
Temple, Henry, *see* Palmerston, Lord
temporal power of the papacy, 281, 368
tender, shortage of, 103
tenute, 100, 150, 157, 159–61, 163, 164
Terence, 304
Terni, 152

Terracina, 110, 153, 172
Terror, the, in France, 64, 68
*Testamento politico d'un accademico*, 102
*testatico*, 102
textiles, 94, 107
theater, French influence on, 304–5
theaters, private, 300–1
theft, 223, 225, 230
Theocritus, 287
Théodon, Jean-Baptiste, 357
theology, 234, 235, 237, 268, 278
thoroughfares, 18–19
Thorvaldsen, Bertel, 364
Tiber, 15, 19, 85, 89, 136, 153, 180, 183, 212, 351
Tiber island, 17, 27, 204
Tiepolo, Giovanni Battista, 354
tillage, 156, 157, 158, 170, 191
Tintoretto, 349
Tischbein, Wilhelm, 260
Tivoli, 36, 171, 205, 212, 306, 313, 314, 323, 324, 356
tobacco, 91, 127
Todi, 107
Tolentino, Peace of (1797), 49, 148, 150, 308, 368
Tolfa, 94, 141–42
Tor Colombano, 314, 319
Tordinona (prison), 225, 227
Torlonia, Giovanni, 49, 110, 142, 150, 367
Torretti, Bernardo, 361
Torrigiani, Cardinal Luigi, 183, 282
tourists, 1, 22, 94, 312, 330, 351, 354; English, 2, 317, 351, 352, 355, 361; French 5–6, 315
Tournon-Simiane, Philippe comte de, 94, 110, 151, 170, 171, 312
Townley, Charles, 315, 320
trades, "floating", 99
tradesmen: bakers, 179, 181–82, 185; bankers, 134; blacksmiths, 92; booksellers, 93; butchers, 92; cabinetmaker, 112; candlemakers, 92; cobblers, 92; coopers, 99; coppersmiths, 99; fishmongers, 92; goldsmiths, 93; innkeepers, 93; scriveners, 234, shoemakers, 92; shopkeepers, 113; soapmakers, 92; *speziali*, 93; tailors, 92; *vermicellari*, 93; waggoners, 99; weavers, 94
traffic congestion, 21
tragedy, dramatic, 292–93, 296–97, 303, 304, 305
transhumance, 170
transit tolls, 90, 169
transportation, 88, 89, 180
Trastevere, 15, 20, 27, 37, 97, 99, 100, 172, 298
Travertine stone, 36
treasurer general, 46–47, 105–106, 109, 145
Trent, Council of, 8–9, 196
Trentino, 99
Trevi fountain, 10, 20, 28–29, 129, 360, 361
Trevisiani, Francesco, 6, 332, 333, 342, 343
tribunal of the annona, 178
tribunal of the Apostolic Chamber, 214
tribunal of the cardinal camerlengo, 24, 223
tribunal of the cardinal vicar, 214, 223
tribunal of the governor of Rome, 214, 220, 221, 223
tribunal of the senator of Rome, 214, 223
Trinità dei Pellegrini (hospice), 25, 200, 209
Trionfetti, Giovanni Battista, 242
Trippel, Alexander, 356
tufa, volcanic, 153
Turgot, Anne Robert Jacques, baron de, 93, 104
Turin, 61, 101, 108, 256, 257, 258, 341
Turks, 143
Turkish "tithe," 130
Tuscans, 27–28, 276
Tuscany, 41, 60, 68, 81, 84–85, 93, 103, 104, 105, 117, 118, 119, 136, 138, 140, 157, 168, 169, 180, 182, 183, 184, 217, 218, 219, 270, 277, 283, 284, 322

*uffici venali vacabili*, 90, 131, 137–38, 150, 151
Umbria, 23, 40, 81, 89, 164, 169, 180, 234
unemployed, 198, 201
*Unigenitus* (1713), 277, 280, 282
*università dei fornari*, 181–82
university faculties, 236
Unterberger, Christoph, 347
Urban VIII, Maffeo Barberini, 9, 52, 53, 87, 118, 134, 148, 179, 332, 360
*Urbem Romam* (1746), 53
Urbino, 40
Ursulines, 233
Utrecht, Peace of, 278
Utrecht, schismatic church of, 282

*vacca romana*, 170, 191
*vaccinari*, 98
vagrants, 59, 60, 64, 198, 199, 200, 202, 274
Valadier, Luigi, 316
Vanbrugh, John, 3, 30
Van Loo, Charles-Andre, 337
Varano, Alfonso, 297
Varro, 155
Vasari, Giorgio, 331
Vasi, Giuseppe, 341, 353–54, 356
Vatican, 17, 18, 205, 248, 311, 321, 323, 324, 369; library, 129, 141, 278, 311, 327, 346; stanzas, 336, 346

Vaudières, de, Marquis de Marigny, 5, 326
*veglia*, 220–21
Velletri, 161, 171
venality of curial offices, 137–38
Venerini, Rosa, 233
vengeance, private, 214, 222
Venice, 55, 62, 68, 89, 170, 180, 234, 258, 283, 284, 300, 302, 338, 354, 355, 362
Venuti, Ridolfo, 310, 311, 312, 316
Vegennes, comte Charles Gravier de, 275
Vernet, Claude-Joseph, 352, 355
Verri, Alessandro, 139, 146, 175, 184, 211–12, 234, 273, 303, 312
Verri, Pietro, 146, 175, 273
Verschaffelt, Peter Anton van, 7
Via Appia, 36, 173
Via Cassia, 17
Via Condotti, 98
Via dei Banchi Vecchi, 98
Via del Babuino, 17
Via del Corso, 17, 19, 98, 259, 286, 351, 354, 360, 367
Via delle Botteghe Oscure, 248, 257
Via del Tritone, 20
Via Flaminia, 17
Via Giulia, 18, 225, 299
Via Gregoriana, 345
Via Lata, *see* Via del Corso
Via Lungara, 18, 35, 210, 227
Via Macelli, 38
Via Pia, 19, 20
Via Ripetta, 17, 38
Via Sistina, 345
vicegerent, 54
Vico, Giambattista, 243, 269, 291
Vien, Joseph-Marie, 348
Vienna, 60, 302, 303, 318
Villa Albani, 324–25
Villa Borghese, 347
Villa d'Este, 324
Villa Medici, 322, 323
Vinci, Leo, 302
vineyards, 100, 164, 172, 194; viniculture, 172
*vino romanesco*, 194
*vini navigati*, 194
Virgil, 169, 268, 287, 289, 306
Virgin Mary, 271, 280
Visconti, Giambattista, 311, 323
Visconti, Ennio Quirino, 306, 310, 311, 312, 353
Viterbo, 97, 177, 233
Vitruvian principles, 323, 326
*Vocabolario della lingua italiana* (1729–1737), 277
Volpato, Giovanni, 316
Voltaire, François-Marie Arouet, 256, 257, 261, 262, 278, 303, 304, 307

wars: Austrian Succession, 43, 144, 260, 326; Holy League of Cognac, 131; Polish Succession, 43; Spanish Succession, 42–43, 127
wars, feudal, 153
watermills, 90
wax, 93
Westminster Abbey, 361
wetnurses, 202–203
Wharton, Philip, 259
Wheughels, Nicolas, 339
widows, 37, 77
Wiedewelt, Hans, 364
Wilson, Richard, 4, 355
Wilton, Joseph, 347
Winckelmann, Johann Joachim, 291, 308, 311, 312, 316, 324, 325, 326, 327, 344, 345, 346, 347, 348, 353, 361, 362, 364, 365
wine, 127, 172, 194; merchants, 93
Wittel, Gaspard Van, 350, 351–52
Wolff, Christian, 257
women, 100, 272; in Arcadia, 289
woodland, 171
Wootton, John, 4
workshops, 90, 91, 92
wormwood, 205
wounds and fractures, 208–9
Wren, Christopher, 30

Ximenes, Leonard, 173

Zaccaria, Francesco Antonio, 262, 283, 287, 285
Zanotti, Francesco Maria, 255, 259
Zappi, Giambattista Felice, 286, 291
*zecca* (Roman mint), 143
Zeno, Apostolo, 302, 303
Zoboli, Giacomo, 345
Zoffoli, Giovanni, 316
Zola, Giuseppe, 282–83
Zuccari, Federico, 345
Zulian, Girolamo, 362
Zurich, 89

# CAMBRIDGE STUDIES IN EARLY MODERN HISTORY

*The Old World and the New, 1492–1650*
J. H. ELLIOT

*The Army of Flanders and the Spanish Road, 1567–1659: The Logistics of Spanish Victory and Defeat in the Low Countries Wars*
GEOFFREY PARKER

*Gunpowder and Galleys: Changing Technology and Mediterranean Warfare at Sea in the Sixteenth Century*
JOHN FRANCIS GUILMARTIN JR

*The State, War and Peace: Spanish Political Thought in the Renaissance 1516–1559*
J. A. FERNANDEZ-SANTAMARIA

*Calvinist Preaching and Iconoclasm in the Netherlands, 1544–1569*
PHYLLIS MACK CREW

*Altopascio: A Study in Tuscan Society 1587–1784*
FRANK MCARDLE

*The Kingdom of Valencia in the Seventeenth Century*
JAMES CASEY

*Filippo Strozzi and the Medici: Favor and Finance in Sixteenth-Century Florence and Rome*
MELISSA MERIAM BULLARD

*Rouen during the Wars of Religion*
PHILIP BENEDICT

*Neostoicism and the Early Modern State*
GERHARD OESTREICH

*The Emperor and his Chancellor: A Study of the Imperial Chancellery under Gattinara*
JOHN M. HEADLEY

*The Military Organization of a Renaissance State: Venice c. 1400 to 1617*
M. E. MALLETT AND J. R. HALE

*Prussian Society and the German Order: An Aristocratic Corporation in Crisis c. 1410 to 1466*
MICHAEL BURLEIGH

*Richelieu and Olivares*
J. H. ELLIOTT

*Society and Religious Toleration in Hamburg 1529–1819*
JOACHIM WHALEY

*Absolutism and Society in Seventeenth-Century France: State Power and Provincial Aristocracy in Languedoc*
WILLIAM BEIK

*Turning Swiss: Cities and Empire 1450–1550*
THOMAS A. BRADY JR

*The Duke of Anjou and the Politique Struggle during the Wars of Religion*
MACK P. HOLT

*Neighbourhood and Community in Paris 1740–1790*
DAVID GARRIOCH

*Renaissance and Revolt: Essays in the Intellectual and Social History of Early Modern France*
J. H. M. SALMON